ETERNITY STREET

ETERNITY STREET

Violence and Justice in
Frontier Los Angeles

JOHN MACK FARAGHER

W. W. NORTON & COMPANY

Independent Publishers Since 1923

New York · London

For information about permission to reproduce selections from this book,
write to Permissions, W. W. Norton & Company, Inc.,
500 Fifth Avenue, New York, NY 10110

For information about special discounts for bulk purchases, please contact
W. W. Norton Special Sales at specialsales@wwnorton.com or 800-233-4830

Manufacturing by Quad Graphics Fairfield
Book design by Marysarah Quinn
Production manager: Anna Oler

ISBN 978-0-393-05136-0

W. W. Norton & Company, Inc.
500 Fifth Avenue, New York, N.Y. 10110
www.wwnorton.com

W. W. Norton & Company Ltd.
Castle House, 75/76 Wells Street, London W1T 3QT

1 2 3 4 5 6 7 8 9 0

FOR MICHELE HOFFNUNG.

Contents

PART TWO

PART THREE

PREFACE

THIS BOOK TELLS A STORY of a violent place in a violent time: Los Angeles and southern California in the mid-nineteenth century. It relates a history of conquest and ethnic suppression. It examines collective disorder and interpersonal conflict, component parts of a culture of violence. It charts a lengthy struggle to achieve justice amid the turmoil of a remote and loosely governed frontier society.

This project began with a personal experience. Several years ago I served as a juror in the trial of a man accused of murder. A woman had been bludgeoned to death in the backyard of an abandoned property in New Haven, Connecticut. The crime scene was only two blocks from the house where my wife and I had raised our three children, which magnified the horror. But what brought home the devastating impact lethal violence has on people's lives was listening to the witness testimony, examining the forensic evidence, and noting the presence and deportment of the members of the victim's family who attended court each day. We the jury labored to make sense of it all, which required us to reconstruct and recount the story of the murder in an attempt to resolve the question of guilt. It was a searing experience, especially when the judge declared a mistrial after we failed to reach agreement. Afterward I found myself reading about violence and justice in literature, social science, and history. I began teaching an interdisciplinary seminar on violence in America. Gradually this study took shape.

Earlier historical work tended to ask a perennial either-or question, "Was the American frontier violent?" I chose instead to investigate the structure, the culture, and the reproduction of violence. Frontiers were the sites of invasion and dispossession. They were beyond the sphere of the routine action of central authorities, places where no state was able to assert and maintain a monopoly of violence. The right of individuals to armed self-defense and the right of communities to enforce "popular justice" were essential elements of the weak-state frontier. Order and a semblance of justice were maintained through honor culture, a kind of middle ground between pure anarchic mayhem and the control of violence by the state. The fundamental underpinning of honor culture was the male domination of women. Domestic violence was commonplace. Violent homes acted as nurseries of violent behavior, training men and women to think of violence as the most appropriate and effective way of resolving social conflict.

This was the perspective I brought to an investigation of the early history of Los Angeles. I was raised in southern California, and while I now reside on the other side of the country, my wife and I go to Los Angeles frequently to visit family and friends. I consider myself a native, and I have long been fascinated with southern California history. According to historians, frontier Los Angeles was a very violent place. But would the historical archives support my approach to the topic? Local librarians and curators directed me to a remarkable collection of judicial records that stretched from the period of Mexican jurisdiction through the first thirty years of American rule. A series of criminal case files offered detailed accounts of homicide and other violent crimes, including court papers, lawyers' briefs, and the affidavits or testimony of witnesses. These sources enabled me to build on the pioneering work of late historian Eric Monkkonen, compiling a comprehensive list of all the homicides committed in the Los Angeles area from 1830 to 1875. Other legal sources, including justice of the peace ledgers and divorce case files, offered harrowing descriptions of intimate and domestic violence. I found a great deal of additional evidence in other official records, as well as contemporary newspapers, personal papers, memoirs, and autobiographies.

Recalling my service as a juror, I chose to narrate this history by telling stories. They are true stories, constructed with evidence drawn directly from the primary sources. Part One recounts the conquest of southern California, first by the Spanish, then by the Americans, noting the ways violence reverberated throughout the frontier social order. Part Two details the struggle of Angelenos to come to terms with that violence through the contending forces of official justice and vigilantism. Part Three explains the triumph of lynch law, with its disastrous consequences, which finally resulted in a turn toward a system of state-sanctioned justice.

Violence is the dark force of our national history. The United States has long had the highest homicide rate of any industrial democracy in the world, an order of magnitude greater than Europe, Japan, or Canada. Our pattern of violence is much closer to our southern neighbor, Mexico. We are a first-world nation with a third-world violence problem. But that problem has historically been associated with particular regions of the country. Numerous statistical studies demonstrate that since the nineteenth century the states with homicide rates higher than the national mean were all located in the West or the South. Los Angeles, settled mainly by migrants from Mexico and the American South, plays an important part in this history.

Violence is chaotic, disruptive, and destructive. But even the most irrational violence has meaning. In the judgment of psychologist James Gilligan, who spent a career working with violent offenders, "all violence is an attempt to achieve justice." What people consider to be just or unjust, of course, depends on their point of view, on the things they value and the values of their culture. And because, as political philosopher Hannah Arendt writes, "violence always needs justification," it tends to generate a complicated and instructive discourse about those values. The residents of frontier Los Angeles argued continually over the nature, causes, and consequences of the murder and mayhem occurring in their midst. Their words and deeds not only reveal a great deal about themselves and their world but speak to the enduring problem of violence in America.

Characters

(in order of appearance)

James R. Barton, from Missouri, sheriff of Los Angeles County, 1851–55, 1856–57

Felipe Alvitre, Californio, outlaw

Pío de Jesús Pico, Californio, ranchero, governor of California, 1844–46

Andrés Pico, his brother, Californio, ranchero and military leader

Andrew Jackson King, from Georgia, settler of the Monte

Benjamin Ignatius Hayes, from Missouri, district judge, 1852–64

David Brown, from Texas, outlaw

Stephen Clark Foster, from Maine, mayor of Los Angeles, 1854–56

Jonathan R. Scott, from Missouri, attorney, judge, vigilante

James S. Waite, from Maine, editor, *Los Angeles Star*, 1854–55

John Ozias Wheeler, from Connecticut, editor, *Southern Californian*, 1854–55

Francisco P. Ramírez, Californio, editor, *El Clamor Público*, 1855–59

John A. Lewis, from Massachusetts, founding editor, Los Angeles *Star*

Juan Bautista Alvarado, Californio, governor of California, 1836–42

José Domingo Féliz, Californio, ranchero

María del Rosario Villa de Féliz, Californiana, his wife

Gervasio Alipás, Californio, her lover, vaquero

Manuel Requena, from Mexico, merchant, alcalde of Los Angeles, 1836–37

Jonathan Temple, from Massachusetts, merchant

María Raphaela Cota de Temple, Californiana, his wife

Victor Prudon, from France, teacher, scribe, political adviser

José Antonio Carrillo, Californio, ranchero, political leader

ANTONIO F. CORONEL, from Mexico, political leader

ABEL STEARNS, from Massachusetts, merchant

JEAN LOUIS VIGNES, from France, vineyardist

JOSÉ ANTONIO CASTRO, Californio, commandant, California militia

BENJAMIN DAVIS WILSON, from Tennessee, ranchero

WILLIAM WORKMAN, from England, ranchero

JOHN A. ROWLAND, from Missouri, ranchero

THOMAS O. LARKIN, from Massachusetts, Monterey merchant

ARCHIBALD H. GILLESPIE, lieutenant, U.S. Marine Corps

JOHN C. FRÉMONT, captain, U.S. Army Corps of Topographical Engineers

KIT CARSON, guide, Frémont's company

ROBERT STOCKTON, commander, U.S. Pacific Squadron

JOSÉ SÉRBULO VARELA, Californio, political leader

JOSÉ MARÍA FLORES, from Mexico, commander, *las fuerzas nacionales*

ISAAC WILLIAMS, from Pennsylvania, ranchero

STEPHEN WATTS KEARNY, commander, U.S. Regiment of Dragoons

JOHN STROTHER GRIFFIN, from Virginia, surgeon

JOHN TRUMBULL (JUAN JOSÉ) WARNER, from Connecticut, ranchero

WILLIAM MARSHALL, from Rhode Island, clerk

EDWARD STOKES, from England, ranchero

ANTONIO GARRA, Cupeño, political leader

AGUSTÍN OLVERA, from Mexico, political leader

JONATHAN D. STEVENSON, commander, New York volunteers

RICHARD B. MASON, colonel, U.S. Army

PETER BIGGS, from Missouri, African American barber

MANUEL CLEMENTE ROJO, from Peru, editor, *La Estrella*, 1851–54

JOHN H. PURDY, from Ohio, city marshal, 1850

G. THOMPSON BURRILL, from New York, sheriff of Los Angeles County, 1850–51

FRANCISCA MARÍA DE JESÚS PÉREZ, Californiana, ranchera

JOSEPH LANCASTER BRENT, from Maryland, attorney, political leader

ANTONIO MARÍA LUGO, Californio, ranchero

JOSÉ DEL CÁRMEN LUGO, Californio, one of his sons, ranchero

José María Lugo, his brother, ranchero

José Francisco "Chico" Lugo, grandson, vaquero

Francisco de Paula "Menito" Lugo, his younger brother, vaquero

Juan Antonio, Cahuilla, political leader

John "Red" Irving, from Texas, outlaw

Joshua H. Bean, from Kentucky, major general, California state militia

Alexander W. Hope, from Virginia, commander, Los Angeles Rangers

Horace Bell, from Indiana, Ranger, memoirist

William B. Osburn, from New York, undersheriff of Los Angeles County, 1851–54

James A. "Jack" Watson, from Scotland, attorney, vigilante

William "Uncle Billy" Rubottom, from Arkansas, innkeeper

David W. Alexander, from Ireland, sheriff of Los Angeles County, 1856

Henry Dwight Barrows, from Connecticut, correspondent, *San Francisco Bulletin*

William Getman, from New York, city marshal, 1856–57

William Wallace, from New Hampshire, teacher, editor, *Los Angeles Star*, 1855

Henry Hamilton, from Northern Ireland, editor, *Los Angeles Star*, 1855–64, 1868–71

María del Espiritu Santo, Cupeño, common-law wife of Sheriff James R. Barton

José Santiago Barton, their son

Francisco "Pancho" Daniel, Californio, outlaw, Manillas gang

Juan Flores, Californio, outlaw, Manillas gang

Andrés Fuentes, Californio, outlaw, Manillas gang

Antonio María "Chino" Varela, Californio, son of Sérbulo Varela, outlaw, Manillas gang

Josephine Donna Smith, from Missouri, schoolgirl, poet

Michael White, from England, ranchero

Tomás Sánchez, Californio, sheriff of Los Angeles County, 1860–68

Edward John Cage Kewen, from Kentucky, attorney and political leader

Hilliard P. Dorsey, from Mississippi, register, U.S. Land Office

Civility Rubottom Dorsey, his wife, daughter of "Uncle Billy" Rubottom

JOHN G. DOWNEY, from Ireland, pharmacist, financier, political leader

CHARLES R. CONWAY, from Minnesota, editor, *Southern News*, 1861–67

ALONZO RIDLEY, from Maine, undersheriff of Los Angeles County, 1860–61

PHINEAS BANNING, from Delaware, transportation magnate

JOSEPH MESMER, from Ohio, schoolboy

FELIX SIGNORET, from France, barber, vigilante

JOHN RAINS, from Alabama, ranchero

MARÍA MERCED WILLIAMS DE RAINS, Californiana, his wife, daughter of Isaac Williams

FRANCISCA WILLIAMS DE CARLISLE, Californiana, her sister

ROBERT S. CARLISLE, from Kentucky, her husband, ranchero

JOSÉ RAMÓN CARRILLO, Californio, ranchero

ROBERT MACLAY WIDNEY, from Ohio, vigilante, California district judge, 1871–74

SAMUEL C. FOY, from Kentucky, saddle and harness maker, vigilante

JAMES FRANK BURNS, from Michigan, sheriff of Los Angeles County, 1868–72

ARMAND MICHEL JOSEF LACHENAIS, from France, vineyardist

CHARLES E. BEANE, from Virginia, editor, *Daily News*, 1871–72

YGNACIO SEPÚLVEDA, Californio, California district judge, 1875–79

SAM YUEN, from China, leader of Chinatown

YO HING, from China, leader of Chinatown

MAPS

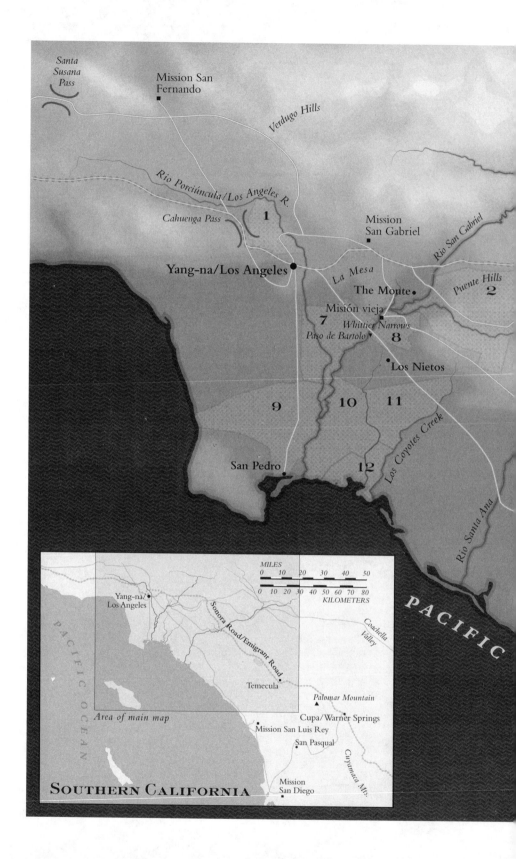

Santa
Susana
Pass

Mission San
Fernando

Verdugo Hills

Rio Porciúncula / Los Angeles R.

Cahuenga Pass

1

Mission
San Gabriel

Rio San Gabriel

Yang-na/Los Angeles

La Mesa

Puente Hills

2

The Monte

Misión vieja

7

Whittier Narrows

Paso de Bartolo

8

Los Nietos

9   10   11

San Pedro

12

Los Coyotes Creek

Rio Santa Ana

PACIFIC

MILES
0   10   20   30   40   50

0 10 20 30 40 50 60 70 80
KILOMETERS

Yang-na/
Los Angeles

Sonora Road/Emigrant Road

Coachella
Valley

PACIFIC OCEAN

Temecula

Palomar Mountain

Cupa/Warner Springs

Area of main map

Mission San Luis Rey

San Pasqual

Cuyamaca Mts.

Mission
San Diego

SOUTHERN CALIFORNIA

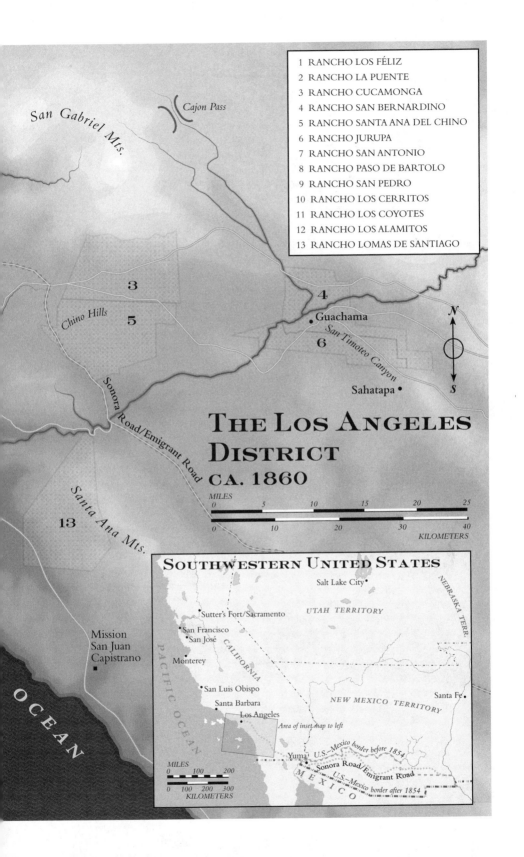

1 RANCHO LOS FÉLIZ
2 RANCHO LA PUENTE
3 RANCHO CUCAMONGA
4 RANCHO SAN BERNARDINO
5 RANCHO SANTA ANA DEL CHINO
6 RANCHO JURUPA
7 RANCHO SAN ANTONIO
8 RANCHO PASO DE BARTOLO
9 RANCHO SAN PEDRO
10 RANCHO LOS CERRITOS
11 RANCHO LOS COYOTES
12 RANCHO LOS ALAMITOS
13 RANCHO LOMAS DE SANTIAGO

San Gabriel Mts.

Cajon Pass

Chino Hills

3

5

4

Guachama

San Timoteo Canyon

6

Sahatapa

N

S

Sonora Road/Emigrant Road

THE LOS ANGELES DISTRICT
CA. 1860

MILES
0   5   10   15   20   25

0   10   20   30   40
KILOMETERS

Santa Ana Mts.

13

Mission San Juan Capistrano

SOUTHWESTERN UNITED STATES

Salt Lake City

Sutter's Fort/Sacramento

UTAH TERRITORY

NEBRASKA TERR.

San Francisco
San José

CALIFORNIA

Monterey

San Luis Obispo

Santa Barbara

Los Angeles

Area of inset map to left

NEW MEXICO TERRITORY

Santa Fe

PACIFIC OCEAN

Yuma

U.S.–Mexico border before 1854

Sonora Road/Emigrant Road

MEXICO

U.S.–Mexico border after 1854

MILES
0   100   200

0   100   200   300
KILOMETERS

OCEAN

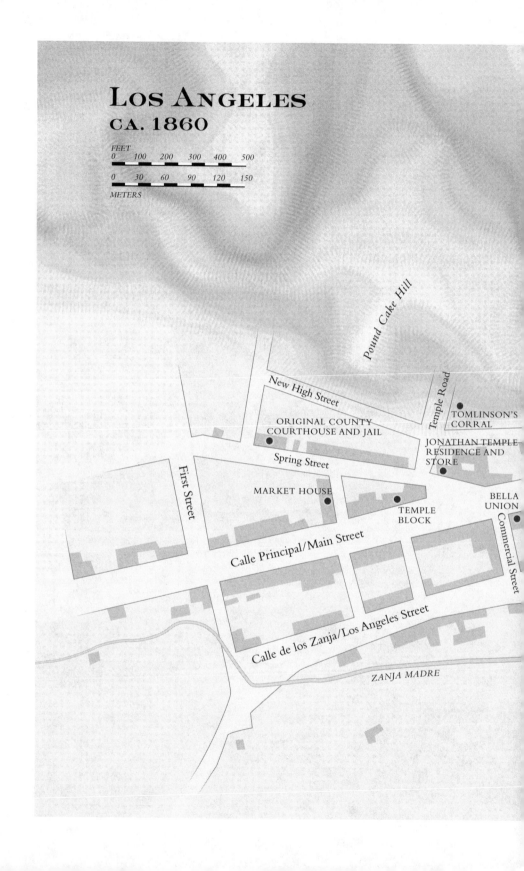

LOS ANGELES
CA. 1860

FEET
0   100   200   300   400   500

0   30   60   90   120   150
METERS

Pound Cake Hill

New High Street

Temple Road

ORIGINAL COUNTY
COURTHOUSE AND JAIL

TOMLINSON'S
CORRAL

JONATHAN TEMPLE
RESIDENCE AND
STORE

Spring Street

First Street

MARKET HOUSE

TEMPLE
BLOCK

BELLA
UNION

Calle Principal/Main Street

Commercial Street

Calle de los Zanja/Los Angeles Street

ZANJA MADRE

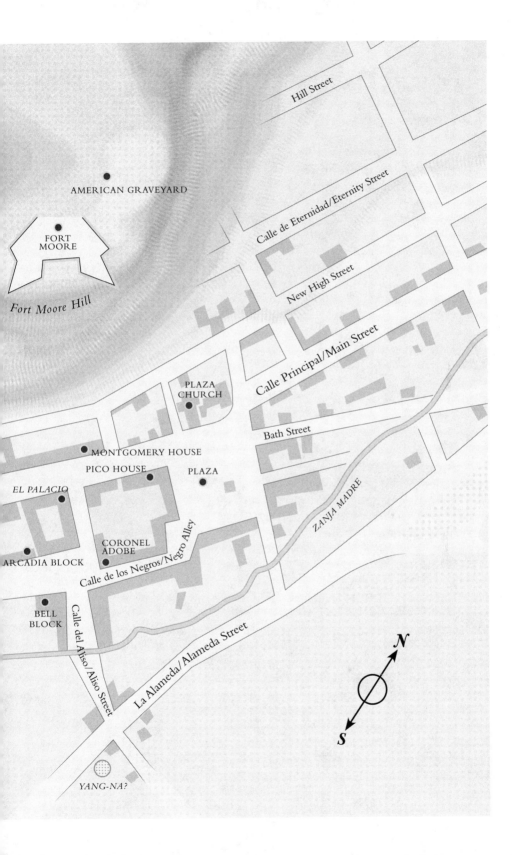

ETERNITY STREET

"My friend," said a certain well-known old resident, to whom we had applied for information, "it is not so much the *known* history of this country that requires to be written, as the *unknown*, the *inside* history. That never has been written and never will be; but if it was—what a rattling there would be among the dry bones."

JOHN ALBERT WILSON,
History of Los Angeles County (1880)

These ugly things in our past history ought to be known. . . . They may not be pleasant to read about. They are not pleasant to write about. They do not reflect on many people who are now living. The rascals whom we downed are now passed away. They are about all dead and buried, and of course they have all gone to heaven, or some other place.

HORACE BELL, "Los Angeles 1882,"
Horace Bell Papers, Huntington Library

· PROLOGUE ·

A Terrible Place
for Murders

Years afterward Angelenos still told of the time Sheriff James R. Barton was called to preserve the peace at Figueroa House, a gambling establishment on Calle de los Negros, center of the pueblo's notorious vice district. There, on the evening of July 4, 1852, Barton had an altercation with gambler Joe Caddick. The two men stepped out to the dusty street, dimly illuminated by lanterns hanging from porch posts and crowded with drunken revelers. "Defend yourself," Caddick shouted, pulling his pistol and firing twice in Barton's direction as bystanders scattered for cover. Barton, displaying little concern for his own safety, raised his revolver and squeezed off three rounds, putting a ball through Caddick's lungs. The gunfight on Negro Alley took place during Barton's first term as sheriff, the year he turned thirty, and it made his reputation as a "brave but reckless" man of the law. He would be returned to office for four successive terms. He would face danger countless times. Yet on the night of January 11, 1855, preparing for what he feared would be a violent assault on the county jail by an angry mob, reckless James Barton sat down and cautiously wrote out his last will and testament.

Sheriff Barton kept an office in a row of old adobes on the west side of Spring Street, an unpaved thoroughfare skirting the rolling hills that defined the pueblo's western boundary. Next door was the county courthouse, a single large room with crumbling walls and leaky roof. Out behind, in the center of a bare yard of swept dirt surrounded by a high plank fence, sat the new jail, the first fired-brick public building in Los Angeles. Behind its heavy iron doors, the dark interior stank of shit and fear. The first floor housed the squalid municipal dungeon, crowded with dozens of drunks every weekend. Upstairs was the county lockup, a large holding tank for ordinary prisoners with half a dozen iron cages for violent felons. On that January night in 1855 those cages held three convicted felons, two of them sentenced to hang the following afternoon. A raging controversy over their pending executions, including threats of violence, was what had Barton spooked.

Angelenos were agitated and fearful, and for good reason. The pueblo was one of the most violent towns in America. "Los Angeles is a terrible place for murders," declared the *Daily Alta California* of San Francisco. "Scarcely a steamer arrives that does not bring an account of one or two." In the five years following California statehood in 1850, Los Angeles County, with some six thousand residents, suffered more than a hundred felonious homicides, twenty-seven of them in 1854 alone. That amounted to a murder rate fifty times greater than New York City, which in 1854 recorded a total of forty-eight homicides in a population of more than six hundred thousand. For every violent death in frontier Los Angeles there were scores of assaults, batterings, rapes, and other acts of brutality. The county's legal justice system proved unable to keep up with the carnage. Over that five-year period the state district court in Los Angeles successfully tried, convicted, and executed but one man for the crime of murder. In the absence of state-sanctioned justice, vigilance committees and lynch mobs hanged at least a dozen suspected offenders. Most violent crime went unpunished. In the absence of formal justice, lethal violence ran rampant and outlaw justice prevailed.

As the new year of 1855 began, however, many Angelenos believed their city had taken a turn for the better. Formal trials in November concluded with the conviction for murder of two desperadoes. There was hope that the public execution of those felons—one a native Californio, the other an Anglo Texan—would affirm the supremacy of the law and the legitimacy of the justice system. But only days before the scheduled executions those hopes had been dashed by the arrival of an official document from the state capital that revived the persistent public controversy over violence and justice, means and ends. Sheriff Barton faced the prospect of an uprising of angry residents. It was enough to make even a reckless man seriously consider his mortality.

CONVICTED MURDERER Felipe Alvitre, a nineteen-year-old *hijo del país*, or native son, freely confessed his crimes. They fit a pattern of Alvitre family violence extending over three generations. The clan went back to the beginnings of Spanish settlement in California. Grandfather Felipe Sebastián Alvitre—a *soldado de cuero* (leather-jacket soldier) of the Spanish crown—served in the 1769 expedition that planted the first colonial foothold. While garrisoned at San Diego, Alvitre and two other soldiers were accused of beating and gang-raping two Indian women, one of whom died. Arrested and confined in irons, Alvitre and his companions were dishonorably discharged and sentenced to permanent exile in the frontier province, which was considered harsh punishment. Alvitre continued his troublesome ways. He relocated to the pueblo of San José in the north, but was banished after engaging in a tempestuous affair with another man's wife. He removed to Los Angeles, where he was arrested and jailed for riotous conduct. Governor Pedro Fages described him as "an incorrigible rogue." Eventually Alvitre married an Indian woman and settled east of the pueblo on the banks of the Río San Gabriel, near where the river squeezes through a gap in the foothills, a place known today as the Whittier Narrows. He and his wife cultivated a small plot of bottomland, herded cattle for the padres at nearby Mission San Gabriel, and raised a large family. Their children married and raised big families of their own on land nearby.

Young Felipe, old Felipe's grandson and namesake, was born in 1835 and raised amid this cluster of extended family. He came of age during the Mexican-American War, when the men of his family, along with virtually all Californios, took up arms in defense of their homeland. The war, officially concluded in 1848, left a bitter legacy. Violent conflict continued between the Spanish-speaking majority and the small English-speaking minority in control of the political system. The institutions of the new American state were weak, and in the absence of credible authority social order depended on codes of honor and vengeance.

As he approached manhood, young Alvitre was witness to a storm of violence within his family circle. During the wedding of a cousin in 1852 an American guest shot and killed one of his uncles. Several months later one of his cousins threatened a bothersome Mexican drifter, who revenged himself by kidnapping the man's three-year-old daughter, cutting her throat, and tossing her body into a swamp. In 1853 a group of vigilantes arrested another cousin, Ysidro Alvitre, Felipe's age-mate, and charged him with the assault and attempted rape of Antonia Margarita Workman de Temple, daughter of Englishman William Workman and the wife of Francis P. F. Temple, two of the most prominent Anglo rancheros in the county. A kangaroo court composed of Anglos and Californios—including Andrés Pico, brother of Pío de Jesús Pico, the last governor of Mexican California—sentenced the offender to 250 lashes "on the bare back" and warned him, on pain of death, to "leave the county as soon as his physicians pronounce him able to do so." The notice was unnecessary. The young man died of his wounds.

Brute force was common in Felipe Alvitre's world, and he felt no hesitation about employing lethal violence himself. His brief but bloody criminal career began on Sunday morning, September 3, 1854. Alvitre and his seventeen-year-old brother, Ylario, accompanied by a Mexican boy named Martín and an Indian girl named Innocencia, were traveling together down the lower valley road, taking turns riding a single horse. About a mile or two east of the Monte, an American settler community on the west bank of the Río San Gabriel, they encountered James Ellington, a recent migrant from Texas, rounding up livestock. The Alvitre brothers somehow persuaded Ellington to dismount, then attacked him with their knives. He ran, but stumbled into a cactus patch, where they dispatched him. The brothers took his buckskin purse containing several hundred dollars, his Colt's Navy revolver, and his black felt hat. Ellington's horse ran off and later showed up at the home place, alerting the family that something was amiss.

They discovered his body several hours later. A local physician, standing in for the county coroner, summoned a jury of six men from the neighborhood and conducted an inquest. His report was explicit. There were "fourteen severe wounds on the body and arms, all thrust wounds, as if made with a spear lance or two edge instrument of some kind. There were two deep wounds just below the left nipple, four on the breast bone, three deep thrusts in the back, and several on each arm." The assault, reported the bilingual *Los Angeles Star,* had been committed by "fiends in human shape." Ellington left a young widow and five children under the age of ten.

The Alvitres struck again the following morning near the settlement of Los Nietos, about ten miles downriver. Charles Moore was on horseback rounding up a drove of hogs, when he saw them in the distance, riding double on an unsaddled horse. The brothers shouted a greeting. Did he have any whiskey? No, Moore replied. They rode in closer. Perhaps he could spare a match? Moore nodded, dug into his pocket, and as he did so, one of the brothers pulled a knife and took a wild swing, ripping Moore's shirt and cutting him superficially. Moore pitched backward off his horse, scrambled up, and took off running as the other brother aimed and fired the Colt. Moore heard four shots whistle past in rapid succession, then the click of the hammer on an empty chamber. He turned, drew his own revolver, and fired one or two ineffective rounds as the Alvitres rode off with his horse in tow.

The residents of the Monte—including local patriarch Samuel King and his three sons, Francis Marion, Andrew Jackson, and Samuel Houston—organized a posse and scoured the countryside. At nearby Rancho La Puente they seized two vaqueros employed by ranchero William Workman and subjected them to harsh interrogation. The "Monte Boys" distrusted Workman, who had supported the Californios during the late war of conquest, and when he vouched for his men, he too was threatened. But cooler heads prevailed and violence was averted.

The gang had fled into the remote canyons of the Puente Hills on the east side of the river, where they hid out for several weeks, supporting themselves by rustling and slaughtering stray cattle. One Sunday in early October, as they scouted for plunder along Los Coyotes Creek, near today's town of Artesia, they encountered a lone rider, a Chilean by the name of Gorgonio Carrera, making his way to Los Angeles after a visit with friends in San Juan Capistrano. Seeing this dirty, ragged band of youngsters approaching, Carrera must have immediately sensed trouble. "Where are your father and mother?" he pointedly asked Felipe, a question he almost certainly intended as an insult. As Alvitre later told the authorities, that was precisely how he took it. The gang surrounded Carrera, and as he swiveled in his saddle to get a good look at them, Alvitre drew the Colt, pressed it against Carrera's back, and fired twice. After stripping the body of clothing and valuables, the Alvitres dragged it into a ditch at the side of the trail. Coyotes and buzzards would ravage the corpse, leaving little more than fragments of hair and bone.

Soon afterward the Alvitre brothers quarreled and parted company. Ylario and the Mexican boy went south to San Diego, leaving Felipe encamped with Innocencia in a ravine near Soquel Canyon in the Chino Hills. A few days later, they were discovered there by a party of mounted Californios, searching for missing stock. Seeing that he was outnumbered, Alvitre tossed the Colt aside and surrendered without resistance. The leader of the party, Ygnacio Palomares, was a prominent ranchero, and Alvitre assumed a deferential demeanor with him.

He was disgusted by what he had done, he told Don Ygnacio, and was ready to be punished for his crimes. Palomares delivered Alvitre and the girl to Sheriff Barton, who brought them to Judge Benjamin Hayes for examination. After hearing Alvitre's confession, Hayes asked him why he had murdered Ellington. He thought he might as well kill as not, the young man answered flippantly. That didn't satisfy Hayes, and when he pressed for an explanation Alvitre turned serious. "*Porque era Americano*," he declared. Because he was American.

ON OCTOBER 13, a week before Alvitre's capture, David Brown was arrested as he ran from a livery stable on Calle Principal, or Main Street, where Pinckney Clifford lay bleeding to death. Like Felipe Alvitre, Brown was no stranger to violence. Born about 1825 in east Texas, he took his lessons in human relations during the settler rebellion of the 1830s. When the war with Mexico commenced in 1846, Brown enlisted in the First Texas Mounted Volunteers, an early iteration of the Texas Rangers. The Texas Mounted scouted for General Zachary Taylor, employing savage tactics that cost the lives of hundreds of Mexican civilians. Taylor was scandalized by their behavior. The Texans "committed extensive depredations and outrages upon the peaceful inhabitants," he reported. "Were it possible to rouse the Mexican people to resistance, no more effectual plan could be devised than the very one pursued by some of our volunteer regiments." Mexicans named the volunteers "*los diablos Tejanos*."

After the war, under the direction of a former officer named John Joel Glanton, Brown and several other hardened veterans took up bounty hunting for the provincial government of Chihuahua. Their assignment was to stalk and kill Apaches, but finding their prey elusive, the gang turned to murdering Mexicans and counterfeiting Apache scalps. By the time the authorities caught on to the trick, Glanton and his men had departed for Gold Rush California, with its abundant criminal opportunities. Arriving in early 1850 at the Yuma crossing of the Colorado River, where hundreds of Americans and Mexicans entered California each month, they forcibly took over the ferrying service, using threat, assault, and murder to eliminate all competitors, including the Quechans (better known in the day as the Yumas), the native inhabitants of the area. Glanton assaulted a Quechan chief, warning him that for every man the Indians ferried over, the gang would kill two of his people. It was no way to make friends and influence people.

In the spring, in need of supplies, Glanton, Brown, and several others traveled to San Diego, 150 miles west on the California coast. Carousing in one of the town's many saloons, Brown shot and killed an American soldier. Arrested and jailed, he bribed his jailer and fled north to Los Angeles. In the meantime his colleagues had returned to the Colorado crossing. The night of their homecoming they drank themselves into a collective stupor, providing the Quechans an opportunity for a sneak attack. Most of the gang were killed, including Glanton, whose head was cleaved open by the vengeful Quechan chief he had roughed up. Two of the gangsters managed to escape and make it to Los Angeles, where their account of the attack stirred up a veritable panic. Later that year, when a volunteer militia force journeyed across the desert, intent on punishing the Quechans, Dave Brown hired on as one of their guides.

Following that campaign, in the fall of 1850, Brown found work as a deputy city marshal in Los Angeles. A criminal complaint by saloonkeeper Charley Burrows in early 1851 suggests something of Brown's approach to policing. Late one afternoon he burst into Burrows's place, claiming to be in hot pursuit of a fleeing criminal. Not seeing the fugitive among the men at the bar, he demanded admission to Burrows's locked stockroom. There's no one in there, Burrows objected, and asked to see some evidence of Brown's authority. Brown drew a large revolver and pushed it into Burrows's face. "Here it is," he said. "I will kill you." Burrows, who was not easily intimidated, began to bellow, and his place quickly filled with curious men from the street outside. Looking around, Brown holstered his weapon and exited, muttering a string of obscenities. Burrows filed a charge of assault, but the county grand jury declined to hand down an indictment, and Brown continued to wear a badge. But in the municipal elections later that year, when he stood as a candidate for city marshal, he was defeated by an overwhelming vote.

A short time later Brown was arrested on a charge of violent assault. He had been among a group of half a dozen drunk Americans who assaulted Juan de Dios Ballesteros, a Californio, returning one evening from the tar pits at Rancho La Brea with a carreta loaded with bitumen or tar, used for waterproofing the flat roofs of the town's adobes. The Americans demanded that Ballesteros drive them out to an Indian encampment on the north side, where they hoped to find willing women. Ballesteros objected that his oxen were too tired, but the Americans piled aboard anyway. Their route took them across the Plaza at the heart of the pueblo, and as they passed the church one of the large wheels caught on a mile post, jolting the carreta and dumping one of the riders into the street. Brown shouted at Ballesteros to control his animals. The American picked himself up and angrily struck at one of the oxen, which jerked away impulsively, jolting the cart again. Erupting in rage, Brown pulled his revolver and fired point-blank at Ballesteros. "He shot four times at my uncle," Ballesteros's nephew testified at the trial, "and catching him by the hair, dragged him out of the cart onto the ground, and while down kept striking him on the head with the pistol." Ballesteros suffered a gunshot wound to his left arm as well as a fractured skull. It was a clear case of assault with intent to commit murder. But intimidated by the presence of several dozen Americans in the courtroom, Ballesteros proved reluctant to make a positive identification, and Brown was acquitted.

After that Brown worked for a time as a vaquero at Rancho Santa Ana del Chino, the largest cattle operation in southern California. On one occasion foreman John Rains, a fellow veteran of the Texas Mounted, dispatched him and a couple of other cowboys to Sonora to purchase cattle. For the return trip they hired several Sonoreños to assist with the drive. According to an Anglo who was present, Brown and one of the Mexicans got into a dispute and Brown shot him dead.

"We buried the poor man, and blamed Brown very much," the man wrote, "for he had no justifiable provocation for the deed." No one bothered to press charges.

Angry, volatile, and homicidal, Brown would not be called to account until he murdered fellow American Pinckney Clifford in the fall of 1854. Young Clifford was a hanger-on among the disorderly crowd of gamblers and shootists who haunted Los Angeles. Unlike most of the others, however, he held a steady job at Acron and Aikin's Livery on Calle Principal. He and Brown shared a room, and the rent was often paid by the admiring Clifford. Late one autumn evening Brown stopped by the livery stable on his way home. It was unseasonably cold, and Clifford suggested that Brown buy a couple of dollars' worth of kindling for the stove in their room. Brown, drunk as usual, took offense at Clifford telling him how to spend his money. He launched into a verbal tirade and quickly worked himself into a frothing rage. The more Clifford attempted to calm him, the angrier Brown became, until suddenly he pulled a knife and plunged it into his roommate's chest. Outraged bystanders seized him and delivered him to Sheriff Barton.

The next day a large procession of Clifford's friends and acquaintances followed the coffin to the American graveyard, a barren, windswept patch of ground atop Fort Moore Hill, adjacent to the crumbling ruin of the fort built by the Americans following the conquest in 1847. There was angry talk at the graveside. The men denounced Brown as a scourge on the community. Since the law proved unable to curb him, the time had come for vigilante action. In an attempt to tamp down the excitement, the authorities called a public meeting at the courthouse for that evening, but their plan nearly backfired. As soon as the meeting began a resolution was proposed and adopted declaring Brown guilty of murder and deserving of death. Speakers began to incite the crowd, and it seemed likely that a lynch mob was about to form.

At that point Mayor Stephen Clark Foster entered the room, mounted a table in front, and called for order. He fully expected, he said, that the county grand jury would indict Brown for murder and that he would be tried at the fall term of district court. Let the legally constituted justice system do its job. Give the authorities "one more chance" to secure justice by legal process. Foster then added a caveat that won the day. If, for whatever reason, Brown escaped conviction or punishment, the people would be fully justified in resorting to popular justice. If Dave Brown was not executed by the state of California, Mayor Foster pledged, "I will resign my office and assist you in hanging him myself."

THE GRAND JURY indicted Brown a few days later, Felipe Alvitre soon thereafter. They were confined to separate cells in the county jail, their arms and legs shackled in irons. When Alvitre's trial began in late November, the courtroom was outfitted with a new judge's bench, jury box, and attorney's desks, as well as benches for the public, which were packed by curious Angelenos. Lacking any physical evidence in the death of the Chilean, District Attorney Cameron E. Thom decided to try Alvitre only for the murder of James Ellington. On the advice of his court-appointed counsel, William G. Dryden, one of the few local attorneys who spoke fluent Spanish, Alvitre pled not guilty, despite his confession. Jury selection took up the first day, and by late afternoon Judge Hayes had seated a panel of six Californios and six Americans. There was no legal requirement for such ethnic balance, but everyone recognized that the credibility of the court was at stake.

The trial commenced the following morning, Saturday, November 26, 1854, with the examination of the prosecution's star witness, the Indian girl Innocencia, granted immunity in exchange for her testimony. With her account and Alvitre's confession, the state's case was open and shut, and Thom rested by midday. Dryden declined to put his client on the stand, so both attorneys made their closing arguments that afternoon. Thom simply reiterated the evidence, but Dryden, alternating between English and Spanish, delivered an emotional appeal focusing on the violent circumstances of Alvitre's upbringing. Jury deliberations began late in the afternoon, and after less than an hour the twelve men delivered a verdict of guilty. Hayes scheduled sentencing for the following Monday and spent his Sunday afternoon working on an address to the prisoner.

Completing his second year as elected district judge, Benjamin Hayes was at the center of efforts to strengthen the county's justice system. Although slight in stature, Hayes projected a fierce determination with his piercing steel-blue gaze. Thanks to Mayor Foster's pledge, Alvitre's trial had become a key test, and the remarks Hayes prepared for the sentencing were so conceived. He intended his address to Alvitre, he noted in his diary, "for the benefit of his young countrymen, who are betraying too many signs of hostility to Americans." Hayes wrote in fluent Spanish but was embarrassed by his poor pronunciation, so before the crowded courtroom on Monday he delivered his address in English, pausing after each paragraph for translation by the court interpreter.

"It is truly worthy of pity," Hayes began, "that one so young would be capable of perpetrating such a bloody and horrible crime." Alvitre's acts were those of a person "hardened and calloused like a stone, without a spark of humanity in his chest." Why had he killed James Ellington? "*¡Porqué era Americano!*" That had been Alvitre's answer. "Why this terrible hatred of Americans?" True, as his attorney had argued, Alvitre had grown up during "tumultuous times." He had been taught to think of violence as the appropriate response to conflict. But none of that mitigated his crime.

Hayes admitted that "too many have fallen into this hatred, under the influence of evil counsel, or perhaps because of small causes, abuses they have suffered, or because their elders have not instructed them in proper conduct." But the time had come to put bitter feelings aside and "learn the ways of peace—to become one and the same family, because we now all live under the same constitution and laws, and our interests and obligations are identical." What the ailing community required was the balm of righteous justice, which only the rule of law made possible. "The law protects all members of the community equally, whether American or not, and punishes the criminal with equal penalties according to the offense, no matter his country, his color, or his race." The trial itself, said Hayes, offered strong evidence of the law's impartiality. The proceedings had been conducted with the utmost fairness, and a jury of Alvitre's peers, half of them Californios, had found him guilty beyond a reasonable doubt. This was what justice looked like.

Hayes expected attorney Dryden to appeal the conviction to California's Supreme Court. "I will set the day of execution with sufficient time that the Court can consider the case." But, Hayes said, this was a mere formality, and he cautioned Alvitre not to be deceived. "I beg you not to foster illusions of hope, thinking you may escape justice," he told the young man. "I firmly believe everything was done right here. The sentence I will pronounce is not in my name, but in the name of the law, and the sentence will be carried out without fail." Then, after counseling the prisoner to spend his remaining days in prayerful contrition and penitence, Hayes formally delivered the sentence. "It is the judgment of this court that you, Felipe Alvitre, be returned to the County Jail of Los Angeles, to remain there until Friday, the 12th of January, on which day at 3 P.M. you will be taken to the place appointed for your execution, and there you shall be hanged by the neck until your life is extinguished. *Y que Dios tenga misericordia en vuestra alma.* And may God have mercy on your soul."

David Brown's trial began that same afternoon. To defend him Brown's friends had retained Jonathan R. Scott, Judge Hayes's former law partner, acknowledged to be the best defense attorney in Los Angeles. Scott immediately moved for a change of venue, charging that the local press had embittered the public mind against his client. He pointed to the remarks of editor John Ozias Wheeler in the weekly *Southern Californian* of Los Angeles, instructing "every officer of the court" to heed the people's demand for justice. "Should Brown be released," Wheeler had written, "we would not vouch for the consequences." After conducting a hearing on the matter, Hayes denied

Scott's motion, ruling that while the "tone of the press" was unfortunate there was not a shred of evidence that the views of the county's residents had been tainted. Scott continued to press the issue of prejudice, closely questioning prospective jurors and rejecting a number for cause. But by Tuesday afternoon a jury of nine Americans and three Californios had been seated.

The trial itself commenced and concluded the following day. There were several eyewitnesses to the crime, so the state's case was easily made. The jury retired in midafternoon and quickly returned with a verdict of guilty. Hayes pronounced sentence the following morning. In this instance, he felt no need for a lengthy statement from the bench, but he reinforced his argument about equality under the law by setting Brown's execution for the same day and time in January as Alvitre's. Hayes was proud of the accomplishment. Despite the threat of a lynching on the night of Brown's arrest, the system had been allowed to work, with Brown "duly tried and convicted."

"THERE IS NO ROOM left for cavil or doubt," editor James S. Waite, a staunch Democrat, wrote in the *Los Angeles Star*, "either as to the integrity of our courts, or to the determination of various officials to do all in their power to secure the ends of justice without fear or favor." In the rival *Southern Californian*, John Wheeler, a Whig and soon-to-be Republican, wrote that "the District Court has set an example. . . . We hope the convictions, and the certainty of an ignominious death, will forever hereafter have a tendency to put a stop to the reckless habits of many of the young men of our community."

The hopeful rhetoric ended on January 4, 1855, when the steamer from the north arrived with an official stay of execution for David Brown signed by Chief Justice Hugh C. Murray of the California Supreme Court. Suspending the execution of a condemned American while proceeding with the execution of a condemned Californio fed the worst suspicions of the Spanish-speaking majority. "So Alvitre is to be hanged alone," wrote Francisco P. Ramírez, young editor of the

Spanish-language section of the *Star*. He could hardly believe it. "If Brown's case was appealed, why not Alvitre's? Are not both equally guilty?" In the English-language pages of the same issue, editor Waite echoed the frustration of his young colleague. "There has been quite an excitement among the native Californians," he reported. "They say if Brown is worthy of a reprieve and a new trial, Alvitre is also entitled to the same." Waite believed they were right. Caution should be the watchword of the hour. Neither man should be hanged until the confusing circumstances were clarified.

Editor Wheeler did not share Waite's qualms. A Connecticut Yankee, he held strong beliefs regarding racial and ethnic justice. There could be only one reason why Brown had received a stay and Alvitre had not, he declared. "One happens to be an American, the other a Californian." Wheeler was also an enthusiastic vigilante, and he embraced the rhetoric of incitement. "Citizens of Los Angeles, it is for you to say whether this gross and outrageous partiality shall be allowed; whether you will permit so flagrant and glaring an evidence of the omnipotence of birth and conditions to operate in widening still further the breach that already exists between our native and foreign population, so prolific of future disaster to this community, . . . which we may all live to regret—perhaps in blood and tears."

On Thursday, January 11, the evening before the scheduled execution, a mass meeting of several hundred Angelenos, the majority of them Californios, adopted a resolution demanding that both Alvitre and Brown "be executed at the same time and on the same drop." A committee of three, delegated to meet with Sheriff Barton, found him in his office about midnight. If he did not agree to execute Brown, they explained, the residents of Los Angeles would mount a violent assault on the jail and hang him themselves. But Barton would not agree, insisting that he would follow the order of the court. Felipe Alvitre would hang, David Brown would not. "The Sheriff is determined to do his duty in carrying out the law at all hazards, having yesterday made his will and prepared himself for every emergency," the *Southern Californian* reported in an unusual extra edition rushed out the following morning. "Some fifteen or twenty men are prepared to stand by him to the death."

IN THE STANDARD TELLING, Los Angeles history begins with the first stirrings of the modern metropolis in the late nineteenth century. The city's earlier years are recalled, if recalled at all, as part of a familiar frontier narrative. Los Angeles, the mother of all western cow towns, flourishing a quarter century before the halcyon days of Dodge City, Kansas. Raucous saloons and gambling houses teeming with crowds of Indians and Californios, Mexicans and Americans. Violent men ambling down dusty streets, armed with Colt's revolvers and Bowie knives. Sheriffs and judges contending with vigilance committees and lynch mobs as well as rustlers and highwaymen. But a closer look reveals those characters acting in unexpected ways. A newspaper editor advocating lynch law in the name of racial justice, and hundreds of Spanish-speaking Californios massing to attack the county jail, determined to lynch an Anglo hooligan from Texas.

> *'Tis strange—but true; for truth is always strange;*
> *Stranger than fiction; if it could be told,*
> *How much would novels gain by the exchange!*
> *How differently the world would men behold!*

To fully tell this story—the triumph of a culture of violence in the struggle between official and outlaw justice—return to the origins of frontier Los Angeles. Fashioned not once but twice by violent conquest and occupation. Conceived in an assault of native homelands by men marching under the banner of heaven, then torn asunder by invaders pursuing their "manifest destiny to overspread the continent." With a diverse mix of peoples linked in relations of dominance and subordination. With structures of order so weak and ineffective that even the most enlightened men came to rely on mob rule and lynch law. What was the possibility for justice in such a place?

Murder and mayhem in edenic southern California. John A. Lewis, founding editor of the *Star,* was struck by the contradiction in 1853.

> There is no brighter sun, no milder clime, no more equable temperature, no scenes more picturesque, no greener valleys, no fairer plains in the wide world, than those we may look upon here. There is no country where nature is more lavish of her exuberant fullness; and yet, with all our natural beauties and advantages, there is no country where human life is of so little account. Men hack one another to pieces with pistols and other cutlery as if God's image were of no more worth than the life of one of the two or three thousand ownerless dogs that prowl about our streets and make night hideous.

LA noir *avant la lettre.* This self-crafted narrative, drawn from direct experience, is one of the oldest stories Angelenos tell about themselves.

PART ONE

· CHAPTER 1 ·

A PEOPLE ANGRY AND ARMED

IN 1836, when Los Angeles was under the jurisdiction of the Mexican republic, Angelenos organized the pueblo's first *comité de vigilancia* and carried out an extralegal execution in response to the murder of a fellow citizen. News of the incident spread rapidly through California. The governor, outraged at this gross circumvention of legal procedure, threatened the vigilantes with jail or worse. But in the end no action was taken against them. Indeed, the spokesman for the vigilantes became an aide to Juan Bautista Alvarado, a Californio from Monterey who later that same year led a political revolt against Mexican authority and was chosen by his fellow revolutionaries to be their new governor. Alvarado heaped praise on the Los Angeles vigilantes, arguing that their independent spirit had inspired his movement, inaugurating what he called "a new era in California history."

According to Alvarado, the people were "like a sleeping lion," peaceful and contented in slumber, but fierce and unconquerable if rudely awakened. When red tape or corruption prevented the prompt punishment of vicious criminals, he counted on the people to rise up. *Justica popular*, he declared, was something he had always supported. By the time Alvarado expressed those views, in the memoirs he dictated in 1876, near the end of his life, the roar of popular justice had been heard hundreds of times in California, resulting in the excution by vigilance committees or mobs of nearly three hundred individuals, more than fifty in Los Angeles County alone.

The man whose murder provoked that first episode of lynch law in Los Angeles was José Domingo Féliz, a Californio born in 1805 at Mission San Gabriel and raised to manhood in the family adobe at Rancho Los Féliz, where the foothills slide down to the Los Angeles River, known then as the Río Porciúncula. In those days Los Angeles and the surrounding countryside was a hardscrabble place, home to several thousand Indians and a few hundred Spanish-speaking settlers. In 1829, at the age of twenty-three, Don Domingo married María del Rosario Villa, familiarly known as Charo, the fourteen-year-old daughter of an upstanding family. During the first three years of their marriage she bore two children, both of whom died in infancy. After that there were no more births. Trouble had developed between husband and wife, and in 1834, after five years of marriage, nineteen-year-old Charo left Rancho Los Féliz and took up with Gervasio Alipás, a Californio who worked at Rancho Los Alamitos on the coast, thirty miles south. Her husband had driven her away with his philandering, she explained to friends. But the claim generated little sympathy. Men might be sexual aggressors, but wives, nonetheless, had to be submissive. Yet Charo flaunted her relationship with Alipás, marking her as a *chingada*, a whore, in the eyes of the community.

For nearly two years Don Domingo tried to persuade his wife to return. But she scorned him and delighted in humiliating him in the presence of her lover. On one such occasion, at a tavern in the rural community of Los Nietos, the two men came to blows. Alipás was a thickset vaquero, or cowboy, virile and vigorous, Féliz a slight caballero, or gentleman, afflicted with a pronounced limp, the result of a childhood injury for which he acquired the cruel nickname of "*el güilo*," the gimp. To the surprise of everyone present, however, before they were pulled apart it was Don Domingo who drew first blood. Alipás swore to have his revenge.

Divorce was not permitted under Mexican law. Civil authorities were empowered to compel husband and wife to live together "*como Díos manda*," as God commands. Reaching the limit of his patience, in the early spring of 1836 Féliz sought and received a warrant from Alcalde Manuel Requena, chief civil officer of the pueblo, authorizing him to bring his fugitive wife home. Early on the morning of March 24, accompanied by his brother Antonio, Féliz rode to Mission San Gabriel and presented the warrant to the mission's civil administrator. It was the mission's annual feast day, featuring food, acrobatic performances, and plenty of dancing. Féliz expected his errant wife and her cowboy lover to be there, and it pained him to think of them parading his shame before the community. He found her alone—Alipás had not yet arrived—and despite her resistance he and his brother forced her to accompany them back to the pueblo. On their way they were overtaken by Dámaso Alipás, brother of Charo's lover. Several years earlier the Alipás brothers had participated in a revolt that overthrew the Mexican governor, and they enjoyed a reputation for reckless violence. But seeing that it was two against one, Dámaso contented himself with making an obscene gesture and shouting a threat: "*¡Hoy las Féliz mueres!*" Today the Félizes die!

Not long thereafter the Féliz brothers arrived at the Los Angeles home of their maternal aunt, María Luisa Cota de López, widow of the late *mayordomo* of Mission San Gabriel, a woman celebrated for her hospitality as well as her cooking. She greeted Charo with open arms and prepared a sumptuous feast in honor of "the lost lamb who has been found." Don Domingo's father, Francisco Féliz, joined them for the meal, which proceeded with surprising equanimity. In the meantime, Gervasio Alipás had arrived at the neighboring adobe, which belonged to his uncle, and that evening he managed to signal his presence to Charo. At midnight, supposing everyone was asleep, she attempted to leave the house but was stopped by her father-in-law. In a fateful decision, Don Francisco chose not to mention the incident to his son.

The following morning the estranged couple visited with Assistant

Alcalde Tiburcio Tapia, a wealthy merchant and ranchero who resided in a townhouse facing the Plaza. Tapia scolded Charo for her scandalous conduct, but he urged Don Domingo to forgive her, advising the couple to patch up their differences and reestablish domestic "peace and harmony." Both pledged to do their best and departed together. As they made their way back to Doña Luisa's, they were watched by Alipás, who was lurking in the shadows of an adjacent garden. He returned to his uncle's house in an ugly mood. Pulling a large knife from his boot, he began to sharpen it on a whetstone, mumbling to himself that he would "make a party for Charo and her gimp."

Early the next day Don Domingo made preparations to depart with his wife for Rancho Los Féliz, some eight miles upriver. Brother Antonio had to run an errand, and fearful of an assault by the Alipás brothers he requested that Don Domingo wait for his return that they might ride together. But as soon as Don Antonio departed Charo began to pester her husband. "Why wait for your brother? I suppose you're afraid, but what can happen? Let's go." Doña Luisa urged them to linger over a leisurely breakfast, but indulging his wife, Don Domingo harnessed his mare, looped his sash over the pommel of his saddle to form a makeshift stirrup, and lifting his wife into position, seated himself behind on the mare's rump, a common way for young married couples to ride. Doña Luisa bid them goodbye as they headed off. She watched as her nephew removed his sombrero and gallantly waved farewell. She saw him place the hat on his wife's head to protect her from the morning sun. She noted the silk bandana tied about the crown of his head in the fashion of the day. The details long remained vivid for her, since it was the last time she saw her nephew alive.

LATER THAT AFTERNOON a boy discovered the mare, still fully saddled, grazing in a field beside the river, about two miles north of the pueblo. Recognizing the animal as Doña Luisa's, he led it back to her casa. Sitting under her arbor, the elderly woman saw them approaching and immediately feared the worst. "My heart tells me Don Domingo is dead, that he has been murdered," she cried. The alcalde was summoned, and he raised a search party. Several hours later they discovered Don Domingo's mangled body in a shallow gully between the river and the *zanja madre*, the pueblo's main irrigation ditch. His face was disfigured with frightful gashes, his bandana soaked with blood, his neck badly bruised. Weeping bitterly, family and friends placed his body in a sling and slowly carried it back to the pueblo.

Gervasio Alipás was the obvious suspect. Several witnesses reported seeing him earlier that day, riding furiously in the direction of the crime scene. While authorities organized a posse, members of the Féliz family clustered about the victim's body in the church rectory, surrounded by burning tapers. Late that evening their mourning was interrupted by the sound of horsemen on the Plaza. The posse had returned with Alipás, whom they found hiding in the rolling hills north of town. An angry crowd formed. The treacherous murder of such a important person, the people cried, demanded immediate punishment. Don Domingo was a direct descendant of the pueblo's founders, the maternal great-grandson of original settler Roque Jacinto Cota, the paternal grandson of Corporal José Vicente Féliz, known as "the little father of the pueblo," who for his service to the community was granted the seven thousand acres of rolling hills and grassland that became Rancho Los Féliz. The extended Féliz-Cota family included some of the most important people in Los Angeles.

"Death to Gervasio!" the crowd shouted. "Death to the monster!" But a minority of those present objected. They urged patience and argued that the manner in which guilt or innocence was established was as important as the punishment itself. The community required justice not vengeance. No one yet knew the fate of María del Rosario Villa. Had she too been murdered and her body hidden, or was she an accomplice to the crime, as many suspected? Let passions cool and allow the law to guide the people toward righteous justice. Those arguments succeeded in calming the crowd. Alcalde Requena ordered Alipás clamped in irons and secured in the adobe jail on the Plaza, beside the church.

The following day was Palm Sunday, the commencement of *semana santa*, Holy Week, when all parishioners were expected to attend confession and receive communion. Most families came in from the countryside for church services, and many remained for Don Domingo's funeral the following morning. The horror of the crime and the prominence of the victim attracted one of the largest crowds in living memory. Following a requiem mass at the Plaza church, the shroud-wrapped body was laid on a wooden slab and carried to the adjacent *campo santo* (graveyard), where it was placed in a coffin and lowered into the grave. The priest delivered the final benediction to the accompaniment of a chorus of weeping and wailing women. Following the burial, the victim's kinsmen lingered at the graveside, scarcely able to contain their anger and frustration. Charo was still missing and Alcalde Requena had yet to open an official investigation. After heated discussion the men present agreed to an oath: "We swear by the bloody remains of our compatriot to exterminate the odious villains who murdered him at the risk of our honor and our lives." The desire for vengeance was strong.

The following morning searchers found Charo, wandering aimlessly in the hills north of town, disheveled and frightened. Alcalde Requena ordered her secured in a private house, then proceeded to interrogate the suspects separately. Both confessed their parts in the murder. Alipás told of his rage as he watched Charo depart for Rancho Los Féliz with her husband. He had taken a shortcut through the rolling hills and hid in the chaparral by the side of the road, waiting for them to come up. Charo admitted to hoping for rescue by her lover, but also her shock when Don Domingo was suddenly jerked from the rear of the mare by Gervasio's *reata*. Looking back she saw her husband writhing in the dust, her lover standing over him, knife in hand. His intention, Alipás told Requena, was to kill them both, but that suddenly changed when he heard Charo urge him on. "Strike, Gervasio, strike," she cried, "I shall be your reward." Whipped into a frenzy by those words, Alipás hacked at the defenseless husband, reducing his face to a bloody pulp. Charo acknowledged helping Alipás drag the body into a gully before they fled to a hiding place in the hills. There they remained, barely speaking to each other as afternoon turned to evening. Finally, hearing the approach of the posse, Alipás allowed himself to be captured, leaving Charo hidden in the chaparral, hoping she might find a way to escape. It was his single act of gallantry.

THE KINSMEN OF DON DOMINGO had little expectation of satisfaction from the drawn-out process of the law. Alcalde Requena, whose office combined executive and judicial responsibilities, was charged with carrying out the investigation, compiling the evidence, then conducting a hearing during which he questioned witnesses, made a determination of guilt, and pronounced sentence. An educated man from the Sonoran port of Guaymas, Requena operated a retail establishment near the Plaza and enjoyed a reputation for fair dealing. Angelenos trusted his judgment, but they knew that whatever his decision, it would not be final. In cases of homicide the law provided for automatic appeal. But since there was no higher court in California, the case would be heard in Mexico City, nearly two thousand miles away, a process that would take months, if not years. That was unacceptable. Justice delayed was justice denied. The murderers had confessed, and the family wanted a speedy hearing and summary punishment.

By Good Friday the public agitation had become so pronounced that Alcalde Requena convened an extraordinary meeting of the ayuntamiento, the town council, and persuaded the regidores, or councilmen, to adopt a resolution: "Whomsoever shall disturb the public tranquility shall be punished according to law." The agitators responded, promising not to "shed blood so impure during the period when the Savior of the world poured forth his blood most holy." But they accompanied that assurance with a call for a public meeting at the conclusion of Holy Week, making it clear that they had no intention of dropping their demand for summary justice. A spring storm blew up on Easter Sunday and heavy rain continued for several days, forcing postponement of the meeting. But the weather finally cleared, and on Thursday morning a group of several dozen Angelenos assembled at the house of merchant Jonathan Temple, a naturalized Mexican citizen from Massachusetts and husband of María Raphaela Cota, first cousin of the victim.

The meeting opened with the selection of schoolmaster Victor Prudon as presiding officer. Chosen for his skill with words, Prudon did not disappoint, with an opening address that staked out the moral high ground. "I am a foreigner," he told the assembled Angelenos, "born in the free land of France, distant from your own. I reached manhood in Mexico City, the capital of your country, where I passed the florid years of my youth, my inborn sentiments of liberty and philanthropy made strong by the examples offered on the part of the Mexican people." After a period of wandering, searching for a place to make his fortune, he had landed in California. "I have adopted as my own this land of yours," Prudon said. "I wish to share your lot and I support your view of things."

Unrestrained violence in the community, he declared, threatened public security, "the shield of protection for our rights, families, and possessions." Decisive action was required. They could no longer afford legal formalities. Violent men must be shown that Angelenos would no longer tolerate their crimes. Their common objectives were "beneficent, just, and necessary," and Prudon proposed that the assembled men constitute themselves as a *junta popular*, a committee for the defense of public safety, to ensure that justice was secured in Los Angeles. The men endorsed his proposal by acclamation. To avoid any charge that they were motivated by private vengeance rather than public justice, they selected as their leaders three men without any family connections in the community: Prudon as chairman, a Mexican attorney named Manuel Arzaga as secretary, and a retired army officer named Francisco Araujo as sergeant at arms.

Prudon managed to keep the meeting orderly despite some incendiary speakers, and after an hour of debate the Angelenos cast a unanimous vote in favor of the immediate execution of the murderers.

Prudon and Arzaga prepared a petition addressed to Alcalde Requena to which fifty-five men affixed their signatures or marks. Don Francisco, the victim's father, signed first, and many of those who followed were relations of the extended Féliz-Cota family. But a slim majority were unrelated to the victim. They included former municipal officials and prominent rancheros. Jonathan Temple, informal leader of the small émigré community and host of the meeting, enlisted the support of a score of extranjeros (foreigners), including a number of Americans, most of them married to daughters of the country. The signing completed, Prudon and Arzaga left to deliver the petition to the ayuntamiento, which was already meeting in emergency session, while Araujo marched the men to the pueblo's small armory, ordered the door forced open, and supervised the distribution of arms.

It was two in the afternoon when Alcalde Requena read the junta's petition aloud to the seven members of the ayuntamiento. Prudon had inscribed it with a Latin motto taken from French political philosopher Montesquieu: "salus populi suprema lex est"—the welfare of the people is the supreme law. Acting in the name of the people, the petition read, the undersigned citizens declared María del Rosario Villa de Féliz and Gervasio Alipás guilty of the brutal murder of José Domingo Féliz. While they took no pleasure in superseding the institutions of the Mexican republic, their action was necessitated by the frequency of lethal violence in Los Angeles, which threatened "a state of anarchy where the might of the strongest is the only law." The petition continued,

> The blood still reeks of other unfortunate victims. . . . Their bloody ghosts cry out for vengeance. Their trembling voices re-echo from the grave. The afflicted widow, the forsaken orphan, the ancient father, the mourning brother, the inconsolable mother, and the general public all demand speedy and solemn justice. We swear to have it today or die trying. The blood of the murderers must be shed today, or ours will be, to the last drop. The world shall know that if judges in Los

Angeles tolerate murder, there are virtuous citizens willing to sacrifice their lives to insure those of their countrymen.

If Alcalde Requena declined to execute the "infernal couple" in the name of the state, the junta demanded that he hand them over to be executed in the name of the people themselves. Requena had one hour to decide. "If no answer has been received by then, he will be responsible before God and the public for what will follow. Death to the murderers!"

As Requena finished reading, the regidores heard a clamor on the Plaza and, looking out, they saw a large assembly of armed citizens. Assistant Alcalde Tapia went out to confront them. What was the meaning of this gathering under arms? Victor Prudon stepped forward. They had come in pursuit of justice, he said. The law made no provision for the direct intervention of the people, Tapia responded. Prudon declined to debate the point. The petition speaks for itself, he said. Tapia returned to the chamber. The regidores fretted, but they had neither the moral nor the physical authority to enforce their will. After some time Prudon sent in a note reminding them that the hour had nearly passed. "An immediate answer is desired, and if it is not forthcoming, the junta shall be obliged to take extraordinary measures." Left without options, the regidores passed a resolution rejecting the junta's demand and authorizing Requena to prepare a full report to the governor. Then they adjourned and went home. Juan Bautista Alvarado put it succinctly in his memoirs. The ayuntamiento "chose not to wage a lonely struggle against a people angry and armed"— *airado y armado*—"in defense of their rights."

Prudon then ordered his men to surround the jail and disarm the guard. They found Alipás in his cell, shackled in irons. A blacksmith was summoned, and he quickly discovered that the prisoner, using a small file hidden in his boot, had nearly cut through the chain connecting his handcuffs. "You did well not to delay," said Alipás with a smile. "Had I more time I would have cut my chains, and when the jailer came with my meal I would have delivered the stroke and secured my freedom." Prudon read aloud the junta's verdict, then ordered a detachment to escort the condemned man to the place chosen for the execution, at the summit of the hill behind the church.

Angelenos thronged the Plaza and crowded the flat roofs of the surrounding adobes to catch a view of the spectacle. Alipás did not resist, and a twelve-man firing squad completed the execution without ceremony. Prudon then sent several men to fetch María del Rosario Villa de Féliz. For the crime of husband-murder the junta had sentenced her to gaze upon the body of her dead lover for an hour before she too was executed. But she was so overcome with fear that the vigilantes took pity on her. They dragged her up the hill and dispatched her without delay.

Thus ended the first episode of popular justice in Los Angeles. As the crowd watched in silence, the men carried the bodies down the hillside to the Plaza and laid them on the ground before the jail, exposing them to public display in the fading light of the spring afternoon. The following morning they were interred in the *campo santo* beside the church. Father Pedro Cabot, Franciscan missionary at Mission San Fernando, some twenty-five miles northwest of the pueblo, tersely recorded their deaths in the parish register. "Both died by execution," he wrote, "without receiving the sacraments."

· CHAPTER 2 ·

REDUCED TO OBEDIENCE

THE ARCHIVE OF MEXICAN LOS ANGELES, although incomplete, records five homicides committed in the pueblo and vicinity during the two years preceding José Domingo Féliz's murder in 1836. For a community of only several hundred residents, that amounted to an alarmingly high frequency of homicide, at least three times the rate of the more established communities of the Mexican heartland, an order of magnitude higher than that in the most violent of American cities today. High enough to rouse the sleeping lion.

People kill other people for all kinds of reasons. For big causes, for petty trifles, or just for the hell of it. But social forces contribute to the frequency of homicide. Frontiers throughout North America were characterized by rampant conflict, and Mexican Los Angeles was no exception. The conquest of Indian homelands left a bitter legacy of continuing struggle, not only between indigenous peoples and colonizers, but among the colonizers themselves, who grew habituated to bloodshed. Ineffective law enforcement and feeble institutions of justice on the periphery of the nation-state meant that disputes were often settled privately, resulting in ongoing feuds and vendettas. In the absence of state authority, social order was more often a function of honor than of law, and honor frequently amounted to little more than one man's ability to dominate other men, to live by the declaration, as Mexicans put it, "*a me no me manda nadie*"—no one orders me around.

Interpersonal violence also increases during periods of rapid social change, when institutions are challenged and communities transformed. And despite the persistent fiction that Mexico was a "lax, lazy, land of *mañana*"—a place where everything was put off until the morrow—during the two decades that preceded the American conquest, Mexican California experienced a remarkable social and economic transformation. Some months before the Féliz murder Alcalde Requena conducted a census of the Los Angeles region—from the mountains to the sea, from the jurisdiction of Santa Barbara in the north to San Diego in the south—and counted a total of 2,228 residents. Although that number is minuscule compared with the great metropolis that would later arise, it marked a growth of more than 60 percent in only six years. Californios were very fertile and their families quite large, but that had long been true, and it did not account for the growth over such a short period.

The surging population was part of the social and economic revolution overtaking the region. California's Franciscan missions were undergoing "secularization"—their lands transferred to private ownership and their labor force, the converted mission Indians, or *neófitos*, released from bondage. Emancipados, as former mission Indians were called, were going to work for the rising landowing class of rancheros and vineyardists. The number of Indian workers residing in and around the pueblo more than doubled from 1830 to 1836, by which time they accounted for nearly a quarter of the population. The convulsive birth of a market economy also attracted migrants from the south, and by 1836 migrants from Sonora made up some 20 percent of the district's residents. Educated men such as Manuel Requena or Victor Prudon were welcomed warmly by Angelenos. But vagabonds and unemployed vaqueros were regarded with a wary eye.

Californios attributed the increasing violence in their community to emancipated Indians and migrants. "I am disgusted to see my country so much under the influence of these devils," one ranchero wrote. They were "out of control," another agreed, "committing robberies and other crimes." The case files of the alcalde's office support these concerns. Emancipados were responsible for considerably more than their proportional share of violent crime, although for the most part they targeted other Indians. Mexicans were even more combative, and what was worse, much of their violence was directed at Californios. "There are here a greater number of scamps than of honorable men," one official reported from Los Angeles a few weeks before the Féliz murder. "They will stick the blade and hilt into us, so long as the administration of justice remains paralyzed."

DESPITE THE FOCUS OF ANGELENOS on the increasing incidence of murder, lethal violence had long been part of their experience. It originated in the turmoil of colonial conquest. Fearful of encroachments by the British or Russians, Spaniards invaded California with plans to transform the region into a buffer colony to protect the silver mines of northern Mexico. Lacking the large, mobile settler populations of the British colonies on the Atlantic coast, their strategy was to transform indigenous Indian peoples into a colonial workforce. The natives of California, Spanish monarch Carlos III decreed in 1770, should be "taught Christianity and reduced to obedience to my Royal officials." Missionaries of the Franciscan order, supported by soldiers of the frontier army, were to concentrate the *gentiles*—the Spanish term for unconverted Indians—at mission compounds, where they would be converted to the Catholic faith and taught to labor in the fields, transforming them into what one early governor of California described as "useful vassals for our religion and state."

The Spaniards assured themselves that the conquest and incorporation of native peoples into the empire was righteous and just because it provided them with temporal civilization and heavenly salvation. In the words of one missionary: "Shall we think that God created these men merely to condemn them to Inferno, after passing in this world a life so miserable as that which they live?" The theory was that once the Indians had been Christianized and Hispanicized, they would be restored to their original position as the lawful proprietors of the soil, with all the privileges and responsibilities of other subjects of the Spanish crown. To the natives, who expressed no discontent with the existing state of their world, the justice of the conquest was not so clear. The promised return of their lands in the distant future offered slight consolation. Yet it was a pledge they would remember. The manner in which Spanish authorities operated the missions, as well as the manner in which Mexican authorities would decommission them, exposed the promise for the lie it was.

In 1771 Franciscan missionaries founded Mission San Gabriel Archángel, the fourth of what would become a string of twenty-one California missions stretching from San Diego to Sonoma. Over the subsequent half century the mission fathers at San Gabriel baptized some twenty-five thousand converts. The *Gabrieleños*, as the missionaries called the *neófitos* of San Gabriel, not only produced their own sustenance but provided abundant material support for the entire colonial enterprise in California. By 1821, the year Mexico won its independence from Spain after a decade of violent struggle, the *neófitos* at San Gabriel tended large herds of cattle and horses, worked extensive fields of wheat, corn, and beans, as well as vineyards and orchards, and labored in workshops producing leather, pottery, bricks, candles, soap, and other domestic goods. Under the direction of Father José María de Zalvidea and his *mayordomo* Claudio López—uncle of José Domingo Féliz—Mission San Gabriel won a well-deserved reputation as the very model of Indian productivity.

But that achievement came at the cost of significant violence, reproduced over several generations. The local inhabitants had permitted the missionaries to establish their first outpost at the narrows of Río San Gabriel, but soon they fell victim to the violence of frontier soldiers. According to Junípero Serra, father-president of the California missions, "the soldiers, clever as they are at lassoing cows and mules, would catch an Indian woman with their lassos to become prey to their unbridled lust." The soldiers thought of native women as the spoils of conquest, and they "shot down with bullets" any native man who dared to intervene. The soldiers were incorrigible, Serra complained. "Even the young boys who came to the mission were not safe from their baseness." The terror at the narrows did not abate until 1775, when a powerful winter storm turned the river into a torrent, destroying the mission compound and forcing the Franciscans to relocate to higher ground, several miles northwest. The Indians who resided at *el misión vieja*, the old mission site, as the area became known, celebrated the move as a liberation. They remained implacable foes of the padres.

FOR THE NATIVE PEOPLES of southern California, who spoke half a dozen languages and dialects and lived in hundreds of autonomous rancherías, organizing a unified resistance to the Spanish invasion proved impossible. "They had little basis for recognizing or understanding the colonial structure which eventually engulfed them," one historian concludes. In exchange for food, clothing, and other goods, Indians went to work for the missionaries, constructing buildings, digging irrigation ditches, and planting crops. Initially few showed any interest in conversion and baptism, but over time many became devout Catholics. Their theological understanding may have been deficient, but no more so than that of ordinary parishioners elsewhere in Christendom.

The native people of southern California were also pushed to the mission by an ecological crisis set in motion by colonization. Over millennia the Indians had used fire to keep down the growth of trees and encourage the abundance of grasses on the hillsides and plains, creating a landscape suited to their gathering economy, which utilized grasses, tubers, nuts, and small game. But that environment turned out to be perfect for the livestock economy of the Spaniards. Rapidly multiplying herds of cattle voraciously consumed and trampled native plants, crippling the indigenous economy in a very few years. By itself this would have been a disaster, but accompanied by the introduction of previously unknown diseases—waterborne bacterial and viral infections like typhoid and hepatitis, as well as sexually transmitted diseases such as gonorrhea and syphilis—it amounted to a catastrophe. By the late 1770s irrigation agriculture was producing abundant crops at Mission San Gabriel, and the availability of food was the single greatest inducement for Indians who, in the words of one Franciscan, were "very poor on account of the scarcity of wild seeds and game." Desperately hungry Indians, in the candid words of another missionary, were "usually caught by the mouth." As for disease, there was simply nothing to be done about it. Sickness and death cast an everlasting pall over the missions.

There was sporadic resistance. A rebellion at Mission San Diego in 1775—provoked by the abuse of native women—cost the lives of three Spaniards, including a priest. Ten years later the residents of several rancherías near Mission San Gabriel organized another uprising, planning to enter the mission at night, overwhelm the guard, and murder the mission fathers as they slept. But the rebels were betrayed by one of their own. The largest revolt took place among the Chumash people of the Santa Barbara vicinity in 1824. Buildings were sacked and hundreds of *neófitos* fled to the interior before Mexican soldiers succeeded in crushing them.

Conversion, the Franciscans insisted, was voluntary. Yet once natives agreed to baptism they lost their individual independence. At San Gabriel *neófitos* were required to live in cramped dormitories, with unmarried women segregated in a separate, locked facility to protect their chastity. They were required to wear a common costume, shirts of drab woolen or cotton cloth that hung below their thighs. They were obligated to schedule their lives by the tolling of mission bells that summoned them to the fields, to their meals, their prayers, and their nightly curfew. Mission life required a radical break with traditional ways, and it comes as no surprise that many Indians suffered buyers' remorse and attempted to escape. Fugitivism decimated the ranks at Mission San Gabriel. The most determined runaways joined resisting bands in the mountains or deserts. The Franciscans treated fugitivism as a serious problem, for not only did it deprive them of converts and workers, but it encouraged others to do likewise. So the missionaries instructed the soldiers to bring the runaways back by any means necessary. *Neófitos* hauled back to the mission were subjected to severe punishment.

Franciscan punishment included short rations, solitary confinement, and public humiliation, but the most common penance was flogging. The lash was the universal symbol of discipline in Hispanic culture. Missionaries beat Indians, just as masters beat servants, husbands beat wives, and parents beat children. *Neófitos* were whipped not only for running away but for shirking work, missing chapel, or violating the European sexual mores so dear to the celibate Franciscans. Father Zalvidea of Mission San Gabriel, a dedicated pastor and brilliant manager, believed deeply in the value of corporal punishment. A ranchero described Zalvidea as "a man of talent," with a mind "as ambitious as it was powerful, and as cruel as it was ambitious." Not only did he punish the Indians severely, "but he was, in his chastisements, most cruel." He "must assuredly have considered whipping as meat and drink to them, for they had it morning, noon and night." Zalvidea saw evil lurking everywhere, including his own soul. "He struggled constantly with the devil," one *neófito* testified, and in an attempt to overcome his wicked impulses "constantly flogged himself, wore haircloth, drove nails into his feet, and, in short, tormented himself in a manner most cruel."

In the Spanish rhetoric of empire, the Indians of California were "reduced to obedience." The program succeeded all too literally. Historians estimate that when Spanish colonization began in the 1770s coastal California was home to some 60,000 native people. Over the subsequent half century that number fell by nearly two-thirds. At Mission San Gabriel the death rate outpaced the birthrate by two to one, meaning that from the beginning the survival of the mission community depended on the recruitment of new converts. Eventually the supply of unconverted Indians ran short. The number of *neófitos* at San Gabriel peaked at 1,701 in 1817 and fell precipitously thereafter. Even the Franciscans had to acknowledge the pathos of their project. "The Indian population is declining," the father-president of the missions wrote in 1820. "They live well free, but as soon as we reduce them to a Christian and community life they decline in health. They fatten, sicken, and die."

THE PUEBLO OF LOS ANGELES arose in the shadow of the mission at San Gabriel. It began as a project of the Spanish military, skeptical of the ability of the missions to supply the soldiers garrisoned at California's four presidios. The advantages of the site where the pueblo was planted were first noted by Franciscan missionary Juan Crespi, a diarist with the Gaspar de Portolá expedition of 1769. "We entered a very spacious valley, well grown with cottonwoods and alders," he wrote, "among which ran a beautiful river from the north-northwest, and then, doubling the point of a steep hill, went on afterwards to the south." The river he christened *Nuestra Señora de los Angeles de Porciúncula*, in honor of the Italian birthplace of the Franciscan order. Even during the dry summer, when Crespi first saw it, the river ran high as it passed through the notch in the hills. That would be a good location for a dam diverting water for irrigation, he reasoned. Continuing southward, the river fanned out across the floodplain, depositing rich sediment that invited cultivation. "The soil is black and loamy, capable of producing every kind of grain and fruit which may be planted," Crespi wrote. The site, he concluded, had "all the requisites for a large settlement."

Indeed, a village called Yang-na, with several hundred residents, was already located there. From the east side of the river, Crespi saw several dozen dome-shaped structures scattered amid stands of timber along the river's west bank. As he and his companions surveyed the scene, a group of eight men, "as naked as Adam in Paradise before he sinned," emerged from the trees and made their way across a shallow ford in the river, chanting songs and smoking clay pipes. They bore gifts, grass baskets brimming with pine nuts and strings of beautiful shell discs. "We gave them a little tobacco and glass beads," Crespi noted, "and they went away well pleased."

Yang-na was still there a dozen years later, on September 4, 1781, when soldiers from Mission San Gabriel, under the command of Corporal José Vicente Féliz—grandfather of José Domingo Féliz— escorted the original group of pobladores, or settlers, to the site. The eleven families—twenty-three adults and twenty-one children—had come overland from northern New Spain several weeks before. Following instructions issued by the military governor, Féliz oversaw the laying out of *el pueblo de la Reyna de los Angeles*—the town of the Queen of the Angels—immediately north of the ranchería, and remained with the settlers to supervise the location of a plaza, the distribution of house lots and fields, and the construction of a dam and the *zanja madre*, the mother ditch channeling water from the river for irrigation and domestic use. Having proved his talent for administration, Féliz won appointment as *comisionado*, charged with oversight of the security of the new pueblo.

Almost immediately the residents of Yang-na went to work for the pobladores. Although they would suffer many of the same negative effects of colonization as the *neófitos*, these people continued to enjoy their own autonomous community life. They labored in the fields planted along the river and worked as muleteers, water carriers, or domestic servants. Social mixing between Indians and settlers was common and extensive. The pobladores themselves, classified in official documents as *mestizos* and *mulattos*, were the offspring of several generations of mixing in Mexico, although they claimed status as *gente de razón*, people of reason, a term that said less about race than about culture. Indians were classified as people without reason, *sin razón*, but that certainly didn't prevent colonists from engaging with them. Some pobladores learned the native language, and a number of men married native women. That kind of easy sociability worried the authorities. Military governor Pedro de Fages objected to "the pernicious familiarity prevailing in the pueblo with the *gentiles*," and introduced rules designed to separate the two groups. Indians would no longer be permitted to enter the homes of pobladores and would be required to return to their ranchería at night. Such rules were honored more in the breach than in the observance.

The Franciscans didn't like what was transpiring at the pueblo any better than the military authorities. The Angelenos were "a set of idlers," one missionary complained. "For them the Indian is errand-boy, vaquero, and digger of ditches—in short, general factotum. Confident that the *gentiles* are working, the pobladores pass the day singing. The young men wander on horseback through the rancherías soliciting the women to immorality." There was truth to the complaint, but it also reflected a resentment about *gentiles* who might avoid the mission yet enjoy the benefits of civilization by working for the settlers. The Indians of Los Angeles "should have been the first to receive Holy Baptism," another Franciscan grumbled, yet they "still abide in the shadows of paganism."

The chorus of complaint continued as long as the Franciscans remained in California. "If there is anything to be done, the Indian has to do it," Father-President Narciso Durán wrote after a visit to Los Angeles in 1831, the pueblo's fiftieth anniversary. "If he fails to do it, nothing will be done. Is anything to be planted? The Indian must do it. Is the wheat to be harvested? Let the Indian come. Are adobes or tiles to be made, a house to be erected, a corral to be built, wood to be hauled, water to be brought for the kitchen? Let the Indian do it." Meanwhile, for Angelenos "it is walk about, play the gentleman, eat, be idle, generally at the cost of the Indian's hard labor, so that in reality it seems as if nature had destined the Indian to be the slave of the *gente de razón*." It was an ironic conclusion, coming as it did from the chief executive officer of an institution founded and maintained on the forced labor of *neófitos*.

THE HARD DEMOGRAPHIC FACTS of the California missions—the exceptionally high mortality and low fertility of *neófitos*—determined that the recently converted, most of them deficient in civilized comportment, were always in the majority. In theory, the missionaries held Indian property in trust against the day when *neófitos* were judged capable of autonomous life, at which time they were supposed to be emancipated, provided with their fair share of mission land and other property, and organized into self-governing pueblos, a process known as *secularización*. But under the prevailing circumstances Franciscan missionaries could not envision a future in which their "Indian children" would be sufficiently mature to govern themselves. "According to the laws, the natives are to be free from tutelage at the end of ten years," the governor noted in 1796. "But those of California, at the rate they are advancing, will not reach the goal in ten centuries."

The pressure to secularize the missions came from the rising generation of California colonists, the sons of soldiers and territorial officials. After Mexico won its independence from Spain in 1821, this new generation began to refer to themselves as *hijos del país* and Californios. Many of them embraced the values espoused by Mexican liberals—individualism, republicanism, and free trade. The new Mexican congress swept away the mercantile restrictions of the Spanish period and opened California's ports to the world. Strong international demand for shoe leather and candles stimulated a booming trade in cattle hide and tallow. Why should all that revenue go to the church? The time had come, these young Californios argued, to privatize mission land, emancipate the Indians, then set them to work for a new class of landowners. Secularization of the missions was their prime objective, the Californio version of liberty.

The initial attempt at secularization in California came from José María Echeandía, the first appointed governor following the adoption of Mexico's 1824 republican constitution. A well-educated military engineer, secular in outlook, Echeandía actively encouraged liberal values among young Californios. He promoted the establishment of local ayuntamientos as well as a territorial *diputación*, or legislature. He introduced a process of indirect election for councilmen and legislators in which *gente de razón* voted for *commissarios*, who in turn made the selections for office. These institutions became the political classroom for the rising generation of politically active Californios. In an attempt to "remove the yoke" from the backs of the Indians, as Echeandía put it, he launched a plan for the emancipation of *neófitos*, appointing civil administrators to assume control over the missions and assigning them the task of shutting down operations and distributing land and other productive property to *neófitos* and Californios.

But before his program got fully underway, conservatives seized power in Mexico City, and Echeandía was replaced by Manuel Victoria, a fervent supporter of the church. In 1831, immediately upon his arrival, Victoria suspended secularization and announced his intention of governing without the legislature, which he condemned for supporting what he characterized as Echeandía's "scheme of spoliation." Outraged Californios complained loudly. In Los Angeles the leader of the protests was José Antonio Carrillo, the wealthy and influential son of the former commander of the Santa Barbara presidio. Determined to brook no opposition, Victoria ordered Carrillo and his followers arrested. At least a dozen men were imprisoned in Los Angeles, and Carrillo was forced into exile in Baja California.

With liberal Angelenos muzzled, the center of the resistance shifted south to San Diego, where former governor Echeandía was living in retirement. The leader of the liberals there was Pío de Jesús Pico, Echeandía's political protégé and brother-in-law of the exiled Carrillo. In many ways Pico was typical of his generation. Born into the family of a soldier garrisoned at San Gabriel in 1801, he spent his early childhood at the mission and at the presidio in San Diego. His father died prematurely when Pico was eighteen, and shouldering the responsibility of supporting his mother and seven younger siblings, he enlisted in the military and spent nearly ten years as a subaltern. He quickly learned that success depended on building a network of personal relations with officers, officials, and merchants, as well as arranging advantageous marriages for his numerous sisters. A garrulous man of serious purpose, Pico was highly successful despite the burden of a clownish nickname—*la breva aplastada*, the squashed fig—which poked fun of his enlarged facial features, likely the symptom of a glandular disorder.

Pico later recalled the moment of his conversion to liberalism. He was assisting Captain Pablo de la Portilla, commander of the presidio, in an investigation of a Los Angeles merchant suspected of misappropriating official funds. But the merchant refused to cooperate. "No Mexican citizen ought to answer before any military authority," he declared. "Mexican citizens constituted the sacred base of the nation, not the military." For Pico, who had been taught to grant ultimate respect to superior officers, this was a stunning assertion. Yet the more he thought about it, the more he found himself in agreement. "From that date," he later wrote in his memoirs, "I began to know the sacred rights of a citizen." Soon thereafter he left military service, determined to pursue a political career. He won a term on the San Diego ayuntamiento, then was chosen as a delegate to the legislature. He supported the secularization plan of Governor Echeandía, who rewarded him with a substantial grant of former mission land. Pico's path to success was echoed by the careers of dozens of other young Californios. What distinguished him was his single-minded ambition.

Angered by the banishment of Carrillo, who had married one of his sisters, Pico authored a letter of protest and distributed it among kinsmen and friends. The letter provoked public agitation in Los Angeles and was followed by the arrest of more young Angelenos, including Pico's brother Andrés. For Pico that was the last straw. In association with his brother-in-law Carrillo and San Diego merchant Juan Bandini, another member of the dismissed legislature, Pico worked up a pronunciamento denouncing Governor Victoria's "criminal abuse" and calling for his overthrow. The three men denied that their rebellion had anything to do with secularization. But in his memoirs Pico was more candid. "I was determined to end the mission system at all costs," he wrote, "so that the properties could be bought by private individuals."

Recruiting a dozen supporters, the rebels armed themselves and late one evening in November 1831 boldly marched on the presidio, disarmed the guard, and seized the armory. Captain Portilla, Pico's old commander, put up token resistance but soon joined the rebellion. A day or two later, he and Pico led a force of some fifty mounted soldiers and a couple of dozen rebels north to Los Angeles, where they freed all the political prisoners. Joined by liberal Angelenos, the rebel force expanded to more than one hundred and fifty men, and Captain Portilla readied them for a confrontation with Governor Victoria.

INFORMED OF THE REVOLT, Victoria headed south from the capital at Monterey with an armed force of Mexican soldiers and Californio militia, vowing to execute Pico. On the morning of December 5, 1831, approaching Cahuenga Pass in the Santa Monica Mountains, several miles northwest of Los Angeles, he found Portilla and his rebel Mexican soldiers and Californios commanding the high ground. The men on both sides knew each other well, the soldiers having served together and the Californios sharing kinship connections. Surprised to see such a large number of fighters arrayed on the ridge, Captain Romualdo Pacheco, commanding the governor's force, advised Victoria to withdraw until they could secure reinforcements. The governor was a brave soldier who had compiled a distinguished record of service during the war of Mexican independence. But he was also an impulsive hothead, and he dismissed Pacheco's suggestion as evidence of cowardice. "Officers in skirts," he said scornfully, "should move to the rear." Pacheco, an accomplished military officer with an unblemished record of his own, jerked to attention and shot back a reply: "I'm a man with *cojones,* as you'll soon see."

Scanning the ranks of his opponents on the ridge before him, Victoria recognized Captain Portilla, whom he had met upon his arrival in California. "Leave that pack of scoundrels and join me!" he shouted, and began to advance. Portilla responded with a single word. "Halt!" It struck Victoria like a thunderbolt. His right forearm shot up impulsively in a vulgar gesture of contempt. "I'm no man to be halted!" he sputtered, and barked out an order for his men to open fire. They responded with a ragged musket volley aimed over the heads of their opponents. No one was hit, but the blast unnerved Portilla's soldiers and most of the Angelenos. They wheeled their horses and retreated in disorder, and soon riders were streaming into the pueblo. Among them was young Andrés Pico. This was his first armed engagement, and he later admitted to having been so frightened that he rode straight through the Plaza to a vineyard near the river, taking cover beneath an arbor and remaining there until late in the day when hunger and thirst drove him back to the Plaza. There he learned that the battle had not concluded as he had expected.

When Victoria saw that his soldiers had aimed high, he flew into a foaming rage. He was not accustomed to commanding "men in petticoats," he stormed. For Captain Pacheco, the taunt was a match applied to his short fuse. Thinking with his *cojones* rather than his *cabeza*, he drew his sword and galloped forward toward the enemy. His charge was answered by José María Ávila, a prosperous ranchero and former Los Angeles alcalde, as well as an accomplished horseman and noted daredevil. The men of both sides silently watched as the two champions sped toward each other. Ávila carried a lance, the standard weapon of Mexican mounted cavalry, and he thrust it at Pacheco, who swerved adroitly to avoid it. As the jousting riders passed, Ávila pulled a pistol from his sash and fired wildly over his shoulder at Pacheco, and by chance the ball found its mark, tearing into the officer's back and hurling him from the saddle. He was dead before he hit the ground. Ávila galloped on, his lance extended, bearing down on Governor Victoria himself.

Accounts differ about precisely what happened next. The sources all agree that Ávila was shot and killed by musket fire, but not before Victoria suffered several grievous wounds to his face and chest. Seeing their colleague dead on the ground, the remaining Angelenos retreated. But with Captain Pacheco dead and Governor Victoria severely wounded, there would be no pursuit. Victoria's aides hurried him to Mission San Gabriel, where he received emergency medical treatment. He survived his wounds, but was finished with California. As soon as he was fit for travel, he returned to Mexico by vessel.

It was a decisive moment. Despite their cowardice in the face of battle, the Californios had successfully deposed the sitting governor. For the first time in their history they were in charge of their own destiny. The legislators reconvened in Los Angeles and, exulting in their newfound power, appointed Pico acting governor. In order to administer the oath of office they needed a bible, a chalice, and other objects from the Plaza church, but the priest refused them entry. Juan Bautista Alvarado, secretary of the legislature, climbed onto the roof and through a skylight, bringing out the items they needed, an act of improvisation that would be long remembered. But former governor Echeandía, who had remained in San Diego, objected that by appointing one of their own the Californios had taken things a step too far, and in deference to his mentor, Pico agreed to step down. There followed a year of political infighting that kept California politics in turmoil until early 1833 and the arrival of Victoria's appointed successor, Brigadier General José Figueroa.

There had been another shift of the political winds in Mexico City, and Figueroa turned out to be a secularist who was sympathetic to the Californio cause. He granted full pardon to all the rebels. "Let peace return to occupy her seat in this delightful country," he declared. He also restarted Echeandía's program of secularization. Characterizing the missions as "entrenchments of monastic despotism," Figueroa placed ten missions, including all those in southern California, in the hands of civil administrators who were charged with converting mission lands, livestock, and tools to private use. It had required systematic violence to transform the indigenous inhabitants into a mission workforce. It would require yet more violence to transition to the new order. Secularization would be midwife to the contested birth of capitalist California.

· CHAPTER 3 ·

A COUNTRY ENTIRELY ALTERED

WHEN THE *NEÓFITOS* of Mission San Luis Rey, ninety miles south of Los Angeles, learned of Governor Figueroa's secularization program, they laid down their tools and refused to work. "I am not an animal to be made to work for bosses who are not to my liking," one of them complained to the governor's assistant. "Set me free if you are a just man!" They remembered the promise of eventual emancipation. "These Indians will do absolutely no work nor obey my orders," wrote Captain Pablo de la Portilla, who had been appointed civil administrator of the mission as a reward for his role in the rebellion against Victoria. Hundreds of Luiseños, as the *neófitos* of San Luis Rey were known, abandoned the mission and headed for their ancestral rancherías. "We are free!" they shouted. "It is not our pleasure to obey! We do not choose to work!" Scores marched north to Mission San Gabriel, where they agitated among the Indians there and assaulted Father José Bernardo Sánchez when he confronted them. "He was filled with sorrow because of what the Indians had done," the padre's housekeeper later recalled. Sánchez retired to his room, lamenting "the time I wasted in behalf of these unfortunates." He died several weeks later.

Recent converts, tied by kinship and community to sacred sites and old gathering spots, were eager to get away from the missions. Many joined *gentile* bands in the mountains and deserts, on the periphery of southern California, and some participated in raids on ranchos and mission estancias, stealing horses and cattle for subsistence. In December 1834, a large group of emancipados from San Gabriel, in league with the unconverted, desert-dwelling Cahuillas, raided the mission outpost at San Bernardino, seventy miles east of Los Angeles, taking captives and spreading destruction. A force of mounted Angelenos hurried to the scene, but arrived to find more than a dozen *neófito* corpses amid the smoking ruin. Indian violence directed at the missions inevitably meant the death of other Indians. As the raiding intensified, rancheros organized reprisals, seeking not only vengeance but captives to replace lost workers. Although captive taking was illegal according to Mexican law, local authorities justified it by arguing that Indian raiders were outlaws. Whatever the rationalization, these forays continued the old mission policy of grabbing fugitives to augment the labor force.

Not all emancipados abandoned the missions. A minority, mission born and bred, knew no other life, and they pinned their hopes on the promised distribution of land and livestock. But for the most part the new civil administrators ignored Indian rights and practiced corruption on a lavish scale. Antonio F. Coronel, an educated Mexican who migrated to Los Angeles in the mid-1830s and held numerous civic offices over the years, was among the few who were critical. "Huge tracts of land were given away to private individuals," he later wrote, "leaving the Indians with nothing." Most administrators began their terms with little property, he noted, "but in no time they were the owners of the most valuable ranchos, with great herds of horses and cattle."

Once again, Pío Pico exemplified the type. Appointed by Governor Figueroa to succeed Portilla as administrator of Mission San Luis Rey, Pico and his extended family established a harsh regime that quickly alienated the remaining Luiseños. "I dedicated myself with great zeal to the job," Pico later recalled, "and in a short time succeeded in bringing order out of chaos." He did so at the expense of Indian liberty. Figueroa's secularization plan authorized administrators to compel emancipados to labor on mission lands during a period of transition, and Pico exercised that authority liberally, sending armed men to drag Indians back to the fields. The Luiseños hated him for it. "Pío Pico, as well as those who followed him, were despots," one of them declared. "All that San Luis Rey Mission produces," another complained "was not enough for the administrator, his brothers, and brothers-in-law." Pico expropriated mission livestock for his own use, but when he attempted to graze the animals on range reserved for the Luiseños he was besieged in his headquarters by several hundred angry men. Arming himself with a brace of pistols, Pico went out to confront them, threatening to fire if they did not disperse. Laughing, the Luiseños dared him to go ahead, warning it would be his last act on earth. Pico was eventually replaced, but not before he had crushed the hopes of hundreds of men and women. Shortly after he left the post the governor rewarded him with a grant of more than 133,000 acres of Mission San Luis Rey land.

Through policy, fraud, and coercion, a new landowning class took shape and took over. Governor Figueroa began the process of dividing mission lands into private ranchos, a project completed by his successors, the last of whom was Pío Pico himself. Between 1834 and 1846 nearly 1.4 million acres of prime southern California property, virtually all of the former mission estate, was transferred to private ownership. The grants went to a small minority of California's *gente de razón*, a self-perpetuating elite made up of former army officers and sergeants, public officials, and their extended families. In the Los Angeles district the great ranchero families could be counted on two hands—Carrillo, Cota, Domínguez, Féliz, Lugo, Pico, Sepúlveda, Tapia—with fingers to spare. Not only land was distributed, but labor as well. Grants were drawn to include the sites of native rancherías, whose residents were told they must labor for the new owners or move on. Despite their liberation, emancipados realized very little improvement in their working lives. Laboring under various forms of servitude, thousands of Indians became vaqueros, field hands, or domestic servants for the new ruling class.

SOME VAQUEROS were Californios, quite a few were Sonoreños, but following secularization most were Indians. "They were the ones who broke the horses," ranchero José del Cármen Lugo recalled. "Some rode with saddles and some rode bareback." But most emancipados adopted the equestrian tradition brought to California by Mexican soldiers, a style of riding known as *á la jineta*, which Spaniards had picked up from the Moors, their opponents in the centuries-long struggle for control of Iberia. In contrast to heavily armored knights who sought to project brute force, Moorish cavalry depended on speed and maneuverability. The *jineta* rider rode with knees bent, feet directly below, squatting in the stirrups. He controlled his horse with a signal bit, designed to send instructions with the slightest movements of the reins, which the rider held loosely in his left hand, reserving his right for a lance, a short sword, or a coiled reata and lasso. Roping an animal, the vaquero quickly turned the reata two or three times around the short, thick neck of the saddle horn, using it like a fisherman's reel, "playing" his catch until it tired, making the work of both rider and horse considerably easier. Indian vaqueros made this equestrian tradition so much their own that when a horseman, regardless of ethnic background, performed some act of special skill—an effective turn of the reata, perhaps, with the rope whizzing around the horn and smoke rising from the singed leather—his fellow vaqueros would say of him, "*se crió entre los indios*," he must have been raised by the Indians.

The standard vaquero outfit also came from cavalry tradition. Broad-brimmed, flat-crowned sombrero, short jacket worn over an open-collar shirt, *chaperrejos* of hide to protect the legs, and colorful sash into which was tucked the ever-present dagger, unless it was concealed in the leather *botas*, to which were attached heavy spurs with enormous rowels. "When he walks (which he seldom does)," wrote an English visitor to California, the vaquero looks "as if he has a couple of mimic wheelbarrows trailing at his heels." This working outfit was common across class lines, although on fiesta days, when everyone dressed up, rancheros donned silk jackets, embroidered waistcoats, and velvet *calzoneras* with silver buttons down the legs, while vaqueros wore "whatever they could afford." The vaquero cut a romantic figure, and foreign observers expressed awe at his riding skill, "flying like the whirlwind over the valleys, racing up and down the steep hillsides, plunging down crumbling barrancas, tearing through chaparral— wherever the maddened cattle sought to escape." These men and their horses were exquisitely prepared for mounted warfare, as American dragoons would learn by painful experience.

The officers and sergeants among the Mexican soldiers achieved their positions of leadership by their martial charisma, their demonstration of fighting skill and valor. The same could be said of the culture of rancheros and vaqueros. Any gathering of them might become an occasion for riding or roping competitions. An *hombre real* was a man who refused to be dominated, who stood up for himself, who responded to the least sign of disrespect with an immediate counterstroke. To gain the esteem of their men, rancheros had to be skilled in the practice of violence and fearless in the face of opponents.

SECULARIZATION CHANGED THE RULES. Rancheros replaced missionaries as the principal suppliers of hides and tallow to foreign traders, most of them Americans. Hide broker Alfred Robinson of New England, representing the Boston trading firm of Bryant & Sturgis, quickly mastered the new game. Missionaries purchased basic commodities, but rancheros wanted fancy goods—Chinese silks, Brussels carpets, East Indian spices—things that distinguished them from the hoi polloi. Robinson's business took off. "The country has entirely altered and the taste of the people has become more refined," he informed his employers in 1835. "The richer the goods & finer, the more readily they sell." Rich textiles and fancy clothing were the things most prized. "He or she that can make the greatest show in dress or fashion is noted as the gentleman or lady. We have *dandies* here as well as at home."

American merchants dominated retail trade just as they controlled foreign commerce—the two went hand in hand. Trading vessels from the United States brought young men in search of their fortunes to southern California. Men like Jonathan Temple, a native of Massachusetts, who opened the pueblo's first general merchandise store in the late 1820s, stocking his shelves with goods obtained through connections developed over several years in the Hawaiian sandalwood trade. Temple quickly adapted to life in Los Angeles, converting to Catholicism, applying for naturalization, and eventually marrying María Rafaela Cota, a cousin of José Domingo Féliz. Temple devoted himself to his business, earning a reputation, as Los Angeles merchant Harris Newmark put it, "as one of the wealthiest, yet one of the stingiest men in all California."

Temple's most formidable competitor was fellow Yankee Abel Stearns. Orphaned at an early age, Stearns went to sea, rising from cabin boy to master of his own schooner. After several years of itinerant trading in Mexico, he was drawn to California by secularization and its economic opportunities. Purchasing a lot south of the Plaza, he opened a store that catered to the whims of ranchero families. Stearns was a shrewd trader, famous for driving a hard bargain. In 1835 he got into a fight with a dissatisfied customer, a saloon keeper from Kentucky, who complained that Stearns had sold him a barrel of sour wine. The angry man slashed Stearns with a Bowie knife, leaving him with a badly scarred face and a permanent speech impediment. Known thereafter as *cara de caballo*, or horse face, Stearns shrugged it off, remaining sociable and gregarious, generous with his friends, and deeply engaged in local politics. He seized on every opportunity to expand his business. At San Pedro, the undeveloped harbor twenty-five miles south of the pueblo, he purchased an abandoned warehouse and within a few years made himself into the dominant commercial middleman in southern California. "I firmly believe that the future of the pueblo is toward the sea," Stearns declared. "Blessed with a genial climate and surrounded by one of the most productive soils in the world, it will in the future be a place of great importance. But we must prepare a means of exporting our products, in order that we may get the benefit of our natural advantage."

The man who exploited that advantage most effectively was French immigrant Jean Louis Vignes. A cooper and distiller from Bordeaux, Vignes spent several years running a distillery in Hawaii before teetotaling Protestant missionaries chased him off the islands. In the early 1830s he relocated to Los Angeles, where he purchased an old vineyard, imported cuttings and skilled vineyardists from his native France, and dedicated himself to the production of quality wines. Vignes was the first Los Angeles grower to raise oranges commercially, transplanting cuttings from abandoned groves at Mission San Gabriel. Like Stearns, he was a visionary. "With my knowledge of vine and orange cultivation, I foresee that these two are to have a great future," Vignes told a friend. "This is just the place to grow them to perfection."

If the mild climate was a crucial asset, cheap labor was even more important. With secularization, hundreds of emancipados from nearby missions found their way to Los Angeles, increasing the Indian population of the pueblo by 50 percent between 1836 and 1844. A surplus of workers kept wages low. Cheap labor allowed Vignes to develop more land and expand his operations, and within a few years he counted over forty thousand vines in cultivation and several vintages aging in his cellars. He employed a regular crew of skilled French vineyardists, and an army of temporary Indian workers for the harvest and the pressing. Other growers followed his lead. The ayuntamiento cooperated by authorizing an expansion of the zanja irrigation system, while owners put Indians to work clearing away the remaining timber along the river, making way for the expansion of production. By 1836 dozens of operations were producing for the local market, and large producers like Vignes were shipping casks of wine abroad. Soon trade was booming.

LIKE THE RANCHEROS, Temple, Stearns, and Vignes represented the new ruling order. Yet they sought inclusion in the traditional elite culture of California. Vignes enclosed his vineyard with imposing adobe walls, broken by a wide gateway that opened onto a vine-covered arbor, leading past his cellars to the river beyond. He named his estate El Aliso, in honor of a towering alder or sycamore that shaded his wine cellars. Years earlier the great tree had marked the center of the ranchería of Yang-na. Less than a mile away, just south of the Plaza, Jonathan Temple built a townhouse with a sala large enough to accommodate the assembly of fifty-five vigilantes in 1836. Nearby was *el palacio*, the Stearns mansion, renowned as the finest dwelling in all of California. Rancheros such as José Antonio Carrillo and Pío Pico also built fine townhouses near the Plaza during those years. But successful extranjeros (foreigners) turned the trick by purchasing ranchos of their own, for in Mexican California, the highest social position was reserved for the owners of the great landed estates with grazing cattle on a thousand hills. Stearns bought Rancho Los Alamitos and Temple acquired Rancho Los Cerritos, twin estates fronting the south-facing Pacific coast in what is today the city of Long Beach, making themselves into rancheros as well as *capitalistas*.

Many an extranjero was seduced by Californian joie de vivre. Dancing was part of nearly every social occasion. If the ranchero's house was too small to accommodate a crowd, he might order his workers to raise a *ramada*, or arbor, enclosed on three sides. Women seated themselves around the perimeter while the men, many on horseback, clustered at the entrance. Once the small musical ensemble—guitar, violin, and perhaps harp—began to play, the *tecolero*, or master of ceremonies, would approach a young señorita and with a clap of his hands invite her to dance. If she accepted, she would stand, lift her petticoat or gown slightly to reveal feet and ankles, and swaying in time to the music take two or three turns about the arbor to the applause of spectators. When the *tecolero* announced the *contradanza*, men descended from their saddles, took off their spurs, and entered the arbor, hats in hand. Couples formed a line in order of social position, rancheros, elders, and honored guests in front, vaqueros and their partners to the rear, and when the music began—a slow and dignified tempo in 3/4 time—the *tecolero* would call out the figures and turns. The dance ending, the men escorted the women back to their seats and returned to their horses. According to Horace Bell, who resided in Los Angeles for more than half a century, "the women excelled in dancing to as striking a degree as did the men in horsemanship."

The traditional California fandango was open to all classes, Indians excepted. But in the 1830s the nouveaux riches began holding exclusive balls of their own. One of the first of those occasions in Los Angeles was the 1834 reception hosted by José Antonio Carrillo at his townhouse on the Plaza, celebrating the marriage of his brother-in-law Pío Pico to María Ignacia Alvarado, a kinswoman of Juan Bautista Alvarado. Governor Figueroa served as Pico's best man. "As soon as the bridal pair arrived," one participant recalled, "the fun commenced, which consisted of dancing, music, singing, and feasting. The bride was dressed magnificently. During the first evening of the fiesta she changed her dress at least three times. Her dresses were of the finest silk, beautifully made. . . . The groom was dressed in knee pants of velvet, trimmed with gold lace; his coat was also of velvet and gold." The party went on for eight days and became legendary as the single most sumptuous and spectacular affair in the history of Mexican California. In effect, the event announced the arrival of a new ruling order.

The increasing wealth and status of the few sometimes roused the jealousy of the many. Angelenos typically celebrated Mexican independence day—*el dieciséis de Septiembre*, the sixteenth of September—with a public celebration on the Plaza on the eve of the holiday, an occasion that included patriotic speeches, fireworks, and dancing, with a recitation at midnight of *el grito de Dolores*, the legendary shout said to have commenced the Mexican independence struggle from Spain in 1810. Independence day was a holiday intended for all the people. So when Abel Stearns invited prominent Angelenos to a private independence eve celebration at his townhouse in 1840, ordinary residents were deeply offended. A group of inebriated celebrants from the festivities on the Plaza marched on *el palacio*, throwing stones and breaking windows, "angry at being treated with such contempt," in the words of one observer.

THE MOST COMMON source of disorder in the pueblo was the hundreds of Indians who came to Los Angeles for work. There were always more emancipados than there were jobs, which kept wages low and resentment high. Indian men and women alike worked the vineyards and groves or took jobs as domestic servants in the households of *gente de razón*. Indians in Los Angeles, president of the missions Narcisco Durán reported to Governor Figueroa, "live far more wretched and oppressed lives than those in the missions. There is not one who has a garden of his own, or a yoke of oxen, a horse, or a house fit for a rational being."

On Saturday evening, to celebrate the end of the workweek, large crowds of emancipados gathered at the cantinas and dives clustered along the short street known as Calle de los Negros, southeast of the Plaza. Fueled by aguardiente—cheap, rotgut brandy—the raucous partying continued through the night and into the next morning. Public drunkenness led to brawling that frequently turned lethal, provoking an outcry from *gente de razón*. But rather than restrict the sale of alcohol—a profitable business for vineyardists and saloonkeepers, and the principal source of municipal tax revenue—the ayuntamiento authorized the roundup of drunken Indians, who were herded into an open corral to sleep it off. On Monday morning the offenders were summarily fined, with those unable to pay sentenced to forced labor, repairing the zanjas or sweeping the streets.

Indian disorder and violence—reflecting the broken promise of secularization—provoked some Angelenos to call for a pueblo without any Indians at all. But this was impossible, since vineyardists and other employers relied almost exclusively on their labor. Instead, the ayunta-miento instituted a policy of residential separation, setting off an area near the vineyards where all Indians were required to live. *Ranchería de poblanos,* as the barrio was known, soon became the principal vice district, a center of prostitution and gambling, and a favorite resort of dissolute Angelenos. In response to continuing complaints, the regi-dores instituted a more comprehensive policy of de jure segregation, ruling, for example, that "dirty and filthy" Indians be confined to the back rows of the Plaza church during mass and that the Indian dead be buried in an isolated section of the new graveyard opened at the terminus of Calle de Eternidad, in the rolling hills north of the pueblo. Finally, in 1845, the ayuntamiento voted to require the relo-cation of all native households across the Río Porciúncula to a place that became known as *el pueblito.* Vineyardists purchased the site of the Indians' former barrio and converted it to the production of more grapes, wine, and aguardiente.

None of these measures had any significant effect in reducing emancipado violence. The records of the alcalde's office document an accelerating pace of Indian assaults, rapes, and homicides. Over the fifteen years from 1830 to 1845 at least twenty-five Indians were mur-dered in the Los Angeles district, most of them by Indian perpetrators. Many of those crimes took place in the vicinity of Calle de los Negros, a short walk across the Plaza from the church. "The sign of Indian murder," one observer wrote, was "heads mashed beyond recogni-tion." Death-dealing blows to the head—delivered in the belief that this would drive the spirit from the physical body—was the forensic hallmark of Indian assault. José Domingo Féliz was the victim of a native Californio, not an Indian. But his mutilated head and face were dramatic evidence that the *gente de razón* had been infected by the plague of Indian violence.

WITH CALIFORNIA SOCIETY in the midst of rapid change, the code of honor took on even more significance. The deadly struggle between Gervasio Alipás and José Domingo Féliz came as no surprise to anyone. It was a violent contest for honor, a zero-sum game between two men over a woman. *Ni modo,* what can be done? Alipás was an assassin and he deserved to die. No, what made the Féliz case extraordinary was the role played by Don Domingo's wife, that "abominable monster," in Victor Prudon's florid prose, "who cruelly destroyed her unfortunate husband that she might give herself over to her immoral passions." When wives murder their husbands, men take notice. The execution of María del Rosario Villa could not await the lengthy process of law. Honor demanded her immediate death.

Matters of gender and honor came up frequently in Mexican Los Angeles. Women were victims in a fifth of all the cases of criminal violence considered by the alcalde. In 1842 María Ramona Véjar appeared before Alcalde Manuel Domínguez to report frequent attacks by her husband, Tomás Urquides. "He has hit me so many times with a reata or whatever else he can find," she testified, "that I can not recall the exact number." Summoned to explain his conduct, Urquides admitted beating his wife, but argued he did so only "when she gives me cause." An honorable man ought to temper his passion, but what he did in his own house to his own wife was his own business.

That point was made forcefully in the case of Enrique Sepúlveda, charged in 1835 with the murder of Juan Jenkins, an English extranjero who operated a carpenter's shop in the pueblo. The altercation began when María Pascuala García, Jenkins's twenty-three-year-old wife, appeared on the veranda of the Sepúlveda house seeking refuge. Her face was bruised and bloodied, the result of a severe beating she said had been delivered by her husband. Sepúlveda, a prominent but quarrelsome man whose family owned Rancho de los Palos Verdes, accompanied the young woman back to her home and confronted Jenkins, who told Sepúlveda to mind his own business. The confrontation threatened to turn violent, but neighbors separated the men and Sepúlveda returned to his casa. A short time later Jenkins appeared at his door, brandishing a knife. Sepúlveda knocked the weapon from his hand, but Jenkins grabbed a club and smashed his opponent in the head. Reeling from the blow, Sepúlveda drew a short sword and plunged it into Jenkins's belly. He died after several hours of agony. Sepúlveda argued he had acted in self-defense, but after a lengthy trial Alcalde Francisco Javier Alvarado found him guilty of manslaughter and sentenced him to five years in prison. By intervening in what was *"un asunto de su familia"* (a family matter), Alvarado ruled, Sepúlveda had become the aggressor.

Patriarchal authority was founded on the control of women. On this, all men agreed. No one questioned the extralegal execution of María del Rosario Villa, murderess and adulteress. When Alcalde Requena commenced an investigation of *"los linchamientos,"* the men of the junta stood together in solidarity. If any were guilty, they insisted, all of them were. Requena's report, which he submitted to the territorial authorities in early May 1836, consisted of little more than a transcription of the junta's petition, accompanied by the names of the men who signed it.

GOVERNOR FIGUEROA died unexpectedly in the fall of 1835. Californios deeply mourned his passing, for he had championed the secularization policies they favored. They felt quite differently about his successor, Colonel Mariano Chico, who arrived in California only a few days after the vigilante executions in Los Angeles. Governor Chico was a committed militarist with an authoritarian personality, cut in the mold of Manuel Victoria, whom he claimed as a mentor. "He was a man of very bad temper," one Californio wrote, "and he arrived like someone who comes to conquer a lawless country." Reading Alcalde Requena's report on the Los Angeles vigilantes, Chico was outraged. Those "scandalous events," he declared, were signs of anarchy and treason. At that same moment, in the Mexican province of Texas, American settlers and Spanish-speaking Tejanos were rising in revolt against the central government in Mexico City, and those unfolding events colored Chico's thinking. Usurping state authority to impose summary punishment, he believed, was but a pretext for a movement by "anarchical spirits" to "overthrow the government." On his orders, Lieutenant Colonel Nicolás Gutiérrez, the highest-ranking military officer in California, arrested the leaders of the junta and clamped them in irons, and when Chico arrived in the pueblo a few weeks later, he threatened them with banishment or worse. He even railed at Alcalde Requena, accusing him of violating his sworn duty to protect the laws. But Chico's thundering only consolidated Angeleno support for the vigilantes and encouraged their growing contempt for the government. Finally realizing that virtually all the residents of the pueblo backed the junta, the governor beat a quick retreat and pardoned the vigilante leaders. The incident proved a template for his short term as governor. By July 1836, after only four months in office, his pattern of furious attack and humble retreat had so thoroughly alienated the legislature, it demanded his resignation. Governor Chico followed Victoria's example and returned to Mexico, promising to return with an armed force to punish the unruly Californios. But he never did.

With Chico's departure Lieutenant Colonel Gutiérrez became acting governor, and he continued to rule in the same arbitrary style. The legislature, led by Juan Bautista Alvarado, opposed him as strenuously as his predecessor, and Gutiérrez responded by locking out the delegates and ordering Alvarado's arrest. The legislators fled to the interior, where they met in rump session and passed a resolution declaring Gutiérrez unfit to govern. Then, with the support of some 150 armed men, Alvarado and his colleagues marched on Monterey and in a bloodless engagement overthrew Gutiérrez and issued a declaration of independence, declaring their homeland the "free and sovereign state of Alta California." His action, Alvarado later claimed, had been inspired by the example of the Los Angeles vigilantes. The legislature chose Alvarado to be acting governor, and he hired Victor Prudon, principal spokesman for the vigilantes, as his aide. Prudon had the rare pleasure of watching as the Californios escorted Gutiérrez, the man who had ordered and supervised his incarceration, onto the vessel transporting him back to Mexico.

WHEN GOVERNORS OVERSTEP their authority, José Antonio Carrillo once remarked to a group of Mexican citizens, "do what we do in Upper California." When we dislike a governor's policies or character, "it's Moor overboard." And if "another one comes and behaves badly, the same thing is repeated, and the Government approves everything." Overthrowing Mexican officials had become something of a tradition for Californios.

Juan Bautista Alvarado's declaration of independence, however, was less a line in the sand than a bargaining chip, and the Mexican national state proved amenable to negotiation in the aftermath of its loss of Texas that same year. Elevated from the status of a territory to that of a department, which provided for greater local autonomy, California rejoined the *patria madre* with Alvarado officially installed as governor. In a proclamation likely written by Victor Prudon, Alvarado expressed hope for his homeland. "The benignity of our climate, the fertility of our soil, and—I say on your behalf—the polish of your customs and excellence of your character are so many privileges with which the Omnipotent has favored us in the distribution of His gifts. What country can count so many advantages as ours? Let us then strive to give it in history a place as distinguished as that which it occupies on the map."

But if the political prospects appeared brighter, the violence in Los Angeles grew considerably darker. From 1836 to 1846, despite a leveling of population growth, the volume of violent criminal complaints heard by the alcalde more than tripled. Angelenos focused attention on the disorder among Indians and Sonoreños, but violence between *gente de razón* also climbed to disturbing new levels. In the ten years following the murder of José Domingo Féliz, a total of nine Californios suffered violent deaths in the Los Angeles district. The vigilantes of 1836 had insisted on the importance of local justice, swiftly administered, and with California's elevation to the status of a department came the authorization to create an expanded justice system, with a superior court qualified to make final rulings in capital cases. Governor Alvarado divided the department into districts and appointed a prefect for Los Angeles whose duty it was to regularize local judicial proceedings. But with very few lawyers and virtually no judges in California, the creation of a functioning judicial system languished. In 1837 and 1838 three Californios accused of murder in Los Angeles were tried, convicted, and sentenced to death by the alcalde, but in the absence of an appellate court their appeals were forwarded to Mexico, and two years later the three prisoners were still awaiting the outcome of their appeals. For Angelenos, there was no closure, no sense of justice being served.

Their frustration came to a head in the aftermath of a particularly brutal murder in 1841. Nicolás Fink, a forty-year-old German cobbler who operated a shop near the Plaza, was reported missing by his neighbors. Alcalde Ygnacio Palomares investigated and found Fink's body in a back room, lying in a pool of dried blood, his skull horribly crushed and his goods rifled. A few days later some of the stolen items turned up in the possession of a young woman, and after intense interrogation she fingered three male accomplices who had committed the cold-blooded murder. Palomares prepared for trial, but he faced an angry public, well aware that there was no likelihood of punishment anytime soon. There were public calls for a revival of the *junta popular*, the vigilance committee. Palomares issued a ban on public meetings, declared a nightly curfew, and posted soldiers from the presidio at Santa Barbara as a guard around the jail. Then, in a short but seemingly fair proceeding, he found the accused guilty and sentenced the woman to banishment, the men to death. He wrote Governor Alvarado, requesting permission to proceed with the executions, despite the men's right to an appeal. Surely California's newly secured autonomy included the authority to mete out local justice. How otherwise would they stem the tide of violent crime? Palomares's letter was endorsed with the signatures of thirty-three prominent Angelenos.

But Governor Alvarado balked. Although he had publicly endorsed the objectives of the 1836 vigilante movement, he did not possess the legal authority to comply with the alcalde's request. Finally, realizing that if he failed to act, Angelenos would take the law into their own hands, Alvarado authorized the executions under cover of his military authority. On April 7, atop the hill behind the Plaza church, on the same spot where the murderous lovers had been executed in 1836, a firing squad of Mexican soldiers carried out the sentence. Alvarado later boasted of his enthusiasm for popular justice, for letting the people themselves decide. But coming face-to-face with the awakening lion, he did what he could to protect the authority of the state. For the moment Angelenos were satisfied. But they remained without a legally-constituted system that could ensure both order and justice.

It was during these turbulent years that Los Angeles gained a reputation as the "wickedest town in California." *El pueblo de los angeles*, wrote George Simpson, governor of the British Hudson's Bay Company, was situated in perhaps the loveliest and most fertile district on the entire Pacific coast of North America. But, he added, the pueblo was also "the noted abode of the lowest drunkards and gamblers in the country." Simpson may have been the first observer to note in print the dramatic contrast between the pueblo's idyllic setting and the terrible things that took place there. But his sentiments were shared by others. Cosme Peña, whom Governor Alvarado appointed prefect of Los Angeles in the late 1830s, served for less than a year. But in that short time he got his fill of the troublesome Angelenos. In his letters and reports he christened *el pueblo de los angeles* with a name he thought more appropriate, *el pueblo de los diablos*—the city of demons.

· CHAPTER 4 ·

EXTRANJEROS

IN EARLY APRIL 1840 Alcalde Tiburcio Tapia received a dispatch from Governor Alvarado instructing him to investigate the foreign residents of the Los Angeles district, detaining all those who were undocumented. Tapia discovered that half the approximately fifty extranjeros in his jurisdiction lacked official papers authorizing their presence in California, and following further inquiry into their employment and marital status, he sent fourteen foreigners under guard to the presidio at Santa Barbara. After additional interrogation by military officers, eight were released and six loaded aboard the government barque *Joven Guipuzcoana*, which had sailed down from Monterey with several dozen foreigners from the north. On the morning of May 8 the vessel weighed anchor and set sail for Mexico with a total of forty-seven deportees—twenty-four Americans and twenty-three Britons. "We were all crammed down in the hold," one of them later recalled. It was a warm day and the atmosphere below deck was stifling. "Such of the prisoners as were able broke the silence that reigned in horror around us by singing 'Rule Britannia' or 'Hail Columbia.'" Others joined in, their voices rising in crescendo, until "the sides of the old barque resounded with the songs of battle."

The expulsion marked the first crackdown on undocumented immigrants in California history. Mexican law allowed for immigration and offered foreigners a pathway to citizenship, but required that they register with the authorities. But officials in Los Angeles were lax, often not bothering with paperwork for the outsiders who began trickling into the pueblo following Mexican independence in 1821. Those who came with plans to settle generally played it by the book, voluntarily registering with the alcalde, applying for naturalization, and frequently marrying daughters of the country. By the mid-1830s Los Angeles had a small but thriving émigré community. But the foreigners who found their way to the pueblo included plenty of vagabonds— deserters from the whalers and trading vessels that anchored at San Diego and San Pedro, or trappers from the mountains—who came to enjoy the mild climate, consume the cheap beef and fresh oranges, and earn a few reales to spend in the cantinas. It was men of this type who were deported in 1840. They had little in common with grandees such as Jonathan Temple, Abel Stearns, or Jean Louis Vignes, or with the craftsmen and day laborers who made up the majority of the émigré community. Governor Alvarado labeled the vagabonds *"malditos extranjeros,"* wicked foreigners, some of whom, he claimed, belonged to "a sordid and mercenary faction" that sought "to strip us of the richest of our treasures, our country and our lives."

Alvarado's fears originated in the role foreigners had played in the 1836 revolution that brought him to power. He and his principal collaborator, Captain José Antonio Castro of the California militia, assembled an armed force that included a company of twenty-five or thirty foreigners known as *los rifleros americanos* made up mostly of American frontiersmen, as the name suggests. Isaac Graham of Kentucky, their leader, had arrived at Los Angeles in 1834 with a party of trappers. During the two years Graham and his associates hung around southern California, they developed a poor reputation among assimilating foreigners. American ranchero Benjamin Davis Wilson described Graham as "a bummer, a blowhard, and a notorious liar, without an atom of honesty." In the census of 1836 Graham and his companions were listed as "transients." Later that year they all relocated to the Monterey area, where Graham opened a distillery and grogshop that became a favorite gathering place for local ruffians. When Alvarado and Castro were organizing for their confrontation with Gutiérrez, they recruited allies wherever they could find them, and the armed Americans constituted an important addition to their force. Although the rifleros saw no action during the short revolution, their presence thoroughly intimidated Gutiérrez and his Mexican lieutenants.

Alvarado quietly made promises of some sort to the rifleros, probably a pledge to officially recognize their land claims. For their part, the Americans proclaimed their conviction that Alvarado should declare California independent of Mexico, opening the way for annexation by the United States. That was what American settlers had done in Baton Rouge in 1810, when they declared the district of West Florida independent of Spain and requested incorporation by the United States. And that was what American settlers had done in Texas, where they were fighting for autonomy from Mexico. In both those cases the American cause was symbolized by a lone star flag, and Isaac Graham supplied Alvarado with an identical lone star banner to raise over the presidio at Monterey. Alvarado declined to use it, presumably alerting the Americans to the fact that he did not share their objectives. Later, however, after Alvarado negotiated an agreement with authorities in Mexico City that kept California within the Mexican union, Graham and the rifleros howled that they had been misled. At Graham's distillery they raised their glasses to the independent Republic of Texas, concluding their toast with the cheer "California next!" Bringing California under American authority would give them easy access to land and power. Increasingly alarmed at the danger these men posed to his regime, Governor Alvarado determined to be rid of them.

In the spring of 1840 the governor learned from a Catholic priest that a recently deceased American had made a deathbed confession of his part in a conspiracy organized by Graham to seize the capital, declare California's independence, and request the protection of the United States. Many Americans, no doubt, had talked about doing precisely that, but even Alvarado's associates were skeptical about the existence of an actual conspiracy. Alvarado nevertheless seized the opportunity, issuing orders for the immediate arrest of all undocumented extranjeros in the department. Soldiers under the command of Captain Castro raided Graham's place, seriously wounding one American and arresting several more, including Graham himself. Over the next several days officials rounded up several dozen men, and by the end of the month the jail at Monterey was filled with more than seventy extranjeros, both Britons and Americans. Nothing tied foreigners in southern California to the alleged plot in the north, but Alvarado concluded that the time had come for a clean sweep.

News of the deportation circulated quickly among Pacific traders, and in June 1840 the American sloop of war USS *Saint Louis*, boasting a crew of 124 men and twenty large guns, sailed into Monterey Bay. Captain French Forrest demanded an explanation for what he characterized as the "very cruel outrage" committed against the Americans. Justice had been done, Alvarado replied. The deportees were "vagabonds, deserters, and horse thieves," all were in California illegally, and some were suspected of conspiring to overthrow the government. His answer did not satisfy Captain Forrest, who demanded that Alvarado present himself for interrogation, but he was informed that the governor was unavailable.

That was increasingly the case. Alvarado was no longer the brash young revolutionary. According to one British trader, a diet of rich food and strong wine had transformed him into "a plump and punchy lover of singing and dancing and feasting." Actually, it was considerably worse than that. Alvarado's excessive drinking had nearly destroyed his family and seriously disrupted his political career. When intoxicated, wrote an acquaintance, the man "lost all judgment and no power could keep him within bounds." He often turned to drink on the most stressful occasions—and Captain Forrest's visit to Monterey was one of them. There would be many more such days to come.

Following a miserable voyage, the deportees were unloaded at the Mexican port of San Blas, then marched overland to the provincial capital of Tepic. Twenty-eight were immediately deported as illegal aliens and the rest bound over for trial, charged with insurrection. But largely through the efforts of the British consul, who threatened trade reprisals, the charges against the rifleros were eventually dropped. In truth, there was little evidence against them, and in an attempt to resolve the matter with the British, the authorities agreed to pay damages and return the deportees to Monterey at government expense, teaching the Californios a hard lesson about the inconstancy of Mexican support. In July 1841, fifteen months after their departure, nineteen deportees made their return. Isaac Graham reveled in his vindication, proclaiming his hatred of Alvarado and Castro.

Press coverage of the deportation in the United States was extensive, if superficial and prejudicial. "Outrage on American Citizens in California," read a typical headline. Travel writer Thomas Jefferson Farnham, who arrived in Monterey just as the roundup was getting underway, appointed himself advocate for the American deportees and soon afterward published a melodramatic account of the episode, assigning California officials stock roles as ethnic villains: Governor Alvarado, the corrupt Spaniard, a schemer who "smiled graciously at us with one corner of his mouth while he cursed us with the other." Captain Castro, the malevolent mestizo, with sinister mustache and dark, shifty eyes. In this confrontation between Californio and American, Farnham claimed to read the future. "No one acquainted with the indolent, mixed race of California will ever believe that they will populate, much less for any length of time govern the country," he asserted. "The old Saxon blood must stride the continent, . . . [and] erect the altar of civil and religious freedom on the plains of California." Race was destiny and destiny was justice. Farnham invented neither the stereotypes nor the rhetoric, which went back decades, but he was the first to apply them to California. Reading his book— which appeared in several editions and was excerpted in numerous newspapers throughout the country—Americans learned to despise the Californios as cruel, treacherous, and unworthy of their beautiful homeland.

THE EXTRANJERO PROBLEM was not going away. The return of the deportees in the summer of 1841 was followed that autumn by the arrival of two large companies of American immigrants, sentinels of a great overland migration that before 1860 would bring more than two hundred thousand Americans across the plains, deserts, and mountains to California. In early November thirty-four settlers from the vicinity of Missouri straggled into the outpost of Swiss empressario Johann Augustus Sutter, located at the junction of the American and Sacramento Rivers, site of present-day Sacramento. John Bidwell, the leader of the group, came with Texas on his mind. "To take the country and annex it," he later wrote, "that was what sent me to California." After becoming personally acquainted with Californios, however, Bidwell had a change of heart. He was shamefaced, he later wrote, "that I ever entertained the idea of making a kill upon a people who have never done me any harm." Bidwell may have soured on conquest, but a number of the men who accompanied him to California would become leaders of the American settler uprising known as the Bear Flag Revolt. That fact alone made Bidwell's the better remembered of the two settler companies of 1841.

The other, which arrived at Mission San Gabriel in the fall, was the larger of the two, numbering some sixty-five persons, including several extended families. The company's well-to-do leaders, Missourian John A. Rowland and Englishman William Workman, had resided in New Mexico for the previous fifteen years, partners in a milling and distillery business in Taos. Converts to Catholicism and naturalized Mexican citizens, both men had married New Mexican women and raised large families. The Rowland-Workman party followed the route of the annual trade caravan that carried New Mexican woolens to California to exchange for horses, and included several New Mexican families, who planted communities on the upper Río Santa Ana, near what are now the cities of Riverside and San Bernardino.

Shortly after his arrival in California, Rowland traveled to Monterey and applied for a grant of land, offering Governor Alvarado a "personal donation" of $1,000 in consideration of the favor. Rowland presented papers testifying to his wealth and good citizenship, and Alvarado awarded him a large tract in the eastern portion of the San Gabriel Valley known as Rancho La Puente, which he and Workman managed together until they partitioned the property some years later. Rowland then returned to New Mexico to retrieve his wife and children, who had remained behind, bringing them back with the trade caravan in late 1842. Traveling with the party were several young Missourians, including the future sheriff of Los Angeles County, twenty-one-year-old James R. Barton.

Barton hailed from Howard County, Missouri, near the bustling market town of Franklin, jumping-off place for the Santa Fe Trail. His parents had migrated from Virginia about 1800, settling at American Bottom on the east bank of the Mississippi in the Illinois Country, where they farmed, purchased slaves, and raised a large family. In 1820, shortly after the admission of Illinois as a free state, the family moved across the river and settled in Missouri, where slavery remained legal. When young Barton came of age he went west to Santa Fe, where he found a job with John Rowland, originally from Howard County. Barton continued in Rowland's employ after his migration to California.

In the spring of 1845 Tomás Esténaga, missionary priest at San Gabriel, recorded the marriage of "Santiago Barton" to seventeen-year-old Margaret, "legitimate daughter of Don Juan Rolenes, native of the United States of North America." Barton and his bride settled near her parents and her married sisters, but the marriage lasted only a few months. "We are all well here," Rowland wrote to a friend in New Mexico less than a year later, "only I had the misfortune to lose one of my children named Margaret, consort of Mr. James Barton, [who] is now lamenting her loss together with her parents. But what can we do? My old friend, we must have patience and hope that the almighty will be merciful to us one day if we are good Christians."

GOVERNOR ALVARADO granted passports to every one of the arriving immigrants of 1841 who requested one. But expecting that they would be followed by hundreds more, he wrote his superiors in Mexico, urging a tightening of the borders with the United States and appealing for manpower sufficient to patrol them. Alvarado was wary of Americans who might attempt to play the Texas game in California. His concerns were seconded by the department's military commandant, Mariano Guadalupe Vallejo. Blood relatives, Alvarado and Vallejo grew up as virtual brothers. Brilliant students, they both became avid liberals. Vallejo followed his father into the military, joined the revolt against Governor Victoria in 1831, and during Governor Figueroa's tenure won a grant to a huge spread that encompassed the incomparably rich Napa and Sonoma Valleys north of San Francisco Bay. Appointed director of colonization for el frontera del norte, he waged war on resisting Indian communities and founded the pueblo of Sonoma, where he built a sprawling adobe mansion. Vallejo was in favor of American immigration to California, arguing that it offered the Californios the best chance for the development of their northern frontier. He later recalled how gratified he was to see "numerous parties of industrious individuals come and settle among us permanently." But he agreed with his kinsman Alvarado that they must try to control the tide of settlement. California, he believed, required a more orderly system of immigration, so he too wrote to Mexico City, appealing for men and arms to better protect the homeland.

Nothing was heard of those requests until the late summer of 1842, when a messenger arrived at Monterey with news that several vessels had landed at San Diego carrying a battalion of 250 Mexican soldiers under the command of Brigadier General Manuel Micheltorena. Both Alvarado and Vallejo had been sacked and Micheltorena appointed to a unified civil and military command with instructions to prevent California from becoming the next Texas. But the Mexican state was nearly bankrupt, and it provided Micheltorena with neither regular troops nor material support. Instead, he was given raw recruits and told to provision them as best he could with resources procured in California. Yankee hide trader Alfred Robinson watched as Micheltorena's force disembarked in San Diego. "They presented a state of wretchedness and misery unequaled," he wrote. "Not one individual among them possessed a jacket or pantaloons." The men were accompanied by dozens of camp followers, including wives and children. "The females were not much better off," Robinson observed, "for the scantiness of their mean apparel was too apparent for modest observers." The soldiers, he wrote, "appeared like convicts," and indeed many were convicted felons, released from prison and granted official pardon upon their enlistment.

Upon their arrival in Los Angeles, Micheltorena and his battalion were greeted with pomp and ceremony. The new governor delivered a speech from a platform erected in the Plaza, and there was dancing in the streets. But even as Angelenos celebrated, Micheltorena's needy soldiers were pilfering from local gardens and vineyards. "If I told of all their crimes in detail I'd never be done," wrote Antonio Coronel, who was serving as assistant alcalde at the time. The governor "lamented his precarious situation," said Coronel, "abandoned by the central government and struggling with the depravity of the troops given him. He was aware that their conduct reflected unfavorably on himself, in spite of his earnest desire to win the esteem of the Californios by good government."

After several weeks in Los Angeles, Micheltorena and his convict army finally packed up and headed for Monterey. But after only a day's march, encamped for the night in the San Fernando Valley, several soldiers from Monterey rode into his camp with an urgent message from Alvarado, dated October 19, just five days before. Two American warships had anchored at Monterey, and Commodore Thomas ap Catesby Jones, in command of the U.S. Pacific Squadron, had demanded the surrender of the department. "Without doubt," Alvarado wrote, "Monterey will be tomorrow occupied by the enemy." Governor Micheltorena dashed off a series of messages to local authorities, urging a militant defense. "Would that I were a thunderbolt to fly and annihilate the invaders," he wrote. But instead of flying northward, he turned around and marched his battalion back to Los Angeles.

COMMODORE THOMAS AP CATESBY JONES (*ap* meaning "son of" in Welsh) had been appointed to the command of the Pacific Squadron in 1841. His official instructions were "to protect the interests of the United States" while exercising "great prudence and discretion," a vague directive that was fleshed out in private conversations with Navy Secretary Abel P. Upshur. The United States, with large trading interests in the Pacific, had long expressed an interest in the acquisition of California with its great port at San Francisco. President Andrew Jackson tendered an offer to purchase the department in 1836, but angered by the revolt of American settlers in Texas the Mexicans refused to consider it. President John Tyler, Secretary Upshur's boss, renewed Jackson's bid, but he too was rebuffed, the Texas question continuing to divide the two nations. Mexico refused to recognize the independence of its former territory, and warned the United States that annexation would be considered an act of war. If the two nations did indeed go to war—which Secretary Upshur thought inevitable—Jones was instructed to seize Monterey and lay claim to California by right of conquest. Upshur's instructions were aptly summarized by a contemporary observer: "That Texas was to be annexed, that Mexico was to go 'on the rampage,' that finally war was to be proclaimed, and then California would be fair game for the American squadron on the Pacific."

In early September 1842, anchored with the Pacific Squadron at the Peruvian port of Callao, Jones received a letter from the American consul at Mazatlán, alerting him to the rapid deterioration of relations between the United States and Mexico. Jones concluded that "war was not only inevitable, but that hostilities must have already commenced." His concern was amplified by the sudden departure of the British Pacific Squadron and the rumor that Mexico had ceded California to Great Britain. Since the War of 1812, in which Jones served as a young lieutenant, he had carried a British musket ball in his shoulder, and he nursed an abiding hatred of everything British. Vowing they would not beat him to the punch, he immediately set sail for Monterey.

The frigate USS *United States* and the sloop USS *Cyane*, boasting a total of seventy-eight guns and upwards of seven hundred men, entered Monterey harbor on the afternoon of October 19. Commodore Jones made no bones about his intentions. "My approach to the shores of California," he wrote, "was in battle array, with lighted match and cannon pointed against the flag and troops of Mexico." To his relief, he found no British vessels in the harbor—Great Britain, historians have since concluded, had no interest in acquiring California. Jones anchored his vessels within firing distance of the presidio's *castillo* and sent one of his captains ashore with an ultimatum. The Californios had until the next morning to surrender the department or suffer the destruction of their capital. "Señor Alvarado was in shock as he read the note," wrote a Californio who was present, "his face suddenly became pale and then immediately turned red, as if blood was about to burst from his eyes." With fewer than thirty able-bodied men and a few old artillery pieces mounted on rotting carriages, resistance was out of the question. Alvarado dispatched riders to General Micheltorena, and late that evening, after delaying as long as he dared, he sent a delegation out to the frigate to arrange the capitulation. Then he locked himself in his office and drank himself into a stupor.

Having spent the majority of his career in the peacetime Navy, Commodore Jones was determined to make the most of this rare opportunity for glory. The next morning he ordered a contingent of 150 sailors and marines ashore to raise the flag, and following a salute from the big American guns, an officer read a proclamation, addressed to the people of California. "Although I come in arms as the representative of a powerful nation," Jones had written, "I come not to spread desolation." As long as the inhabitants remained at home in the peaceful pursuit of their occupations, he would guarantee the security of life and property "from the consequences of the unjust war into which Mexico has plunged you." With the raising of the American banner, he declared, California had become a possession of the United States. "Those stars and stripes, infallible emblems of civil liberty, now float triumphantly before you, and henceforth and forever will give protection and security to you, to your children, and to unborn, countless thousands."

But the American flag flew over Monterey for less than thirty hours. When Jones came ashore the following morning, Thomas O. Larkin, a young American merchant from Massachusetts who had resided in Monterey for ten years, handed him copies of the most recent Mexican newspapers, none of which made any mention of war with the United States. Jones spent some time stewing before finally admitting that he had acted precipitously. He ordered the Mexican flag rehoisted, recalled his marines and seamen, and dispatched a perfunctory note to Governor Micheltorena in Los Angeles. This note has been described as an apology, but it was hardly that. "I have received new communications from Mexico," Jones wrote disingenuously, "which induce me to believe that friendly relations have been reestablished between the two nations." In fact, relations had never been broken. Micheltorena received the note on October 26, the day his battalion returned to the pueblo, and he replied immediately. The honor of Mexico and California "require that satisfaction should be public," he wrote, and he demanded that Commodore Jones meet him in person in Los Angeles to settle the affair honorably.

Jones took his time getting there. After spending some weeks in Monterey, indulging his men in an extended shore leave, he took the opportunity to visit San Francisco Bay and Honolulu before sailing to San Pedro, arriving in mid-January 1843. He was met by a Mexican officer in command of a cavalry company who escorted the commodore and his small entourage of officers and midshipmen over the twenty-five miles of rough road that led to the pueblo, depositing them at *el palacio*, the townhouse of Abel Stearns. The next day the commodore and the governor sat down to reason together. Micheltorena demanded the payment of an indemnity as well as a formal apology from the United States, which Jones said he did not have the authority to grant, but would communicate to his superiors. Nothing came of it. Eventually the Mexican minister in Washington delivered a formal note of protest, demanding a public reprimand. "Does Commodore Jones esteem the peace of nations so lightly," he asked, "that on the strength of a mere rumor of some printed paper, in which war with his country is spoken of, he should consider himself authorized to act in arms against a friendly nation?" But rather than censuring Jones, the navy secretary praised him for his "ardent zeal" and his "elevated principles of duty."

The seizure of Monterey doomed President Tyler's proposed purchase of California while greatly stimulating the American interest in acquisition. Jones and his officers spoke enthusiastically about the department, particularly Los Angeles. While in the pueblo they had attended a brilliant ball at an elegant townhouse, where they danced with the wives and daughters of the rancheros. Jones was particularly taken with Arcadia Bandini, young wife of Abel Stearns, who "for beauty, amiability, and accomplishments would not lose by comparison with our own fair countrywomen." The Americans chuckled at the nickname Angelenos used for Stearns and his lovely bride—"*la bella y la bestia*," beauty and the beast. They toured El Aliso, the vineyard and cellars of Louis Vignes, sampled his wines, and expressed astonishment at the golden fruit hanging from his orange trees in the midst of winter. Los Angeles, they declared, was "the Eden of the earth." Even more important, it was a paradise vulnerable to conquest. An effective defense of this priceless territory seemed far beyond anything either Mexicans or Californios could muster. Governor Micheltorena drew the same conclusion, writing to Mexico City that he despaired of holding the department against another American assault. Mexico, he wrote, must immediately find a way of "preventing it from being overrun by the North Americans and declared independent by them and the native Californians."

GOVERNOR MICHELTORENA remained in Los Angeles until the fall of 1843, when he finally relocated his command to Monterey. The Montereños resented the governor's convict army as much as the Angelenos did. But when Micheltorena, in keeping with his conservative politics, announced a policy designed to strengthen the missions by restoring a portion of their lands, resentment turned to outright opposition. In fact, Micheltorena's plan never had a chance. The mission system was a skeleton of its former self, and while the governor "might rattle its dry bones," as one California historian puts it, "to give it the breath of organic life was impossible." The mere aspiration to revive the missions, however, precipitated another rebellion among the Californios, for whom the overthrow of appointed Mexican governors was an established tradition.

By the fall of 1844 a full-scale revolt was underway, led once again by Juan Bautista Alvarado and José Antonio Castro. The campaign revived Alvarado, a natural-born agitator and orator. Traveling through the countryside outside of Monterey, he succeeded in rallying some two hundred mounted vaqueros, whom Castro organized into a rough military force, and in November they confronted Micheltorena's battalion near the pueblo of San José. The governor—who trusted neither the capacity of his officers nor the courage of his troops— avoided bloodshed by agreeing to negotiate. But, as he later admitted, he intended no change of course but was simply playing for time while he recruited support among extranjeros in the north, including Alvarado's old nemesis, Isaac Graham. When Alvarado and Castro learned that Micheltorena had enlisted *los rifleros americanos*, just as the two of them had done eight years before, they feigned outrage. "Sir, you have aroused the country," they wrote to Micheltorena. "The sons of California will do us justice, and we will shed our blood rather than permit our country to endure this infamous oppression." Outnumbered by the governor's newly augmented battalion, in early 1845 the two leaders fled south with a force of mounted men, hoping to enlist Angelenos in their cause.

But for the moment Angelenos remained loyal to Governor Micheltorena. When negotiation failed to change their minds, Captain Castro led a detachment in a surprise assault on a small company of soldiers garrisoned at the rectory of the Plaza church. The intense fighting claimed several lives on both sides, and it was with some difficulty that Castro was able to restrain his troops from wreaking vengeance on Andrés Pico, the garrison's commander. Over the next couple of weeks Alvarado employed a combination of threat and persuasion to bring leading Angelenos over to his cause. Castro's protection of Pico turned out to be critical, for the tipping point came when Pico's brother, Don Pío, senior member of the *diputación* and the leading politician of the south, announced his support of the rebellion. On February 15 the legislature convened in rump session, deposed Micheltorena, and appointed Pío Pico as his successor. The principal charge against the governor was his reliance on the American rifleros. Yet, with the active support of the Pico brothers, Castro had already enlisted immigrant William Workman to recruit a rifle company among American émigrés in southern California, a force that included Workman's partner, John Rowland, and Rowland's son-in-law James Barton.

Three days later Governor Micheltorena arrived in the San Fernando Valley with a force of three hundred men. Some two hundred rebels, under the command of Captain Castro, marched out of the pueblo and over Cahuenga Pass to confront him. The engagement began on the morning of February 20, not far from the spot where the Californios had halted Governor Manuel Victoria fourteen years before. Micheltorena had three field guns, the Californios had two, and deploying these along the *barrancas*, or gulches, that crisscrossed the bed of the Río Porciúncula, the combatants began a lengthy artillery duel that continued throughout the day.

The sound of the barrage could be heard back at the pueblo, and many residents climbed the rolling hills on the north side of town to observe the battle. William Heath Davis, an American merchant trader, joined them there and was struck by the scene. "Women and children with crosses in their hands, kneeling and praying to the Saints for the safety and protection of their fathers, brothers, sons, husbands, lovers, cousins—that they might not be killed in the battle, indifferent to their personal appearance, tears streaming from their eyes, their hair blown about by the wind." The firing ceased at sunset and the people made their way back down to their homes. "The night that followed was a gloomy one," wrote Davis, "caused by the lamentations of the women and children."

But there was no reason for grief, since no one had been killed in the firing. Americans ridiculed the lack of casualties. The Californios "uniformly preferred delay to fighting," wrote Thomas Farnham, choosing "to massacre time instead of men." Californio cowardice would be a consistent refrain among Americans, who had little appreciation for the art of bloodless warfare. In the internecine battles that pitted relatives against each other, the Californio objective was not outright victory so much as it was the defense of honor and eventual arbitration.

The following morning the artillery was repositioned and the barrage resumed, but soon Americans on both sides found an opportunity to fraternize. Workman, leading the southern rifleros, declared that this was not their fight and that all of them should withdraw together. When the northerners, Isaac Graham among them, objected that Micheltorena had promised to honor their land claims, Workman arranged for Pío Pico himself to speak to them. "I will give you my word of honor as a gentleman," he told the Americans, "that I will protect all and each one of you in the land that you hold now." Castro spoke as well, saying he hoped "to unite the Californians and foreigners and then declare the country independent of Mexico." Those promises proved decisive. The Americans agreed to lay down their arms, and when Micheltorena realized he had lost the support of his rifleros, he raised the white flag. Following a brief negotiation with the Californios, he marched his convict army to San Pedro, and they returned to Mexico as soon as transport could be arranged.

"The Californians have succeeded," reported Thomas O. Larkin in Monterey. "Upper California, from Bodega to San Diego, is once more under its own command." Pío Pico—who resided in a townhouse on the Plaza, built with the wealth accumulated during his administration of Mission San Luis Rey—declared his intention of governing the department from Los Angeles. The *norteños* demanded their due, however, and in a compromise the legislature selected Castro as the department's *commandante militar* and Alvarado as chief customs inspector, both positions based at Monterey. All these appointments were later confirmed by Mexican authorities, demonstrating once again their inability to control events in distant California.

But over subsequent months the regional and personal jealousies among the Californios continued to break out in persistent conflict. Larkin's initial enthusiasm was considerably dampened. "The Californians are now free to govern themselves," he wrote in September, "which freedom they exercise by not governing at all." Leading Californios were divided among themselves at what turned out to be the moment of their greatest peril. "There is little to prevent the Americans from making this land another Texas," observed a French diplomat. "California will undoubtedly belong to whatever nation is willing to send out a man-of-war and 200 men."

· CHAPTER 5 ·

THE TEXAS GAME

IN MARCH 1845, as Californios attempted to take charge of their homeland, President James K. Polk entered the White House, determined to take it from them. Fifty years old, married but childless, Polk was devoted to politics, "aside from which," according to his biographer, "he had no aspirations, intellectual interests, recreations, or even friendships." A protégé of Andrew Jackson, former Speaker of the House of Representatives and governor of Tennessee, Polk prevailed in a close presidential election after waging a spread-eagle campaign calling for "the reoccupation of Oregon and the reannexation of Texas," language suggesting that the nation had a preemptive claim to those territories, implying that expansion was, in the legendary phrase of a Democratic Party propagandist, "the fulfillment of our manifest destiny to overspread the continent." Expanding the nation's boundaries, Polk declared in his inaugural address, "is to extend the dominions of peace over additional territories and increasing millions." Conquest was justice. "The world has nothing to fear from military ambition in our Government." There would be ample opportunity to test his proposition.

A few days before Polk's inauguration, Congress passed a joint resolution offering statehood to Texas, and by the time the new president took the oath of office, he was considering further extensions of the national domain. He shared his views in a private conversation with his new navy secretary, historian George Bancroft, an avid supporter of continental expansion. "In the clearest manner and with the utmost energy," Bancroft later recalled, Polk declared that "the acquisition of California for the United States" would be a principal goal of his administration. He hoped to accomplish it through negotiation, but was willing to wage war if necessary. Polk hoped to lure Mexico into making a hostile move providing him with a casus belli. The commander of the Pacific Squadron received the same standing orders given to Commodore Jones in 1841—seize California at the first news of a declaration of war between the United States and Mexico.

In the meantime Polk devised a covert operation aimed at securing California more directly. His plan required an agent, and with Secretary Bancroft's assistance he selected Lieutenant Archibald H. Gillespie, an ambitious young Marine Corps officer, known for his shock of red hair, his fluency in Spanish, and his familiarity with the Pacific region, having served several tours in that theater as commander of the marine guard aboard several American warships. Gillespie was briefed by Secretary Bancroft, then by Polk himself in a private interview at the White House. His assignment was to get himself to California as quickly as possible, traveling incognito across central Mexico to the Pacific port of Mazatlán, then catching a lift to Monterey on an American naval vessel, in order to deliver secret instructions to two Americans in California.

The first was merchant Thomas O. Larkin, the man who tipped Commodore Jones to his mistake in 1842 and the following year was appointed American consul at Monterey. Larkin enjoyed excellent relations with influential Californios, including Alvarado, Vallejo, Castro, and the Pico brothers. Gillespie carried instructions from Secretary of State James Buchanan naming Larkin a "confidential agent" of the American state and instructing him to do everything in his power to encourage the Californios in their struggle for autonomy. "Should California assert and maintain her independence," wrote Buchanan, "we shall render her all the kind offices in our power as a sister republic." And if the Californios "should desire to unite their destiny with ours, they would be received as brethren." Larkin's task was to persuade California's leaders to seek annexation by the United States.

Gillespie's second contact was Captain John C. Frémont of the Army Corps of Topographical Engineers, celebrated as the "Pathfinder" for his leadership of two official government explorations of the trans-Mississippi West. In the summer of 1845 Frémont departed on a third expedition, guided by mountain man Kit Carson and accompanied by a private company of sixty or seventy well-armed men. His official instructions were to explore and survey the front range of the Rocky Mountains, but President Polk told Gillespie he would find the explorer in California. As Frémont later put it, in making arrangements for his expedition "the eventualities of war were taken into consideration, . . . the contingencies anticipated and weighed." He was privately told to lead his men to the Pacific coast, assigned the task of watching, waiting, and, if expedient, "carrying the war now imminent with Mexico into the territory of California." Polk provided Gillespie with what he characterized as additional "secret instructions" for Frémont, oral directives that were not committed to paper. According to Bancroft, Gillespie was to inform Frémont of "the new state of affairs and the designs of the President," namely his determination "to take possession of California." But by what means?

Polk was a secretive man. He hinted at what he had in mind, though, in a conversation with Samuel J. Hastings, an experienced California trader who visited the White House shortly after Gillespie's departure and reported what he learned in a letter to Thomas Larkin. "I am now going to give you some advice, and I have good grounds to go on," Hastings wrote. "Carry on your business exactly as you would if you had been in Texas ten years since and knew at that time things would turn out as they have." The president, in other words, expected the Texas game—an uprising of American settlers—to be played in California. "American agents and American capital," Hastings continued, "will be at the bottom of it." The most important of those agents was John C. Frémont.

Polk's clandestine California operation played both ends against the middle. Gillespie carried two sets of instructions promoting two seemingly incompatible objectives. Larkin was to conciliate the Californios and persuade them to request American protection, while Frémont was to encourage insurrection among American settlers. The incongruity of the two aims led early California historian Josiah Royce to wonder how a "sane government" could have simultaneously pursued both goals. But in attempting to shape the outcome of events by covert means, nation-states often choose the most expedient rather than the most rational course. Polk sought to create turmoil in California and thereby opportunity for the United States. It mattered little to him which plan succeeded, as long as one of them did.

LIEUTENANT ARCHIBALD H. GILLESPIE arrived at the Gulf coast port of Vera Cruz in early December 1845 and set off across central Mexico. At about the same time Captain John C. Frémont arrived at Sutter's Fort on the Sacramento River, following a swift march across the Rockies and the Great Basin. Frémont took a small party to Monterey, where he paid his respects to Californian officials and met with Thomas Larkin. Commandante Castro was suspicious, but Frémont assured him that his visit was peaceful and scientific. That must have been something of a hard sell. Neither Frémont's personal entourage of Delaware Indian scouts nor the frontiersmen who made up his company looked like peaceful, scientific types. Frémont told Castro he planned a survey of the lower Río Colorado, and in anticipation of a hard journey he requested permission to spend a few weeks grazing his horses and mules in California's Central Valley. Castro reluctantly agreed. But instead of departing for the San Joaquín, Frémont and his company spent the late winter exploring the coastal valleys near Monterey, the department's most thickly settled region. Frémont was following Polk's instructions, playing for time, watching for signs of war between Mexico and the United States.

In early March 1846 a Mexican officer and two guards rode into

Frémont's camp with a summons from Commandante Castro. "You and the party under your command have entered the towns of this department," it read, "and such being prohibited by our laws, . . . you will immediately retire beyond the limits of this same department, such being the orders of the Supreme Government." Frémont had no business being where he was. In fact, he was engaged in spying. As the guest of a foreign nation, he ought to have responded respectfully. But, as Frémont would demonstrate numerous times throughout his career, he was disdainful of authority. He was also impulsive, and bristling at Castro's threatening tone, he reacted in knee-jerk fashion. "I peremptorily refused compliance to an order insulting to my government and myself," he later explained. Having provoked the challenge, Frémont's sense of honor compelled him to meet it.

Breaking camp, he led his men into the hills east of the Salinas River, mounted a commanding summit, and hoisted the American flag, thereby raising the stakes considerably. Castro immediately issued a proclamation. "*Bandoleros* commanded by a captain of the United States Army, J. C. Frémont, have without respect to the laws and authorities of the department daringly introduced themselves into the country." It was imperative, Castro declared, that the authorities "lance the ulcer," for if the Americans got away with such outrageous conduct, it would threaten "our liberties and our independence."

Consul Larkin wrote to both Castro and Frémont, counseling moderation, and his intervention may have prevented a clash. On March 9, after a three-day standoff, Frémont retreated under cover of darkness, leading his men east to the Central Valley, then north toward Sutter's Fort. News of the confrontation preceded him, and when Frémont and his men arrived at the Sacramento River, dozens of American settlers were there to offer support. That demonstration of sentiment proved more disturbing to California officials than Frémont's bravado. With a sense of mounting crisis, Castro called prominent Californio military officers together for what Consul Larkin described as "a council of war."

They assembled at Monterey in late March. All those attending—

including former governor Juan Bautista Alvarado and former commandante Mariano Guadalupe Vallejo—knew California was on the verge of extraordinary change. What course should they pursue? For Commandante Castro, fear of the Americans was the overwhelming sentiment. "We find ourselves suddenly threatened by hordes of Yankee emigrants," he told his colleagues.

> Already have the wagons of that perfidious people scaled the almost inaccessible summits of the Sierra Nevada, crossed the entire continent, and penetrated the fruitful valley of the Sacramento. What that astonishing people will next undertake, I cannot say; but in whatever enterprise they embark they will be sure to prove successful. . . . We cannot successfully oppose them by our own unaided power, and the swelling tide of emigration renders the odds against us more formidable every day.

Their best hope, Castro believed, was to request the protection of France or Great Britain. "Is it not better that one of them should be invited to send a fleet and an army, to defend and protect California, rather than we should fall an easy prey to the lawless adventurers who are overrunning our beautiful country?"

Vallejo respectfully disagreed. As a liberal, he admired the United States for its political system, particularly for the promise of economic liberty and the legal protection of property rights. "We are republicans," he argued. "So far as we are governed at all, we at least profess to be self-governed. Who, then, that possesses true patriotism will consent to subject himself and his children to the caprices of a foreign king and his official minions?" He dared his colleagues to consider the option of "annexation to the United States."

> Why should we shrink from incorporating ourselves with the happiest and freest nation in the world, destined soon to be the most wealthy and powerful? Why should we go abroad for

protection when this great nation is our adjoining neighbor? When we join our fortunes to hers, we shall not become subjects, but fellow-citizens. . . . Look not, therefore, with jealousy upon the hardy pioneers who scale our mountains and cultivate our unoccupied plains; but rather welcome them as brothers, who come to share with us a common destiny.

Vallejo had long held such views, but this was the first time he had made them known in a public forum. Earnest discussion followed, but the Californios found themselves unable to agree on a way forward.

Vallejo's perspective was shared by a surprising number of prominent men in the southern part of the department. Los Angeles merchant Abel Stearns had family and many friends among the elite. "The majority of the people in this quarter," he wrote to Thomas Larkin, "particularly the land holders and the most respectable part, would willingly and anxiously join the United States if they were sure of immediate protection against the Mexican Government. I often hear them say, *ojalá que toma esta los Americanos*"—I hope the Americans take us. The "vast majority of Californians would be glad and anxious to throw themselves into the hands of the United States," reported Jonathan Trumbull Warner, another Yankee, the proprietor of a southern California rancho who counted the Pico brothers among his closest associates. "This opinion I believe to be almost universal."

ON APRIL 17, shortly after the adjournment of the Californio council of war, Archibald Gillespie arrived in Monterey aboard the sloop of war USS *Cyane,* which he had boarded in Mazatlán after a short meeting with Commodore John D. Sloat, commander of the Pacific Squadron. Gillespie immediately went to Larkin's residence with Secretary of State Buchanan's dispatch, which Larkin read with delight. His new assignment would pay him six dollars a day for continuing to do what he was already doing—encouraging the Californios to consider the United States their friend. He remained confident that a process of peaceful annexation was possible, despite Frémont's unfortunate provocation, about which he informed Gillespie.

Larkin deplored Frémont's adventurism, but Gillespie found it exhilarating. In a report to Washington he applauded Frémont's "bold and chivalrous manner" and condemned Commandante Castro as "a treacherous and cowardly knave," language drawn almost word for word from Thomas Farnham's account of the deportation of the American rifleros. At least three hundred American settlers, Gillespie reported, were "ready at a moment's warning to rally in defense of their new homes and firesides." The Californios were "cowardly and inert," powerless to stop them. He expressed his strong conviction—based on old prejudices rather than new intelligence—that "the government of California must soon fall into the hands of a very different set of men than those who direct its destinies at present." Despite Larkin's instructions to conciliate the Californios, Gillespie put the emphasis on violent confrontation.

That evening he attended a ball at former governor Alvarado's Monterey townhouse, honoring the American officers of the warship *Cyane.* The leading Californio officials suspected the young lieutenant was a spy, but they did not dare detain him for fear of rousing the enmity of the U.S. Navy. Alvarado plied him with drink, but despite Gillespie's strong taste for spirits he managed to keep his head, and shortly before midnight he left the ball and departed for the village of Yerba Buena on San Francisco Bay, where he hoped to arrange transport for his pursuit of Frémont. The following day the sloop USS *Portsmouth* arrived at Monterey from Mazatlán with the news that President Polk had ordered an army of several thousand American soldiers into the disputed border region between Texas and Mexico. Captain John B. Montgomery predicted that within days Commodore Sloat would arrive to take possession of California. Larkin dispatched a messenger who found Gillespie at Yerba Buena and conveyed the new information. That following morning Gillespie left in search of Frémont.

That same day, April 25, 1846, some two thousand miles away on the north bank of the Río Grande, Mexican troops attacked a U.S. Army patrol, killing sixteen American soldiers and wounding five more. The news of the deadly skirmish, which reached Polk on May 9, provided him with the justification he had long sought. As he put it in his war message to Congress, "Mexico has passed the boundary of the United States, has invaded our territory and shed American blood upon the American soil." Polk had deliberately ordered his troops into harm's way, conniving to have them fired upon. But for the moment skepticism over the outbreak of the conflict was trumped by the patriotic necessity of supporting the troops. Congress declared war on May 13.

By then Gillespie had located Frémont in southern Oregon, some three hundred miles north of Sutter's Fort. He conveyed the president's verbal instructions and Frémont resolved to act. Commandante Castro had "humiliated and humbled" him, as he wrote in a letter home, and returning to California in arms offered an opportunity to "justify my own character." What made the difference was Gillespie's assurance that Frémont would be acting with Polk's blessing. "A grand opportunity now presented itself," Frémont later wrote, to "make the Pacific Ocean the western boundary of the United States." He interpreted the president's instructions as discretionary. "My proper course," he wrote, was to "take advantage of any contingency which I could turn in favor of the United States." He would do what he could to raise an insurrection among the American settlers, hastening the prospects for American annexation.

While Gillespie hurried back to Yerba Buena to procure funds and stores from American naval vessels anchored in San Francisco Bay, Frémont returned south to agitate among the American settlers. He circulated a notice among them, falsely claiming that several hundred mounted Californios under Commandante Castro's command were "on their way to the Sacramento Valley, destroying the crops, burning the houses and driving off the cattle." It was a complete fabrication, but effective propaganda. "Captain Frémont invites every freeman in the valley to come to his camp immediately," the notice concluded. Dozens of American settlers responded, many fearing for their lives and property, some simply spoiling for a fight. They must not wait to be attacked, Frémont counseled them, but should seize the initiative, striking at the nearest center of Californio authority and taking hostages. He would provide clandestine support. On June 14 a motley band of several dozen Americans invaded the settlement of Sonoma, imprisoned several prominent Californios, including Mariano Vallejo and Victor Prudon, who was working as Vallejo's aide. The Americans declared California an independent republic and raised a flag featuring the crude image of a grizzly bear and a lone star. They were playing the Texas game, urged on by Frémont.

Over subsequent days there were several violent confrontations. Californios riding with José Ramón Carrillo, Vallejo's brother-in-law, tortured and killed two American rebels. Americans commanded by Frémont dispatched three Californios in cold blood. Controversy over the responsibility for those deaths would haunt both men during their subsequent careers. Such things happen in the course of war. But responsibility for the armed conflict rested solely on Frémont's shoulders. "He brought war into a peaceful department," wrote historian Josiah Royce. "His operations began an estrangement, insured a memory of bloodshed, excited a furious bitterness of feeling between the two peoples that were henceforth to dwell in California." It was all unnecessary, since many prominent Californios favored union with the United States. But thanks to Frémont, all that goodwill went up in smoke. The Bear Flag insurrection came as a shock to Thomas Larkin. The uprising, he wrote to Secretary of State Buchanan, "completely frustrated all hopes I had of the friendship of the natives to my countrymen."

· CHAPTER 6 ·

A TERRITORY OF THE UNITED STATES

AFTER THE CONFRONTATION with Frémont, Commandante José Castro concluded that an American invasion of California was inevitable. He attempted to persuade Governor Pío Pico to leave Los Angeles and come north with men and matériel to reinforce the defenses around Monterey, but Don Pío refused in the belief that Castro was attempting to isolate him from his base of support. He had reason to be concerned. Castro had made numerous military appointments, including José Antonio Carrillo to succeed Andrés Pico as commander of the Los Angeles district. Although Don José was Don Pío's brother-in-law, he had become one of the governor's fiercest political opponents. Carrillo was driven by pure ambition, which he pursued with considerable skill. A master political strategist with something of the common touch, he built a following among ordinary Angelenos, and in November 1845 he attempted to overthrow Pico's government, but failed. The shocked governor exiled his kinsman to Mexico, just as Governor Victoria had done years before, but Don José found his way to Monterey, where he joined forces with Castro. After this betrayal, Don Pío's distrust of the *norteños* became an obsession. Even after receiving a warning from Mexico City that war with the United States was only a matter of time, he continued to fix his attentions on Castro. "What can I do?" he replied when asked about his plans for the defense of the department. "I have not a dollar or a soldier. Castro at Monterey has got up a party against me and is trying to displace me."

Both men bore responsibility for the lack of unity, but Castro, if only by virtue of his location, proved considerably more attentive to the impending crisis. "War is preferable to peace," he declared to American consul Thomas Larkin, for then "affairs will at once be brought to a close and each one know his doom." In early June, only days before the Bear Flag insurrection, he appealed to Don Pío a final time. "I have notified you over and over again of the risk which the country runs, and of the necessity of taking steps for its defense," he wrote. Unless the governor responded immediately with arms and men, "I shall be absolutely compelled to declare the department in a state of siege and martial law in full force." The threat got Pico's attention. Within days of receiving Castro's letter, he had raised a force of several dozen men, including a company of eight or ten American rifleros, and on June 16, with brother Don Andrés by his side, Pico marched his little army out of Los Angeles, toward Monterey. His intention, however, was not to join in the defense of the homeland but to confront and defeat Castro, his rival for power. "I was convinced that Castro and I could not exist at the same time in the department," Pico later explained, "and that one or the other had to go."

Arriving at Santa Barbara on June 23, Pico was met by a messenger from Castro with news of the Bear Flag insurrection. At first he thought Castro was trying to trick him, but confirming reports soon arrived, and in haste Pico issued a proclamation addressed to the people of California. "A gang of North American adventurers, with the blackest treason that the spirit of evil could invent," he announced, "have invaded the town of Sonoma, raising their flag, and carrying off as prisoners four Mexican citizens." There could be no doubt that the insurgents were agents of the United States, which had first "stolen the Department of Texas and now wishes to do the same with California." He fired off an angry dispatch to Larkin, condemning the consul's "extraordinary indifference" in the face of this treachery, and warning that he would be held responsible for the actions of Frémont and his men.

Pico's letter reached Larkin shortly after the July 2 arrival at Monterey of Commodore John D. Sloat in the frigate USS *Savannah*. Sloat had learned of the fighting along the Río Grande on May 31, but being a cautious man, did not set sail for California until June 7, after learning that American naval forces had established a blockade of the Gulf port of Vera Cruz. Larkin had no power to constrain Frémont or the Bears, as Pico demanded, but he did succeed in persuading Sloat to delay coming ashore for several days while he made an attempt to get Alvarado and Castro, who had fled to the interior, to voluntarily place the department under American authority. Larkin understood that the events at Sonoma made it exceedingly difficult for them to cooperate "and still keep untarnished the national honor," but he feared that if they continued in resistance "the Bears may destroy them." Larkin's effort at persuasion, however, proved futile.

On the morning of July 7, under intense pressure from his own officers, Sloat sent Captain William Mervine ashore with a force of 250 sailors and marines to raise the flag. "We must take the place," Sloat told Larkin. "I shall be blamed for doing too little or too much—I prefer the latter." But Sloat's reputation was already ruined. He would be criticized precisely for doing too little, too late—for waiting too long at Mazatlán, then again at Monterey. Navy Secretary Bancroft would later characterize Sloat's caution as "shameful."

Sloat was also criticized for being too magnanimous in the proclamation in which he announced his intentions. The government of Mexico had attacked the United States and the two nations were at war, he asserted, and just as he had hoisted the American flag at the capital, so he would "carry it throughout California," which henceforth was to be considered a possession of the United States. He came in arms but hoped Californios would consider him their friend. He guaranteed the safety of all peaceable inhabitants, promising U.S. citizenship for all who chose to remain in California, and for those who wished to leave, the opportunity to remove without hindrance. Sloat wrote to Governor Pico and Commandante Castro in the same spirit, demanding their surrender, but also inviting them to return to Monterey to negotiate articles of capitulation, offering his personal assurance that they would be received "with all the respect due to your distinguished situation." Their compliance, he wrote, would "prevent the sacrifice of human life and the horrors of war, which I most anxiously desire to avoid." Sloat's sentiments, greatly influenced by Larkin, were conciliatory. In the opinion of his critics, they were deficient in martial fortitude.

Sloat said nothing about the Bears, which he considered an embarrassment, and in his response Castro insisted that the silence on that point presented an insurmountable difficulty. Armed Americans under Frémont's command had taken control of the department's northern frontier. "As he cannot believe that they belong to the forces commanded by the Commodore," Castro wrote, employing the formal third-person voice of diplomacy, "he will be obliged to him if he will be pleased to make an explanation on this subject in order that he may act in conformity with his reply." There could be no negotiations until Sloat assured the Californios that Frémont and the Bears had been brought under his command and control.

That same day Larkin received a melancholy note from Alvarado, his good friend for many years. The former governor expressed the hope that the conflict between their two countries might be resolved peacefully. But in the meantime, he wrote, he was duty-bound to follow the lead of Commandante Castro. Overriding even that allegiance was his patriotic duty to *la patria*, which he expected Larkin to understand. "The history of your country holds in remembrance the efforts of the immortal Washington," wrote the man who had championed the independence of California. "Although I know myself unworthy to compare with that hero, I would desire you to have the goodness to be the judge and decide what you would do in my case." By the time

Larkin received this letter, Alvarado and Castro had departed for the south to join forces with Governor Pico. The Californios would once again make their stand at Los Angeles.

AT SONOMA ON JULY 5 Frémont assumed formal command of the Bears and enlisted some two hundred American settlers to join the original members of his expedition in a force he christened the "California Battalion of Mounted Rifles," their term of service lasting "as long as necessary for the purpose of gaining and maintaining the independence of California." Frémont was planning a war of conquest, and he led his men back to Sutter's Fort to ready them for the campaign. A few days later a Navy lieutenant and a small company of marines arrived with the news that Commodore Sloat had taken possession of California for the United States. The lieutenant raised the American flag over Sutter's Fort and told Frémont that Sloat required his immediate presence.

The California Battalion entered Monterey eight days later, Frémont in the lead, surrounded by his entourage of Delaware Indians and followed by the men of his expedition, each balancing a rifle across the pommel of his saddle. "They are principally backwoodsmen," wrote a British naval officer who witnessed the parade, "the class that produced the heroes of Fenimore Cooper's best works." Behind them in a disorganized mass came the American settler volunteers. They were "a rough set," said the officer, adding that their "private, public, and moral character had better not be too closely examined." While the battalion bivouacked in a clearing at the edge of town, Frémont and Gillespie were ferried out to Sloat's frigate, expecting the commodore to applaud their actions and muster the California Battalion into the service of the United States.

But Sloat met them with stern questions. His orders were merely to occupy California's ports, and from his point of view the insurrection at Sonoma had made that assignment far more complicated than it ought to have been. He assumed, however, that Gillespie had brought

secret instructions from Washington that explained Frémont's conduct, and he insisted on hearing the details. "I know nothing," Sloat
protested, and "I want to know by what authority you are acting."
Frémont, who may have been under orders not to reveal President
Polk's secret instructions, responded defensively. "I acted solely on my
own responsibility, without any authority from the government," he
said, in a tone of passive aggression. Astonished by this response, Sloat
angrily dismissed both men.

But Sloat's tenure as commander in chief was about to end. Months
earlier he had written to Secretary Bancroft, complaining of failing
health and requesting that he be relieved. Bancroft complied, ordering
Captain Robert F. Stockton to set sail for the Pacific as Sloat's replacement. By happenstance Stockton arrived in Monterey the day following Sloat's interview with Frémont. After assuming command the new
commodore called Frémont to his quarters. In dress blues with gold
buttons and epaulets, his face framed by flowing curls and heavy mut-
tonchops, Stockton presented a striking contrast with the plain and
dour Sloat. A flamboyant advocate of American expansion through
naval power, he was as aggressive as Sloat was cautious. After listening
to Frémont's account, Stockton offered an enthusiastic endorsement
and ordered the California Battalion mustered into service under his
command. Together Stockton and Frémont developed a plan to carry
the American conquest to southern California. Stockton would sail
to San Pedro, Frémont to San Diego. With a detachment of sailors
and marines, the commodore would march on Los Angeles, confronting the forces of Castro and Pico, while Frémont blocked the passage
leading to Sonora. Sloat sailed for home on July 29, and that same day
Stockton issued a proclamation of his own, addressed to the people of
California.

The circumstances required nothing more from Stockton than an
announcement of his command. Instead, he used the occasion to intro-
duce an entirely new theory of the conquest, one deeply influenced
by Frémont. The military occupation of California by the United
States, Stockton asserted, was directed at obtaining redress from the

Three views of the Plaza, looking east from Fort Moore Hill,
in 1852, ca. 1865, and ca. 1871.

Mission San Gabriel, depicted by the German artist Ferdinand Deppe in 1832, showing a dome-shaped native dwelling in the right foreground.

Above: Two elderly Indian women near Mission San Fernando, ca. 1890.

Left: An emancipado, or emancipated mission Indian, 1839.

The church and the Plaza, ca. 1865.

Looking north across Sonoratown toward the cemetery and
the Stone Quarry Hills (today's Elysian Park), ca. 1870.

Angelenos pose before an adobe near the Plaza, ca. 1870.

The Lugo family at the Vicente Lugo residence, ca. 1890.

A contemporary sketch depicting the lynching of the five men taken from the Los Angeles jail in November 1863.

A crowd assembles on Poundcake Hill to witness the lynching of Josef Lachenais in 1870.

Lachenais hangs from the beam above the gate.

Samuel C. Foy (with the white beard), a leading vigilante, stands before his harness shop.

Residents of Chinatown, ca. 1875.

The bodies of seventeen murdered Chinese lie on the ground of the jail yard the morning following the riot, October 25, 1871.

The head of Los Angeles Street, Coronel building in the center distance,
Negro Alley to the right, site of the Chinese massacre of 1871.

Corner of Main and Commercial Streets, hardscrabble center of the
Los Angeles business district, ca. 1870.

Bird's-eye view of Los Angeles, 1857, looking north from about First Street, surrounded by illustrations of local businesses and residences.

government of Mexico for the crimes committed by Commandante Castro, who had "violated every principle of international law and national hospitality by hunting and pursuing Captain Frémont." Castro had "deluded and deceived the inhabitants of California," Stockton declared. "He came into power by rebellion and force, and by force he must be expelled." Every day brought new reports of "rapine, blood, and murder" committed by Castro's forces, and Stockton vowed he would bring "these criminals to justice." In the meantime the inhabitants, including all civil officers, were warned to remain in their homes. Otherwise "they will be treated as enemies and suffer accordingly."

It was an extraordinary argument. The United States had invaded and occupied California, Stockton asserted, because of the actions of the Californios themselves. That was a bald-faced lie, directly contradicted by Commodore Sloat's proclamation of three weeks before, but it provided Stockton with a justification for the conquest in the event that war with Mexico was not forthcoming. California's leaders, whom Sloat had addressed with respect, were now to be regarded as "criminals," hunted down and punished under the banner of American justice. Stockton's proclamation was, in effect, a declaration of martial law. Larkin was nonplussed by the document, unable to explain "where Commodore Stockton obtained the statements it contains." Commodore Sloat, handed a copy as his vessel weighed anchor, found it shocking. "It does not contain my reasons for taking possession," he reported to Secretary Bancroft, "or my views or intentions towards that country, [and] consequently it does not meet my approbation." Frémont and Gillespie, on the other hand, were delighted. As Gillespie put it, with Stockton now in charge, there would be no more of Sloat's "half way measures."

ON JULY 12 Commandante Castro and his body of men met Governor Pico and his force at San Luis Obispo, the midpoint between Monterey and Los Angeles. Pico later recalled the moment. "We embraced, and all manifested great enthusiasm for the cause of our country." The two leaders issued a joint declaration, boldly vowing to repel the American invaders. In fact, the bitter rivalry between them was not so easily forgotten, and to forestall open conflict between their supporters they traveled separately to Los Angeles, where both arrived ten days later. Pico was pessimistic. "No matter how great our patriotism," he reported to the authorities in Mexico City, without additional men and matériel "we shall never be able to reconquer what is lost nor avoid losing the rest." He ordered all male Californios between the ages of fifteen and sixty to arm themselves and assemble at the pueblo, but the response was disappointing. Most ordinary Angelenos were outraged at the American invasion, but the elite of rancheros, vineyardists, and merchants expressed more ambiguous sentiments. A number of prominent individuals openly welcomed annexation by the United States, and the division of opinion led to confusion and apathy. By the end of the month fewer than two hundred men had enlisted in defense of Los Angeles.

By that time Frémont and the California Battalion had taken possession of the presidio at San Diego without firing a shot. Rancheros in the surrounding country did what they could to keep livestock out of American hands, and it took more than a week to round up a sufficient number of horses, but with that accomplished, Frémont set out for Los Angeles with 120 men, leaving San Diego under the control of a small garrison commanded by Archibald Gillespie. Castro learned of Frémont's advance the same day he received news that Stockton had landed with 360 men at San Pedro. Knowing his paltry force would be unable to resist such an onslaught, Castro wrote to Stockton, expressing his willingness to enter into negotiations and proposing a cease-fire.

His dispatch was carried to San Pedro under a flag of truce by Captain José María Flores, a Mexican officer on Castro's staff. Stockton received Flores and his delegation imperiously and, ignoring diplomatic protocol, forced them to stand on the beach while he withdrew to his campaign tent to read the dispatch and compose a response.

Reemerging, he handed Flores a sealed note for Castro and announced he would never agree to a cease-fire. "I will either take the country or be licked out of it," he declared, then peremptorily dismissed the delegation with a wave of his hand. Flores was deeply insulted, as was Castro when he read Stockton's reply. His plain duty, Stockton had written, was to press the fight until California ceased to be part of Mexico. The only alternative to war was unconditional surrender. "If you will agree to hoist the American flag in California, I will stop my forces and negotiate the treaty."

Castro replied in an angry letter. "You offer me the most shameful of propositions, to hoist the American flag in this department. Never, never, never!" Stockton might succeed in raising his banner over Los Angeles, but "it will not be by my acquiescence, nor by that of my compatriots, but solely by force." Alvarado, who had accompanied Castro to Los Angeles, considered this the moment of no return. "If Stockton had sent a commission to confer with Castro and myself," he wrote, "a treaty satisfactory to both sides might have been arranged." Instead, the commodore insisted on capitulation without honor. The refusal to negotiate, Castro warned Stockton, "makes you responsible for all the evils and misfortunes that may result from a war so unjust as that which has been declared against this peaceful department."

Castro concluded that retreat was his only option. "I can count on only 100 men, badly armed, worse supplied, and discontented," he told Pico, and "have reason to fear that not even these few will fight when the necessity arises." Honorable withdrawal to Sonora was better than ignominious defeat in Los Angeles. Not everyone agreed. "If the Spaniards had thought like you when Napoleon Bonaparte invaded," one of Pico's aides told Castro, "we would be French." But on the evening of August 9, after instructing his men to return to their homes and families in the north, Castro fled south, accompanied by a small group of Mexican officers. The following morning, at an emergency meeting of the legislature, Pico read Castro's parting proclamation to the delegates. American intentions, Castro charged, had been treacherous from beginning to end. The government of the United

States, which initially denied any complicity with the insurgents at Sonoma, had in fact joined with them in perpetrating this "iniquitous invasion." But it got worse. "Not only do our oppressors wish to make us tributary slaves, but moreover they have the effrontery to order that we should voluntarily proclaim this slavery ourselves." The Americans might take their country but not their honor. "The lack of resources to carry on the war against a powerful nation will perhaps make it triumph over our weak forces, but nevermore over our hearts."

Los Angeles was defenseless, Pico told the delegates, and he asked for their advice and counsel in this dire emergency. Quickly they reached a consensus. "The best thing," reported Antonio Coronel, "would be for Pico to leave as well, since with neither civil nor military governor at hand the enemy couldn't impose severe terms of surrender on them." Together they agreed to dissolve the department government. That decision made, Pico delivered an impromptu address. "My friends, farewell!" he said, shedding bitter tears. "I abandon the country of my birth, my family, property, and everything that a man holds most dear, all to save the national honor." There would be hard days ahead, but he trusted the courage and loyalty of the *hijos del país* would frustrate the conqueror's designs. "The Supreme Being that guards over the future destiny of nations will provide us the glorious day in which we shall again see our dear Fatherland free and happy," he declared. "That will be for me, beloved compatriots, the fulfillment of all my happiness and the only thing to which my heart aspires, in the midst of the bitter sorrow that it feels in telling you good bye!" Then the legislature voted to adjourn for the last and final time. That night a stream of functionaries, officers, and common soldiers abandoned Los Angeles, leaving Angelenos to their fate.

NEWS OF THE AMERICAN UPRISING at Sonoma and the occupation of Monterey created considerable anxiety among extranjeros in Los Angeles. The hostility of Californios toward resident Americans became so intense that a number of them abandoned the pueblo and sought refuge in the countryside. Governor Pico attempted to reassure them, declaring that their lives and property would be protected as long as they remained neutral. Most hunkered down, kept quiet, and were not disturbed. Abel Stearns, who had served in Pico's administration, left with his young wife shortly after Stockton landed at San Pedro. They sat out the war at Rancho Los Alamitos, his coastal retreat.

A number of Americans, however, lent active support to the conquest. They were organized by Alexander Bell, a middle-aged Pennsylvanian who in 1844, after nearly twenty years as a successful merchant in Mexico, had settled in Los Angeles and established a flourishing business, trading in hides, tallow, and general merchandise. Bell built a house and storefront on the southeastern side of the Plaza, married into an elite Californio family, and became an active parishioner of the Plaza church. But he declined to become a Mexican citizen. "The United States will come to me," he predicted to American friends shortly after his arrival in California. When Stockton landed, Bell assembled a group of two dozen like-minded Americans, including James R. Barton, and led them to San Pedro, where Stockton enrolled them as a volunteer rifle company with Bell as their captain.

Despite their years in Mexican California, Bell and his men still considered themselves Americans. For other extranjeros, however, the question of loyalty was more complicated. Benjamin Davis Wilson of Tennessee had spent ten years working as a trapper and trader in New Mexico before coming to Los Angeles with the Rowland-Workman party. He found himself beguiled by both the country and the people. "Receiving so much kindness from the native Californians," he wrote, "I arrived at the conclusion that there was no place in the world where I could enjoy more true happiness and true friendship than among them." Using accumulated savings, he purchased Rancho Jurupa, situated on the banks of the Río Santa Ana, sixty miles east of the pueblo, where the city of Riverside would later rise. He married Ramona Yorba, the fifteen-year-old daughter of Bernardo Yorba, wealthy owner of Rancho Santa Ana, downstream from Wilson's property. And in 1845 he accepted Governor Pico's appointment as deputy alcalde in charge of the eastern frontier of the Los Angeles district. Like Bell—and unlike most of his fellow Americans—Wilson chose to maintain his American citizenship. But in contrast to Bell, he remained neutral, which pleased neither side. Falling under the suspicion of both American and Californio neighbors, he was compelled to resign his post. If he was permitted to remain unmolested on his rancho, Wilson wrote to Governor Pico, "I would pledge my word to be peaceable and do no act hostile to the country."

The night before Pico fled Los Angeles, he summoned Wilson to his headquarters and asked him to carry a message to Commodore Stockton. "Tell him of my intention to abandon the country," Pico said, "and that I hope he will not ill treat my people." On the morning of August 11, accompanied by his friend John Rowland and several other Americans, Wilson left for San Pedro. A few miles from the harbor they encountered Stockton at the head of his "web-feet regiment" of approximately three hundred sailors and marines. Hauling four large guns, taken from the *Congress* and mounted on carretas, they were making slow progress. Wilson delivered Pico's message, and when Stockton learned Los Angeles was without defenders, he sent half his men back to their vessel. The Domínguez family, owners of Rancho San Pedro, had provided Wilson with a beautiful saddle horse for the commodore, and he presented it with an invitation that Stockton accompany his party back to the pueblo. They arrived in the afternoon and found the place deserted. Wilson took Stockton to Government House on Calle Principal, south of the Plaza, vacated by Pico only hours before. Later that afternoon a marine detachment from the *Congress* arrived after a forced march and established a defensive perimeter around the new American headquarters.

The main force of American sailors reached the southern outskirts of the pueblo two days later, about midday on August 13. Stockton and the marines came down to greet them and were soon joined by Frémont and his mounted rifles who had ridden up from San Diego. At four in the afternoon approximately three hundred Americans entered

Los Angeles in triumphant formation, led by a brass band playing "Hail Columbia!" The procession resembled more "a parade of home guards than an enemy taking possession of a conquered town," wrote Frémont. They hoisted the American flag from a staff on the Plaza while small clusters of Angelenos observed from the summit of the hill behind the church. As the band continued playing, a few brave souls drew nearer. "At first the children on the hill ventured down and peeped round the corners of the houses," wrote William Dane Phelps, captain of an American merchant vessel, who had joined Stockton's sailors in their march. "A few lively tunes brought out the 'vivas' of the elder ones, and before closing for the day quite a circle of delighted natives surrounded the musicians." Californios loved music and dancing, but few had ever heard a full brass band. Captain Phelps found himself standing next to the priest from the Plaza church. "Ah!" the old man exclaimed, "that music will do more service in the conquest of California than a thousand bayonets." The band continued to hold concerts in the Plaza every evening for the next several days.

Gradually the pueblo came back to life, as first the children and the elderly, then the women, and finally the men returned to their homes and occupations. On August 17 a messenger came up from San Pedro with the first definitive word of the American declaration of war against Mexico three months before, and later that day Stockton issued a proclamation declaring that henceforth California would be "a Territory of the United States." Until a civil government could be organized, he declared, the country would remain under martial law. All civil and military officers of the old regime would be required to swear an oath not to take up arms. Frémont's men had already been dispatched in pursuit of Castro and Pico, both of whom successfully evaded capture and escaped to Mexico. But the Bears took other Californios into custody, and a number more came in of their own volition. Andrés Pico, José Antonio Carrillo, José María Flores, and others surrendered to the Americans and took an oath, solemnly swearing, "That I will not take up arms against the United States of North America, that I will not do anything, or say anything, or write anything that may disturb the peace and tranquility of California, *so pena de muerte*," under penalty of death. They were then released on parole.

Los Angeles, that turbulent pueblo, had been occupied by the forces of the United States without bloodshed. The Americans misinterpreted the lack of resistance as a sign of the Californios' timidity and cowardice, but it was, in fact, the result of their divided leadership. A hatred of the American invaders would continue to simmer among ordinary Angelenos, but for the time being they remained leaderless.

B. D. Wilson decided the moment had come to return to his rancho and resume his business, so he went to Stockton to bid goodbye. "I should have someone on the frontier watching events," the commodore said, and he asked Wilson to take the job. When Wilson objected that he was a civilian, Stockton replied with a laugh. "That is nonsense. You have a ranch on the frontier and there is no other person in whom I can trust who knows the people or understands their language. Therefore accept a captaincy from me and make up your own company of as many men as you please." Wilson reluctantly agreed, and when he returned to the upper Río Santa Ana, he recruited some two dozen settlers, including both Americans and New Mexicans, to his ranger company.

On August 26 Stockton composed an ebullient dispatch to President Polk. He had routed and dispersed the Californio forces and secured the country for the United States. In a few days he would return to Monterey, resupply the Pacific Squadron, and extend naval operations south to the Pacific coast of Mexico. He planned to appoint Frémont territorial governor. "All is now peaceful and quiet," he wrote. "My word is at present the law of the land. My person is more than regal. The haughty Mexican cavalier shakes hands with me with pleasure, and the beautiful women look to me with joy and gladness as their friend and benefactor. In short, all of power and luxury is spread before me, through the mysterious workings of a beneficent Providence." In the words of the psalmist, pride goeth before destruction, and an haughty spirit before a fall.

· CHAPTER 7 ·

¡ABAJO LOS AMERICANOS!

IN EARLY SEPTEMBER, Stockton and Frémont decamped for Monterey with their forces. Archibald Gillespie and a company of fifty American rifleros, including a score of Bear Flag veterans, remained to enforce martial law in Los Angeles. From his headquarters at Government House on Calle Principal, Gillespie ruled with a heavy hand. Stockton had granted parole to all Mexican and Californio officers who agreed to lay down their arms, but Gillespie jailed those he deemed troublesome. He issued arbitrary rules prohibiting Angelenos from congregating in public, riding horses on public streets, or conducting business after sunset. He dispatched his rifleros to ransack private homes in search of weapons and other contraband.

On Mexican independence day, the sixteenth of September 1846, there were no public celebrations. Gillespie refused to lift the curfew, forcing Angelenos who wished to commemorate the holiday to assemble in small groups behind locked doors. On the evening of the fifteenth a number of men gathered at Ylario Varela's, and as the midnight hour approached, José Antonio Carrillo rose to lead them in the *grito*. Politics was Carrillo's passion. "A remarkable fellow he was," wrote Horace Bell, "standing six feet four inches tall, weighing about two hundred and forty pounds, and bearing a perfect resemblance to the statues of some of the old Roman senators." One early Los Angeles historian described Carrillo as "the Machiavelli of California politics," the reigning master of political intrigue. That evening at Varela's, he was working his craft.

"*¡Los Mexicanos!*" he began. "*¡Viva la independencia!* Long live the heroes who gave us our homeland!" The other men joined in, reciting the familiar phrases, but their words rang hollow. Mexico had done nothing to protect them from the American invaders. Even the leaders of California, their *patria chica*, had abandoned them. Don José paused, fighting back tears, then departed from the standard script. "There is not one among us who deserves to call himself the son of those great men," he said. "We are craven cowards for allowing ourselves to be so shamefully conquered."

Cobardía—cowardice. Angelenos were haunted by the charge. The American occupiers taunted them with it. Commodore Stockton, in a bombastic speech to a crowd of Americans at Yerba Buena in the north, characterized the conquest of Los Angeles as a test of honor the Californios had failed. He had challenged Castro and Pico to a "fair fight," Stockton exclaimed, giving them the choice of "when and where this great matter was to be settled." They responded with pronunciamentos, something they were very good at doing. But after all their threats, he scoffed, "they would not under the most favorable circumstances strike one manly blow for their capital or their country." Californios deeply resented such talk. They considered themselves men of honor. Honor was the prime regulating force in their world. Yet among themselves they had to admit their shame at the conduct of leaders who, in the words of one patriot, had "disgraced the country" by running away.

The men greeted Carrillo's words with silence until finally Sérbulo Varela rose to speak. He and his brother had arranged this occasion with Carrillo. The Varelas were native Angelenos, *gente de razón* but not elite, although Don Sérbulo's marriage to a woman of the Ávila family had raised his social status considerably. Described as tempestuous by all who knew them, the brothers had a long history of political activism in Los Angeles, having played a role in virtually every protest in the decade since the vigilante episode of 1836. They developed a reputation as charismatic and popular leaders of ordinary Angelenos, often working in conjunction with Carrillo, the Varela brothers providing the street smarts, Don José the respectable connections. In 1845, only a year before, they had joined Carrillo in his attempt to overthrow Governor Pico. And in the aftermath of the American conquest, Don Sérbulo immediately got himself into hot water, fined for violating an American regulation against gambling in public. Rather than submit, he went into hiding. He told friends he would rather die than live as he was.

That night Don Sérbulo vowed he would no longer tolerate the charge of cowardice. "I swear by the love of my homeland this will not be said about me." In an effort to reclaim Angeleno honor, he would mount a challenge to the American occupiers. The other men present that evening responded with enthusiasm. There was a great deal at stake for them. They wanted to throw out the invaders, but even more they wanted to resuscitate their honor. "We are with you," they exclaimed, "but what can we do?" There is only one way, said Don Sérbulo, "*armarse y combatir*"—take up arms and fight. They must risk all or nothing. That night the group assembled at Varela's swore an oath: that as soon as they had assembled a sufficient force, they would strike at the Americans, *pase lo que pase*, come what may.

DURING THE HOLIDAY WEEK the cantinas along Calle de los Negros filled to overflowing with Californios and emancipados but also with off-duty American rifleros—eager for a drink, a chance at the monte table, or the company of one of the pueblo's loose women, the *hijas de puta*. The vice district created no end of trouble for Captain Gillespie. His garrison included "some very good men," he reported, "but many very bad." They were unaccustomed to military control, and proved themselves "perfect drunkards whilst in this ciudad of wine and aguardiente." In the evenings, when Angelenos were forced back to their homes by the curfew, the rifleros headed across the river to the *pueblito*, which never closed. On any given evening half the garrison could be found carousing at the Indian ranchería.

Gillespie was expert at commanding a Marine company aboard a Navy frigate, but entirely at sea with these independent frontiersmen. "Every means in my power were tried to enforce discipline," he reported, "but the men whom I depended upon would not do a soldier's duty." He sent several incorrigibles packing, but that sparked protest among the remaining men. He dispatched an officer with ten of the rebellious rifleros to guard Warner's Pass on the Sonora Road, some 125 miles to the southeast, but the trouble did not end there, and a few days later he was forced to jail several men for "mutiny, drunkenness and using disrespectful language towards the flag and officers." Angelenos, he feared, understood the character of his rifleros all too well. "They were men for whom the Californians could have no respect," Gillespie wrote, "and whom, from the spirit of insubordination they constantly evinced, the Californians thought they could overcome."

Before dawn on the morning of September 23, Gillespie awoke to the report of firearms. Rushing up a ladder to the flat roof of Government House, he found his sentries firing down at what they insisted was a force of several dozen heavily armed men. Angelenos later claimed the group included no more than a handful of hooligans, most of them drunk, armed with several old *escopetas*, or shotguns. Led by Sérbulo Varela, they gathered at the rear of the building, beating drums and chanting, "*¡Abajo los Americanos!*"—Down with the Americans! More a protest than an attack, their demonstration turned violent when the Americans opened fire and the insurgents took cover behind an adobe wall. The two sides exchanged shots until one of the Californios suffered a minor wound and all of them retreated.

At first light Gillespie dispatched Lieutenant Samuel J. Hensley's mounted company—among them James Barton, future sheriff of Los Angeles County—to locate and arrest the offenders. The Americans barged into homes, confiscated weapons, and seized half a dozen men suspected of "aiding the party in arms." While investigating some adobes on the pueblo's south side, they fell into an ambush by a small group of mounted Angelenos, hidden in a field of corn. "*¡A las armas, muchachos!*" the riders cried as they charged through the tall, dry stalks. The Americans scattered, but not before one of them was knocked from his horse and mortally wounded by a lance.

Outraged, Gillespie ordered the roundup and arrest of every paroled officer in the pueblo, including such prominent men as Andrés Pico and José Antonio Carrillo. It was an ill-considered move, for it so angered the Californios, as one of them later testified, "that even those who had recognized the American conquest out of fear joined with those who had started the uprising." Sensing his error, Gillespie released the officers later that day, but the damage was done. Leaving the American headquarters, the paroled officers joined Varela and his band of insurgents at their encampment at Paredon Blanco, the white bluffs along the east bank of Río Porciúncula, across from the pueblo. By day's end more than three hundred men had congregated there. Gillespie's response to Varela's challenge had sparked a popular uprising.

THE FOLLOWING DAY, September 24, the insurgents issued a carefully written pronunciamento, an appeal that detailed the justice of their cause.

> Fellow Citizens: For a month and a half we have been subjugated and oppressed by an insignificant force of adventurers from the United States of North America, the result of the regrettable cowardice and incompetence of the department's chief authorities. They have placed us in a condition worse than slavery. They dictate despotic and arbitrary laws and burden us with onerous levies. They seek to destroy our industry and agriculture, and compel us to

abandon our property, which they intend to divide among themselves. Shall we permit ourselves to be subjugated and to accept in silence the heavy chains of slavery? Shall we lose the soil inherited from our fathers, which cost them so much blood and sacrifice? Shall we leave our families victim to the most barbarous servitude? Shall we wait to see our wives violated, our innocent children beaten by American whips, our property sacked, our temples profaned, to drag out a life full of shame and disgrace? No, a thousand times no! Compatriots, death rather than that! Who among you does not feel his heart beat with violence? Who does not feel his blood boil? Who is not willing to rise up in arms to destroy our oppressors? We believe none are so vile and cowardly. We, the majority of the inhabitants of this district, justly indignant at the tyrants, raise the cry of war, arms in hand, and with one voice swear to the following articles.

A list followed. The insurgents declared their determination to remain a "free and independent" department of Mexico, and vowed to drive the invaders from their soil. They called on all male Californios to report in arms, and warned that anyone failing to respond would be "declared a traitor, under penalty of death." Extranjeros who assisted the invaders would be subject to the same punishment. All citizens of the United States were to be arrested and dispatched to Mexico, their property confiscated and sold to support the defense of the homeland. The pronunciamento concluded with the signatures or marks of more than three hundred citizens, nearly half the male residents of Los Angeles, men both ordinary and elite. "There was not a soul who did not rise up against the North Americans," wrote Manuel Clemente Rojo, a young Peruvian attorney and journalist who moved to Los Angeles after the American conquest and devoted himself to collecting the wartime stories of Californios.

After consulting with the paroled officers, Don Sérbulo appointed Capitán José María Flores commander in chief of what would henceforth be known as *las fuerzas nacionales*, the national forces. Flores, a native of Sonora, had come to California in 1842 as a young officer in Governor Micheltorena's battalion. Some time later he married the daughter of a ranchero, and when Micheltorena was forced out in 1845 Flores remained behind with his wife and children, joining the staff of Commandant José Castro. He fled to Los Angeles with Castro following the American invasion of Monterey. In August 1846 he delivered Castro's proposal for a truce to Stockton, and was deeply insulted by Stockton's verbal abuse. Captain Flores was an intelligent officer and a righteously angry opponent of the United States. To Californios, however, he remained *un mexicano de la otra banda*—a Mexican from the other shore—and eventually that would create problems.

But before it did so, Flores displayed his organizational skill. He divided the insurgent forces into three squadrons, two commanded by Californios José Antonio Carrillo and Andrés Pico, the third by a Mexican officer. Fewer than half the volunteers had firearms, and there was very little lead or gunpowder. But owing to the forethought of an elderly woman, Flores found himself in possession of a valuable artillery piece. For years this brass swivel gun had been used for firing ceremonial salutes on feast days and special occasions. When Stockton began his advance on the pueblo in August, the widow María Cota de Reyes enlisted her daughters and nieces to help bury it in the garden behind her adobe, declaring that the Americans should not have the cannon. Learning of it, Flores ordered the weapon exhumed, and Angelenos christened it *"el pedrero de la vieja,"* the old woman's gun. A blacksmith hammered out a number of iron cannon balls, and Doña María's niece María Rafaela Cota de Temple contributed several kegs of gunpowder, expropriated from the storehouse of her husband, merchant Jonathan Temple.

Temple himself was holed up at Government House with virtually every other American remaining in Los Angeles, a total of fifty or sixty men. Well stocked with hunting rifles and an ample supply of ammunition, they also had access to several rusty iron cannons that had been spiked and abandoned after the battle with Governor Micheltorena in

1845. Gillespie ordered his men to drill them out and collect scrap iron for shot, then had them drag one of the guns up the hill behind the church, where it commanded the Plaza, making it impossible for the insurgents to attack without serious risk. But the Americans remained besieged, with no way to break out of the pueblo.

Gillespie received a copy of the insurgents' proclamation on the evening of September 24 and immediately dispatched a courier to Stockton in the north. For this desperate mission he selected a man named John Brown, better known as Juan Flaco or Lean John, a Swede who had resided in California for some fifteen years. While they waited for nightfall to provide him with some cover, Brown's fellow rifleros treated him to champagne plundered from a local cellar. Finally, when it was dark, he mounted up. "I then requested Jon Temple to open the gate and give the password so that I could pass the sentinels," Brown recalled. Instead, Temple shouted out, at full voice, "Don't shoot the man on the white horse!" Brown felt as if a target had been slapped on his back. "I put spurs to my horse and went off kiting, followed by a pack of dogs barking," he remembered. The Americans heard the Californio guards shouting to one another and mounting up in pursuit. The chances of Brown's making it out of town, let alone reaching Monterey, seemed remote. In a memoir, Brown described Temple's shout as "impudence." Had the Americans known that Temple's wife, Doña Rafaela, had provided powder to the insurgents, they might have considered his loud mouth something worse. Temple was one of many for whom the war created difficult personal dilemmas.

LATE IN THE AFTERNOON of September 25, on a bear-hunting expedition in the Palomar Mountains with the men of his ranger company, Captain Benjamin Davis Wilson was overtaken by an exhausted rider with an urgent message from ranchero John Rowland and several other extranjeros, warning "that there was a general revolt of the Californians and Mexicans against Gillespie and all Americans, and that there was the devil to pay generally, and to hasten down." Wilson turned his men around and, after traveling down mountain trails in the dark of night, arrived the next morning at Rancho Jurupa, his home place on the upper Río Santa Ana, where they found Rowland and two others waiting. "Gillespie's course towards the people had been so despotic and in every way unjustifiable," explained Rowland, "the people had risen to a man against him." The "shout of insurrection" now sounded throughout the countryside, "and rumor was that they would spare not the life of any extranjero." Wilson's wife had fled with their child to her father's rancho downriver. The Indian women who kept his house told Wilson that his vaqueros had taken all the horses and joined the insurgents at Paredon Blanco. "They are going to drive the Americans out of the country," they said.

Americans were a small minority among the several hundred residents—Californios, New Mexicans, and Indians—who lived and worked along the upper Río Santa Ana. Wilson and his company were vulnerable, so he decided to lead his men west some twenty-five miles to Rancho Santa Ana del Chino, where American ranchero Isaac Williams, known to Californios as Don Julián, was said to have ample stores of gunpowder and lead. Spread the word to rendezvous at Chino, Wilson told Rowland, as he and his rangers rode off. They would gather there, then attempt to penetrate the Californio lines and join Gillespie's force.

Within an hour of Wilson's departure José del Cármen Lugo arrived at Jurupa with ten or fifteen of his vaqueros. Lugo, Wilson's upstream neighbor, operated Rancho San Bernardino with his two brothers. For several years the Lugos and Wilson had maintained neighborly relations, dividing their cattle at the annual rodeo and defending each other's stock against desert raiders who swept down Cajon Pass, the notch in the mountains separating southern California from the desert badlands beyond. But the war divided neighbors, and fearing a preemptive attack by Wilson's ranger company, Lugo chose to take the offensive.

From the Indian women at Wilson's casa he learned that the Americans were headed west to Chino. Lugo knew Rancho Santa Ana del

Chino well, for it was part of his family's patrimony. He also knew its proprietor intimately. Born in Pennsylvania, Isaac Williams had came to California in the early 1830s after several years as a fur trapper and trader in the Rocky Mountains. He settled in as a merchant, became a naturalized Mexican citizen, and in 1839 married María de Jesús Lugo, daughter of Antonio María Lugo, one of the wealthiest rancheros in the Los Angeles district. Rancho del Chino, some 22,000 acres sixty miles east of Los Angeles, was the father's wedding present to the couple. Don José del Cármen was Don Julián's brother-in-law. Doña María, his sister and Don Julián's wife, had died in childbirth several years before, after bearing three children. The families were close.

The ranch house at Chino was heavily fortified against attack by Indian raiders, equipped with heavy wooden doors and shutters, gun ports, and a bulwark of ditches and walls, making it a logical place for the Americans to make a stand. Wilson's rangers arrived in the midafternoon and were soon joined by Rowland and several more extranjeros, raising their number to twenty-five or thirty men. But it turned out that Don Julián had almost no ammunition—his stores, like Wilson's horses, had been confiscated by Californio insurgents—and Wilson estimated that with what they had in hand they could hold out for no more than a few hours in a siege. Better to leave immediately and find a back way into Los Angeles, he advised his men, but they scorned the suggestion. "The majority of them, being new in the country, had a very contemptible opinion of the Californian's courage and fighting qualities," Wilson later recalled, "and seemed to be of the unanimous opinion that a few shots would suffice to scare away any number of them that should come to attack us." A few went so far as to question Wilson's nerve, which raised his dander. So be it, he exclaimed. He would stay and fight with the rest, and "we would see where the real courage was."

Wilson sent one of the rangers out to scout, and after a few minutes they heard the sound of gunfire, and the man came running back with a ball lodged in his shoulder. The compound was surrounded by nearly a hundred Californios, he reported excitedly, inflating the size of Lugo's party by a factor of five. For his part, Don José del Cármen also overestimated. He dispatched a courier to Los Angeles reporting that at least fifty Americans were inside his brother-in-law's casa and begging for reinforcements. Lugo's fear was that Wilson's men might commence a fight before the Angelenos arrived. "They would have finished us," he later recalled, "since we had no more than four or five guns and a few pistols, plus one or two lances and a few Indian arrows." His men made camp in a willow grove not far from the compound, and both sides spent a restless night exchanging sporadic gunfire.

Early the next morning, thirty Angelenos arrived under the command of Sérbulo Varela. Many were indignant, as one later recalled, that the Americans, "most of whom had solicited and obtained Mexican citizenship, who had married the daughters of the country, and had made their fortunes under the Mexican banner, should show themselves such ingrates toward those who had loaded them with benefits." Lugo requested that Varela hold off on any attack while he made a final attempt to persuade Wilson to surrender. He was concerned that Don Julián's three children—his nephew and nieces—might still be in the house.

As the two men stood talking, a boy on horseback suddenly bolted from a corral at the backside of the ranch house, a pair of mounted Californios took off in pursuit, and someone inside the adobe began firing at them through the gun ports. The fight was on. Shouting to his men to follow him, Lugo mounted and charged toward the adobe. His horse jumped a moat, but the horse of the man riding beside him, Carlos Ballesteros, stumbled, throwing the rider to the ground. Ballesteros jumped up and was instantly hit in the temple with a slug fired from an American rifle. Lugo heard him cry out, with his last breath, "*¡Adelante, adelante, compañeros!*" Forward comrades! Lugo and several others made it to the adobe. They jumped from their horses and crouched against the outer wall, below the gun ports, where the Americans firing from inside could not get at them.

Ballesteros's death enraged them. "*¡Mueran los Americanos!*"—Death to the Americans!—one cried. "*¡No hay cuartel!*"—No quarter! One or two men reached up and grabbed the barrels of the rifles protruding through the ports, then rose and fired their pistols point-blank into the dark interior. "*¡Incendiar la casa!*"—Burn the house!—another Californio shouted. "*¡Hacerles asado!*"—Let them roast!

Like virtually all adobes in southern California, Don Julián's was roofed with cane and covered in a thick coating of water-resistant but flammable bitumen or tar. Hurriedly gathering grass and cornstalks, the Californios twisted them into makeshift torches, while Don José, braving a barrage from the American rifles, galloped to the adjacent ranchería of Don Julián's Indian workers, and brought back a burning faggot from a cooking fire. The torches were lit and tossed onto the roof, igniting the tar and producing thick clouds of black smoke.

A few moments later, through the smoky haze, the Californios saw the form of a man on the roof of the adobe. It was Don Julián, a daughter in each arm, his frightened son clinging to his knees. "Don't shoot! Don't shoot!" he cried. "Quarter for my motherless children!" Lugo was suddenly overcome with panic. In his passion for the fight he had forgotten his nieces and nephew, and now they were in deadly peril. He hurried to the backside of the house, where the adobe wall of an adjoining corral provided a step up to the roof, and shouted to his brother-in-law to hand the children down.

By that time, overcome by the acrid smoke, the Americans had ceased firing, and Don Sérbulo was conducting negotiations with Wilson through the locked front door. "I am your friend," he shouted. "Neither you or any of your friends shall be injured." Suddenly the door swung open and the Americans spilled out, coughing and spitting. Several had been seriously wounded. As they lay on the ground, recovering from the ordeal, Lugo approached his brother-in-law, Don Julián. "I told him that he should thank me for saving his children," he later recalled, "but neither he nor they gave me any sign of thanks afterward. The little boy, who then was eight years old, died soon after. The girls are still living and care nothing about their uncle." The war divided families as well as neighbors.

That afternoon the Californios and the Americans mounted their horses and began the journey to Los Angeles. They had traveled only a little distance when the column suddenly halted. Wilson and Varela, riding together at the rear, saw men dismounting ahead. "There's some deviltry going on there," said Don Sérbulo, and with Wilson following he charged forward. Ranchero Diego Sepúlveda, responding to the general clamor of his men, was preparing to execute a number of the prisoners. Don Sérbulo jumped from his saddle, drew his short sword, and placed himself between the Americans and Don Diego. He had given the extranjeros his personal guarantee of safety, he declared, and would kill the first man who attempted to harm them. For a moment the two Californios stood facing each other; then, without a word, Don Diego turned and remounted. The crisis passed quickly, but Wilson never forgot it. "His voice was stentorian," he wrote of Varela, "his deportment very gallant, and his conduct on that occasion made him worthy of our admiration and respect."

BY THAT EVENING the Americans were imprisoned in a cell at Paredon Blanco. The following morning Wilson was summoned by Commandante José María Flores, who asked that he compose a note to Captain Gillespie. "Say to him that General Flores is a Christian as well as a soldier," he instructed, "and wishes to avoid the spilling of blood unnecessarily. That my men are very anxious to attack him, and one charge from them would cause the destruction of himself and all his soldiers." Looking around at the Angelenos assembled at Paredon Blanco, Wilson saw the truth of what Flores said. Elated by their victory at Chino, they were certain they could defeat Gillespie. Flores had the upper hand, but he proposed an honorable capitulation. If Gillespie would agree to evacuate Los Angeles, he would guarantee the safety of all the Americans. He would permit them to march out with their arms and ammunition and proceed unmolested to the port of San Pedro, where they would be required to embark on the first vessel headed north. Wilson wrote what Flores told him and added a personal postscript, urging Gillespie to accept the offer, "in the interest of himself and all Americans in the country, whether prisoners or not." Otherwise Wilson feared the worst. "Many of the old Californians who had been ill treated by Gillespie felt revengeful," he noted. They were drinking heavily and taking bets on which of them would have the luck to kill the American commander.

Wilson's note forced Gillespie to face the hopelessness of his situation. That afternoon negotiations began between his representatives and Angeleno leaders at El Aliso, the vineyard of Luis Vignes. The bone of contention proved to be the artillery Gillespie had found at Government House, which he insisted on hauling to San Pedro for the protection of his men. Finally the negotiators arranged a compromise. Flores would permit the Americans to take the guns as long as Gillespie agreed to abandon them on the beach before his embarkation. The truce, signed late on the afternoon of September 29, was followed by an exchange of prisoners, twelve Californios held by Gillespie for twelve Americans held by the insurgents. Wilson and most of the prominent captives, however, remained in Californio custody for the duration.

The following morning, as hundreds of Angelenos lined the road heading south to San Pedro, the Americans marched out of the pueblo, drums beating and flags flying, every man in arms, cannons loaded and primed, with slow matches burning. "I marched out of the city with colors flying," Gillespie reported, "having endured more suffering in those seven days, than my service of seventeen years could equal." Flores supplied carts and horses, which enabled a full evacuation in a single long day of travel. The advance guard arrived at San Pedro just after sunset and established a camp on the bluffs in the enveloping evening fog.

The following morning the Americans awoke to find the merchant vessel *Vandalia* at anchor in the roadstead. The articles of capitulation stipulated that their stay be "only long enough to prepare for embarkation for Monterey," but Gillespie had other intentions. "Hoping that my courier might have reached Commodore Stockton," he wrote, "I determined to remain a few days at San Pedro roads, for the arrival of one of the ships from the north." In direct violation of the agreement he had signed, Gillespie unlimbered his guns and positioned them in battery. Flores sent a note of protest and ordered Carrillo's squadron to take up a position a mile or so distant. But not until October 4, when Carrillo began pressing forward, did Gillespie finally issue an order for his men to begin loading their baggage onto the vessel. Even then he planned to remain in port, again in violation of the truce, hoping for the arrival of relief. That strategy, however, created a problem, for he feared the Californios would use the abandoned cannons to bombard the vessel. Gillespie called a council of officers to consider the situation, and they decided to render the guns "perfectly useless." They were spiked, packed hard with gravel and sand, and rolled into the sea. Gillespie did not consider himself honor bound by an agreement made with "dishonored men." The hard feelings created by American disrespect and contempt would cost the lives of many men and produce a postwar environment of distrust and suspicion.

· CHAPTER 8 ·

THE OLD WOMAN'S GUN

AGAINST THE ODDS, Gillespie's courier made it to San Francisco Bay, riding more than five hundred miles in only six days and delivering his intelligence to Stockton, who later that same day dispatched the USS *Savannah*, with 350 sailors and marines under the command of Captain William Mervine, on a rescue mission to San Pedro. The Los Angeles insurgents had fallen on "our little band of brothers," said Stockton, "like cowards, like miscreants, like assassins." Have no fear, he proclaimed to a crowd of Americans, "the Sons of Liberty are on the way," and "we go this time *to punish* as well as *to conquer.*" Later that evening, after several rounds of toasts at a banquet held in his honor, Stockton spoke even more bluntly. If any of Gillespie's company had been harmed, he vowed to "wade knee-deep in my own blood to avenge it." The *Californian* of Monterey, the territory's first newspaper, applauded those sentiments. The uprising, it informed its readers, amounted to "lawless violence." But "retribution will follow fast on the heels of crime." The ringleaders of the revolt were doomed. "There is only one resting place for them in California, and that is in the grave." There could be no negotiations with such men.

The *Savannah* entered San Pedro harbor on the afternoon of Octo-

ber 7 to the cheers of the Americans aboard the *Vandalia*. Gillespie
ferried over in a launch and met with Captain Mervine. A large man
of imposing bearing, with a record of nearly forty years of service,
Mervine expressed scorn at Gillespie's evacuation of Los Angeles.
He intended to seize victory from the jaws of defeat, he announced,
immediately marching on the pueblo and striking the Angelenos decisively. Gillespie cautioned that such an operation would require vehi-
cles and draft animals to convey ammunition and baggage, as well as
to evacuate the dead and wounded during the inevitable engagement.
The Angelenos, he informed Mervine, possessed a troublesome artillery piece, and he suggested mounting the six-pounders from the *Vandalia* on carretas and hauling them along to even the score. That would
take far too long, answered Mervine. His sailors and marines would
manage with what they could carry on their backs. Mervine shared
Commodore Stockton's view that the Californios were cowards and
would flee at his approach. There was "nothing to fear," he declared.
His men would retake the city, where "all the necessary means could
be procured to enable me to sustain myself." He issued orders for his
sailors and marines to disembark at dawn.

The following morning the entire force of 379 men, including
Gillespie's company, was on the road to Los Angeles. Small detach-
ments of mounted Californios appeared on the ridges of the Palos
Verdes Hills to the west, but they scattered when the rifleros fired on
them, confirming Mervine's expectations. Leaving the hills behind,
the Americans continued north across a flat alluvial plain, overgrown
with tall stands of wild mustard. The road was rough and proved
heavy going. Few men carried canteens, and they found no source
of fresh water along the way, "for the want of which we suffered
greatly, render[ing] our situation truly miserable," wrote Midshipman
Robert C. Duvall. At two in the afternoon, after marching fourteen
miles, the advance guard came to a cluster of adobes on a hillside,
the headquarters of Rancho San Pedro, owned by the Domínguez
family. The site included a spring as well as cleared ground suitable
for an encampment. Mervine wanted to press on, but when Gillespie

objected that the men were too exhausted to march farther, he agreed to remain there for the night.

The American rear guard had not yet come up when José Antonio Carrillo and a force of fifty or sixty mounted lanceros presented themselves on elevated ground some three hundred yards west of the American camp. Don José had orders to harass the Americans but avoid a general engagement until Commandante Flores arrived with the old woman's gun. Gillespie's rifleros advanced on the Californios, taking potshots and scattering them. But with nightfall that tactic proved impossible to sustain. Circling the perimeter of the American encampment on horseback, filling the air with shrill cries and the occasional blast of their pistols, the Angelenos kept the exhausted Americans from getting any rest. Sometime after midnight Flores and thirty or forty lanceros arrived with the artillery piece, which they deployed on the rise overlooking the Domínguez compound. "Let us give the morning salute, boys," said Don José, and his gunners fired off a round that smashed through one of the adobe walls. No one was injured, but the blast announced to the Americans that they would face artillery fire in the morning.

REVEILLE SOUNDED at first light, and after a cold breakfast the Americans dragged themselves into formation, "quite as much fatigued as when we arrived from San Pedro," according to Gillespie. "For myself," he continued, "I was so stiff and lame I could scarcely walk." The sailors formed into columns by platoon, with marines and rifleros on the flanks, acting as skirmishers. They had proceeded north about two miles when, according to Midshipman Duvall, "the enemy appeared before us, drawn up on each side of the road, mounted on fine horses, and armed with a lance and carbine each man." At the center was the old woman's gun, lashed with rawhide thongs to the forward axle of a wagon and drawn by the reatas of several horsemen, who handled the piece as they might wrangle a bull.

Mervine called out an order to advance, with skirmishers firing at will. When the Americans were still several hundred yards away, Carrillo gave the signal and his gunners fired the swivel. With no means of aiming but line of sight, their first shot went high, passing well over the heads of the Americans, who continued their advance, shouting jeers and catcalls. The Angelenos wheeled and retreated several hundred yards farther north, repositioned, reloaded, and as the Americans came within range, fired a second round. This ball too passed over the sailors' heads, shattering a pike held aloft by one of them. "Bejabers, I'm dismasted!" the man shouted in jest as the Americans roared their approval, confident now that the gun could do them no harm.

Again the Angelenos withdrew several hundred yards. "*¡Muchachos!*" Carrillo shouted, "*¡vamos a divertirnos!*"—let's have some fun!—and he ordered his lanceros to charge. At a distance of perhaps a quarter mile, it would take no more than thirty seconds for the horsemen to reach the Americans. Mervine barked out the order for his men to "form squares," the standard infantry defense against a cavalry charge, in which troops assumed a rectangular formation, the front rank kneeling, and presenting their bayonets or pikes to repel the enemy, the second rank standing directly behind with rifles aimed at the horsemen, ready to fire off a volley when they came within range. But untrained in infantry maneuvers, Mervine's sailors and marines had only the roughest idea of what they were doing. Instead of forming ordered ranks, they pressed together in a compact mass as the lanceros bore down on them. Then, when the riders were no more than a hundred yards away, they veered off, and at the same moment Don José shouted an order to fire. This time his gunners aimed low, and the ball struck the hard ground some distance in front of the Americans, shattering and sending chunks of iron shrapnel careening into their crowded ranks. One man was killed instantly, his leg torn away. Two or three others were mortally wounded.

The Americans hesitated, but Mervine cried out an order to advance, and the officers pushed the sailors forward again, the Angelenos giving ground before reforming their line once more. As the Americans closed the gap, the lanceros charged again. The use of "flying artillery" against infantry squares was a classic cavalry maneuver, and Don José executed it brilliantly, not once but several times. "Shot after shot told upon the Marines and sailors with dreadful havoc," wrote Gillespie. The running fight continued for three miles, at which point the road passed over the dry bed of a small watercourse, today's Compton Creek. As the Angelenos pulled the gun across, the wheels stuck in the sandy bottom and Gillespie's skirmishers nearly captured it. But bending low over the backs of their mounts, as the balls whistled past them, the riders spurred their horses and succeeded in pulling it away.

It was a moment of extreme frustration for the Americans. With another ten miles to Los Angeles, how many more men would fall to the old woman's gun? Mervine's strategy had proven an abject failure. He ordered the bugler to sound retreat, and the Americans turned back, abandoning much of their equipment on the field, including a battle flag. Piling the dead and wounded into a carreta they had confiscated from the Domínguez compound, the men retreated south as Gillespie and the rifleros protected the rear. The Californios positioned the old woman's gun on a rise to the west and lobbed grapeshot at the retreating Americans, mortally wounding another sailor. With two or three blasts of the gun, they consumed the last of their powder.

Several Californio officers wanted to attack the retreating Americans with their lances. "Let's eat some Yankee meat!" one of them exclaimed. But Don José refused. "Let us content ourselves with what we have done," he said. "We own the ground." No Californios had been killed in the battle, although a number were seriously wounded and two died some days later. The lanceros returned to Los Angeles in triumph. The enemy "left behind weapons, equipment, food, tobacco, and a flag that I have the honor to place at your disposition," Don José announced in his official report to Commandante Flores. "When it is convenient, you can take the flag to the supreme government as proof of the triumph of ninety volunteer horsemen, showing that Californios are no disgrace to the Mexican people." Disputing the charge of cowardice, defending the honor of his people, remained uppermost for Carrillo. "I feel the need to recognize the courage and enthusiasm manifested by the citizens that accompanied me," he wrote, "all of whom displayed their patriotism."

The Americans reached San Pedro at sundown. "We presented truly a pitiable condition," wrote Duvall, "many being barely able to drag one foot after the other from excessive fatigue." It was the young midshipman's first taste of battle. The slaughter horrified him, but he found the conduct of the sailors and marines inspiring. "I can assert that no men could have acted more bravely," he wrote. "Even when their shipmates were falling by their sides, I saw but one impulse and that was to push forward, and when the retreat was ordered I noticed a general reluctance to turn their backs to the enemy." Two Americans had been killed on the battlefield and nine seriously wounded, three of whom died before day's end. The five bodies were buried on a rocky outcropping at the harbor's entrance known thereafter as Dead Man's Island. Mervine had promised them grapes in Los Angeles, the men joked darkly, but all they got was grapeshot, and they afterward referred to the engagement as "the Battle of Captain Mervine's Grapes, vintage 1846." Mervine comforted himself with the thought that it could have been far worse. Had Carrillo "made use of the advantages he possessed over us," he wrote in his report, "not a man could have escaped. By his cowardice alone were we saved." That idée fixe died hard.

IN THE WAKE OF THEIR VICTORY, Angelenos prepared for the struggle to come. The Americans controlled the seas and the ports, and occupied the northern half of the department. They would surely make another assault on Los Angeles. The Californios would make no attempt to expel them, but by guerrilla tactics would seek to prevent them from obtaining horses, confining the Americans to the ports while they awaited assistance from Mexico or word of negotiations to end the war. There were few available firearms, so Flores focused on equipping his squadrons with the lances traditionally carried by Mexican mounted cavalry. The call went out to local blacksmiths to produce as many lance points as possible from available scrap iron. Those ten-inch blades were attached to eight-foot shafts, cut from stands of willow or ash in the surrounding hills. Within weeks Angelenos were equipped with more than four hundred of those deadly weapons. Women crafted colorful *banderolas*, or pennants, which they attached to the lances of husbands, sons, and lovers. Antonio Coronel, appointed quartermaster by Flores, managed to salvage two of the cannons left by Gillespie in San Pedro harbor, but the only gunpowder he had was of local manufacture and unreliable. The artillery would be reserved as a last means of defense if the Americans succeeded in mounting an assault on Los Angeles.

In the meantime, while the invaders languished aboard the *Savannah*, still anchored at San Pedro, the trading vessel *Vandalia* sailed north with the melancholy news of defeat. Stockton had already departed San Francisco with a full complement of sailors and marines, scheduled to stop first at Monterey, where he would shore up defenses before continuing south. Frémont and the men of the California Battalion took sail at the same time in a merchant vessel, planning to land at Santa Barbara, where they were to round up horses and supplies and head south for San Pedro and a rendezvous with Stockton. But on his way down the coast, Frémont encountered the *Vandalia*, and learning of Mervine's defeat, as well as the success of the Californios in keeping horses out of the hands of the Americans, he made the decision to return north where horses were more plentiful. He would make an overland trek to Los Angeles.

When Stockton arrived at San Pedro, he was shocked to learn what had happened. Consulting with Gillespie, he concluded that the "very bad defeat" had resulted from Mervine's "haste and confusion." From the deck of his frigate he could see mounted Californios swarming the adjacent Palos Verdes Hills, and he estimated the size of the rebel force at better than eight hundred men. In fact, Carrillo's squadron numbered under one hundred and fifty, but by mixing hundreds of riderless horses among his mounted lanceros, and keeping them in constant motion, he created the impression of many more. Stockton was outraged by the "boasting insolence" of the Californios, and he vowed to land a force of marines "to hoist the glorious stars in the presence of their horse-covered hills." But planting the flag on the beach proved easier than moving his men inland. "The enemy had driven off every animal, man, and beast, from that section of the country," Stockton wrote, "and it was not possible by any means in our power to carry provisions for our march to the city." Without word from the absent Frémont, he reembarked his marines and sailed south for the sheltered harbor at San Diego, still under the control of a small American force. There he would make the preparations necessary for an advance on Los Angeles.

Stockton urgently needed horses and cattle for transport and sustenance, and the Californios did all they could to prevent him from obtaining them, taking advantage of their mobility to drive livestock away from the coast and annoy the Americans with sniper attacks and running assaults. In mid-November, after weeks of skirmishing, Carrillo led his squadron south and attacked San Diego in an attempt to force Stockton back onto his vessels. But he found the Americans too heavily entrenched. In truth, many of the Californios at San Diego had aligned themselves with Stockton and were providing him with critical intelligence. They guided a company of Americans south into Baja California, where they located herds of livestock. The horses and mules were in bad shape, however, and Stockton estimated it would take until the turn of the year before they were fit for battle service.

If the Americans needed livestock, the Californios were equally desperate for arms and ammunition. Shortly after Carrillo's failed attack on San Diego, Commandante Flores dispatched Quartermaster Antonio Coronel to Mexico with the captured American flag and detailed reports of the victories at Chino, Los Angeles, and San Pedro, hoping that these triumphs would persuade the authorities to send additional men and matériel to assist in the defense of the department. Accompanied by a small party and several dozen saddle and pack animals, Coronel traveled the Sonora Road southeast across the mountains and desert, arriving on November 21 at the crossing of the Colorado River, where he was greeted by an excited group of Quechans, the native residents of the area. A large American force was approaching from the east, they warned. Coronel was unable to confirm the report, but he realized that this was intelligence Commandante Flores must know. Entrusting the dispatches to a reliable scout, Coronel turned his men and animals around and headed back across the desert toward Los Angeles.

THE FIRST REGIMENT of U.S. Dragoons had pulled out of Fort Leavenworth five months earlier, commanded by Brigadier General Stephen Watts Kearny, a veteran officer with thirty-five years of Army service. "General Kearny is a man rising fifty years of age," wrote one admirer. "His height is about five feet ten or eleven inches. His figure is all that is required by symmetry. His features are regular, almost Grecian. His eye is blue, and he has an eagle-like expression." More to the point, "he appears the cool, brave, and energetic soldier."

Kearny received his orders from Secretary of War William L. Marcy in late May 1846, two weeks after the declaration of war on Mexico. His instructions were to raise a half dozen companies of several hundred volunteers, including a battalion recruited from the thousands of Mormon migrants who at that moment were preparing for a trek across the plains and mountains to Great Salt Lake. Kearny was to add these forces to his command, henceforth to be known as "the Army of the West," and lead them down the Santa Fe Trail to New Mexico, which he was to secure for the United States. Then he was to press on to California, where he would assume command of American ground forces, suppress all remaining resistance, and organize a temporary territorial government. The Mormon Battalion would follow in his wake, opening a military wagon road from Santa Fe to southern California. Additional troops, arms, and provisions would be sent by vessel around Cape Horn. "Much must necessarily be left to your own discretion," Marcy instructed Kearny, but "in your whole conduct you will act in such a manner as best to conciliate the inhabitants and render them friendly to the United States." The assignment presented the general with the greatest challenge of his career, but also his greatest opportunity for advancement and glory.

The Army of the West—1,701 soldiers and teamsters, 1,556 supply wagons, and several thousand horses, mules, oxen, and cattle—took possession of Santa Fe, New Mexico, without resistance in August. A month later, leaving the volunteer companies to garrison that province, Kearny set out for California with 300 dragoons hauling two mountain howitzers. As one of his officers put it, it was "a leap in the dark of a thousand miles of wild plain and mountain." Less than two weeks out of Santa Fe, the company met Kit Carson, Frémont's chief of scouts, returning east with a party of 15 men, carrying dispatches for officials in Washington. Carson and company had departed Los Angeles shortly after it fell to the Americans but before the insurrection of the Angelenos, about which they knew absolutely nothing. "The American flag was flying from every important position in the territory," Carson reported to Kearny, and "the country was forever free from Mexican control, the war ended, and peace and harmony established among the people." Few of Kearny's officers were happy at that news. "The general feeling was one of disappointment and regret," regimental surgeon John S. Griffin wrote in his journal. "Most of us hoped when leaving Santa Fe that we might have a little kick-up with the good people of California, but this totally blasted all our hopes." Griffin needn't have worried. There would be plenty of kick.

Acting on Carson's intelligence, Kearny sent three companies of dragoons back to Santa Fe, reducing his force to two companies of 50 each, a total of 121 men including officers, teamsters, and servants. And hearing Carson's description of the hard travel ahead on the Gila River trail, Kearny ordered the scout to turn about-face and guide him to California. Carson was anxious to see his wife and family, only a few days away in Taos, New Mexico, but he followed orders. Pushing westward, the travel indeed turned difficult. "It surprised me to see so much land that can never be of any use to man or beast," Kearny wrote. The horses and mules were pressed to their limit and many dropped in their tracks, leaving a trail of carcasses marking the route west. By the time they approached the Colorado River in late November, nearly eight hundred miles from Santa Fe, most of the dragoons were afoot.

At the crossing they encountered a party driving a herd of two or three hundred horses and mules to Sonora, part of the Californio plan to keep horses out of American hands. Kearny requisitioned several dozen unbroken animals for his men and interrogated the vaqueros. They were evasive, but after being plied with brandy one of them boasted of the insurrection in Los Angeles. Carson refused to believe it. The following day, however, while still encamped with the vaqueros, the Americans captured Coronel's scout and discovered the Mexican dispatches and the captured American battle flag, which confirmed everything the vaquero had said and more. Seeing the distress this created for Kearny and his officers, the vaqueros turned joyful, "bragging like the devil of having whipped some 450 sailors with 80 Mexican dragoons," according to Griffin. A serious reversal of fortune had taken place following Carson's departure. "The young men of the country are perfectly furious," one vaquero bragged. "They are fiends incarnate." This rekindled Griffin's martial interest. "I suppose we may expect a small chunk of hell when we get over there," he wrote happily.

ON NOVEMBER 25 the dragoons forded the Colorado and began the trek across the desert. After five days of hard travel, with neither grass nor water for the animals, they began the gradual ascent of the Cuyamaca Mountains in an early winter storm. "We are still to look for the glowing pictures drawn of California," Lieutenant William H. Emory complained in his diary. "As yet, barrenness and desolation hold their reign." But on the afternoon of December 2, traveling in the face of a stiff, cold wind, they crested a pass in the mountains and descended into a beautiful, grass-covered valley fringed with live oaks and tall pines. A few miles more and they came to a cluster of adobes, the headquarters of Warner's Ranch, named for its proprietor, Jonathan Trumbull Warner, a Connecticut Yankee who came west as a trapper and trader in 1831, became a Mexican citizen under the given name of Juan José, and married into the Pico family, which resulted in the grant to him of this strategic piece of property.

That evening and the following day the dragoons enjoyed a well-deserved rest. "Poor fellows!" wrote Captain Abraham Johnston, Kearny's aide-de-camp, after conducting an inspection. "They are well-nigh naked—some of them barefoot—a sorry looking set." Warner's Ranch was famous throughout southern California for the nearby *agua caliente*, or hot springs, and some of the dragoons spent time soaking their weary bones in the steaming, sulfurous pools. Meanwhile, Kearny and his officers spoke with William Marshall, an American *extranjero* who ran a store at the Indian ranchería of Cupa, located at the springs. Marshall reported that Warner, owner of the rancho, had been arrested after refusing to provide the Americans with any information on the whereabouts of his kinsman Governor Pico. At Kearny's insistence, Marshall went to fetch a neighboring ranchero named Edward Stokes, an Englishman married to the daughter of José Joaquín Ortega, proprietor of nearby Rancho Santa Maria.

They returned several hours later. Stokes was dressed in the fashionable costume of the country—black velvet jacket with matching pantaloons, open to the knee, exposing drawers of spotless white, leather chaps and deerskin boots, with a pair of oversize silver spurs. He greeted Kearny and the officers in a friendly, open manner, but told them candidly that his social position required that he remain neutral in the conflict. The Californios controlled the countryside, he warned. "The country people," added Marshall, were exhibiting "vastly more courage than they did at the commencement of difficulties." Stokes said he planned a trip to San Diego the following day and would be happy to carry a message from General Kearny to Commodore Stockton.

Rancheros like Stokes and Warner, John Griffin noted in his diary, lived "in feudal style," employing the Indians from nearby rancherías to do their bidding. Lieutenant Emory conversed in Spanish with some of the emancipados at Cupa. Following the arrival of the Spanish, they told him, the Franciscan missionaries from Mission San Luis Rey had established an outpost near the hot springs. Working for the mission fathers, they said, all the Indians had been "comfortable and happy." But "since the good priests had been removed, and the missions placed in the hands of the people of the country, they had been ill-treated." With secularization the property had passed into the possession of the Pico family, who exploited them mercilessly, then to Warner, who treated them little better. The Indians knew Warner, who stood six foot three, as Juan Largo (Big John), as much for his imperious style as his height. Under Warner's management, wrote Captain Johnston, the Indians were "stimulated to work by three dollars per month and repeated floggings." Griffin, a native of Virginia, believed the Indian workers were treated "worse by far than the worst treated slaves in the United States."

The headman at Cupa, whose Christian name was Antonio Garra, spoke to Kearny in Spanish, with Emory translating. The Californios were their oppressors, he explained. If the Americans had come to wage a just struggle against his enemies, then they were his friends, and friends must be supported. Garra proved his point by supplying Kearny with some useful intelligence. A day or two earlier, he reported, a company of Californios with a large herd of horses and mules had taken refuge in a mountain canyon a few miles northwest. Garra did not know it, but it was the party of Quartermaster Antonio Coronel, hurrying back to Los Angeles with the intelligence of Kearny's arrival in California. As the winter storm continued to rage, Kearny dispatched an officer and twenty-five dragoons to attack the Californio camp and seize the animals.

Coronel was sitting before a campfire in his drawers, waiting for his soaked clothing to dry, when he heard the approach of the American dragoons. He quickly climbed a cottonwood and watched undetected as they stormed into camp, arrested his companions, and confiscated everything in sight, including his trousers and shoes. Once they departed, Coronel fled into the forest and after several hours of barefoot travel reached an isolated Indian ranchería. The headman provided him with blankets and sustenance, but noting the suspicious looks and whispers of the residents, Coronel concluded that the people "were getting restless, wanting to go over to the Americans." Supplied with sandals and an old horse by the headman, he set out for Los Angeles, to report the unexpected ground invasion of southern California by an American army. The situation of the Californios was now desperate.

· CHAPTER 9 ·

SAN PASQUAL

COMMODORE STOCKTON had been alerted to the imminent arrival of the First Regiment of Dragoons a month earlier in a dispatch from Washington. It nevertheless came as something of a shock when Stokes arrived with Kearny's note on the evening of December 3. Stockton dispatched Captain Archibald Gillespie with thirty-seven mounted volunteers—some of the same men who had served with him at Los Angeles, including James Barton—as well as two naval officers in charge of a brass field piece. Gillespie carried a message from Stockton. He had received intelligence from his spies that an enemy squadron of Angelenos had positioned themselves somewhere along the route from San Diego to Warner's Ranch. "If you see fit," Stockton wrote, "endeavor to surprise them."

Eighty lanceros commanded by Andrés Pico had come south to monitor American movements. Pico was well acquainted with the southern countryside, having served several years at the San Diego presidio, and like Stockton, he relied on a network of spies. Within hours of Gillespie's departure for Warner's, Pico knew the size and composition of the force. The American must be in search of horses, he reasoned, and would likely make camp at Edward Stokes's Rancho

Santa María. To keep a watchful eye on them, Don Andrés moved his squadron to the adjacent valley of San Pasqual, where an ancient Indian ranchería could provide succor for his men and horses. Soon after his arrival there, Pico's Indian hosts told him that Gillespie's company was encamped across a range of hills, only a few miles away.

Pico's men loathed Gillespie—the tyrant of the American occupation, the man who had broken his solemn oath on the beach at San Pedro—and were spoiling for a fight. But Don Andrés ordered his men to pasture their horses in a grassy meadow some distance from the ranchería. He had no intention of engaging the Americans. He was, in fact, rapidly losing confidence in the Californio cause. Before departing Los Angeles, he had quarreled with Commandante Flores over the disposition of the American prisoners, Wilson, Rowland, and the others. Flores wanted to send them to Mexico, precisely what the insurgents had threatened in their pronunciamento. But Pico and other Angeleno leaders objected. A number of the prisoners were married to local women and counted kinsmen among the Californios. It was one thing to confine them for the duration, something else altogether to send them hostage to Mexico. What if the Americans retook Los Angeles? Flores could beat a hasty retreat to the mother country, but Angelenos would have no place to hide. The outraged Americans, Don Andrés worried, "would send them all to Cape Horn." Pico's dispute with Flores dampened his ardor and intensified his caution.

Unchallenged, Gillespie's company departed for Warner's Ranch the following morning in the midst of a winter storm, and at midday ran headlong into Kearny's column, descending the mountain trail. While the enlisted men and volunteers exchanged hearty greetings, Kearny huddled with Gillespie, who conveyed Stockton's message regarding Pico's company. From Cupeño headman Antonio Garra Kearny had already learned about the Angeleno squadron, and he required little persuading. General Kearny's determination to attack the enemy, Gillespie wrote, was "received with great pleasure by all parties." The combined force of Americans, now numbering 179 men, followed the trail back down to Stokes's ranch.

Across the ridge of hills at San Pasqual, Indian spies informed Pico that the Americans had returned to Rancho Santa María. *"Ellos son mas muchos,"* they are very many, one of them reported. But Don Andrés refused to believe it. His previous intelligence indicated that Gillespie commanded a relatively small company, and he remained ignorant of the arrival of the American dragoons. "Be careful, Don Andrés," one of the Indians warned, "they are very close, and may catch you unawares." But Pico took no special precautions.

LATE THAT EVENING Kearny convened a council of war in his tent and requested the opinion of his officers regarding their next move. Captain Benjamin Moore proposed an immediate surprise attack on the Angeleno camp. They would likely be caught sleeping, separated from their horses, he said, and "to dismount them is to whip them." A general discussion followed. Navy Lieutenant Edward F. Beale, who had accompanied Gillespie from San Diego, strenuously objected to Moore's plan. The dragoons appeared "wan, thin, and used up," he said. The weather was uncooperative, the men were cold and hungry, and their arms were soaking wet. Better to press on to San Diego, join forces with Stockton, and begin preparations for the march on Los Angeles. Kearny had remained silent, but Beale's argument roused him. "No sir," he responded, "I will go and fight them." But first he would send a scouting party to reconnoiter their camp.

Lieutenant Thomas Hammond, assigned to lead the party, reported back to Kearny about two in the morning. He had located the enemy encampment across the hills at San Pasqual. It contained eighty or a hundred men, most of whom were sleeping, and were unprepared for an attack. But, he added, his party had been detected by the camp guards. The Californios knew they were here. The element of surprise was lost. But that fact did not alter Kearny's resolve. "I then determined," he wrote in his official report, "that I would march for and attack them by break of day."

That fateful decision is difficult to justify. "We were on the main road to San Diego, all the 'by-ways' being in our rear," wrote Lieutenant William Emory in his journal. "It was therefore deemed necessary to attack the enemy and force a passage." But that was simply not true. There was an alternate route, the one Gillespie had taken from San Diego two days before, and going that way the Americans would have avoided Pico completely. Kearny was not forced to confront the Californios; he chose to.

He had adopted the view of Kit Carson and Archibald Gillespie. "The native Californians would not fight," Carson told him. "All the Americans had to do was to yell, make a rush, and they would run away." Gillespie made light of Californio valor, claiming that "Californians of Spanish blood have a holy horror of the American rifle." Lieutenant Beale of the Navy held a different view. His experience in California with Stockton had convinced him that the Californios were "numerous as well as brave, and not to be despised as enemies." But Kearny rejected Beale's counsel. He was determined to attack. Then why not wait for daylight in order to survey the enemy encampment and the valley terrain from the hills, gathering as much information as possible, before committing his men to the fight? For that matter, why not commence the engagement with an artillery barrage from the highlands, which might scatter and confuse the Californios? Because Kearny did not want them scattered. He believed he possessed the power to defeat them decisively. He wanted the First Regiment of U.S. Dragoons to enter California in martial glory.

Kearny did not know it, but his opponent, Andrés Pico, was a reluctant combatant. "He did not want to fight," one Angeleno later recalled, but "was forced to do so by circumstance." One of the first historians to write about Kearny's decision got it right. "If General Kearny had marched into the valley of San Pasqual in open daylight and according to military rules," wrote Benjamin Hayes after interviewing participants from both sides, "his advent would have been the signal for a treaty of peace and prompt submission to his authority. At any rate, he would have reached San Diego, it is easy to believe from all the circumstances, without the loss of blood on either side." But that was not to be.

It was three or four in the morning when Kearny ordered the bugler to sound "boots and saddles," the signal to mount up, and the dragoons began the ten-mile ride to San Pasqual. The cold, drenching rain continued, slowing their pace. By the time the first of them reached the ridge separating the valley of Santa María from San Pasqual, dawn was breaking and the skies were clearing. The valley floor below was shrouded in fog, but through the mist the Americans could see the flickering light of the enemy's fires. The blue flannel uniforms of the dragoons were soaking wet, and the cold wind from the mountains chilled them to the bone.

Kearny called a halt and addressed the men from his saddle. "Be steady," he shouted. "Obey implicitly the orders of your officers. Your country expects you to do your duty." He laid out the plan of attack. Captain Abraham Johnston, accompanied by Kit Carson and a dozen hand-picked dragoons, mounted on the best available horses, would lead the assault. He and Lieutenant Emory, with a dozen riders, would go next, followed by Captain Moore and his brother-in-law Lieutenant Hammond, accompanied by another two dozen dragoons. All the officers were mounted on horses, most of the enlisted men on mules. Gillespie and his rifleros would bring up the rear, with the artillery. About half the men would be held in reserve, guarding the baggage. Once they reached the valley floor the men were to "charge as foragers," that is, to advance at full gallop in open formation, each man choosing opponents at will, vanquishing as many as he could. Remember, Kearny concluded, "one thrust of the saber point is far more effective than any number of cuts." Then he gave the order—"Forward!"—and the Americans began to descend the hill.

WITH THE DISCOVERY of the American scouts Don Andrés ordered immediate preparations for a defense. As the Californios ran for their horses, they cursed their commander for his unpreparedness. But as it happened they had plenty of time to deploy. Don Andrés directed most of the men to hunker down on horseback in the gullies on either side of the road, while with a small contingent he took the center, hoping to draw the Americans into an ambush.

The dragoons came down the hill in good order, flushed with

anticipation. In their enthusiasm, Captain Johnston and the advance guard got considerably ahead of the others. Kearny, still descending the hill, called out an order, "Trot!" But as Johnston reached the valley floor he saw two mounted men some distance ahead, riding in the direction of the Californio encampment. They were Pico's scouts, and Johnston resolved to cut them off. "Charge!" he cried, and his group took off after them. Johnston's shouted order reverberated back to Kearny. "Oh, heavens, I did not mean that!" he cried. But the die was cast, and as soon as they completed the descent, Kearny and Emory also took up the charge, followed by their men, most of them mounted on uncooperative mules and unable to match the pace of the officers on horseback.

The Californio scouts rejoined the lanceros only seconds before the Americans arrived. One of Pico's officers shouted out the rule of engagement: "*Un tiro, y a la lanza!*"—One shot, then the lance! They had very little powder, only enough for one or two rifle volleys. They could hear the sharp clang of sabers in scabbards echoing across the valley, "like so many alarm bells," Gillespie thought to himself, "to give notice of our approach." The clamor roused the sleeping Indians at the ranchería, who rushed from their huts. "The clouds hung low so that at first we could see nothing for the mist," recalled Felicita, daughter of the community's headman. "But soon there came the figures of men like shadows riding down the mountain. As they drew nearer we saw that they too were soldiers, wearing blue coats."

As they galloped toward the encampment, Captain Johnston and Kit Carson saw Pico and several other mounted men blocking the road ahead. Carson was leveling his rifle when suddenly his horse stumbled and went down, throwing him to the ground and breaking the stock of his weapon. As he rolled to one side to avoid the onrushing riders, he saw the flash of the Californio guns. Captain Johnston was caught in the first volley. A ball smashed into his forehead and blew off the back of his skull. Carson rushed into the fray, retrieved Johnston's rifle and cartridge box, then retreated to an outcropping of rocks and began firing on the mounted Californios. He saw the dragoons enveloped and assaulted by the lanceros. The Americans were overpowered and confused. None of them had any experience fighting lanceros.

Within moments Kearny, Emory, and other officers charged up, followed by a stream of enlisted men on mules. Now it was Pico's turn to be surprised, for there were far more Americans than he expected. He shouted a command and his lanceros wheeled and retreated at full gallop, taking the road westward along the curve of the hills that marked the valley's northern perimeter. Captain Moore was first to follow in hot pursuit. Thanks to Pico's caution, the Californio horses were rested and well fed, and they quickly outpaced the tired mounts of the Americans. As the lanceros pulled ahead, the pursuing dragoons stretched out in a long, straggling line.

About a mile west of the ranchería the road took a sharp right around a rocky point, and making that turn Don Andrés shouted another order and once again his men wheeled and halted, this time to face the oncoming Americans. Captain Moore was first to clear the point and confront them. Looking about and realizing he had outpaced his men, Moore pulled his pistol, fired a single ineffective shot, then drew his saber, put spurs to flanks, and charged directly at Pico, who parried the blow and made a counterthrust with his own sword. Simultaneously two Angelenos pierced Moore with their lances. He toppled from his horse and was dispatched with a pistol shot to the head by Lieutenant Tomás Sánchez, who a decade later would be elected sheriff of Los Angeles County. At that moment Lieutenant Hammond rounded the point and saw what was happening. "For God's sake, men, come up!" he shouted, and he charged forward towards where Moore lay. Pierced by a lance driven deep into his side, Hammond fell near his brother-in-law, mortally wounded. For years Californios would tell the tale of *"el valiente Morin,"* the valiant Moore, the American who dared to single-handedly charge their line in a mad but courageous assault on their commander.

Dragoons began arriving by twos and threes, officers first, then enlisted men, and as they did so the Angelenos charged into them. *"¡Aqui vamos hacer matanza!"* they shouted to one another, Here we go to the slaughter! From their hiding place on the rocky hillside, the Indians saw it all. "We trembled as we watched," remembered Felicita. "The Americans did not shoot their guns many times; perhaps the rain had made the powder wet. They struck with their guns and used the sword, while the Mexicans used the long lances and their reatas. The mules that the Americans rode were frightened and ran all through the willows by the river. After them rode the Mexicans on their swift horses, striking with the lances and lassoing with the reata; it was a very terrible time." Within minutes the ground was covered with dead and wounded Americans. General Kearny himself was lanced in the backside and grounded. In the words of historian Manuel Clemente Rojo, who spoke with many Californio veterans of the fight, "this was no battle, but a massacre."

Gillespie, Barton, and the other rifleros were among the last Americans to arrive at the scene of the carnage. They met the dragoons falling back along the road toward the ranchería. Gillespie attempted to turn them around. "Rally men, rally, for God's sake," he cried. "Show a front, don't turn your backs, face them, face them!" But the panic-stricken men ignored him and continued their retreat, pursued by the Angelenos. Gillespie found his way to the thick of the fight. "Such an affray can hardly be conceived," Navy Lieutenant Beale said afterward. "Men, horses, and mules were intermixed and rolling on each other. No one could tell whom he was grappling with, for the day had not broken and there was a dense fog." One lancero was thrown to the ground when a dragoon on foot shot his horse out from under him. The Californio struggled up and charged forward, reaching the American before he could reload. The two were engaged in fierce hand-to-hand combat when another Californio rode up and ran his lance through the dragoon, instantly killing him. "*Asi se hace!*" he shouted, that's how it's done.

Suddenly a group of mounted Angelenos recognized Gillespie. "*¡Ya es Gillespie,*" one shouted. "*¡Adentro, hombres, adentro!*" At him, men! Gillespie dashed away, bending low along the neck of his horse, but one of the lances found him, grazing his back, catching his collar, and hoisting him out of the saddle and onto the rough ground with a crash. He staggered to his feet just as his assailant—ranchero Francisco Higuera, a tall, powerful man, known to everyone as *el güero* (blondie), because of his light coloring—turned and charged again. This time Higuera's lance caught Gillespie directly under his left arm, tearing a gaping wound in his side and puncturing a lung. The impact spun Gillespie around, into the path of another charging lancero, who struck a glancing blow to the American's mouth, splitting his lip, breaking several teeth, and knocking him backside. Dazed, prone on his back, Gillespie prepared himself for the coup de grâce, but the moment passed. Struggling to his knees, he saw Higuera and several other Angelenos in pursuit of his fleeing horse, with its fine New Mexican blanket and silver-mounted saddle and tack. Blood gushing from his wounds, Gillespie staggered up, grabbed his saber, and swinging it wildly, cleared a path to the rear.

The artillery had finally come up, but under furious assault the American gunners had great difficulty unlimbering the weapons. The mules harnessed to one of the howitzers panicked and bolted, and the Angelenos captured the weapon. Gillespie found his way to the other two field pieces, where several officers and a dozen dragoons were making a stand around General Kearny, who was on the ground amid a pool of blood. The men had successfully positioned and loaded one of the guns. "Where's the match?" one of them called. "There is none," another shouted back. One of the officers attempted to ignite the charge by firing his pistol at the touch hole, but without success. Gillespie, swooning from loss of blood, reached into his pocket and pulled out a *mechero*, a flint and steel cigar lighter, struck it, fired the gun, and fainted. Using the *mechero*, Lieutenant Beale got off a second shot, but by then Pico and his men had abandoned the field.

SURGEON JOHN GRIFFIN surveyed the carnage. The Battle of San Pasqual, which lasted only fifteen or twenty minutes, cost the lives of eighteen Americans and left nineteen wounded. Griffin and two medical assistants spent the entire day attending the torn bodies of the injured, several in critical condition. Three would die, with another man missing in action and presumed dead, for a total of twenty-two lost in the fight. "This was an action," Griffin concluded, "where decidedly more courage than conduct was showed." Gillespie, despite being severely wounded, survived, Higuera's lance missing his heart by only an inch or so. The gash on Kearny's buttocks, while painful and humiliating, was not critical. William Dunne, a participant in the fight, later recalled that many of his fellow dragoons thought the general got what he deserved, some even declaring "it would have been well if they had killed him." Dunne himself was bitter about Kearny's decision to attack. "It was a disgrace, because if he had waited for daylight, no man would have suffered. They would have seen how to defend themselves."

Kearny acknowledged no such mistake in his official report, in which he claimed a technical victory, since the Angelenos left the field first. Many later commentators ridiculed that claim. "Another such victory," wrote one, "would have been disastrous." His men paid a high price, Kearny conceded, but he was certain the enemy had suffered comparable or greater losses. He was wrong about that. Pico, in his report to Flores, bragged that his men had left many Americans dead on the field "without other casualty on our side than eleven wounded, none seriously." Angeleno participants later revised Pico's account, acknowledging the death of one man on the battlefield and another several days later. But casualties among the Californios were minor compared with the devastation suffered by the Americans, for whom San Pasqual was the costliest battle of the California conquest.

After the remainder of the dragoons came up with the baggage, the Americans took refuge in the hills north of the battlefield, making a dry camp behind a breastwork of rocks, fearful of another assault by the Angelenos. They watched throughout the day as Pico's men gathered and dispersed on the opposite side of the valley, but the feared attack never came. Pico kept his distance, wary of the American artillery. That evening, after a long day of worry, the dragoons buried their dead in a common grave. With Kearny incapacitated, the command fell to the next most senior officer, Captain Henry Smith Turner, who composed a letter to Stockton, providing a short account of the battle. "We are without provisions," he wrote. "I have to suggest to you the propriety of dispatching, without delay, a considerable force to meet us on the route to San Diego." Alex Godey, an experienced trapper from Frémont's expedition and one of Gillespie's rifleros, volunteered to take the letter to Stockton in San Diego, and about midnight, under cover of darkness, he and two other rifleros crept out of the camp. Earlier that day, Pico had dispatched a rider to Los Angeles with a request of his own for reinforcements.

The following morning, December 7, dawned clear. Reassuming command, Kearny painfully mounted a mule and warily led his men in the direction of San Diego, transporting the wounded by means of improvised *travois*, blankets or hides stretched between willow poles lashed to the flanks of the mules. Thus encumbered, their pace was excruciatingly slow. The Angelenos kept their distance for much of the day. But late in the afternoon Pico ordered an assault on the American column, his men charging down from the cover of a ravine. The dragoons mustered a spirited defense, their powder now dry and their carbines firing effectively, and wounded two or three lanceros. The Americans seized possession of a small hill, where they unlimbered their artillery, which kept the Angelenos at bay. But they had traveled no more than six or seven miles that day, and Kearny knew that without relief from Stockton they would be hard pressed to continue the remaining thirty miles to San Diego. Their food supply was exhausted, and he issued orders for the men to begin slaughtering and eating their mules. It looked bad. Yet Kearny's success in establishing a camp on what became known as Mule Hill was the cause of considerable demoralization among the Angelenos, who feared they had lost their opportunity to crush the Americans.

Later that evening a rider from Los Angeles brought a dispatch that depressed the spirits of Pico's men even further. There would be no reinforcements. Four days earlier, on the night of December 3, an armed group led by José Antonio Carrillo and Sérbulo Varela had staged a mutiny against Commandante Flores. The ostensible issue was the continuing conflict over Flores's plan to send the American prisoners to Mexico, which Carrillo and most of the Angelenos opposed. But the deeper conflict was the continuing antagonism between Californios and Mexicans. From the adobe near Government House where the Americans prisoners were housed, Benjamin Davis Wilson and the others could hear "the firing with cannon and small arms in the street, which was kept up for many hours." Finally, in the wee hours of the morning, the shooting stopped, and ranchero William Workman, who had remained loyal to the Californio cause, rushed in to inform the Americans that Flores had been arrested.

He remained under guard for two days until December 5, when Antonio Coronel arrived with the news of Kearny's presence in California. In light of that intelligence, Flores abandoned his plan of transporting the prisoners and was restored to his command. He sent orders to Pico to return to Los Angeles to assist in the preparation of a defense. It must have been a moment of great frustration for Don Andrés. He had been a reluctant warrior, but the confrontation had gone his way. Kearny and his dragoons were within his grasp. Defeating them and taking prisoners might change the outcome of the struggle considerably. The insurgents might then negotiate from strength. But divisions among them now prevented Pico from delivering the fatal blow. The hopes of his fighters faded. That night, by ones and twos, they began deserting camp.

Early the following morning Californio sentries captured Alex Godey and his two companions, returning from their mission to San Diego. Pico, thinking that some of his missing men might be in American hands, sent an emissary to Mule Hill under a flag of truce to propose a prisoner exchange. In fact, Kearny was holding just one Californio prisoner, whom he swapped for one of the captured messengers. The redeemed men brought bad news to both camps. Francisco Higuera had bragged about killing Gillespie, which had been the occasion for considerable celebration among the Angelenos in Pico's squadron. Now they learned from their returned compatriot that Gillespie was alive, if seriously wounded.

Thomas Burgess, the prisoner released by Pico, also delivered an upsetting report. The three men had gotten through to Commodore Stockton and delivered Captain Turner's message, he said. But "Stockton refused to send us a reinforcement." The commodore had given them a letter addressed to Captain Turner, but Pico had confiscated it. Navy Lieutenant Beale refused to believe the story, which cast his superior officer in a very bad light. Beale declared he would go to San Diego himself and summon relief. Kit Carson volunteered to accompany him. Neither of them was familiar with the countryside, but the headman of San Pasqual ranchería—whose Christian name was José Panto—was at that moment in the American camp offering assistance, and he agreed to act as their guide.

The men departed late that night. Carson and Beale removed their shoes and fastened them to their belts, and the three of them bellycrawled through the Angeleno lines. "We could see three rows of sentinels, all a-horseback," Carson recalled. Somehow they lost their shoes and "had to travel over a country covered with prickly pear and rocks, barefoot." The men agreed to split up, in the hope that one of them might get through. As soon as the three had departed, Kearny ordered his men to burn all nonessential property. If they were overpowered, he wanted no booty for the Californios to plunder. A feeling of "last stand" permeated the American camp. They were unaware that Pico had already received orders to withdraw.

Headman Panto was first to arrive in San Diego, early on the afternoon of December 9. Beale came in that evening, Carson an hour or two later. Shortly after midnight on the morning of December 10, a relief force of 215 sailors and marines, commanded by Lieutenant Andrew Gray of the U.S. Navy, departed for San Pasqual. They arrived at Mule Hill some twenty-four hours later to the cheers of the stranded Americans. Lieutenant Gray had been prepared to fight his way through the Angeleno lines, but found himself unopposed. The reason why became clear at daybreak. The Angelenos were gone. Pico and the core of his squadron had returned to Los Angeles, while many other men had simply drifted away. The Americans began their journey to San Diego that morning and arrived the following afternoon, the First Regiment of U.S. Dragoons finally completing their 2,000-mile trek across the continent.

STOCKTON WAS LATER REQUIRED "to vindicate his official conduct" in not sending relief sooner to Kearny and the dragoons. According to his sworn testimony, he first learned of their dire situation on the evening of December 6, the day of the battle, from ranchero Edward Stokes, who had watched the fighting—at least what he could see through the fog—from the hills overlooking San Pasqual. "General Kearny had lost a great many killed and wounded, and one of his guns," Stokes reported to Stockton. Yet the commodore did nothing. The following day he received the letter from Captain Turner, reporting eighteen Americans dead, many wounded, and provisions exhausted. The letter persuaded him to send relief, Stockton testified, but unsure of the size of Pico's squadron he decided he had to send a very large company, which required a correspondingly large number of animals. Assembling such a force took time, and it was still not ready to depart by the time José Panto arrived two days later. Panto, however, provided Stockton with an accurate count of the enemy force, persuading him to risk sending a smaller company on foot. They were quickly mustered and dispatched.

What, then, of Thomas Burgess's claim that Stockton had refused outright to send assistance, and had said so in a letter? Pico had taken possession of that document and sent it to Los Angeles for translation. Many years later, when it resurfaced among the papers of Antonio Coronel, the letter revealed that Stockton had lied under oath. "I have thought it most wise to postpone the march of my men till I can hear from you again," he had written to Captain Turner, "as they will only consume provisions without being of any use." His delay in sending relief had placed American lives in jeopardy, something Stockton was loath to admit. So he concocted testimony that was less discomfiting. Just as Kearny's reckless decision to attack Pico may be explained by his desire to claim the martial glory for himself—the Army pulling the Navy's chestnuts from the fire—so Stockton's delay in providing assistance may have been rooted in his expectation that Kearny would be his competitor for the heroic role as conqueror of California.

WHEN KEARNY AND HIS MEN arrived in San Diego, they were greeted by Stockton, who offered the wounded general the use of his own quarters and ordered his naval surgeons to attend the wounded dragoons, many of whom were suffering from what a later generation would label posttraumatic stress. "They all had the utmost horror of Californians," wrote American merchant William Heath Davis, who visited the injured men in the infirmary. "The attack upon them had been sudden and vigorous, and they had been pursued by the Californians relentlessly." While Davis was speaking with a young dragoon "with an intelligent face," the wounded man suddenly turned delirious and cried out in terror, convinced the lanceros were upon him once again. Other men salved their wounded psyches with fantasies of violent retribution. The dragoons he spoke with, said Ordinary Seaman Joseph Downey, "burned to get a chance to revenge the death of their comrades," eager for the opportunity to win back their lost honor.

Kearny was equally anxious for the vindication of battle. He presented Stockton with his commission and instructions from President Polk, which authorized him to assume command of the ground campaign in California and begin the organization of a military government. This was precisely what Stockton had feared, and he responded aggressively. The Navy had already completed the conquest, he assured Kearny, and was in the process of putting down an insurrection against American authority. He had already begun the establishment of a government, he continued, and planned to appoint John C.

Frémont as governor. Kearny bristled at this news but chose not to argue. Stockton commanded hundreds of sailors and marines, Kearny merely a small company of battle-damaged dragoons. "Our General has no force at his command," Griffin noted in his diary, "and he seems low spirited."

But additional U.S. Army forces would soon arrive in California. The Mormon Battalion, some five hundred men commanded by Captain Philip St. George Cooke, was trailing Kearny overland across the southwestern desert and was expected any day. In addition, Washington had promised a regiment of New York volunteers, eight hundred officers and men, who were being sent around Cape Horn. Kearny felt sure he would prevail once these additional forces were under his command. In the short term, however, defeating the Californios meant relying on Stockton's webfoot infantry. So Kearny suffered in silence and bided his time.

JOHN C. FRÉMONT had been at Monterey since late October. He spent several weeks rounding up horses and signing up recruits for the California Battalion from the large number of overland immigrants arriving at Sutter's Fort. The insurgent Californios enjoyed a great deal of support around Monterey, but the only armed engagement of any consequence in the north took place in mid-November at Rancho Natividad, near present-day Salinas, when a group of *norteños* attacked a detachment of 50 American volunteers, killing 3 and wounding 7. A few days later, on November 29, Frémont began his march south with an estimated 350 fighting men. "To arms, Colonel Fremont!" sang the editor of the Monterey *Californian*, "now arm thy battalion, and humble the foe."

But Frémont decided to cast himself in a different kind of role. Stockton had promised him the governorship of California, so Frémont shifted course midstream, seeking to win friends and influence among the Californios he expected to govern. On the eve of his departure for the south, he issued orders that all American officers were "to abstain from any further offensive proceedings against the Californians residing and being in the Northern Department." The time had come, he proclaimed, for "conciliatory measures."

His first opportunity to apply this policy arose in mid-December, when his force occupied the town of San Luis Obispo, 150 miles south of Monterey. Some thirty Californio fighters were rounded up and jailed, including their leader, Alcalde José de Jesús Pico, a cousin of the Pico brothers of Los Angeles. Alcalde Pico had been paroled the previous August, but following the uprising in September he joined the insurgents, violating his oath. Frémont ordered him tried before an American military tribunal. "I denied nothing," Pico later recalled, even acknowledging his participation in the attack on Americans at Natividad the month before. Found guilty of breaking his parole, he was sentenced to death, with the execution to take place the following day. That morning Frémont was in his quarters speaking with an aide when the two of them heard a commotion in the adjoining room, and suddenly, in the aide's words, "a lady with a group of children, followed by many other ladies, burst into the room, throwing themselves upon their knees, and crying for mercy for the father and husband. It was the wife and children and friends of Pico." Frémont listened to their pleas, then dismissed them and ordered Don Jesús brought from his cell.

"I thought they were taking me to the gallows," Pico recalled, but instead he was escorted to Frémont. He entered the room, in Frémont's words, "with the gray face of a man expecting death, but calm and brave." Frémont pointed out the window at the troops parading in the square, preparing for the execution. "You were about to die," he said, "but your wife has saved you." Pico's repressed emotions suddenly erupted and he dropped to his knees, but Frémont told him to stand. There was a condition, he said. Don Jesús must agree to accompany him on the march to Los Angeles. Pico feared that once they were a safe distance from his wife and family he would be shot. But Frémont wanted Pico as an intermediary, utilizing the man's personal and political connections to assist in opening negotiations with the Californios. "The impression at the time was that the colonel was acting with too much clemency," a riflero in the California Battalion testified. But "the result proved that he acted wisely." Frémont was once again demonstrating his skill as a master opportunist.

Warned of a potential ambush by Californios along the road to Santa Barbara, Frémont directed his men over mountain trails in the midst of an extended winter storm, taking eleven days to travel a distance of one hundred miles. Reaching the town on December 28, the Americans found it deserted and undefended. Frémont dispatched a short letter to Stockton. "Bad weather and poor horses have harassed and impeded our movements, making our advance extremely slow." But now he planned to move in for the kill. "I shall march directly to the pueblo de los Angeles, and if not met by the enemy on the road will attack him at the town."

· CHAPTER 10 ·

Poor Californios

AMONG CALIFORNIOS, popular enthusiasm for the war was
waning rapidly. In the weeks after the Battle of San Pasqual, a steady
trickle of men came in to surrender to the Americans at San Diego.
"We have had many flags of truce and Mexicans coming in and delivering themselves up," wrote army surgeon John Griffin, including
"some the very rascals who were in the fight at San Pasqual." Stockton authorized the creation of a squadron of Californios in support
of American forces. This showed "too much leniency," Griffin worried. "These fellows suppose that they can make war as long as it is
convenient—and when they get tired of it, come in and be paid high
wages for little or no services." Griffin had served during the Seminole
War in Florida, an experience that hardened him. The fight must be
pursued, he believed, until the enemy had been ground into the dust
and was begging for mercy.

Most Californios did their best to keep as far away from the action
as possible. Veterans of the fight at San Pasqual—as traumatic for the
Californios as for the Americans—hoped to sit out what they expected
to be the war's violent conclusion. One group of eleven men left the
lines around Mule Hill and headed for an isolated rancho in the foothills of the Pauma Valley, about eighteen miles from the coast on Río

de San Luis Rey. They made their way across the country in the traditional manner of *soldados*, expropriating whatever they needed from
the Indian rancherías along the way. But with the Americans on the
scene, that was something the Indians were no longer willing to tolerate. In early December an armed band of Luiseños attacked the adobe
in which those Californios were holed up, seizing and killing them
all. When news of the massacre reached Los Angeles, Commandante
Flores ordered ranchero José del Cármen Lugo of far-flung Rancho
San Bernardino to punish the perpetrators. With a company of fifteen
Californios and fifty Cahuilla Indian allies, Lugo lured the Luiseño
fighters into an ambush near Rancho Temecula in the waning days of
December 1846. "We made a great slaughter," he reported, "and falling on them from the rear killed many." The precise toll is unknown,
but Lugo claimed to have killed more than a hundred men, which
would make the fight at Temecula the deadliest fight of the entire war
in California. The violent struggle between Indians and the Spanish,
which had begun with the conquest seventy-five years before, continued unabated through the closing days of Mexican rule.

While the violence played out among local actors, Flores received
a letter from José Castro, the former commandant of California who
had fled to Mexico. "Do not wait for any aid from the state of Sonora,"
Castro wrote. "This country is in ruins and funds are not sufficient
to cover even the most necessary expenses." Thus was the last hope
of the Californios dashed. Despite a series of brilliant tactical victories against a vastly superior enemy, they plainly saw they were about
to be overwhelmed by converging American forces. "Destiny's cold
hand directed the path they had to follow," wrote historian Manuel
Clemente Rojo. "It was decreed that they had to submit, and that
submission was not long in coming. Poor Californios! So generous,
so courageous, and so unfortunate." Flores concluded that he had no
option but to make peace with the Americans.

ON DECEMBER 29 the Americans moved out of San Diego,
headed north for Los Angeles. Lieutenant William Emory noted the

size and composition of the force: 521 fighting men, mostly sailors and marines acting as infantry, but including 60 mounted rifleros, 25 mounted Californios, and 57 dragoons afoot; six artillery pieces and ten carretas carrying provisions; as well as a herd of several hundred cattle to supply the daily ration of beef. The 140-mile march began in a fierce rainstorm, and the weather continued wet and cold for most of the journey. "Our men were badly clothed, and their shoes generally made by themselves out of canvas," Stockton reported. In fact, many of the sailors were barefoot. "It was very cold and the roads heavy. Our animals were all poor and weak, some of them giving out daily, which gave much hard work to the men in dragging the heavy carts." Yet the Americans were in high spirits. "We were actuated and led on by a craving desire to win back our lost honor," wrote Seaman Joseph Downey, determined "to plant the Stripes and Stars once more in the square of Los Angeles." Downey's journal provides the best account of the final campaign of the conquest.

General Kearny asked Stockton for command of the troops, which the commodore granted, while retaining the rank of commander-in-chief for himself. He had spent the month of December drilling his webfoot infantry in battlefield maneuvers—marching, counter-marching, and forming hollow squares on command—determined that there be no repetition of the fiasco at Rancho San Pedro. Stockton understood that the enemy retained the capacity to deliver devastating mounted attacks. Receiving Frémont's dispatch from Santa Barbara, he responded with a note of warning. "Keep your forces in close order; do not allow them to be separated, or even unnecessarily extended," he wrote. The Californios "will probably try to deceive you by a sudden retreat or pretended runaway, and then unexpectedly return to the charge after your men get in disorder in the chase. My advice to you is, to allow them to do all the charging and running, and let your rifles do the rest. In the art of horsemanship, of dodging and running, it is in vain to attempt to compete with them." Stockton had learned the lessons of Mervine's and Kearny's defeats.

Several days into the march, near Mission San Juan Capistrano, the Americans were met by a delegation of three mounted men under a flag of truce—William Workman, Charles Flügge, and Domingo Olivas, an Englishman, a German, and a Californio—bearing a letter from Commandante Flores addressed to Stockton. In his capacity as the military governor of the Californios, Flores wrote, he had authorized these men to negotiate a cease-fire. He flattered himself that Stockton shared his determination "to avoid the useless effusion of human blood and its terrible consequences." He was willing to capitulate, but would not agree to a dishonorable peace. If Stockton proved unwilling to proceed on this basis, Flores wrote, "may the terrible consequences of your want of consideration fall on your head." The Californios had resolved "to bury themselves under the ruins of their country, fighting to the last moment, before consenting to the tyranny and ominous discretionary power of the agents of the government of the United States of North America." Stockton should have no doubt about their resolve. "Deeds of arms prove that they know how to defend their rights on the field of battle."

Stockton was barely able to control his rage. He was aware of no such person as "Governor Flores," he declared, although he knew a rebel who went by that name, a man "whom I had captured and held as a prisoner, and whom I had released on his parole of honor." That man had violated his sacred oath by arming himself and leading an insurrection against American authority, and "could not be treated as an honorable man." This scene had been played before, when Stockton rejected Castro's offer of negotiations on the beach at San Pedro, insulting Flores, who had delivered the proposal. Now, four months later, after a great deal of violence and suffering on both sides, Stockton rejected yet another offer to negotiate and once again insulted the emissaries. He would not treat with the representatives of a disreputable regime, he told them. But they could deliver a message to the man who had sent them—"that he was a rebel in arms, and if I caught him I would have him shot."

Dismissing the delegation, Stockton then issued a proclamation to the people of California. It had come to his attention, he wrote, that many of the insurgents were desirous of laying down their arms and returning to their homes. He welcomed their peaceable intentions and would gladly declare "a general amnesty to all persons," but only on the condition that José María Flores "be forthwith delivered into my hands as a prisoner." If Stockton knew anything, it was that the Californios would not do this dishonorable thing. He was deliberately pouring salt on their wounds.

Traveling at the rate of ten or twelve miles a day, the Americans had by the afternoon of January 6 reached the crossing of the Río Santa Ana, less than forty miles from Los Angeles. They forded the river the following morning and continued in a northwesterly direction along the main road, a route that parallels today's Interstate 5. As they approached a group of low hills on the north, they caught their first glimpse of the enemy, arrayed along the ridge line. The Americans continued their advance and the Californios, shouting and gesturing rudely, rode off. At the verge of the hills the Americans came upon a cluster of adobes, the headquarters of Rancho Los Coyotes. Stockton sent an officer to request permission to camp, which was granted by the lady of the house, María Francisca Uribe de Ocampo. All the men were gone, but the women had remained behind, trusting the Americans to treat them honorably. From one of them Stockton learned that the Californios planned to make their stand at the crossing of the Río San Gabriel, some twelve miles ahead. The decisive battle for the control of Los Angeles would take place the following day.

After supper Stockton sent his brass band to serenade the women at the ranch house with his compliments, and Doña María invited the officers inside. "Ladies were soon whirling around in the giddy mazes of the waltz," Lieutenant Emory recorded in his diary, "their taper waists encircled by arms which on the day following would beyond a doubt be dealing death blows upon perhaps friends and relations. But it made no odds to the ladies. There was music and there was a chance for dancing, and it went on as if this was the last night in the world."

FRIDAY MORNING dawned bright and clear. After taking their breakfast and packing another meal in their haversacks, the Americans took their places in the line of march. General Kearny then addressed them from horseback. This day they would meet the enemy at the Río San Gabriel, he shouted in a booming voice that all could hear. "I want you all to understand distinctly that we have got to cross that river, and more than that, we have got to whip the enemy, and plant our colors in the pueblo." He had full confidence in them all, he said, even including the sailors. "I have got the sole charge of you jacks," he said, "and if I don't put you on the track that will run you straight to the arms of victory, call me no soldier." There was one last thing he wanted to say, Kearny told them. "I want you to remember what day it is. This is the glorious Eighth of January, memorable in our country's history," the anniversary of the Battle of New Orleans, when Americans under the command of Andrew Jackson had turned back the British assault, a day of glory, celebrated by several generations of Americans. "Now let every man of you think of this day and strive so to conduct himself that the anniversary shall never be disgraced and that the Eighth of January 1847 may be placed in the calendar of fame alongside of the Eighth of January 1815." A spontaneous cheer erupted from one end of the line to the other. Then the command was given, and the Americans moved out.

The Californios, some five hundred mounted men with two field pieces—the old woman's gun along with the howitzer captured at San Pasqual—positioned themselves at Paso de Bartolo, the upper crossing of the Rio San Gabriel. They placed their guns in battery on a forty-foot bluff running along the right bank, which provided a clear view of the crossing. The river, fifty or sixty yards across, was running heavy because of the recent storms, surging down a floodplain more than four hundred yards wide.

The Californios caught their first sight of the Americans about 2 PM, emerging from the thickets of willow and cottonwood on the east bank. Kearny called a halt, and as the officers reconnoitered the site and planned the crossing, the men ate their cold dinner. "Before we had fairly finished," Joseph Downey reported, "the enemy were seen in considerable numbers in advance of us." A company of mounted Californios came splashing across the ford, taking ineffective potshots at the Americans with their standard-issue carbines. A company of mounted rifleros, armed with much superior Kentucky rifles, went after them, and the Californios retreated back across the river. With the officers barking out orders, the Americans then assumed formation and began the crossing, dragoons in the lead pulling the two field pieces. From his position, Downey could see parties of Californios "dodging and flying about among the hills" on the opposite shore, "their lances and sabers glittering in the sun."

The Californio battery opened fire, raking the river with grape-shot, as the Americans waded in. Their feet sank into the porous sand, and it required strenuous effort to lumber ahead. Downey realized his vulnerability the moment he entered the water and saw the splash of the grape on both his right and left sides. "Do or die," he thought to himself, "each moment might be our last." Preoccupied with the struggle to cross, the Americans made no attempt to return fire. The mounted Californios remained in formation on the bluff, out of range. Observing the difficulty his men were having, and concerned lest the artillery get stuck in the sand, Kearny ordered it returned to the left bank and unlimbered. He would begin a barrage from there, covering the crossing of the men. But suddenly Stockton charged up and countermanded Kearny's order. "There is quicksand!" Kearny exclaimed. "Quicksand be damned!" Stockton shouted back, and jumping from his horse he put his own shoulder to the wheel of one of the gun carriages. "Pull for your lives, boys," Downey heard him shout. "Your Commodore is here, don't desert him, and don't for the love of God lose these guns." His action inspired the men and they labored ahead. Within fifteen minutes the artillery and most of the sailors had made it across, at the cost of two wounded, one seriously. The surprisingly low number of casualties was attributable to the inferior gunpowder of the Californios, which failed to propel the grapeshot with lethal momentum.

As the remainder of the American force continued to cross with the baggage and cattle, Stockton ordered the artillery unlimbered, then began directing devastating fire at the Californio battery. Antonio Coronel was on the receiving end, atop the bluff. "They aimed chiefly at our two guns, so accurately it was difficult to return their fire," he recalled. The barrage went on for some time, eventually scoring a direct hit on the old woman's gun, destroying its carriage and rendering it useless. Finally, after nearly all the Americans had crossed the river, Kearny ordered his jack tars to assault the bluff, and they rushed forward, bayonets fixed, shouting, "New Orleans! New Orleans!" They were halfway across the floodplain when two squadrons of mounted Californios charged down from the bluff and prepared to assault their left flank. Kearny ordered his men to form a square, a manuever they executed perfectly. Downey, in the front rank, watched the Californios riding at him. "Down they came, in one long line, their red blankets, black hats, and bright lances glittering in the sun. On they came and death seemed to stare us in the face, for what could stay the power of that tide of horse and human flesh that was rearing toward us?" Over the din of battle Downey heard Kearny's command. "Steady my jacks, reserve your fire," he cried, "front rank, kneel to receive cavalry." The men in front, including Downey, dropped to one knee, and planted the butts of their muskets in the sand, their bayonets projecting outward at a threatening angle, while the men directly behind them leveled their guns. "For a single moment they stood, and then came the word 'Fire,' and at the word a sheet of fire flew along that line." Several riders fell from their saddles while the others veered off. The charge had been broken.

"Now, jacks, at them," shouted Kearny. "Charge and take the hill!" The men dashed forward, Stockton in the lead, Downey in the thick of it, scrambling up the side of the bluff. When they reached the summit, the Californios could be seen retreating northward, toward the nearby Merced Hills. Stockton "raved and stormed and shouted like a madman," said Downey. "There were no bounds to his joy and satisfaction— he laughed, and danced, and cut up all sorts of monkey-shines." He called for his brass band, and after a few minutes its members arrived, the conductor "puffing and blowing like a porpoise, from his uphill journey." Stockton ordered them to play. "Fix your pipes," he shouted, "keep your eyes on them yellow devils, and give them the damnd'st blast of 'Hail Columbia!' they ever heard." Californios later recalled the "strange emotions" they felt as they retreated to the sound of Stockton's music.

The Americans camped on the bluff that night. They had lost two men killed, one accidentally shot by one of his mates, the other struck by an artillery round in the neck, which nearly decapitated him. They were buried that night in a common grave. Eight men had been wounded, two critically, one of whom later died. According to Downey, "no matter who was killed, it was but a moment's work to say 'poor fellow, well he is gone, he was a good shipmate, and I hope he is better off,' and then he was forgotten." That might seem cold-hearted, Downey admitted, but "after the danger is passed, if we did not pass the joke and enjoy the laugh we would be no sailors." Kearny had promised the men a good fat bullock for supper, and they enjoyed their ration of beef, but joked that the officers must have gotten the fat, since all they had was the lean.

Californio losses were not officially recorded, but two lanceros were killed in the failed charge, which was marred by contradictory commands and considerable confusion. José Antonio Carrillo, who was supposed to join the charge with his squadron, held his men back and was later condemned for cowardice. Yet the outcome might have been much worse. Coronel registered his astonishment that the casualties were so light. "I thought we were going to take terrible losses, charging head on at a well-barricaded and well-armed foe, but fortune spared us." More likely, it was the poor aim of the sailors. The Californios found refuge several miles northwest in Aliso Canyon, adjacent to *misión vieja*, the original site of Mission San Gabriel. "We had no blankets and we didn't dare build a fire," said Coronel, "so we suffered a great deal." It was a night of painful reflection for them. Flores proposed they make another attempt to stop the Americans in the morning, but everyone knew the struggle was all but over. That night many men deserted. Those who remained believed that Stockton had given them no honorable choice other than to fight to the last man.

THE FOLLOWING MORNING the Americans took up the line of march for the pueblo, less than ten miles away. The road, today's Whittier Boulevard, ran across an elevated plain Angelenos knew as La Mesa. About noon, after traveling some five miles, the American advance guard saw the Californios blocking the road ahead. Flores had brought up two old cast-iron nine-pounders, probably the ones Gillespie abandoned at San Pedro, positioning them in a shallow ravine, and he began lobbing round shot at the Americans. Kearny turned his force and made a rapid movement southwest, as Stockton unlimbered the American artillery and answered Flores with a barrage of his own. The exchange went on for some time and left several men wounded on both sides.

Eventually the Californios exhausted their powder and the firing ceased. Several hundred lanceros emerged from the ravine and pursued the Americans, who assumed a defensive formation. Nearly all the riders were Angelenos, and many had outfitted themselves and their horses in finery. According to Agustín Olvera, who was among them, their engagement of the enemy was "solely on a point of honor." If this was to be their last stand, they were determined to make it memorable. Remaining just out of rifle range, the Angelenos began encircling the Americans, searching for a vulnerable position in their line, a spot to make a charge. Settling on the left flank, they marshaled themselves in a single long line, leveled their lances, then charged forward at full gallop. The Americans waited until the lanceros closed to about fifty yards, then let loose with a volley of deadly fire. The Angelenos wheeled and retreated.

"We all considered this as the beginning of the fight," said Lieutenant Emory, "but it was the end of it." The plain was littered with men and horses. The Americans held their fire while their opponents collected their dead and injured and withdrew north toward Los Angeles. From beginning to end the engagement had lasted less than three hours. Although some time remained before sunset, Stockton chose to postpone the occupation of the pueblo. "The town, known to contain great quantities of wine and aguardiente, was four miles distant," wrote Emory. But "from previous experience of the difficulty of controlling men when entering towns, it was determined to cross the river, halt there for the night, and enter the town in the morning with the whole day before us." That evening there was a mass evacuation of residents from the pueblo, leaving it in possession of the rabble. From their encampment that night the Americans could hear the sounds of anarchy. "They kept up the pow wow until 3 the next morning," wrote Downey, "and then only knocked off, as we were told, because they were too drunk to make any more noise."

Early on the morning of the tenth, a party of three Californios under a flag of truce appeared at the American camp with a verbal message from Commandante Flores. He would not contest the American occupation of the capital, he wrote, and he trusted Stockton to respect Angeleno lives and property. Stockton nevertheless took the precaution of marching his men out of camp in full battle array. They came up the Alameda through the vineyard district, turned onto Calle Principal as they entered the pueblo, then headed toward the Plaza, colors flying and brass band playing. "The streets were full of desperate and drunken fellows," wrote Emory, "who brandished their arms and saluted us with every term of reproach." When a disturbance broke out among some of the drunks, several sailors fired on them, and one Angeleno was slightly wounded, but otherwise there was no violence. Reaching Government House on Calle Principal, Stockton dismounted and called for Gillespie, who came forward with the flag he had hauled down when he abandoned Los Angeles in September, and as the band played he hoisted it once again.

The sailors and marines encamped on the Plaza, while the dragoons and rifleros distributed themselves in small companies throughout the pueblo. The plundering soon began. Downey described the scene. "No sooner were their quarters assigned than parties were out, all over town, foraging. And woe betide the house that had no occupants for it was sure to be ransacked from clue to earring, and everything that was useful or ornamental carried off to the barracks." A number of Angelenos later filed official complaints of stolen property. One woman testified that she fled so quickly she had no time to secure her important documents. "All I could do was to lock the doors of my house." But the Americans broke in and "carried off everything I had in it, including the title papers, thus leaving me today without any safeguard to protect my property rights." The principal object of the looters, however, was wine and aguardiente. "Stroll from quarters to quarters, and you would see drunken men on all sides," Downey observed. "Nor were the men alone in this spree, the officers had all imbibed their juice, save only the Old General and the Commodore." Marine Lieutenant Henry Watson was disgusted. "We have marched one hundred and fifty miles, fought two battles in both of which [we] were victorious, taken the city, and are now in the wildest scene of confusion, for nearly one half of the army are drunk."

DESPITE THE LOSS of Los Angeles, the Californios retained the advantage of mobility. Walter Colton, editor of the *Californian* of Monterey, explained the situation to his readers. "The forces of the Commodore were on foot, and of course unable to follow up their brilliant successes. The enemy were mounted, and might have held the country around. If attacked, they had only to retreat, and return again on the retiring footsteps of their foes." To secure the conquest, Stockton required Frémont and his mounted California Battalion. He had hoped to link up with them before the final assault on the pueblo, but as John Griffin recorded in his diary on January 11, there was "nothing heard from Frémont."

In the early afternoon of that same day, Frémont and the California Battalion entered the northern reaches of the San Fernando Valley, some forty miles northwest of Los Angeles. Within minutes his advance guard was met by two mounted Californios under a flag of truce. They had come from their headquarters, carrying a message similar to the one conveyed to Stockton a week before, proposing an armistice and negotiations. A few minutes later another rider arrived, a Frenchman from Los Angeles, carrying a dispatch for Frémont from General Kearny. "We are in possession of this place with a force of marines and sailors," Kearny had written. "Join us as soon as you can." The note ended with a request: "Please acknowledge the receipt of this." But Frémont chose not to respond. Neither did he rush to Los Angeles to provide Stockton and Kearny with the mounted support they needed. Instead, he elected to act on his own initiative, pursuing the offer of negotiations with the Californios. It was a most extraordinary thing for a junior officer to do, but for Frémont, entirely in character.

Directing his men into camp on the grounds of Mission San Fernando, Frémont dispatched José de Jesús Pico, the captured alcalde of San Luis Obispo, to the encampment of the defeated Californio force, holed up in the Verdugo Hills, northeast of Los Angeles. To Commandante Flores, his cousin Don Andrés, and other Californio leaders, Don Jesús recounted his personal story of Frémont's mercy as proof of his intention of "conquering by clemency and justice." Historian Justin Smith best summarized Frémont's transformation in his classic history of the Mexican-American War: "The arch-ruffian of the Bear cult reappeared as a fairy godmother to save and bless the Californians."

Flores wasn't buying it. Stockton had vowed to shoot him on sight, and he was understandably reluctant to trust the word of a junior officer with a history of violent confrontation with Mexicans and Californios. Flores instead decided that the time had come for strategic retreat to Mexico, and he urged Andrés Pico and other Angeleno officers to join him in flight. The Californios had expected this. They told Flores they were staying. Not because they thought they could win. "I no longer flattered myself that we might attain a victory," Pico admitted. Fewer than one hundred and twenty poorly armed Californios remained to face more than a thousand well-armed Americans. "I nevertheless wished to give the last impulse to save the country, and to guarantee the lives and property of the inhabitants." He sent his cousin back to Frémont with the message that he was ready to negotiate a capitulation "as long as it was honorable in every sense of the word." Flores was angry about Pico's decision, but he signed a document officially turning over command of the Californio forces. Then he departed for Sonora with a party of some thirty Mexican officers.

The following morning a delegation of Californios appeared at Frémont's camp to open negotiations. "We are ready to abandon this strife," they declared. They had attempted to negotiate a truce with Stockton, they said, but "we were taunted as cowards and told we [would] dare not strike a blow for our country." Their course throughout the war had been directed solely by the dictates of honor. And rather than accept Stockton's disgraceful terms, "they would take to the hills and make a guerrilla war of it." Don Jesús, however, had assured them that Frémont would treat them honorably. In which case "we agree to submit and live peaceably under the laws established, but our leaders must be included in the amnesty. Otherwise we will stand by them, see our ranchos burnt, and sacrifice our lands for them."

This corresponded perfectly with the course Frémont had already adopted. As a gesture of goodwill, he declared a cessation of hostilities and invited the Californios to bring their wounded to Mission San Fernando, where his surgeon would attend them. That afternoon three officers of the California Battalion sat down with José Antonio Carrillo and Agustín Olvera, former secretary of the California assembly, to negotiate the terms. At Pico's suggestion, they agreed to meet the following morning at Cahuenga Pass to sign the agreement. The choice of location was highly symbolic. For Californios it was a place of honor, the site where they had defeated Governors Victoria and Micheltorena in defense of their independence.

On the morning of January 13, 1847, in an old adobe within sight of Río de Porciúncula, Andrés Pico, in his capacity as commander in chief of the California forces, and John C. Frémont, claiming the title of "Military Commandant of the Territory of California," signed what became known as the Treaty of Cahuenga. The Californios agreed to surrender their artillery and public arms to the Americans and "return peaceably to their homes, conforming to the laws and regulations of the United States, and not again take up arms during the war between the United States and Mexico, but will assist in placing the country in a state of peace and tranquility." The Americans agreed that until a treaty of peace was signed, ending the war with Mexico, Californios would enjoy equal rights and privileges with citizens of the United States; that they would be permitted to leave the country "without let or hindrance;" that they would not be required to take an oath of allegiance; and "that they shall be guaranteed protection of life and property, whether on parole or otherwise." This final guarantee resolved a major sticking point, Stockton's insistence that by rising up against Gillespie's tyranny Californios had violated their parole of honor, a capital offense punishable by death under the law of nations. Just in case that language was not clear enough, a supplemental article to the treaty explicitly stated that "the paroles of all officers . . . are by this foregoing capitulation cancelled, and every condition of said paroles from and after this date are of no further force and effect, and all prisoners of both parties are hereby released."

A courier carried a copy of the treaty to the pueblo that afternoon. It was Frémont's first communication with his superior officers since his arrival in southern California. "I have the honor to report to you," Frémont wrote to Kearny, that the Californios "have this day laid down their arms and surrendered to my command." Both Kearny and Stockton were shocked by the treaty's liberal concessions but even more so by the junior officer who negotiated it behind their backs. But they decided that the best course was to endorse it. Other Americans remained skeptical. "The junior officers have opinions of their own," wrote surgeon John Griffin, "and like all Americans will express them. They are decidedly opposed to the treaty and the terms granted to the Californians as not a man among them believes it will be observed on the part of the Californians with good faith." This would not be the end of the conflict, Griffin predicted. "The people will rise again."

In a letter to his brother, exiled governor Pío Pico, Don Andrés gave expression to his own sentiments. "This was the end, Excellent Sir, of the struggle carried on by the inhabitants of California against the invaders of our Country." In more than four months of struggle they had upheld the honor of the country "by dint of great sacrifices," and without any other assistance "than that of Divine Providence, who seemed to protect the sacred cause that was heroically defended by a handful of men who spring to arms to recover their lost liberty." Those were heartfelt words, and they summarized the thinking of many Angelenos, who believed that despite their losing struggle to maintain their independence, they had vindicated their honor. The fight had been costly in blood and treasure, a toll that might have been avoided if, at San Pedro in August 1846, Stockton had adopted the course Frémont chose at Cahuenga in January 1847. Memories of a harsh occupation, of dead and maimed fathers, husbands, and sons, would continue to haunt Los Angeles for years to come.

· CHAPTER 11 ·

THE GRAB GAME

THE AMERICANS had badly mishandled the first occupation of Los Angeles in August and September of 1846. Establishing order after the reoccupation in January 1847, amid the hostility, resentment, and chaos resulting from several months of armed conflict, promised to be difficult. They needed to proceed with clear rules of operation and clear lines of authority. But American rule began inauspiciously, with a dramatic conflict among the conquerors over who would direct the occupation authority.

Brigadier General Stephen Watts Kearny had arrived in California with instructions from the secretary of war naming him commander of American ground forces and chief administrator of the military occupation. Commodore Robert F. Stockton, however, had already claimed those roles for himself, and he jealously refused to recognize Kearny's authority. Reluctantly but quietly, Kearny submitted to Stockton during the operation to retake Los Angeles, but with that task completed he expected naval personnel to retire to their vessels, leaving the Army in control on land. "As long as you are here, you are commander in chief," he told Stockton. "After you are gone, I will be."

To reinforce his claim, however, Kearny needed armed might.

With the regiment of dragoons severely weakened by its devastating loss at San Pasqual, his only immediate recourse was the California Battalion, commanded by Frémont. Frémont had been conducting operations under the authority of Commodore Stockton of the Navy, but he was a lieutenant colonel in the Army. Kearny was his superior officer, and he expected that Frémont would now come under his command. But when Frémont arrived in Los Angeles with his mounted rifleros, he reported first to Stockton and gave Kearny no indication of his support. Among American officers in the pueblo there was great uncertainty about where Frémont would plant his flag. "There is something going on between General Kearny, Commodore Stockton, and Lieutenant-Colonel Frémont of an unpleasant character which has not yet leaked out," Marine Lieutenant Henry Watson noted in his journal. That "something" was the fundamental question of who would be in charge of the military occupation of California. It leaked out soon enough and became a matter of public controversy, with serious consequences for the establishment of law and order in Los Angeles.

On the morning of January 16, two days after Frémont's arrival, Stockton announced the organization of an occupation government for California, with Frémont as governor. Kearny was outraged. "I am informed that you are now engaged in organizing a civil government and appointing officers for it in this Territory," he wrote to Stockton. "As this duty has been specially assigned to myself by orders of the President of the United States, I have to ask if you have any authority from the President, from the Secretary of the Navy, or from any other channel of the President, to form such government or make such appointments. If you have such authority, and will show it to me, or furnish me with a certified copy of it, I will cheerfully acquiesce in what you are doing. If you have not such authority, I then demand that you cease all further proceeding." Stockton dashed off a response. "I need say but little more than that which I communicated to you in a conversation at San Diego, that California was conquered and a civil government put into successful operation before your arrival in the Territory." He ignored Kearny's demand that he provide a copy of the orders authorizing his assumption of power. In fact, he had none. The conquest of California did not turn on orders or instructions, but on power. And for the moment Stockton had it, in the form of more than a thousand sailors and marines. He concluded his response to Kearny with a twist of the knife. "I will only add that I cannot do anything, nor desist from doing anything, nor alter anything, on your demand— which I will submit to the president and ask for your recall. In the meantime, you will consider yourself suspended from the command of the United States forces in this place." In the phrase of one naval officer on the scene, Stockton was "playing a grab game."

Stockton expected that Kearny's next move would be an order to Frémont "to terminate his connection with me as a volunteer under my command, and to report to him for orders," and that is precisely what Kearny did, instructing Frémont that from that moment he was to do nothing without Kearny's explicit authorization. But Frémont responded that he considered Stockton his commanding officer. Since the previous summer, he wrote, Stockton had exercised the functions of military commandant in California. All the operations of the California Battalion took place under cover of that authority. On his arrival in Los Angeles only a few days before, he had found Stockton still exercising command, with all American officers, including Kearny himself, acknowledging his authority. "With great deference to your professional and personal character," Frémont concluded, "until you and Commodore Stockton adjust between yourselves the question of rank, where I respectfully think the difficulty belongs, I shall have to report and receive orders, as heretofore, from the Commodore."

Kearny was stunned. If Frémont insisted on pursuing this course, he countered, "he would unquestionably ruin himself"—meaning that Kearny would do everything in his power to destroy the young man's military career. If, on the other hand, Frémont would take back and destroy the note, he would gladly forget about the whole thing. But Frémont refused. It was a question of honor, he insisted. "I had contracted relations with Commodore Stockton, and I thought it neither right nor politically honorable to withdraw my support." As one early historian quipped, "there is, or should be, honor even among filibusters." Others viewed Frémont's stand as a matter less of honor than of opportunism.

The implications were clear enough for Kearny. "I am not recognized in my official capacity, either by Commodore Stockton or Lieutenant Colonel Frémont, both of whom refuse to obey my orders or the instructions of the President," he reported to Washington, "and as I have no troops in the country under my authority, excepting a few dragoons, I have no power of enforcing them." He left for San Diego the following morning, writing to Stockton that he did so to prevent "a collision between us and possibly *a civil war* in consequence of it." That was an extraordinary prospect, Americans battling each other over California spoils. But it was something Stockton also foresaw. "I should not only have felt it to be my right, but a matter of imperative duty," he wrote in justification of his conduct a short time later, "to assert and maintain my authority, if necessary, *by a resort to force.*"

The fears of violence between the two branches of the American military establishment was not confined to private correspondence. According to one report, Frémont called the officers of the California Battalion together and solicited their support in his opposition to Kearny, "thus trying to *incite a civil war,*" thought Marine Lieutenant Henry Watson, "for which in my opinion he should be hanged." Naval surgeon Marius Duvall recorded gossip that the Californios had offered to join Frémont in fighting Kearny. No independent evidence supports that rumor, but Kearny apparently took it seriously. On the eve of his departure from the pueblo, he summoned ranchero Benjamin Davis Wilson to his quarters and requested that he muster a group of armed and mounted American civilians to accompany his small troop of dragoons to San Diego. "Frémont has a large force with him of undisciplined men," said Kearny, "and I hear all kinds of rumors of his intentions and acts." Wilson complied, but was appalled at the prospect of an attack by one American commander on another. "I was much surprised," he later recalled, to find Kearny fearful "of *foul play to his person* by some of the Frémont party."

STOCKTON DEPARTED Los Angeles soon after Kearny, leaving Frémont and the California Battalion in control. Frémont established headquarters in Alexander Bell's two-story adobe mansion, from where he issued a circular proclaiming order and peace restored throughout the country. According to Antonio Coronel, "Frémont deliberately set out to win over the Californios." He adopted the rancheo costume—pantaloons, sash, and flat-crowned sombrero—and invited local leaders to meet with him at his quarters. Some Angelenos refused—José Antonio Carrillo prominent among them—but others came, often reluctantly. José del Cármen Lugo later recalled receiving a summons from Frémont. He arrived with trepidation, he said, but was immediately put at ease, Frémont flattering his vanity by telling him that when it came to matters on the eastern frontier, everyone insisted that he must consult with the Lugos. Lugo escorted Frémont on a tour of the upper Río Santa Ana countryside, concluding with a visit to San Gabriel, where a ball was held in the American's honor. "The young women danced and talked with him," said Lugo, "and he returned to Los Angeles pleased and happy." Although Coronel and Lugo understood the expediency of Frémont's policy, they preferred the opportunism of the open palm to the disdain of the closed fist.

Frémont reveled in the attention, and his letters reveal an inflated sense of self-importance. "Throughout the Californian population," he wrote his father-in-law, Senator Thomas Hart Benton of Missouri, "there is only one feeling of satisfaction and gratitude to myself." He reported Californios greeting him on the streets with the phrase "*viva usted seguro, duerme usted seguro*"—live safe, sleep safe—and young boys singing his praises:

> *Viva los Estados Unidos,*
> *Y viva el Coronel Frémont,*
> *Quien nos ha asegurado las vidas*

Long live the United States,
And long live Colonel Frémont,
Who has secured our lives.

A little of this went a long way, but Frémont laid it on thick, in the process alienating a number of Americans, who viewed his conduct with suspicion. "He wears the sombrero and other things, and makes himself ridiculous," one of them noted. "He gave rowdy balls, and so became popular with the lower classes," said another. The most persistent rumor concerned Frémont's philandering. "Frémont's a low fellow," Benjamin Davis Wilson told a visitor to the pueblo, "and patronized common prostitutes in public." When, in 1856, Frémont stood as the first nominee of the Republican Party for president of the United States, allusions to those stories were published in an attempt to sully his character. Henry Hamilton, editor of the *Los Angeles Star*, mouthpiece of the local Democratic Party, wrote of Frémont's "harem, publicly established and maintained in this city, where sisters, mothers, and daughters were indiscriminately collected, [to] the shame of the American people." Hamilton claimed to possess "facts, names, and dates," but he never produced them.

The differing views of Frémont's policy during his short tenure as governor are illustrated by two encounters at one of the many balls he hosted at his headquarters. As Frémont was greeting the guests, across the room he saw a Californio named Geronimo López, the young messenger who had carried the note from Andrés Pico that initiated the negotiations resulting in the Treaty of Cahuenga. Frémont strode over to López with an outstretched hand, congratulating him on his role in ending the conflict. The gesture impressed the Californios who were present, among them Francisco Higuera, *el güero*, the man who had attacked and wounded Archibald Gillespie at San Pasqual. In the spirit of the moment, Higuera approached Gillespie, introduced himself, and said he wished to return the saddle and blanket he had taken during the battle. Gillespie turned beet red. "You damned rascal!" he exclaimed, "keep the property and welcome!" He turned his back on Higuera and stomped off. Gillespie was explicit about his feelings in a letter to Thomas Larkin. Frémont "favors the country people in every particular, and I think to the injury of the foreign residents." Had he been in charge, Gillespie wrote, American policy would be far different. "I would make every one of these rascally Californians pay most dearly for every drop of American blood they have spilt, through their treachery and want of faith." Frémont had shifted with the tide, Gillespie had not. This incident would be the parting of the ways for the former confederates in conquest.

KEARNY ARRIVED in San Diego on January 23. The following day he received word that the Mormon Battalion—some four hundred men under the command of Lieutenant Colonel Philip St. George Cooke—had arrived at Warner's Ranch, completing a five-month trek of nearly two thousand miles. Recruited as part of Kearny's Army of the West, the Mormons had followed in the wake of the First Regiment of Dragoons. Kearny noted their arrival with pleasure. "I will, agreeably to the instructions of the President, have the management of affairs in this country, and will endeavor to carry out his views in relation to it." At last his fortunes were rising.

A week later he sailed for Monterey, where to his delight he found Commodore William Bradford Shubrick, sent to relieve Stockton as commander of the Pacific Squadron. When Stockton received the news of his replacement, he was crestfallen. "You see how transitory all my high sounding titles have proven to be," he wrote his brother-in-law back in the states. "I have in one moment's time been reduced to plain Captain Stockton." Little more than two weeks after his dramatic standoff with Kearny in Los Angeles, Stockton quietly retired from the California stage.

Frémont did not go so easily. With Stockton's fall he lost the cover of official authority for his claim to be California's governor. But with the armed power of the California Battalion to back him, he continued to stand his ground. "Viewing my position and claim clear and indisputable," he wrote, "I cannot permit myself to be interfered with by any other, until directed to do so by the proper authorities at home." That directive arrived within days, explicitly confirming

Kearny's command. On March 1 Kearny published a circular proclaiming himself military governor, appointing Lieutenant Colonel Cooke as commander of the southern military district, and ordering Frémont to muster the volunteers of the California Battalion into regular service under Cooke, discharging all who refused.

Three weeks later, on March 23, Cooke rode into Los Angeles at the head of the Mormon Battalion. Beside him was Stephen Clark Foster, Yankee graduate of Yale College (1840) who would later be elected mayor of Los Angeles. Foster had spent the previous six years in a peripatetic search for a career, teaching school in Virginia and Alabama, attending medical college in Louisiana, and practicing medicine in western Missouri, before heading to New Mexico with a trading caravan in 1845. He was clerking at a store in Santa Fe, "waiting for something to turn up," in his words, when the Mormon Battalion passed through on its way to California. Foster, who had acquired a fluency in Spanish, hired on as Lieutenant Colonel Cooke's translator. Years later he recalled his arrival in Los Angeles after the long trek across the desert. "My place in the column as interpreter was with the colonel at the head," he wrote, "and I rode with my rifle slung across the saddle, powder-horn and bullet-pouch slung about my shoulders. My beard rivaled in length that of the old colonel by whose side I rode, but mine was as black as the raven's wing, and his was as grey as mine is now."

They forded the river, passed through the vineyards and groves on the east side of town, and entered the pueblo on Calle del Aliso, named for Louis Vignes's estate. It was Foster's first glimpse of the people of Los Angeles, among whom he would spend the rest of his life. Several hundred Indians, taking a respite from their labors, crowded together at the foot of Calle de los Negros. A group of women, heads covered with rebozos, exited the Plaza church and formed a small funeral procession along Calle de Eternidad to the *campo santo* at the base of the rolling hills north of town. Thirty or forty Californios, in their distinctive short jackets and breeches, lined Calle Principal. They greeted the Americans in silence. The only sound Foster heard was the battalion's fife and drum playing "The Star Spangled Banner" as they paraded past Government House, then the loud huzza from the men when Cooke ordered them to break ranks and stack arms. They pitched their tents in the corral at the rear of Jonathan Temple's townhouse.

Neither Frémont nor the California Battalion was present to greet them. Frémont had departed for Monterey the day before, intent on challenging Kearny's orders. He had relocated the California Battalion to San Gabriel. Cooke found one of Frémont's officers, who told him that the rifleros had refused to be mustered into regular service, and that Frémont would not allow their discharge. His commander, he said, considered it "unsafe at this time, when rumor is rife with a threatened insurrection, to discharge the Battalion, and will decline doing so." No evidence of any such a threatened insurrection exists. Without the volunteers of the battalion, Frémont would have been powerless, which was his reason for keeping them in service.

Cooke had orders from Kearny to take possession of Frémont's artillery and ammunition, but when he went to San Gabriel the quartermaster there told him he had direct orders from Frémont to release the weapons to no one. Cooke was flabbergasted. "I told him that the government authorities, the general of the army and governor, had committed the command here to *me*," he reported, "and I asked him if he did not acknowledge the authority of the United States Government." He would acknowledge no authority but that of his commanding officer, the man replied. "The President of the United States, in person," he declared, "would fail to get the artillery until Lieutenant-Colonel Frémont gave permission!" Cooke wrote to Kearny. "If these Americans are taught not to obey the legal authority of the government, what dangerous impression must have unavoidably been imparted to the late enemy." He considered Frémont's conduct treasonous, but was unwilling to press the issue. "I sacrifice all feeling of pride to duty, which I think plainly forbids any attempt to crush this resistance of misguided men." Such a challenge, he feared, "would be a signal for revolt" among the Californios, who were paying close attention, soaking it all in.

FRÉMONT WAS PLAYING FOR TIME, hoping the next set of dispatches from Washington would acknowledge him as the "conqueror of California" and grant him what he considered his due, the governorship. But at Monterey he learned of the arrival at San Francisco of the New York Regiment of Volunteers, nearly eight hundred men under the command of Colonel Jonathan D. Stevenson. The Polk administration had sent them as military backup, but also as colonizers. Most were young bachelors from the vicinity of New York City who enlisted with the explicit understanding that they would remain in California after the war, forming a nucleus for the Americanization of the territory. "There were men of pretty much every class except the most opulent," one of the volunteers later remembered, "a large proportion of steady mechanics of all trades, with a smart sprinkling of the b'hoys of New York City, and not a few intemperates and ne'er-do-wells." Stevenson's regiment had sailed from New York in three vessels in September 1846 and arrived six months later, in March 1847. They provided Kearny with overwhelming force, and he treated Frémont accordingly, ordering him to return to Los Angeles immediately, to discharge the men of the California Battalion. He was then to accompany Kearny back to the states.

Frémont rejoined the California Battalion at San Gabriel at the beginning of April. During his final weeks in southern California his behavior became increasingly desperate. There was bad blood between the men of the California Battalion, many of them Missourians, and the men of the Mormon Battalion, many of whom had experienced a violent expulsion from Missouri in 1838. Frémont played up that antagonism, encouraging his men to confront the Mormons whenever they visited the pueblo, while also attempting to arouse ill-feeling toward them among Angelenos. A number of Californios reported that Frémont himself told them that "the Mormons were cannibals, and especially fond of eating children."

Relations between the two battalions grew so tense that Cooke decided to take defensive measures in case of attack. He ordered his men to begin the construction of an earthenwork fort on the hill behind the Plaza church, in fear not of the Californios but of the California Battalion. "Last night we were called up and ordered to load and fix bayonets," Private Henry Standage wrote on the morning of April 26. "The colonel had sent word that an attack might be expected from Col. Frémont's men before day." There was no attack, but the fear was real, and the conflict among the Americans could not be hidden from Angelenos. "With the prospect of the Mexicans again rising and the low murmurings of civil war hardly ceasing to salute our ears," wrote Sergeant Daniel Tyler, "what the end would have been is difficult to say."

General Kearny sent Colonel Richard B. Mason to Los Angeles with a demand that Frémont disbanded the battalion. Frémont treated Mason with contempt, on one occasion showing up several hours late for a scheduled meeting. "Sir," said Mason, "when I send for an officer whom I rank and command, I expect him to obey me." Frémont bristled. "My business was closed to you, Sir, was my reason for not coming." (Los Angeles gossips claimed that Frémont's "business" was an assignation with a young woman; one man claimed he had never seen "so much fuss made about a whore.") "None of your insolence," Mason snapped back, "or I will put you in irons." Frémont immediately asked whether Mason would stand personally accountable for those words, and when Mason replied that he would, Frémont dashed back to his quarters and wrote out a formal challenge. Mason adhered to the script, and arrangements were made for a duel the following morning. But at dawn Frémont received a note from Mason saying he had been called back to Monterey and proposing that they meet there to conclude their affair of honor. When Kearny learned of the dispute, he ordered both men to stand down, which they did, agreeing that they would meet in the states later to settle accounts. But that never happened.

Finally realizing that if Frémont was to be removed he would have to do it himself, Kearny went to Los Angeles, accompanied by Colonel Stevenson and two companies of New York volunteers. "I this morning started Lieutenant-Colonel Frémont to Monterey to close his public business there before he leaves for Washington," Kearny reported to the adjutant general in Washington. "His conduct in California has been such that I shall be compelled, on arriving in Missouri, to arrest him, and send him under charges to report to you." Frémont's court-martial on a charge of mutiny, which took place the following winter, brought the principal American commanders of the California conquest together a final time. Their testimony exposed a sordid contest for power characterized by egotism, calumny, and recklessness. It was certainly no way to begin the complicated military occupation of a hostile country. Frémont was found guilty and sentenced to dismissal from the service, which many considered a mild punishment. The reputation of all the players was badly sullied.

Within a year Kearny would be dead, struck down by yellow fever, contracted in Mexico. Stockton resigned from the Navy, served a term as senator from his home state of New Jersey, then unsuccessfully sought the presidential nomination of the nativist American Party, campaigning under the banner "Americans Should Rule America." Gillespie developed a drinking problem, resigned from the Marine Corps in disgrace, and ended up in San Francisco, where he became infamous for his frequent outbursts against his former colleague-in-arms. "Frémont disappointed everybody," he declared bitterly. Frémont himself led two more exploring expeditions—one simply a failure, the other a complete disaster—then became one of the first two senators from the state of California, the first of numerous high assignments, notably as the first presidential candidate of the newly formed Republican Party in 1856. Over a long career he remained the brilliant opportunist, always with a fatal tendency to overplay his hand.

· CHAPTER 12 ·

MILITARY OCCUPATION

DESPITE PRESIDENT JAMES K. POLK'S determination to seize California, his administration had given no thought to how the Mexican department would be governed for the duration of the war. Stockton had no instructions at all, but that did not prevent him from declaring California "a Territory of the United States" in his proclamation of August 17, 1846. When Polk released that document to the public four months later—as part of a cache of state papers on the conduct of the war—his congressional opponents were outraged by what they considered the president's infringement on their constitutional authority to "make all needful rules and regulations" for territory acquired by the nation. On the floor of the House of Representatives, Whig congressman Garrett Davis of Kentucky itemized the list of offenses. "Foreign countries occupied by our army and navy, . . . officers of our Government proclaiming themselves governors of provinces, appointing subordinate officers, fixing their salaries and the duration of their offices, establishing, in a word, the whole machine of civil government." By what authority had Polk sanctioned such actions? "What! Was our American President an emperor, sending forth his Agrippa and his Marcellus, his proconsuls, to establish and to govern the provinces they might conquer by force of arms?"

Polk might have shifted the blame to Stockton had he not explicitly directed Kearny to do much the same thing. The general's hastily prepared instructions authorized him, once California was firmly in American hands, to establish a civil government "similar to that which exists in our territories," one in which the Californios would "exercise the rights of freemen in electing their own representatives to the territorial legislature." Such a policy was entirely without precedent. There was no provision in the Constitution for the establishment of an American empire. Polk's men were making it up as they went along.

In early January 1847, in an attempt to clarify the character of the occupation authority, the administration issued new instructions to the military command in California. "The possession of portions of the enemy's territory, acquired by justifiable acts of war, gives to us the right of government during the continuance of our possession," but "only such right as the laws of nations recognize." That is, a government strictly military and temporary, with no conveyance of the constitutional rights of American citizens to the inhabitants. The occupation authority was to recognize and enforce existing Mexican law until California had been legally joined to the United States by congressional action. American officers were obligated to protect the lives and property of the inhabitants, guarantee their freedom of religion, and permit them to select their own officials to make, execute, and enforce local laws. These instructions drew a fine line between the prerogative of the conqueror and the protection of the conquered—just how fine a line would be revealed in practice.

Receiving these instructions, Colonel Richard B. Mason, who became military governor upon General Kearny's departure, made his own attempt at clarification. "This is a military government," he declared, responsible only for such duties "as are necessary to the full enjoyment of the advantages resulting from the conquest, and to the due protection of the rights of persons and of property of the inhabitants." The war with Mexico dragged on, and the situation in California remained volatile. The inhabitants "dislike the change of flags," Mason reported to Washington, and Californios in the Los Angeles district "would rise immediately if it were possible for Mexico to send even a small force into the country." He expressed confidence that the United States would ultimately prevail, but until the war was concluded, military rule of the Californios would remain his principal assignment. "Nothing keeps them quiet but the want of a proper leader and a rallying-point," Mason wrote. "We must keep up a show of troops, however small in numbers."

Colonel Jonathan D. Stevenson of the New York Regiment of Volunteers was sent to command the garrison in Los Angeles. The Mormons departed at the end of the year of service to which they had agreed, but that left Stevenson with nearly four hundred men—two companies of New York volunteers and another of dragoons. A big man, with a square face and a jutting jaw, Stevenson presented himself as a hard but fair ruler. Shortly after he arrived, he called together a group of Angeleno leaders to announce his intentions. As long as they "preserved a quiet and peaceful deportment," Stevenson said, he would "protect them in all their rights and property." Their municipal institutions—alcalde and ayuntamiento—would continue to function without American interference. But at the first sign of resistance, he warned, he would "treat them as a conquered province under martial law." He intended to "rely upon their word of honor," Stevenson said, until the people of Los Angeles gave him cause "to doubt their good faith."

THE CALIFORNIOS LOVED DANCING. The ordinary fandangos and elite balls often went on well into the early morning hours. Those evenings became the occasion for regular social contact between American enlisted men and officers and Angelenos. "No doubt the Society of Los Pueblanas will in some measure reconcile you to a longer residence in California," an American officer wrote to army surgeon John S. Griffin, posted in Los Angeles with the dragoons. "War you have tasted of—women and wine are still left to you."

On the Fourth of July, with the construction of the earthenwork fort atop the hill nearing completion, Stevenson invited Angelenos to a dedication ceremony, to be followed that evening by a gala ball for officers and prominent Californios. The entire garrison paraded up to the fort and assembled around a towering pole as the flag was raised and the regimental band played "The Star Spangled Banner." Stevenson gave an interminable speech, dedicating the fort in honor of Captain Benjamin Moore, killed at San Pasqual, followed by ceremonial readings of the Declaration of Independence in both English and Spanish. Stevenson reported only one problem: "no Californians came." He had wanted the event to be an occasion for reconciliation, yet seemed oblivious to the contradiction of holding it on an American patriotic holiday. The Angelenos would obey Stevenson's command to remain peaceful and orderly, but that did not mean they would participate in this American ritual. "It is very evident from the state of feeling," Stevenson wrote, "that we shall have as much as we can do with our small force . . . to keep possession of this post."

The ball that evening got off to a bad start when Angelenos arrived to find the hall decked with the symbols of American nationalism, including the same large flag hoisted on the hill that morning. In attendance was José Antonio Carrillo, the outspoken squadron commander who had humiliated the Americans at the Battle of Rancho San Pedro, and throughout the evening he kept up a running commentary on the boorishness of his American hosts. At midnight a jury of American officers announced a competition to select the "belle of the evening," and after all the women had promenaded they chose beautiful María Guadalupe Zamorano, the fourteen-year-old sister of María Dolores Francesca Zamorano de Flores, wife of the exiled former commandante of the uprising, José María Flores. A number of Angelenos claimed to be insulted. Carrillo took particular offense at the competition among American officers for a chance to dance with the young woman. At one point she was escorted to the dance floor by Captain Jefferson Hunt, a grizzled Mormon at least three times her age. Hunt proved himself especially clumsy at the waltz, and Carrillo remarked scornfully that he "danced like a bear."

That comment circulated quickly among all the American officers, and when Hunt caught word of it the next morning, he declared that Carrillo must either apologize or provide him with satisfaction. "When this was communicated to me," Stevenson later reported, "I considered it a very good opportunity to let the turbulent spirits know that they were understood." Carrillo was "a great knave, and undoubtedly one of the shrewdest men in California," commanding "great influence with the lower order of his countrymen," so Stevenson instructed Stephen Foster, principal translator for the Americans, to go to him with a demand that he make a public apology at a special meeting of American officers and prominent Angelenos called for later that day. Foster approached Carrillo with trepidation, but Don José received him graciously and without a moment's hesitation agreed to attend and deliver the apology. "When a man was convinced he was wrong," he told Foster, "he ought to take back what he said." He had given the matter a great deal of thought and had concluded that his comparison was "unfair to the bear, the better dancer of the two." Not daring to challenge Carrillo, Foster merely reported to Stevenson that Don José had agreed to attend and hoped for the best.

Americans and Angelenos began assembling around noon at the home of vineyardist Nathaniel Pryor, where the meeting was being held. Pryor set out an ample selection of his wines, and plenty had been consumed by the time Carrillo arrived. Stevenson embarked on another windy speech, reminding the Californios that his mission was to retain possession of the country, that he was attempting to do that by promoting peace and harmony, and that he would not tolerate conduct promoting conflict. Carrillo was then introduced, but as he began to speak he was rudely interrupted by Captain Hunt, deep in his cups. It was outrageous, Hunt declared, that he and his fellow officers should be forced to suffer the insults of "an unregenerate Mexican with the blood of Americans still red on his hands." The room erupted in pandemonium. Carrillo left in a huff, remarking to Foster on his way out, "*sus paisanos son un atajo de pendejos y borrachos*"—your countrymen are a bunch of idiots and drunks. It was for the best, Foster concluded, for "if Carrillo had continued speaking, I am sure that he would have made the same remarks that he did to me, and there would have been the devil to pay."

WHILE THE ELITE attended the officers' ball, ordinary Angelenos and common soldiers celebrated at a fandango sponsored by American enlisted men. In the early morning hours of July 5, as several American soldiers made their way home from the event, they literally stumbled over the body of a man lying dead in the dusty street. It was Julien Bartolet, a young Frenchman employed as a cooper at one of the vineyards, killed by a blow that smashed his head like a pumpkin. Alcalde José Salazar opened an investigation. Bartolet had left the fandango in the company of a Californio and several American soldiers. One of the Americans had been seen arguing with Bartolet in a dark alley, but his fellow soldiers provided him with an alibi. There Salazar's investigation stalled.

Excluding the American occupation force, the French made up the largest group of foreign born in Los Angeles, providing the skilled labor required in winemaking. During the fighting in 1846 most of them remained neutral and attempted to maintain good relations with both Californios and Americans. With no indictment or any prospect of one, a group of French residents petitioned Colonel Stevenson, asking that he press Alcalde Salazar "to act with all rigor and formality prescribed by the laws of the courts in the prosecution of so important a case." Stevenson summoned the alcalde and ordered him to arrest the Californio who had gone off with Bartolet that night, which Salazar refused to do. The investigation quickly became mired in mutual suspicion. Criminal violence was common in Los Angeles, John Griffin noted, and "the worst of it is, there seems to be no means of finding out who are the authors of the crimes." Local officials, he thought, were quick to place the blame on Americans. "So long as the alcaldes supposed that it was a dragoon who committed the murder, they were excessively energetic—but the evidence being clear that the man was not guilty, no further prosecution was had in the case."

RATHER THAN BRINGING Americans and Californios together, as Stevenson intended, the celebrations on the Fourth had led to further estrangement. A few days afterward, Angelenos commenced the celebration of their own traditional summer festival. The Americans were invited to attend, but fearing violence Stevenson ordered them confined to quarters at Fort Moore. From their perch atop the hill, the men watched as Angelenos indulged in several days of feasting, dancing, and bullfighting. They fumed when they saw Andrés Pico and other former officers of *las fuerzas nacionales* parade through the Plaza in their military finery, including the very lances they had carried into battle at San Pasqual. "I have a guard of about twenty volunteers and ten dragoons on the heights with two pieces of artillery," Lieutenant John McHenry Hollingsworth noted in his journal, "ready for a fight at any time the Californians want it."

Throughout that summer and into the fall there were continual rumors of insurrection and invasion. Soldiers on patrol frequently overheard Angeleno women chanting a little ditty *en español*, very likely aimed at raising American anxiety:

> *Poco tiempo*
> *Viene Castro*
> *Con mucho gente.*
> *Vamos Americanos.*

> *In a little while*
> *Castro will come*
> *With many people.*
> *Goodbye Americans.*

There was never any chance of that. Neither José Antonio Castro nor Pío Pico, the exiled leaders of the department of California, had the least success in getting a hearing for their cause in Mexico. Rather, the taunt signaled the deteriorating relationship between Angelenos and the occupiers. By the late autumn of 1847, things had grown so tense that Stevenson issued a curfew order, confining his men to barracks after eight o'clock each evening. There would be no more fandangos, no more fraternizing in the cantinas. "Everything is quiet," Lieutenant Hollingsworth noted in early December, "though I think that the country is in a very unsettled state."

On December 6, the anniversary of the Battle of San Pasqual, an argument between Americans and Californios on the Plaza turned violent, and several men were injured, though none seriously. The next morning Stevenson received intelligence—faulty intelligence, it turned out—that Angelenos were planning a general uprising for that night. He doubled the guard and ordered his whole force to be on the alert. "As night came on," wrote Hollingsworth, "I could not but feel anxious." At midnight he armed himself and accompanied by another officer took several turns about the Plaza. Everything appeared normal, so they returned to the fort and retired to bed. About an hour later Hollingsworth was jolted awoke by a powerful explosion that rocked the entire pueblo like an earthquake. The guardhouse had been blown to bits, and after investigation an explanation was pieced together. A nervous sentry had challenged what he thought was an approaching horseman—in fact a wandering cow—and receiving no reply, fired blindly into the night. The guard formed to repel the attack, the call to arms sounded, and in the subsequent excitement a soldier accidentally dropped a lighted match into an open chest of ammunition, touching off the blast. Four Americans were killed, and ten or twelve badly wounded. The explosion "cast a gloom over us all," wrote Hollingsworth, but "the Californians are much delighted at our misfortune."

That accident, the product of suspicion and mistrust, was the most important event to take place at Fort Moore. The construction of a cannonaded fortification on the hill, conceived as protection for the Mormon Battalion against Frémont's rifleros, was in truth an unfortunate mistake. As Archibald Gillespie and his men discovered in 1846, the hill was impossible to hold for the simple reason that there was no water there. At the conclusion of the military occupation of Los Angeles, Fort Moore would be abandoned.

TEN DAYS AFTER THE EXPLOSION Angelenos held their annual election for new municipal officers, resulting in the selection of José Loreto Sepúlveda and Ygnacio Palomares as alcalde and assistant alcalde, respectively. Both men were rancheros with long records of public service. But Stevenson considered them incorrigible rebels, men of "the worst class," as he wrote to Governor Mason, elected solely because of their opposition to American rule. With Mason's compliance, Stevenson nullifed the election. The entire ayuntamiento resigned in protest. Mason appointed official translator Stephen Foster alcalde *pro tempore*, and he was installed in an improvised ceremony during which he swore "to administer justice in accordance with Mexican law." That was going to be difficult, Foster later wrote, since "I then knew as much about Mexican law as I did about Chinese."

But he proved a quick study, served well not only by his fluency in Spanish but also his native talent for diplomacy. He also raised his credibility with elite Angelenos by marrying María Merced Lugo, the widowed daughter of wealthy ranchero Antonio María Lugo. Foster's legitimacy in the eyes of ordinary Angelenos, however, came none too readily. In December 1848, after serving a full year, he announced another election for municipal officers. "But no attention was paid to my proclamation," he later recalled, "so I was directed to continue as alcalde until the people were willing to act." He would continue to serve until the final departure of American military forces from the pueblo.

During the occupation, which ran from January 1847 to May 1849, nine murders were recorded in the Los Angeles district. Six of the victims were Indians, four of them killed by Californios. In one of those cases a ranchero was accused of murdering a military leader of the Cahuillas, a crime with political implications. The mangled body of Captain Yerbabuena, with several gaping wounds and a knife still lodged in his throat, was found in the foothills near Mission San Gabriel in April 1847. A young Indian woman named Acahual reported that she and Yerbabuena had been walking together when two Californios approached them on horseback. Acahual hid in the chaparral and watched as the Californios confronted her friend, accusing him of supporting the Americans during the late war. No, Yerbabuena replied, "*yo establa con los Californios*"—I was with the Californios. The Cahuillas, known for their fierce loyalty to the Lugo family of Rancho San Bernardino, had joined José del Cármen Lugo in attacking and massacring the pro-American Luiseños at Temecula. Yerbabuena was a Cahuilla "captain," so the charge these Californios made against him was scarcely credible. But the men were angry and had no intention of arguing the point. Acahual saw one of them lasso Yerbabuena and drag him away. After considerable investigation the alcalde ordered the arrest of Felipe Ballesteros, brother of the Californio killed during the fighting at Chino. Young Ballesteros denied having anything to do with the murder, although Acahual positively identified him as one of the attackers. The alcalde found Ballesteros guilty, but ordered his release on bond while the verdict was appealed. And there the record falls silent.

With Foster as alcalde and thus judge, American procedure began to slip into Mexican legal process. In September 1848 Pedro Pacheco was indicted for the murder of José María Machado. According to Pacheco, the conflict between them began with a dispute over a card game at Negro Manuel's tavern. Machado called Pacheco a "motherfucker" and other epithets that, in Pacheco's words, "naturally provoked a response." They began to fight but were separated by bystanders. Later, as Pacheco rode down the street, Machado struck him with a club, knocking him from the saddle. Pacheco picked himself up, charged Machado, and thrust a knife into his side, inflicting a mortal wound.

He claimed self-defense. The prosecutor argued that he had armed himself, evidence of malice aforethought, but Pacheco, representing himself, countered that he always carried a knife, which he used in his trade as a cobbler. This was one of the first criminal trials in Los Angeles to proceed according to the adversarial model of the common law, with prosecutor, defense attorney, and a jury of "six legal and impartial neighbors." They found Pacheco not guilty. The case marked a transition in the legal administration of justice in Los Angeles.

THE NEWS OF THE DISCOVERY of gold in the Sierra Nevada reached Los Angeles in late March or early April of 1848, and within weeks Angelenos were leaving for the north in droves. Stevenson had enormous difficulty holding on to his soldiers. They were "deserting rapidly," Lieutenant Hollingsworth wrote in July. "There is great excitement among the men—we much fear that many more will go." By that time, the summer of 1848, the fighting in Mexico had ended and a treaty negotiated ceding California and New Mexico. Word of ratification by the respective governments of the United States and Mexico was expected at any time. "The gold fever is raging now and there is a great disposition to desert among the men and much dissatisfaction," Hollingsworth wrote in early August. "The news of the peace has made the men the more impatient to be discharged."

A few days later Governor Mason received official word of the ratification of the Treaty of Guadalupe Hidalgo. "Americans and Californians will now be one and the same people," he proclaimed optimistically, "subject to the same laws, and enjoying the same rights and privileges." There would be "a new order, . . . a firm and stable government, administering justice with impartiality, and punishing crime with the strong arm of the law." This was little more than wishful thinking. In fact, the end of the war placed Governor Mason in an impossible position. The New York volunteers, who had enlisted for the duration, now clamored to be discharged, and rather than risk mutiny, Mason took steps for their orderly release.

That left the military government supported by a few hundred dragoons and sailors, and they too were deserting at a rapid clip. Moreover, Mason had to wonder, under what authority could military rule be continued following the ratification of the treaty ending the war? Yet how could it be disbanded? There was neither a civil government to take its place nor hope of one anytime soon. Congress was sharply divided over the question of slavery in the territory ceded by Mexico, and the Polk administration had no backup plan. Not until October did Secretary of State James Buchanan announce the administration's position, declaring that until Congress acted, "the great law of necessity" justified the continuation of military rule in California as a "government *de facto*." Mason had already presumed as much and had acted accordingly. But without troops, his government de facto was, for all practical purposes, no government at all.

The New York volunteers departed Los Angeles on September 18, 1848. They were replaced by a regiment of dragoons under the command of Major Lawrence Graham. During the time Graham's men were stationed in Los Angeles, more than ten thousand Mexicans passed through town on their way to the northern goldfields. "The pueblo has changed much since you left," John Griffin wrote from Los Angeles to Colonel Stevenson in Monterey. "It is now thronged with soldiers, quartermaster's men, Sonoranians, &c., the most vicious and idle set you ever beheld. Gambling, drinking, and whoring are the only occupations, and they seem to be followed with great industry."

Graham's dragoons were supposed to preserve order, but the streets were not at all orderly. "Our men seem inclined to keep peace among themselves," wrote Griffin, "and the Sonoranians and Californians seem very much afraid of them. A Californian is a rare sight now in the streets. You never see them parading about on their fine horses as formerly." Even this rough order began to break down as the dragoons deserted for the goldfields. The official report of their conduct was scathing. "It is known that these deserters committed many outrages upon the property and it is feared on the persons of the inhabitants they encountered on their route to the mines," it read. In an attempt to hold on to the few enlisted men who remained, Major Graham was reassigned to San Diego, hoping that the greater distance from the mines would lessen the temptation to desert. And so, on May 17, 1849, the military occupation of Los Angeles finally ended. Whether Americans and Californios would succeed in becoming "one people," as Governor Mason hoped, remained to be seen.

PART TWO

· CHAPTER 13 ·

Mob Law

BENJAMIN HAYES caught his first glimpse of Los Angeles on the road from Mission San Gabriel late on the morning of Saturday, February 2, 1850. Fording the Los Angeles River, formerly known as Río Porciúncula, he came down Calle del Aliso, passing El Aliso, the winery of Luis Vignes, marked by its towering sycamore. At the intersection with Calle de la Zanja (soon renamed Los Angeles Street) he passed Alexander Bell's impressive two-story adobe on his left, then the entrance to Calle de los Negros with its saloons and brothels on his right, before coming to Calle Principal. A left turn brought him to the Bella Union Hotel, which occupied the adobe previously known as Government House. It was the dinner hour, so Hayes tied his mule to a post, went inside, and seated himself in what passed for the dining room, crowded with Californios, Mexicanos, and Americans. Los Angeles was a rest stop for hundreds of men headed for the mines.

Hayes looked about for a familiar face, but recognized no one until a large black man named Peter Biggs ambled over to his table. Hayes had known Biggs as the slave of an old friend back in Liberty, Missouri. He had journeyed to Los Angeles with a new master, Lieutenant Andrew Jackson Smith, an officer with the Mormon Battalion, and after the war, when Smith was posted back to the states, he made Biggs an offer he couldn't refuse: his freedom if he would agree to remain behind, saving Smith the cost of his transport. In a ramshackle shed next door to the Bella Union, Biggs opened the "New Orleans Shaving Saloon," the pueblo's first barbershop. Known to Californios as "Don Pedro," to Americans as "Nigger Pete," Biggs was acquainted with virtually every resident of Los Angeles, and he obligingly directed Hayes to other Missourians in town. Hayes spent the afternoon wandering the dusty streets, greeting old acquaintances, and picking up interesting tidbits of news. "I remained a few hours in the pueblo, long enough to learn that an infinite amount of gambling was going on, and that the price of a small loaf of bread was 25 cents," nearly ten times what it cost back in Missouri.

Benjamin Ignatius Hayes, a man in his midthirties, had grown up in a Catholic household in Baltimore, the eldest son of an enterprising master mechanic who served a term as the city's sheriff. Hayes attended St. Mary's, a seminary dedicated to the education of young men for the priesthood. Although Hayes would remain spiritually and intellectually engaged by Catholicism all his life, he turned to the law. He went west to make his fortune and spent several years as an attorney on Missouri's western border. In 1848 he married Emily Chauncey of St. Louis, planning to make a home in Liberty, now a suburb of Kansas City. Not long after their wedding, however, Hayes was swept up in the excitement of the Gold Rush.

"I threw myself alone upon the road to 'El Dorado,'" he wrote in his diary. There would be plenty of work out there for lawyers, he reasoned, and he would send for Emily as soon as he found a favorable position. His first day on the road was a series of small disasters. By noon he had "burnt" his right hand from the friction of the new rope running through it, and unable to use it effectively, "I found myself going over the head of my mule, my gun going one way, and the mule another." Distracted, he took a wrong turn and got lost. At twilight he spied a light, and heading toward it he came to a cabin, whose occupant agreed to put him up for five dollars, a princely sum, but Hayes was desperate. The next morning his host guided him back to the main road, three or four miles distant. As they rode along, the man gave Hayes a sidelong glance and out of the blue remarked, "How easy I could kill you now, and nobody would ever know it!" Hayes was cradling a double-barreled shotgun in his arms and had an "Allen's revolver," a mean-looking little six-shooter known as a "pepperbox," tucked in his coat pocket, but the weapons made him feel no safer. This inauspicious beginning gave Hayes pause. "Last night, as I lay wrapped in my blanket, I dreamt of home and my dear wife," he wrote to Emily. "How much I desire success for your sake. You must always pray for me, dearest."

At Council Grove on the Kansas prairie, 150 miles from home, Hayes joined a company of travelers. From that point the trail was crowded with men headed for California. Hayes had read accounts of the march of General Kearny's dragoons as well as the Mormon Battalion, so he was not surprised by the hard traveling along the southern trail. He completed it unscathed, maintaining throughout the journey a lively interest in the things he saw and the people he met. He found New Mexicans "a polite, kind, mild, well-meaning people, respecting the laws, and eminently religious in their feelings," which appealed to his own Catholic piety. At Warner's Ranch he enjoyed several days of recuperation, soaking in the hot pools, "surrounded by squaws and muchachos, all naked, dabbling in the water." Hayes spoke a little Spanish—he could read and write the language quite well—and he conversed with some of the Cupeños. "One Indian told me the people are *todos Cristianos*," he reported, but "sadly corrupted" by alcohol, gambling, and prostitution. Hayes noted this as "an example of 'Anglo-Saxon progress.'" Hayes himself had a drinking problem. He had taken the temperance pledge and been sober since his wedding day.

He arrived at Rancho Santa Ana del Chino on January 30, 1850. A company of immigrants from Missouri had just come in, ending a grueling trip across the desert from Great Salt Lake, and Hayes compared notes of travel with several of the men. The next morning he pressed on, stopping midday at John Rowland's Rancho La Puente, where he found more immigrants encamped. "Rowland is married to a New Mexican lady, whose manners are very agreeable, a delightful little woman," Hayes noted. "They have several interesting little children, live well." Nearby were the residences of Rowland's sons-in-law, John Reed and James Barton, volunteers under Archibald Gillespie and veterans of the battles at Rancho San Pedro, San Pasqual, Paso de Bartolo, and La Mesa. Rowland provided Hayes with an account of his imprisonment in Los Angeles during the fighting.

By the time Hayes arrived at Mission San Gabriel, the bells were announcing vespers. "Twilight had just gone, lights were flickering in the various rooms of the mission; men, women, and children flocking around; and from the whole neighborhood the murmurs of voices indicated a populous village." He attended chapel and found himself deeply moved.

> The whole scene, American by the side of Mexican (to adopt the language of the day), Indian and white, trader and penitent, gayety, bustle and confusion on the one side and religious solemnity on the other, was singular to me. A beggar at the door, as we sallied out, at the conclusion of the service, struck my attention, although I did not understand the language in which he now chanted and again prayed, as many in passing placed their alms in his hand.

It was a world untold, but with the familiar, comforting universality of the mother church. Hayes had come to California with every expectation of looking for work in the north. But the south appealed. After his initial visit to the pueblo, he decided he would take temporary lodgings and inquire into the local prospects for a lawyer.

HAYES SOUGHT OUT the only practicing attorney in Los Angeles, a young Peruvian named Manuel Clemente Rojo, who graciously introduced him to local notables, including the patriarch of Angeleno politics, José Antonio Carrillo. Don José invited Hayes to visit his home at the southwest corner of the Plaza, where in 1834 he had hosted Pío Pico's grand wedding ball. Carrillo proudly displayed the lance he carried as a squadron commander and spoke about his military career. Hayes was appropriately admiring, and Don José responded with the offer of room and board in his house for thirty-one dollars a month. Hayes accepted and over the next several months became a familiar figure in the Carrillo household.

The previous fall Carrillo had been a reluctant delegate to the state constitutional convention. Congress, divided over the issue of slavery in the territories, had failed to establish a territorial authority. American settlers in communities throughout California agitated for a provisional republican government. In Los Angeles, those efforts were supported by a number of leading men, including Agustín Olvera, Antonio Coronel, Andrés Pico, and other Californios who joined forces in an informal group, or *junta*, with Americans such as Abel Stearns, Benjamin Davis Wilson, and Stephen Clark Foster. Carrillo, however, was strongly opposed, fearing the loss of the familiar governmental institutions the Californio elite had utilized to achieve their rise to power. At one such gathering Carrillo denounced the agitation, declaring that he could neither countenance nor support a movement that aimed to overthrow the existing system. "And thereupon," wrote John S. Griffin, who was present, "he left the meeting in high dudgeon."

But the movement for home rule was unstoppable, and bowing to the pressure, California's military governor called an election for delegates to an officially sanctioned constitutional convention. Southern California was apportioned five delegates, and the Los Angeles junta, in the words of ranchero Benjamin Davis Wilson, "held a public meeting and selected the best men we could find." Three Anglos—Abel Stearns, Stephen Foster, and Hugo Reid, each married to a daughter of the country and sympathetic to Californio concerns. And two Californios—Manuel Domínguez, proprietor of Rancho San Pedro and a longtime supporter of American annexation, and José Antonio Carrillo himself, the most prominent critic of the American occupation, who had been persuaded by fellow rancheros that his presence would be critical to the credibility of the proceedings. The slate was endorsed in a election notable for its low turnout. "So little interest was felt," wrote Foster, that "only forty-eight votes were polled," most of them cast by members of the junta.

When the constitutional convention opened in Monterey in September 1849, it seated a total of forty-eight delegates, only eight of them Californios. The remarkable thing, delegate Charles Botts of Monterey declared, was not that there were so few but that there were any at all. "It has been the custom of other nations to trample to the dust the rights of the conquered," he said. "But what do you see here? You see these gentlemen admitted to exactly the same platform that you occupy yourselves—taken to your hearts as friends and brothers. . . . Is not that a guaranty—a sufficient guaranty—that they who have done this will never do them wrong?" With this bit of self-congratulation, the conquerors moved to create a state structured entirely in the American mold. William M. Gwin, who would join John C. Frémont as one of California's first two senators, expressed the prevailing point of view at the opening session. "It was not for the native Californians we were making this Constitution," he declared, but "for the great American population, comprising four-fifths of the population of this country."

His comment elicited a retort from the sharp-tongued Carrillo, who "begged leave to say, that he considered himself as much an American citizen as the gentleman." It was the first time Carrillo had publicly accepted the fact of the conquest. He had strong views on many issues, but the Californios had no power at the convention and had almost no impact on the outcome. Carrillo came home in a funk and thereafter played no role in local politics. During the time Hayes roomed at his house, Don José was rarely home, but off with his cronies rehearsing old struggles.

MANUEL CLEMENTE ROJO also introduced Hayes to Abel Stearns, who was serving a term as the pueblo's assistant alcalde. Stearns had declared himself neutral during the late war, which left him unscathed. When Hayes arrived at the alcalde's office, Stearns was in the midst of a court proceeding adhering to Mexican legal protocol that Hayes had difficulty following. Once the hearing was adjourned the two men spoke. Hayes asked about the prospects for an attorney in the pueblo, and Stearns inquired about his visitor's background. Learning that he was literate *en español*, Stearns offered to hire him as an assistant. Hayes went back to Carrillo's with a Mexican law book under his arm.

Stearns needed help dealing with the increasing disorder in Los Angeles. The war had ended two years before. Congress remained deadlocked over the question of statehood, but the proposed state constitution had been ratified at the polls, and men throughout California were engaged in the formation of state, county, and municipal institutions. For the time being, however, Los Angeles continued to be governed under Mexican law, with locally elected alcaldes and council. Preconquest governance was weak, ineffective, and discriminatory, particularly when it came to Indians, who made up a considerable portion of the population and performed much of the necessary labor.

After the conquest, with bodies and souls still wounded and broken, the task of administering justice became even more difficult. Crowds of migrants passed through Los Angeles on their way to and from the mines. Mexicans and Americans—Sonoreños and Texans, mostly—established encampments on the outskirts of town, and each night men thronged the saloons and brothels along Calle de los Negros. Violent mayhem became a regular occurrence on what English-speakers called "Negro Alley" (or sometimes "Nigger Alley"). Yet Alcalde Stearns had neither a police force nor an effective court system at his disposal.

Two violent incidents stood out as particularly threatening. One Friday evening in January, about a month before Hayes arrived, a group of drunken Americans emerged from a saloon shouting epithets at passing Californios and Mexicans. Such behavior was commonplace. But this time the situation got out of hand. Placido Yeasa was minding his own business, pissing against the adobe wall in front of Benjamin Davis Wilson's casa, when one of those men, a curly-headed Texan named James Ollin, charged up on horseback, clubbed him with a pistol, and took a potshot at Maxiano Oliveras, who was unloading a carreta nearby. The ball entered Oliveras's right arm and passed into his chest, lodging against a rib. He had no idea, he told Stearns from his sickbed the next morning, why the American had shot him. Family and friends demanded action, but Ollin and his American companions were nowhere to be found.

Several nights later a group of Californios, bent on revenge, exchanged blows with another group of Americans on the street, but the affray ended without the display or use of firearms. Some hours later, however, as the Californios relaxed at Santiago Monnet's saloon, a group of Americans charged in with guns blazing, wounding several men. Examined by Alcalde Stearns, Dionisio Alipás, brother of the late Gervasio Alipás and a veteran of the Battle of San Pasqual, testified that they had been attacked "without any provocation." The Americans, he said, were creating a "public havoc." But Stearns declined to prosecute. Some time later Alipás was involved in another violent exchange with an American who took offense after Alipás called him a "gringo." Two years after the end of the war the hostility between Californios and Americans appeared as strong as ever, driven not only by ethnic antagonism but by lawless behavior.

In February 1850, at the same time he hired Benjamin Hayes to help with these cases, Stearns recruited John H. Purdy, another American, as town marshal, in charge of a small constabulary. Purdy, a single man in his early fifties who had just arrived in an overland caravan from Ohio, impressed Stearns as a tough customer. He proved it several days later when called to a saloon where a drunk by the name of Patrick Mooney was creating a public disturbance by indiscriminately firing his pistol. As Marshal Purdy entered the establishment, Mooney rose from the monte table and drew his weapon. Purdy fearlessly rushed forward and grabbed the gun by the barrel, demanding that Mooney surrender it in compliance with the municipal law prohibiting the carriage of fireams within the city limits. That ordinance had been passed by the ayuntamiento some years before, but this was the first time anyone had attempted to enforce it. The two men continued to struggle until one of Purdy's deputies rushed in and overpowered Mooney, who was dragged off to jail. Later that night the prisoner escaped with the assistance of two friends, who threatened the jailer with a pistol.

Stephen Clark Foster, serving as prefect of the Los Angeles district, dispatched an urgent message to Governor Peter Burnett, who had been elected California's first American governor the previous autumn. "Our town has been some three months infested with a gang of rowdies and gamblers who alike set law and order at defiance," Foster wrote. "They have rendered the place a very unsafe one for the peaceable inhabitants," and he requested the governor to dispatch a military company to the pueblo. Burnett might well wonder, Foster admitted, why a town of several thousand persons could not muster a sufficient force to put an end to such disorders. "The answer is this," he wrote. The vast majority of the permanent residents were Californios, while nearly all the rowdies were transient Americans. "The native population, unaccustomed as they are to our laws, if called on would certainly be led on into excesses that would arouse national hatreds and lead to far worse evils. . . . Already, in two instances, sectional fights where firearms have been used have taken place between Californians and Americans, and we know not the hour when the difficulties of 1846 may not be renewed."

IN THE TRANSITION between Mexican and American governance, the authority of local officials came under assault, and Benjamin Hayes soon was directly involved. Shortly after he began working for Stearns, Hayes was approached by Stephen Cribbs, a young black man recently arrived in Los Angeles. Cribbs and his father, both free men of color, had come from Arkansas in the employ of an American, a Dr. Josiah Earl, a friend and associate of Benjamin D. Wilson's. The elder Cribbs took sick and died, and when the son attempted to claim his father's property, which included a valuable team of mules, Earl refused, declaring that Cribbs had been his slave and thus the mules belonged to him. The trouble began when Hayes agreed to represent the younger Cribbs in a suit to recover his inheritance. Although slavery had been banned in Mexico since 1829 and was outlawed by California's new constitution, many southerners brought slaves overland, intending to utilize them in the mines. Los Angeles teemed with "sons of the sunny South," in Hayes's words, and many of them regarded the suit he brought on Cribbs's behalf a direct threat to their interests.

A day or two later Marshal Purdy learned that three black men, including Stephen Cribbs, had been brutally assaulted. A passerby heard cries for help coming from the courtyard of an adobe, and investigating found Colonel Thomas Thorne of Texas whipping two black men. They were his slaves, Thorne said, and were being punished for refusing to accompany him to the mines. He believed they had been inspired by Cribbs's lawsuit. That same night another witness reported seeing a group of half a dozen men attack Cribbs with clubs, shouting that this was payback for what he had been saying around town. Cribbs, described as "a tall and powerful black man," broke away from the group and vaulted over an eight-foot wall as his assailants fired their pistols at him. Had they caught him, a witness heard one of the men exclaim, "they would have killed him as dead as a herring."

Before coming to California from Ohio, Purdy had been an antislavery activist who founded and edited an abolitionist newspaper. He had no intention of letting this matter drop. He collected the statements of witnesses and filed a police report with Stearns. But the southerners were not about to submit either. On March 4 they held a meeting, and afterwards a delegation of them confronted Purdy at his office, saying they had been appointed to deliver a message. "They told me," Purdy reported to Stearns, "that I was required to leave the city within the space of 24 hours, at my peril, which I distinctly understood to mean the peril of my life." The next day one of the southerners pulled a revolver on Purdy. The marshal reacted in character, seizing the gun with one hand and the attacker with the other. "He cocked and discharged one barrel at me and attempted to cock it again," said Purdy. "I held his hands so as to prevent his re-cocking it." Assisted by one of his deputies, Purdy succeeded in getting control of the weapon, but his assailant escaped with the aid of two accomplices.

Most of the Americans in Los Angeles hailed from the South and were accustomed to the brutalities of slavery. They directed their anger at Hayes and Purdy for standing with Cribbs. In fear for his life, Hayes kept a loaded shotgun by the side of his desk and the pepperbox in the pocket of his coat. But the primary target of the southerners was Purdy. Several dozen men assembled in the Plaza and threatened to storm the jail, where the marshal and his deputies were holed up. They took over a meeting of the ayuntamiento, threatening a revolution unless the regidores agreed to eliminate the constabulary Alcalde Stearns had created. Thoroughly intimidated, the councilmen did as they were told, voting to dismiss the deputies, leaving the marshal to face the mob alone. "Poor Purdy was thus left in the lurch," wrote Hayes. As the meeting was about to break up, Purdy appeared in the doorway, rifle in hand. It looked as if there would be another violent confrontation, but according to Hayes, some of the "northern men" present persuaded Purdy to stand down. The next morning he left for San Francisco, where he became a crusading editor of the *Pacific Statesman*, a newspaper that opposed the state's prosouthern Democratic political establishment.

In the aftermath of Purdy's departure, Prefect Stephen Foster wrote again to Governor Burnett, who had failed to respond to his first appeal. "Our city has been harassed for the last four months by various disorders," he wrote. "Quite an excitement has been caused within a few days by an attempt on the part of some slaves introduced from Texas to assert their rights to freedom." The town marshal, "with more zeal than judgment," had attempted to defend them, provoking a violent opposition. The ayuntamiento had buckled under pressure, leaving the marshal no choice but to abandon the pueblo. "*Mob law,* to use the harsh but truthful term, is triumphant," Foster wrote. The authority of municipal government had crumbled, anarchy prevailed, and his only recourse was to appeal for a military force to reestablish order in Los Angeles. Two weeks later he received a response, not from the governor, but from a lowly second lieutenant at the garrison in Monterey. His application for military assistance had been rejected.

· CHAPTER 14 ·

VIOLENCE BEGINS AT HOME

IN THE LATE WINTER OF 1850—as Los Angeles churned with the violent confrontation between Marshal Purdy and the Americans—Benjamin Hayes joined "a secret junta of all the leading Californians at the residence of Don Agustín Olvera." Several Americans—including Abel Stearns (who brought Hayes along), Jonathan Temple, and Benjamin Davis Wilson—were in attendance, although, as Hayes put it, "native Californians were then in the ascendancy." Thus commenced a political machine that would dominate Los Angeles politics for the next thirty years. The junta nominated a slate of candidates, Californios and Americans, for the first election to fill county offices. Hayes was tapped for the post of county attorney. The junta's ticket won without opposition.

The first order of business for the new officials, especially given the violent turmoil in the pueblo, was setting up and staffing the basic institutions of law and order. The first county sheriff was G. Thompson Burrill, a native of New York who had spent a decade living and working in Mexico before moving to Los Angeles at the conclusion of the war. Burrill was fluent in Spanish and comfortable with Mexicans and Californios. According to Benjamin Hayes, he was "punctilious, perhaps formal" but an effective officer. He hired two deputies, and the three of them made up the totality of the county's law enforcement authority.

Oversight of the judicial system was in the hands of County Judge Agustín Olvera, a man in his early thirties. Before the war Olvera had served as secretary of the California legislature, during the war as an officer in *las fuerzas nacionales,* and he was one of the commissioners who negotiated the Treaty of Cahuenga. It was his responsibility to supervise the six county justices of the peace chosen at the same election. Each justice was allowed to hire a constable to serve warrants and arrest suspects. Justice court was where most of the everyday work of adjudication took place, and where most cases of violent assault—and there were dozens of those during the county's first few months— were originally heard. Violent felony crimes such as attempted murder or homicide were referred to the county grand jury for indictment, then to the court of the state's First Judicial District, which covered all of southern California and was presided over by Judge Oliver S. Witherby, who rode the circuit between Los Angeles, San Bernardino, and San Diego.

Witherby gaveled his court into session in the pueblo for the first time in June 1850. Four attorneys, including Benjamin Hayes, were admitted to the practice of law. And there being no further business, the court adjourned. Despite the extraordinary level of violent conflict in the community, despite a dozen murders in Los Angeles and vicinity since the termination of military occupation, Witherby's court heard no violent felony cases. Sheriff Burrill simply did not have the wherewithal to investigate or pursue perpetrators.

Not until January 1851, when Judge Witherby convened the winter session of district court in Los Angeles, was he asked to render judgment in a case of violent assault. It came in the first suit for divorce heard in Los Angeles County, filed by Francisca María de Jesús Pérez against her estranged husband, Mariano Silvas. Speaking through her attorney, Joseph Lancaster Brent, Doña Francisca told the court that in the twenty years she had been Silvas's wife, she had lived with him faithfully as a good and virtuous wife.

But notwithstanding her aforesaid behavior and affectionate bearing towards him, he has treated her in a cruel and unkind manner and has been for a long series of years accustomed to whip and beat her with extreme violence without any cause or provocation whatsoever; that at last on or about the 10th of July last, he drove her from his house without any provocation, and has since that time, up to this date, abandoned and ceased to live with her or to provide her with the necessaries of life, although possessed of considerable property.

Doña Francisca prayed the court to award her a "divorce from bed and board," the common-law term for a legal separation rather than an absolute dissolution of marriage. The California legislature had yet to pass a divorce law, so Brent chose to argue the case on common-law grounds.

Mariano Silvas, Doña Francisca's husband, was an ordinary vaquero, but something of a local hero, renowned for his fearless conduct at the Battle of San Pasqual. He was also a notorious wife beater. In 1844, three years before the war, the alcalde had summoned him to answer charges of assault filed by his wife. A physician, sent to their house to investigate, found Doña Francisca in bed vomiting blood, with bruises to her head and shoulders and an ear nearly torn off. She had been resting in her room, she said, when her husband suddenly burst in, and "using offensive words questioned my decisions in drawing up the will." Doña Francisca had been born into the minor gentry, and along with her four siblings, she stood to inherit a portion of her father's Rancho Paso de Bartolo, on the east bank of the Río San Gabriel. It was a comparatively modest piece of property, but situated in a valuable location, at the ford of the river where the Americans under Stockton and Kearny had fought their way across in 1847. By Mexican law, married women retained title to their own property, and Silvas was agitated about his wife's plans for her inheritance.

"He dealt me three blows," she said, "pulled me out of bed, and dragged me by my hair, leaving me on the floor, bathed in blood." It was not the first time he had beaten her, she claimed, and she wanted the full weight of the law brought down on him. Silvas admitted striking and pushing his wife to the floor, infuriated, he said, by the disrespectful tone she used with him. The alcalde promised further investigation, but within days Doña Francisca withdrew her complaint, saying that she and her husband had reconciled. "He has expressed regret," she said, "and promises me a new life."

It was a promise Silvas did not keep, and in Judge Witherby's court in 1851 he attempted to defend himself. For the entirety of their marriage, he testified, his wife had tested his patience with her "gross and abusive language." He argued that "corporal chastisement" was required for domestic peace, but was something he resorted to only when it "was necessary to check her violent and unladylike conduct." The laws of Mexico, Silvas reminded the court, had "allowed of no divorce," and "it would have been impossible for him to have lived with her without inflicting the chastisement aforesaid, and defendant avers that such was the custom of the country."

THE JUDICIAL RECORDS of frontier Los Angeles include the voices of hundreds of women and men, protesting and defending the "custom" of intimate violence. The consistent assumption was that a husband had every right to control and discipline his wife, even using violence if necessary. When Jesús Valdes complained to a local justice that her husband, Miguel Soloma, "whipped me severely with a reata without any cause or provocation," Soloma readily admitted his guilt. "I whipped my wife as charged," he told the court, "but I done it because she ran away." Corporal chastisement was a husband's prerogative, and virtually every man charged with domestic violence asserted the same privilege. María Juana Oliveras complained that her husband had attacked her in a drunken rage. "He tied me to an oak tree and whipped me with a piece of reata," she said. "My whole body is marked up with blows resulting from his cruelty." She warned him that if he didn't stop she would file a complaint against him, but he laughed in her face. "He said that I could do nothing if I did, as he had all authority in his favor, that I was a woman, and the justice would not believe me."

Male prerogative was not always linked to marriage. Francisca Silvas, a single woman in her midtwenties, employed as a laundress, brought a complaint against young José Sérbulo Varela, nephew of his locally famous namesake. She was washing clothes on the bank of the zanja when Varela approached her. They had been seeing each other, but she had broken off the relationship when he began ordering her around. He had left a sash at her house, Varela said, and wanted to retrieve it. Together they walked to her place, and when they arrived, she told the court, "he gave me a severe blow and knocked me down, and kicked me on both knees." The justice asked her to lift her skirts that he might see, and noted for the record that both her legs were badly bruised. "I had two plaits of hair," she continued, and "he cut them off with a butcher knife." As Varela left he shouted at her. "Go ahead, fuck the Americans, you whore, go fuck the Americans." Varela appeared in court to answer the charge. "I know Francisca, I have mounted her in my house, she is a whore," he testified. "I have the rights of a man who keeps a woman, and for whatever fault she commits, I have the rights of the man. I have no more to say."

"The rights of the man"—that was what Doña Francisca challenged in her suit for divorce. At the same time she filed a civil complaint against Pío Pico, the last governor of Mexican California, for unlawfully taking possession of her portion of Rancho Paso de Bartolo. Her father, Juan Antonio Lazaro Pérez, had died in 1847, and the property was partitioned among his five children. That same year Don Pío returned from Mexico, determined to make a new start under the American regime. What he needed, he decided, was a rancho close enough to Los Angeles for him to efficiently conduct business, but distant enough to serve as a retreat. Rancho Paso de Bartolo met his requirements perfectly. He negotiated successfully with the other siblings, but Doña Francisca refused to sell, and after her husband threw her out of their house in the pueblo, she took up residence in an adobe on the rancho, spending several months there in "the peaceable and quiet possession and enjoyment of her property." But in the fall of 1850 Don Pío "entered upon and took possession of her aforesaid rights in and to the said rancho and ejected her from the same," claiming the property "by virtue of a pretended bill of sale of her said rights and property, made to him by the husband." She had authorized no such transfer, Doña Francisca said, and her estranged husband had "no right to sell without her permission and authorization." She asked the court to declare the sale null and void and require Don Pío to pay her damages.

Judge Witherby's ruling crushed Doña Francisca's hopes. He summarily dismissed both suits, declaring that she had proven neither case. She was ordered to pay court costs as well as the attorney fees of both Silvas and Pico. Witherby issued an order of execution to the sheriff. "You will proceed to sell sufficient of the personal property of said Francisca Pérez de Silvas to satisfy said costs and if sufficient personal property be not found, then to satisfy the same out of her real estate." Attorney Brent appealed, but without success. By the time the order to sell was finally executed, James R. Barton had become sheriff. "At the court house door in the City of Los Angeles," he reported to the court, "I proceeded to sell all the right, title, and interest of the said plaintiff in and to 'Rancho Paso de Bartolo,' now known as El Ranchito and occupied by Pío Pico." Doña Francisca's share of the property was promptly conveyed to Don Pío. "The rights of the man" had prevailed.

WOMEN WERE VICTIMS in a quarter of the cases of criminal violence recorded after the American conquest. Frequently there was a sexual dimension to the assaults—a violent quarrel between lovers, the rejection of a man's attentions, or the selection of a lone woman as a target of opportunity. María Cañedo, a married woman of about forty years, was walking home from the house of a friend one evening in 1852 when she was attacked by four men. "I cried out for help," she said, but "they struck me on the head and dragged me to the ground."

As one of her attackers stood guard with a cocked pistol, she was raped a total of nine times.

The cases included sexual assaults on several young girls. The record of one featured the voice of the young victim herself. In 1853 thirteen-year-old Jane Mulkins was sent by her mother to fetch Doctor Thomas Foster so he could examine her sick sister. According to the girl's testimony, she knocked on Foster's door, he opened it a crack, and seeing who it was, pulled her inside. "He shut the door and fastened it," she told the justice, then "put me upon his bed and pulled up my clothes against my will and consent, and put his hand upon my mouth." She struggled with Foster as he forced himself on her, tearing the paper collar of his boiled shirt. "I was much scared," she said. She had been absent for nearly half an hour by the time her mother went looking for her tardy daughter, knocking on the doctor's door and, when there was no response, going to his neighbor, a butcher named William Smith, to ask whether he had seen the girl. As they were speaking, Foster's door opened and Jane came out, in the words of her mother, "her face much flushed and her clothes much disordered."

While mother and daughter left to report the incident, another neighbor, attorney Ezra Drown, went to check on Foster. He found the doctor lying on his bed, so drunk he nearly fell as he attempted to get up. Drown assisted him to the basin, where Foster washed his face and changed his shirt, which was spotted with blood. Then the two of them went next door to the butcher shop, where, according to Drown, "Mr. Smith, Foster, and I joked considerably about the occurrence." For these men the rape of this young girl was a laughing matter. The age of consent in California (and most of the United States) was only ten years, so there was no thought of this being a case of child abuse. Mrs. Mulkins filed charges of rape, but Foster's attorney argued that she and her daughter were "women of easy virtue," bent on extorting money from the good doctor, and the grand jury declined to hand down an indictment.

Dr. Foster had come to Los Angeles in 1849 and established the first regular medical practice in the pueblo. People considered him a man of accomplishment and attainment, noted for his extensive library and fine clothes, never appearing in public without starched shirt, frock coat, and silk hat. There was gossip about the rape charge, but it did little to tarnish Foster's reputation. Two years after the incident he was elected mayor. In 1856 he was joined by his wife, Catherine, and their two daughters. "We congratulate the Doctor on the consummation of his happiness," read a notice printed in the *Star*, "and hail the advent of the ladies as a boon conferred on the society of our locality." But the Foster home was not a happy one. "I am sorry to tell you how Dr. Foster has treated his wife and family since their arrival," Benjamin Wilson wrote to his wife. "He has been drunk ever since, and they say he has whipped his wife and drawn a pistol on her several times." Foster was a lonely, unhappy, violent man, one of many in frontier Los Angeles. Traveling to San Francisco on the steamer in 1862, he committed suicide by throwing himself overboard.

He was not the only violent husband in Los Angeles who took his own life. Nicholas Blair came to the pueblo as a private with the New York Regiment of Volunteers and remained after the war, opening a tailor's shop. In 1851 he married María Jesús Bouchet, the fifteen-year-old daughter of a French widow who owned a substantial vineyard. Several months after the wedding, in the late stages of pregnancy, Doña María filed a common-law suit for divorce. Her husband began mistreating her shortly after their marriage, she told the court, and the torment had grown intolerable. One night, as she was sleeping, he stormed into her room and "violently tore her from her bed by the hair of her head, tore her clothes off her person, then beat her violently with his fist on her face and breast, proceeded to tie her wrists with a reata, and inflicted on her person several severe blows with a horse whip." As soon as she was able Doña María fled back to her mother's house.

Blair was served by Sheriff Barton, and the same day he penned a pathetic letter to his estranged wife. "We enjoyed ourselves," he wrote, "until this sad affair occurred, which has caused me much trouble both night and day." He noted that she had asked the court for damages. "You cannot collect one cent of me," he said, but "I'm willing to give it." He had left a package with papers and some money for her and the child with Abel Stearns. "You shall certainly never see me more," he concluded. "Good by, good by, I say to my once wife and partner, but now and forevermore a stranger." The following day, Blair killed himself. Violent men go after not only their wives but other men, and sometimes themselves.

IN 1853 BENJAMIN HAYES was elected to succeed Oliver Witherby as judge of the First Judicial District. Hayes was much more sympathetic than his predecessor to the women who petitioned for divorce. "The California ladies are an interesting race of females in many respects," he wrote to a friend. "They are a kindhearted, amiable, industrious set of women. I like them much better than I do the men." Shortly before Hayes took the oath of office, the legislature enacted a liberal divorce law, and he used it to grant relief to nearly every woman who petitioned him for the dissolution of marriage. One of the first cases he decided was Francisca Sepúlveda de Carrillo's suit for divorce from her husband, José Antonio Carrillo. Boarding with the family during his first months in Los Angeles, Hayes had seen firsthand just how difficult life with Don José could be. He granted the divorce and ordered a lien placed on Carrillo's townhouse to secure the payment of alimony, attorney fees, and court costs.

Doña Francisca did not charge her husband with cruelty or violence, but with habitual drunkenness and failure to provide support. But violence figured prominently in many of the divorces granted by Judge Hayes. One of the most challenging cases for him was that of Rosaria Díaz. When she was fourteen, in 1850, she married Felipe Rheim, a German immigrant in his late thirties, the owner of Dos Amigos, a saloon near the Plaza that catered to the Indian trade. Doña Rosaria soon discovered that her husband was an alcoholic with a violent temper. Only five weeks after their wedding, she filed a complaint in one of the justice courts. "Felipe Rheim has assaulted and threatened to beat affiant," read her complaint, "and has used various vulgar and indecent epithets towards affiant such as calling her a whore, a street walker, and has threatened to break affiant's head with bottles and sticks." The justice fined Rheim $10, ordered him to pay court costs of $40 more, and sent him home. Seven years later Doña Rosaria filed for divorce in district court. By then she was a mother of three. "While laboring under the influence of intoxicating liquors," she complained, Rheim "had grossly and violently inflicted severe and cruel corporal punishment upon her, using guns, knives, and any weapons and instruments within his reach." She had been forced to leave the house to save herself and the children from his "merciless attacks and assaults." Yet only a week after she filed her complaint, Doña Rosaria withdrew it.

"Violence, like charity, begins at home," in the words of psychologist James Gilligan. A man who practices domestic tyranny may carry his sense of brutal entitlement into the larger community. Merchant Harris Newmark recalled encountering Rheim one New Year's Eve, "gloriously intoxicated and out for a good time." The German pulled out a pistol and aimed it at Newmark's head. "Treat, or I shoot!" he exclaimed. Newmark treated. "After this pleasing transaction," wrote Newmark, "amid the smoky obscurity of Ramón Alexander's saloon, Felipe fired his gun into the air and disappeared." He took his drunken violence home.

Dona Rosaria was back in court little more than a year later. It no longer mattered whether Rheim was drunk or sober, she testified, his conduct toward her was consistently brutal and threatening. In front of the children, the neighbors, and her friends, he called her a common prostitute and other terrible names, "in a manner that makes marriage life a burden." He beat her with his fists, with clubs, with whips, and often drew and cocked his pistol, threatening her life. But most shocking to Doña Rosaria was the night when, in the midst of a foaming rage, Rheim took all her clothes, piled them in the street before the house, and set them afire. His conduct had been "so outrageous, brutal, and inhuman," she said, she had suffered a miscarriage, and "she now lives in continual fear of him and dread of her life." But once again, after several weeks, Doña Rosaria withdrew her complaint and went back to her husband.

The record of the past can reveal much but hide even more. Beyond the general understanding that divorce was contrary to cultural and religious norms, that it might leave an indelible stain upon a woman's reputation, and that the relationship binding spouses is always complicated, the legal archive offers no explanation for Doña Rosaria's choices. Women frequently return to abusive husbands and lovers. But six months later Doña Rosaria was in Judge Hayes's court again with a new complaint, one that detailed even more abuse, violence, and terror. By then she had separated from Rheim and was refusing him access to the children, about whose safety she was worried sick. This time she did not withdraw her suit. When Hayes heard the case in the spring of 1860, Rheim failed to appear and was declared in default. There was to be a final hearing, during which Hayes declared the marriage dissolved. But it proved unnecessary. Rheim killed himself with an overdose of laudanum.

Despite the years of abuse and terror, the story of Rosaria Díaz and her children does not end unhappily. In 1866 she married Ygnacio García, a native Angeleno employed as confidential clerk by merchant Jonathan Temple. García formally adopted Doña Rosaria's children, and the couple had several more of their own. The couple played an active role in the social and cultural life of the pueblo. García was a leader in several *mutualistas* and fraternal organizations, and Doña Rosaria frequently took part in musical events in town. She was said to have a beautiful, resonant voice, accompanying herself on the guitar, and she filled the lives of her children with music and song. Two of her daughters became accomplished musicians, and at the turn of the century one of them made wax cylinder recordings of several dozen songs taught to her by her mother. In those songs, perhaps, the voice of Doña Rosaria can yet be heard.

> *Even though you love a man more than your life*
> *Don't show it, for then you are lost.*

¡Ay¡ Mononina mia, because men,
Even when they say they love you, don't mean it.

I loved a man and he told me
That if I forgot him he would die.
¡Ay! Mononina mia, this is not true,
Because I forgot him and he hasn't died yet.

· CHAPTER 15 ·

THE LUGO CASE

ON JANUARY 29, 1851—as Francisca Pérez and Pío Pico tangled in district court over the ownership of Rancho Paso de Bartolo—a detachment of soldiers on patrol at Cajon Pass discovered the mangled bodies of two men near their abandoned wagon. The victims had been shot and dragged through the chaparral. The soldiers buried the bodies in shallow graves and returned to their post at Rancho Santa Ana del Chino to report the discovery. Cajon Pass was within the jurisdiction of Los Angeles, although the pueblo was more than seventy miles distant, and it took nearly a month before County Coroner Alpheus P. Hodges and a jury of eight men arrived at the scene to hold an inquest over the bodies. Disinterred, the victims were identified as Patrick McSwiggen and his Creek Indian partner Sam, teamsters who had been hired in Los Angeles to haul heavy equipment to a mining operation in the Mojave Desert. The bodies were reburied, and Hodges returned to Los Angeles to continue his investigation. This murder case would join the predictable with the improbable, igniting the most explosive episode of violence since the conclusion of the war, challenging the trust that both Americans and Californios placed in the system of justice.

The murders occurred in the wake of a raid by a large band of desert Indians, Utes and Mojaves, who swept down Cajon Pass and made off with several hundred horses from ranchos on the eastern frontier, including seventy-five highly trained "gentle horses" from the *caballada* of José María Lugo of Rancho San Bernardino. Don José María hastily assembled a posse and took off in pursuit of the rustlers.

Coroner Hodges first assumed the murders had been committed by the Indians, but he changed his mind after interrogating the men who rode with the Lugos. The vaqueros acknowledged encountering the teamsters, who reported seeing the Indians earlier that day, driving a large herd of horses toward the desert. The raiders, the teamsters reported, appeared to be lightly armed, without firearms. The posse continued on and later that evening made camp on the bank of the Mojave River, in the vicinity of present-day Victorville, expecting to overtake the raiders the following day. But as the men slept the Indians staged a surprise attack, firing down on the camp with rifles, killing one of the vaqueros in the first barrage. Overpowered and demoralized, the posse turned back, passing the teamsters again on the way home. Hodges believed that members of the posse had committed the murders, angry over the misinformation they had received. The vaqueros admitted being very upset about the death of one of their number, but to a man they denied any knowledge of the crime.

Relations between the Spanish-speaking majority and the Anglo minority in southern California were already at a low point. Thousands of Mexicans continued to pass through the region on their way to and from the northern mines, and there were frequent reports of affrays with itinerant Americans. In the fall of 1850, a group of Sonoreños attacked an American family in their home on the upper Río Santa Ana, brutally murdering the proprietor and his hired man and leaving several others critically injured. Los Angeles county sheriff G. Thompson Burrill arrested several suspects, but they escaped from the poorly secured county jail.

If Americans felt generally fearful and suspicious of Mexicans and Californios, toward the Lugos in particular they were overtly hostile.

In large measure their feelings reflected the persistent bitterness of the late war. José del Cármen Lugo had led the attack on Benjamin Davis Wilson's rangers at Chino and directed the campaign against the Luiseños, who favored the Americans. A more recent incident exacerbated the ill will. The deaths of John Glanton and his gang at the hands of Quechan Indians at the Colorado crossing in the spring of 1850 stirred up considerable outrage, and California's governor authorized a counterattack by a force of volunteers. In need of horses to outfit the expedition, the militia officer in charge commandeered them from local rancheros. But when he attempted to expropriate animals from the Lugos, he ran into serious difficulty. According to a report in the *Daily Alta California* of San Francisco, the "sons and assistants" of José María Lugo "valiantly made a charge and retook the animals." Coroner Hodges suspected that those very same "sons and assistants" were responsible for the murder of the teamsters.

In early March the coroner's jury ruled that the teamsters had come to their deaths "by the hands of some person or persons of a party or parties that went after a band of Eutow [Ute] Indians." Coroner Hodges issued a warrant for the arrest of several young men from Rancho San Bernardino, including two sons of Don José María—twenty-three-year-old José Francisco, known as Chico, and his brother, nineteen-year-old Francisco de Paula, known as Menito or Junior.

PATRIARCH ANTONIO MARÍA LUGO celebrated his seventy-fifth birthday in 1851. The son of a *soldado de cuera* present at the founding of Los Angeles, Lugo followed his father into military service but retired after winning a land grant to Rancho San Antonio, a huge swath of territory on La Mesa, southeast of the pueblo. Lugo proved as tough as the arid environment, with growing herds and an expanding family. Exploiting his military, political, and kinship connections, he won other grants—to Rancho Santa Ana del Chino, which he gifted to daughter María de Jesús on the occasion of her marriage to American Isaac Williams, and Rancho San Bernardino, seventy miles east of the pueblo, which he placed under the management of three sons. With a total of nearly ninety thousand acres, the Lugos controlled a vast landed empire. In 1851 *el viejo Lugo*—or "Old Man Lugo," as Americans knew him—was living in retirement at his Los Angeles townhouse and was frequently seen about town, mounted on one of his splendid gentle horses, tall and erect in his silver-plated saddle, his sword strapped beneath his left leg. He was, in the words of Horace Bell, "the beau-ideal of a horseman and the envy of all the young dons, who were emulous of acquiring the style and carriage known and designated as *el cuerpo de Lugo*," literally, the body of Lugo.

Lugo's sons inherited their father's style as well as his tenacity. In the early 1840s brothers José María, José del Cármen, and Vicente settled with their families at Rancho San Bernardino, and soon they had large herds of cattle and horses grazing on the extensive grasslands of the inland valleys. But the more they prospered, the more tempting a target they became for raiding desert Indians. For assistance in protecting their assets they first turned to the scouts and muleteers who accompanied the annual trade caravan from New Mexico, bringing woolen goods to southern California to exchange for horses and mules. Their route traversed the desert homelands of Utes, Mojaves, and Shoshones before crossing Cajon Pass, and these men became experienced Indian fighters. In 1842 the Lugo brothers offered a group of them bottomland along the upper Río Santa Ana if they would agree to settle there and act as a frontier guard. Several dozen families from New Mexico founded a thriving colony, but following a disagreement with the Lugos over access to water, they relocated several miles south to Rancho Jurupa, where they established a settlement called Agua Mansa.

To replace them the Lugos invited Juan Antonio, leader or "captain" of a large band of Cahuilla Indians, to establish a ranchería on the site. The Cahuillas, with a proud warrior tradition, had resisted missionization and retained their own spiritual worldview. Supplied with horses and equipment by the Lugos, Captain Antonio's Cahuillas made a highly effective constabulary, and with their protection

Rancho San Bernardino thrived. In turn, the horses and arms supplied by the Lugos greatly strengthened Captain Antonio's power and authority. A diminutive but commanding man in his late sixties, he began styling himself "Chief of the Cahuilla Nation," a role that was grudgingly acknowledged by the leaders of other Cahuilla bands. At the height of his power, Juan Antonio was able to call upon nearly a thousand fighting men. When the Lugos organized the posse to go after the rustlers in January 1851, at least half the riders were Cahuillas.

IN EARLY MARCH 1851 the Lugo brothers traveled to Los Angeles to retain an attorney to defend Chico and Menito Lugo. The young lawyer Joseph Lancaster Brent was standing at the door to his office, an old adobe on Calle Principal, when he saw the Lugos coming down the street from the Plaza. They were mounted on horses "pretty as Arabians," Brent later recalled, dressed in "rich jackets and trousers trimmed with silver bullets or buttons, and mangas or riding cloaks fringed with heavy gold." The demand for beef in the mines had driven commodity prices to unprecedented levels. Cattle were going for thirty to forty dollars a head in southern California, ten times the price of a year or two earlier, and rancheros like the Lugos suddenly found themselves fabulously wealthy. Brent was surprised and delighted when the brothers stopped in front of his place, dismounted, and asked to speak with him. They had come on the recommendation of friends, said Don José María, to inquire whether Brent would be willing to represent his sons.

Like almost every American in California, Brent had been drawn west by the Gold Rush. The climate in the north didn't suit, however, and he relocated to Los Angeles. Like Benjamin Hayes, Brent was a native of Baltimore. He studied law at Georgetown College in Washington, then practiced for several years in Louisiana, where he became fluent in French, enabling him to acquire a competency in conversational Spanish rather quickly. Like Hayes, Brent was a practicing Catholic. For those reasons—and also because he genuinely admired

Californio culture—he found the majority of his clients among the Californio elite. Soon after his arrival, in January 1851, he represented Francisca María Pérez in both her divorce proceeding and her suit against Pío Pico. Three of Don Antonio María's children were married into the Pérez family, and it was probably Brent's work in that case that caught the Lugos' attention. They agreed to pay him a very large retainer, twenty thousand dollars according to Horace Bell, the equivalent of half a million in today's money.

Brent would represent many of the elite in defense of their lands. In 1851 Congress passed legislation and established a Public Land Commission to consider all claims of title to California land granted under the Spanish and Mexican regimes. The complicated legal process established by the law placed the burden of proof on claimants and created lucrative opportunities for attorneys. Brent was one of the few whom rancheros felt they could trust. His willingness to take on the Lugo case earned him enormous respect. In a letter to a brother in Baltimore, he boasted that his practice was "rapidly rolling me along the path of wealth," and that "among the Spanish portion, who constitute four fifths of the population, I am regarded without a rival in the most flattering way."

In early March, in a makeshift courtroom in the Bella Union Hotel, Brent stood before Justice Jonathan Scott representing Don José María's two sons as well as six vaqueros who had ridden with the posse. Brent moved for immediate dismissal of the charges, arguing that there was no direct evidence linking any of his clients to the murder, and county prosecutor Benjamin Hayes had to agree. Sheriff Burrill, however, recognized one of the vaqueros, a Sonoreño named Ysidro Higuera, as a suspect in a case of horse theft. Higuera was jailed, but Scott ordered all the others released on their own recognizance.

Two days later, though, county jailer George Robinson notified Justice Scott that Higuera wished to make a statement, and Hayes took his deposition. After passing the teamsters on the way back to Rancho San Bernardino, Higuera swore, most of the posse dispersed into small groups, but he remained behind with the two Lugo grandsons and their friend Mariano Elisalde. Chico, the elder brother, was steaming, convinced that the teamsters had been in cahoots with the Indians. "Let's kill those two men," Higuera heard him exclaim. The four of them waited for the teamsters to come up. It was about midday when they finally saw the wagon approaching, McSwiggen riding on the back of one of the draft mules, the Indian Sam sitting in the wagon, holding the reins. Higuera saw Sam reach down and grab his rifle. Chico Lugo hailed him in Spanish. Nice rifle, he said. How about swapping for my pistol? Chico pulled a piece from his sash. Sam shrugged his shoulders, indicating he did not speak Spanish. Suddenly, without warning, Lugo leveled the weapon and fired point-blank, and Sam fell from the wagon, dead. McSwiggen jumped from his mule and took off running, but Lugo rode up from behind and dispatched him with a single shot to the back of the head. Higuera helped drag the bodies into the chaparral. "Don't say anything about this affair," Chico warned him.

The details in Higuera's deposition lent it credibility, but Brent argued that his story was improbable. "The witness confessed himself to have participated in a murder of people whom he did not know, without any motive whatsoever except to comply with a mere request from two boys with whom he was not especially intimate, who offered him nothing for his assistance." Hayes asked Higuera what motive he had for participating in such a cold-blooded crime, to which the vaquero answered that he had simply done as he was told, that Chico Lugo "was the captain of the company," and that he was duty bound to obey. Brent found that answer hardly credible, but Justice Scott saw it differently, ruling that Higuera's deposition established a presumption of guilt sufficient to arrest and hold the Lugo brothers and their friend Elisalde. Brent objected that it was unreasonable "to allow the uncorroborated testimony of one man, a confessed accomplice, to overbalance that of twenty men," the members of the posse examined by Coroner Hodges. But again Scott overruled him and ordered the four men jailed and bound over for trial. Brent requested bail, but that too was denied.

Don José María was incredulous. "It was an impossibility that the boys had taken part," he exclaimed. During the posse's trek over the pass they had never been out of his sight. Jailer Robinson must have coerced a false confession from Higuera. But why would he do such a thing? asked Brent. Because of bad blood between Robinson and the Lugos, Don José María replied. A year earlier Robinson had been involved in a violent affray with the family at Rancho San Bernardino, and he was bent on revenge.

KENTUCKIAN GEORGE D. W. ROBINSON had arrived in southern California by wagon with his bride, Jane Sutch Robinson, fifteen months earlier. He was thirty and she nineteen when they married at Council Bluffs in the spring of 1849, shortly before commencing their overland journey. Arriving at Salt Lake too late in the season to risk the crossing of the Sierra Nevada, they joined nearly two thousand other immigrants on the trail southwest across the desert, the route followed today by Interstate 15, and in January they reached Rancho San Bernardino in destitute condition. Don José María offered them aid and comfort, as the Lugos did for many of the immigrants coming over Cajon Pass that winter.

Robinson was headed for the mines and the Lugos invited his wife to remain with them during his absence. During her stay she became a favorite of Don José María's wife, Doña Antonia. Robinson had little success in the goldfields, and by summer he was back in Los Angeles. He accepted an offer to become the new county's first jailer, and in July he returned to Rancho San Bernardino for his wife. It was an unhappy reunion. In the privacy of Mrs. Robinson's room, the couple quarreled. Don José María was absent, but Doña Antonia and the servants heard shouting, then a scream, and investigating they found Robinson, a straight razor in hand, standing over his wife, who was bleeding from a nasty gash across her nose. When she accused her husband of trying to kill her, he hurriedly made his exit and returned to Los Angeles alone.

Several days later he was back in the company of Luis Robidoux, justice of the peace for San Bernardino township. This time Don José María and his sons, Chico and Menito, as well as several vaqueros, were at the house. They were protective of Mrs. Robinson and wary of her husband. Robinson requested a private conversation with his wife, and the couple withdrew to her room. Again, it did not go well. According to Robinson's own testimony, "I spoke to Mrs. Robinson harshly, took hold of her, she became frightened and hallowed or screamed." Don José María rushed in and saw the two of them struggling. "*¿Qué escándalo es éste en mi casa?*" he exclaimed. What scandal is this in my house? Robinson pulled a revolver from his coat pocket, leveled it at Lugo, and holding him at bay fled the house and took off running down the road. Lugo's sons and several vaqueros went after him, and several minutes later they returned with the man in tow, bound with a reata, his face bloodied. As the Lugo sons and associates stood by with their pistols cocked, "ready to plug me," as Robinson later put it, Robidoux negotiated a truce. Don José María allowed Robinson to leave without his wife.

Eventually Jane Robinson reconciled with her husband and rejoined him in Los Angeles. But soon thereafter Robinson filed a criminal complaint against Don José María for assault and battery, as well as a civil suit for false imprisonment, seeking $30,000 in damages. He was represented by Jonathan R. Scott and Benjamin Hayes, later the justice of the peace and county attorney in the prosecution of the Lugo grandsons. Was it any wonder that Don José considered Higuera's confession part of a conspiracy?

FOR THE NEXT SEVERAL WEEKS the Lugo boys and their friend Elisalde remained in the custody of jailer Robinson. "His bearing towards them was harsh and cruel," recalled Brent. "He refused to allow the boys to see anyone except myself, and availing himself of the plea that the walls of the jail were not very strong, he kept the prisoners heavily ironed day and night." Brent planned to file a writ of habeas corpus and petition for bail in district court, but he had to await the commencement of the court's spring term. In late April, Judge Oliver S. Witherby heard Brent's motion and ruled that the defendants were entitled to bail, which he set at $10,000 apiece—a great deal of money, but certainly not beyond the means of the Lugo family. The law required the bondsmen to undergo examination in open court regarding their personal worth, and Judge Witherby granted Brent a continuance while he made the necessary arrangements.

As Brent left the courtroom, he could feel the scorn of fellow Americans. Most were convinced of the Lugos' guilt, a belief Brent attributed to "race feeling rather than a fair consideration of the circumstances." There was talk of a lynching if the suspects were released on bail. That was no idle threat. Los Angeles remained vulnerable to what Prefect Stephen Foster had described the previous year as "mob law."

For several weeks a gang of some twenty-five heavily armed Americans, commanded by a former Texas Ranger named John "Red" Irving, so named for the color of his unkempt hair and beard, had been camped in a sycamore grove in the Arroyo Seco, just north of the pueblo. "They say that they are going to prospect the Gila," a correspondent reported in the *Daily California Alta*, but "the real object of the expedition is a descent upon Sonora." In Mexico men like these were known as *filibusteros*—filibusters or freebooters—violent and ruthless land pirates, intent on plunder. "These bands are composed generally of deserters from the United States army and other desperate adventurers, whose careers commenced with the Mexican War, and who after the treaty came to this country ready for any deeds of robbery or blood." That description perfectly described Irving's gang, which took over the streets of the pueblo, defying the authorities and intimidating residents, especially Californios. Their voices were among the loudest in the angry calls for immediate and summary punishment for the Lugos. It turned out there was motive in their madness.

When Brent returned to his office from the bail hearing, waiting for him was George Evans, Red Irving's lieutenant. He had come to discuss the Lugos, Evans said. "Our boys have been given the job of taking them out of jail, and now we hear the judge is going to turn them loose, and we don't intend to stand it." Brent had no idea what Evans was talking about. The Lugos had made a deal with his boss, Evans explained. In exchange for a payment of several thousand dollars, his men were to liberate Brent's clients and deliver them to safety in Mexico. Shocked and disgusted, Brent ordered the man from his office. "They think it is cheaper to buy the judge and district attorney than us," Evans said as he left. "But those boys will never get out alive except with our consent, and they had better know it."

When the Lugo brothers arrived with the bondsmen later that afternoon, Brent confronted them. He was withdrawing from the case, he said, because he couldn't stomach the pact they had made with Irving. The Lugos firmly denied any knowledge of the deal and quickly convinced Brent of their sincerity. The *Star* later reported that Irving had approached patriarch Antonio María Lugo, demanding a payment of $50,000 to ensure the safety of his grandsons. It was a classic case of extortion, which Don Antonio had simply ignored.

As Brent and the Lugos were conversing, they heard a commotion, and looking out saw a number of Irving's men ride up the hill to where the jail was located and surround it. This uncontested seizure in sight of the entire town offered proof that Irving could count on what Brent termed "the sympathy of the American population." He would prefer to proceed by legal remedy, he told the Lugos, but under the circumstances the only way to ensure the safety of his clients was to mobilize an armed force of Californios. "If the matter was to be determined by fighting," said Don José María, "they were willing to so settle it, and they could get plenty of men." By early evening several dozen armed Californios had placed themselves in the ravines near the jail, with orders to attack Irving's guards if they perceived any threat to the prisoners.

Brent had little faith in the capacity of Sheriff Burrill. But Burrill was determined not to be undercut like Marshal Purdy. Shortly after the arrival of Irving's gang in Los Angeles, he had sent a request for help to U.S. Army Major Edward H. Fitzgerald, in command of a garrison of fifty dragoons in San Diego, and Fitzgerald responded by bringing his men north on what he said was a routine patrol. When Irving's gang seized the jail, Fitzgerald was encamped only a few miles away from the pueblo. Burrill dispatched a messenger with an appeal for immediate assistance. The following morning, as Brent prepared for the continuation of the bail hearing, he heard the tramping of horses and saw Major Fitzgerald and his dragoons riding up Calle Principal. "If the men had descended from Heaven," Brent wrote years later, "my surprise and my pleasure could not have been greater. There marched law and order, and the physical power to support them." Fitzgerald directed his men to the Plaza, where they dismounted and watered their horses.

A few minutes prior to the court session, scheduled for 2 PM, Brent armed himself with a revolver and walked over to the Bella Union. The street was filled with a milling crowd, including Irving's men, conspicuous in their red flannel shirts, with pistols and knives tucked into their belts. But the crowd also included dozens of armed Californios with orders to target the outlaws at a signal from their leader, who was off to the side, surveying the situation from horseback. The air was thick with morbid excitement. Entering the makeshift courtroom, Brent noted that both Judge Witherby and county attorney Hayes were armed with pistols. At Witherby's order the clerk opened the doors and the crowd surged in, including Irving and a dozen of his men, all of them "armed to the teeth," according to Hayes. Finally Sheriff Burrill marched in with the prisoners, surrounded by a detachment of dragoons. Irving jerked to attention. He had not figured on military intervention.

After Judge Witherby carefully examined the sureties, he approved the bonds and ordered the release of the prisoners. They rose, were immediately surrounded again by Sheriff Burrill and the dragoons, and escorted out of the Bella Union and up the street to the Plaza, where a group of mounted Californios waited. Within minutes they were gone. Through the remainder of the afternoon and into the evening the streets surrounding the Plaza were thronged. "A great deal of liquor was consumed and many ugly threats made," wrote Brent, "but no violence took place." That evening as he was finishing his supper in the dining room of the Bella Union, Red Irving approached his table, drunk and angry. For a moment he loomed over Brent. "Young man, I don't blame *you*," the outlaw finally said. "You did your duty." But for the Lugos, he continued, he had nothing but contempt. "I solemnly swear, I will have their hair, or be in hell."

THE IRVING GANG remained in Los Angeles until the third week of May, when they packed up and left town, headed for Sonora, they said. Three days later, on May 25, Sheriff Burrill received an urgent message from the officer in charge of the small army contingent garrisoned at Rancho Santa Ana del Chino, forty miles east, reporting that Irving's men were stealing horses, killing cattle, and intimidating residents throughout the countryside. "They had threatened to ravish the females, and men, women, and children had left the ranchos and fled," he reported. According to ranchero Isaac Williams, Irving said that his men were "determined to take from the native Californians whatever they wanted." They were "well armed with Colt's revolvers," Williams wrote, "and outnumber the troops three to one. The whole country is entirely at the mercy of these highway robbers." Brent dispatched a messenger to San Bernardino, warning the Lugos to be on their guard. Sheriff Burrill, armed with warrants for the arrest of the gangsters, organized a posse of some fifty men, nearly all of them Californios, and departed with them early the following morning.

By the time Burrill's men arrived at Chino, the Irving gang had already departed for Rancho Jurupa. Formerly the property of Benjamin Davis Wilson, it had been purchased by Luis Robidoux, who was standing on the veranda when he saw a dozen men riding toward the house. He recognized Irving, whom he had seen in the pueblo several weeks before. Where were they headed? Robidoux asked as Irving drew near. Sonora, he replied. About half his men had gone ahead to Warner's Ranch, he said, and he planned to meet them there after he and his party had attended to important business at San Bernardino. Each of his men carried a brace of revolvers. "They made some inquires about Lugo's ranch," Robidoux later testified, "the distance to it, and where the troops were stationed." Robidoux figured they were up to no good. "They were bad men," he later told the authorities. Yet he made no attempt to warn his neighbors, the Lugos. They had taken separate sides during the war, and had been further estranged by the affray with George Robinson. Irving and his men camped in the yard, and Robidoux saw him off the following morning.

At about that same time Brent's messenger located the Lugos, who were supervising a roundup of stock, some eight or ten miles from their residences. Don José María and his brother Don Vicente rushed back to warn their families and associates, while Don José del Cármen and Ricardo Uribe, his *mayordomo*, rode to an outpost of volunteer militia near the entrance to Cajon Pass, stationed there to guard against the incursions of Indian raiders. Most of the volunteers had departed for Chino, responding to the alarm over the depredations of Irving's gang, leaving only a small force under the command of a young lieutenant. The gang was threatening his family, Lugo explained, and he required assistance. He was not authorized to leave the encampment, the lieutenant replied, but the Lugos could bring their families to him for protection. "His offer was of no value to me," Don José del Cármen later recalled. Sending Uribe to rouse Captain Juan Antonio and his Cahuillas, Lugo set off on a mad dash for home, at least twenty miles and more than an hour's ride away.

At about ten in the morning, as vaquero Jesús Castro was working outside the family compound of Don José María's place, he saw the gang approaching. They were riding "in military order, armed with pistols," he later testified, which meant trouble. Castro shouted a warning to the women, children, and servants inside, and they fled to a thicket at the rear of the house. Castro remained behind, determined to keep the gang from finding the family.

Riding up, Irving immediately came to the point. "Where are the boys?" he demanded. "*En el pueblo*," in town, Castro lied. What about

Don José María and his brothers? "*En el rodeo*," rounding up stock. Irving ordered Castro to saddle fresh horses for his men, and while a couple of them pushed the Californio toward the corral at gunpoint, the others barged into the house. By the time Castro had transferred the saddles to new mounts, the gang was exiting with several sacks of booty. They packed up and immediately headed east in the direction of Don José del Cármen's place, at the site of the old mission estancia, a place the Indians called Guachama, some five miles away. Castro went inside and found trunks broken open, furniture overturned, and household goods scattered about. A few minutes later Don José María charged up on a frothing horse and was greatly relieved to see his wife, daughter, and a number of grandchildren emerging from the thicket. Minutes later Ricardo Uribe arrived with Captain Antonio and two or three dozen Cahuillas, some mounted, others on foot, and with Don José María in the lead they set out in pursuit of the outlaws.

The gang showed up at Guachama around noon. Hired man Alexander Martino was working in a field nearby, and seeing their approach he climbed into the branches of a large cottonwood and hid there as the men broke into the house. They rifled trunks and stole valuables, including two silver-plated saddles and bridles. They had packed up and were about to depart when the Cahuillas appeared, Captain Antonio and Ricardo Uribe in the lead. Uribe hailed the outlaws in Spanish, but they answered with a volley from their revolvers, then took off in an easterly direction, the Cahuillas on their heels. After a few minutes the outlaws wheeled and fired a barrage at their pursuers. "The Indians did not retreat," Martino testified, but "held up their horses and bent their bodies over, as if dodging, and then pushed on again." This maneuver was repeated several times. Irving's men had plenty of ammunition, including extra cylinders loaded with cap and ball, which they were able to snap into their revolvers. Martino watched as the chase advanced across an ascending plain, later the site of the town of Redlands, leading toward a range of low-lying hills.

REACHING THE RIDGE LINE, the gangsters looked out on the Yucaipa Valley. In the near distance, about a mile ahead, they saw the adobe of Diego Sepúlveda, a cousin of the Lugos, who grazed his stock on this eastern section of Rancho San Bernardino. Spurring their horses forward, in a few minutes they arrived at the building, which was unoccupied, and took the opportunity to water their parched horses while the Cahuillas closed in. Irving was completely unfamiliar with the country. Robidoux had advised him to take the trail through Yucaipa and watch for a turnoff leading south through the hills, which would bring them to Temecula and the Sonora Road to Warner's Ranch. Looking about, Irving spied a trail cutting south along the bank of Yucaipa Creek, a few hundred yards away. George Evans, his lieutenant, didn't believe it was the right road, and he advised going farther on. But Irving, "as if doomed," as Evans put it, "turned into the mountains along the path which led into the fatal trap." Evans was right. The southbound trail Robidoux had told them to watch for was another ten miles ahead.

Irving must have realized his error within minutes, for the creek and the trail turned westward. But with the Cahuillas in hot pursuit there was no turning back. After another four miles of rough riding across a desiccated landscape, the trail made a rapid descent into a narrow valley known as San Timoteo Canyon. On the canyon floor, by a flowing stream, they came to an adobe with a fenced cornfield and a corral. By then it was late in the afternoon and the men were exhausted. They had been engaged in the running fight with the Cahuillas for a couple of hours and more than a dozen miles. Using the house and fence for cover, they skirmished with the Indians. Their ammunition was running low, but only by continuing to fire were they able to keep their pursuers at bay. They succeeded in hitting two or three Indians, including the brother of Captain Antonio, who was mortally wounded. That sealed their fate. The sound of fire attracted the attention of another group of Cahuillas at a ranchería some distance upstream, and more warriors came running. Soon the Americans were facing more than a hundred men. There was only one option open to them. A cart trail behind the adobe led through an opening in the hills. Perhaps it would take them to safety.

Within a few hundred yards, however, the canyon walls began to narrow and the Americans realized they were trapped in a blind canyon. Ricardo Uribe shouted for them to lay down their arms and give themselves up. "They replied that they would not surrender," Uribe later testified, "and uttered oaths and words in English which I could not understand." As the Americans pushed farther into the canyon, George Evans, Irving's lieutenant, deliberately fell back, and when the moment was right he slipped from his horse, dived into a crevasse, and hid. As the lone survivor, he would provide an eyewitness account of what happened next. The Cahuillas swarmed up the hillsides of the canyon. Evans heard several more gunshots, then an ominous silence. "The Indians first shot them down with arrows, and then beat in their skulls with stones," he said. From his hiding place he watched as the Cahuillas stripped the bodies of his eleven colleagues, leaving them for the coyotes and buzzards. He saw them pile the booty atop the horses and lead them back out of the canyon. He remained in the crevasse until after dark, then crept out and followed the watercourse downstream for several miles until he found himself once again at Guachama, having made a twenty mile loop. There he stole a mule and escaped.

Sheriff Burrill's posse, mostly Californios, arrived at Rancho San Bernardino the following morning, accompanied by the militia volunteers, nearly all of them Americans, who had come back from Chino under the command of General Joshua H. Bean of the state militia. Bean was a Kentuckian who came to California in 1849 with his brother Roy Bean, later notorious as the eccentric Texas saloonkeeper who advertised himself as "Law West of the Pecos." In California in 1851, however, it was the older brother who enjoyed the fame. Bean opened a store in San Diego and in 1850 served as the city's last alcalde and first mayor, before being named major general of the California state militia by Governor Peter Burnett. Following the trail of the outlaws, Bean and his men, along with the posse, reached the scene of the slaughter about midday. "I saw the bodies," said Stephen Foster, who was riding with the posse. "They were naked, and the men appeared to have been killed with arrows, and their heads beaten with stones." Buzzards circling overhead had already plucked the eyes from some of the bodies. The Californios expressed their satisfaction, saying justice had been served. But according to Brent, the Americans "resented the gloating over the dead of their race by the Spaniards." Bitter words led to drawn pistols. The leaders—including Burrill, Foster, and Bean— "rode between the angry and separated lines, and quieted the outburst of what would have been a bloodier fray than that before them." The two groups cooperated in burying the eleven bodies in a mass grave before leaving the canyon separately.

Over the next several days the anger and resentment among Bean's militia volunteers continued to fester. Back at their encampment, near the entrance to Cajon Pass, many were eager to punish the Cahuillas. "The volunteers were almost in a state of open mutiny," one correspondent wrote, "and had declared their intention of attacking the Indians, notwithstanding the most strict and positive orders had been given by the General that no man should leave the camp." Bean met the trouble head-on. He ordered his men to assemble, then announced that "they would have to pass over his dead body before they left that ground." The crisis passed. But learning of the incident, and fearing for the lives of his people, Juan Antonio led his Cahuillas into the mountains.

Bean understood the calamity that would have resulted had Captain Antonio, in control of the most powerful military force in southern California, turned from friend to foe. Los Angeles County officials did what they could to bring the Indian commander back into the fold, issuing a statement praising him for his efforts on behalf of law and order. "He can return with his people to their homes," they announced, "with a guaranty that no harm shall be done him, either by individuals or by the county authorities, because all consider him as a good friend, and will not consent to let him be injured." They presented him with "a beautiful sword, a silver-mounted scabbard, and a belt with a general's epaulets," as well as a wagonload of presents for his people. A few days later a coroner's jury exonerated the Cahuillas, declaring that the killing of Irving and his men was justifiable homicide. Nevertheless, Captain Antonio soon relocated his ranchería to a place the Cahuillas called Sahatapa in the San Timoteo Canyon. With the loss of their constabulary, the Lugos decided it was time to get out, and in September 1851 they sold Rancho San Bernardino to a group of Mormon colonists.

A FEW WEEKS AFTER THE MASSACRE of Irving's gang, the *Daily Alta California* of San Francisco offered some reflections on the episode. Although Americans had succeeded in conquering southern California, they had failed to establish a system of law and justice, leaving the Californios at the mercy of the "lawless and reckless scum of our own country." In early 1850 "a band of desperados put all law at defiance and committed whatever crimes suited their depraved appetites, with impunity," even running the marshal out of town at gunpoint. More recently Red Irving and his men had "roamed about the country, laying the different proprietors under such contributions as their needs, or caprice, or malignity dictated." The state of affairs in Los Angeles was "execrable beyond anything we have experienced here." That was saying a good deal. Only days before, San Franciscans had organized a committee of vigilance which had summarily hanged its first victim. If southern California was to avoid the same fate, the paper argued, civil authorities needed to act energetically "to put an end to the outrageous acts of the desperadoes who have ruled so long in that garden spot of California."

But the suspicion and hostility between Americans and Californios, with all the attendant threats and acts of violence, continued unabated. In the fall of 1851 the grand jury handed down indictments charging Chico Lugo, Menito Lugo, and Mariano Elisalde with murder. Justice Scott revoked their bond and issued warrants for their arrest. But by that time Brent had lost confidence in the county's justice system.

"Behind these efforts," he believed, "was a strong and resolute organization to hang the Lugos if they were ever brought to town." He advised the family to keep the brothers hidden, which they did.

The violence cut both ways. One night in November, as Benjamin Hayes worked in his office, he heard the sound of horsemen outside. Expecting that it was some of his friends come to pay him a visit, he opened the door and was greeted by a pistol fired in his face. The ball grazed his cheek and smashed into the back wall, leaving Hayes terribly shaken but unhurt. Despite the efforts of Sheriff Barton to track the assailant, he was never identified, but the shooting was generally considered payback for Hayes's role in the Lugo case.

By year's end, however, Brent sensed that the local passions were moderating. "Other American settlers came into the county," he wrote, people "who had no feelings at all in respect to the Lugos." In December he arranged for the surrender of his clients to the sheriff, and they were immediately released again on bond by County Judge Agustín Olvera. At Brent's request the district court undertook a review of the case, and in early 1852 Judge Witherby tossed out the indictments, ruling that county authorities had failed to follow "the most ordinary and necessary regulations of the law." Some months later, Judge Olvera finally dismissed the case. It would long be remembered by both Californios and Americans as evidence of the failure of the justice system. By Californios for the unjust prosecution of the Lugos, by Americans for the failure to convict and punish according to law.

José Francisco "Chico" Lugo later married a ranchero's daughter and settled at Rancho San Antonio on La Mesa with the rest of the extended Lugo family. His friend Mariano Elisalde lived nearby with his wife and children. But brother Francisco de Paula "Menito" Lugo refused to settle down. Over subsequent years he was arrested numerous times and served a term in the state penitentiary at San Quentin, where a photograph was taken of the handsome but stern-faced young man. Shortly after his release he was implicated in another murder. Menito Lugo's ultimate fate is unknown.

· CHAPTER 16 ·

WAR FOR A WHOLE LIFE

THE DESTRUCTION OF THE IRVING GANG by the Cahuillas in May 1851 was a harsh reminder of the demographic facts. In southern California some four thousand Californios and perhaps a thousand Americans and other immigrants (in popular parlance lumped together as "Anglos") were outnumbered by some ten thousand native inhabitants, among whom the Cahuillas were the largest and most powerful organized group. Anglo vulnerability tamped down the outrage over the killing of eleven white men at the hands of "savages."

The Cahuillas were "undomesticated" *gentiles* in the Spanish lexicon. But southern California was also home to approximately six thousand "domesticated" Indians, emancipados living in autonomous rancherías or on the outskirts of Los Angeles and San Diego. In 1849, when the pueblo's total population was about fifteen hundred, Alcalde Stephen Clark Foster estimated that four or five hundred Indians were at work in Los Angeles.

The important role played by Indian workers in the local economy was made plain in a report written in 1852 by Benjamin Hayes for Benjamin Davis Wilson, who had been appointed federal agent for the Indians of southern California. "Let us remember," Hayes wrote,

"Indians built all the houses in the country, and planted all the fields and vineyards." They possessed all kinds of practical knowledge, "how to make an *adobe* (sun-dried brick), mix the *lodo* (mud mortar), put on the *brea* (pitch) for roof[ing], all of these recondite arts to the new beginner, yet very important to be known when there are no other building materials." Indians could read local weather signs and they understood "the mysteries of irrigation." Without them the production of wine, the pueblo's most important commodity, would have been impossible. "Most of our vineyard labor," wrote winemaker Matthew Keller, "is done by Indians, some of whom are the best pruners we have, an art they learned from the Mission Fathers." The vineyards—the *Star* counted 104 in the county in 1851, most within the city limits—hired large crews of Luiseños and Cahuillas for the spring pruning and the fall harvest and pressing.

On Saturday afternoons, at the conclusion of the workweek, several hundred Indian workers congregated in the vicinity of Calle de los Negros for their *juegos*, or pastimes—drinking, gambling, and fighting—a custom that had originated years before the American conquest but grew thereafter, with the expanding number of vineyards and vineyard workers. Horace Bell, who arrived in Los Angeles in 1852, witnessed the bacchanal on his first weekend in town. The area southeast of the Plaza, Bell wrote, was "crowded from morn till night with Indians, males and females of all ages, from the girl of ten or twelve, to the old man and woman of 70 or 80." By Sunday afternoon the streets were overflowing "with a mass of drunken Indians, yelling and fighting. Men and women, boys and girls, tooth and toe nail, sometimes, and frequently with knives, but always in a manner that would strike the beholder with awe and horror." At sundown the city marshal appeared with his Indian deputies. Swinging their canes, they charged into the crowd, driving men and women alike into a large corral near the jail, where they spent the night in the open air. The next morning those unable to pay their fines were auctioned off to the highest bidder.

The practice of arresting drunk or vagrant Indians and sentencing them to forced labor began in the 1830s. On the occasions when the supply of prisoners grew too large for available public works projects, the alcalde hired them out to private employers. The Americans formalized that system. In August 1850 the common council of Los Angeles, successor to the ayuntamiento, enacted a set of "Police Regulations" authorizing the city marshal to arrest Indian vagrants, auctioning them for a week of labor. Vineyardists and rancheros in need of temporary workers gathered at the jail every Monday morning for the prisoner auction. "I wish you would deputize some one to attend the auction and buy me five or six Indians," the manager of Rancho Los Alamitos wrote his boss, Abel Stearns, in 1852. The bidding rarely went higher than three or four dollars for a week's work, at the conclusion of which the convict worker would be paid an additional dollar or two, often in the form of a bottle of aguardiente, ensuring another crop of prisoners for the subsequent week. "Los Angeles had its slave mart, as well as New Orleans and Constantinople," wrote Bell. "Only the slave at Los Angeles was sold fifty-two times a year as long as he lived, which did not generally exceed one, two or three years, under the new dispensation."

For every fine paid, the city marshal received a commission of eight bits (one dollar) and his Indian deputies shared one bit (twelve and a half cents), with the remainder going into the city's coffers. The Indian auction became a lucrative source of municipal revenue, second only to the license fees collected from the pueblo's ubiquitous drinking and gambling establishments. A cash-and-carry operation, the auction was easily corrupted. In 1852 the county grand jury charged that "Indians arrested for intoxication, disturbing the peace, etc., are taken to the jail and are there sold out to the highest bidder—without even as much as the form of a trial—and that the proceeds of the sale are divided between the mayor and the city marshal." According to state law, before Indians could be legally auctioned there needed to be some semblance of adjudication. Mayor John G. Nichols, a Democrat who served four terms during the 1850s, dismissed the allegation, insisting that he was merely following the practice of his predecessors. In

1853 District Judge Benjamin Hayes ruled the slave mart "unlawful" on similar grounds, but his decision was either reversed or ignored, because the auctions continued, not ending until the early 1870s, by which time Indians had ceased to be an important component of the pueblo's working class.

THE SUBSTANCE ABUSE, the debauchery, and especially the violence among emancipados were symptoms of social dysfunction if not social disintegration. These patterns had been developing for many years and were accelerated by the American conquest. Indians contributed to the general mayhem in Los Angeles as much as any group. But unlike Californios and Anglos, who were equal opportunity perpetrators, Indians directed virtually all their aggressions at their own people. With the important exception of the destruction of the Irving gang, there is no recorded instance of an Indian killing a Californio or an American during the entire decade of the 1850s. Yet the record overflows with instances of Indians killing Indians. Juan Pelon, a Cahuilla, stabbed and killed Calletano, a Luiseño, during an angry dispute over a card game. The Indian José "took an axe and smote one Salvador," a fellow Gabrieleño, inflicting a mortal wound. Juan Chapo, a Luiseño, struck and killed a native woman named Anselmo during a "drunken frolic" on Calle de los Negros. The identification of the killers in these cases was the only thing unusual about them. Most Indian perpetrators and victims went unidentified. "On Monday, Justice Mallard held an inquest upon the body of an Indian woman found dead near the new jail," read a typical report in the *Star*. The coroner believed she had been killed on Saturday evening, her body lying undiscovered in a ravine for nearly two days. "There were several fresh wounds upon her body and her skull was broken, as if stones had been thrown upon it. A verdict of death by violence was rendered—but, as usual in such cases, all endeavors to discover the murderers have been unsuccessful." City and county authorities expended very little energy investigating Indian homicides.

The greatest mayhem came during episodes of Indian communal violence. Bitter feelings between the Luiseños and Cahuillas, originating in the wartime violence, led to persistent conflict between members of the two groups, who together made up a majority of the Indian residents of Los Angeles. One evening in April 1851 a large group of Cahuillas went after a smaller group of Luiseños with clubs and stones. Five men were killed on the spot, with five more dying later of their wounds. A few weeks later leaders of the two peoples staged a match of *churchurki*, better known to Angelenos as *peon*, a game in which two teams of Indians sat facing each other, singing and drumming, and as the men on one side surreptitiously passed a small white stick from hand to hand, the men on the other side attempted to keep track of it. At a signal from an umpire, the singing stopped and wagering began on which man was holding the stick. A game of *peon* "produced enormous excitement and extravagant betting," wrote attorney Joseph Lancaster Brent. "The bystanders took sides, including the women, who were desperate gamblers." Accompanied by heavy drinking, the matches frequently ended in disputes and fights. This particular event, played on the slope of Fort Moore Hill behind the Plaza church, attracted several hundred Californio and Anglo spectators and went on late into the night, when an affray broke out among the players. Brent awoke to the "awful shrieks and war whoops of the combatants," and the next morning he and others found the bodies of thirteen men on the hillside. At its next meeting, the city council banned the playing of *peon* within the city limits.

Several months later, in late October 1851, the Cahuillas held another *peon* match near the graveyard, outside the city limits at the northern terminus of Calle de Eternidad. Late in the evening a player named Coyote got into a dispute with Guadaloupe Ybarra over the price she was charging for aguardiente at a stand near her casa, resulting in a fight between a group of Cahuillas and Californios. The county sheriff was summoned, and by the time he arrived with an armed posse, a mob of Cahuillas was attempting to torch the Ybarra house. The sheriff ordered his men to fire on the unarmed crowd, and the Indians fled in all directions. The following morning authorities found a number of bullet-riddled bodies. "How many of the Indians were killed is not positively known," reported the *Star*. "It is supposed that others must have been conveyed away and secretly buried during the night." The sheriff arrested twenty-one Cahuillas on charges of riot and attempted arson, and a justice of the peace sentenced them to twenty-five lashes apiece. But before punishment could be meted out, Cahuilla headman Juan Antonio arrived, arranged to have the prisoners released to his custody, and departed with them in a huff. Reports of the deaths of a great many Cahuillas at the hands of the sheriff circulated widely among the Indian communities of southern California.

JUAN ANTONIO had saved Los Angeles from the outlaws terrorizing the county. He had offered assurances of his continued support. Yet he and his people got no respect. Only a few weeks before, southern California Indian leaders including Captain Antonio had been summoned to Rancho Santa Ana del Chino for a treaty conference with "the big men sent by the President." Congress had authorized the appointment of commissioners to negotiate with the California tribes, who were asked to cede title to their lands in exchange for permanent reservations and promises of perpetual peace and friendship. The commissioners had already signed treaties with many tribes in the northern portion of the state. Captain Antonio and the leaders of the Luiseños dutifully appeared at Chino in mid-July 1851 and waited for most of a week, but the commissioners never appeared. Ranchero Isaac Williams furnished the delegations with plenty of beef, and attempted to mollify them with presents, but they left in bad humor. For Captain Antonio it was another in what he considered a long train of abuses. Angelenos feared the consequences. "Nothing could be worse for this country," opined the *Star*, "than a serious disaffection on the part of this tribe towards the inhabitants." But as it happened, Captain Antonio would once again play a role as savior of the pueblo.

The real threat came from another corner of Indian country.

Also present at Chino was Antonio Garra, headman of the Cupeños. Garra, raised at Mission San Luis Rey, impressed the missionaries with his intelligence and his facility for languages, and they placed him in charge of the mission estancia at the hot springs in Valle de San José. The Indians who worked there—Luiseños, Quechans, and Cahuillas— became known as the Cupeños under his leadership. Garra skillfully guided the community through the turmoil of secularization, and they made significant economic progress, raising subsistence crops, grazing cattle, and herding sheep in the grassy valleys of the Santa Rosa Mountains.

Many Cupeños worked for ranchero J. J. Warner, owner of Rancho Valle de San José or Warner's Ranch, by virtue of a Mexican land grant. Warner, whom everyone knew as Juan Largo, was a harsh taskmaster as well as a covetous neighbor, often encroaching on the Cupeños' prime grazing land as well as their hot springs, a site with both practical and ceremonial significance for them. Frustration with Warner led Garra to befriend General Kearny when he arrived in December 1846. Garra, wrote the editor of the *San Diego Herald*, "is regarded by all who know him as a man of energy, determination, and bravery. As one of the most outstanding chiefs, his power and influence among the Indians is almost unbounded."

But the route into southern California along the old Sonora Road crossed through the Cupeño homeland, and during the Gold Rush the people were overrun by Mexicans and Americans who pilfered their crops, slaughtered their livestock, and squatted on their land. Garra appealed to American officers for protection, but very little assistance was forthcoming. The outlook grew even bleaker after the organization of the state government. The legislature explicitly authorized taxing the property of "Christianized" Indians. Los Angeles County made no attempt to tax emancipados, but San Diego County did. Garra was outraged. He believed his people should be exempt from supporting a government that denied them the franchise, barred them from the protections of the law, and refused to provide them with basic government services. When the Cupeños declined to pay, the county sheriff threatened to impound their livestock. Coming on the heels of the aborted negotiations with federal officials, and left with no one to whom he could appeal, Garra concluded that his only remaining recourse was violent resistance.

He had demography on his side, if only he could unite the fractious tribes of southern California. Garra approached Indian leaders in San Diego and Los Angeles Counties and made a special effort to recruit Juan Antonio of the Cahuillas. He dispatched a delegation north to organize among the Chumash and another south to stir up the native peoples of Baja California. He attempted to rouse the Quechans of the Colorado River, who had a long history of resistance to intruders. He also seems to have shared his thinking with a number of Californios who were unhappy with Anglo dominance. Garra proposed a coordinated strike at American centers of power throughout southern California. The uprising would begin with a Quechan attack on Fort Yuma, the American military outpost at the Colorado crossing, with the goal of closing the Sonora Road. The Quechans and the Diegueños (former *néofitos* of Mission San Diego, also known as the Kumeyaay) would then join in an assault on San Diego, while the Chumash fell on Santa Barbara. Finally, a joint force of Cupeños, Luiseños, and Cahuillas would beseige Los Angeles. Californio supporters were to act as a fifth column.

In early November, Garra and his personal guard traveled east across the desert and joined the Quechans in an assault on Fort Yuma. It was a small garrison, but defended with heavy artillery, and the Quechans quickly lost heart. To humor them, Garra and his men participated in the ambush of a party of sheep herders, killing four or five Americans and stealing several thousand sheep. But when the Quechans fell to quarreling over the spoils, Garra realized the first phase of his plan had failed. Returning home he was greeted with more bad news. The Chumash had declined to join the uprising, having just signed a treaty of peace with the Americans. Moreover, the Luiseños were badly divided. Many sought refuge from the anticipated uprising in San Diego and from those refugees the Americans had caught wind of Garra's plans. Aside from his own people at Cupa, the only solid support came from their Cahuilla neighbors at the ranchería of Los Coyotes, in the mountains several miles east of Cupa, a community that had experienced a similar disruption of its homeland by migrants. Garra decided to press ahead nevertheless, hoping that forceful action on his part might inspire other Indians.

On Friday evening, November 21, 1851, four invalid Americans bathing at the hot springs near Cupa were murdered in cold blood by Cupeños commanded by Garra's twenty-year-old son, Antonino. The next target was ranchero J. J. Warner. "On Saturday morning, about sunrise," Warner later recalled, "I was awoke by the war-whoop." Looking out he saw twenty or thirty Indians from the ranchería of Los Coyotes, armed with bows and arrows. "The Cahuillas are on us!" his Cupeño servant boy exclaimed. Warner sent the boy out to parlay, but he joined the rebels. Anticipating trouble, Warner had already dispatched his wife and children to San Diego and had taken the precaution of saddling several horses and leaving them tied next to an outbuilding at the back of the house. His only hope was to get to them before the Cahuillas did. Grabbing a revolver, and pulling another servant along behind, he threw open the door and began firing. "I succeeded in killing one, and shortly afterwards shot another while running from my house to the outhouse." Warner jumped on one of the horses, pulled his servant up behind, and charged off amid a shower of arrows. The Cahuillas declined to pursue him, but instead began methodically plundering and vandalizing Warner's ranch.

Later that day the Cupeño and Cahuilla attackers rendezvoused at Los Coyotes, where Garra had established his headquarters. They brought along the American William Marshall, who operated a store at Cupa, whose life had been spared because he was married to a Cupeño woman. Garra told Marshall he was counting on the support of several prominent Californios, including the Lugos of San Bernardino, who he said "were in his favor." That same day he dispatched a runner with a note to José Antonio Estudillo, a wealthy ranchero living in San Diego. "The moment has arrived to strike the blow,"

Garra wrote. The mountain Cahuillas had joined his uprising, and he was about to depart for the assault on Los Angeles. "You will arrange with the white people and Indians," he concluded, "and send me your word."

Word of the attacks reached San Diego the following evening, followed the next day by Warner himself, who estimated that Garra was in command of a force of four or five hundred men. But, Warner warned, if Juan Antonio's Cahuillas joined in, that number could jump to several thousand. Even as residents came to terms with that sobering observation, sentries captured the runner carrying Garra's note to Estudillo. Its contents were made public, which greatly raised Anglo suspicions of Californios. At a mass meeting, Major General Joshua H. Bean of the state militia called for volunteers for an immediate counterattack. "The tocsin of war sounds," merchant Thomas Whaley, who joined up, wrote to his mother. "We momentarily expect to be attacked by the Indians who under their great chief Antonio Garra are swarming by thousands into the south. The town of San Diego is proclaimed under martial law. Every man is enrolled a soldier."

Well, not exactly every man. Although Californios supplied horses, mules, and rations for the expedition, none served in the volunteer force, which was a thoroughly Anglo operation. Forty men under the command of Major George B. Fitzgerald of the U.S. Army marched out of San Diego headed for Cupa, leaving the town, which was overflowing with refugee Luiseños and Californios, in the hands of some three dozen armed vigilantes. "The native Californians were backward in volunteering to punish the Indians," reported the *San Diego Herald*, apparently referring to their lukewarm support of the campaign. "It was deemed prudent, under the circumstances, to bring them under strict military discipline."

GARRA'S UPRISING presented the first major challenge for Los Angeles County sheriff James R. Barton, elected the previous September to succeed G. Thompson Burrill, who declined to stand for a second term. Barton, who fought with Alexander Bell and Archibald Gillespie during the late war, enjoyed a reputation as a fearless combatant and an ardent southerner. He was well-known and generally well-liked. It was Sheriff Barton who ordered the slaughter of the unarmed Cahuillas during the October riot at the *peon* match. Afterward Angelenos had expected trouble from the Cahuillas. But county authorities learned otherwise in a letter from ranchero Isaac Williams. He had spoken with a Mexican who claimed to be the sole survivor of the Quechan attack on the sheep herders at the Colorado crossing. Antonio Garra had spared his life, the man reported, saying that he was rising against the Anglos but did not wish to harm Mexicans or Californios. Los Angeles, Don Julián feared, was in imminent danger of attack by Garra's pan-Indian army.

Sheriff Barton and two deputies rode east to investigate and returned several days later with General Bean. On Friday evening, November 28, a week after the murder of the Americans at the hot springs, Barton and Bean spoke at a mass meeting in Los Angeles. An Indian uprising had indeed begun, they reported. At San Bernardino, 150 Mormon settlers were holed up in a stockade. Los Angeles was in equal or greater danger, said Barton, and he stressed the "urgent necessity for speedy preparations for defense." Bean called for volunteers to serve under his command. The county government had neither arms nor funds, so the meeting empowered a committee of prominent Angelenos to cooperate with Bean in procuring weapons, ammunition, horses, and equipment, by seizure if necessary. Andrés Pico raised a company of 50 Californio lanceros, and an equal number of Anglos volunteered. But Bean was not optimistic. If the Cahuillas joined the Cupeños, he wrote the governor, they would be capable of mustering a force of several thousand men. "It would strain the energies of this county to their utmost tension to resist so formidable a combination, if it could be resisted at all."

At almost the same moment, Antonio Garra was attempting to persuade Juan Antonio to join him in an attack on Los Angeles. He dispatched a runner to Captain Antonio's ranchería with a written message. "If we lose this war, all will be lost," he wrote, "the world if we gain this war—then it is forever, never will it stop—this war is for a whole life." His syntax may have been awkward (at least in the *Star*'s literal translation of the Spanish original, which was not preserved), but Garra's meaning was clear. For him and his followers, the war was a struggle for justice. To win, Indian peoples had to stand and fight together, and without the support of the Cahuillas, the uprising was doomed. If that were to happen, Garra would go down fighting. "I have a good strong hold here," he declared in an angry challenge to the Americans, issued from his mountain redoubt. "Tell them that I have plenty of money, horses, mares, sheep. And tell them to come on." A few days later Captain Antonio responded to Garra, proposing that the two of them meet to make joint plans at a ranchería in the Coachella Valley. That same day the Cahuilla leader dispatched a note to Los Angeles County judge Agustín Olvera, pledging that if Angelenos required his assistance, "he was ready to join them with his whole force." As a token of his support, Captain Antonio provided a copy of the letter Garra had sent him. He was playing a treacherous game.

When Captain Antonio arrived for the meeting with Garra, he found the Cupeño chief and a small delegation waiting. He immediately ordered Garra seized and bound, instructed his followers to return home and make no further mischief, and dispatched a messenger to summon General Bean and his men. When Bean arrived he spoke with Garra, whom he knew personally, and somehow persuaded him to call on his son and his other lieutenants to voluntarily surrender. There may have been promises of amnesty, compounding the treachery. When young Antonino and four of his associates arrived, they were immediately arrested.

Juan Antonio taunted the young man for falling into the trap. "I am your prisoner," Antonino declared, "but I will not permit you to insult me," and pulling a knife from his sash, he lunged at Captain Antonio, but succeeded only in slightly wounding him. Cahuilla guards jumped the assailant, but Bean intervened, holding Captain Antonio to his promise to surrender his prisoners. His job, the Cahuilla headman acknowledged, was to "catch bad men, not to hurt them," an obvious reference to the lesson learned from the Irving affair. Over the next day or two General Bean and Captain Antonio negotiated a treaty of friendship between the state of California and the Cahuilla nation. For so long as relations with the Cahuillas remained friendly and pacific, the state pledged to defend their right to their homeland. Bean then departed with the prisoners. The uprising was over. The executions were about to begin.

THE SAN DIEGO VOLUNTEERS reached Cupa and the hot springs on December 1. After burying the bodies of the murdered American health seekers they torched the entire ranchería. William Marshall and a Mexican companion named Juan Verdugo, returning from Los Coyotes, were arrested on suspicion of collaborating with the enemy. Many Anglos, citing Garra's letter to José Antonio Estudillo, believed that Californios had encouraged if not supported the uprising. But Don José was a wealthy ranchero as well as an elected county officer, and the Anglo establishment in San Diego did not feel strong enough to challenge him. Instead, the Anglos focused their rage on Marshall and Verdugo. "These prisoners are now hourly looked for," a correspondent wrote from San Diego. "It will be short work after they are brought in." A makeshift gallows was in place before they arrived, and their execution was a foregone conclusion. They were tried by vigilantes on charges of murder and treason. Verdugo acknowledged his support of the uprising, but Marshall insisted on his innocence. He had learned of the plan to murder the Americans at the hot springs, he admitted, and failed to warn them for fear of his own life. "It was not my intention to take any part in the war," he said. "I say this as my dying declaration." Both men were found guilty and hanged side by side before a large crowd.

That same day, December 13, three volunteer companies of Americans from San Francisco arrived in San Diego on the steamer. "We shall soon number some four or five hundred strong, more than a match for all the Indians in California," wrote Thomas Whaley. "We must exterminate them." Under the command of Major Samuel P.

Heintzelman of the U.S. Army, and guided by J. J. Warner, the volunteers marched into the mountains in severe winter weather and attacked the rebels at Los Coyotes. A short but bloody engagement ensued in which a large number of Cahuilla combatants were killed and four of their leaders captured. There were no American casualties. A drumhead court-martial convicted the leaders of murder, arson, and robbery, and on Christmas morning, blindfolded and kneeling before their open graves, they were executed by firing squad. "To have done less, after they knew we were aware of their guilt," wrote one observer, "would have been fraught with evil."

Meanwhile, at Rancho Santa Ana del Chino, another military court found Garra's son and two associates guilty of treason and murder. One of them, a mere boy, was sentenced to twenty-five lashes, but Antonino and the other Cupeño were executed by firing squad before a crowd of volunteers from Los Angeles. On December 30 General Bean and a small party departed for San Diego with the senior Garra in custody. He had been saved for public trial and execution.

Antonio Garra's court-martial on charges of treason, murder, and robbery was held in early January. Garra pled guilty to only one charge, the theft of sheep at the Colorado crossing. He testified in his own defense, and named several prominent Californios as co-conspirators, including Estudillo, who he said had promised to "join with us and help me drive the Americans from the country." Major Justus McKinstry, assigned as Garra's defense counsel, demanded that his client be allowed to confront Estudillo, but the court refused. McKinstry then raised a strong challenge to the charge of treason. Garra was the leader of an independent Indian nation and "owed no allegiance to the State of California," he argued. "Therefore, under no circumstances could [he] be guilty of the crime of treason." McKinstry moved that Garra be considered a prisoner of war, but the court denied his motion and the trial proceeded. None of the testimony directly connected Garra with the murder of the Americans, but that didn't matter. On January 10 he was convicted of murder and sentenced to death. The charge of treason was quietly dropped.

A few hours later Garra was led to the graveyard, where the execution by firing squad was to take place before a crowd of several hundred. "His whole deportment evinced the brave man prepared to meet his fate," reported the *San Diego Herald*. The priest accompanying him urged Garra to pray, but he refused. "What's the use?" he said. Reaching the place of execution, he was asked whether he wished to make a statement. No, he replied. The priest remonstrated with him, insisting that as a Christian he must make a public profession of his sins and his hope of forgiveness. Relenting, Garra finally lifted his eyes and looked directly at the crowd. "Gentlemen," he said, a contemptuous smile breaking across his face, "I ask your pardon for all my offenses, and expect yours in return." Blindfolded, he knelt at the head of his open grave, and the twelve-man squad fired on command. According to some observers, Garra died chuckling at his own joke.

IN LATE DECEMBER, Oliver M. Wozencraft, one of the federal Indian commissioners appointed to make treaties with the California tribes, met with Juan Antonio and other Indian leaders at Temecula to negotiate compacts of peace and friendship with the United States. Captain Antonio was not happy about sitting down with Luiseño and Cupeño headmen, whom he considered mortal enemies, but he did as he was asked. In the Treaty of Temecula, signed January 5, 1852, the Indians agreed to acknowledge the sovereignty and protection of the United States, to preserve peace with their neighbors, and to conform to the regulations of the federal government. In exchange for their willingness to cede their aboriginal claims to land in southern California, a large inland territory would be set aside as a homeland in perpetuity. Several weeks later Captain Antonio paid a visit to Los Angeles with a hundred of his men. "They came to collect presents for their conduct in the late war," reported the *Star*. "Juan appears to be a prompt business man as well as a cunning chief, and a debt due by his white brethren is not soon forgotten."

In fact, they forgot quickly and completely. When the Treaty of

Temecula was sent to the U.S. Senate for ratification, along with seventeen other treaties negotiated with California tribes, Anglos and Californios alike made clear their opposition. "To place upon our most fertile soil the most degraded race of aborigines upon the North American continent," opined the *Star*, "to invest them with the rights of sovereignty and to teach them that they are to be treated as powerful and independent nations, is planting the seeds of future disaster and ruin." The California senate appointed a committee to consider the matter, and they voted to scrap the treaties and demand that the federal government remove all Indians from the state. One member of the committee opposed that conclusion—J. J. Warner, who shortly after the uprising had been elected to represent San Diego County in the legislature. "Where will you locate them?" Warner asked.

> On the desert and sterile regions east of the Sierra Nevada, that they may die of starvation? . . . Better, far better, drive them at once into the ocean, or bury them in the land of their birth. . . . Is it not our duty to devise some measure, dictated by a policy which, while it may not be onerous on our citizens, may lean to the side of justice in favor of the Indian? . . . Will it be said that the land is not broad enough for them and us? Or that while our doors are open to the stranger from the uttermost parts of the earth, we have not spare room for the residence of the once sole inhabitants of our magnificent empire? Shall future generations seek in vain for one remaining descendant of the sons of the forest? Has the love of gold blotted from our minds all feelings of compassion or justice?

Warner was no friend of the Cupeños. But unlike the other members of the committee, he actually knew what he was talking about.

Vehemently opposed by California's congressional delegation, the treaties were tabled by the U.S. Senate and never reconsidered. No one bothered to inform the Indians that they had no legally binding title to their homelands. Numerous times Captain Antonio complained to state and federal officials of Anglo squatters on Cahuilla territory. In 1856 he signed a letter of protest addressed to the commissioner of Indian affairs. "We have been encroached upon by the white settlers who have taken possession of a large portion of our best farming and grazing lands and by diverting the water from our lands depriving us to a great extent of the means of irrigation." Captain Antonio met with Captain Henry S. Burton of the U.S. Army. The squatters were not breaking any laws, Burton told him, and there was nothing he could do about them. "You must remain quiet, and keep your people so," he warned. "The government is watching you, and if you do wrong you will be punished."

In 1863 a smallpox epidemic swept through southern California, infecting thousands of people and killing hundreds. At the Cahuilla ranchería of Sahatapa, many were stricken, including Captain Antonio. Those who could fled, leaving their leader and other sufferers behind. According to Cahuilla legend, Juan Antonio died regretting he had not joined forces with Garra twelve years before.

· CHAPTER 17 ·

LA LEY DE LINCH

WHILE ANGELENOS OCCUPIED THEMSELVES with the threat
of Indian violence, the number of lethal assaults occurring in their midst
continued to rise. Five murders in 1849, ten in 1850, twelve in 1851 (not
including the killing of Red Irving and ten members of his gang), and
a staggering twenty-four in 1852. From 1850 to 1859 more than two
hundred homicides took place in Los Angeles County, which counted
five to ten thousand residents. Los Angeles was one of the most lethal
places on the planet, with a murder rate comparable to that of Mexican border towns in the first decade of the twenty-first century, at
the height of the violence between warring drug cartels. Calling
attention to the huge number of murders, John A. Lewis, editor of
the *Star*, asked the question that surely troubled many Angelenos.
"Who today can name *one* instance in which a murderer has been
punished?"

In the summer of 1851, when Lewis posed that question, his paper
was focusing on developments in San Francisco, where residents had
organized a celebrated committee of vigilance in response to the ineffective enforcement of law and order. In June San Francisco vigilantes executed a man convicted of grand larceny in an extralegal trial.

Lewis, a native of Boston who had edited a San Francisco paper before coming to Los Angeles, was highly critical.

> We are told that the members of the Committee are men of integrity, and that they were impelled to the course they took from a conviction that the criminal laws are totally inadequate to protect society. Yet we cannot perceive that their course has a tendency to gain for the Law any additional respect. On the contrary, the supporters of Law and Order have great cause to despond. Where is all this to end? It commenced with the hanging of criminals; it may end in the death of the innocent. The zeal of these men may lead them into some mistakes, or individuals of less integrity may find a place upon the Committee. The Days of Terror will then come upon us.

If half the energy that went into the organization of the vigilance committee went instead into efforts to strengthen law enforcement, Lewis argued, "a result would have been obtained that they would never have occasion to regret."

Since 1850, when county government was organized, law enforcement in Los Angeles had consisted of the county sheriff, his under-sheriff and deputy, as well as the city marshal and his two deputies. Both the sheriff and the marshal were frequently preoccupied with other duties—the sheriff with the collection of county taxes (out of which he took a share), the marshal with the roundup and auction of vagrant Indians (for which he received a commission). The suppression of criminal violence was a secondary concern. Left essentially unprotected, besieged by the ongoing disorder, Angelenos were drawn to vigilantism equally as much as San Franciscans.

In response to calls from private citizens for the organization of a real police force, the common council of Los Angeles voted in July 1851 to establish a volunteer patrol "to watch over the security of the inhabitants and the preservation of peace, in conformity with the laws of the state." Dr. Alexander W. Hope, medical doctor and veteran of the late war, was appointed chief, operating under the executive authority of the mayor. According to the *Star*, a total of eighty-three men, including twenty-six Californios, signed on immediately. Wearing ribbon badges inscribed "Police/Policia" provided by the city, the volunteers enjoyed semiofficial authority. But unlike the city marshal or the county sheriff, they were not officers of the court. As historian Hubert Bancroft put it, the Los Angeles volunteers "might be called a vigilance committee organized under the auspices of the law." But, he added, "we may be sure that such a body would never let law stand greatly in their way."

Despite his previous warnings about the dangers of vigilantism, editor Lewis of the *Star* endorsed this proposal, which he considered "admirably calculated to preserve peace and good order." His support provoked Manuel Clemente Rojo, editor of *La Estrella*, the *Star's* Spanish-language section, to wonder in print whether Lewis had changed his opinion of vigilantism. Lewis responded in the same issue of the paper. "Our views upon the subject have not in the least degree changed," he assured Rojo. What Lewis found attractive about the plan, he explained, was the creation of a police "without being at any expense for its maintenance." Something for nothing—the sure sign of a devil's bargain.

THE FIRST TEST of the new law enforcement regime came in the summer of 1852 when two men—Benjamin Franklin McCoy, twenty-one, and his partner, a German identified only as Ludwig—went missing under suspicious circumstances. They had taken the steamer from San Francisco to San Diego, purchased saddle ponies, and set off across the countryside with several hundred dollars in gold, intending to purchase cattle to drive north and sell at inflated prices. They had last been seen in the company of a Californio named Doroteo Zabaleta, who had recently escaped from the Los Angeles county jail, where he had been held awaiting trial on a charge of petty theft. Zabaleta later showed up at a cantina in San Gabriel, spending lavishly and exhibiting a buckskin purse full of gold coins. Sheriff Barton and his under-sheriff left town looking for him.

While Barton was absent, a group of Anglos from Santa Barbara arrived with Zabaleta and two other prisoners, Sonoreños Jesús Rivas and Francisco Carmello. The three had been arrested on suspicion of horse theft. But under intense examination, Carmello broke down and implicated the other two in the murder of the cattle buyers. Since the sheriff was unavailable, the prisoners were turned over to the volunteer patrol. There was intense public pressure for summary justice. "In accordance with the wishes of our citizens," the *Star* reported, "it was deemed proper that a committee should be chosen to hear any statements that the prisoners might be inclined to make." That committee operated outside the established procedures of the county's justice system. The volunteers had become vigilantes.

The committee counted both Californio and Anglo members, including editor Manuel Clemente Rojo of the *Star*, who acted as interpreter. The three suspects were examined separately. Carmello repeated his confession, and when it was read aloud to Zabaleta he broke down and made a confession of his own, blaming Rivas for the murders. When informed what his partner had said, Rivas insisted that Zabaleta had been the instigator. In fact, the question of who planned the murders mattered little to the vigilantes. Zabaleta led them to the scene of the crime at the lower crossing of the San Gabriel River, where they found what remained of the victims' corpses after the coyotes and buzzards had finished their work.

Nearly a hundred Angelenos assembled in the lobby of the Bella Union for the vigilante trial. A jury of twelve men, six Anglos and six Californios, returned a verdict of guilty and a sentence of death for both men. Francisco Carmello was turned over to Sheriff Barton. The executions took place the following morning before a large crowd made up predominantly of Californios and Sonoreños.

Both men spoke from the gallows. Neither expressed any remorse. Zabaleta played the victim, blaming the murders on Rivas. He had committed many crimes, he admitted, but nothing that justified the penalty of death, and he expressed anguish over the shame it brought on his family. Rivas condemned the bad luck that had brought him to such a miserable end. "Young men, consider my fate!" he exclaimed. "Never join with so-called friends if you plan to commit a crime!" The executioner then slipped canvas bags over the heads of the two men, stepped back and pulled a lever, releasing the trapdoor. The drop was too short, and both men struggled violently against the ropes as they strangled to death, the crowd watching in silent horror. The bodies were left suspended for an hour or more on the brow of the hill where, as one observer recalled, "everyone could see them swinging in the air until they were cut down for burial."

The gallows speeches and the botched execution disquieted many, and over the next few days editors Lewis and Rojo of the *Star* heard plenty of criticism from Californios, who blamed Anglos for proceeding in too great haste. Rojo responded, reminding his readers that Californios had participated actively in the investigation and trial, which had been conducted in emulation of legal process. "Justice was the goal," he concluded, "and justice was achieved." Yet, as Lewis had warned the year before, the proceeding did nothing to strengthen the legal justice system. Zabaleta and Rivas were plainly guilty of murder. How much better it would have been had the law been able to take credit for their punishment. The next case would prove far more difficult.

LATE ONE NIGHT in the autumn of 1852, Ana Benites awoke to the sound of gunfire outside the San Gabriel home of Juan Ávila Rico, where she and her lover were sleeping. "Rico! Rico! Rico!" a man cried. One of her children opened the door to the house, and the man stumbled inside. "*Madre*," the child cried out, "*es general Bean.*" Joshua H. Bean, major general of the California state militia, had been shot by an unknown assailant as he walked home following a performance of *las maromas*, a traveling tent show of acrobats, ropewalkers, and clowns. The ball tore into his chest, ripped through his right lung, and exited his upper back, a mortal wound. Bean spent the next twenty-four hours drifting in and out of consciousness before finally succumbing to the loss of blood.

A coroner's inquest convened the following morning, Monday, November 8. General Bean was well-known and widely admired by Americans. "His death," reported the *Star*, "has created a deep sensation in this community." After Garra's uprising Bean had relocated from San Diego to San Gabriel, opening a popular saloon in an old mission building. There were no witnesses to the shooting, at least none who came forward. As he was dying, Bean had mumbled the names of two men, but his meaning was unclear. One of them was ranchero Juan Pacifico Ontiveros, the other Ontiveros's son-in-law, Felipe Reid. At the inquest both men testified that although they were in San Gabriel that evening to watch the *maromas*, they knew nothing of Bean's murder. Don Pacifico, proprietor of a large rancho, was a man beyond reproach. Reid, the son of a Scots father and a Gabrieleño mother who worked as an account clerk for Abel Stearns, was widely considered a ne'er-do-well, but he provided what the *Star* called "a perfect alibi." The coroner's jury ruled that "the deceased, Gen. J. H. Bean, came to his death by a shot received from some person or persons unknown."

That was a conclusion Bean's American friends refused to accept, and constrained by neither due process nor social deference they took the matter into their own hands. A group of men led by Alexander Hope, chief of the volunteer patrol, questioned Don Pacifico again, and under intense interrogation he provided them with a list of names that led to the detention of several individuals, including Ana Benites. According to Antonio Coronel, Hope's men subjected them to the third degree and "even applied torture," which terrorized the small Californio community in San Gabriel. "The matter became so serious, Anglos and Californios alike were alarmed," Coronel recalled, and "it was agreed, therefore, to name a committee to investigate and make the results public." The hope was to prevent the formation of a lynch mob by organizing a more formal vigilance committee that included both Anglos and Californios. On Friday, November 26, the prisoners were transported to Los Angeles and turned over to this committee.

Editor John Lewis of the *Star* was enthusiastic about these developments. The prisoners, he wrote, belonged to "a gang of desperadoes . . . some one of whom, there is every reason to believe, was guilty of the murder." In fact, not a shred of evidence linked any of the suspects to Bean's death, but Lewis was nevertheless ready to begin their trial. "These persons will be tried by a people's court and the guilty ones punished as they deserve," he announced. "There can certainly be no objection to this mode of procedure, when we hear our very court officers acknowledge that the law is utterly incapable of bringing them to justice." Lewis was deliberately dissembling. The problem was not the incapacity of the law, as he implied, but rather its insistence on evidence and proof. Lewis had come a long way since his expression of concern the year before, although a faint echo of his earlier caution reverberated in the final sentence of his editorial. "It is to be hoped," he concluded, "that passion will not get the better of justice and judgment, but let everything be conducted in a manner worthy of an American community."

The vigilance committee kept up the pressure. Ana Benites was held incommunicado for more than a week at the home of William Osburn, undersheriff of Los Angeles County and a prominent supporter of vigilantism. Osburn was married to a Mexican woman and fluent in Spanish, and eventually he persuaded Benites to talk. One of his sons later recalled that "father one night dressed her up in men's clothes and took her to an acrobatic performance given in Nigger Alley," and "while there she pointed out one of the gang," a Sonoreño named Reyes Féliz, about fifteen years old. After several hours of interrogation, Féliz made a confession. "I belonged to the company of Joaquín Murieta," he said, using a name that meant little to Angelenos at that moment but would soon become infamous. After committing a murder during a robbery near Stockton, the Murieta gang fled south to Los Angeles, a bounty hunter named Harry Love hot on their trail.

Love caught up with one of the gang and shot him dead, but Murieta, Féliz, and several others found refuge in "Sonoratown," the name Anglos applied to the predominantly Mexican neighborhood on the north side of the pueblo. Ana Benites knew about his past, Féliz said, because she was Murieta's mistress and had been in bed with him the night of Bean's murder. But in regard to that crime, he insisted, "I know nothing."

Féliz acknowledged a murderous past, so the vigilantes convened what the *Star* called "a people's court" at the Bella Union to consider his fate. Horace Bell attended and provided an eyewitness account. "The place was packed to suffocation, with a dense crowd outside," he wrote, with "Old Horse-Face," Abel Stearns, presiding. Féliz's statement was read aloud, and afterward Stearns asked whether anyone wished to make a motion. According to Bell, "a ferocious looking gambler mounted a bench, and said: 'I move that Reyes Féliz be taken to the hill and hanged by the neck until he be dead.'" Stearns gravely called for a vote, the crowd shouted its approval, "and Reyes Féliz was a doomed man." The following day, November 30, Féliz was conducted to the gallows on Fort Moore Hill at noon, and before being "launched into eternity," as the *Star* put it, he addressed a few words to the large crowd, advising the young men "never to put faith in woman!"

Cherchez la femme. Ana Benites made no attempt to deny her relationship with the outlaw Murieta, who had already returned north to begin a crime spree that would end in his death at the hands of bounty hunter Harry Love the following year. In fact, Benites was proud of her connection and the purchase it provided. After further examination by the vigilance committee she implicated yet another Sonoreño, a young man named Benito López. Knowing that she was intimate with Murieta, and hoping to get on her good side, López had given her some of the booty stolen from a couple he had murdered near Cahuenga Pass. Seized by the vigilantes, López confessed to the crime and led his captors to the scene, where they discovered the moldering bones of his victims. So much for López.

By this point Ana Benites's credibility was soaring. What more did she know? After more interrogation she provided them with precisely what they wanted. Before he left town, she said, Murieta had confided that Bean's murderer was a poor San Gabriel shoemaker by the name of Cipriano Sandoval. Shortly after leaving the performance of the *maromas*, Sandoval saw Bean assaulting an Indian woman in a dark alley, and outraged by this demonstration of Anglo arrogance, he pulled a pistol and shot Bean dead. Sandoval had previously denied any knowledge of the murder, but confronted with Benites's accusation he changed his story. He had indeed heard the gunshots, he admitted, and then the sound of someone running. Suddenly a man crashed into him headlong. It was Felipe Reid. "I have just shot Bean," Reid exclaimed. "Here is five dollars; take it, say nothing about it, and when you want more money come to me and get it." The vigilantes questioned Reid again, but he vociferously denied Sandoval's charge. They reinvestigated his alibi, and it held up. They concluded Sandoval was lying. Benites's testimony against him was hearsay at best, evidence inadmissible in a court of law. But that was not where Sandoval's fate would be decided. Some members of the committee, including Antonio Coronel, had qualms. But, said Coronel, "Dr. Hope was determined on revenge at all costs" and insisted that "Sandoval should be hanged."

The outcome of the "trial" of Benito López and Cipriano Sandoval, held at the Bella Union on Sunday morning, December 5, was a foregone conclusion. Both were declared guilty and sentenced to death, with the execution scheduled for that same afternoon. As the vigilantes were finishing their work, a group of Americans arrived with an intoxicated Mexican named Juan Moran who they said had just killed one of his countrymen in an affray on Negro Alley. Since the people's court was already in session, why not try him as well. "The proof in the case being perfectly clear," opined the *Star*, "it was not deemed advisable to deliver him to the civil authorities, but to punish his offence summarily; and as the men Cipriano and López were to be executed in the afternoon, he was condemned to the same fate and at the same time." Come one, come all! It was a confirmation of the ill-considered nature of the entire proceeding. Yet editor John Lewis of the *Star* reported it with a straight face.

That afternoon the condemned men made the long walk to the top of the hill, accompanied by Father Anacleto of the Plaza church. They mounted the gallows, were trussed and noosed, then given the opportunity to make a final statement. López acknowledged the justice of his punishment, and like Féliz the week before he cautioned the young men in the crowd to avoid "bad women." Moran made what the *Star* called "a lengthy speech," condemning the absence of due process and addressing his fellow Sonoreños in the crowd. "We made a mistake in coming to this country, amigos," he said. "Go back, every one of you to Sonora and obey the laws, or you will soon be travelling this same road." The cobbler Sandoval maintained his innocence but stoically accepted his fate. Providence had ordained that this would be the way he met his death, he said, and he was prepared to meet his maker. Undersheriff William B. Osburn, serving as executioner, carefully provided ropes of an appropriate length and adjusted the nooses correctly to avoid any mishaps. "Do your worst, you son of a bitch," Moran said to him in Spanish. The condemned "met their fate with great calmness," reported the *Star*, "and with a courage worthy of a better cause."

Many Angelenos doubted Cipriano Sandoval's guilt. Manuel Clemente Rojo, Lewis's editorial colleague at the *Star*, was a member of the vigilance committee, but he opposed the verdict and condemned the "inhuman execution." According to Benjamin Hayes, "none of the Californians ever believed that Sandoval was guilty." Hayes later learned the truth from a number of Indian woman who lived near the mission. Joshua Bean and Felipe Reid, they told him, were involved with the same Gab鼋eño woman. The night of his murder, Bean accosted her on the street and demanded she go home with him. When she refused, he grabbed her by her hair and began dragging her toward his adobe. Reid, hiding in the shadows, stepped forward and fired point-blank at Bean. Afterward the murderer spread plenty of money around in a successful effort to cover up the crime. Several years later, however, as Reid lay dying of smallpox, he called Hayes to his side and made a full confession.

Horace Bell was in the crowd when Sandoval, López, and Moran were executed. "Heavy clouds over-spread the sky," he wrote, "as though an angel had in charity thrown its mantle over the scene to shut out the horrid spectacle from the face of heaven." What he had witnessed, Bell thought, was a travesty of justice. "In the minds of unprejudiced persons at the time, the hanging of the poor village cobbler of San Gabriel was considered an unmitigated and deliberate murder." Bell returned to his rooms that evening "pondering sadly and solemnly over the events of the day and could not refrain from thinking," as he later wrote, "that humanity would have been greatly benefited, if about four-fifths of that mob had been disposed of in the same way as had been the hapless Mexicans who were hung."

CALIFORNIOS JOINED Alexander Hope's volunteer patrol and took part in the vigilance committees that tried and executed Zabaleta and Rivas. But Hope's zeal in the investigation of Bean's murder alienated many of them. In the summer of 1853, several months after the executions, Hope and his officers reorganized the volunteer patrol as a mounted cavalry company, which they named the Los Angeles Rangers. Hope applied to the state government for recognition of his company as an arm of the California militia, which was granted, providing state subsidies for the purchase of arms and equipment. The Rangers held their first muster at the El Dorado Saloon near the Plaza, a place noted as a "white man's rendezvous," where Californios and Mexicans were not welcome. Reorganizing the force was necessary, argued the *Star*, because Los Angeles was faced with "peculiar obstacles" in the maintenance of law and order, namely "the habitual concealment of offenders and the repugnance to give information to the authorities of which a large class of our population is justly accused." That veiled criticism of the Spanish-speaking majority was made clearer in the list of officers and members published by the *Star*. It included not a single Hispanic name.

The conflict between Americans and Californios on questions of law and order, simmering since the Lugo case of 1851, arose once again in October 1853, when the Rangers arrested a gang of Californios suspected of horse theft and murder. The gang had been tracked to Los Angeles by the sheriff of San Luis Obispo County, some two hundred miles north, and he requested the assistance of the Rangers. Horace Bell, who like most young Anglos in town had joined the group, participated in the capture of the suspects at their encampment in a cornfield outside of town, an engagement Bell described enthusiastically as "one of the most exciting pleasures that it is possible to conceive. . . . The pop, pop, pop of the revolvers, the answering yell and hurrah of the intercepting Rangers, the defiant *carajo!* of the robbers, and the crashing of the breaking cornstalks." Bell and the others captured three men and a young woman, "as pretty a little brunette as ever excited the lustful desires of a Mormon missionary," according to Bell. The suspects were brought into town, where a public meeting was convened to consider their fate. No thought was given to turning them over to Sheriff Barton.

The first sign of trouble came when Andrés Pico declined to serve as the meeting's chairman. He was replaced by the ever available Abel Stearns. At the encampment the Rangers had found a *caballada*, the horses displaying a variety of brands, as well as a cache of silks and other dry goods, presumably stolen from a peddler reported murdered during a highway robbery. Stearns selected a jury of six men to examine the evidence and render a judgment. After deliberating for a few minutes, they returned with a verdict of guilty and a sentence of death. Stearns called for discussion, and it was quickly moved and seconded that the sentence be approved and the three men and one woman be hanged the following morning.

But it immediately became clear that most of the Californios in attendance were opposed. Manuel Clemente Rojo mounted a table in the front of the room and gave a speech attacking the practice of vigilantism. This meeting, he declared, constituted an illegal assembly. Matters of guilt and innocence were the exclusive province of the legally constituted courts, not irregular combinations of vindictive and excited men. Several Americans attempted to shout him down, but Rojo refused to be silenced. The law, he declared, existed for the good of the whole community. If Angelenos abandoned the law, the result would be anarchy. Several Americans rushed forward and tried to push Rojo out of the room, but Californios challenged them and Rojo held his position, declaring he would not be "choked off." The crimes of which these individuals were accused had taken place in another county, he said, and that was where they should be tried. At that moment Rojo was joined by his law partner, Isaac S. K. Ogier, who had just been appointed U.S. attorney for the southern district of California. He agreed with Rojo, Ogier said, and was unalterably opposed to lynch law. With that declaration, Anglo solidarity in the face of Californio objection crumbled. Stearns called for a vote, and the motion to support the jury's decision was defeated by a wide margin. Ogier moved that the prisoners be sent to San Luis Obispo for trial. His motion was seconded and passed. The prisoners were dispatched on the next steamer.

Rojo devoted nearly the entirety of *La Estrella* that week to a detailed summary of the meeting as well as a passionate editorial. He was appalled by the conduct of the Americans. "The bad feeling, even hatred, was palpable," he wrote, and the meeting "appeared to us like a battlefield." The Anglos had armed themselves with revolvers in an obvious attempt to intimidate the Californios, who refused to be scared off. "If an attempt had been made to subject the prisoners to *la ley de linch*," Rojo wrote, "there would have been a disastrous scene." He recalled the events of the previous year. "We cannot forget the lynching of Cipriano Sandoval. . . . His death, ordered by a barbarous people who watched him die on the scaffold, was a lesson to us." At these so-called "people's courts," he wrote, it was too easy to "commit an injustice like the one that, in our judgment, was committed against the hapless Sandoval." Lynch law was not the solution to the problem of crime and violence in Los Angeles.

Rojo then offered an argument that masterfully summarized the choice faced by Angelenos. If the police are ineffective in enforcing the laws, find new men to take their place. If the courts are ineffective in convicting criminals, place new judges on the bench. If the laws are ineffective, pass new ones that work. "Are we a people who must submit to the immorality, barbarism, and disorder of lynch law? Are we capable of being shamed into making good use of our freedom? Must we commit injustice when we have the recourse to remedy all our needs?" Rojo's questions would haunt Los Angeles for years to come.

The four Californios the Angelenos shipped off were met at the San Luis Obispo landing by a dozen Anglo vigilantes, who hustled them to the first available tree and hanged them all without ceremony. Rojo printed that news in *La Estrella* and accompanied it with yet another plea for the sanctity of the law. "Should we not let justice take its course, let criminals be tried by our courts and punished under the law?" he asked. These would be his last printed words in Los Angeles. Soon thereafter Rojo, who had lived and worked in the pueblo for nearly five years, relocated to the coastal town of Ensenada, south of the border in Baja California. There he practiced law, ran for political office, and was responsible for founding the territory's public education system. Years later, asked why he chose to leave Los Angeles, he responded sharply, *"No me pude aclimatar"*—I could not acclimatize.

· CHAPTER 18 ·

THE CULT OF VIOLENCE

BENJAMIN HAYES WAS PROUD of his electoral victory in
November 1852. He was a lifelong Democrat, but believing the court
should be above politics he stood for the open position of judge of
California's First Judicial District without his party's endorsement.
Yet he outpolled the Democratic candidates for all other local offices.
"So as you see," he reported to a friend in Missouri, "I am considerably ahead of the party." He was happy to give up his private practice
of bickering clients and petty suits. As district judge, he would be
required to ride circuit between Los Angeles, San Diego, and San
Bernardino, the seat of a new county being carved from the other two.
"The counties are large," Hayes conceded, and "I shall have my hands
full." Yet the work was critical. As presiding judge of the highest court
in southern California, he envisioned leading Los Angeles "to better
order and more perfect security."

His wife, Emily Chauncey Hayes, supported her husband's decision
but worried about his stamina. "His health in truth is far from being
good," she wrote a relative, "he cannot stand as much as I can." Hayes
disagreed. "I consider myself to be in excellent health," he countered.
"A ride for a day or two on horseback renews my strength." Indeed,

"one reason why I felt desirous to quit the practice of law for the judgeship was to get time for exercise, of which I have sometimes had too little, as well as to take Emily out riding, so advantageous to her." Emily was in fact the frail one, suffering from a pulmonary disorder (probably tuberculosis) that often left her coughing uncontrollably and struggling for breath. After a journey across the Isthmus of Panama that taxed every ounce of her strength, she had joined her husband in Los Angeles in early 1852.

It was a welcome reunion for the young couple. They settled into a small adobe on the slope of Fort Moore Hill, a few steps from the Plaza church. "I do not think there could be a more lovely spot," Emily declared. From her front door she enjoyed a view looking east across the broad valley to the rugged San Gabriel Mountains. Together the couple strolled the grassy foothills and meandered along the banks of the zanja, a word which Anglo tongues pronounced *sankey*. "Today we walked out to a vineyard, about a mile and a half," Emily wrote after one of their excursions. "I was weak, but it did me a great deal of good. Whilst there I had two oranges and some dried grapes, which helped me, I think. . . . I intend to walk out there often in the fruit season, should I live." Both she and Hayes were devout Catholics, and despite the language barrier—unlike her husband, Emily spoke no Spanish—she grew fond of the local women who crowded the church on Sunday mornings. They fussed over her, bringing her little gifts of fruit, embroidery, and advice. Learning she was childless, they offered reassurance. "Ah, no matter, *California es muy fertil*, you will have many yet." In the spring of 1853 she delivered a son, John Chauncey Hayes, whom she pronounced "the sweetest thing in the world." Two years later she suffered the loss of an infant daughter, who died after only a few hours of life. But in the meantime two of her husband's sisters relocated from Missouri to Los Angeles, providing the couple with a circle of family in addition to their growing network of friends.

Los Angeles became home. But there were aspects of pueblo life Emily Hayes did not appreciate. "The site of Los Angeles is lovely," she thought, "but the city is very ugly. Most of the houses are built of mud." That included her own casa, with its dirt floor and leaky roof. She pleaded with her husband for floorboards, but it was several months before he procured them from a mill in San Bernardino. Emily kept her distance from the raucous doings down on Calle de los Negros, although she got a taste when with Hayes she attended the Fourth of July festivities on the Plaza. "They were to have had a procession through the town," she wrote, "but this turned out to be a few men on horseback, racing through the streets, nearly all drunk." The couple retreated to their home on the hillside, but the sound of gunfire kept Emily awake late into the night. A few weeks later, the first of the vigilante executions took place at the summit of "Gallows Hill," as Fort Moore Hill had become known, a hailing distance from her back door. Emily was horrified when the first hanging was followed by another several months later, and yet another a few weeks after that.

Hayes himself was more forbearing. He estimated that there were three or four hundred Americans in the pueblo, perhaps half of them transients—miners on their way to or from the diggings or gamblers out to fleece them. But they were gradually giving way to more respectable settlers, "a clever, manly population, such as you find on the frontiers of Missouri, . . . well-disposed citizens, peaceful and seeking the prosperity of the country," not the "bloodthirsty horde" critics made them out to be. True, they had resorted to lynch law, which Hayes staunchly opposed, although he had to admit that since the vigilante episodes of the previous year "there has been felt generally a great sense of safety." Among Anglos anyway, if not among Californios. The trick, Hayes thought, was to use this moment of calm to build up support for the legally constituted justice system. When Hayes took the oath of office in January 1853, he was generally upbeat. He would soon have reason to feel otherwise.

TO CELEBRATE THE ANNIVERSARY of George Washington's birth on February 22, a group of prominent Americans and elite Californios invited what attorney Joseph Lancaster Brent described as "the better class" of Angelenos to a ball at *el palacio*, the Abel Stearns mansion. Some Americans of the vagabond class professed to be deeply offended. Such national occasions, they insisted, should be celebrated democratically, and they denounced the pretentions of "the aristocrats." Something quite similar had happened several years before the American conquest, when ordinary Angelenos protested a gathering of the Californio elite at *el palacio* on Mexican Independence Day.

On the night of the ball a crowd of drunken protesters gathered on the Plaza. There were incendiary speeches. A group of a dozen men or more commandeered an old artillery piece that sat on the Plaza, pushed it down Main Street, and positioned it in front of the entrance to *el palacio*. Then, loading it with stones and a small charge of powder, they fired it off, producing a loud report though doing relatively little damage to the house. Then the men staged a "shivaree," banging tin pans, shooting off firecrackers, and singing patriotic songs. Eventually the guests inside decided the foolishness had gone on long enough, and once the women were secured in a back room the men marched to the foyer and threw open the heavy double doors. Myron Norton and James A. "Jack" Watson stepped into the doorway and faced the crowd. Both were armed. Norton, an attorney who had come to California as an officer with the New York volunteers, was a large man with a commanding presence. Watson, who had fought with the Texas Mounted during the war, was short and slight. He was a "game little fellow," wrote Horace Bell, with "a battery of Colts buckled to him, either of which was nearly as large as himself." It is not clear which side fired first, but Norton was hit in the first round and went down with what turned out to be a minor wound. Watson "sallied out alone," both revolvers blazing, and brought down two protesters. The rest of the mob fled, leaving the wounded men writhing on the ground. Both were dead within the hour.

Writing in the *Star*, editor John A. Lewis strongly criticized all the participants in the affray. How could the protesters have thought it acceptable to attack the private residence of a respectable citizen?

Why hadn't the men inside summoned the marshal or the sheriff? Lewis believed he knew the answer. Men on both sides, including shooters and victims, had been active participants in the recent vigilante activities. "Men have become so accustomed to acting as judges, jurors, and executioners," he wrote, "they have come to think justice will lose a victim unless they swing him off or flog him themselves." In frontier Los Angeles, where state-sponsored institutions of justice were extraordinarily weak, men of all classes and backgrounds considered the offenses of other men as insults to themselves rather than as offenses against the community. Justice was personal. Men followed the precept of former president Andrew Jackson, who famously quoted his mother's advice on how he should handle challenges to his reputation or honor. "Always settle them cases yourself!"

Norton and Watson surrendered to the authorities and were examined by Judge Hayes. Watson claimed the first fire came from the mob, but he took full responsibility for the deadly shots fired in response. Norton had gotten off a round, but Watson was confident that he had fired the shots that killed the two men because both died of wounds to the belly. "It is my habit when I shoot a man at night, to aim just below the belt," he told Hayes. "In the day time you can pick your place to shoot, but at night I make it a rule to aim at the stomach." Hayes ruled the killings to be justifiable homicides.

The public reputations of both men were greatly enhanced by the episode. Soon thereafter Norton was elected county judge, succeeding Agustín Olvera. Watson established a lucrative legal practice, served three terms in the state assembly, and married María Dolores Domínguez, an heir to Rancho San Pedro. "He was the gamest man and the best fighter that I ever knew," an associate wrote after Watson's death some years later. "The little chap didn't provoke difficulties, but I verily believe he enjoyed fighting for its own sake, and odds didn't figure with him once he concluded to go into a melee. His long suit was shooting, and a deadlier shot never fingered a revolver."

Jack Watson was a devotee of the cult of violence, a sect with its own set of symbols and rituals. The Colt was his cross, stand your ground his creed, the glory of defying risk his reward. The shootist, observed Peter Burnett, a Missourian who served as California's first American governor, was "essentially selfish, and therefore he heeds not the ruin he produces. The cry and distress of the widow and the orphan never reach his dull, cold ear, or affect his stony heart." Burnett's opinion of gunfighters was "that most of them are atheists, whose moral conduct depends upon the sliding scale of the times, and who have no strict moral principles independent of public opinion." Watson was a lifelong Catholic who married in the Plaza church and had his children baptized there. But he was also a practicioner of the cult of violence.

LOS ANGELES WAS AWASH IN GUNS, many carried west by soldiers and immigrants, others imported for sale by merchants. The private armory of residents included military muskets and hunting rifles, single- and double-barreled shotguns, carbines, and pistols of all shapes and sizes, an increasing proportion of them outfitted with percussion ignition. Firearms manufacturer Samuel Colt utilized the percussion cap in his patented "revolving gun," featuring a cylinder with multiple chambers that rotated into place with the cock of the hammer, enabling the discharge of several rounds without reloading. Introduced in 1848, Colt's Dragoon six-shooter, also known as an Army revolver, was a large .44-caliber horse pistol weighing four and a half pounds, designed to be carried in a saddle holster. Two years later Colt began manufacturing more compact models, the Navy and Pocket revolvers, which could be tucked into a belt or concealed in a coat pocket. Wildly popular with the public, those were the guns that made the Colt brand famous. Hundreds of thousands were manufactured over the subsequent quarter century. Within months of their initial introduction, Los Angeles merchants were advertising the availability of "Colt's Army and Navy Pistols."

Revolvers were ubiquitous in Los Angeles by 1852 when Horace Bell arrived. "The patrons who came and went from the Bella Union bar during that time," he wrote, "were the most bandit, cut-throat looking set that the writer had ever sat his youthful eyes upon. Some were dressed in the gorgeous attire of the country, some half *ranchero*, half miner; others were dressed in the most modern style of tailorship; all, however, had slung to their rear the never-failing pair of *Colts*, generally with the accompaniment of the Bowie knife."

Some Angelenos had tried to prevent that. In the summer of 1850, at one of the first meetings of the Los Angeles common council, two members proposed a regulation prohibiting the carriage or discharge of firearms within city limits. This would have extended the life of the ordinance passed by the ayuntamiento before the conquest, which Marshal Purdy had tried to enforce but was ignored by virtually everyone else. Passing and enforcing a ban on firearms would have been a bold move, but not an unprecedented one. Several states adopted restrictions on firearms, and in later years a number of notable frontier towns—Dodge City, Tombstone, and Fort Worth among them—passed local ordinances banning handguns. But after considerable discussion, the council rejected the restriction. Enforcing the ordinance would have required hiring more deputy marshals or creating a real city police, which in turn would have necessitated an increase in fees and taxes on businessmen and property owners, something a majority of councilmen were loath to do. On several subsequent occasions the common council would again reject proposals for a city police force operating at taxpayer expense. As a result, as Benjamin Hayes put it, "the revolver seems to have been the law about this time."

THE ANNALS OF FRONTIER LOS ANGELES are crowded with instances in which Anglos of "the better class" resorted to guns to settle disputes. In September of 1852 William A. Cornwall, private secretary to Governor John Bigler, in Los Angeles on political business, assaulted newspaperman Andrew C. Russell after he published a column in the *Star* accusing Cornwall of corruption. Cornwall found

Russell standing at the crowded bar in the Bella Union. He came up from behind, a cocked Colt's Navy in one hand and a Bowie knife in the other. "Clear the way," he shouted. Russell spun around and Cornwall struck him in the face with the handle of his knife. "Defend yourself," he exclaimed. He raised the Colt but in his excitement discharged it prematurely, literally shooting himself in the foot. Russell ran for the door, simultaneously drawing a Colt Pocket revolver and firing wildly over his shoulder, miraculously hitting no one. Cornwall came after him, hopping and cursing. He caught Russell as he paused to reload in the middle of Main Street. The men clinched and fell, biting and kicking like two fighting dogs before being pulled apart. The county grand jury later indicted Cornwall for assault with intent to commit murder, but he had returned to Sacramento and was never brought to trial.

Brawls like these among prominent Anglos were common. Isaac S. K. Ogier, U.S. attorney and later U.S. district court judge for southern California, and Hilliard P. Dorsey, register of the Federal Land Office, both cultivated reputations as street fighters. One late evening the two got into a dispute during a boozy supper at the Montgomery House Hotel. Ogier tossed a bowl of hot soup in Dorsey's face, and with barely a hesitation Dorsey vaulted across the table and onto Ogier. "It was a genuine Georgia affair," reported the *Daily Alta California*, "bite, cut, and gouge." Dorsey suffered second-degree burns to his face, but left Ogier with an eye hanging from its socket and the tip of a nose that had to be reattached. Dorsey, wrote Horace Bell, was "an out-and-out man-of-war. He could wield a Bowie, was quick on the draw, struck square out from the shoulder, and could gouge out an eye or bite off a nose in such a style and manner as would excite the envy of the most fastidious backwoods fighter."

If Bell's description hints at admiration, that is because he was a true believer in the efficacy of violence. Born in 1830 in frontier southern Indiana, Bell had imbibed the aggressive values of his Scots-Irish father. Raised to be a fighter, he was ever eager to set things aright with fists or guns. During more than a half century in Los Angeles, Bell took part in dozens of street fights and bloody encounters. The first on record occurred on New Year's Day, 1854, when he confronted Horace Zebulon Wheeler, proprietor of a hardware store and brother of editor John Ozias Wheeler of the *Southern Californian*. In its account, the *Star* did not detail the nature of the dispute, but reported that Bell challenged Wheeler's manhood and shouted that "one of us must die." Wheeler got the upper hand, however, subjecting Bell to what the *Star* characterized as "a horse whipping." Bell refused to cry uncle, and when he came back for more, Wheeler drew a pistol and shot him in the shoulder. Fortunately it proved a minor wound, though a major injury to Bell's pride. Because Bell had started the fight, Wheeler was not charged. "One justice of the peace has told us that had the shot proved fatal," the *Star* reported, "he would have discharged Mr. Wheeler upon the ground of justified homicide." Self-defense was a very broad category, a cover for violence of all kinds.

THE CULT OF VIOLENCE drew disciples from all classes and ethnicities, although the ritual observances of the hoi polloi rarely garnered the rapt attention paid to the elite. The *Star* might devote a few lines to the everyday conflicts of ordinary people, but generally failed to give them extensive coverage. An exception to that rule was the attention lavished on a spectacular gunfight that took place on Calle de los Negros one Sunday morning during the spring of 1854. For the principals in this pathetic melodrama, the day began at the Montgomery House Hotel, on Main Street. Merchant clerk George Dyke arrived about eight, planning to have something to eat. But at the bar he found his friend Tom Smith, a tough character who had drifted into town several weeks before. "We got to drinking together," Dyke said, "taking two or three drinks apiece, and knocking around." At Smith's suggestion the two men left the Montgomery and walked uptown "to a whorehouse kept by three white women," a new addition to the pueblo's demimonde.

Shortly after they departed, gambler Frank Dana came in for

breakfast. He ate quickly. What's the rush, asked the manager. "I'm obliged to go over to Nigger Alley," said Dana. "I have a game going on and I must hurry." With his partner Levi Jackson, Dana operated a monte table at Moore & Alvarta's saloon. He was gone by the time Dyke and Smith returned from their visit to the brothel and resumed their stations at the bar, soon joined by Sterling Lester and Bill Foster, two more Americans of the vagabond class. "Let's go over to Nigger Alley," one of them suggested. Smith liked that idea. "Come on, Dyke," he said to his friend. The four men left the Montgomery and proceeded east down a muddy lane to Moore & Alvarta's, located in an old adobe owned by Antonio F. Coronel, at the southwest corner of Calle de los Negros.

Monte (or montebank), a card game brought back from Mexico by American troops, was the most popular form of losing money in a town as famous for its gambling as its gun fighting. In monte the players (called "punters") bet against the "banker" who operated the table and who by custom keep his entire stake or "bank" in plain view. After an initial shuffle of the deck, the banker drew one card from the top and another from the bottom, placing both face up on the table. This was the "layout." Punters then placed bets on whether the next card drawn would match the suit of either layout card. Once the bets were on the table, the banker turned the deck over to expose the bottom card. He paid one-to-one for pairs and swept up all losing bets. The three face cards were then discarded and the banker dealt another layout, continuing until the deck grew short, when he would reshuffle the cards and begin again. The game was simple, fast, and addictive, and Horace Bell was astounded at the quantity of money that changed hands. "Each table with its baize cover," he wrote, was "literally heaped with piles of $50 ingots, commonly called 'slugs.' Betting was high. You would frequently see a ranchero with an immense pile of gold in front of him, quietly and unconcernedly smoking his cigarrito and betting twenty slugs on the turn, the losing of which produced no perceptible discomposure of his grave countenance." Not everyone, however, took the losses with such equanimity.

It was a Sunday morning, but Moore & Alvarta's was crowded when the four men arrived from the Montgomery. Lester found his way to the bar while the other three sat down at the table where Levi Jackson was dealing. His partner Frank Dana stood behind him, monitoring the action. Tom Smith bet on several layouts, losing each time until he ran out of money. "Foster, lend me $50," he said to his friend, who ignored him. Over the previous several days Smith had lost a pile to Dana and Jackson, and he believed it was time for his luck to change. "Hand me $50!" he barked again, and Foster reluctantly dug into his pocket and tossed two $20 double eagles onto the table. Smith played them both on the next layout and lost again. Jackson began another deal, but Smith grabbed the first card and tore it in two. No one said a word. Smith was a notorious troublemaker, and no one wanted to be on his bad side. Jackson discarded the old deck, broke the seal of a new one, sorted the cards, shuffled, and began again. Suddenly Smith rose, leapt onto his chair, then mounted the table, simultaneously drawing his revolver. He kicked at Jackson's bank with his boots, scattering the coins and ingots. "Tom, don't do that," Jackson said calmly. Smith stopped, stared daggers at Jackson for a moment, then stepped down. Putting his pistol back in its scabbard, he left the table and walked toward the large double doors opening onto Calle de los Negros.

Frank Dana had not said a word. He too left the table and walked over to the bar, and noticing him out of the corner of his eye, Smith turned and approached, at the same time reaching beneath his coat and drawing a large Bowie knife. He waved it in Dana's face. "What do you look so white about?" he declared. Dana remained silent for a few moments, then responded. "Tom," he said, "what have you got against me?" According to shopkeeper Joe Cummings, who was standing next to them at the bar, Dana "spoke pretty spunky—pretty sharp—did not appear to be afraid." Tom Cavanaugh, a tailor who was also standing at the bar, did not catch the words but immediately understood the tone of the exchange. "There was going to be something more than words," he thought to himself, then turned and quickly left the establishment. "You are a damned little shit ass," Smith said to Dana, "and

I can whip you any way that men fight." Dana looked him straight in the face. "I suppose you can," he said, "you're big enough." That ended the verbal contretemps, with Smith the apparent victor. He put his knife away and turned heel on Dana.

Pedro Alvarta, one of the owners of the place, was tending bar. At the coroner's inquest he testified that he understood very little English, but enough to know that "shit ass" meant trouble, which was why he ducked behind the bar. As soon as Smith turned, Dana went for his revolver. Smith's friend Lester was standing off to the side, watching. "Tom," he shouted, "Dana's drawing," and simultaneously he pulled his own revolver. Smith wheeled as he too went for his gun. The three men fired at almost the same moment. "I could see the fire roll out of Dana's pistol," said Joe Cummings. His ball missed its mark, but Lester's did not. "I could see the coat and dust fly up on the right side of Dana's coat," said bricklayer William Winters. The ball plowed into Dana's chest and through one of his lungs. Smith's shot went wide and he continued firing wildly, a total of four rounds, wounding two bystanders seriously. The crowd rushed for the doors. Dana staggered into a back room, turned, and fired again, but he was reeling, and his shot wounded another bystander. Bleeding profusely, Dana stumbled out a side door.

Along with nearly everyone else in the saloon, Smith assumed that one of his shots had hit Dana. Lester knew different, but he wasn't saying. Smith stood surveying the room, the smoking revolver still in his right hand. He turned and walked toward the doors leading out to the alley, crowded with frightened men, then out onto the veranda, in a sort of euphoric daze. "I'm the best man who ever stood in leather," he crowed in a loud voice, then holstered his revolver. The ritual had concluded.

Meanwhile, Dana was staggering back toward Montgomery House, leaving behind a trail of blood. He collapsed at the muddy corner of Main Street and several pedestrians hurried over and lifted him up. "Tom Smith has killed me," he said. By the time a doctor arrived a few minutes later, Dana was indeed dead. The doctor also attended the three other victims, one wounded in the thigh, the other two in the buttocks. They all recovered. Sheriff James Barton was summoned, and he arrested Smith and Lester, whom he found wandering aimlessly near the Plaza. Smith, who claimed to have fired the fatal shot, was jailed. Lester, who said nothing about his role, was released. Before the truth emerged at the inquest, he had departed for parts unknown. Smith also avoided a reckoning. Before he could be brought to trial before Judge Hayes, he and three other prisoners overpowered the jailer and escaped into the night.

BENJAMIN HAYES FIRMLY BELIEVED that "better order and more perfect security" would be most lastingly achieved through the firm and fair application of the law by the courts. Yet his first year as district judge in 1853 offered little evidence in support of that proposition. By late November county authorities had recorded a total of fourteen homicides for the year. That was a considerable decline from the year before, but few of those cases came before Judge Hayes. Several were ruled justifiable homicides. Others failed to go to trial because of an absence of reliable evidence or the reluctance of witnesses to testify. In at least two cases the suspects were killed during their attempted apprehension. In others the perpetrators remained unknown. Hayes heard one case in which the self-defense defense resulted in swift acquittal. A final case remained to be heard, which Hayes scheduled for Thursday, December 8.

The day before that trial began Los Angeles suffered the fifteenth homicide of the year. Deputy city marshal Jack Whalen was killed by a Sonoreño named Gabriel Sanate, whom Whalen was attempting to arrest on an outstanding warrant for assault. Whalen, a veteran of the New York volunteers, was well-known and well-respected. "He was brave and reckless," read an account of the murder in the *Star*, "and has lost his life through a careless indifference to the desperate character of the man he arrested." Whalen's funeral took place the following day, and Hayes adjourned his court in respect. As was so often the case on such occasions, angry men gathered at the graveside. "There was much excitement," the *Star* reported, "and many threats were uttered against the whole mixed race," meaning the Mexicans. The murder had occurred in a tent camp on the north side, and there were plenty of bystanders, most of them Sonoreños, not one of whom had offered assistance to Whalen during the confrontation or information to Sheriff Barton after the fact. The Los Angeles Rangers mobilized and scoured the county in search of Sanate. The homes of many Californios were subjected to rough searches.

The trial of Ygnacio Herrera for the murder of Nestor Nartiago took place in this crisis atmosphere. Hayes was determined to proceed with deliberation and care, and he gave defense attorney Myron Norton wide latitude to call numerous witnesses who spoke to Herrera's good character. The defendant took the stand in his own defense, testifying that he and Nartiago had been friends but found themselves competing for the attention of the same woman. Nartiago started the fight, Herrera claimed, and he had drawn his knife only after being attacked. Plenty of men in frontier Los Angeles had been acquitted under similar circumstances, but not this time. After Norton rested his case, Hayes instructed the jury with a reading of common-law doctrine that was much stricter than the one he had applied earlier that year in the case of Jack Watson. To acquit, Hayes ruled, the jurors must find that Herrera had done everything possible to avoid the fight, resorting to deadly force only when his own life was in imminent peril. So instructed, the jury found Herrera guilty of murder, and Hayes sentenced him to death. It would be the first judicial execution to take place in southern California.

THE NEW YEAR OF 1854 opened with the Rangers still hunting for Gabriel Sanate. They covered all of southern California, from the Tehachapi Mountains in the north to Warner's Ranch in the south, "following the will-o'-the-wisp of some false alarm without any important result," according to Horace Bell, a Ranger himself.

Joseph Lancaster Brent wrote of taking part in the raid of an isolated adobe northeast of town. "We surrounded the house and rode down upon it at full speed," Brent wrote, but inside found only an ordinary Californio and his family, "who received us with black looks and scant courtesy."

The Rangers' inability to find their man made it all the more humiliating when, late on the evening of January 19, the hoodlum Sanate and several armed accomplices commandeered the recently opened American brothel on Bath Street, robbing both the women and their clientele of cash and jewelry before fleeing into the night. The gang moved on to the house of Martin Lelong, a Frenchman who lived in the midst of his vineyard with his young wife and their infant son. Awakened by the barking of his dogs, Lelong was still in his nightclothes when the gang burst into his house, demanding his money or his life. They bound him to a chair and took their time ransacking the place, taking money, clothing, and jewelry. And then, as Lelong watched in helpless horror, "they each proceeded to inflict the last injury upon him, by committing diabolical outrage upon his defenseless wife," María Josepha Alanis de Lelong.

Two days later Sheriff Barton published a notice in English and Spanish, offering a reward of $500 for the apprehension of Gabriel Sanate "*vivo o muerto*"—dead or alive. Hayes opposed posting the reward, arguing that it would provide more incentive for vigilantism. "I remonstrated with the Sheriff," he noted, but Barton went ahead anyway. Several days later a man drove up to the sheriff's office with a carreta piled with the bodies of Sanate and a member of his gang. Claiming the reward was Anastacio Moreno, a shopkeeper who had been unaccountably absent from the pueblo for several weeks. Sanate's gang had kidnapped and held him prisoner, he claimed. But finally, finding himself alone with the bandit chief and another gangster, he grabbed a sword and killed them both. "The death of these two villains caused universal joy to our citizens," reported the *Star*, and Moreno was celebrated as a hero. But two weeks later he was arrested after attempting to sell some of the loot stolen from Martin Lelong.

Lelong then identified Moreno as one of the men who robbed him, but added that he had not participated in the rape of Doña Josepha, a fact that saved Moreno's life. He made a full confession, admitting he had been a member of the gang and murdered his companions to collect the reward. Tried and convicted in district court, he was sentenced to fifteen years in state prison.

On February 13, the day designated for Ygnacio Herrera's execution, Sheriff Barton and Undersheriff Osburn conducted themselves with appropriate solemnity and propriety. A scaffold was erected in the yard behind the jail, rather than atop the hill, where the vigilante executions had taken place. Fearful of a demonstration, Barton deployed an armed detachment of Rangers. The crowd was large but orderly. At the appointed hour Barton and Osburn emerged from the jail with the condemned man, then mounted the scaffold, accompanied by Father Anacleto. Herrera was allowed to make a short statement. "To me it has fallen to be the first man executed by the district court of this county," he said. "I have been convicted as a murderer, but God, in whose presence I will be very soon, knows that I have not murdered, but only killed to defend my own life." As a Mexican citizen and a former soldier, he believed he deserved a better fate than this. Herrera's last words amounted to a stinging rebuke to Judge Hayes. "There was no justice."

Although the first legal execution in Los Angeles proceeded without complications, it failed to be the affirmation of the law for which Hayes had hoped. The opera buffa of the Moreno episode made the authorities look foolish, and the strict definition of self-defense Hayes applied in Herrera's case struck many Californios as discriminatory. The day following the execution Hayes awoke in a sour mood. It was his thirty-ninth birthday. That evening Emily would make him a party, attended by his sisters and a small circle of friends. There would be singing and laughter and memories of home, back in the states. But Hayes would not be able to get Ygnacio Herrera off his mind. That morning, from the front door of their adobe on the slope of Gallows Hill, he and Emily watched as several hundred mourners exited the Plaza church and slowly ascended Eternity Street to the mournful strains of a martial band, following Herrera's body on its journey to the *campo santo*, at the foot of the rolling hills on the north side of town.

· CHAPTER 19 ·

CITY OF DEMONS

IN THE SUMMER OF 1854 a new newspaper, the *Southern Californian*, began publication in Los Angeles. Determined to distinguish his weekly from the *Star*, editor William Butts took up the pueblo's most pressing issue, the problem of violence. He reported speaking to prospective settlers who expressed delight with the climate and excitement at the economic prospects, but declined to relocate for fear of their personal safety. "This place will not do for me," Butts quoted one of them. "There is no security here—I dare not venture out after the dark of night has set in." Peaceable men were repelled by the lawlessness and disorder, while desperadoes were attracted. "Americans profess to be a Christian people," Butts wrote, but those who came to Los Angeles seemed to have "left their precepts at home." He lamented that the principal contribution of the local culture was the introduction of "ever more formidable weapons of death and destruction."

Lethal violence in Los Angeles took a turn for the worse in 1854. During the previous year fifteen homicides were recorded for Los Angeles County, a large number for such a sparsely settled region but a considerable decline from the twenty-four of 1852. In 1854, however, the pace picked up significantly, and on September 17, with the death of farmer James Ellington at the hands of the Alvitre brothers, the toll for the year reached sixteen, exceeding the total of the year before. By the end of November the list of victims had grown to a record high of twenty-seven, including twelve Anglos, twice the number killed the preceding year. The October 13 murder of Pinckney Clifford by David Brown focused public attention on violence within the Anglo community. Angelenos were "appalled at the frequent and enormous crimes constantly perpetrated in our midst," wrote James S. Waite, who had taken over as editor of the *Star.* "All the slumbering energies of the people are being aroused to the intensest state of excitement."

Following Brown's arrest, Stephen Clark Foster, mayor of Los Angeles, persuaded an incipient lynch mob to allow the legally constituted justice system "one more chance." But less than a month later vigilantism threatened again in response to a murder in the Monte, the American settler community on the upper San Gabriel River. Ownership of the area—formerly part of the Mission San Gabriel estate—was in dispute. The lack of clear title encouraged settlers from Missouri, Arkansas, and Texas to stake out squatter's claims, but also contributed to rampant conflict over boundaries. Samuel Knox, a recent arrival in the community, was appalled. "What a selfish creature man is," he declared. "I have never seen so much of it as since I came to this place. There are scarcely any two men that pull the same way, and some there are who think they know it all, and when they have their mind made up it would seem that all creation could not change it."

On November 8, during a dispute such as Knox described, William B. Lee shot and killed his neighbor Frederick Leatherman. Hearing the report of her husband's double-barreled shotgun, Lee's wife, Martha Johnson, came running from the house. "What have you done," she cried, "what have you done?" Lee attempted to calm her. "Hush, honey," he said. "I did not shoot him to kill, I only shot him in the legs." But the load of buckshot had torn into Leatherman's belly, and he suffered a long, painful death. After Sheriff Barton arrested Lee, he was taken before Judge Hayes for examination, as an angry crowd milled about outside. Hayes ordered the accused jailed without

bond while the grand jury considered his case. Lee "seems very indifferent as to result," observed the Reverend James Woods, who was
present in the courtroom. He "probably expects to be acquitted."

The Reverend Woods, a Presbyterian missionary, was attempting to organize the first Protestant congregation in Los Angeles. He
had come from the mining supply town of Stockton in California's
Central Valley, where he had witnessed his share of frontier violence.
But the turmoil in Los Angeles shocked him nonetheless. "This is a
rough country, even for California," he wrote in his journal. "Today
I saw a young man, apparently a farmer, about leaving town. On his
belt, conspicuous from having on no coat or vest, hung a revolver and
bowie knife, and in his hand he carried a double barrel gun. Most of
the people go armed for safety, some for fear, and some for fashion."
Editor James Waite of the *Star*, addressed himself to "newcomers" like
Woods, who couldn't understand why everyone carried arms. "Our
roads are safe enough, if men will go armed and be prudent as to their
associates," wrote Waite, and he advised all residents to carry firearms
and keep a watchful eye. Woods found that argument appalling. Surely
the causes of violence could not be remedied by a resort to arms. "The
name of this city in Spanish is the City of Angels," he wrote, "but with
much more truth might it be called at present the City of Demons."

JOHN OZIAS WHEELER replaced William Butts as editor of the
Southern Californian in the fall of 1854, but he continued his predecessor's campaign against violence. Wheeler, who would soon declare
himself a Republican, announced his support of a municipal firearms
ban, the measure the common council had rejected four years before.
"We cannot but condemn in the strongest terms," Wheeler wrote,
"the practice of daily packing about the streets of our city a *park of
artillery*." Young men stalked the town like the hero of Donnybrook
Fair—a character in a popular ballad of the day—who deliberately
let his coattails drag on the ground in the hope that some fool would
trample them, giving him an excuse to thrash the man. "How often

has it been ours to witness the melancholy results of this practice in our city?" wrote Wheeler. "How often has what otherwise would have been a trifling dispute ended in a bloody affray?"

Despite his advocacy of a weapons ban, Wheeler was a champion of popular justice. He rode with the Los Angeles Rangers and served proudly on the vigilance committee. When the legal justice system failed, Wheeler argued, the people had the right, indeed the duty, to administer justice in their own rough way, precisely the same argument made by Victor Prudon in 1836. The people—Juan Bautista Alvarado's sleeping lion—must wake up and take charge. "Is it not incumbent upon us to be up and doing," asked Wheeler, "to arm ourselves *en mass* for individual and general protection?" He endorsed a proposal made by Captain Alexander W. Hope of the Rangers to expand their mission, giving them the authority to arrest troublemakers.

When that plan came to naught for lack of volunteers, a number of Angelenos once again petitioned the common council for the organization of a regular police force paid from the public treasury. The *Star* published a series of opinion pieces supporting that proposal, including two unsigned columns contributed by Judge Benjamin Hayes. "We do not agree with the few who are in favor of what is called a 'Vigilance Committee,' nor with those who insist upon something they style a 'Voluntary Police,'" Hayes wrote. "Experience has shown that it is impossible to subject them to responsibility." That was precisely the problem with the Rangers. The plague of violence in Los Angeles would not end, Hayes argued, until the council took positive action. But when the proposal came before the councilmen the following week it was tabled, and Hayes responded with a scathing anonymous commentary. The council declined to act, he believed, because of the opposition of property owners who wished to avoid higher taxes. "We hold that *life* is more precious than *property*," Hayes declared. "Let the council consider the happiness of the many—not yield to the selfishness of the few."

Editor James Waite of the *Star* agreed. "Lynch law will not help," he argued. "Lynch law has not improved San Francisco nor the mines, yet it has been tried there over and over again. Crime of the blackest dye is rampant as ever. Our true remedy is in electing faithful, industrious and vigilant officers." He celebrated the good sense Angelenos had shown in endorsing Mayor Foster's appeal for legally constituted authority. "It is but another evidence that our citizens are a law-abiding people," he wrote. "We believe one judicial execution of more value than ten executions effected by the people outside of the law." Waite remained confident that justice could be secured through legal process. "Our only hope is the strong arm of the law."

In the *Southern Californian,* Wheeler was more begrudging, welcoming the decision to try Brown in district court but also praising the vigilante impulse "to no longer wait for the tardy, tricky operations of the law—which had too often and too long robbed justice of her dues, by setting villains afloat in the midst of our people." The people, he wrote, would not allow quibbling lawyers, lax judges, or corrupt juries to frustrate the ends of justice. "Should Brown be released from the charge by any neglect of the proper authorities," he warned, "we would not vouch for the consequences."

On November 23, the day before the opening of Felipe Alvitre's trial, Wheeler published a letter from a pseudonymous correspondent. "We are at a terrible crisis," it began. "Murder and outrage have so long held sway in our midst that we are fast becoming a hissing and a byword." Violent criminals went unpunished in Los Angeles because of the inefficiency and corruption of the justice system. "Are criminals to be punished by our constituted courts, or are we to form ourselves into one good *Vigilance Committee,* and Judge Lynch to visit every crime with prompt and condign punishment?" The writer sincerely hoped Judge Hayes's court would secure justice. But, he cautioned, "if the time for action should come, let the merchant leave his ledger, the mechanic his shop, the farmer his plough, and come up to work." The letter concluded with an extravagant peroration.

> By the bones of the traveler bleaching on our plains; by the
> cry of the widow and the fatherless, as the bloody corpse of

a husband and father is brought before them; by the young man cut down in the morning of his days and hurried to the presence of his God; by the young mother and her unborn babe, pierced by the bullet of the midnight assassin; by all the holy ties that blend mankind together, thus rudely severed by the red hand of *Murder*; by the outraged feelings of the community, and the violated laws of the land; by our love to those nearest and dearest, *let us be ready when the time comes to act.*

FELIPE ALVITRE AND DAVID BROWN were found guilty by juries of their peers and sentenced to death by Judge Hayes. Both trials epitomized the orderly working of the American justice system, with carefully selected juries, strong representation for both the prosecution and the defense, a calm and rational presentation of evidence, and the examination and cross-examination of witnesses.

With those proceedings concluded, Hayes took up the case of farmer William B. Lee, charged with the first-degree murder of Frederick Leatherman. It began with defense attorney Joseph Lancaster Brent's motion for a change of venue, following the lead of Jonathan R. Scott, who had made the same motion during his defense of David Brown. Sensational coverage in the local press, Brent argued, made it impossible to seat a jury untainted by prejudice. Judge Hayes and attorney Brent had been friends and associates since their arrival in Los Angeles four years before. Both were natives of Baltimore, practicing Catholics, and committed Democrats. But when Hayes denied Brent's motion—as he was bound to do, having previously denied Scott's—their friendship came to an abrupt end. By virtue of his sterling credentials in the Californio community and the votes he could muster there, Brent had become the political boss of Los Angeles Democrats. Over the next several years he would do what he could to undercut Hayes's authority.

The trial proceeded with the defense taking exception to Hayes's ruling, and on December 11 the jury returned a verdict of guilty. Hayes pronounced judgment the following day, sentencing Lee to death and setting his execution for February, a month after the scheduled hanging of Alvitre and Brown.

These three murder trials, James Waite wrote in the *Star,* had "done more toward establishing the supremacy of the law and inspiring the confidence of this community than all the precedents which can be found recorded on the criminal docket of this county since it has been organized." In the rival *Southern Californian,* John Wheeler predicted the verdicts would have "the desired effect upon this community in deterring, by the certainty of punishment, the commission of crime, creating a feeling of security in life and property, restoring and maintaining order and quietness, and redeeming our escutcheon from the blighting pall which has heretofore enshrouded it."

That was setting too high a standard. But in regard to murder, at least, the month of December exceeded Wheeler's hopes. Heavy rain had blanketed the region during the trials, but once the verdicts were rendered the skies cleared, the days turned warmer, and Angelenos began the celebration of the approaching holidays with the usual round of bullfights, fandangos, and nightly performances of *los pastores*—groups of children, portraying the shepherds and the wise men, making the rounds of the townhouses near the Plaza, singing Christmas hymns and begging for sweets. "Peace and quietness reign on all hands," Wheeler noted. "No single disturbance has come to our knowledge during the past few weeks, and we believe that the future will be as bright as the past has been mournful."

The calm ended abruptly in early January with another violent affray in the Monte that claimed the lives of two prominent American settlers. The King and Johnson clans had been feuding for some time over what John Wheeler in the *Southern Californian* described as "an old grudge," almost certainly a dispute over land. The Johnsons had come from Kentucky in early 1852 and settled on the west bank of the upper San Gabriel River. Some weeks later they were followed by the Kings of Arkansas. Patriarch Samuel King purchased land from a ranchero who claimed title, then surveyed a site for a town he called Lexington. King's speculation "enjoyed the good will of all," wrote Wheeler, "with the exception of a few isolated persons, whose enmity were manifested towards him during the past two or three years in consequence of his steadfast adherence to the laws of *meum and tuum*." Wheeler was not an impartial observer, for he had invested in King's real estate venture. King's challengers included the Johnsons, who believed they had established squatter's rights to the location prior to King claiming it for himself.

Prominent among King's enemies was Micajah Johnson, a man with a reputation for violence as well as boorish behavior with women. Josiah Hart was one of several men who complained that Johnson had "interfered" with their wives. Hart confronted Johnson but he reacted aggressively, pulling his six-shooter from its scabbard and spinning the cylinder with his thumb. Hart got the message. He went home, armed himself with a double-barreled shotgun, and went looking for Johnson. He found him at a local tavern, and without so much as a word of warning, he let loose with a load of buckshot. Hart defended his conduct before a local justice of the peace. "I believed that he would have crawled up on me through the wild mustard and killed me privately," he said, "and I thought I might as well die in defense of my life." Fortunately for both men, Hart's shot went wide. Samuel King stood bond for him, and Hart was released pending action by the grand jury, which declined to indict him, despite the premeditated nature of his attack.

On Sunday morning, January 7, 1855, Johnson was sitting with a small group of men at a local tavern when Samuel Houston King, the youngest of Samuel King's sons, walked in. Johnson began taunting him, denouncing his father and the entire King clan in vile and obscene language. The young man refused to take the bait and quickly left, candidly declaring as he exited the tavern that "he did not consider himself man enough for Johnson," but adding that "he would find one who would." A short time later, as Johnson was leaving, he saw Samuel King approaching on horseback with his three sons—not only the youngest, Houston, but his older brothers, Francis Marion and Andrew Jackson King, as well—all strapping young men. Johnson put spurs to his horse and took off, extending his middle finger at the Kings in a vulgar gesture of contempt. Not a man to be denied, the elder King pulled a pistol and fired a round in Johnson's direction, missing his mark but spooking the horse, which reared and threw Johnson to the ground.

He picked himself up and scrambled into a nearby house, positioned himself at a window, and taking deliberate aim with his six-shooter put a ball through the left side of Samuel King's chest. The elder King calmly dismounted and collapsed onto the ground. "Boys, he has killed me!" he exclaimed to his sons. "Now, if you have any of my blood in your veins you will not let him live." The three brothers rushed the house, braving Johnson's fire and dragged him out, beating and kicking him mercilessly. Johnson struggled free, but the Kings pulled their revolvers and shot him repeatedly as he writhed on the ground. Johnson suffered four gunshot wounds, including one in the forehead that was instantly fatal. Samuel King, on the other hand, suffered for two days before dying. The King brothers were given leave to attend their father's bedside, then they voluntarily surrendered to Sheriff Barton and were arraigned before Judge Hayes, who released them on bond. "Much excitement and feeling was manifested in their favor," Wheeler wrote in the *Southern Californian*, "their house being guarded by some fifty men during the night, there being some fear that Johnson's friends might attempt to revenge his death." But the King brothers had plenty of supporters, and the grand jury declined to indict them.

"We had hoped that a new and brighter era had ushered itself upon us," wrote Wheeler, "but the late tragedy in the Monte shows the fallacy of our too eager expectations." Micajah Johnson, it turned out, was the father-in-law of convicted murderer William B. Lee, a fact that amplified the shock. The Reverend Woods rode out to the Monte and sat with Lee's pregnant wife. "Poor woman," he wrote, "her husband about to be hung, her father shot dead on the spot, and she about to be confined. May the Lord have mercy on her." These deadly conflicts all originated in the struggle over land. "Land is a natural element that no man can live without," declared prominent Monte resident Daniel Sexton in a letter to the *Star*. "I have not words to express my contempt of them who will not defend their right to it. The greatest fertilizer that ever was sown broadcast over the land is the blood of those that try to suppress its cultivation."

Ten days later, in a vineyard near the river, the corpse of an unidentified man was discovered, his head crushed with heavy stones and his body stripped of all but his socks. Nothing had changed. Tranquil December was forgotten as Angelenos began the new year of 1855, which would be the most violent year yet for Los Angeles County. Public fear found expression in a smoldering rage that threatened to rise to the point of ignition.

ALVITRE, BROWN, AND LEE sat in the iron cages installed in the new county jail, their arms and legs shackled in irons. The Reverend Woods, who visited frequently to minister to the inmates, saw them there, "chained up like wild beasts." Woods kept his distance from Alvitre, a "low Mexican" as well as a "Catholick, without the knowledge of God," but he requested permission to minister to Brown and Lee. Brown refused, saying he would sooner invite a grizzly into his cell, but Lee was amenable. Woods flattered himself that their conversations might have an indirect effect on Brown in the adjoining cell. Yet as the fateful day of execution approached, the condemned man showed no sign of softening. One afternoon Woods spent an hour praying aloud with Lee. "Brown was asleep, or pretended to be," he lamented. "Poor fellow, he does not believe in a future."

More likely, he was calculating his chances for survival. Three days before, on January 4, a stay of execution for Brown, signed by Chief Justice Hugh C. Murray of the California Supreme Court, had arrived on the steamer from San Francisco. Several days later the weekly mail brought a stay for Lee. The attorneys for all three convicted men had filed appeals and requested stays from the state's highest court, but nothing arrived for Alvitre. Angelenos had no way of knowing it, but Chief Justice Murray had ordered the stay of all three executions. Alvitre's papers, however, got delayed in transit. They would arrive, but too late.

During the days and hours remaining before Alvitre's scheduled execution on Friday, January 12, Los Angeles experienced the greatest public turmoil since the American conquest. The absence of a stay for Alvitre, wrote Judge Hayes, "inflamed the native Californian and Mexican portion of the population." According to Horace Bell, Californios "raised a public clamor, claiming that when a Mexican was convicted of crime he was always promptly punished, but that an American in like circumstances always escaped." Bell had to agree with them.

Francisco P. Ramírez, hired by James Waite to edit *La Estrella*, the Spanish-language section of the *Star*, provided a Californio perspective on the crisis. Ramírez, only seventeen, was the son of an established Angeleno family of modest means. His mother, Petra Ávila de Ramírez, was the daughter of wealthy ranchero Francisco Ávila. His father, Juan Ramírez, of more humble background, made a living growing grapes and selling them to his neighbor Luis Vignes, Francisco's godfather. The boy, known as Pancho, received no formal schooling but was exceptionally bright. In addition to his native Spanish he learned French from his godfather and English from the Americans. An organic intellectual, self-educated but well-read in the classics, Ramírez responded thoughtfully to the stirrings of the world around him. At fourteen he went to work as a compositor at the *Star*, assisting Manuel Clemente Rojo, who assumed a role as the young man's intellectual mentor. In 1852 Ramírez left Los Angeles to train for a career in journalism, studying with Jesuit teachers in San José and apprenticing for a Catholic newspaper in San Francisco before taking a job as a reporter for a paper in the mining town of Marysville. In the fall of 1854 he returned to Los Angeles to revive *La Estrella*, dormant since Rojo's departure the year before. Ramírez launched a lengthy career in journalism and politics in frontier Los Angeles with his coverage of the public clamor over Alvitre and Brown.

Ramírez reviewed the history of Alvitre's case. When the man was first arrested, he wrote, Californios considered him a vicious criminal who had "committed crimes unworthy of a rational man." Californios captured him, and Californios made up half the jury that convicted him. But with the stays for Brown and Lee the sentiment of the community shifted. According to Ramírez, Alvitre had become a symbol of their discontent, attracting the sympathy "of the great mass of the Hispanic population." Why no stay for the Californio? Ramírez thought it might be explained by the politics of Chief Justice Murray, a public advocate of white supremacy who had authored judicial opinions upholding and extending the legal restrictions on the rights of people of color. This looked like more of the same. "When you start playing that way," Ramírez wrote, "better that the people take the law into their own hands, using lynch law to secure their rights and achieve their goals." Writing in the English-language section of the *Star*, James Waite agreed with much of what his young assistant editor wrote. But he parted company on the question of extralegal action. Better that both executions be postponed, Waite argued. In any event, he would not condone lynch law.

The exchange between the editors of the *Star* was temperate in tone and reasoned in argument. But editor John Wheeler of the *Southern Californian* employed the rhetoric of incitement. Were Angelenos "ready to take the life of the groveling, ignorant, half-civilized Alvitre, and at the same time fear the responsibility of carrying out their own verdict upon an individual who, to our own disgrace, claims a kindred tongue and nation with us?" If that was the case, wrote Wheeler, "better that we henceforth give ourselves over to utter contempt, and nevermore prate of law, order, or justice." The time had come to act. Lynch law should be employed in the service of racial justice. "Citizens of Los Angeles, it is for you to say whether this gross and outrageous partiality shall be allowed; whether you will permit so flagrant and glaring an evidence of the omnipotence of birth and conditions to operate in widening still further the breach that already exists between our native and foreign population, so prolific of future disaster to this community, which we may all live to regret—perhaps in blood and tears."

On the evening before the scheduled execution a mass meeting of citizens to consider what should be done convened at the Montgomery House Hotel. Several hundred men, a majority of them Californios, filled the dining hall and overflowed onto Main Street. Numerous individuals spoke their minds, but the most important was Mayor Stephen Clark Foster, who "unequivocally proclaimed himself in favor of hanging Alvitre and Brown together," and reaffirmed his pledge that "if justice was not done, he would resign his office and assist the people in carrying out the wishes of the public." Adopting a resolution to that effect, the meeting chose a committee of two Anglos and a Californio to present it to Sheriff Barton. They found him at his office around ten that night. Barton listened respectfully but told them he was determined to carry out the law. The committee returned to the Montgomery, where they joined the others in making plans for an assault on the jail the following day.

FRIDAY, JANUARY 12, 1855, was one of those mild, picture-perfect winter days for which Los Angeles is famous. Following the precedent set at the Herrera execution, Sheriff Barton ordered a scaffold erected in the yard behind the jail. The view from the street was blocked by a tall plank fence, but spectators mounted the slope of Pound Cake Hill, which overlooked Spring Street. All the town's shops and businesses closed for the occasion, and although the execution was scheduled for three in the afternoon, by midmorning hundreds of men, women, and children were swarming the hillside. On the grass, luxuriant from the rains of early December, families spread blankets and opened picnic baskets. From the western heights they commanded a majestic view of the surrounding landscape. The glistening Pacific to the south, the snow-capped San Gabriels to the northeast, and due east the willows and sycamores that marked the course of the Los Angeles River, as it rounded the narrows and flowed south, carrying snowmelt from mountain to ocean and providing irrigation for the city's vineyards and orchards. In the foreground, spectators had an unobstructed view of the jail yard and the gallows.

The previous day Sheriff Barton had issued a call for volunteers to join him at the jail to assist in upholding the rule of law, but only about a dozen armed men showed up. The Rangers were notably absent. At noon, with the crowd continuing to swell in size, the committee met once again with Barton. "Extensive and determined preparations are being made," they told him. The Rangers had an armory where they stored rifles, ammunition, and several artillery pieces, which Barton had taken the precaution of having spiked. But the committee ordered the armory seized and the guns drilled out. Friends urged Barton to compromise in order to avoid "the effusion of blood," but he remained intransigent, insisting he would stand by his oath to uphold the law. What was most feared, according to Francisco Ramírez, was a violent confrontation along ethnic lines, Californios battling Anglos. A rumor circulated that a group of *hijo del país* had stockpiled dozens of loaded cylinders they could snap into their revolvers in case of an extended gun battle. As the appointed hour approached, angry and armed militants filled the streets surrounding the jail.

Shortly before three the heavy iron door to the jail opened, and Barton and his undersheriff William Osburn emerged with Alvitre between them, his arms bound behind his back. They were surrounded by an armed volunteer guard. Ramírez was standing near the gallows. "Alvitre was just a boy, of good appearance," he observed. "It is a pity that one so young should have drenched his hands in the blood of his victims." Barton and Alvitre climbed the scaffold, accompanied by Father Lestrade of Plaza church, chanting the last rites. Given the opportunity to make a statement, Alvitre spoke a few words in Spanish. No one outside the jail yard could hear him, but Ramírez reported that he asked forgiveness from all he had injured. When he finished, Barton adjusted the rope around his neck and pulled a canvas sack over his head. Alvitre did not so much as flinch. Barton stepped back and released the trap.

Alvitre dropped. But the noose slipped and he crashed to the ground. A low moan rose from the crowd. A few individuals cried out. "*¡Arriba, arriba!*" Get him up! Rescue him! A few stones were thrown from the hillside. Frightened deputies cocked and presented their rifles, fearing a rush to the gate of the yard. But it did not happen. The crowd seemed frozen in place, shocked by what they had seen. Alvitre, suffering from acute shock, "half-dead" in the words of one account, was dragged back up the scaffold by Osburn and Deputy Charles E. Hale. He was steadied, the noose tightened and placed around his neck, then the trap released again. This time the knot held, and the hard drop snapped Alvitre's neck. "In a moment," Ramírez wrote, "he was launched into eternity." The crowd watched the entire spectacle in awed silence.

The body remained suspended for some minutes before being cut down and taken back inside the jail. Only then did the crowd awake to the realization that the official events of the day had concluded. The tension built as men milled about the streets surrounding the jail yard. They required a leader to focus their energy. A call went out for Mayor Foster, and he came forward, climbed atop a barrel, and addressed the crowd in Spanish. He immediately identified himself with the *hijos del país*. "Señores," he began, "being what might be called a Californio, my sympathies are with you." Foster was married to a daughter of the country, and he had seved as their alcalde.

> When Brown committed his murder during the days when crime eclipsed the flame of justice, the citizens of this town came together to punish him. Everyone wanted to execute him immediately, but I opposed such violence, declaring we should allow the law to fulfill its duty. We have all seen how Alvitre and Brown were tried and sentenced by the same judge to suffer the same penalty of death on the same day, thus uniting their destinies. We now see, my fellow citizens, that

this will not happen, blocked by order of the Supreme Court to suspend Brown's execution. This is an injustice, Señores, and I, who have given my word, feel the infringement of the law more than anyone else.

He had officially tendered his resignation as mayor, Foster told them, and was ready to lead them in hanging Brown if that was what they wanted. The time had come for the people to make their decision. Would they allow the legal process to continue? Would they allow Brown to live so the Supreme Court could hear his appeal? Or would they take justice into their own hands and hang him now? The crowd roared its response. "¡*Ahorcar!*" Hang him! Foster waited for the shouting to die down. "And now," he said, "there is nothing to do but bring Brown out and hang him. And I will die with all of you."

As his closing words suggested, Foster had every expectation that what would follow was an armed confrontation with Sheriff Barton and his deputies. But as a group of men began to batter the outer gate with heavy timbers, neither fire nor shouts of warning issued from inside the jail. Men poured into the yard and attacked the jailhouse door. Still no response from inside. Encouraged, other men came forward with axes and crowbars. It took time and effort, but the heavy iron door was finally forced open. The most daring men entered and soon their shouts could be heard. Sheriff Barton and his men had abandoned the building, leaving by an unseen exit and taking refuge in the courthouse, leaving Brown to his fate. "Words fail to describe the demeanor then of that mass of eager, angry men," wrote Benjamin Hayes, who witnessed the entire episode from the hillside. Ramírez, inside the jail yard, compared the mob to a raging river.

Brown had to be freed from his shackles by a blacksmith, and it was well after four in the afternoon by the time the crowd finally dragged him from the jail, out of the yard and across Spring Street to the gate of a corral directly opposite the sheriff's office. A rope was tossed over the crossbeam and Brown, bound hand and foot, was lifted to a standing position on a chair with the noose around his neck. Pale and trembling, he looked out at the tumultuous mob and somehow regained his composure. "He evinced the utmost coolness," reported the *Southern Californian*, "recognizing and speaking to his acquaintances in the crowd." He had no memory of killing Pinckney Clifford, Brown said, "but if I did, I am ready to give my life in retribution." His only objection, he declared, was to being strung up by a "lot of Greasers," and he requested some American step forward to do the job. According to the *Star*, none did. A blindfold was tied over Brown's eyes, and as he stood there, swaying slightly from side to side, the crowd fell silent. Someone tugged at the chair, and feeling the movement Brown jumped off on his own volition, swinging in a wide arc, his body violently convulsing in a macabre dance as he slowly strangled to death.

In the gathering twilight of the January afternoon, the spectators drifted away as family and friends attended to the remains of the executed men. Their destinies had indeed been bound together, if only at the end. The next morning they made their final, separate journeys. Friends loaded David Brown's coffin on a carreta and hauled it up *cañada de los muertos* at the backside of Gallows Hill to the Protestant graveyard at the summit. Meanwhile, at the Plaza church, Father Anacleto celebrated a requiem mass for Felipe Alvitre. Then the body, rolled in a shroud and laid on a wide plank, was carried up Eternity Street to the *campo santo*.

"THUS ENDED THIS FEARFUL TRAGEDY," wrote editor James Waite. "God grant that our citizens never witness the like again." Waite's was one of the few critical voices. John Wheeler's reaction in the *Southern Californian* was more typical. "The omnipotence of justice has been vindicated in this city. We hope that hereafter its solemn and impressive lessons may have their effect in convincing the evil disposed that there is a power greater than all law, vested in the unity and purpose of an entire people." Francisco Ramírez likewise celebrated the outcome. Californios, he wrote, "wished to see the law applied equally between Spanish and Americans, and it does not require great perception to understand their just reasons." They had acted on principle. The episode, Ramírez thought, laid down a marker. "This was the only occasion in which the people"—by which he meant the Spanish-speaking majority—"have demonstrated their supremacy, and it will live long in the annals of Los Angeles."

When the mob broke into the jail, while the blacksmith removed Brown's shackles, convicted murderer William B. Lee lay cowering in the adjoining cell, terrified that he too would be seized and hanged. After Brown was dragged away, Lee heard the pulsing excitement of the crowd outside. He survived the episode, but remained in a state of fevered and anxious apprehension for the next several months, awaiting the ruling of the Supreme Court on his motion for a new trial. In July 1855, in an opinion written by Chief Justice Murray, the court remanded his case back to district court, ruling that Judge Hayes had erred in not granting attorney Joseph Lancaster Brent's motion for a change of venue. Public prejudice in Los Angeles had made a fair trial impossible, Murray argued. "No man should be put upon his trial in a community thus excited. It would be a judicial murder to affirm a judgment thus rendered, when the reason of the people of a whole county was so clouded with passion and prejudice as to prevent mercy, and deny justice."

Hayes granted the change of venue at the next term of his court and transferred Lee's case to the jurisdiction of Santa Barbara. But when he came to trial there in December 1855, the uninformed and uninterested county prosecutor failed to summon the state's witnesses, and in the absence of direct testimony the charges against Lee were dismissed and he was released. "Lee has returned to his family at the Monte," reported the *Star*. "No one, we believe, regrets his acquittal. His confinement for more than a year in our jail, among vile criminals, and in a loathsome atmosphere, has debilitated his system to such a degree that he will probably never recover. His punishment has already been very severe, and the success of his counsel in freeing him from prison and from merited death will, we hope, make him a wiser and better man." David Brown's appeal had been the model for Lee's.

Had Brown's life been spared, he too would have been the beneficiary of Justice Murray's logic. The lesson was not lost on Angelenos. They had looked for a turning point—and they got one. But rather than strengthening the legally constituted system of justice, it broadened the power and appeal of lynch law. The calamitous consequences of this turn would become apparent all too soon.

· CHAPTER 20 ·

VINDICTA PÚBLICA

THE MONTE, the American community on the east bank of the San Gabriel River, was the fastest-growing settlement in Los Angeles County during the 1850s. "Within four or five years past," a visitor reported in 1855, "it has rapidly filled up with American families, almost exclusively from the extreme South and West of the Atlantic States." William and Ezekiel Rubottom came from the town of Spadra on the bluffs of the Arkansas River. "Uncle Billy," as the elder brother was universally known, opened an inn that became locally famous for "plain country fare, well cooked, and plenty of it." He planted the grounds of his place with seeds, slips, and rooted scions brought from home and took pride in conducting tours of the property. One admiring guest compiled a list of the exotics he found growing there. "Red and slippery elm, ash, black mulberry, Chickasaw plum, black walnut and chestnut, and blackberry vines, the roots of which first drew their sustenance from Missouri and Arkansas soil, all testify to the pains the old man has taken to renew the surroundings of his youth." Arkansas on the banks of the Río San Gabriel.

The settlers of the Monte grazed their cattle and horses on the open range of the San Gabriel Valley. When rustlers helped themselves to the livestock, the settlers responded with traditions of order and justice also imported from the South. They were experienced in the methods and means of vigilantism. So when, in the spring of 1855, a turncoat rustler provided a justice of the peace in the Monte with information regarding the whereabouts of his compatriots, instead of turning the matter over to the county sheriff, the justice alerted his friends and neighbors, who formed a vigilante posse. Early one morning they attacked the gang's hideout deep in the mountains, capturing four men and bringing them back. After harsh interrogation—including the torture of one prisoner who had suffered a serious wound in the affray—the men confessed. They were part of a "large organized band" of three hundred men, one of them boasted, led by a Texan claiming to be the brother of David Brown, whose lynching he vowed to avenge. The braggadocio infuriated the Monte Boys, and they decided to hang the rustlers themselves.

The prisoners were placed in a carreta, hands bound behind their backs and nooses around their necks, and driven to the base of a large tree in Willow Grove, a central gathering spot for the community. A crowd assembled, but a number of residents objected to the proceeding, arguing that the rustlers should be turned over to the proper authorities. The prisoners were locked in a shed for safe keeping until the issue was resolved. But later that evening a group of masked men overwhelmed the guard and announced to the captives that the time had come for them "to say their prayers." Two were selected to go first. It was a moonless night, and in the darkness both men slipped their bonds and escaped. While a number of vigilantes scoured the countryside in search of the fugitives, the rest went back for the other two. The wounded man, lying semiconscious on a pallet, was dispatched with a single shot to the temple. His companion was wrestled outside, ineptly strung up from the branch of a tree, and finished off with a fusillade of gunfire as he struggling against the rope. Meanwhile, one of the fugitives succeeded in stealing a horse and fleeing back to the mountains, while the other found his way to Los Angeles, where he filed a formal complaint of murder against four of the vigilantes he was able to identify by name.

Judge Benjamin Hayes was determined that this episode of lynch law—the first in the county since the hanging of David Brown four months earlier—not go unchallenged. He issued warrants for the arrest of the men identified by the fugitive—E. P. Robinson, William Burt, John Ward, and Ezekiel Rubottom—all upstanding citizens of the Monte. A few days later, as Hayes was walking to his courtroom for the preliminary hearing, he was overtaken and surrounded by several dozen mounted men from the Monte, one of whom bent down and handed him a sealed note. "We the undersigned," it read, "have been informed that some of our best citizens have been arrested," charged with the murder of the two prisoners. "It having been satisfactorily proved that the above mentioned men were connected with a band of robbers & thieves numbering about three hundred, we therefore approve of those of . . . ." The bottom half of the surviving note is torn away, truncating the message and removing what Hayes said were several dozen signatures. Someone, perhaps Hayes himself, decided it was better that they not be identified in the record. The final lines of the note warned Hayes "to lookout for your personal safety."

Hayes forwarded the complaint against the Monte Boys to the district attorney, who declined to prosecute, exasperating Hayes. He was even more distressed when he learned that another posse from the Monte had pursued the fugitive rustler into the mountains, capturing him along with Brown, the reputed leader, and hanging them both on the spot. These lynchings, Hayes believed, further weakened public support for the law.

JOHN O. WHEELER saw things differently. "We have, during a residence in this county for the last half dozen years," he wrote in the *Southern Californian*, "become somewhat intimately acquainted with lynch law or, as it is sometimes called, 'mob law,' and we have scarcely ever seen it wrong." Popular justice, he argued, had served Los Angeles well. "Whatever security to life, liberty, and the pursuit of happiness which have in times past been vouchsafed to us has been owing wholly and entirely to the retributive justice meted out by the people."

Wheeler applauded "the late efforts of Judge Lynch in the Monte" as an inspiring example for all county residents. Good riddance to the rustlers who plagued the county. Good riddance to the Brown brothers and their criminal ilk. "So the work goes bravely on," Wheeler concluded. "A few more examples of this sort will clean the land of all such *gente*."

Wheeler had long supported popular justice, but previously his views had been contested by editor Waite of the *Star*. Following the lynching of David Brown, however, Waite shifted position. The residents of the Monte, he wrote, had done a commendable job and "we wish them every success." It was a quiet admission of defeat but a capitulation nonetheless, and it left the impression that his opposition to mob law might depend on the character of the people who made up the mob. Waite's had been a lone public voice opposing lynch law in Los Angeles. And then there were none.

Yet Waite conveyed none of Wheeler's bluster. He was a reluctant supporter of popular justice. He held a view similar to that of his young colleague Francisco Ramírez, editor of *La Estrella*, who soon after Brown was hanged opened an editorial column with the declaration that "lynch law reigns supreme in California." But like Waite, Ramírez considered this an unfortunate fact. He regretted the absence of an effective urban police or a rural constabulary. "Law without arms is like a body without a soul," he wrote. "One is not possible without the other." If and when the authorities demonstrated a capacity to effectively enforce the laws, he felt certain that the people would abandon their support of vigilantism. But in the meantime, as Ramírez put it, "we must satisfy public vengeance."

With his literary savvy and his sharp reporting, Ramírez proved an effective replacement for Manuel Clemente Rojo. "The editor of the Spanish pages of the Los Angeles *Star* is a native Californian named Francisco Ramírez, only fifteen years of age," noted the editor of San Francisco's *Daily Alta California*. "Those versed in the Castilian language say that *La Estrella* is a model for purity of style." Ramírez was actually eighteen at the time, but that made him no less precocious. He learned on the job, and the pressures of responding to the complicated events of his time and place sometimes led him to take contradictory positions. But his idealism showed through consistently, as it did in a column he wrote lambasting the nativist American Party (scornfully known by their critics as the "Know-Nothings," a label inherited from a secret society from which the party emerged), whose opposition to immigrants and Catholics Ramírez considered not merely distasteful but ill informed. "Our country," he wrote of the United States, "is not only the home of men from all nations, but of their ideas. . . . Our religion is from Palestine; the hymns we sing in our churches were heard for the first time in Italy, some in Arabia, and others on the banks of the Euphrates; our arts came from Greece, our case law from Rome, our maritime code from Russia; England taught us the system of representative government, and the noble republic of the United Provinces bequeathed to us the idea of tolerance." The Know-Nothings lived up to their name—*los ignorantes.*

Ramírez's success at the *Star* inspired him to begin an independent Spanish-language newspaper of his own. James Waite encouraged the young man's aspirations, offering Ramírez his list of Spanish-language subscribers and advertisers. The *Star* was operating in the red, and Waite hoped that freeing up the back pages for more advertising might generate more revenue. He even allowed Ramírez to promote his new venture in the *Star.* In June Ramírez published the first issue of *El Clamor Público*—the public outcry—"devoted exclusively to the service and interests of native Californians." Over the next four and a half years, he would use the paper to argue for his liberal principles, including racial equality and political rights for all citizens.

The three weeklies—the *Star*, the *Southern Californian*, and *El Clamor Público*—competed for readers through the second half of 1855, but Los Angeles was not large enough to support them all. In December the *Southern Californian* went out of business, and a few months later Waite sold the *Star* to Henry Hamilton, a partisan Democrat who made the paper over into the mouthpiece of the local party machine, which was led by Joseph Lancaster Brent. About the same time Ramírez declared his support for the new Republican Party, inaugurating an intense political competition between the two weeklies.

SATISFYING PUBLIC VENGEANCE—*vindicta pública*—was something local authorities had difficulty doing. In 1855 Los Angeles County recorded a total of thirty-three murders, more than any other county in the state, including San Francisco, which was nearly ten times larger. With less than 3 percent of the population, Angelenos accounted for more than 6 percent of California's homicides, making for a murder rate that was double the state average. Yet most violent perpetrators in Los Angeles went unpunished.

David Brown's hanging further undercut the authority and morale of the county's legal justice system. After his humiliating capitulation to the mob, Sheriff James R. Barton announced he would not stand for another term. David W. Alexander, his elected successor, focused most of his attention on his freighting business, operating as something of a part-time sheriff, leaving most matters in the hands of Undersheriff William Osburn. That was unfortunate, because the state of affairs in the county required strong leadership. Lawbreakers were emboldened and officers of the law responded aggressively, resulting in a number of confrontations, including a wild shootout on the Plaza in the spring of 1855 between a group of Sonoreños and Undersheriff Osburn.

The California legislature had passed a law authorizing the arrest and incarceration of vagrants, singling out for special attention, in the words of the statute, "all persons who are commonly known as 'Greasers,' or the issue of Spanish and Indian blood." The statute authorized officers, in effect, to stop, question, disarm, and detain any suspicious-looking Mexican or Californio, without distinction of citizenship. Juan Sepúlveda, a man who had held many civic offices in Los Angeles over the years and was then serving as county treasurer, published an outraged open letter in response. "A portion of the people, which ought to enjoy equal rights with the rest," he wrote, "has been contemptuously treated by a body of would-be enlightened gentlemen, meeting in the name of the entire people." The treaty ending the war had guaranteed full rights as citizens to all Mexicans who chose to remain in ceded territory. "Why is it now," Sepúlveda wanted to know, "that we should be marked out as fit objects for defamatory taunts and branded with special legislation to our injury? . . . We can look upon it only as a step towards excluding us from all the rights enjoyed by other citizens." Francisco Ramírez agreed. The Greaser Law, he wrote "widens the barriers that have long existed between *extranjeros* and *nativos*."

IN THE SPRING OF 1856 Angelenos were closely following developments in San Francisco, where a committee of vigilance had hanged two men for murder and seized political control of the city, events extensively reported in newspapers throughout the state and nation. "Though rather distant from the exciting scenes of San Francisco," a correspondent from Los Angeles reported in the San Francisco *Daily Evening Bulletin*, "the almost universal opinion is that the San Francisco Vigilance Committee have commenced a glorious work, and they are earnestly requested to continue their labors." The events in the north served to further legitimize popular justice in Los Angeles. Ramírez made the connection explicit in *El Clamor Público*. What was taking place in San Francisco, he wrote, had occurred the year before in Los Angeles, when outraged citizens hanged David Brown. "*Bien hecho*," Ramírez declared. Well done. "Murderers still march through the streets with impunity and arrogant pride," he admitted, but the remedy was at hand. "We hope the people know what to do when it comes to punishing criminals."

But popular justice was parochial. It reflected the interests and values of particular groups, not the community as a whole. In the spring of 1856 the residents of the Monte organized another vigilance committee to address the continuing problem of livestock theft, this time focusing attention on a gang of Mexican and Californio rustlers. A few weeks later the mangled body of Cruz Montoya, a longtime resident of San Gabriel, was found in a ravine near the mission. "Cruz was looked upon by Americans as the chief of a band of robbers," reported the *Star*, "the community can well bear the loss of his company." That was coded language strongly suggesting a vigilante killing. Montoya had been ambushed by a group of mounted men, tortured with a knife, and dragged through the chaparral, before being riddled with bullets. His mangled body was intended to terrorize others.

Ramírez took the occasion to stand up for a universal standard of justice. "We are all linked together in society," he wrote. "Californios! Americans! Citizens of all origins and classes! Unite to obey the laws and see that our officers have the help they need." But that was aspirational, and as a practical matter Ramírez found himself returning to the nostrum of vigilantism. There must be no delay in finding those responsible for Montoya's death and administering retributive justice, he wrote. "*¿No necesitamos aqui un comité de vigilancia?*" Do we not need a vigilance committee here? What Ramírez had in mind was a vigilance committee composed of Californios, a committee that would protect *hijos del país* from Anglo vigilantes.

RAMÍREZ RAISED THAT QUESTION in the issue of *El Clamor Público* for Saturday, July 19, 1856. The morning of that same day, Constable William Jenkins appeared at the Eternity Street home of María Candelaria Pollorena with an order of attachment for an unpaid fifty-dollar debt on the property of Antonio Ruiz, a Mexican citizen who was living there. Although it was still early in the day, it was already intensely hot, and Jenkins found Ruiz sitting with Doña Candelaria in the shade of the adobe's front veranda. Jenkins, who spoke fluent Spanish, produced a court order and spoke with Ruiz for a few minutes. Then they went into the house together and emerged with Jenkins holding a guitar that belonged to Ruiz. The constable turned to leave, but Doña Candelaria stopped him. She had placed a letter from her mother inside the instrument, she said, and she wished to retrieve it. "*Por favor*, let her have the letter," said Ruiz. No, Jenkins replied, he couldn't do that, for the guitar was now the property of the court. "Give it to me, it's mine," said Doña Candelaria. She grabbed the guitar with one hand and thrust the other through the *boca*, or sound hole, in an attempt to retrieve it. "Give her that letter," Ruiz demanded, and he grabbed Jenkins from behind. Jenkins instantly pulled a revolver from his belt, pointed it blindly over his shoulder, and fired.

City marshal William Getman was nearby when he heard the gunshot. Hurrying to the scene, he found Ruiz lying on the ground, surrounded by neighbors attempting to stanch the blood flowing from a wound to his chest. Jenkins was pacing up and down nervously, the revolver still in his hand. Getman took it from him. He had been forced to fire in the execution of his duty, Jenkins said, and was "sorry for having done so." Ruiz was carried inside, where he was examined by a physician, who called for a priest. Getman escorted Jenkins to the office of a justice of the peace and swore out a complaint against him for assault. He was then released on his own recognizance.

William Willoughby Jenkins, a lanky young man of twenty-one, had immigrated from Ohio with his mother and stepfather six years before. He grew to manhood on the streets of Los Angeles during its most turbulent period and was considered among the toughest of the young Anglo toughs. He joined the Rangers and later became a constable. The man Jenkins shot, Antonio Ruiz, was a Sonoreño in his early thirties who had resided in Los Angeles for less than two years. Well educated, with the deportment of a scholar, Ruiz earned his living as a tutor and a music instructor. He took an interest in civic affairs and the previous September had been the featured speaker at Mexican independence day festivities. He was admired by Californios and Mexicans alike, and as word of his shooting circulated through the community a steady stream of friends and associates made their way to the house on Eternity Street to pay their respects.

Ruiz died Sunday afternoon. Judge Hayes issued a warrant for Jenkins's arrest on a charge of homicide. Jenkins surrendered voluntarily and was released again a few minutes later. Los Angeles schoolteacher William Wallace worried in his diary that this pattern was all too familiar. "He who commits an assassination or murder is uniformly greeted with a verdict of justifiable homicide, which amounts to an acquittal," Wallace wrote. "And the slayer goes forth again having gained some renown for his exploits. He holds his head more erect than ever and almost demands the deference of the people. . . . Jenkins has accomplished his fame, he has shed blood, and now he may aspire to office." Recognizing the negative impact Jenkins's release would have among Mexicans and Californios, Hayes remonstrated with Sheriff Alexander, who ordered Jenkins arrested and jailed again.

The requiem mass for Ruiz on Monday afternoon concluded with what Francisco Ramírez characterized as the largest funeral procession in the history of the pueblo. A double column of mourners stretched along Eternity Street from the church to the graveyard. As had been the case so many times before, a crowd of men, including Sonoreños, Californios, and a large contingent of Frenchmen, remained at the graveside following the burial, arguing over what was to be done. One of the speakers, a young French vineyard worker named Fernando Carriaga, with a striking red beard, urged the crowd to march to the jail and hang Jenkins just as they had hanged David Brown. But several prominent Californios spoke in favor of allowing the justice system take its course. The men settled on a compromise, naming several Californios to a *comité de vigilancia* and charging them with ensuring that the case was handled impartially and effectively. Then the crowd resolved to march on the jail to demonstrate their determination. Two members of the *comité* stopped at the home of Judge Hayes, and he agreed to accompany them to the jail.

They arrived to find the situation rapidly spiraling out of control. Hearing reports of the agitation at the *campo santo*, a posse of several dozen armed Anglos had surrounded the jail, determined to protect Jenkins. Francisco Ramírez was among the marching protesters as they turned down Spring Street, and he could see the Anglo guard ahead, cocking their weapons and "making other bellicose demonstrations." Hotheads on both sides began hurling insults and challenges across the divide, and the demonstration degenerated into a near riot, with the protesters, according to Hayes, "evincing a deep emotion that might have been mistaken for the excitement incident to violence." Sheriff Alexander finally appeared and announced that Judge Hayes would open the judicial process the following day, which calmed things down considerably. By then it was nearly sundown, and the crowd gradually dispersed.

H AYES CONVENED Jenkins's preliminary hearing the next morning. The owners of the city's shops and businesses shuttered their establishments in anticipation of trouble, but the saloons remained open and the streets were crowded with armed men. Unruly spectators thronged the courtroom, forcing Hayes to order it cleared, allowing only those whose presence was vital to remain, including the Californios of the *comité*, whom he seated in the jury box, thinking that was the appropriate spot for them since they were there to determine whether or not "the Judge did justice." Jenkins was ushered in, surrounded by an armed guard of no fewer than a dozen men. After hearing the testimony of several witnesses, Hayes adjourned, saying that he would announce whether there was sufficient evidence to charge Jenkins with a crime the following morning.

Great excitement prevailed for the remainder of the day. "The population of the city," reported Francisco Ramírez, "was divided into two different factions," a split that fell along ethnic lines. Late in the afternoon Hayes heard an unconfirmed rumor that a number of Sonoreños were planning a general attack on the city that night, planning to "destroy all the Americans." He hurried to the homes of the men on the *comité* to see what they knew. All of them claimed ignorance, although they took the rumor seriously, one of them cautioning Hayes that it was dangerous for him to be out and about and that he "might be fired on from the corner of any of these streets." Hayes hurried home, and late that evening, as darkness fell on the still quiet town, he reassured himself that, after all, rumors were just rumors. But about ten thirty, just after the rising of the moon, a man arrived at his door with an urgent message from Sheriff Alexander. Numerous men had been seen gathering at the summit of Gallows Hill. Hayes roused his wife and child and headed for the jail, where most of the town's Anglos had preceded him and were preparing a stout defense.

The sheriff enlisted two trusted Californios to investigate what was happening on the hill, fearing that sending his own Anglo deputies would provoke the crowd. By the light of a bright moon, Juan Padilla and Pedro Romo ascended the footpath leading up a ravine behind the church to the ruins of the earthenwork fort at the summit. To the rear was the "American graveyard," a plot of city land used as the burying ground for non-Catholics, and there Padilla and Romo saw some two hundred men, many of them armed. They were Sonoreños mostly, but included a surprising number of Frenchmen. Romo reported seeing only one Californio, the old agitator Ylario Varela, who insisted he had only come to observe and quickly departed. Padilla and Romo circulated among the men, urging them to return to their homes. They were determined to hang Jenkins, the insurgents said, but they intended no harm to others. Jenkins was closely guarded, Romo told them, and "they should consider that the sheriff was obliged to do his duty."

The conversation was interrupted by the Frenchman Fernando Carriaga, who by virtue of his stand at the graveyard had become de facto leader of the insurgents. "In this country," he declared, "the law is not administered equally to the poor and *Mexicanos*." Ruiz's death demonstrated that violence threatened them every day, and "they were persuaded it was better to die together than be killed one by one." The Sonoreños nearby shook their heads in agreement. "I am French," Carriaga declared. "But at this moment I am Mexican like the others." "*¡Viva México!*" the men cheered. "*¡Viva México!*" Then Carriaga gave the order. "Let's go!" he shouted. "Now is the time!" Padilla and Romo took that as their cue to depart.

The intelligence from Gallows Hill stiffened the resolve of the men at the jail, many of whom had brought their families. Marshal Getman and his deputy, William H. Peterson, armed themselves with shotguns, and mounting their horses they rode up Main Street to reconnoiter. Coming to a little wooden bridge over a branch of the zanja at the entrance to the Plaza, they dismounted, and keeping to the shadow of an adobe wall they slowly walked their horses to the backside of the church. In the moonlight they could see a column of men streaming down the hill and assembling at the northwest corner of the Plaza, some twenty-five or thirty yards ahead. Suddenly one of the insurgents spied them and Peterson heard a cry, "¡Vámonos!"—let's go!—immediately followed by gunfire. "We heard the balls whistling by us," Peterson later testified, and he and the marshal hastily retreated back to the wooden bridge.

"Go raise the alarm," said Getman. Deputy Peterson took off, but hearing a clamor looked back and saw ten or fifteen horsemen dart out from behind the church. Getman leveled his shotgun and slowly walked his horse toward them. "¿Quien vive?" he called. Who's there? "¡Carajo!" a voice shouted back, Fuck you! Peterson heard the discharge of revolvers, then the blast from Getman's shotgun. He dismounted and ran back to the bridge. Getman was on the ground, knocked from his horse by a ball that had grazed his scalp, burning a bloody crease across the right side of his head, a painful but thankfully superficial wound. Peterson helped him back to the jail. Sheriff Alexander dispatched a company of forty men, who cautiously made their way to the Plaza, but found it completely deserted.

The insurgents had scattered in all directions. "The truth is," Hayes wrote later, "they came, they saw, and left." Wine and aguardiente flowed freely on the hill, and Hayes believed that many of the men "got so drunk that the original seriousness of their project lost its influence on them." Their plan had been to hang Jenkins, Hayes said, "just as they had done before with Brown." The current instance, however, "fell under the stigma that attaches to a mere mob." Why the difference? Hayes thought he knew the answer. "In this business, as in other things, *success* seems to be the test of merit."

———

EARLY WEDNESDAY MORNING handbills appeared through-
out the pueblo calling for a public meeting of all citizens at 10 AM in
front of Montgomery House. A mostly Anglo crowd assembled at the
clang of the triangle that hung from the veranda of the hotel, used to
summon guests at mealtime. As the meeting was getting underway,
some three dozen riders came charging down Main Street and pulled
up directly in front of the Montgomery. The previous evening Sheriff
Alexander had sent out a call for emergency assistance, and the Monte
Boys had ridden to the rescue. The Anglo crowd greeted them with
sustained cheering. The significance was lost on no one. These were
the vigilantes Judge Hayes had tried to corral.

The meeting began with County Judge Myron Norton presiding.
The town's elite had caucused and agreed on the necessity of a show
of unity, and Norton's first item of business was to call Andrés Pico
forward to act as cochair. Pico was received by cheers from the crowd.
Don Andrés, along with his brother, the former governor, had grown
wealthy in the cattle business. Both had townhouses fronting the
Plaza. Don Andrés was a political insider, a former state senator and a
member of the Democratic junta in control of local politics. He and
Norton spoke to the crowd in Spanish and English, delivering a common message. The events of the previous night, they said, had demonstrated once again the inability of local law enforcement to maintain
order, and in the current emergency they proposed the formation of a
vigilance committee representing all the people, empowered to arrest
and disarm all "disorderly or suspicious persons." Ramírez reported
that many Californios worried that the phrase was a euphemism for
Spanish-speakers, but not wanting to be tarred with defending the
insurgents, they decided to go along, in effect "agreeing to their own
persecution." There was only one public dissenter, a young attorney
named William Handlin who argued in favor of proceeding according
to law, but he was shouted down and threatened with violence. Some
time after the meeting Handlin was assaulted and beaten senseless.
There was no room for dissent.

The meeting approved the Pico-Norton proposal by acclamation and appointed a "Committee of Twenty," made up of both Anglos and Californios, including Agustín Olvera and Antonio Coronel, Abel Stearns and Benjamin Davis Wilson, Stephen Clark Foster and John S. Griffin. The committee in turn authorized several volunteer companies, including the Los Angeles Rangers, to search out, arrest, and interrogate any and all men suspected of participating in the disorders of the previous two days. "We will not take away the life of any man unless he is found resisting the proper authority," the committee pledged, although that does not seem to have been the general understanding. "Companies are now organized to go out," reported the Los Angeles correspondent for the San Francisco *Daily Evening Bulletin*, "and to hang upon the spot every Spaniard they can find who has been connected with this movement."

Hayes refused to attend the public meeting. "Being myself a rival of Judge Lynch," he wrote, "I was never, of course, admitted within their holy of holies." Instead, he reconvened the preliminary hearing at the courthouse and announced his decision regarding the charges against William Jenkins. The testimony made it clear, Hayes said, that Constable Jenkins had killed Antonio Ruiz in the heat of passion, "without deliberation and without malice, either express or implied." It was a clear case of manslaughter, and he forwarded the case to the grand jury, setting bond at three thousand dollars, which several friends of Jenkins quickly posted before spiriting him away to a secret location.

By that afternoon the Rangers had rounded up several dozen Mexicans and a handful of Californios. The vigilance committee reserved the power of interrogation to itself, but Hayes interposed. "I passed the next day," he wrote, "examining and discharging (to the infinite disgust of the marshal's friends) the numbers of innocent and harmless persons with whom, by their random and half-frantic exertions, they filled the jail." Andrés Pico, at the head of a company of twenty mounted Californios, brought in Fernando Carriaga, whom they discovered hiding near the old mission in San Gabriel. Hayes intervened again, filing charges against the Frenchman for assault with intent to commit murder and consigning him to the protection of the sheriff.

The following morning Hayes convened a preliminary hearing for Carriaga, and after examining several witnesses to the events of Tuesday night, he announced his decision. Great caution was required, he began, when a single individual was charged with the criminal conduct of a multitude. That was particularly true in this case, which Hayes characterized as "the first prosecution in this state, I believe, for acts done in those popular movements too common amongst us, bearing the designation of 'Lynch Law' or 'Committee of Vigilance.'" On three memorable occasions over the previous five years, he reminded the men in the courtroom, organized bodies of Angelenos had inflicted extralegal execution on a total of seven men. In the eyes of the law, every person who actively participated in those executions was guilty of the crime of murder, yet not a single one had been arrested or tried. When David Brown was lynched six months earlier, the perpetrators, a majority of them Californios and Mexicans, had been "sustained by universal public sympathy." That precedent, said Hayes, impressed those who sought to lynch Constable Jenkins with "an undue confidence in their power." The entire community, including the frustrated lynchers themselves, ought to feel great relief that they had failed. If Mexicans or Californios believed they suffered as a distinct class of people, there were remedies for their redress within the legal justice system. Popular justice offered them no protection and could only lead to disaster. "Violence, in kindness say it, will only terminate in their utter ruin."

The plan for a lynching had miscarried, but the insurgents had committed a serious crime when they fired on the marshal, who was present in the discharge of his duty. Each individual engaged in riot is responsible for every act done by the rest, said Hayes, and "it appearing to me that the offense of an assault with intent to commit murder has been committed, and that there is sufficient cause to believe the within named Fernando Carriaga guilty thereof, I order that he be held to answer." Hayes set bond at two thousand dollars, which was posted by several French vineyardists later that afternoon.

That concluded the formal hearing, Hayes said. But before

adjourning the court he hoped he might be indulged "in a further remark or two."

> Good men should occupy themselves at once in the endeavor to subdue the spirit of anarchy which, I fear, of late has diffused itself widely in our county, owing to various palpable causes— among which [is] a deep sense of the enormity of our own local evils which thus far the law has not been able to eradicate. A certain impatience of legal routine has affected, more or less, all the different classes or nationalities (so to speak) of which our community is composed. . . . How long shall we labor through this anti-social distrust, and this painful sense of insecurity of property and life? Shall the law be left nearly powerless for want of adequate cooperation on the part of the people with the efforts made by the officers for its enforcement? Must each man provide for his own safety? This cannot be. To me it seems that the events of the past week afford a sufficient admonition of the perils we have run and must run again, by listening to the voice of sudden passion and giving way to the impulses of every momentary excitement. The best course is to be found in a firm and constant reliance upon the laws of the land, and in upholding them.

TWO WEEKS LATER the grand jury indicted William Jenkins for second-degree murder. His trial took place in mid-August. Defense attorney Jonathan R. Scott aggressively challenged every Californio among the forty-eight prospective jurors, and succeeded in seating an all-Anglo panel of twelve men. The prosecution's case, presented by District Attorney Cameron E. Thom, rested on the eyewitness testimony of María Candelaria Pollorena, and Scott's strategy was to discredit her. His first question to the first defense witness revealed his line of attack: "What was her general character, good or bad?" Thom objected that the question was irrelevant, but Hayes ruled to allow testimony bearing directly on her credibility. Scott then called a parade of prominent Anglos, including Benjamin Davis Wilson, John Ozias Wheeler, and Undersheriff William Osburn, all of whom testified to Doña Candelaria's bad reputation.

Their testimony was entirely unsubstantiated. But virtually everyone in the courtroom, especially including Hayes, knew that the preceding year Doña Candelaria had sued her husband for divorce in district court, claiming that he had taken up with "an Indian woman or squaw." Her husband had answered with the countercharge that it was Doña Candelaria who was the adulterer. He had hired a tutor for his children named Antonio Ruiz, he said, who boarded with the family, and while living there Ruiz had seduced his wife. She wanted a divorce, he told the court, "to gratify her lusts and desires with Antonio Ruiz." Before the divorce case could be concluded, Doña Candelaria's husband died of natural causes, and soon thereafter she and Ruiz began living together. If there was substance to the charge of bad character, that was it. María Candelaria Pollorena was a willful woman.

In his closing argument District Attorney Thom ignored that distraction and focused on the stark facts of the case, which clearly established, he argued, that Jenkins had demonstrated a reckless disregard for human life and was guilty of murder in the second degree. Scott countered that Doña Candelaria's testimony could not be trusted and ought to be rejected as "false in every detail." The purpose she and Ruiz had, Scott said, was not to retrieve a letter but to seize the guitar, an attempt at robbery, pure and simple, justifying Jenkins's use of deadly force. A tendentious argument, perhaps, but one that provided members of the jury with the cover they needed. They retired after receiving the instructions of Judge Hayes—which plainly indicated that no officer of the law could be justified in using deadly force to enforce a civil seizure—and returned fifteen minutes later with a verdict of not guilty. Angelenos braced for an angry response, but it did not materialize. Less than two days later the grand jury terminated the case against Fernando Carriaga by declining to indict him. An equality of injustice.

The entire episode forced Francisco Ramírez to rethink his support of vigilantism. "Everyone knows it was a murder—nothing more, nothing less," he wrote of the Ruiz killing. But "the assault on the jail was out of bounds," and served to further the division between Anglos and Californios. Ramírez now took the position that "there is nothing more unfortunate than the people taking the law into their own hands." He now recognized that vigilantism offered no guarantee of universal justice. It arose from people's deepest fears and exaggerated their prejudices. The rule of law, not the rule of individual men, offered the only sure way forward. "Let us work together in a common spirit to enforce the laws," he wrote. "Let the hatred that pits race against race be transformed into the most sincere friendship. That's what is required by the times in which we live."

The outcome gave Benjamin Hayes reason to hope for better days. "Ruiz is in his sepulcher," he wrote in an unsigned essay published in Spanish in *El Clamor Público*. "Nothing will change the eternal destiny of the man by whose hand he fell." No one would deny the ill effects the episode had on the community. "But time will erase them, and we will return to living in harmony, working to firmly establish and perpetuate the fraternal feelings that must reign in every orderly society." Hayes could not have been more wrong.

PART THREE

· CHAPTER 21 ·

WE HAVE GOT YOU NOW,
DON SANTIAGO

AT THE CONCLUSION of his fourth term as sheriff, in October 1855, James R. Barton retired to his ranch, 170 acres of prime land near Los Nietos, some ten miles east of the pueblo on the west bank of the San Gabriel River. He bred horses, tended what one observer described as a "large and flourishing orchard," and set out the first planting of English walnuts in a district that would later be celebrated for them. The property was valued at more than ten thousand dollars—the equivalent of several million in today's money—placing Barton in the elite class of the county's ranchers and farmers. While serving as sheriff he kept a room in Los Angeles, but Barton Ranch, which he purchased in 1853, was his permanent home. Living with him there was María del Espiritu Santo, a young Cupeño woman born and raised at Mission San Juan Capistrano. She and Barton were not legally married, but in the spring of 1854 she delivered a son, José Santiago, whom Barton acknowledged as his offspring in a legal document executed several months later. A gentleman farmer living in common-law marriage with "an Indian girl" and their child was not uncommon in southern California during those years.

But people would talk. Horace Bell repeated a story about Barton and his consort that clearly expressed contempt. "He was an uncouth, illiterate man," Bell wrote. "He had lived for years prior to his death in illicit intercourse with a Capistrano Indian woman." But one day, because of "some alleged ill treatment," the woman took her things as well as her child to the home of her mother, who lived in a ranchería on the east side of the Los Angeles River. "The high sheriff of Los Angeles County," wrote Bell, "went to the Indian settlement to recover his woman. She refused to return to him. After long argument he seized her by her scalp lock and started to lead her away." But Barton was immediately challenged by a young *medio indio*, or "half breed," named Andrés Fuentes who, according to Bell, was María del Espiritu Santo's brother and "a desperate sort of fellow given to the use of his knife on slight provocation." Under the circumstances Sheriff Barton did the wise thing and retreated. But two days later, Bell reported, he had Fuentes arrested on a trumped-up charge of horse theft, for which he was convicted and sentenced to two years in San Quentin. The sheriff was present when the young man, manacled hand and foot, boarded the stage taking him to prison. "You put this job on me," Fuentes said to Barton "I will return and kill you."

There is no corroboration for Bell's story, which he claimed to have heard from Fuentes himself some years later. Whether or not he was María del Espiritu Santo's brother—his name is not among those of her siblings on the parish register—he nursed a bitter grudge against Barton, the man who set him up. Fuentes was convicted during the summer of 1854, shortly after the birth of Barton's son but before Barton's formal acknowledgment of paternity. Perhaps that was what Barton and María del Espiritu Santo were fighting over. One thing seems clear. Once Barton made his declaration, which had significant implications for the child, his mother returned to Barton Ranch.

BARTON WAS NOT ONLY a man of property but a man with considerable power. Elected county sheriff four times on the Democratic ticket, he became a fixture of the party's local leadership. He resigned from law enforcement in the autumn of 1855, but not from politics. The following spring he was elected to fill a vacancy on the county's governing board of supervisors and he served as a delegate to the party's annual state convention. He kept a low profile during the crisis following the killing of Antonio Ruiz, when Sheriff David W. Alexander, his successor, came in for a great deal of criticism for his weak leadership. Alexander resigned shortly afterward, his term completed by Deputy Charles Hale. Party colleagues and friends, arguing that the office required Barton's experienced hand, urged him to stand for sheriff once again. That was all the encouragement Barton needed, and at summer's end he resigned from his post as supervisor and announced his candidacy for county sheriff in the upcoming November election.

"Bloody Kansas" was the commanding item of national news during the summer of 1856, and that autumn's political contest, which focused on the question of slavery in the western territories, promised to be equally turbulent. John C. Frémont, presidential nominee of the nascent Republican Party, ran on a "Free Soil" platform, while Democrat James Buchanan endorsed the principle of "Popular Sovereignty," leaving the decision over slavery for territorial residents themselves to decide. The contest had local resonance. A group of notable Californios—led by Pío Pico and including representatives of the Lugo, Yorba, Ávila, Sepúlveda, and Carrillo families—announced their endorsement of Frémont's candidacy, which stirred up a great deal of political backlash among Democrats. Californio José Rubio, who supported the Republicans, reported that Democrat Antonio Coronel, a consummate political insider, had been harassed by Anglo members of his own party when he showed up to vote at a special municipal election held in October. "Here comes another Greaser vote," the Anglos had shouted, "here comes another vote for the Negro. If the Negro Coronel comes to vote, don't let him." That's the way it would always be with the Democrats, Rubio warned his fellow Californios. They sang the praises of the *hijos del país* as long as the community followed them blindly, but "now that you want to vote for Frémont, they cannot find words despicable enough to condemn you." Francisco Ramírez proclaimed that the outcome of the election would determine whether Californios moved forward together under the banner of freedom and independence, or remained under the thumb of the Democrats, "whose vile 'Greaser' laws have weighed on us so ignominiously."

The Democrats carried Los Angeles once again. But Buchanan's electors captured only a bare majority of the votes cast. Editor Henry Hamilton of the *Star* was upset at the number of Californios who cast their ballots for Frémont, and he blamed Ramírez, accusing him of deliberately stirring up ethnic hostility in order "to produce a rift between them and their Democratic brethren." For his part, Ramírez was scornful of Hamilton's assumption that the Democratic Party was the natural home for Californios. "What name will the Democrats use for us now," he wondered, "Mexicans or Greasers?" Buried in the debate over the outcome of the election was the news that James R. Barton had won a fifth term as county sheriff, outpolling the national ticket, with more than two-thirds of all the votes cast.

SHORTLY AFTER the presidential election in November, a notorious outlaw gang arrived in the Los Angeles vicinity from the north. The putative leaders, Francisco "Pancho" Daniel and Juan Flores, were young Californios from the vicinity of San José. Daniel, the older of the two, was a career criminal who survived by avoiding the limelight. He had a ferocious reputation but an unassuming appearance, looking for all the world like "an ordinary appearing little Mexican," in the words of an Anglo who knew him. Flores was the flashy one. Horace Bell described him as "a dark complexioned fellow of medium height, slim, lithe and graceful, a most beautiful figure in the fandango or on horseback."

Flores had been to Los Angeles before. In the spring of 1855 he and an associate had been convicted and sentenced to two years in prison for stealing a team of horses from the Hardy brothers, teamsters who operated a livery stable southeast of the Plaza. According to Antonio Coronel, after Flores was sentenced, he swore that "whenever he got out he'd wreak vengeance on the person responsible." That was Garnett Hardy, the man who testified against him in court, earning Flores's everlasting enmity. Flores met Pancho Daniel at San Quentin, where they were both serving time, and in October 1856 they joined several other convicts in a spectacular breakout, hijacking a brig from the prison's dock and sailing it into San Francisco Bay. Guards fired into the ranks of the several dozen prisoners who jumped aboard, killing a number of them. But the ringleaders, still in handcuffs, successfully piloted the vessel to the eastern shore and escaped. Calling themselves *los Manillas* (the Handcuffs), Flores and Daniel recruited a peripatetic band of followers, including Andrés Fuentes, Sheriff Barton's nemesis, who had been released from prison several months earlier. Fuentes agreed to join the gang, he told Horace Bell, "on condition that they would help him to murder Jim Barton."

The Manillas were responsible for a number of attacks committed in the Los Angeles vicinity. But both Fuentes and Flores were preoccupied with revenge. On a Sunday afternoon in mid-January 1857, one of the gang observed Garnett Hardy leaving town with a wagonload of goods intended for a merchant in San Juan Capistrano, sixty miles southeast, about halfway to San Diego. It was an opportunity for Flores to wreak vengeance, and he gathered his men and set out in pursuit. Hardy made a cold camp somewhere along the road that night, and in the darkness the Manillas missed him. They arrived at San Juan before him the following morning, and spent the next several hours visiting the drinking establishments and bragging of their criminal accomplishments. By the time Hardy pulled in, most of the gang were sleeping it off. Warned that someone named Flores was looking for him, it all suddenly came back to Hardy. He wrote a short note of warning to his brothers and arranged for a rider to carry it express to Los Angeles. Then he unhitched his horses, abandoned his wagon, and set out for home, taking a circuitous route to avoid being overtaken by the gang.

Flores discovered Hardy's wagon some time later and flew into a rage. Suspecting that local residents had warned him, he unleashed his men on the town. They plundered several stores, including the retail establishment of Jewish merchant Michael Kraszewski, who saved himself by hiding under a large clothes basket. "I looked upon myself as lost," Kraszewski recalled, "but did not lose my presence of mind." He sat without moving a muscle while the Manillas shot and wounded his clerk, then proceeded to loot the place, loading the booty onto their horses. They departed late that night, but were back the following day to continue the plunder of other shops. George Pflugardt, a German who operated a tavern and grocery, armed himself and warned them not to enter, but Flores and two accomplices pushed their way inside and shot Pflugardt dead. Across the street was the old mission compound, which had been converted into the palatial home of ranchero John Forster, brother-in-law of Pío Pico and proprietor of several large properties in the area. Many townspeople had taken refuge there. As the gang members prepared to leave with their loot, they fired a few random shots at Forster's place. They would return, they shouted, and when they did "they would kill all the San Juanians."

That same day in Los Angeles Alfred Hardy received his brother's note of warning and immediately went to Sheriff Barton. San Juan Capistrano was within Barton's jurisdiction—Orange County would not be hived off until 1889—and the news that the town had been invaded by an armed gang of desperadoes under the command of two escaped convicts was alarming, to say the least. Barton organized a small posse consisting of Deputy Frank Alexander and Constables William Little and Charles Baker. Anxious over the fate of his brother, Alfred Hardy volunteered to go along, as did Charles Daley, a blacksmith who worked for him. Barton arranged for a guide, a Frenchman identified only as "François," who had worked as a vaquero at Rancho Santiago de Santa Ana and knew that part of the county as well as anyone in the pueblo. The preparations of the posse were observed from a distance by Andrés Fuentes, who had remained behind when the Manillas took off in pursuit of Hardy. Watching and listening, he soon learned where Barton was headed, and as the sheriff prepared to depart, he mounted a horse and set off at a furious pace for San Juan.

The news of what was taking place in San Juan Capistrano spread around town. According to Harris Newmark, Anglos were "seized with terror." He recalled the moment Louis Hayes Griffin—sister of Benjamin Hayes and wife of Dr. John S. Griffin—burst into the Newmark house in panic. Lock the doors and bolt the windows, she cried, "the outlaws are on their way to Los Angeles to murder the white people." By Thursday evening most of the town's Anglo women had been relocated to the heavily defended armory on Spring Street, while armed men took up positions at key defensive points throughout town.

The fear of attack was understandable, but there is little or no evidence that the Manillas gang was targeting "white people." John Forster noted that "they are down upon the Americans particularly," but virtually all accounts agree that the gang attacked indiscriminately, threatening and assaulting any and all who stood in their way, without regard to ethnicity or race. That did not prevent commentators from repeating the claim that the violence had ethnic and political overtones. Horace Bell wrote that the Manillas "raised the standard of revolt," declaring that their intention was to "rid the country of the hated gringos." According to Hubert Howe Bancroft, the gang "threatened the extermination of the Americans." But aside from Forster's offhanded comment, there is absolutely no firsthand evidence to support those claims.

More recently this notion has mutated into an argument that the Manillas were "quasi-revolutionary," as one historian puts it, that they were "social bandits" who sought to reverse the conquest and enjoyed the popular support of ordinary Californios and Mexicans. The only contemporary evidence for such an interpretation, however, comes from the terrified imaginings of Anglos. Henry Dwight Barrows, who had been in Los Angeles barely two years, reported that "the Sonoreans and Mexicans, many of them, succor and assist the villains, either through fear or sympathy." Barrows offered no support for his claim, because he didn't have any. It was a slander against ordinary Mexicans and Californios, most of whom were simply trying to get along. Anglos at the time, and historians after them, considerably exaggerated the gang's size, something Flores and Daniel themselves encouraged. "The robbers use every means to impress the idea of their superior force," wrote John Forster. "But I notice that the very same individuals have been engaged in every action." He estimated that the Manillas numbered no more than ten or fifteen men. The exaggeration and the attribution of motive was driven by politics, not evidence.

SHERIFF BARTON AND HIS POSSE left Los Angeles at dusk, and after traveling some forty miles, at about one in the morning, they arrived at the crossing of the Santa Ana River, where they made a cold camp. A short ride of two or three miles the next morning brought them to El Refugio, the home of José Andrés Sepúlveda, proprietor of Rancho Santiago de Santa Ana, where they fed their horses and breakfasted. Don Andrés's vaqueros had told him of the troubles at San Juan, and he warned Barton that the Manillas were said to number fifty men or more. Barton dismissed that figure as implausible. "The party made light of it and proceeded on their journey," the *Star* later reported.

Friday, January 23, was a clear, dry day, quite warm for midwinter, even by southern California standards. It was still early in the morning when the men left El Refugio, and by ten they had traveled approximately twelve or thirteen miles, about half the distance from the rancho to San Juan. They rode by ones and twos, strung out along the road for several hundred yards, so those behind could avoid the dust kicked up by those ahead. As they rounded a projecting spur of the San Joaquín Hills on their right, Constables Little and Baker, riding point with the guide François, saw a horse and rider emerge from a ravine several hundred yards ahead and gallop briskly away from them. Curious, the three men picked up the pace, ignoring Barton's call to stay close. They had their eyes fixed on the distant rider, who was in fact a decoy, when suddenly off to their right they heard the sound of gunfire. Turning in that direction they saw a party of a dozen men riding down on them through a gap in the foothills. Andrés

Fuentes had arrived in San Juan and alerted the Manillas of Barton's approach, and they had staged this ambush expertly. "There is Juan Flores, boys!" shouted François. "There are the *ladrones*! Fire! Fire!" And then, wheeling his horse, the Frenchman tore off in the opposite direction. "Run for your life, boys!"

Little and Baker did not panic, but calmly drew their revolvers and got off several rounds before both of them were hit. Baker took a ball to the forehead and fell dead. Little was wounded in the stomach. He tumbled to the ground, crawled into a gully, and commenced firing with a second revolver as Barton and the other three men came charging up. The posse was outnumbered two or three to one, but in the first exchange three Manillas were hit and killed. Pancho Daniel saw Barton and bore down on him. "We have got you now, Don Santiago, God damn you," he shouted. "And I reckon I've got you too," Barton shouted back. According to Frank Alexander, the two men fired at the same instant. Daniel was hit in the leg, Barton's shot penetrating the top of his leather boot and shattering the bone, a serious though not a life-threatening wound. But Daniel's shot was decisive, tearing into Barton's chest, a mortal blow. He fell hard, breaking his left arm. Barton quickly pulled a second revolver from his belt and continued firing.

Hardy and Alexander saw him go down. Hardy had lost his pistol in the melee and was defenseless. He signaled to Alexander, and suddenly the two men retreated at full speed. They were pursued by several Manillas all the way back to El Refugio but escaped with their lives. Their flight was made possible by Barton and Little, who kept the rest of the gang occupied for several critical minutes. Eventually Little stopped firing from the gully. A Sonoreño named Juan Catabo crept over and peered in. Little was reloading his revolver with powder, cap, and ball. Catabo shot him dead.

"Barton fought like a lion," one member of the gang later reported, "and kept the whole gang at bay by his terrible defiance." They circled him at a safe distance until he had finally emptied his revolver. Then Andrés Fuentes dismounted and slowly advanced toward him on foot. Barton raised himself on his left elbow and hurled his empty revolver at the outlaw. "Now kill me, God damn you!" he said. According to

Horace Bell, who had it from the shooter himself, Fuentes walked up to Barton and fired point-blank at his face. "Thus ended the massacre," wrote Bell. "Taking the arms, equipment and horses of the murdered gringos, the murderers returned to San Juan in triumph."

AFTER A CHANGE OF HORSES, a quick bite, and a stiff drink, Hardy and Alexander started back, riding together until they reached the San Gabriel River, not far from Barton Ranch, at which point Alexander turned north for the Monte, while Hardy continued west toward the pueblo. Darkness had fallen by the time Hardy arrived, but his distressing intelligence spread like wildfire, provoking intense anxiety and excitement. Marshal Getman immediately raised a party of thirty or forty men, rode out of town before midnight, and arrived at the scene of the disaster early the following morning. He found the bodies of the four men scattered along the road, bloated and blackened after a full day in the sun. Barton had three gunshot wounds to the chest and a bloody cavity where his right eye had been. The other bodies displayed similar wounds, apparently inflicted after death— Little and Baker in the right eye, like Barton, Daley in the mouth. Their pockets were turned out and all their money and valuables were gone, along with their boots, belts, and firearms.

Posting several men to stand watch until the wagons and coffins arrived from the pueblo, Getman directed the rest of his men on toward San Juan. Spying a group of riders on the ridge of a nearby hill, he led a charge on their position, but the mounted men vanished. Unprepared for an extended chase through the chaparral, Getman and his posse moved on to San Juan. While the men refreshed themselves in the grogshops, Getman went to John Forster to learn what he could. Forster was unimpressed. "I am sadly afraid they will do no good," he reported to a correspondent, "on account of their apparent disorderly arrangement." The Manillas remained in the general area, Forester believed, but capturing them would require a force with considerably more discipline. He was right. After several days spent chasing shadows, Getman led his men back to the pueblo. "His party returned having accomplished nothing," noted schoolteacher William Wallace. "They came in sight of the robbers once, but they would not attack them until they had had their coffee!"

The bodies of Barton and his men were brought back to Los Angeles on Sunday, and the funeral took place the following morning. An elaborate procession wound through city streets and up *cañada de los muertos* to the American graveyard on Gallows Hill. None of the victims were Catholic, and there wasn't a single Protestant clergyman in Los Angeles, so there would be no religious service. Barton and Little had been members of the Masonic order, and their brother Masons conducted a short ceremony beside the graves, including Baker and Daley in the ritual as a matter of courtesy. Henry Barrows found the occasion disheartening. "We poor Americans in Los Angeles," he wrote, "are liable to die, as many of us have lived, as though there were no God."

The thoughts of most Anglos were far from God. "There is a call for blood revenge," wrote Wallace. "No demand is made for sheriffs or constables—the only demand is for rifles and pistols." The *Star* published a poem calling for action, written by a fifteen-year-old Los Angeles schoolgirl named Josephine Donna Smith.

> *Parents, brothers and sisters will mourn for the lost,*
> *For, alas, they can never regain them,*
> *And in heart-breaking sorrow will pray to their God*
> *For revenge on the ones who have slain them.*
>
> *Aye, revenge on their murderers! Is there no true man,*
> *Not one, to act as the avenger*
> *Of the four noble beings who lost their own lives*
> *In defending this people from danger?*
>
> *Go, seek for the inhuman, ruffianly horde,*
> *Nor strive, as ye do, to avoid them,*
> *Go forth in the names of the brave men they've killed,*
> *And rest not until you've destroyed them.*

And they, *who are sleeping in death's cold embrace,*
Time can n'er from our memory estrange them;
Then, O! while the sod is yet damp on their graves,
Go forth, in God's name, and avenge them.

Marshal Getman had learned from John Forster that most of the Manillas were Californios, one of them an Angeleno. That was Antonio María Varela, known as Chino (Curley), the sixteen-year-old son of Sérbulo Varela. Some months earlier young Varela had gone on record, complaining that he "could not stand to live under American rule." If the son of a man so widely admired by Americans had turned outlaw, what did that say about Californios in general? Anglos began to suspect that many were in cahoots with the Manillas. Californio leaders understood the importance of proving them wrong, as Francisco Ramírez did in an editorial addressed to his fellow *hijos del país*. "We are bound by indissoluble ties with the Americans," he wrote, and "now is the time to prove that we are loyal to the homeland, that we are good citizens, and like everyone else we desire public peace and the welfare of our families."

Californios! We know that this gang of thieves is without principle, without mercy, without religion, stealing and killing everyone they encounter. They steal from both the Americano and the Californio, they target both the French and the Jew! . . . We are sure none of our good citizens harbor the slightest sympathy with them. Put aside any animosity, forget the misfortunes of the past, and think only of the future of our families!

Motivated by such sentiments, Andrés Pico organized a mounted company of fifty-one lanceros, and on Monday afternoon, at the conclusion of the funeral, he led them out of the pueblo, toward San Juan. The Californios would bring the Manillas to justice.

———

"IN THE MATTER of the Estate of James R. Barton." The notice of probate, naming Barton's brother-in-law John Reed as executor of the estate, appeared in the *Star* in late January. "Since his death," the paper noted, "we find that all Mr. Barton's property has been left to his eldest son." That would be José Santiago Barton, his only son, the child of María del Espiritu Santo. Like so many other individuals of Indian ancestry, the mother disappeared from the record and her ultimate fate is unknown. But when the federal census enumerator made his rounds in 1860, he found the son, not once but twice: listed first as "James Barton," living at Rancho La Puente with John Reed and his wife, Nieves Rowland Reed, a couple the boy surely considered his aunt and uncle; then as "José Santiago Barton," living in the pueblo at the home of Bailio and María Jurado, in a neighborhood of Californio, Mexican, and Indian families. Perhaps young Barton's dual residency—like the Spanish and English versions of his name—was an aspect of his mixed parentage. In 1870, at the age of sixteen, he enrolled as a student at St. Vincent's, a Catholic high school in the center of the pueblo.

Five years later, turning twenty-one, he registered to vote under his legal name, José Santiago Barton. But an adult life was not something he would be granted. The following year he died of unknown causes at the tender age of twenty-two. He may have been suffering from a chronic disease, for he seems to have anticipated an early passing in a last will and testament he signed some months before his death: "This is to show that if anything should happen to me, and I should fail suddenly, I, the undersigned, will all my property to William and Joseph Perdue, brothers." They were the children of William Perdue, who came to California with James Barton in 1842 and married another of the Rowland daughters. With the son's death, his father's estate was finally liquidated. Put up for sale in 1878, Barton Ranch was described as a bountiful property that included a orchard of mature English walnut trees producing large crops of excellent nuts that fetched top dollar in the San Francisco market.

· CHAPTER 22 ·

THE CRIME MUST BE AVENGED

WITHIN HOURS of Sheriff Barton's death, self-appointed groups of vigilantes began patrolling the county's roads in search of the perpetrators. One was led by William B. Osburn, who had served for years as Barton's undersheriff and was his close personal friend. "When the word came," Osburn's eldest son later recalled, "my father was greatly disturbed." He packed a bag and told the boy to saddle his favorite horse. "I am going away and may never come back again," he said. "The crime must be avenged."

Osburn had known Barton since his arrival in Los Angeles as a hospital steward attached to the New York Regiment of Volunteers. Osburn was older than the typical volunteer, and he brought along two of his three children, boys aged ten and six. His youngest son he left behind with his wife in upstate New York. There was surely a complicated backstory there, which must remain untold in the absence of evidence, but it would appear to be the tale of a man looking to start his life over, for at war's end Osburn remained in Los Angeles with his two sons. There is no record that he ever divorced his wife in New York, yet he soon married a Mexican woman in Los Angeles, who became stepmother to the boys. With no training other than his wartime experience, he advertised himself as "Dr. Osburn," and Angelenos accorded him the respect due a regular physician. In addition to practicing medicine and acting as undersheriff, Osburn served a term as justice of the peace and was the pueblo's first postmaster. He was credited with a number of other "firsts," like teaching the first English common school and opening the first photography studio, which made him a favorite subject of antiquarians. He and Barton served as officers in a local temperance organization and went into business together drilling for artesian wells. After Barton declined to run for reelection, Osburn relocated to San Gabriel, where he purchased two hundred acres and opened the county's first commercial nursery, raising and marketing the first ornamental roses cultivated in southern California. He was elected to serve as a justice of the peace. Benjamin Hayes described Osburn as a "most useful man." He was also a well-practiced vigilante, although local historians said little or nothing about that.

On the morning of January 29, 1857, some days after Barton's death, Osburn and a party of Americans were patrolling the roads not far from Mission San Gabriel when they came upon two mounted men who roused their suspicions. When confronted, the pair sped off at a gallop, the Americans in hot pursuit. In a running gunfight one of the men, a Mexican later identified as José Santos, received a mortal wound. The other, a Californio named Miguel Soto, jumped from his horse and plunged into a *ciénega*, or marsh, attempting to hide among the tules. The Americans burned him out, and one of the King brothers from the Monte brought him down with a rifle shot. The body was dragged out, and a quick search of the man's pockets produced a Masonic ring thought to belong to Sheriff Barton.

The Americans—ten or fifteen men from San Gabriel and the Monte—reacted like angry wasps from a disturbed nest. Assuming that Santos and Soto were somehow connected with the local Californio community, they swarmed through the neighborhood surrounding the mission, rousting residents from their homes and driving them at gunpoint to a small plaza in front of the mission, where they were forced to witness a terrifying spectacle orchestrated by William Osburn. The body of one of the dead men was brought up in a carreta and dumped on the ground. An eyewitness described what happened next. Osburn "came forward, knife in hand, rolled up his sleeves, and with one hand took the dead man's head by its long hair, cut it from the body, and tossed it aside; thrust his dagger into the heart of the corpse, then kicked the head into the midst of the crowd as they shouted and cheered." Hilliard P. Dorsey, another resident of San Gabriel and register of the U.S. Land Office, then stepped forward and did the same with his own knife, followed by several other Americans. In the words of a further witness, they acted "with a brutality rarely seen among barbarians." Savagery and sadism inevitably accompanied mob law, and would recur for as long as vigilantism was tolerated.

But the vigilantes were just getting started. During their rampage through the village, they had seized three young Californios—Juan Valenzuela, Pedro López, and Diego Navarro—on suspicion of aiding and assisting the two dead men. In the *Star*, editor Henry Hamilton reported that "a number of arrests were made at the time by the people, who afterwards organized a court, tried the prisoners, and sentenced them to be hung." In *El Clamor Público*, Francisco Ramírez told a different story. The Americans, he reported, "threw themselves on a few miserable victims, like voracious lions with unchecked appetites." As residents watched in horror, the three men, their hands bound behind their backs, were wrestled to the center of the plaza. "All this was happening before our eyes," said one Californio. "We could not imagine that they would hang those poor men so suddenly, without a formal trial and no evidence of their crime." There was only Osburn's call to the mob—"all in favor of hanging the prisoners will hold up their hands"—and shouts of "Death! Death!" from the Americans. Osburn distributed ropes, nooses were tied and placed around the necks of the three men, and they were pulled up from the branches of an overspreading oak. The hanging proved a messy business. The legs of the victims were not bound, and their bodies convulsed violently as they strangled to death. A rope snapped, and one of the men crashed to the ground, the noose still around his neck. His wife rushed to his side as vigilantes finished him off with their pistols.

José Santos, the man who died in the running gunfight, was later confirmed as one of the Manillas. His associate, Miguel Soto, in whose pocket the vigilantes found Barton's ring, was apparently not affiliated with the gang, although he had a long criminal record. No evidence, however, connected either of them to the three men hanged in front of the mission. Henry Hamilton, generally uncomfortable with vigilantism, nevertheless defended the justice of the San Gabriel lynching on general grounds. Juan Valenzuela, he wrote, was "an old offender" with a record of many robberies, Pedro López a thief, "never known to work," and Diego Navarro "a man of general bad character, and dangerous to be permitted to live in any peaceable community." Ramírez responded to Hamilton's wretched argument with righteous indignation. Ad hominem attack did not change the facts. The three Californios had been murdered by an American mob. He insisted the county grand jury take up the matter. "Nothing less than a complete and impartial investigation will satisfy the public mind," he wrote. But there is no indication that there was an official investigation of any kind.

Michael White, an English immigrant in his midfifties and a long-time resident of San Gabriel, witnessed the entire episode. He tried to stop the killing before it started, insisting that the man hiding in the ciénega be captured alive in order that he be interrogated. White was also among a small group of Anglos who attempted to prevent the lynchings, but were pushed aside. "We will not forget their noble conduct," wrote Ramírez. During the late war, White had been among the Anglos captured at Rancho Santa Ana del Chino and imprisoned for several months by the Californios. He understood the emotional necessity of revenge. But he could not comprehend why those three Californios in particular had been hanged. He had known them since they were boys, and whatever their faults he was certain they had nothing to do with the Manillas. Later that afternoon, standing over their bodies, he asked an old friend why they had been singled out. He didn't know, the man admitted. "Neither did I," White later recalled, "except that I was convinced that they were killed because they were Spanish and their murderers willed it."

WILLIAM WALLACE was teaching the boys' class at the school-house in Los Angeles when a friend rushed in with a report of the violence at San Gabriel. "I had to adjourn immediately," Wallace wrote in a dispatch to the *Daily Alta California* of San Francisco, "for in these times, when everybody is so bloodthirsty, I can't bear to be locked up." He found the streets thronged with excited men, pre-dominantly Anglos. There were few Californios and Mexicans to be seen, something quite unusual. Wallace wholeheartedly approved of the San Gabriel lynchings—"Osburn was judge, and his conduct of the cases was characteristic and satisfactory"—but he wondered where the retribution for the deaths of Barton and the three mem-bers of his posse would end. "There is not dark blood enough in all California to pay for the four murdered men. God grant that in this crusade against crime we do not prove ourselves devils." Wallace soon heard a second report—"that the natives of the mission were to join the natives of the pueblo and ravage and murder indiscriminately." He did not quite believe it, but the rumor kept popping up, embellished with new particulars in each successive telling—that a large number of Mexicans and Californios had already left San Gabriel, marching for the pueblo; that the residents of Sonoratown, north of the Plaza, were stockpiling arms; that their leaders had vowed to wipe out all gringos. Fear of retribution by defeated natives is the worst nightmare of colonizers. Vengeance breeds fear, and fear provokes the need for further vengeance.

Early that evening, at a torchlight meeting held on the street before Montgomery House, Anglo residents organized what they called, in a reference to the American Revolution, a "Committee of Safety." To lead it they appointed Dr. John S. Griffin, the hardheaded sur-geon who had come to southern California with General Kearny's dragoons. Retiring from military service after the war, Griffin settled in Los Angeles, where he established a medical practice and eventually married Louisa Hayes, sister of Judge Hayes, who taught the girls' classes at the pueblo's single public school. Despite being Hayes's brother-in-law, Griffin was an enthusiastic vigilante, and as the pueblo's newly appointed commandant he turned security over to several Anglo volunteer companies, tasking them with establishing a defensive perimeter on the city's eastern outskirts. The watch for the invading army from San Gabriel was kept up all night with no sign of an attack. "There was really more danger from friends than enemies," wrote Wallace, "from careless shooting."

Fear of an attack faded with the sunrise, and Griffin turned his attention to the supposed enemy within, ordering his men to surround Sonoratown and block every avenue of escape, after which Marshal Getman conducted a sweep of the neighborhood. "He entered each house," Wallace reported, "and as he found a villain, quietly tapped him on the shoulder and motioned to the guard, who silently marched him off to jail." How Getman distinguished villains from ordinary villagers, Wallace didn't say, but by the end of the day the county jail was crowded with several dozen men. According to Ramírez, most of them "were there simply for being poor and friendless."

Wallace, who participated in the operation, oscillated between eager anticipation and anxious worry. "No one shall escape," he exclaimed. "What a joyous time we will have hanging the rascals!" But he also expressed concern. "There is much anxiety among the Californians," he reported. "The thirst for blood increases, and as each new prisoner is carried to jail, his name and acts are made known and magnified. There is little sober judgment in the people, but they have resolved that there is no protection in the courts or the law, and they are now about to make some notable examples." This was about revenge, not justice. The mass arrests stunned the Californio community. Ramírez's muted response in El Clamor Público reflected their shock. "We hope," he wrote, "that those arrested are examined by competent authorities, that the innocent are released, and the wicked receive their deserved punishment."

Pío Pico with his wife and two nieces, ca. 1850.

Andrés Pico, ca. 1860.

Benjamin Hayes, 1849.

Emily Chauncey Hayes and son
Chauncey, ca. 1857.

Andrew Jackson King, ca. 1865.

Stephen Clark Foster, ca. 1890.

James S. Waite, ca. 1860.

Francisco P. Ramírez, 1855.

John O. Wheeler, ca. 1860.

Juan Bautista Alvarado, ca. 1850.

José Castro, ca. 1845.

Raphaela Cota de Temple, Jonathan Temple, and their son-in-law Gregorio de Ajuria, ca. 1860.

Manuel Requena, ca. 1855.

José Antonio Carrillo, ca. 1850.

Antonio F. Coronel, ca. 1880.

Abel Stearns, ca. 1860.

Jean Louis Vignes, ca. 1860.

Benjamin D. Wilson (third from left) with his second wife, the widow Margaret Hereford Wilson, and her two sons, ca. 1855.

David Alexander and William Workman, ca. 1860.

John Rowland, Alberta Rowland, and child, ca. 1860.

John C. Frémont, 1850.

Robert F. Stockton, 1839.

Stephen Watts Kearny, ca. 1845.

John Strother Griffin, ca. 1870.

Jonathan Drake Stevenson, ca. 1847.

Richard Barnes Mason, ca. 1850.

Antonio María Lugo, ca. 1855.

Francisco de Paula "Menito" Lugo,
ca. 1855.

Joseph Lancaster Brent, ca. 1860.

Horace Bell, ca. 1865.

James Alexander Watson, ca.
1865.

William "Uncle Billy" Rubottom,
ca. 1870.

Henry D. Barrows, ca. 1865.

Henry Hamilton, ca. 1870.

Josephine Donna Smith (Ina Coolbrith), ca. 1870.

Melvina Prater, ca. 1870.

Tomás Sánchez, ca. 1865.

Edward John Cage Kewen, ca. 1860.

Phineas Banning, ca. 1865

Charles Wilkins, ca. 1860

María Merced Williams, Margarita Chata Bandini, and Francisca Williams, ca. 1860.

John Rains, ca. 1860.

Robert Carlisle, ca. 1860.

José Ramón Carrillo, ca. 1860.

Above: Manuel Olegario,
ca. 1870.

Left: J. J. Warner with Cahuilla
leaders, including Chief Manuel
Largo, with mustache, ca. 1875.

Henry T. Hazard, ca. 1875.

James Francis Burns, ca. 1875.

Robert M. Widney, ca. 1870.

Ygnacio Sepúlveda, ca. 1875.

Anglo vigilantes conducted similar searches for "villains" throughout the county. William Osburn's company continued to terrorize the Spanish-speaking residents of the San Gabriel Valley, invading homes, arresting suspects, and threatening a repetition of the horror they had perpetrated at the mission. A number of Anglos objected to Osburn's methods, but like the Californios most remained silent. Michael White of San Gabriel was one of the few who did not. Learning that Osburn had seized a young Californio whose family lived and worked at his rancho, White swore he would rescue the boy. Friends warned he might suffer the same fate as the Californios if he challenged Osburn, but White didn't care. "I was determined to have the boy if it cost me my life," he later recalled. Arming himself with a pair of revolvers, he rode to the encampment of Osburn's vigilantes. As White approached, he could see the boy sitting in the midst of the Anglos, his head in his hands, weeping. White dismounted and was immediately challenged by Osburn. "I want that boy and I will have him," White said. The two men glared at each other for a moment before Osburn stepped aside and White took the boy home.

ANDRÉS PICO and his fifty-one lanceros, in pursuit of the Manillas, arrived in San Juan Capistrano on Tuesday, January 27, and the following day were joined by a company of twenty-six Americans from the Monte under the command of Dr. Frank Gentry. Pico and Gentry were well acquainted, having served together on the executive committee of the local Democratic Party, and they agreed to work in concert. Their cooperation was in dramatic contrast to the violent ethnic conflict taking place in San Gabriel and Los Angeles, about which both men were ignorant. On Thursday, Luiseño scouts reported the discovery of the gang's hideout, in a ravine near the head of Santiago Canyon in the Santa Ana Mountains, some twenty-five miles north of San Juan, and that evening the combined force of Californios and Anglos headed out together. Traveling at night to avoid detection, they made their way up Trabuco Creek to the mouth of the canyon that led to the Manillas' lair, where they made a cold camp.

Don Andrés had a plan. Once again he dispatched his Luiseño scouts, this time with instructions to make contact with the young Angeleno outlaw Antonio María "Chino" Varela, the son of Sérbulo Varela, Pico's comrade-in-arms during the war of conquest. In exchange for Varela's betrayal of the gang, Don Andrés offered his personal guarantee that the young man would be neither harmed nor prosecuted. Late on Friday the Luiseños returned with good news. One of them had managed a few secret words with Varela, and he indicated his readiness to surrender. Pico and Gentry agreed the Californios would make the initial advance, while the Americans blocked Trabuco Pass, the escape route north over the Santa Anas.

Don Andrés and his men began their ascent of the canyon at first light on Saturday and reached their destination by midmorning. Varela had been instructed to watch for an opportunity to join them and provide information on the precise whereabouts of the rest of the gang. But as Pico's men were taking up position, they heard a clamor on a ridge above, and looking up they saw the Manillas escaping into the mountain fastness. The Californios had been discovered. According to the Luiseños, the gang's only avenue of escape was by a rugged trail leading ten or twelve miles down Santiago Canyon. Dispatching a runner to inform Gentry, Don Andrés and his men set off in hot pursuit.

The chase continued for several hours, and it was late afternoon by the time the Manillas reached the mouth of the canyon, the Californios still on their heels. The trail before them wound around the base of an isolated peak that rose nearly a thousand feet. A mile or two beyond, the plains of the valley floor offered the opportunity to scatter. Then they saw Gentry's men, who had arrayed themselves along the trail ahead, blocking their passage. The outlaws had nowhere to go but up the side of the peak. It was a moment of desperation, and in the confusion Chino Varela managed to break away, surrendering to the oncoming Californios. He was quick to volunteer information and prove his loyalty. Only five of the gang remained, he told Pico. Three had been killed in the fight with Barton's posse, and five more—including José Santos, Andrés Fuentes, and the seriously wounded Pancho Daniel—had fled for parts unknown immediately after the shootout. A few minutes later another Manilla, Sonoreño Juan Catabo, gave himself up, declaring his fear of climbing that peak.

Pico and Gentry assessed the situation. Four Manillas had ascended the northwestern slope, pulling their horses up behind them, but the peak's southern face dropped off precipitously. It looked as though they would have to come down the way they had gone up, so that was how the leaders positioned their men. One option was to simply wait them out, running the risk that with nightfall one or more of the outlaws might slip through their lines. But going up after them would expose the men to fire from above. Tomás Sánchez, Pico's lieutenant, nevertheless declared his willingness to lead an assault. He was joined by Bethel Coopwood, second in command of the American company. With a party of half a dozen men, they cautiously ascended the peak on foot, keeping their eyes fixed above as they climbed. None of the outlaws appeared and there was no shooting. Reaching the summit, they still saw no Manillas.

Sánchez led the men across the rocky pinnacle to its southern face, which fell off at a steep angle. There, some fifty feet down the slope, they saw four horses and one of the outlaws, a Sonoreño named Francisco Ardillero, looking back at them with his hands high in the air. Their revolvers cocked and extended, Sánchez, Gentry, and the others cautiously made their way toward him. Ardillero was standing at the edge of the cliff, and immediately it became clear that the other outlaws had used their reatas to lower themselves down the rock face. Ardillero, who had been too frightened to make the drop, was sent back under guard. Sánchez tested the ropes and found them securely fastened. Placing his knife between his teeth and taking hold with both hands, he slowly made his way down. At the bottom he found a broken gun but no Manillas. Neither the Californios nor the Americans had expected the outlaws to come down on that side, and with the way clear, they had made their escape into the thick chaparral.

The light was already failing, so the two companies made camp.

The following morning Sánchez and a number of Americans started for Los Angeles with Chino Varela, who promised help in locating the Manillas who had left earlier. Pico and Gentry divided their companies into smaller parties and began scouring the area for signs of the fugitives. That afternoon Gentry's party discovered their trail, several miles down Santiago Creek, and pursuing it his men caught sight of them. "We galloped upon them," said Pedro Rivera, riding with Gentry, "and they jumped into a ravine." There was an exchange of gunfire, and one of the Americans was wounded before the outlaws finally gave themselves up. First to surrender was Leonardo Lopez, a Mexican, who asked for water and tobacco. He was followed by Californio José Jesús Espinoza and finally by Juan Flores himself, suffering from a gunshot wound to his left arm, inflicted when his revolver had accidentally discharged during the perilous descent of the cliff. In his pocket was Sheriff Barton's gold watch.

Gentry dispatched a messenger to Pico with the news, then turned homeward with his prisoners. It was late Sunday afternoon, and the Americans had been in the saddle for nearly a week. Five or six miles brought them to the headquarters of Rancho Lomas de Santiago, where they camped for the night, tying up the prisoners and locking them in an outbuilding. Accounts differ about what happened next. According to one report, in deference to his wound, Flores was not bound quite as tightly as the other two, and he was able to wiggle free. According to another, he used his teeth to loosen the ropes of the others. When, about midnight, the sentry unlocked the door to check on the prisoners, they struck him unconscious and fled into the night. By the time the sentry recovered his senses and raised the alarm, the Manillas were long gone.

A messenger carried the news to Los Angeles that same day. "The town is in a perfect rage at the escape of the three prisoners," William Wallace reported. "And worst of all, they escaped from our own men," meaning the Americans. Since the troubles of the previous summer, the Monte Boys had been lionized by Angelenos. "But the Monte is not popular just now," Wallace wrote, "because just at the moment when they were desired to be ferocious, they took a freak of being kindhearted." A report of the escape reached Don Andrés as he and his Californios made the trek down Santiago Canyon with outlaws Juan Catabo and Francisco Ardillero in custody. According to Wallace, Pico "tore his hair, swore a thousand *carajos*, seized his two prisoners, marched them back into the canyon, and hung them from the branches of a tree." The large sycamore from which they were hanged still stands in Precitos Canyon, near Irvine Lake. Pico ordered the dead men's ears cut off, proof that the Californios had done their duty, even if the Anglos had not.

THE FOLLOWING MORNING, Tuesday, February 3, two men guarding the trail over Santa Susana Pass, in the northern part of Los Angeles County, some seventy miles from Rancho Lomas de Santiago, observed a lone rider slowly approaching from the valley side. Stepping from behind a rock with their revolvers leveled and cocked, they caught him unawares and commanded him to dismount. Dressed in ragged clothing and without arms, the man identified himself as an emancipado from Mission San Fernando, scouting for stray stock. He had not expected to find anyone on this little-used trail, he said. The guards had been stationed there the day before by ranchero James Thompson, proprietor of nearby Rancho del Encino, who suspected that one or more of the Manillas gang might head that way, and ordered his volunteer company to close off all the roads leading out of the San Fernando Valley. The guards had orders to bring in anyone who tried to cross, so they escorted their prisoner back down to Rancho del Encino. Californios there identified the man as Juan Flores.

A large and boisterous crowd watched as Thompson escorted Flores into Los Angeles on Thursday afternoon. Taken directly to the county jail, a blacksmith spent the better part of an hour manacling his arms and legs in heavy irons. "He rests quietly and seems unconcerned about the fate that awaits him," Francisco Ramírez reported. "A throng of onlookers crowded around to see such a brave man who had accomplished such daring feats." Among them was William Wallace, who readily admitted his admiration of the man's skill at eluding capture. In less than thirty-six hours Flores had made his way from the far south of the county to the far north. "He has run the gauntlet the whole distance—his escapes are marvelous—but his industry and perseverance are not appreciated here." Anglos were eager for summary justice. "Now for a hanging," Wallace announced.

Outside the pueblo the lynching of suspected accomplices continued apace. Marshal Getman reported the discovery of three unidentified Mexican bodies near Los Nietos, two hanging from the branches of a tree, a third at the bottom of a ravine nearby with a bullet in his brain. Another two Mexicans were lynched near Fort Tejon, in the Tehachapi Mountains. It is unlikely these victims had anything to do with the death of Sheriff Barton. Mob law provided a cover for the violent resolution of old disputes, and Mexican bodies swinging from the sycamore trees sent a message of terror to the Spanish-speaking community.

A company from the Monte, led by the old vigilante Ezekiel Rubottom, returned from the north to report that they had executed two men near Mission San Buenaventura. One had nothing to do with the Manillas, but the other was José Jesús Espinoza, a Californio who escaped with Flores. Espinoza's confession, printed in the *Star*, offered a candid thumbnail history of the gang. "We, the thieves and murderers, are but ten persons," he said, supplying a list of names that corresponded precisely with the one provided by Chino Varela. "Our organization dates back one month or a little less, in which time we committed four murders near San Juan, and one murder in that place. We have stolen from three stores in San Juan, taking away goods and money, which with that taken from the murdered persons, I think might exceed $120, and about ten horses. This is the truth, which I sign with a cross before my name, as I cannot write." There was nothing "revolutionary" about the Manillas.

Four members of the gang remained at large, including Pancho Daniel and Andrés Fuentes. Four had already died at the hands of vigilantes, while Juan Flores and Chino Varela were in the custody of the committee of safety, awaiting their fate along with the fifty-two men jailed during the dragnet of Sonoratown. Over the next several days the clamor for summary justice increased among Anglos, and by Tuesday, February 10, with the arrival in the pueblo of a large contingent of Monte Boys eager for a hanging, it looked as if the situation might spin out of control. That afternoon the committee summoned the town to a public meeting chaired by attorney Jonathan R. Scott, who assured the crowd that the prisoners were secure and proposed a public trial on the upcoming Saturday, providing a few more days for those prisoners "to prove their innocence." Scott's comment inadvertently highlighted one of the critical distinctions between vigilantism and the law, which considered suspects innocent until proven guilty. Scott's motion was carried by a majority of those present, although many of the Monte Boys objected that when it came to hanging, there was no time like the present.

Chino Varela presented a special case since he had surrendered with the promise of a pardon. In a letter to the *Star*, Frank Gentry and Bethel Coopwood declared themselves "honor bound" to uphold that agreement because it had been made by Andrés Pico, "who in every action was honorable and acted in good faith towards the Americans." Honoring that promise was only just, Franciso Ramírez argued in *El Clamor Público*, because Varela had joined the gang under "threats of violence." But no evidence supports that contention. According to witnesses, Varela had participated enthusiastically in the invasion of the shops in San Juan and was triggerman in the murder of shopkeeper George Pflugardt. Pico made his offer of pardon not because Varela was a victim but because, as Antonio Coronel put it, the young man was "very respectably connected," with kinship ties to several elite Californio families. Influential Americans endorsed the deal not only out of respect for Don Andrés but because Varela's father, Don Sérbulo, had risked his life during the war of conquest to save the American prisoners from execution.

Varela's fate was the subject of some debate, but there was virtual unanimity about what should be done with Flores. Ramírez was among the few dissenters. "Let us not stain our hands with the blood of our brothers," he cautioned. He remained opposed to vigilantism. "Let the authorities carry out their responsibilities. If we do not respect the law, we renounce all sense of honor and respectability." Henry Hamilton, editor of the *Star*, counterpunched. If the prosecution of Flores was left to the state, he feared, he would be "patted on the shoulder and told to go away home and be a good boy." In a matter of such importance, Hamilton insisted, it was meet and proper that the decision be left to the people. "God bless the people, we say—they may be deceived and deluded for a while, but in the end they make all things right." The most bellicose counsel came from Henry Barrows, local correspondent for the San Francisco *Daily Evening Bulletin* and a leader of the county's nascent Republican Party. Barton's assassination, Barrows declared, "was the fatal result of not hanging Juan Flores and his companions two years ago," when he was arrested for horse theft. The people should not pass up the opportunity to rectify that error.

SATURDAY MORNING dawned cloudy and cool, the aftermath of a heavy rainstorm the previous day that turned the pueblo's streets into seas of mud. At ten the clang of the triangle summoned a crowd of some several hundred men to the street in front of Montgomery House. Among them were a number of volunteer companies from the pueblo, including one from the French community, another from the Monte, and two or three made up entirely of Californios. Those who arrived on horseback remained mounted, while those on foot were forced to stand in mud up to their ankles. The meeting was chaired by Judge Scott. "Old Scott rose," Wallace reported, "and proposed that in the proceedings of the day, the will of the majority should govern the whole." The crowd roared its approval. Scott, always an enthusiastic vigilante, did not raise the option of turning the case against Flores over to the courts, but immediately began presenting it to the crowd. The evidence was read aloud in three languages, Spanish, French, and

English. Ramírez knew what was coming. "It was of course proposed that Flores be hung, his crimes being well documented, and of course the crowd cheered its approval without dissent." Wallace's account was more enthusiastic. "This, I think, was one of the most magnificent spectacles ever witnessed by man," he wrote. "The whole people, of all colors, rose up together as one and said: 'Let him be hung.' The cold-blooded murderer was beyond the pale even of friendship. Not a human voice was raised in his behalf. He was not fit to live even in this community, and you may well conceive that a man who is not fit to live in *this* community must be a very bad man."

What of the suspects who remained in jail? Over the previous several days their number had been whittled down to some twenty men. According to Ramírez, "before being released, each had to undergo a kind of inquisition in which they were asked about their lives and occupations—and if at any time they had committed an offense for which they had been punished." Those who remained incarcerated were suspected of various crimes, but none were linked to the Manillas, and Scott proposed that their cases be turned over to the legally-constituted authorities. The crowd indicated its approval by voice vote, with Henry Barrows on the losing side. "It was generally expected that there would have been several of the compadres of Flores hung with him, and there is a good deal of dissatisfaction expressed because they were not," he reported. "A great ado is made, talking, voting, excitement, and it all ends in smoke."

Dissenters like Barrows refused to let the question die. Several men harangued the crowd with the evidence against two Mexicans who the previous day had been arrested on suspicion of stealing horses. Someone moved that they be hanged alongside Flores, and Scott called for a show of hands: there were 257 for summary execution and 395 for leaving the matter for the courts to decide. According to Wallace, "the Americans were for hanging, believing that a severe example was needed to check crime." The opposition came from the French and the Californios. Ramírez was "shocked and horrified to see so many people in favor of sacrificing some unhappy Mexicans alongside the bandit Flores for simply stealing a horse. But," he added, "we must rejoice that the great majority of thinking people rejected violence. Sad to say, we had feared the worst."

By then it was nearly noon and the crowd was growing restless. A man rose in his stirrups and called for attention. "All who are in favor of hanging Flores, follow me!" he shouted. The crowd responded immediately. Everyone turned south and followed the mounted companies to the jail. Neither the undersheriff nor the county jailer put up the slightest resistance, so the crowd remained orderly. A delegation went inside and found Flores in his cell, praying with two priests from the Plaza church. His irons were removed and he was escorted out, surrounded by a heavy guard. He had dressed for the occasion in white linen trousers, white collarless shirt, and embroidered vest, over which he wore a fashionable black merino sack coat. "There was nothing in his appearance," noted the *Star*, "to indicate the formidable bandit which he had proved himself to be."

Sunshine broke through the clouds as Flores, accompanied by the priests and surrounded by guards, ascended Gallows Hill, followed by the large crowd. The surrounding hills were covered with spectators, including women and children. Reaching the summit, Flores, the priests, and the executioner mounted the ungainly gallows hastily erected that morning. Flores was offered a cigarillo, which he smoked as the priests prayed. Then he addressed the crowd. He spoke in a calm, firm voice, his words translated into French and English by an interpreter. He was ready to die, he said. He had committed many crimes but harbored no ill will against anyone, and hoped none would bear ill will toward him. The executioner bound his arms and legs, adjusted the noose around his neck, and tied a white handkerchief over his eyes. The priests descended the platform and the executioner made ready as Flores stood silently before the crowd for several moments, his body trembling slightly.

The latch was pulled and Flores dropped, but the fall did not kill him. His body bucked and convulsed, the cord binding his arms slipped, and they flailed wildly in a vain attempt to grasp the rope and stop the agony. "He was hung very much like a dog," reported William Wallace, "and the way he dangled in the air afforded a disgusting spectacle to the people." It was thirty minutes before the attending physician declared Flores dead. He had been hanged with the reata of one of the men slain with Barton, and it had proved far too short. "Those who seek vengeance," observed Ramírez, "dote on the most insignificant of details."

A FEW DAYS LATER California governor J. Neely Johnson issued a proclamation offering a large cash reward for the apprehension of the Manillas still at large, provoking an intensive manhunt that lasted many months. The murderers of a county sheriff could not be allowed to remain free. Angelenos soon learned that Andrés Fuentes, the man who killed Barton, had fled to Mexico, beyond their reach. Pancho Daniel and Leonardo López, however, had remained closer. In early December the sheriff of Santa Clara County in the north arrested López after a desperate gunfight that left him seriously wounded. William Getman, elected to succeed Barton as county sheriff, brought López back on the steamer. He was tried in district court with Judge Hayes presiding and found guilty of the murder of George Pflugardt. Asked whether he wished to make a statement before sentencing, López gave what William Wallace characterized as a brave speech. He was innocent of Plugardt's murder and everyone knew it, he said. Indeed, the testimony clearly indicated that Chino Varela had fired the fatal shot. But, López continued, "inasmuch as they had resolved to hang him, he did not comprehend why they should torment him by keeping him two or three months in jail, exposed to the curiosity of any impertinent person who might come to look at him. Why not hang him at once, as they had the other Californians? He was ready to die, and didn't ask any favors." When López finished, Hayes pronounced sentence, setting the execution for two months hence, the soonest the law would allow.

A few weeks later the same sheriff who captured López arrested

Pancho Daniel, who was also brought south and placed in a cell next to his compatriot. In the meantime, Los Angeles had suffered another shocking act of violence, the cold-blooded murder of Sheriff Getman by a deranged Anglo. In the excitement that followed, there were calls for hanging all the inmates of the jail, but cooler heads prevailed, and on February 16, as Daniel remained in his cell, López was executed in the jail yard alongside another murderer, an Anglo convicted of cold-blooded murder. In his gallows declaration, López advised young men to take caution from his example. If any of his creditors were present, he joked, he would happily write them a bank draft. James Thompson, acting sheriff, appointed to fill out Getman's term, had made careful preparations, and the double hanging came off without a hitch. "It was a happy day for society," wrote Ramírez. "Let us hope that the terrible spectacle of death, presented so often before the eyes of the people, will serve as an example."

When Pancho Daniel came to trial in March 1858, court-assigned defense attorney Columbus Sims requested a postponement until he could arrange for witnesses from San José he claimed would prove that Daniel had been in the north at the time of Barton's murder. Hayes granted the request and set a new trial date for the court's next term. "Considerable uneasiness was manifested at this continuance," wrote Wallace. Henry Barrows was more explicit. "There is here a quiet but deep feeling," he wrote, "that if the law should fail to mete out justice, the PEOPLE will not. It is this very certainty that gives us security. The source of all power in human society is in the PEOPLE; law is merely their organized representative. When that becomes inactive or inadequate, it is their duty to come to its rescue, and in desperate cases to act directly and instantly."

The trial began in July. Hayes issued venire for ninety-six prospective jurors, and Sheriff Thompson supervised their selection from the county's register of voters. Most of them were present when attorney Sims challenged the entire panel on the grounds of bias, arguing that Sheriff Thompson—a good friend of Barton's and renowned as Flores's captor—had tainted the process by publicly declaring that Daniel was guilty. The prosecution objected, and rather than rule on the question himself, Hayes selected three lawyers as triers to investigate the charge. After interviewing Thompson they decided in favor of Sims. Hayes ordered that another panel of prospective jurors be summoned by County Coroner J. C. Welsh. But once that panel had assembled, Sims challenged Welsh's objectivity as well. Hayes appointed another three triers, who again found for Sims. "It will be next to impossible to find a jury in the county who have not expressed opinions," Barrows reported. Virtually every public official in Los Angeles was on record excoriating Pancho Daniel. The legal maneuvering took up an entire month. Judge Hayes was due to open the summer term of district court in San Diego, so for a second time he postponed the trial, and placed it on the calendar for the autumn. Bewildering procedural delay was the cost for following the rule of law. But it confused many people and encouraged them to support alternatives that promised more immediate satisfaction.

BENJAMIN HAYES was nearing the end of his six-year term as district judge. The preceding year he and his wife, Emily, had debated whether or not he should stand for another. Her consumption had grown much worse, often confining her to bed for days at a time. She required considerably more care, and although Hayes made arrangements with friends and relatives, both of them dreaded the weeks he rode the circuit, away from the family. They talked it over one afternoon as they strolled the vineyard district, returning home with a basket of peaches and ripe figs, on which they made their supper. It was then that Emily Hayes made her declaration. "I hope you will not again be a candidate for judge," she said. "I never wish you to be electioneering and treating, as when you were a candidate before." Hayes recorded the conversation in his diary before bed that evening. "My father once told me that he had often lost greatly in life by not taking my mother's advice. What if Emily be right on this occasion? The matter will have to be thought of carefully." In the succeeding months

Hayes indeed thought about it a great deal. But he and Emily never spoke of it again, for the following day she suffered a hemorrhage of the lungs and died within minutes.

Hayes was disconsolate. His sisters were there to help with his son, Chauncey, and he had many supportive friends, but in his despair he turned back to the bottle. Alcoholism would remain a problem for the rest of his life and may be what led to his premature death in 1877, an old man at the age of just sixty-two. About the judgeship, Hayes remained undecided for some months. What persuaded him to run again was the opposition to his candidacy from within the Democratic Party. Hayes had studiously kept out of the increasingly partisan political contests in the county, which infuriated local party boss and former friend Joseph Lancaster Brent, who openly solicited other candidates for district court judge, men Hayes considered far less scrupulous than himself. With vigilantism in ascendance, Hayes became convinced that southern California required his continued presence on the bench. He issued a formal announcement of his candidacy several months after Emily's death, in July 1858. "All my life I have been a Democrat," he wrote. "But I beg leave to add that, in my opinion, the office of Judge should be maintained free forever from any influence of mere party politics." He sought reelection as an independent, "without reference to the proceedings of any cabal, committee, or convention." He would stand for another term, despite Emily's dying wish, but would honor her memory by declining to campaign. The Democrats, sensing a losing fight, did not run a candidate of their own. The Republicans put up Columbus Sims. In the September election Hayes was reelected by a large majority, which he interpreted as a vindication for the authority of the law, although it seems likely that many voters cast their ballots against Sims, the defender of Pancho Daniel, rather than in favor of Hayes.

When the Daniel trial reconvened in November, Hayes appointed Antonio Coronel to summon a panel of prospective jurors. Sims objected once again, but Hayes overruled him. Coronel, a consummate politician, had been careful to keep mum during the crisis following Barton's death. But when Hayes directed that the trial proceed with the selection of a jury, Sims filed for a change of venue, forcing a hearing on the matter. It revealed, to the surprise of no one, that many Angelenos believed that if the court failed to convict, the people should act. Four years before, Hayes had denied similar motions from Jonathan Scott and Joseph Lancaster Brent, representing David Brown and William Lee, and had been rebuked by the California Supreme Court. On November 24 he granted Sims's motion and reassigned the case to the district court in Santa Barbara.

Six days later, shortly before sunrise on the morning of November 30, the county jailer was on his way to market when he was waylaid by a group of eight or ten armed men, who forced him back to the jail and demanded the keys. Seeing that resistance was useless, he handed them over. The men opened the gate to the yard and were immediately joined by several dozen more who had concealed themselves in a neighboring corral. Henry Barrows may have been among them, for his report of the event reads like an eyewitness account. The leaders unlocked the door and entered the jail, emerging some time later with an ashen-faced Pancho Daniel. "He rather broke down at first," wrote Barrows, but "then recovered and told them to bid his wife good-bye; said he was ready, and stood up to his fate like a hero—or bravado, as he was." Daniel was hanged without ceremony from the crosspiece over the gate posts. It took a long time for him to die.

The news quickly spread through town and a large crowd gathered. "Some turned away and said nothing," wrote Barrows, "but most said, in words, in looks, or in acts, 'Amen—it is well!' Some few of the lower class of Californians or Sonoranians vowed vengeance on his murderers, as they call his executioners. But they will hardly undertake any overt act. If they do, they may find it a terrible business for themselves." After an hour or so the body was taken down and delivered to Daniel's wife, who had come down from San José for the trial. An inquest over the body was held later that day at the house where she was staying. The coroner's jury concluded that Daniel had been "accidentally hung through the carelessness of some American citizens."

Pancho Daniel was the fourteenth and final lynching in the aftermath of the fatal attack on Sheriff Barton's posse, and as in the other summary executions there was nothing at all careless about it. The lynching had been carefully planned and executed by what the *Star* called "a committee acting on behalf of a larger body of citizens." Barrows celebrated their accomplishment. The day previous to the lynching the vigilance committee had planted a false report that Andrés Fuentes had been seen near San Gabriel. Sheriff Thompson and his deputy went to investigate, getting them "out of the way." The vigilantes met in secret and were careful to cover their tracks. "The execution," Barrows wrote, "was so well planned and executed that scarcely a person in town knew of word of it till it was all over." This was vigilantism of a new, secretive type, and for the next dozen years it would dominate Los Angeles. "Justice, though tardy, had been done at last," wrote Barrows. "The criminal has met that terrible and summary retribution which the murderer will ever meet in every community where, as here, there is a power behind the law that is swift to execute the spirit of the law, and which will not see justice foiled by the accidents or frailties of the letter of the law."

· CHAPTER 23 ·

DUELING, SHOOTING,
AND KILLING

THE LYNCHING OF PANCHO DANIEL left Francisco Ramírez
heartsick. "We can not find expressions strong enough to condemn
the conduct of those who consummated their atrocity under cover of
darkness." Ramírez expected an outpouring of protest from Californios, but it was not forthcoming. "News of the barbaric and diabolical
lynching that was perpetrated in this city has fallen on deaf ears," he
wrote, "and it will soon be forgotten, like so many other appalling
and horrifying events." The Spanish-speaking community had been
silenced by the terrorism in response to Barton's death, but Ramírez
wasn't cutting his people any slack. "You, imbecile Californios!" he
raged in *El Clamor Público*. "You must take the blame for the tragic
events we are seeing. We are tired of saying, 'Open your eyes, it's time
to uphold your rights and interests.'"

Henry Barrows responded in the San Francisco *Daily Evening Bulletin*. Ramírez was "a young man of promise, a Spanish, French, and
English scholar, and a *gentleman*," Barrows declared. But his opposition to vigilantism was "a great wrong—not alone to Americans, nor
to the society at large in which he lives, but *to his own people and race*

throughout California, for whom he volunteers to act as champion and defender." Had Ramírez forgotten the role Californios played in the lynching of David Brown? They had been justified then, argued Barrows, just as the Anglos who hanged Pancho Daniel were justified now. Ramírez stubbornly opposed vigilantism "when he knows—as all know—that justice, otherwise, *will not be done*, . . . that no one can be safe in life and property *unless the people do rise*, as they did in this county of Los Angeles."

Barrows acknowledged that when the sleeping lion awoke and the people acted, excesses sometimes occurred. "It is indeed awful that any innocent person should suffer with the guilty," he wrote. But he thought that an acceptable cost for social peace. "What would have been the condition of society if the people had not acted? Intolerable." Let the law take its course, let the courts do their job. But when the justice system failed, as it sometimes did, allow the people to do what was required. The citizens who hanged Pancho Daniel "did not desire to subvert the law," he averred. "They would gladly have been spared the duty of an exceptional breach of its *letter* to fulfill its *spirit*—for Justice must be satisfied." Murder, rape, and rapine "would have continued till nobody knows when, if our people had not banded together." But by their decisive action, "the bloody flood was stayed, and now we may live in peace." Vigilantism, Barrows argued, produced a deterrent effect, reducing the incidence of lethal violence. It had proved its worth. "We have had quiet, peaceable times since."

He overstated his case, for Los Angeles did not suddenly turn quiet and peaceable following the terror. But judging solely by the numbers, Barrows had a point. Significant episodes of vigilantism occurred in 1852 (when there were seven lynching executions), 1855 (six), and 1857 (thirteen). In each instance the number of homicides dropped significantly in the subsequent year, by a quarter in 1853 and 1856, by 40 percent in 1858. At the end of the decade the homicide rate was less than half of what it had been several years before.

Even so, Los Angeles remained a violent place, and Angelenos remained acutely aware of the problem. "Matters and things about town present the usual characteristics which later years have rendered peculiar to this people," Henry Hamilton wrote in the *Star*.

> There is the same delightful uncertainty of life, both animal and vegetable, which has served to render us peculiarly susceptible to the enjoyments of the present—meager as they may be—without hazarding our peace by speculations upon a future, which experience has taught us, defies our calculation. Possessed of a climate which challenges competition with the most favored of localities, its salubrity unsurpassed, yet the children may become familiar with the sciences of reading and writing from the numerous and ever-recurring Probate Notices, which, with their huge plethoric capitals, stare out from the walls and awning posts upon the passers by.

One of those children, sixteen-year-old Josephine Donna Smith— whose poem calling for vengeance in the aftermath of the killings Hamilton published in the *Star*—was repelled by the disorder. "This is an awful, awful town to live in," she wrote to a cousin. "I don't believe there is another place in the world so small as this town is that has more crimes committed in it every day." For Henry Barrows, the persistent high level of criminal violence simply demonstrated the necessity for more lynch law. "There has been considerable shooting and cutting in our midst of late," he reported in late 1859. "Our people will have to make an example of some of the desperadoes lurking about." If all the bad guys were lynched, crime would be eliminated.

In that year, 1859, the grand jury of Los Angeles County handed down thirty felony indictments for violent crime, but only four men were convicted. Barrows, a member of the county's Republican central committee, blamed the Democrats in control of county government since 1850. Horace Bell likewise denounced county officials as "foragers at the public crib," more interested in advancing their personal interests than in promoting collective order and justice. By California law the compensation for county officials came from the fees they collected in the course of their duties, which could add up to considerable sums. The office of sheriff in Los Angeles County was said to be worth $10,000 annually, propelling James R. Barton into the ranks of gentleman farmers.

But county officials were not simply in it for their own enrichment. They were operatives in a political machine. The opportunity to stand for county office as a Democrat was a favor bestowed by local party boss Joseph Lancaster Brent. With friendly presidential administrations in Washington after 1852, Brent also had a considerable say in the federal patronage—the appointive positions for the post office, the land office, the office of Indian affairs, the customs service, and the federal judiciary. Dozens of subordinates, appointed by county and federal officers, made up a veritable political army that mobilized at each election. The result was the dominance of "the Democracy," as the machine was known in the day. For Barrows, the Democracy was the problem. There was more to it than that, of course. The county's criminal justice system was underfunded and understaffed. Juries were extraordinarily sympathetic to claims of self-defense. The courts, undercut by vigilantism, lacked legitimacy and authority. Yet again, Barrows had a point. County officials were often incompetent and corrupt. Moreover, most were men of violence.

CONSIDER THE MAN elected district attorney of Los Angeles County in 1859, Edward John Cage Kewen, universally known as E. J. C. Kewen, or sometimes "Alphabet" Kewen, although never to his face. Kewen was one of those hot-tempered gentlemen popularly associated with the chivalrous traditions of the Old South. Born in Mississippi in 1825, he imbibed the code of honor from his Irish father, a decorated veteran of the Battle of New Orleans, who died in a duel when his son was only eight years old. Kewen was slightly built, "somewhat undersized," in the words of an acquaintance, but "every ounce of his anatomy was filled with Southern fire."

He attended university, read law, and was admitted to the Mississippi bar at the age of nineteen. The law carried him into politics. Kewen's political hero was Senator Henry Clay of Kentucky, perennial Whig candidate for president, and it was while stumping for Clay in 1844 that Kewen discovered his talent for political oratory. Politics became his lifeblood. He relocated to St. Louis, where he opened a law practice and edited a political journal until 1849, when he joined the Gold Rush at the age of twenty-four. Brash, self-confident, and full of himself, Kewen was not everyone's piece of cake. He was one of those men, wrote an associate who rode with him on the trail to California, "whom I would like to buy at *my* estimate of their worth and sell at *theirs*."

Kewen opened a law practice in Sacramento, invested in city lots, and grew wealthy. He defended the claims of speculators against the protests of settlers, and was an officer in the militia company that dispersed protesters during what became known as the Squatters' Riot of 1850, which earned Kewen the honorific title of "colonel." The following year he was joined by his two younger brothers—Achilles and Thomas—both recently returned from a failed filibuster invasion of Cuba. Kewen lent his support to their efforts to recruit Californians for another invasion of the island, and in the autumn of 1851 the two brothers departed Sacramento with a company of volunteers. The invasion never came off, and in 1853 Achilles Kewen returned to California with the news that brother Thomas was dead, the victim of a tropical disease.

By that time E. J. C. Kewen had married and relocated his practice to San Francisco, where he became a leader of the city's Whigs. In 1854 he transferred his allegiance to the nativist Know-Nothings, becoming one of their "big guns," although he was the son of an Irish emigrant. That contradiction didn't seem to bother Kewen, but his brother Achilles proved more sensitive. When, during a boozy saloon dispute, a belligerent Texan accused him of being "a damn Know Nothing," the younger Kewen punched the man in the nose. Kewen immediately offered an apology for his instinctive response, but his opponent insisted on satisfaction. In a duel fought with rifles before several hundred spectators, the Texan was killed. Politics and violence went hand in hand.

Several months later Achilles Kewen left San Francisco to join the filibustering expedition of William Walker in Nicaragua. He was shot and killed in one of his first engagements. The deaths of both his brothers, Kewen told a friend, "drove him almost to despair." He sought to avenge them in late 1855 by organizing a military company of some eighty volunteers and joining Walker in Nicaragua. He participated in several minor skirmishes and was twice wounded before Walker appointed him principal spokesman and fund-raiser for the cause, a task for which Kewen was far better suited.

Filibustering enjoyed wide support in California. William Walker fought under the "lone star" banner of American expansionist tradition. In the *Star*, Henry Hamilton celebrated the "new fields of glory" Walker had opened in Central America "for adventurous spirits." One of those spirits was Horace Bell, who enthusiastically enrolled as an officer in Walker's army in early 1856. Bell loved the camaraderie and saw a good deal of action—suffering a serious wound in one engagement—but found the experience deeply disillusioning. The turning point for him came during a conversation with a fellow officer after a particularly bloody fight. "Look here, my friend," the man told Bell, "do you know that we are in the wrong? We are trying to rob these people of their property and country. They are fighting for all they hold dear—and right always prevails over wrong." Filibustering, Bell concluded, was "the spirit of conquest run riot."

Walker suffered ignominious defeat in 1857, and Kewen returned to California. His wife had been staying with her parents in southern California, and he relocated his legal practice there, moving the family into a palatial adobe in San Gabriel. By that time Kewen had abandoned the Know-Nothings for the Democrats. In political philosophy, he explained, he remained "a Whig of olden time—a disciple of Clay." But times had changed. The critical political choice of the day, he delared, was between "Democracy and Black Republicanism," and there was no doubt where Kewen stood on that divide.

Local Democratic leaders welcomed him enthusiastically into their ranks.

A NOTHER LEADING MEMBER of the southern California Democracy was Hilliard P. Dorsey, a Mississippi native who had moved to Los Angeles to assume a patronage appointment as register of the U.S. Land Office. Dorsey located near Kewen in San Gabriel, and they became fast friends. Dorsey was "a fighter from way back," Horace Bell recalled, "a pistol fighter, a knife fighter, and away up in rough and tumble." He joined William Osburn in the terrorist assault on the Californio community at Mission San Gabriel in the aftermath of Sheriff Barton's death. But it wasn't only Californios who were wary of Dorsey. His no-holds-barred fight with U.S. Attorney Isaac S. K. Ogier was only one of his many brawls with fellow Anglos. "The greater portion of the neighborhood in which he lived was in constant dread of him," wrote a contemporary, "and would yield to almost any terms to prevent a difficulty with him."

In 1857 Dorsey married Civility Rubottom, youngest daughter of William "Uncle Billy" Rubottom of the Monte, and the following spring she delivered a son they named Kewen, in honor of their neighbor. But Dorsey's violent temper ruined the marriage. "My daughter was high-spirited," recalled Rubottom, and Dorsey "didn't know how to treat a woman." The bickering and fighting increased after the birth of their son. During an argument one evening Dorsey flew into a rage and violently forced his wife from the house. She showed up at her parents' place late that night, bloody and bruised, in fear for her own life, and frantic over the child. Rubottom rode to Kewen's place and asked him to intervene.

Kewen went to Dorsey's the following morning and found his friend, he testified, "promenading the parlor with the child in his arms." He was on a mission of reconciliation, Kewen said, but Dorsey would have none of it. "Where's my wife?" he demanded. When Kewen told him, Dorsey put down the child and began to load an assortment of firearms. "I'll have my wife here today or I'll die," he declared. She would come home willingly, said Kewen, if only Dorsey would allow her to see the child first. "Not unless stained with its father's blood," Dorsey replied. He "spoke in a voice so calm, so composed, and so full of determination," Kewen testified, that "his words sounded upon my ears like the premonitions of destiny." Hoping to forestall violence, Kewen immediately left for Rubottom's in his buggy, but was soon overtaken and passed by Dorsey, mounted on a fast horse.

When Dorsey arrived, Rubottom later told Horace Bell, "I was sitting on my front porch with a double-barreled shotgun across my knees." Noting that his son-in-law was packing a Colt's revolver, Rubottom called out a warning. "Dorsey, I have but one request to make, and that is that you do not enter my gate." Dorsey responded with cold determination. "I'll come in or die," he said. "We'll end it right here." Then, reaching up, he absent-mindedly plucked a leaf from the hedge surrounding the front yard, placed the stem between his gritted teeth, and pushed open the gate. "He didn't hesitate one instant but walked right in, revolver in hand," said Rubottom. Dorsey cocked and leveled his piece, and as he did so Rubottom dropped to one knee. The two men fired simultaneously. Dorsey's shot went high, slamming into the wall of the house. But Rubottom's double load of buckshot found its mark. When Kewen arrived, minutes later, he found Dorsey on the ground, "a bleeding and gasping corpse."

Friends of the family upheld both men. "It had to be," they said, "what else could either do?" The conviction that lethal violence offered the only possible resolution of this family dispute spoke volumes about the honor culture of frontier Los Angeles.

VIOLENCE AND THE RHETORIC OF VIOLENCE permeated political discourse both before and after the American conquest. That was particularly true during the gathering national storm over the expansion of slavery in the western territories. The Democrats split into two querulous factions. The dominant bloc, known as the "Chivalry" in California because so many of its leaders had come from the South, was aggressively proslavery. In Los Angeles the Chivs were led by Joseph Lancaster Brent of Baltimore and New Orleans, and supported by the oratorical E. J. C. Kewen of Mississippi. The opposition free-soil faction was led by John G. Downey, naturalized immigrant from Ireland and Los Angeles pharmacist who made his fortune lending money to needy rancheros at usurious rates. The most prominent free-soil spokesman was J. J. Warner, who relocated from San Diego to Los Angeles, purchasing the press of the defunct *Southern Californian* and commencing publication of the *Southern Vineyard*, an avowedly free-soil weekly.

Both factions of the Democracy fielded candidates for the statewide election of September 1859, and the campaign that summer was a vituperative, no-holds-barred affair. Warner ran for an open seat in the state assembly, Kewen for county district attorney, but they expended most of their energy attacking each other rather than their specific opponents. Warner went after Kewen's filibustering past, consistently referring to him as "the citizen corporal of Nicaragua." Like a bandit in the night, Warner declared, Kewen "sneaked into a country with his accomplices for the avowed purpose of despoiling the inhabitants of their goods, chattels, lands, and homes." Kewen responded by digging up the old accusation that Warner had favored the Californians during the war of conquest and thus was "a traitor to his country." He was "so notoriously corrupt and villainous," Kewen declared, "as to wholly exclude him from any consideration except that which prompts a man to kick a snarling cur that intercepts his path." Friends of both candidates worried that the rhetoric would end in actual violence. Murray Morrison, a prominent Democrat and a close associate of Kewen's—he was engaged to the sister of Kewen's wife—took pains to establish a line of communication between the two camps, which may have prevented the candidates from coming to blows, or worse. A violent encounter was by no means inconceivable.

As for the opposition Republicans, local support remained very weak. Francisco Ramírez, Republican candidate for the legislature, had been badly defeated in 1858 but made another attempt in 1859. "I am a Republican from principle," he declared, "believing that the doctrines on which the party is founded are coeval with Liberty and the Rights of Man." The party's local strategy was to break the Chivalry's lock on the Californio vote. But despite endorsements from a growing list of prominent *hijos del país*—including former governor Pío Pico, merchant Manuel Requena, and ranchero José Ramón Carrillo— the Republicans were completely shut out. John G. Downey won the statewide contest for lieutenant governor and Warner won an assembly seat, but the Chivs took all the other prizes, electing Kewen district attorney, Tomás Sánchez county sheriff, Andrés Pico state senator, and Andrew Jackson King the county's second assemblyman. "It is unbelievable," Ramírez wrote, "that after so many insults and affronts, one still sees the sad spectacle of Hispanic Americans supporting the slavery party with their votes." Several weeks later he closed his shop and ceased publication of *El Clamor Público*.

A few days after the election Senator David Broderick, statewide leader of the free-soil Democrats, was killed in a duel with David S. Terry, a prominent member of the Chivalry and a former justice of the California Supreme Court. Throughout the campaign militant Chivs had tried to gin up a fight with Broderick, an effort in which Kewen was deeply implicated, at one point carrying a formal challenge to the senator. "Dueling, shooting, and killing generally seem to be epidemic in our State just now," Henry Hamilton wrote in the *Star* following Broderick's death, but "we suppose there is little use in protesting against the bloody code." Not long afterward the Democrat-controlled legislature appointed the newly elected Chivalry governor to fill the vacancy created by Broderick's death, and John G. Downey became governor, the first Angeleno to fill that office since Pío Pico in 1845–46.

Kewen assumed his duty as Los Angeles County's chief prosecutor, although it remained to be seen how a man with such a violent temperament might handle that responsibility. The answer came a few weeks later. An anonymous letter appeared in the press criticizing

Kewen for his conduct of a pending criminal case. The publication of such complaining letters was commonplace, but Kewen could not abide personal censure of any kind. He concluded that it must have been written by Columbus Sims, opposing defense counsel for the case in question. In court the following day Kewen launched into a rhetorical assault on Sims with all the verbal vitriol at his command. Finally, working himself to an emotional climax, he picked up a parcel of papers and flung them at Sims, who instinctively grabbed a tumbler and returned fire. The missile went wide but Kewen, recoiling in shock, pulled a small pistol from his pocket and cocked it. The courtroom erupted in pandemonium. Two or three men mobbed Kewen, preventing him from firing. But in the melee Kewen's pistol fired and the ball struck a bystander, inflicting a serious wound. There is no record of Kewen's being held to legal account for this criminal outburst, but Hamilton condemned his conduct in the *Star*. "It places the district attorney in a very awkward position," he wrote, "for after this display of lawlessness, how can he consistently demand the punishment of offenders against the law."

L O S   A N G E L E S was one of the most isolated communities in the nation during the 1850s. It took several months for mail to arrive from the East until the commencement of the Butterfield Overland Mail in 1858, which cut the time to three weeks. Entrepreneurs constructed a statewide telegraphic system in the early 1850s, but it was not extended to Los Angeles until October 1860. The telegraphic connection was celebrated with a gala ball held at the Bella Union. The formalities opened with one of Kewen's trademark orations. He was followed by Henry Barrows, local correspondent for the San Francisco *Daily Evening Bulletin*, who sent the first dispatch north: "Here is the maiden salutation of Los Angeles to San Francisco by lightning!" The crowd then waited for a reply. When it arrived, it included a summary of the day's news that shocked everyone in attendance. A fusion ticket of free-soil Democrats and Republicans had triumphed at the polls in the neighboring state of Oregon, resulting in the election of the first Republican senator from the far West.

A month later, on presidential election day, the Los Angeles Democracy was even more shocked when the telegraph delivered the news that Abraham Lincoln, the Republican nominee for president, had won California's electoral votes. Proslavery and free-soil Democrats had fielded separate slates of electors, allowing Lincoln to prevail with a 35 percent plurality. In Los Angeles County, however, the proslavery ticket captured fully 45 per cent of the vote. Henry Hamilton comforted his fellow Chivs in the *Star*. "Whatever disaster may have occurred elsewhere," he wrote, "here our glorious banner flutters in victory."

There was strong secessionist sentiment in southern California following the election. That was only natural, Hamilton argued. "We are on the highway to and from the South, our population are from the South, and we sympathize with her. Why then should we turn our backs on our friends and join their enemies to invade, impoverish, and despoil them?" Judge Benjamin Hayes—who considered himself "southern from nature and association, to say nothing of principle"— was one of the few southern men to declare himself a unionist. The thought of civil war, Hayes wrote to a friend in Missouri, made him "sick at heart." He hoped Angelenos would take advantage of their isolation and remain aloof from the conflict. But Los Angeles would experience its own local civil war.

Secessionist Hamilton of the *Star* and unionist Charles R. Conway of the *Southern News*—a new paper that commenced publication in 1860, using the press of the defunct *El Clamor Público*—sought to incite rather than to calm public passions. Conway had only recently arrived in Los Angeles from the Midwest, but he quickly got up to speed, and it was not long before bad blood had developed between the two editors. Their war of words turned violent shortly after the election, when Conway published an item poking fun at Hamilton's supposed dalliance with a lady of the night. Enraged, Hamilton went looking for Conway, and finding him on the street, charged at the offending editor with a walking stick in his upraised hand. Conway pulled a revolver and fired several rounds, hitting Hamilton, who ignored his wounds and beat Conway severely before fainting from loss of blood. "This grim catastrophe struck me as quite novel and surprising," wrote a visitor to Los Angeles who witnessed the affray. "But the residents found such an occurrence commonplace." Hamilton and Conway were hauled into justice court and fined, then released to the care of their doctors.

While editors battled, partisans busied themselves organizing armed militias. The Los Angeles Grays, a unionist company chartered in early 1861, failed to muster much support. But eighty citizens enrolled in the Los Angeles Mounted Rifles, a secessionist group commanded by Undersheriff Alonzo Ridley. Ridley, a thirty-year-old former miner, trader, and Indian agent, was an avid supporter of the South and slavery. He petitioned the state government for support of the Mounted Rifles, and Governor John G. Downey, catering to the Chivalry faction of the party, personally authorized a full complement of rifles, revolvers, and sabers. "They would be put to good use," Ridley declared. Unionists in Los Angeles wondered just what that use might be, and Ridley was summoned before a federal grand jury to explain. No action was taken against him, but it was a reminder that federal authorities were keeping an eye on secessionists in Los Angeles.

General Albert Sidney Johnston of Texas commanded the Pacific Division of the U.S. Army, headquartered in San Francisco. Learning that his home state had joined the Confederacy, Johnston tendered his resignation and traveled south to Los Angeles, where he and his wife planned to spend several weeks with her brother, Dr. John S. Griffin, before returning east by steamer. While he was staying in San Gabriel, Johnston was approached by Undersheriff Ridley and several associates, who informed him of their plan to use the Mounted Rifles to seize control of southern California and deliver it to the Confederacy. "To all of them he gave the same advice," Johnston's wife recalled, that "nothing could be gained by turning this country into a scene of civil war." If you want to fight, he told them, "go South." Taking Johnston's advice to heart, Ridley offered the Mounted Rifles as Johnston's escort overland to Texas. Under the circumstances it was an offer Johnston could not refuse, and in the spring of 1861, leaving his wife in the care of her brother, and accompanied by at least a dozen former U. S. Army officers who had resigned their commissions, Johnston and the Mounted Rifles departed.

Several Californios joined the company, including Antonio María "Chino" Varela, the well-connected young man who had been pardoned for his criminal association with the Manillas gang. A few months before, Varela's father, Don Sérbulo, had been murdered, his throat cut ear to ear by an unknown assailant. The old rebel, increasingly addicted to drink, had before his death been arrested several times for petty theft and drunken assault. "The deceased was a great favorite with the early American residents of this section," noted the *Star*, "as he once saved their lives, aided alone by his energetic humanity." Chino Varela, his only son, would now fight for the South. The company reached Texas in July after weeks of hard travel. The Los Angeles Mounted Rifles had the dubious distinction of being the only free-state militia that went over to the Confederacy.

BRIGADIER GENERAL EDWIN V. SUMNER, Johnston's replacement as commander of the Pacific Division, was alarmed at reports of secessionist strength in Los Angeles. Nearly every county official was on the record in support of the Confederacy. Concluding that there was "more danger of disaffection at this place than any other in the state," he ordered several companies of volunteers south to garrison the pueblo. "There are people here anxious for a difficulty," Captain Winfield S. Hancock reported from Los Angeles. "Those persons who have heretofore been influential and active leaders in politics, and have exercised great control over the people, are encouraging difficulties here by open avowals of their opinions."

On a Saturday in early May 1861, several hundred secessionists paraded through the Monte under a homemade Bear Flag, their standard of rebellion. (California did not adopt the Bear Flag as the official state banner until 1911.) "We were ready and determined and well organized," remembered William "Tooch" Martin, a resident of the Monte who took part in the protest. The secessionists marched on the home of Jonathan Tibbetts, one of the few unionists in the township. "He was a Black Republican, and we knew he was giving information to the government," recalled Martin. Tibbetts was indeed reporting to federal authoritieson the activities of the Monte chapter of the Knights of the Golden Circle, a secret society that promoted a Confederate victory. The crowd surrounded the Tibbetts place, beating pots and pans and blowing horns. A man mounted a fence and shouted to Tibbetts to come out and fight. Tibbetts responded by flinging open the shutters and leveling the barrel of his rifle at the man. "Get down, Bill," he shouted. "Get down or I'll shoot you off that fence." The man got down and the protest ended without violence.

Captain Hancock was relieved. "There need be no anxiety concerning matters at this place," he reported. Unionist Angelenos were less sure about that. "Secessionists are getting very noisy here," reported U.S. Attorney Kimball S. Dimmick, the new appointee of the Lincoln administration, and "we may have to fight them yet." His appeal for additional troops was seconded by other prominent unionists, including Henry Barrows, J. J. Warner, Abel Stearns, Pío Pico, and Manuel Requena. Sumner responded swiftly and effectively, dispatching several additional companies to southern California and ordering the construction of Drum Barracks, a base near San Pedro where several thousand soldiers were garrisoned for the duration of the war. Army officers encouraged the formation of a civilian home guard, distributing arms to residents who willingly took the oath of allegiance to the United States. Emboldened, supporters of the North organized a "Union Club," which became a kind of shadow county government. "Until very lately all the 'organizing' has been on one side, and that the *wrong* side," Barrows wrote. "Patriots have come to the conclusion that it is time for *them* to organize."

A few weeks later Barrows was named U.S. marshal for the southern district of California, and soon thereafter Warner was appointed deputy provost marshal, responsible for local security. Through an extensive network of spies and informers, they provided Union officers with detailed reports of local secessionist activity. Although the struggle between the two sides continued until war's end, the troops at Camp Drum ensured that Los Angeles remained firmly within the control of the United States. Fifteen years after the war of conquest, turbulent Los Angeles was once again occupied by American troops.

· CHAPTER 24 ·

THE PLAGUE IS UPON US

OPPOSITION TO THE CIVIL WAR in Los Angeles was greatly affected by local conditions. During the war years southern California suffered through four plagues of biblical proportion. First came the flood. The rains began Christmas Eve 1861 and continued for more than a month, dumping nearly fifty inches on the county, better than three times the annual average. The Los Angeles River overflowed its banks, destroying farms, orchards, and vineyards. The San Gabriel and Santa Ana Rivers broke from their channels, creating a vast inland sea, drowning livestock by the thousands. Then came the drought. The next two winters produced less than ten inches of rain, a third of normal levels. The grasslands withered and thousands of cattle starved to death. Rancheros rushed to sell their remaining stock, creating a market glut and collapsing prices. Property values fell by more than 70 percent. The county pressed suits for delinquent taxes, and the sheriff conducted scores of forced sales from the courthouse steps.

Next came the pests. "As misfortunes come in groups and not singly," a correspondent reported in the spring of 1863, "the plague of locusts is also upon us." The black clouds of swarming insects first appeared in the San Fernando Valley, where they attacked and destroyed the vineyards of Andrés Pico, then moved on to feed on the rest of the county. "Gardens or orchards, or grain-fields are invaded," reported the *Star*, "and in a day or two laid bare by these voracious creatures." The swarms finally subsided as the weather turned cooler. But then came the pestilence itself. An epidemic of smallpox began that fall and grew in intensity until it peaked in early 1864. Dozens of victims died each day. Benjamin Hayes, accompanying Antonio Coronel to a burial at the Catholic cemetery at the end of Eternity Street, drove past the shuttered adobes of Sonoratown. "Coronel pointed out to me one house in which eleven had died, in another three, in this two remained sick, in that three, in that one, and so on." At the cemetery Hayes noted "the great number of fresh graves." The rancherías were hardest hit. From 1860 to 1870 the number of Indians enumerated on the census of the county fell from two thousand to little more than two hundred.

During these terrible years the secessionist Democrats of Los Angeles did what they could to mobilize public fear and frustration in opposition to the Union. Before a large crowd at the Bella Union in the spring of 1862, prominent Democrat Andrew Jackson King, who had replaced Alonzo Ridley as undersheriff, excoriated the federal government for taxing the people, proclaimed the Confederacy "the only constitutional government we have," and then, to the sustained cheers of his audience, unveiled a life-size portrait of General P. G. T. Beauregard, hero of the Confederate victory at the Battle of Bull Run. As U.S. Marshal Henry Barrows complained to military authorities, King sought "to give éclat in a disaffected community to the rebel cause." He demanded that King be charged with treason and arrested. Undersherriff King was picked up, interrogated, and released by the military authorities after taking the oath of allegiance to the United States. Barrows protested his lenient treatment. "In what country would the display of portraits of generals of the enemy in war be tolerated," he wrote, "especially in a disaffected community as this is?" Federal authorities promised stricter enforcement.

Later that year the Lincoln administration authorized federal marshals to arrest anyone giving aid and comfort to the Confederacy, suspending the right of habeas corpus in all such cases, and Barrows soon found an occasion to use his new authority. In the state and local elections of September 1862, several hundred soldiers cast their ballots at the polling place nearest their barracks. Virtually all of them were from northern California, and county officials protested that they were ineligible to vote in local contests. E. J. C. Kewen, running for a seat in the state assembly, personally challenged the votes of many soldiers, who reacted with outrage. "Pistols were flourished and threats of every kind made," recalled one observer. Kewen complained of being "abused and menaced in a most wanton and outrageous manner," and finally left when an army officer said he could no longer guarantee his safety. To be sure, the Los Angeles Chivalry, which commanded a large majority in the county, had little to fear from the votes of several hundred soldiers. "Secesh has carried this county again, body and boots, for Dixie," Henry Barrows reported. "For all intents and purposes we might as well live in the Southern Confederacy as in Southern California." Kewen nevertheless filed a formal protest and succeeded in getting the county clerk to throw out the results for the precinct where the soldiers had voted. The Chiv strategy was to keep the pot boiling.

Several days later Barrows ordered Kewen's arrest on a charge of treason. Not only had he interfered with the right of soldiers to cast their ballots, but there were reports he had publicly raised three cheers for President Jefferson Davis of the Confederacy. Kewen was sent north on the steamer and imprisoned at the federal penitentiary on Alcatraz Island. "Arrest a score or two more of the secesh leaders," a local unionist declared, and "they will hush up their seditious talk and their abuse of the Union cause and Union men." Two weeks later Barrows ordered the arrest of editor Henry Hamilton of the *Star* on the same charge, and he was sent north to join Kewen. There was little sentiment for keeping them imprisoned, however, and once both men volunteered to take the oath of allegiance and had posted bond, they were allowed to return to Los Angeles.

LOS ANGELES SECESSIONISTS lost heart as the tide of battle turned in the North's favor during the summer of 1863. When news of Lee's retreat from Gettysburg and Grant's victory at Vicksburg reached Los Angeles, several dozen unionists gathered to celebrate. They were interrupted by a group of armed men from the Bella Union across the street, who vowed that "no demonstration of joy upon this event would be permitted." Voices were raised, shots fired, and two unionists wounded. A detachment of troops came on the double from their temporary encampment, the celebration resumed, and there was no further trouble. But the lieutenant in charge reported that "a very feverish and excited feeling nevertheless prevails," and he recommended that a full company be posted in the pueblo on a permanent basis.

The Chivs remained in control of county government, but with a Republican administration in Washington the federal patronage was controlled by their opponents. One of the biggest beneficiaries was Phineas Banning, who owned southern California's premier transport company, operating the stage line between Los Angeles and San Pedro as well as a large freighting operation into Arizona, Nevada, and Utah. To better his competitive advantage, Banning purchased land from the Domínguez family, dredged a channel farther inland, and built his own wharf and warehouse at the terminus, which became the town of Wilmington, named by Banning in honor of his Delaware birthplace. An outspoken critic of secession, Banning was a founder of the Los Angeles chapter of the Union Party—a fusion of free-soil Democrats and Republicans—and became the preeminent supplier for the U.S. Army in southern California. Before the war was over, Banning made at least a million dollars from government contracts.

Another political beneficiary was Francisco Ramírez, who returned to Los Angeles in 1862, after two years of editing a newspaper in Sonora, and was rewarded for past political loyalty with a series of appointments, including the position of register of the U.S. Land Office, the post formerly held by the late Hilliard P. Dorsey. In 1863 the Union Party nominated Ramírez as candidate for the state senate, running against his old nemesis, editor Henry Hamilton of the *Star*. Although he waged a vigorous campaign, Ramírez was again defeated in what would be his last try for public office. Democrats won all the major contests in the county, although the Union Party was triumphant statewide.

Occasionally, if rarely, unionists prevailed in southern California. In late 1863 Judge Benjamin Hayes announced his candidacy for a third term as district judge. The bench, he wrote, "should be maintained free forever from any influence of mere party politics." Despite the "vexed questions" presented by the war, Hayes had done his best to maintain the independence and impartiality of the court, and if the people supported him for a third term, he promised continued "fidelity to the Constitution and the Laws." Hayes ran as an independent and was opposed by both Democrat and Union candidates. What Hayes considered a virtue—his allegiance to the Constitution—the Chivalry attacked as a vice. "Hayes is no especial favorite of mine," his brother-in-law Dr. John S. Griffin wrote to Benjamin Davis Wilson, one of the county's leading Chivs. But, he explained, constrained by family ties, he could not oppose Hayes publicly. "I cannot aid or assist in his defeat—I hew close to my wife." With weak support from Democrats, however, Hayes was defeated in a close contest by unionist Pablo de la Guerra of Santa Barbara.

UNLIKE THE KNIGHTS of the Golden Circle, said Henry Barrows, he and his fellow unionists organized "not secretly, with grips and countersigns, and what not, but openly, though very quietly." In practice, "quietly" proved little different from "secretly." Outside the inner circle of the Union Club, the work of men like Barrows and Warner was far from transparent. As Benjamin Hayes noted in his diary, "it is difficult to divine what 'notions' are operating at this time on the overzealous dispositions of the leaders of 'Union Clubs' and military chieftains (in embryo) who appear to have the control."

Secessionist Knights and Union Clubs were instruments of the opposing sides of the politically committed. But in late 1861 another semi-secret organization, one enjoying broad support across the entire political spectrum, made a return appearance in Los Angeles. There had not been a lynching since the summary execution of Pancho Daniel in November 1858. But with the ongoing political turmoil, with residents concerned over the possibility of civil violence, and especially with a dramatic increase in homicides—which rose from nine in 1860, to twelve in 1861, to seventeen in 1862, the highest number since 1856—the stage was set once again for an extended episode of vigilantism.

The first indication was a lynching conducted by a mob of Californios at *misión vieja*. José Claudio Alvitre, uncle of the late Felipe Alvitre, was released from county jail after serving a term of four months for beating his wife. He returned home and after taking a few drinks grabbed a butcher knife and slit his wife's throat. Neighbors found her lying in a pool of blood and the perpetrator hiding nearby. "The people decided that as the act needed no investigation he should be punished at once," reported the *Star*. Unlike previous vigilante episodes that often featured some version of a kangaroo court, this one included no pretense of quasi-legal proceedings. Alvitre was bound, a noose placed around his neck, and soon he was "swinging in mid-air" from the branch of a nearby tree. Noting the frequency with which wives were "assaulted and treated in an inhuman manner" by their husbands, editor Hamilton hoped that "the promptness of justice in these parts will soon cure their propensity to abuse or kill women."

Another mob lynching took place several months later. The precipitating event was the brutal murder of Caroline van der Leck, wife of a German shopkeeper, during a botched robbery of the couple's dry goods store by a young Californio named Francisco Cota. The woman's two young children witnessed the brutal knifing. "I touched her and called to her," the daughter later recalled, "and when she did not answer, I knew that something dreadful had happened. I took my little brother by the hand and with my dress covered with blood, I ran crying up the street to the house of some friends." Cota, seen running from the scene, was quickly apprehended. A crowd gathered, and it was with considerable difficulty that the deputy marshal delivered him to the county lockup. "I have never forgotten being carried to the jail on the shoulders of some of the men for the purpose of having me identify the criminal," the daughter recalled. The sight of this innocent six-year-old being carried inside the jail greatly inflamed the crowd, which grew large and threatening. "Bring him out!" people cried. "Hang him!"

A public meeting was held on the street and a committee chosen to meet with Sheriff Tomás Sánchez. He promised Cota's case would proceed immediately with an arraignment by a justice of the peace. About three in the afternoon, surrounded by a hastily formed posse, Sánchez escorted Cota to the courtroom of Justice William H. Peterson, a couple of blocks away. The streets were filled with people. Justice Peterson's small court was packed to overflowing. Sheriff Sánchez read the complaint, Peterson asked Cota how he pled, and he responded "not guilty." Did he have counsel? Cota replied in the negative. He would have until the following morning to obtain representation, said Peterson, who then gaveled an adjournment and ordered the room cleared. There was a moment of stunned silence, then a roar as the crowd rushed forward, fought off Sánchez and his posse, and dragged Cota out to the street.

The mob surged toward the commercial district with their captive. The brutal slashing by a Californio of an Anglo woman in the presence of her children was a crime of such horror it seemed to justify the exaction of communal vengeance. Sheriff Sánchez and his men made a valiant attempt to rescue the young man, but to no avail. Someone threw a noose about Cota's neck, and he was violently pulled ahead. Joseph Mesmer, a mere boy of six or seven at the time, vividly recalled the scene many years later. As Cota was dragged along, Mesmer wrote, people "showered him with blows, pulled his hair, and tore his clothes half off." At the corner of Aliso and Alameda the rope was tossed over the crossbeam of a tall gate, and Cota was hauled up by the neck. His limbs were untied, and they jerked wildly as his body swung in a wide arc. "The air was filled with cries, oaths, and imprecations," Mesmer continued, "but the leaders went about their task with grim visage and determined mien, which brooked no interference. The crowd milled about with that indescribable sound of bodies pummeling each other and striving desperately for advantage. The impression of those sounds that day on my young mind was something which has not been erased through a long life of many other tragic incidents."

The *Southern News* reported the lynching without comment. "Verily the soul of the murderer shall descend with curses to perdition," wrote editor Charles Conway. In the *Star*, Hamilton was somewhat more equivocal. "We have ever been, and still are, opposed to mob law," he wrote. "But if an occasion can arise, when the righteous indignation of a people will prompt them to the instant punishment of an enormity, whose hellish atrocity appalls the stoutest heart, and shocks the moral sensibilities of the most obdurate, or the most obtuse, the present is that occasion." Both newspapers reported on the public meeting, the formation of the leadership committee, and the active participation of those same leaders in the lynching. But neither editor identified a single participant by name. That would remain the editorial policy in regard to lynching for the subsequent decade. The editors and their papers might be on opposite sides of the political divide, but both endorsed vigilantism.

Several weeks later the bodies of four or five Californios or Mexicans were found hanging along a road in the northern portion of the county. "It is supposed they were horse and cattle thieves, were on their way to the upper country with stock," reported the *Star*, "that they had been overtaken on the road by the owners of the cattle, and immediately executed." This time Hamilton refrained from expressing any criticism at all. An extended period of lynching had begun.

FOLLOWING A TWO-YEAR TERM as district attorney, E. J. C. Kewen opened a legal practice specializing in criminal defense. It was a much better fit for him. He defended at least five men charged with murder or attempted murder in 1863 and succeeded in getting four acquitted. In the most controversial case, he represented blacksmith John Buckley, charged with the murder of musician Francisco "Pancho" Cruz, a harp player in a band that performed at Sam McKlasky's saloon on Negro Alley. The two men had been competitors for the affection of a young prostitute named Augusta Cañada. One evening Cruz found her in bed with Buckley, and the men exchanged hard words. Buckley left and Cruz reproached Cañada. "You do not command me," she shot back. The next night, as Cruz tried to make up with Cañada, Buckley approached them. "What do *you* want," Cruz demanded. Buckley drew a revolver and without a word shot his rival in the belly. Cruz died within minutes. According to the district attorney it was an open-and-shut case of murder. But Kewen elicited testimony that Cruz had a small pocketknife in his pocket, which he used to cut the strings of his harp, and planted the suggestion that he might have been attempting to draw the knife before Buckley fired. That was enough for the men of the jury, who concluded that Buckley had acted in self-defense and acquitted him. It was a classic Kewen move, playing on the prejudices of the jurors, exploiting their deep adherence to the honor code.

In partnership with Colonel James G. Howard, another shrewd litigator, Kewen became the most celebrated criminal defense attorney in southern California. So successful were the partners that they roused the ire of the vigilance committee, which continued to meet following the lynching of Francisco Cota. The vigilantes passed a resolution, so the story was told, that both attorneys deserved hanging. Word of the resolution leaked out, and on the street a day or two later Colonel Howard confronted one of the committee's leaders, a Frenchman named Felix Signoret, described as a man huge in frame, with hands the size of hams. Signoret operated a "deluxe" barbershop on Main Street, which he parlayed into the ownership of a saloon, a billiard parlor, and eventually an entire business block. Howard, a very large man, planted himself directly in front of Signoret, his feet spread wide, head and shoulders bent forward. "Signoret," he said in his booming baritone, "I understand you are going to hang Kewen and Howard." The Frenchman responded nervously. "That was our intention," he stuttered. "Come now, Signoret," said Howard, "we are old friends. Be generous, let's compromise. Hang Kewen, he's the head of the firm." The story is apocryphal. But Signoret was indeed a leader of the vigilance committee, which in fact expressed frustration at the repeated acquittal of murderers in Los Angeles. "Lawyers do abound in this city," declared J. J. Warner. "It is well that Justice is blind, for if she could see all that is done in her name she would become a raving maniac."

Late in 1863 Kewen acted as defense attorney for one B. J. Daimwood, arrested for a violent assault on a Los Angeles deputy marshal. Daimwood was a notorious desperado, rumored to have murdered two miners for their gold. Kewen got him admitted to bail, but before Daimwood's bond could be raised, he was targeted by the vigilance committee. On November 20 Sheriff Sánchez informed Judge Hayes that he believed the vigilantes were preparing to strike. Hayes telegraphed the commander at Drum Barracks requesting "aid and protection." But the vigilantes acted before the officer could respond. Early the following day, the jail was swarmed by some two or three hundred men led by Felix Signoret and what Joseph Mesmer described as a group of "old timers who had taken part in other lynchings." Sheriff Sánchez and Undersheriff King barred the iron door of the jail, but using sledgehammers and battering rams the vigilantes broke in and emerged with five men, including Daimwood, accused of an assortment of crimes ranging from attempted murder to horse theft. They were dragged up Spring Street to its junction with Main and unceremoniously hanged from the portico of an old adobe.

Henry Hamilton reminded his readers once again that he was "emphatically opposed to all such proceedings." He also published a proclamation from Sheriff Sánchez, threatening the unnamed leaders with arrest. In response the vigilante "executive committee" issued a public statement, refusing to disband and insisting that their aim was "to help the Sheriff and all officers to execute the law." After that there was no further mention of arrests. J. J. Warner defended the lynchings.

"For the last year highway robberies and murder have become a common occurrence," he wrote, and "the slow process of the law is inadequate to the task, hence the interference of the citizens." Although "this wholesale slaughter may not be sanctioned by the community at large, the citizens of this section have borne the outrages until forbearance ceased to be a virtue." The vigilance committee, he reported, had warned other "suspicious characters" that they had twenty-four hours to get out of town "or take the consequences." It seemed that the vigilance committee had become a permanent institution in Los Angeles.

TWO WEEKS LATER the body of rancher John Sanford was discovered along a lonely stretch of road in the northern portion of the county. Sanford was well-known and well-connected. One of his brothers owned a ranch in San Gabriel; another was a business associate of Phineas Banning, the transportation baron, who was married to Sanford's sister. A week after the discovery of the body, a young drifter named Charles Wilkins, arrested in Santa Barbara on a charge of vagrancy, confessed to the crime. He had been walking along the road, Wilkins said, when Sanford came by in a buggy and hired him on the spot to herd sheep. Wilkins climbed aboard and the two men continued on for a pace until Sanford stopped to relieve himself. "It occurred to me that he might have money," Wilkins said, "and seeing his pistol lying in the bottom of the buggy, I picked it up and shot him while his back was towards me." It was a cold-blooded murder of the worst sort. He was disappointed, Wilkins said, to find only twenty dollars and a gold watch in Sanford's pockets. Asked whether his conscience troubled him, he answered no. "I have killed eight other men and think no more of killing a man than a dog."

Wilkins arrived in Los Angeles in the custody of a deputy sheriff on a morning in mid-December. Benjamin Hayes, concluding the autumn term of district court, was determined to achieve swift justice in the case. A special grand jury was convened, Wilkins was brought before its members, and that very afternoon they handed down an indictment for murder. As Undersheriff King was escorting the prisoner back to the jail, he was surrounded by an angry crowd. King shoved his way through and got Wilkins back in his cell, but that afternoon he dispatched a telegram to the military authorities, requesting the presence of troops. King's plea for federal intervention was ironic, of course, coming as it did from one of the most partisan secessionists in Los Angeles. Later that day he received an official response. "In reply to your telegram of this date stating that the jail of Los Angeles County is threatened by a mob and requesting the assistance of the U.S. troops, I am instructed to say that application should be made to the Governor of this State. . . . It is only upon the requisition of the highest executive authority in the State that the commanding general can act."

The trial before Judge Hayes took place the following day. His term as district judge would end on December 31, and he knew that this would probably be the last capital case he would hear after twelve years on the bench. At midmorning a throng of several hundred watched as Undersheriff King and a large group of armed men escorted Wilkins from the jail to the courthouse. Suddenly a man with a shotgun pushed to the front of the crowd. It was the murdered man's brother, Cyrus Sanford. King and his men rushed forward and prevented Sanford from firing, but in the confusion Wilkins broke from the guard and fled into a nearby house. Found cowering under a bed, he was hustled into the courthouse without further disruption. The proceeding went quickly and smoothly. Wilkins waived his right to a jury trial and pled guilty to murder in the first degree. Hayes pronounced him guilty and announced that sentencing would take place the following morning. Then, ordering King to return Wilkins to jail, he adjourned the court. Suddenly Phineas Banning, the murdered man's brother-in-law, leading a group of his own teamsters, rushed forward, pushed King aside, and seized Wilkins. They dragged the terrified man outside and down the street to Banning's corral, where they hanged him from a crossbeam over the gate.

Henry Barrows made no comment at the time—that would have

been unseemly for a U.S. marshal—but he later wrote about this lynching. "The people were compelled to rise up in self-defense and summarily exterminate the thieves, thugs, and assassins who were preying upon the community," he argued. It demonstrated once again that when the people awakened to the necessity of action, there was no stopping them. "In looking back to those days from this distance," he wrote a quarter century later, "one would say that it would have been better if Wilkins and his fellow murderers could have been hung by law; but that it was better even that they should have been hung as they were, than that they should not have been hung at all."

The lynching of Charles Wilkins concluded the extended episode of vigilantism that began in 1861 and included the extralegal execution of at least fourteen men. "It cleared the atmosphere wonderfully," Barrows wrote. "Justice had been done without any quibbles or elisions or escapes, but swift and sure; the people, who had been stirred up by intense excitement, quieted down as if by magic; and human rights and property rights from that time on, were never safer, and peace and quietness prevailed for a long time." Barrows got what he asked for—and for the next four or five years the number of homicides fell to the lowest level since before the war of conquest.

· CHAPTER 25 ·

MASTER IN THE HOUSE

"MARRIED—AT SAN GABRIEL, April 21st, by Rev. T. O. Ellis at the residence of Mr. D. F. Hall, Mr. Robert B. Carsley to Miss Josephine Smith." The notice, printed in the *Star* on April 24, 1858, was accompanied by a note of congratulation from editor Henry Hamilton. "Cupid, the sly archer, has been winging his shafts pretty freely of late in this locality. Among his conquests, we find enrolled our young friend and highly esteemed correspondent, Miss Josephine Smith, whose compositions, over the signature of 'Ina' have frequently delighted our readers. Entering now on the serious duties of life, we may be permitted to wish her all felicity, and that her future may be as happy as her past has been bright and full of promise." Bob Carsley was twenty-five, Josephine Smith seventeen.

Ina, as she was known to family and friends, was the daughter of Agnes Coolbrith and Don Carlos Smith, born in the Mormon community of Nauvoo, Illinois, in 1841. Her father died of malaria when she was an infant, and the next year her mother married her late husband's older brother, the Mormon prophet Joseph Smith, becoming the seventh of his plural wives. Three years later Smith was murdered by an angry mob, and soon the Mormons were being hounded out of Illinois, just as they had been forced from Missouri several years before. When the faithful departed for the far West in 1846, Agnes Coolbrith Smith chose not to join them. Instead, she married a third time, to attorney William Pickett, not a Latter-day Saint himself, but a man who publicly supported the Mormons' right to practice their religion as they chose. With Ina and her sister Charlotte, the couple relocated to St. Louis, where twin sons were born. In 1851, infected with gold fever, Pickett took the family overland to California, and in 1855 they relocated to Los Angeles, where Pickett hung out his shingle. Ina and her sister enrolled in the girls' class taught by Louisa Hayes Griffin. It was a small world.

She wrote her first poems for Miss Hayes, who sent them to editor Hamilton. He published the first of them in 1856, when Ina was fifteen. The verses proved immensely popular, were reprinted in other papers around the state, and Ina became known as the "Los Angeles poetess." Her revenge poem, published in the *Star* in aftermath of Barton's death, was uncharacteristic. She wrote elegies of separation and loss, sentimental and conventional, but notably sincere. Her perspective reflected her family's history, but also the experiences of her readers, most of them immigrants and transients, far from their homes of origin. Typical was a poem Hamilton published in 1857.

> *We miss thee at home—we miss thee,*
> *Through the long, weary hours of the day,*
> *And wonder how long, as a pilgrim,*
> *In a far distant land thou wilt stray.*

Ina was repulsed by the coarseness of Los Angeles life, which underscored her feelings of estrangement. Yet she was struck by the beauty of the landscape—the rolling hills, the vistas, the diaphanous light. A quarter century later she would recall

> *The long, low vale, with tawny edge*
> *Of hills, within the sunset glow;*

Cool vine-rows through the cactus hedge,
And fluttering gleams of orchard snow.

Those lines suggest her development as a very good poet with a fresh, unforced voice. Years later, publishing under the nom de plume of Ina Coolbrith (her mother's maiden name), she would become a noted California writer, eventually the state's first poet laureate. Life's sorrows and limitations would remain pronounced themes in her work.

But there was nothing melancholic about the young woman herself. Ina Smith was vivacious and exceptionally good-looking. "She might easily have been mistaken for a daughter of Spain," wrote an admirer. "The dark eyes, the luxuriant dark hair, the pure olive skin flushed with the ripe glow of pomegranates, the rich contralto voice." She often entertained visitors to the Pickett home with songs of her own composition, accompanying herself on the guitar. She and her equally attractive sister Charlotte were belles of Los Angeles society and enjoyed an active social life. Ina later recalled attending a fancy dress ball and leading the dancers to the floor on the arm of former governor Pío Pico.

She met Robert Carsley when she was sixteen. After apprenticing as a blacksmith in his hometown of New Bedford, Massachusetts, in 1851, at the age of eighteen, Carsley had signed on to operate the forge aboard a whaling vessel. Thus he found his way to California, settling in San Francisco in 1855. In addition to blacksmithing, Carsley was a part-time professional musician who played in a troupe known as Frank Hussey's Minstrels. During several performing tours of the state he visited Los Angeles, found it to his liking, and in 1857 relocated there, opening a shop that produced custom iron doors, shutters, and railings. Carsley, described as good-looking, with dark hair and eyes, was considered a talented and enterprising young man, and impressed everyone as a good catch.

The young couple set up housekeeping in an adobe not far from Carsley's shop in the center of the pueblo. For a year or two they lived happily together. Ina later recalled the first months of their marriage.

Oh, balm, and dew, and fragrance of those nights
Of southern splendor 'neath a southern sky.
The soft star-closes to the golden days
I dreamed away, in that far tropic clime,
Wherein love's blossom budded, bloomed, and died.

The troubles began in the winter of 1860–61. Their firstborn, a son, died after only a few weeks of life. Infant mortality took a heavy toll in those days. Ina kept active, pursuing a lively social life in the pueblo while Carsley continued touring with Hussey's Minstrels, leaving his shop in the hands of an assistant. Increasingly, however, he returned home in an angry and resentful mood, jealous of the attentions paid to his attractive wife. Carsley had a short temper, often expressed himself incautiously, and soon he was castigating Ina as a loose woman, using vile epithets she found shocking. By the time Carsley left on tour in the autumn of 1861, the two were estranged. When he returned in October he provoked the fight that ended the marriage.

She was staying with her mother and stepfather at their residence south of the Plaza. He returned unexpectedly and confronted her with his broodings over imagined infidelities. Her mother, Agnes Pickett, intervened. "I want to hear nothing degrading to her character," she told him. But Carsley wasn't listening. He had learned from an unimpeachable source that his wife had been intimate with one of the Union army officers stationed in the city, "which proved her to be a whore." Ina denied his outrageous charge, but that only made him angrier. He turned violent, grabbed a kitchen knife and brandished it in her face. Mrs. Pickett heard someone at the door, and assuming it was her husband she told Carsley that he'd better leave, that if Pickett saw what was happening there would be trouble. "I would as soon spill Mr. Pickett's blood as a pig's in the shoot," declared Carsley.

It was not Pickett but attorney E. J. C. Kewen, come to call. A poet himself—he published a volume of his own verse in 1853, the first book of poetry printed in California—Kewen had appointed himself Ina Smith's literary mentor and become a good friend of the family.

Mrs. Pickett asked for his help. Kewen was only eight years older than Carsley, yet he treated him like a boy, instructing him in the ways a husband ought to treat a wife. It was precisely his wife's relationship with men like Kewen that obsessed Carsley, and the more the older man lectured, the angrier the young man became. Kewen, the hot-headed southern gentleman, took offense at Carsley's Yankee insolence. If he refused to leave, Kewen finally told him, he would take it as a personal affront, one that could be settled only on the field of honor. Kewen's reputation for violence was well-known, and the declaration got Carsley's attention. He agreed to leave, and Kewen went on his way, assuming the matter was settled.

But Carsley soon returned, erratically waving a six-shooter. Mrs. Pickett barred the door, but he stood in front of the house, shouting a stream of expletives heard by the entire neighborhood. Mrs. Pickett led Ina and the other children out the back of the house and fled to the nearby Union army encampment. Carsley followed them there, and observing Ina in conversation with one of the officers he went crazy. He rushed up, grabbed his wife, and pressed the revolver to her temple. At that moment William Pickett arrived, and seeing his stepdaughter being held at the point of a gun by her husband, he grabbed a loaded musket from one of the soldiers, leveled it at Carsley, and shouted at him to put the weapon down. Instead, Carsley fired a round in Pickett's direction. He missed, but Pickett didn't. He squeezed off a shot, blasting the revolver from Carsley's grasp, shattering the bones of his hand so badly that it had to be amputated.

Kewen advised an immediate divorce, and the family retained him as Ina's legal counsel. "The said defendant, threatened the said plaintiff with personal violence," Kewen wrote in his brief, "and with drawn weapons, with force and arms, and angry words and gestures, put plaintiff in extreme fear for her personal safety, threatening to take the life of said plaintiff, and compelling her to seek security from threatened violence." The case, heard by Judge Hayes, was a local sensation, although out of respect for the family, neither Henry Hamilton nor Charles Conway made mention of it in their papers. Still, Ina was humiliated by the scandal. Hayes granted the divorce in late December 1861, and the next year she left Los Angeles, relocating with her mother and stepfather to San Francisco, where her career as a poet would take off.

DIVORCE WAS RELATIVELY RARE in nineteenth-century America, and in that regard Los Angeles was little different from the rest of the country. Nevertheless, during its first quarter century the district court heard more than two hundred petitions for dissolution of marriage, creating a substantial archive of testimony by dozens of ordinary men and women about the things that went on behind closed doors. A home could be a refuge. But it could also be a hothouse of rage and tumult, an incubator for the violent behavior that infected the public world. The sights and sounds of intimate violence—a problem widely acknowledged by contemporaries, but usually with a shrug of the shoulders—contributed mightily to the atmosphere of fear and loathing that permeated frontier Los Angeles.

Occasionally women were the perpetrators. Thomas C. Swigart petitioned the court for a divorce from his wife, Serena Keller Swigart, whom he had married two years before, complaining she was "wholly unfit and unreliable in all the duties due from a wife" because of her frequent intoxication, her vulgar comportment, and her ferocious assaults on her husband. When they married both were in their early forties and recently widowed, he with three young children, she with one. The idea of combining households must have seemed a good idea, but it proved a disaster. Although they resided in the Monte, Swigart was co-owner of a hardware store in the pueblo—"Swigart & Huber. Dealers in Stoves, Ranges, Tin, Copper, and Sheet Iron Ware. At the sign of the Big Red Coffee Pot." The business demanded his daily presence, and the children required the stable hand of a mother. But instead Sireny, as she was known to intimates, took to drinking and gallivanting about the neighborhood. She hung around the taverns, begging drinks. She was seen lying in a public road, too drunk to get up. Swigart confronted her, they argued, and she assaulted him. "Several times she knocked me down," he testified. "She was stronger than I was."

The break occurred after Swigart learned that Sireny was sexually involved with Frank Thurman, the brother of his late wife, and a boarder with the family. The revelation came late one evening. "I went to bed with her," Swigart testified, "and she said to me after our connection that it wasn't satisfactory." As he considered this, she announced she was going upstairs to Thurman's room. Swigart heard the sound of them making love through the floorboards. Some time later she returned to their bed. "Frank fucked me before you ever did," Sireny said, as if trying to provide her husband with some context. She had been with many men, she said, and she knew what she liked. Her late husband had known how to please her. "What did he ever do for you, except give you a good beating, as I ought to have done," Swigart exclaimed. But he wasn't that kind of man, he admitted. Sireny laughed. "That's why I married *you*," she said, "you God-damned, black Republican, nigger-loving son-of-a-bitch."

Those were powerful insults to hurl at Swigart, who had been raised in Mississippi. But instead of erupting, he attempted to calm her. "You hadn't ought to talk that way," he said, as he embraced her. But she jerked away, grabbed a heavy object from the bedside table and brought it crashing down on his head. As the blood streamed down his face, she began pummeling him with her fists. "I had to push her over on the bed several times before I could get out of the house," Swigart said. A witness saw him stagger out the door, "his shirt torn and considerably stained in blood." In court, he pointed to a deep scar on his left temple. Swigart got his divorce, and Serena Keller married Frank Thurman.

Intimate violence is typically initiated by the person with the most authority in the relationship, and in the majority of cases that was the husband. Male dominance in marriage generally prevailed without overt conflict. But a man who sensed or imagined resistance from his wife might attempt to dominate her through a series of escalating tactics—

deliberately excluding her from decision making, isolating her from family and friends, humiliating her with vile names, destroying her personal possessions, terrorizing her by look or gesture. Overt violence was usually a last resort. But once the battering began, it often became habitual. Most vicitimized wives—there is no way of knowing how many—suffered in silence. Even those who came forward did so with great reluctance, often after years of abuse.

Mary Ellen Culberson sued her husband, William Culberson, for divorce after what she claimed was seventeen torturous years. He had treated her in a "cruel and inhuman manner" ever since their wedding day, she testified. It began with insulting and demeaning language, moved on to threat and intimidation, and finally to violence. She attempted to cope. When "his looks and manner were excited and savage," she said, "I got out of the way as quick as I could." The last straw came with an incident that left her in fear for her life. Culberson came home drunk, picked a fight and worked himself into a rage, then grabbed a loaded shotgun and pressed the muzzle to his wife's chest. "Damn you, I'll kill you," he said. Then he passed out. The next morning, after he sobered up, she asked what he intended by threatening her with a firearm. Just what I said, he responded. "You better not let me catch you napping." She left him that same day. Culberson denied his wife's accusations but defended his prerogative. "She is my wife," he declared. "I can do as I please with her."

That was the common defense of virtually all would-be patriarchs. Joseph G. Carmona responded to his wife's charge of battering by insisting that it was "only the exercise by him of that authority which it is the duty and privilege of a husband to use in order to prevent his wife from becoming a common scold, a notorious virago, and a constant disturber of the peace in the community." Similarly, Andrés Rubio denied his wife's accusation that he regularly whipped her, yet contended that as "a woman of the most violent and uncontrollable temper," she "deserved such infliction in the most aggravated form." Men had made the same argument for years, before the alcalde prior to the American war of conquest, in the courts thereafter.

TWO YEARS AFTER THE DEATH of her first husband, Augustina Varela, niece of the late José Sérbulo Varela, married longshoreman Hiram Emerson and took up residence with him in a modest cottage in Wilmington, where he was employed by Phineas Banning. Her husband's abuse, she alleged, began the night of their wedding. "He called me very bad, indecent, dirty, abusive names, and began pounding me. He blacked my eyes and bruised me on the shoulder and body by striking me with his boot and with his fists." There was hardly a day afterward, she testified, "that he did not pound and kick and abuse." According to Juliana Redi, a neighbor from across the street who testified in district court, Emerson "was always abusing and ill-treating her. The times are so numerous I can not remember them all. She was always a good wife to him and he had no cause or reason for using her as he did. She was bruised all over her body from the effects of the beatings." Late one night Mrs. Redi was awakened by pounding on her door. It was Mrs. Emerson, seeking refuge after a particularly brutal beating. Her husband was right behind her, "determined to take her away by force," but Mrs. Redi wouldn't allow it. "I took a stick and drove him out of the house." Frank Cowden, a justice of the peace who lived down the block, saw Emerson beating his wife in the street. Cowden confronted him, warned him off in the name of the law, and advised her to seek a divorce. It was granted by the court.

The brutality was not restricted to working-class households. Mary Neal Stoddard, a middle-class woman of twenty, married a prosperous Los Angeles hardware dealer named William M. Stoddard, a widower in his late thirties. Following the wedding, which took place at her parents' home in San Francisco, the couple departed on the steamer for Los Angeles. A remark Stoddard made during the southbound voyage was her first indication that he might not be the gentleman she assumed him to be. He had married her, Stoddard said, because she was young and attractive enough to "keep up his passions." The comment shocked the innocent young woman, but its meaning did not become clear until they arrived at Stoddard's home in the prime Anglo residential district on the south side of the Plaza. After Stoddard had a few drinks he began making remarks she considered indecent. Fearful and tired, she excused herself and retired to the bedroom, locking the door behind her. Stoddard knocked and asked permission to enter, but she pled exhaustion. He pounded, but she refused him entry. So he kicked in the door. "God damn you!" he exclaimed. "I'm going to sleep in this room and you can go to hell." Mary Neal Stoddard's first sexual experience was being raped by her new husband. "I'm master in this house and I'll have my way," he exclaimed. The sexual tyranny continued for the next several nights.

Terrified and alone in a strange town, she sought out an old family friend, an attorney and a "churchman" named Bryant L. Peel who had recently relocated to Los Angeles from San Francisco. Peel found her story so appalling, he urged her to return to her parents immediately. He accompanied her back to Stoddard's house so she could collect her things. Stoddard at first refused to admit them. "If you attempt to enter this house you are a dead man," he threatened Peel. He was there to ensure Mrs. Stoddard's safety, Peel responded. Would Stoddard prefer that he fetched the marshal? Stoddard stepped aside and Mrs. Stoddard pushed past him as Peel waited on the threshold.

"That woman is a God-damned deadbeat," Stoddard said to Peel. "She thought she could play me with her damned ass." He would not stand for such talk, said Peel, but Stoddard kept it up. "She's a young girl," he said, but "as familiar with the act of sexual intercourse as any whore." Perhaps Peel wanted her for himself, Stoddard said, perhaps that was his real motive. "For twenty-five dollars you can sleep with her," he said, "just go ahead and try it." Before Peel could respond to that outrageous comment, he heard Mrs. Stoddard call for his assistance. He entered the house and walked down the hall to where she was standing. "Do you see what he has done?" she said. Her room was a shambles, her clothing strewn about, ripped apart, soiled. "Yes, I done that," said Stoddard. "I busted the damned trunk open and found in it many of my things." Mrs. Stoddard gathered up what she could and left on the steamer that afternoon. Several weeks later Stoddard filed a suit for divorce in Los Angeles, alleging abandonment by his wife. But she had already commenced proceedings in San Francisco. The case was remanded there, and the following year the court granted her petition on the grounds of extreme cruelty.

R EBECCA M. PALMER, thirty-six, with three daughters from a former marriage, petitioned for a divorce from her husband, Nathan A. Palmer, forty-three, alleging his violent conduct toward both herself and her girls. The couple had met when Palmer was a boarder in the house she owned in the mining town of Gold Hill in the northern part of the state. After their wedding they relocated to a small farm southeast of Los Angeles, purchased with the proceeds from the sale of her boardinghouse. But Palmer proved to be a loafer who refused to engage in steady work of any kind. He spent his time at local taverns, drinking up the proceeds of the farm and usually returning home in a foul mood, which he took out on his wife and her daughters. The only certain income came from the sale of Mrs. Palmer's butter, eggs, and chickens. Her oldest daughter had married and was living with her husband in the Monte, and although Rebecca Palmer was desperately unhappy, she told herself she must remain with her husband until the other two girls had finished school and found partners of their own.

But the tipping point came sooner. One day she asked Palmer to take a load of butter into town for sale. When he returned several hours later with the cash, she found it short. It's all there, he assured her, you must have miscounted the rolls of butter in the load. There were twenty-four of them, she insisted, and turned to one of her daughters for confirmation. "Yes mother, that's what you said," the girl replied. Palmer flew into a rage. "Will you listen to that!" he said. "One slut holding up for the other." He began throwing objects about the kitchen, including a clock that sat on the shelf, one of his wife's prized possessions, which he smashed to smithereens. He grabbed hold of the kitchen table, set with the supper dishes, and turned it over. "You lousy whore," he shouted, "I have a good mind to set fire to the house."

The girls were quaking in terror. "Are you crazy?" cried their mother. "Yes, mad crazy," Palmer shouted. "Now get out of my house. This is my house and you shall leave it." Then, seizing his wife by the shoulders, he hustled her to the door and pushed her out with a shove that sent her sprawling to the ground. She picked herself up and stood there for several moments, gathering her wits, then marched back inside. "I worked hard for this home, to make it what it is," she said, "and this is the thanks I get?" Her words fueled Palmer's rage and again he shoved her out the door, then went after the girls, who fled from him and ran out to their mother. "I've suffered you and your damn children ever since we were married," Palmer shouted. "If you do not go away, I will kill you all." He slammed and locked the door. It was a cool evening, and after a few minutes the girls began to shiver. Mrs. Palmer led them around to the rear and opened the back door. Palmer was sitting in a straight-backed chair in the middle of the room with a shotgun across his knees. "He cocked it and took aim," she testified, "and told me that if I stepped further into the house he would shoot me."

At the divorce proceeding in district court the daughters provided detailed corroboration of their mother's story. Their most interesting testimony came during the cross-examination by Palmer's attorney. Didn't your stepfather always treat you with kindness, he asked the youngest. "No sir," she answered. "He would whip us for anything. Sometimes take a stick, shoes, and even hoops. He used to whip me with anything he could get hold of." Corporal punishment of children was commonplace and generally accepted. But a stepfather beating an adolescent stepdaughter with metal hoops crossed the line. The attorney tried a different tactic with the married sister. You must be very fond of your mother, he said. "Yes sir," she replied, "she has been my support ever since I can remember." Then your stepfather's name-calling must have made a lasting impression on you. "Yes sir, rather," she answered. Then the attorney sprang his trap. Can you tell the court the precise times and places, he asked, when he called your mother bad names? The young woman paused to think. "No sir," she finally answered. That seems odd, said the attorney, seeing how important it was to you. But the young woman wasn't finished. "I'll tell you what I do remember," she added. "I do recollect him abusing us girls. I remember *that* very well." There were no more questions. The court granted the divorce.

Intimate violence inevitably injured children. Eleanor Jane Joughin Johnson, the daughter of a prosperous Los Angeles blacksmith and wagonmaker, sued her husband, William Johnson, for divorce, seeking custody of their infant son. When they married she was sixteen, he twenty-one. They moved about ten miles southwest of town to a small ranch, a wedding gift from Eleanor's parents. The abuse, she said, began soon thereafter, when Johnson began cursing her. "He told me I was too damned contrary to live, and meaner than hell. Then that I was a God-damned whore and bitch, and used to tell me every day to go to hell." Meanwhile, Johnson was compiling a record of public violence in justice court, charged with threatening one neighbor with a firearm and assaulting another. The battering of his wife began shortly after the birth of the child. "When the baby was about three months old was the first time he struck me," she told the court. "He took me by the throat, threw me down, and slapped me in the face. He said he would kill me. He swore he would cut my heart out, fry it on the rocks, and eat it." His shouting woke the baby, who began crying. Johnson picked the child up roughly and thrust him into the arms of his mother. "If you don't get away from here," he said, "I'll kill you both." She took the baby that day and returned to her parents' residence in Los Angeles.

Johnson showed up there a few days later. He had decided to sell the ranch, he said, and if she wanted her things she should go collect them before he threw them out. She went down in a wagon with the baby, her mother, and her brother. "We found my clothes all outside the door," she testified. "They were scattered all over and filled full of tobacco juice." She went inside and confronted Johnson. "If I must do my own cooking," he told her, "there will be no room for your damned clothes in my house." The room was strewn with more of her things, and as she bent down to pick something up Johnson delivered a fierce kick that sent her reeling. Then he grabbed the baby from the grandmother's arms and ran out of the house, in the process injuring the child, which frightened everyone, including Johnson. He returned the baby to his wife, and she returned to Los Angeles.

A few days later Johnson again appeared at the Joughin place and asked for some time with his son, which his wife granted. A short while later she announced it was time for the baby to nurse, but Johnson refused to give him up. He was going to take the boy to town, he said, and he walked out with the child, his wife and her father in pursuit. Johnson turned and confronted them. "Stand back," he said to Mr. Joughin, "you have nothing to do with this affair." Then drawing a pistol from his belt and waving it in a threatening manner, he started down the street, trailed by mother and grandfather. Suddenly Johnson spun around, pushed the baby into the mother's arms, then clubbed her father with the pistol, knocking him to the ground. Notwithstanding the testimony detailing this abuse, the court ruled there were insufficient grounds for divorce, and denied Eleanor Johnson's petition.

Johnson expected that with this decision his wife would return, but he was badly mistaken. She remained with the baby at her parents' house, where Johnson continued to pester her, alternately pleading and threatening. Finally, in a crude attempt at revenge, he went to the house on a Sunday morning when the family was attending church and tricked a nursemaid into letting him take the child. In a brief to the court, attorney E. J. C. Kewen, who represented Eleanor Johnson in a second divorce proceeding, revealed what happened next. The father, Kewen wrote, "took the child and carried him away and placed him in charge of a low, vulgar, drunken, and disreputable woman in Los Angeles City, and there kept the said child concealed and secreted until said child came to his death by violence." Beyond this statement, neither the case file nor the local press offers any account of what happened, nor any indication that Johnson was held accountable for the death. But this time the court ordered the marriage dissolved, and along with the resumption of her maiden name, Eleanor Joughin was awarded two-thirds of the community property as well as an additional sum of $2,000 in gold coin from Johnson. Fortunately her life story does not end there. Several years later she married an enterprising rancher and vineyardist, and they became the parents of three children.

WILLIAM JOHNSON was abusive not only with his wife but with his neighbors. Hiram Emerson thought nothing of beating his wife on a public street. Intimate violence and public violence were two phases of the same phenomenon. Melvina Prater filed for divorce from her husband, John B. Prater. "He threatened to kill me," she alleged, "and his treatment was so rough I could not endure it." Prater denied the charge, but several weeks later, just days before the case was to be heard in district court, he assaulted his wife on a public street, and when a bystander intervened on her behalf, he pulled a pistol and took a shot at the man, which fortunately went wild and injured no one. Indicted and tried for assault with intent to commit murder, Prater's defense was that he had been exercising his rights as a husband, an argument Judge Ygnacio Sepúlveda rejected out of hand, instructing the jury that a husband had "no power to commit a breach of the peace upon the person of his wife any more than upon anybody else," and that bystanders not only had a right but a duty "to prevent such breach of the peace." The jury found Prater guilty and Sepúlveda sentenced him to several years in San Quentin. The divorce was granted in his absence.

Judge Sepúlveda was right about the law. But for a husband to be charged with battering his wife in his own home, generally someone from the household had to press charges. In 1870 Mary Golden complained to Justice of the Peace William H. Gray that her husband,

Patrick Golden, had savagely beaten both her and her young daughter. Both were visibly battered and bruised. Her husband had beaten them many times before, Mrs. Golden said. He was arrested and hauled before Justice Gray, who found him guilty of assault and battery and sentenced him to thirty days in the county jail. Mrs. Golden was shocked. How, she asked Justice Gray, was the family to get along without her husband's earnings as a laborer? Gray agreed to allow Golden to post a bond to keep the peace. But Mrs. Golden could find no one willing to put up the money for this incorrigible wife beater. Finally, after what Justice Gray described as a "flood of tears" from Mrs. Golden, he relented and remitted the sentence to a small fine.

There was the problem in microcosm. Most wives were reluctant to press charges against their husbands, on whom they were dependent for support, and only the most desperate were willing to pursue a divorce. It was an inherent feature of patriarchial power dynamics, in which the categories of male and female stood respectively for dominance and subordination.

· CHAPTER 26 ·

A REFINED PIECE
OF VILLAINY

RANCHERO JOHN RAINS left his house at Rancho Cucamonga early on the morning of Monday, November 17, 1862, headed for Los Angeles, about forty miles west. He never arrived. The alarm was not raised until Friday, when concerned friends from the pueblo arrived at Cucamonga asking about him. An exhaustive search along the road led to the discovery of his wagon, hidden in a ravine, his hat and overcoat nearby. But it was another week before Undersheriff Andrew Jackson King and Rains's brother-in-law Robert S. Carlisle, observing buzzards circling over the San José Hills, midway between the rancho and Los Angeles, discovered the body in a dense patch of cactus. The physical evidence indicated that Rains had been lassoed from behind, dragged from his wagon, and shot several times at close range. "It is generally supposed that the deed was done out of pure revenge," merchant Charles Robinson Johnson wrote to Able Stearns, "and that woman is at the bottom of it." The woman Johnson had in mind was the wife of the murdered man, María Merced Williams de Rains.

Doña Merced and John Rains had been married for six years. She was the daughter of ranchero Isaac Williams, better known as Don

Julián, proprietor of Rancho Santa Ana del Chino, 22,000 acres of prime grazing land forty miles east of the pueblo. With her sister and brother, she had huddled in terror with their father on the roof of their burning adobe at the conclusion of the Battle of Chino in 1846. The boy died of unknown causes soon after the war, and the bereft father pampered and spoiled the two daughters. He sent them to English-language school for a brief time, but otherwise hired tutors to educate them at home. Mostly they were taught how to wear expensive clothes, dance fashionable steps, and be an adornment for the powerful men around them. Still, Doña Merced was literate in both Spanish and English. She was passionate, but equally intelligent, combining a hot temperament with a fierce will.

Don Julián was "the most perfect specimen of the frontier gentleman I ever knew," wrote Horace Bell. "With his corps of Mexican assistants and his village of Indian vassals, this adventurous American was more than a baron; he was a prince, and wielded an influence and power more absolute and arbitrary than any of the barons of the middle ages." In addition to his legitimate children, Don Julián fathered six more with two Indian women who lived at the rancho. Only fifty-seven when he died after a prolonged illness in 1856, he acknowledged these illegitimate offspring in his will and left them substantial trust funds. To his legitimate daughters, Doña Merced and Doña Francisca, he bequeathed Rancho Santa Ana del Chino, all its land, livestock, and improvements, valued at the princely sum of $150,000 (tens of millions in today's dollars).

The will named Stephen Clark Foster executor of the estate and guardian of the children during their minority. Foster resigned as mayor of Los Angeles to devote full time to the assignment; it was that important to the family. His wife, María Merced Lugo de Foster, was the daughters' aunt, the sister of their mother—who had died before they knew her—making *tia Merced* the most significant woman in their lives. She was surely the first to learn about John Rains. Doña Merced was seventeen, a minor, and her request to marry Rains was addressed to her guardian, *tio Esteban*.

John Rains was twenty-seven and employed as a foreman at Rancho Chino. He was among several employees who witnessed Don Julián's will. Otherwise Rains's name did not appear in the document, strongly suggesting that the dying man knew nothing about the courtship of his daughter. Before Foster granted Doña Merced permission to marry, he consulted with the family. There must have been a consensus about the importance of settling her under approved male authority. The wedding, held at the Plaza church, took place a day after Don Julián's burial.

Rains had come to California from Alabama after serving in the Texas Mounted Volunteers with David Brown and Jack Watson. He made a name for himself as a top hand, driving livestock from New Mexico and Sonora across the desert and mountains to southern California. In 1854 he went to work for Don Julián. "John Rains was an untamed mustang," wrote Horace Bell, who claimed to have known him well. Rough around the edges, hard-nosed and opinionated, Rains was warm and generous with friends. His relationship with Doña Merced was often stormy, but those who knew them insisted it was a love match. Attorney Jonathan R. Scott recalled the "look of love and joy" that came over her face when Rains entered the room. "She thought more of John than she did of all the world," he said. But the secret courtship and hasty wedding also suggested opportunism. Not that Rains was exceptional in that regard. Both Don Julián and Don Esteban, after all, made their fortunes by marrying Lugo women. As Bell put it, "a rancho girl with a thousand or more head of cattle in expectancy and her share of a huge ranch thrown in was a rich catch for one of those matrimonial sharks."

The sharks were soon circling the younger sister, fifteen-year-old Doña Francisca. "All the young men in town have thrown themselves at her feet," William Wallace noted in his diary. When the young woman indicated her interest in a certain Los Angeles gambler named Joe Fort, a suitor the Lugos considered inappropriate, her brother-in-law was dispatched to quiet the man's pretensions. Rains "got up a quarrel, became very abusive, and wound up by kicking Joe out of doors," wrote Wallace, "leaving a large mark upon his seat of honor." Other suitors took his place, and by the time Doña Francisca turned sixteen she had secured her uncle's permission to marry twenty-seven-year-old Robert S. Carlisle, a strikingly handsome Kentuckian with a thick head of dark brown hair and penetrating steel-blue eyes. Little is known of his background, except that he had come to California during the Gold Rush and resided in the north before relocating to Los Angeles. Carlisle was calculating and vindictive, in contrast to Rains, who was impulsive and gallant. Both were fortune hunters.

THE WILLIAMS SISTERS, their husbands, and their growing numbers of children lived together at Chino for several years. Rains and Carlisle managed ranch operations jointly, but each man felt constrained by the other. In 1858 Rains consulted with Los Angeles attorney Jonathan Scott about selling his wife's share of the inheritance to her sister and investing the proceeds elsewhere. He was considering the purchase of Rancho Cucamonga, a neighboring property of 13,000 well-watered acres in the shadow of the San Gabriel Mountains, which he hoped to develop as a large vineyard and modern winery. Scott pronounced it a good investment, and Rains and Carlisle agreed on a price of $25,000 for Doña Merced's undivided half share of Rancho Santa Ana del Chino, paid in the form of cash, goods, and promissory notes. Rains also sold several thousand head of Doña Merced's cattle. He used the funds to purchase Rancho Cucamonga as well as several other properties, including the northern portion of Warner's Ranch in San Diego County and the Bella Union Hotel in Los Angeles.

Doña Merced later testified that these transactions took place without her knowledge or consent. Neither Rains nor Carlisle consulted their wives, and attorney Scott advised Rains to have the deeds to the new properties executed in his name only. As both men knew, that was a clear violation of California's community property law. Doña Merced made a point of asking her husband several times whether Rancho Cucamonga was registered in her name. "If you don't believe it, just ask old Scott," Rains replied, but according to Scott she never did. Carlisle admitted that Doña Merced asked him to look into the matter for her, but he equivocated. It was none of his business, he said, and he didn't want to "cause a blowup." Carlisle was well aware, as he later testified in court, that Rains "used his wife's property as his own, traded it as he pleased without consulting her." It is likely that Carlisle acted in the same manner.

Over the years Rains used a substantial portion of the proceeds from the sale of his wife's assets to subsidize his expenses as a country gentleman. A lifelong Democrat and a local party activist, with his marriage into the local aristocracy Rains rose to the top ranks of the Chivalry. In 1859 he challenged and nearly defeated Andrés Pico in an election for a state senate seat, and the following year he was chosen to be a delegate at the National Democratic Convention in Charleston, South Carolina, a trip he financed with the sale of more of his wife's livestock. He spared no expense in the construction of the elegant brick ranch house at Rancho Cucamonga, which still stands today, and he delighted in entertaining the personal and political friends who passed by along the stage road. The elaborate irrigation system and the preparation of the vineyard proved considerably more expensive than expected. Rains borrowed heavily, spent freely, and by the end of 1861 was in way over his head. With revenue insufficient to cover his obligations, he was forced to mortgage the properties at usurious rates of interest.

Rains also found himself in political hot water. An avid secessionist, he allowed Warner's Ranch to be used as a staging ground for men returning east to fight for the Confederacy. He supplied horses and beef to Alonzo Ridley and the Los Angeles Mounted Rifles when they rendezvoused at Warner's Ranch before setting off on their march across the desert. Later he and his vaqueros drove horses east for use by the rebels. When Union authorities in Los Angeles caught wind of what Rains was doing, they issued an order for his arrest. In January 1862 a Union officer and twenty dragoons arrived at Rancho Cucamonga looking for him, but he was not at home.

Like other prominent secessionists, Rains must have been required to explain himself and swear the oath of allegiance to the United States, although there is no record of it.

The intelligence about Rains very likely came from ranchero José Ramón Carrillo, who worked as a spy for Deputy Provost Marshal J. J. Warner. Don Ramón, a ranchero in his early forties, had been a prominent defender of the homeland during the American war of conquest. An English traveler described him as "a striking-looking fellow, well-built and muscular," with large brown eyes and an elegantly waxed Vandyke. According to Horace Bell, Don Ramón was "a dashing Hotspur." In 1847 he married a wealthy widow, María Vicenta Sepúlveda, and in the 1850s they purchased Rancho Valle de San José, the southern portion of Warner's Ranch, and relocated there. When John Rains moved a large herd of Doña Merced's cattle to his spread at Warner's, he arranged with Don Ramón to oversee their management. That assignment provided Carrillo with an excellent opportunity for gathering intelligence, something Rains realized after his threatened arrest. In the summer of 1862 he confronted Don Ramón. According to Benjamin Hayes, they had "high words," and Rains "insultingly discharged" Carrillo from any further responsibility for Doña Merced's livestock.

JOHN RAINS was a man on the make, a prominent Chiv and the owner of the Bella Union, which secessionists used as their unofficial Los Angeles headquarters. Rains's murder was widely considered the most dastardly crime since the ambush of Sheriff Barton and his posse five years before. The conflict between Rains and Doña Merced over his finances as well as the confrontation between Rains and Don Ramón were the subjects of a great deal of gossip and speculation. Even before Rains's body was discovered, rumors circulated that Doña Merced and Don Ramón had conspired in the murder. Some suspected the involvement of the Lugo family, resentful over the upstart Anglo who had seized control of Doña Merced's share of the family estate.

Benjamin Hayes, still serving as district judge in 1863, took charge of the investigation. Servants at Rancho Cucamonga as well as friends of the deceased led Hayes to an Indian woman named Semanta who operated a whorehouse in Sonoratown that Rains was said to have "habitually or frequently visited when he came to Los Angeles." Hayes questioned Semanta, and she provided the names of half a dozen Californios she claimed had been involved in the murder, alleging that it all had been arranged by Don Ramón. Hayes issued warrants, but before any arrests were made Don Ramón came in voluntarily and submitted himself for examination. "I am as innocent as yourself," he declared. He convinced Hayes that he had neither the means, the motive, or the opportunity to commit the crime, and Hayes discharged him.

Meanwhile, several of the Californios fingered by Semanta were picked up, including a man named Manuel Cerradel, who shot and wounded a deputy sheriff during his apprehension, for which he was charged with attempted murder. Cerradel made a jailhouse confession, claiming that Carrillo had offered him $500 to murder Rains. A second warrant was issued for Don Ramón's arrest, and once again he volunteered himself for examination by the district attorney, who later declared that "the people of the State of California have no complaint against Ramón Carrillo." Hayes dismissed Cerradel's accusation as fabrication.

Hayes believed these informants had been bribed or intimidated into implicating Don Ramón. He suspected Robert Carlisle, the murdered man's brother-in-law, who was conducting what Hayes called an "extra-judicial" investigation. Carlisle harshly interrogated the servants at Rancho Cucamonga, then announced that the evidence pointed to Carrillo. Hayes was appalled not only by Carlisle's conduct but by the implication of his charge, for his insistence on Don Ramón's guilt carried with it an assumption that Doña Merced was guilty as well. "Some *enemies* have murdered John Rains," Hayes wrote. "And now some *friends* would murder him *again* by destroying the fame of his wife."

For all the talk, not a shred of evidence linked Doña Merced to the crime. The rumors of her complicity, however, made the burden of her husband's death all the harder to bear. Just twenty-three years old, she had four young children to raise and was pregnant with a fifth. There were plenty of servants to do the work, including several half siblings, but Doña Merced was, for the first time in her life, in charge of operations. She soon learned that despite what her late husband had led her to believe, she was not registered as the legal owner of any of the properties.

Her petition in district court for the reregistration of the deeds amounted to a painful acknowledgment of the bitter truth about her marriage. John Rains never had any money of his own, but had used her inheritance, without her consent, to purchase properties he illegally registered in his own name. In his brief to the court, attorney Scott argued that Doña Merced had been "deceived by said Rains," who "fraudulently contrived and intended to deprive her of her separate property and convert it to his own use." Scott, of course, was the man who had advised Rains to ignore his wife's rights in the first place. The law was clear, and Hayes ordered the transfer of all titles to Doña Merced.

The day after the ruling Doña Merced met with attorney Scott, her uncle Stephen Foster, and her brother-in-law, Robert Carlisle, for several hours, going over the tangled finances of the estate. They did not expect her to understand the intricacies, they told her, but they wanted her to grasp the magnitude of the problem. They advised her to protect herself and the children by assigning power of attorney to Carlisle, a man with the expertise to manage both properties. Apparently Doña Merced resisted. The three men remained with her for many hours, using all their powers of persuasion. But not until they assured her that Judge Hayes had recommended this course did she finally relent and sign. Later she learned that Hayes had said nothing of the kind.

The irrevocable power of attorney she signed gave Carlisle complete control of all of her property for a term of four years. Over the next several months Carlisle placed his own men in positions of management at Rancho Cucamonga and sold off real estate, livestock, and the entire first vintage from the winery. He used the funds for his own purposes—having diamonds set in his teeth, for example—and paid none of Doña Merced's debts. Besieged by her husband's creditors, she complained to her sister, begging for provisions to feed and clothe her large household. But Doña Francisca stood implacably by her husband, and soon the sisters were estranged.

IN THIS TIME OF TROUBLE, ranchero José Ramón Carrillo stepped forward to assist Doña Merced. Although Rains had dismissed Carrillo from the management of his wife's cattle at Warner's Ranch, some time after the murder Don Ramón spoke with her about it, and Doña Merced requested that he continue. "I did not abandon my place as superintendent of the stock, and I still hold the position," he wrote to his brother, Julio María Carrillo. "It is for her interest that I am taking care of her property." Carillo's intervention enraged Carlisle, and it is entirely likely that in the zero-sum calculations of male honor, getting one-up on his principal accuser in the John Rains murder case may well have been Don Ramón's prime objective. Carlisle "cannot conduct the business with as much liberty as he could if I was out of the way," Carrillo wrote, adding pridefully, "I am satisfied that while awake he thinks of nothing else but a half chance to assassinate me so that he can do with the widow as he sees fit."

Given the risk, Carrillo's chivalric conduct toward Doña Merced seems quixotic. "I am resolved to protect her if it costs me my life," he declared. Inevitably his self-appointed role as her protector fed public suspicion of them both. In the minds of many Anglos, Doña Merced became a "black widow," and Don Ramón a genteel version of Joaquín Murieta or Juan Flores, supposedly in charge of a "band of cutthroats" who swore vengeance "against the American race." A visitor to Los Angeles in late 1863 reported hearing fabulous tales of Don Ramón's gallantry and ferocity that embraced "all the charms of romance." None of this was even remotely true.

In November, Manuel Cerradel, the Californio who had implicated Don Ramón in his jailhouse confession, was convicted of shooting the deputy sent to arrest him and sentenced to five years at San Quentin. On December 10, 1863, as he was being shuttled by lighter to the steamer that would take him to prison, a small but determined delegation of vigilantes overpowered Sheriff Sánchez, seized his prisoner, and hanged him from the main mast, announcing to all present that Cerradel was paying the price for his role in the murder of John Rains. The lynching came during the epidemic of vigilantism in Civil War Los Angeles, and there was a general expectation that Carrillo would be the next victim.

Once again Don Ramón took preemptive action. He recognized that the vigilance committee had become an ongoing extralegal institution in Los Angeles. "When I learned that government forces here were sustaining the vigilance committee," he wrote, "I resolved to pay a visit to the president of the committee." He didn't say who that was, perhaps the ham-fisted barber Felix Signoret, or the gunslinging attorney Jack Watson, both leading vigilantes. Whoever it was, Don Ramón believed he had made a convincing case for his innocence, just as he had previously convinced Judge Hayes. "Since that time," he wrote to his brother, "I have lived peaceably, attending to my business."

That business included acting as Doña Merced's protector. With Carrillo's encouragement she retained Benjamin Hayes—in private practice for the first time in fourteen years—to sue for revocation of the power of attorney assigned to Carlisle. Hayes announced the suit with a notice in the *Star*, alleging that the assignment had been obtained "by fraud." Carlisle responded in the next issue of the paper. Having seen the notice "published by instigation and at the request of Benjamin Hayes," he announced, "I declare said notice totally false in every respect and pronounce Hayes a low-lived vilifier, liar, and coward." Those were fighting words, and while Carlisle knew full well that Hayes would never respond to his challenge, his language signaled a willingness to use violence to maintain his stranglehold over the widow and her property.

In April, while visiting Doña Merced at Rancho Cucamonga, Don Ramón came down with an illness that kept him laid him up for several weeks. His prolonged presence in her house set tongues wagging. Among Anglos it was taken as a confirmation of their conspiracy. Among Californios, who continued to believe in Don Ramón's honorable intentions, it raised fears for his safety. Several residents in the vicinity reported seeing Carlisle in huddled conversation with the managers of Rancho Cucamonga at an inn operated by "Uncle Billy" Rubottom along the stage road near Doña Merced's ranch house. Rubottom later reported the arrival at his place, about the same time, of a man calling himself Lewis Love, who claimed to be awaiting the arrival of friends from the north and requested accommodations for an extended stay. "He seemed to be killing time around the place," Rubottom said, "going out rabbit hunting a great deal." Friends warned Don Ramón. While at Doña Merced's he wrote to his brother, Don Julio, naming Carlisle as his persecutor. "He does not do it personally, but through others paid by him," Carrillo wrote. "If by bad luck I should happen to disappear, Bob Carlisle will know and he will be the cause of my disappearance and he is the one whom you should prosecute."

ON THE MORNING OF MAY 21, Carrillo, having fully recovered, set out for his home in the south. Doña Merced and one of her half sisters accompanied him on the first leg of his journey. He and a companion were riding horseback, with the women alongside in a buggy. Lewis Love saw them pass Rubottom's inn. "Well, Uncle Bill," he said, "guess I'll go out and get a few more rabbits." Not long afterward Rubottom heard the sound of gunfire. Carrillo was hit in the back. Doña Merced saw him grasp his chest and slump to the side of his saddle. "Don't let him fall!" she cried, as the other rider jumped down, caught the wounded man, and lowered him to the ground. "Leave this place," Don Ramón exclaimed through clenched teeth, fearing there would be more shooting. Doña Merced whipped the horses and the buggy took off, leaving Carrillo alone. He struggled to his feet and staggered back to the inn, where he was carried inside, spitting blood.

Rubottom proposed sending for a doctor, but Carrillo shook his head. "Don't bother, I'm done for," he said. Rubottom was deeply impressed by the man's stoicism. "There came over his face a smile of scorn," he later recalled. "He faced the approach of death with bitter gayety." People had accused him of arranging the murder of John Rains, Carrillo said to Rubottom, but he was incapable of doing such a thing. "If I had been the enemy of John Rains, I would have challenged him face to face." He always prided himself on confronting his enemies. "I never did a cowardly act nor fought a man except face to face," he said. "But for all this, I am murdered from behind!" Rubottom was convinced Carrillo was telling the truth. "A man who could talk like that in the presence of death could not be lying," he said. Could he identify the man who shot him, Rubottom asked. He had seen a man fleeing on foot, Carrillo said, but did not recognize him. But that did not concern him, for he knew who was responsible. He slipped into unconsciousness, but roused himself just before the end. "I'm going to die and I'm going to hell," he said. "I'm going to meet the devil and fight him. And may the best man win!" According to Uncle Billy Rubottom, those were Carrillo's last words.

The murder stirred up a whirlwind of controversy in Los Angeles. "You have little idea of the quiet, deep-seated rage of the Californians," Hayes wrote a friend in San Bernardino County, which encompassed Rancho Cucamonga. "They ask me continually if the authorities . . . are not going to do something in relation to it." A warrant was issued for the arrest of Lewis Love, who disappeared immediately after the shooting. He was arrested in San Francisco several months later and brought south. Two managers at Rancho Cucamonga were accused of conspiring with him, but the grand jury in San Bernardino, citing the absence of any direct evidence, refused to indict them, and all three were released.

Don Ramón's brother, Don Julio, published an angry letter in the press. "I desire," he wrote, "to brand, as it deserves, the foul aspersion upon the name of my brother, Ramón Carrillo, who was recently murdered in a most cowardly manner near Los Angeles."

> Ever since the death of John Rains, one Carlisle, whose designs upon the property of Rains have been crossed by my brother in the interests of the widow, has endeavored to blacken the character of my brother and his friends and has given circulation to the most infamous falsehoods in regard to him. This Carlisle has grown rich and infamous by practicing with superior American cunning upon the too easily and confiding disposition of native Californians, and was now indignant that one intractable subject should be found among those whom he considered the legitimate victims of his rapacity.

Doña Merced never publicly accused Carlisle, her brother-in-law, of the murder, but she cut off all relations with her sister, Doña Francisca. "We are sure that money was what done it," she wrote to Hayes, and expressed fear for the safety of herself and her children. "It is impossible for me," she wrote, "to be amongst so many thieves and murderers."

Rubottom later recounted a story of an attempt on Doña Merced's life. "There were a good many threats made against her," he told Horace Bell, "so that the air was buzzing with things that might happen any time." One day at his inn, he claimed, he had overheard a group of Carlisle's friends conspiring to lynch the widow. Rubottom was widely celebrated for his kitchen, which featured southern cooking, including fried chicken, stewed greens, and buttermilk biscuits. "I served the men at the long supper table myself," he said, "then when they all had their heads well down into their plates I returned, stood at the head of the table and said: 'Now, gentlemen, don't make a move or I'll shoot.' They all looked up with the mouths full of food and saw me standing there with a double-barreled shotgun at ready." He took their guns and sent them packing once they had finished their meal.

"I'd seen enough of lynching in my time," Rubottom told Horace Bell, "and when it came to stringing up a woman without a trial, I wouldn't stand it in my neighborhood." Skeptics argue that the story sounds implausible. But consider the warning Hayes received from the sheriff of San Bernardino County. "I really believe these men are becoming insane," he wrote of Carlisle's associates shortly after Don Ramón's murder. "And you will think so too when you hear of something that has taken place at Cucamonga." The reference is vague, but it lends credibility to Rubottom's story.

Hayes certainly took the threats seriously. He wrote to the commander of Union forces in southern California, requesting protection for Doña Merced. "If I was justified once before, while I held the office of district judge, in asking military intervention to preserve the peace of the county," he wrote, "permit me to represent now that a much stronger case for it exists, arising out of the recent murder of Don Ramón," which he characterized as "the most atrocious crime that has been committed within my memory going back more than fourteen years," the whole of his two terms as district judge. The widow had now been threatened with violence, and for her protection Hayes requested that "a small force of dragoons be stationed at the rancho for a short time." An officer and fifteen men were dispatched and spent several days camped in the vicinity of the ranch house.

While there, one of the dragoons recorded the gossip he heard from locals, very possibly at Rubottom's inn, less than a mile from the ranch house.

> It appears that from what I can hear that John Rains married a woman that was half English and half Spanish and an heiress also, and became a noted man. Report says that he kept one or more spirituals and that his wife became jealous and took a paramour by the name of Ramón Carrillo, which of course caused family trouble, and the husband ordered the paramour to keep away from his house and out of his Eden. The paramour, being possessed of little moral but of great animal

courage, resolved to put the husband out of his way and have the woman all to himself, so he either directly or indirectly assassinated the aforesaid Rains. Then the friends of Rains (acting according to the old proverb that is when you are in Rome you must do as the Romans do) caused the paramour Ramón Carrillo to be assassinated.

This version of the story was in striking contrast to the one related by Don Ramón's brother. It made perfect sense, even if it was completely false.

"Rarely has a woman—defenseless herself—been exposed to such injury as has been visited upon you," Hayes wrote to Doña Merced.

> But *es fuerza* [take strength], as the Californians say. It is not necessary for anyone to advise me of the designs which several had against your property—to accomplish which design the better, they have not spared your reputation—that which is the most valuable thing that can belong to one of your sex. It has indeed been the most refined piece of villainy I have every watched, and I have observed it pretty closely for more than a year.

Her suit against Carlisle would soon come before district court, he assured her, and he was optimistic. But in the meantime he could only counsel patience. "Under a kind Providence you will, I doubt not, come safely out of this severe affliction and trial. Always look for protection from heaven. This never fails. I am sure of it." Hayes tried to be upbeat. "Never forget your usual smile at the cares that sometimes threaten you. . . . There, lively Merced, you have quite a sermon. I suppose you think . . . I would make a better *padre* than an *abogado*."

But Doña Merced was not smiling. Her Anglo husband and then her Californio protector had both been murdered. She was responsible for a large household that included five children and three half sisters. She was in jeopardy of losing her property, her only source of income. She was threatened with violence. Less than two weeks after writing that letter, she married José Clemente Carrillo, a cousin of Don Ramón's, who worked as a constable in Los Angeles. Doña Merced's biographer puts it succinctly. "Merced's only alternative was to remarry. It was a man's world."

DISTRICT JUDGE PABLO DE LA GUERRA was a distant cousin of Doña Merced's, so he recused himself, and her suit was transferred to the district court in San José. The case was not heard until the spring of 1865. Carlisle moved for a continuation of the power of attorney, arguing that Doña Merced was "a woman of impulsive and passionate temperament and character," and that the children of John Rains required protection against the risk that their mother might "come under the influence of a husband who would abuse that influence." A man like John Rains, perhaps? But the judge ruled that the power of attorney had been obtained through fraud. Arguing that a neutral party ought to be appointed to oversee the estate in the best interests of the children, he appointed Undersheriff Andrew Jackson King of Los Angeles County. Hayes applauded the decision. "If a receiver had not been appointed," he wrote, the creditors "would have left little for either mother or children." Carlisle was outraged, of course, and Hayes worried that "further violence on the part of R. S. Carlisle" would be directed at Doña Merced or her husband.

Hayes was right about the potential for retribution. But when it erupted it was aimed not at Doña Merced but at Jack King, who stood in Carlisle's way just as Don Ramón had. The confrontation came some weeks after the ruling, at a wedding reception held at the Bella Union on July 5, 1865, attended by all the Los Angeles elite. Carlisle, who was roaring drunk, was standing at the bar when Undersheriff King and Sheriff Sánchez came in from the ballroom and ordered drinks. Carlisle looked over at them. "Jack King is a damned shit ass," he said belligerently. It was a spontaneous outburst, his anger and frustration bursting out under the effect of the booze. King calmly put down his drink, walked directly up to Carlisle, and slapped him hard across the face with his open hand. Carlisle took a swing and the two men clinched, but were separated by Sánchez. Without a word, King turned heel and returned to the ballroom. Carlisle stood there stewing for several minutes, then followed. King was standing with a small group when Carlisle came up from behind, large Bowie knife in hand, which he thrust into King's side. King staggered away, bleeding profusely, and attempted to draw his revolver. But his gun hand had also been badly cut, so he took the weapon in the other hand and fired twice at Carlisle, both shots going wide and fortunately injuring no one. Dr. Griffin, who was nearby, ordered King carried to his office, where he repaired a severed artery and pronounced him out of danger. But loss of blood kept King confined to bed for more than a week.

His brothers, Frank and Houston King, did not learn of the incident until the following morning. Everyone expected a confrontation with Carlisle, who had remained all night in the barroom of the Bella Union. Sheriff Sánchez stationed himself in a chair on the veranda outside, hoping to cut off the King brothers. Apparently he gave no thought to arresting Carlisle for his assault on King, an attack he witnessed, instead regarding it as a private dispute. Main Street was all hustle and bustle. Dozens of people had come into town for the wedding, and those who had spent the night at the Bella Union or the other hotels on Main Street were checking out, carrying bags, and loading themselves into the coaches and carriages lined up along the dusty street. At noon, with no sign of trouble, Sánchez left his post to purchase a cigar. The King brothers may have been watching, for that was the moment they entered the barroom, revolvers in hand. Carlisle was confering with his attorney. "Your time has come," Frank King shouted. Carlisle drew his revolver, and the three men began firing simultaneously.

The report of their guns came so rapidly people thought it was firecrackers going off. Houston King fell in the first fire with a ball to his chest. Carlisle was hit several times, but continued firing wildly. His attorney was wounded, as was another bystander. A horse standing in front of the hotel was shot and dropped dead in its tracks. Frank King's revolver jammed. He charged Carlisle and began clubbing him on the head with the butt end of the weapon. The two men grappled, dancing violently about the room before bursting through the doors and into the crowded street. People screamed and ran in all directions. Teamsters attempted to steady their rearing horses. Amid the chaos, Sheriff Sánchez charged up and pushed the two combatants apart. Carlisle fell back and crashed against the wall of the hotel. His coat and shirt were soaked in blood. Frank King, who had not been hit, fumbled with his revolver, intent on getting off a shot. Carlisle weakly raised his pistol with both hands, took aim and fired. Struck in the heart, King dropped to his knees and remained upright for a few seconds, before falling on his face, dead. Carlisle was carried inside the Bella Union and laid on the billiard table. In addition to a fractured skull he had suffered three or four wounds to his chest, any one of which would have been fatal. It took two or three hours for him to die. Houston King survived his wounds. Tried for murder, he was acquitted.

Despite prevailing in court, Doña Merced was ultimately unable to satisfy her creditors. Jack King advertised the sale of her properties, but could not to raise the capital required to retire the debt run up by her late husband. She was able to hang on to Rancho Cucamonga for several years more, but in the end the mortgage was foreclosed and the property was auctioned off at bottom dollar. Doña Merced relocated to a working-class neighborhood in the pueblo. In the 1880 federal census she was listed as a "laborer," reduced to taking in laundry. Her sister, Doña Francisca, was more fortunate. After Carlisle's death she found an able ranch manager, the husband of one of her half sisters, and some years later she married a wealthy Angeleno. She resided in one of the city's most fashionable neighborhoods, in a household with several servants. "I hardly think the two sisters can long war with each other," Hayes had predicted shortly after Carlisle's death. But the bitterness of their feud persisted. Doña Merced and Doña Francisca remained estranged for the remainder of their lives.

The shootout at the Bella Union, wrote Henry Barrows, was "one of the most desperate encounters that ever occurred in Los Angeles or anywhere else." In fact it bore a striking resemblance to numerous violent affrays in and around the pueblo, including the gunfight ten years earlier between the King brothers and Micajah Johnson. "This was a quick, sharp, diabolical conflict," wrote Hayes, "and yet, come to look around me, it seems to have been almost inevitable." Inevitable perhaps, but as Los Angeles moved into the postwar world, its likes would not be seen again.

CHAPTER 27

THE HOME GUARD
VIGILANCE COMMITTEE

THE FINAL YEAR of the Civil War was an unhappy time for the Democrats of Los Angeles. Their confidence was badly shaken by Union battlefield victories and the resurgent popularity of President Lincoln. Most were upset over with the national party's presidential nomination of General George McClellan, who supported a continuation of the war. Henry Hamilton, editor and publisher of the *Star*, was so disgusted he turned management over to others and left Los Angeles. The paper struggled on without him for a few weeks, then ceased publication altogether. Lincoln actually outpolled McClellan in the November election, largely because of the votes cast by the troops garrisoned at Camp Drum. Citing irregularities, county officials tossed out several hundred ballots, tipping the vote in favor of the Democrats, although the state electorate as a whole voted strongly Republican and California went for Lincoln.

But the Democrats remained firmly in control of local government, carrying the county for the party in every state and national election before 1880. Democrats continued to control Los Angeles, and former secessionists continued to control the Democrats. After the deadly affray with Bob Carlisle, Jack King left the sheriff's office, read law with Benjamin Hayes, and was admitted to the bar. In 1865 he purchased the Los Angeles *News* and turned it into a mouthpiece for unreconstructed Chivs. Editor King made no apologies for his views. "Call us traitors!" he wrote in one of his first editorials. "We have been and are yet secessionist." His newspaper, he announced, would speak in the name of "six million brave, gallant, and chivalrous people who sacrificed fortune, ease, home and the lives of the flower of their young men in support of a principle that should be dear to the heart of every American." In 1868, after several unhappy editorial posts elsewhere, Henry Hamilton returned to Los Angeles and revived the *Star*. The postwar press of Los Angeles spoke with the southern drawl of the Democrats.

Few of the young men who fought for the Confederacy returned to Los Angeles after the war. Most were originally from the South and were only wayfarers in California. Among those who came back was Cameron E. Thom, former state senator and district attorney, who served in the Confederate army with the rank of captain and fought in numerous engagements, including Gettysburg, where he was wounded. With a pardon from President Andrew Johnson he was allowed to continue the practice of law, and he resumed his place in the Democratic hierarchy, serving once again as district attorney and later as mayor.

Another returned veteran was Horace Bell. The previous ten years had been full ones for Bell. Following his disillusioning experience in Nicaragua, he performed penance of a sort by fighting for Benito Juarez and his liberal forces in Mexico before being called home to Indiana. His father and a brother, who jointly operated a ferry downstream from Louisville on the Ohio River, had been jailed in Kentucky on a trumped-up charge of assisting a fugitive slave to escape across the river. In an adventure worthy of Bell's pen—but one about which he declined to write—he and another brother traveled across the river in the dead of night, rescued the prisoners at the point of their revolvers, and brought them back as a crowd of angry men took potshots at them from the Kentucky shore. The Bell brothers were celebrated as local heroes. But several weeks later Bell was kidnapped by bounty hunters, taken back to Kentucky, and placed in the same jail on felony charges. A group of more than a hundred outraged Indiana residents mustered for an attack, and the incident became national news, with Bell's story reprinted in newspapers all over the country. Kentucky authorities, sensitive to the negative publicity, agreed to release him on bond and quietly dropped the charges.

His Nicaragua and Kentucky experiences converted Bell to the cause of antislavery. He served as a Union scout operating behind enemy lines during the first years of the Civil War, and as a reward for bravery under fire was posted to New York City as a recruitment officer. There he met, wooed, and wed young Georgia Herrick, then was sent to the front in western Louisiana, where he served as chief of scouts, spying on the Confederate cavalry force led by Brigadier General Joseph Lancaster Brent, who had left Los Angeles to serve in the Confederate army.

In July 1866 Bell returned to the pueblo with his wife and the first of their brood of eleven children. They traveled overland across the Southwest, ferried the Colorado River at Yuma, and crested the coast range at Warner's Pass. Bell had promised his wife that they were relocating to paradise, but coming up the stage road past Rancho Santa Ana del Chino, they saw the parched grassland covered with the bones of thousands of cattle, the toll of the drought. Bell purchased a small property southwest of town, built a cottage for his family (on the southwest corner of what would later be the intersection of Figueroa and Pico), dug a ditch from the zanja, and laid out a vineyard and a small orange grove.

"My reception in the pueblo was cold," Bell recalled. With the exception of a few gregarious men like Ned Kewen and Jack King, his old friends turned their backs on him. "I was the first man to reappear in Los Angeles who had fought on the Union side in the war," Bell said, "and as I had gone from this town to do this nefarious thing, I was simply a red rag to the secessionist bulls of the vicinity."

His first violent clash with them came not long after his return.

Bell was shopping at a dry goods store when the clerk told him that a big man was waiting outside with a whip to flog him. "I was quite proud of my war record," Bell wrote, "and was not in the frame of mind to accept discipline from any individual, especially from a stay-at-home scoundrel." He confronted the man, who was accompanied by about a dozen Monte Boys. "Is it me that you're looking for?" Bell inquired. The man glared at him and raised his whip. But before he could use it, Bell put everything he had into a roundhouse punch that laid the man flat. Climbing onto a large wood crate, he came down feet first on his opponent's chest "with sufficient force to break three ribs from his backbone." Then he seized the whip and administered a savage lashing. It was the first of many street fights. "I never did get the worst of it in any of them," Bell bragged. "I always got there first with the most force. That is more than half the fight. When a man knows he has to fight he must get there first—never wait to be assaulted."

Bell remained a true believer in righteous violence. But as a product of his time and place he found his rage difficult to manage. The fighting continued long after he had won the grudging respect of the Monte Boys. In the most serious incident, a confrontation on a lonely road with a drunken Californio, Bell beat the man to death with the butt end of his pistol. He was acquitted of murder in a jury trial, but the affair highlighted his violent proclivities. The local press frequently depicted him as a dangerous brute and that angered Bell. "I want this community to know that I am a peaceable man," he wrote in an open letter to Angelenos, and he defied his critics "to point to one single instance of my having ever been known to speak unkindly to any one or to comport myself in any manner unbecoming a gentleman and a good citizen." When challenged, however, Bell's instinctive response was to strike first.

THE GREAT DROUGHT of 1862–65 destroyed the open-range cattle business in southern California and led to the breakup of the great ranchos. Most rancheros successfully defended their claims before the Public Land Commission or in the courts, but few survived the drought. To pay taxes, service debts, and maintain their way of life, many took mortgages at usurious rates and later suffered foreclosure. In 1865 former governor John G. Downey, who had gained possession of considerable property through foreclosure, announced the subdivision and sale of fifty-acre plots with access to irrigation at ten dollars per acre, credit available. The Pico brothers and members of the Lugo family, with large properties east of the pueblo adjoining Downey's, followed suit, making available hundreds of farm sites along the San Gabriel River. Abel Stearns, with huge holdings in the south county, avoided bankruptcy by selling out to a consortium of San Francisco investors, who paid him several million dollars and placed the land in trust for subdivision and sale. "A great many ranches are being reduced into farms and placed on the market for sale at attractive prices," reported Benjamin C. Truman, Los Angeles correspondent for the *New York Times*. "Look this way, ye seekers after homes and happiness."

A flood of new immigrants in search of land, farms, and homes soon began arriving. "Not a day passes but long trains of emigrant wagons pass through town," the *Star* reported in 1868. Most who came overland hailed from the South, and rural southern California retained its southern character. But increasingly people also arrived from elsewhere in the far West or by vessel from Ireland, Germany, and China. During the ten years following the war, nearly twenty thousand newcomers settled in Los Angeles County, two-thirds of them on farms or in small towns. "Real estate, both improved and unimproved, has advanced within the past ten months at least one hundred per cent," J. J. Warner reported. "An activity in all the productive branches of labor beyond that of any former time is observable in this section." The subdivision of ranchos into farms drove an economic recovery. The appearance in 1870 of the monthly *Real Estate Advertiser*, a listing service published by Robert M. Widney, the first real estate agent in Los Angeles, marked the moment that the sale and development of land became the foundation of the southern Californian economy.

In 1868 county voters passed a bond issue subsidizing the construction of a short-haul railroad connecting downtown Los Angeles with the wharves at Wilmington and San Pedro, and in November 1869 the first steam locomotive pulled into the new Alameda Street rail station. Expanded access to the San Francisco market encouraged farmers to experiment with a variety of new cash crops—cotton, tobacco, sugar beets, even silkworms—but most found it more profitable to stick with corn and barley, or grapes and orchard fruit, especially oranges. The extraordinary profits enjoyed by established growers like William Wolfskill and Benjamin Davis Wilson began a citrus frenzy that would long shape the economy and landscape of southern California. The railroad also made Los Angeles into a distribution point for mining operations throughout the Southwest. By 1874 freight traffic in and out of Los Angeles was running at more than fifty boxcars per day.

In the business district, south of the Plaza, adobes gave way to substantial buildings with metropolitan pretensions. Abel Stearns and Jonathan Temple built the first two-story business blocks in 1859, the Arcadia Block on Los Angeles Street and the Market House between Main and Spring, which became the de facto city hall. Urban building ground to a halt during the years of drought and plague but resumed as the economy recovered. In 1869 the Pico brothers built the first hotel in Los Angeles with indoor plumbing and gas lighting on the southwest corner of the Plaza, where the Pico and Carrillo townhouses had once stood. Pico House was located at what was then the city center, poised between Sonoratown on the north and "downtown" on the south. It was intended to revitalize the Plaza area, but instead became a marker of the northern perimeter of urban development.

Pico House was followed by a score of notable new buildings and business blocks stretching several blocks south, including the new Catholic Cathedral of St. Vibiana, which opened on South Main Street in 1876. The movement south of diocesan headquarters, even as the majority of the city's Catholics continued to reside in the north, was a sign of the uneven nature of postwar development, which aggravated existing disparities of wealth and power. As new residential neighborhoods with domestic water and sewer systems expanded south and west, Sonoratown remained in the adobe age. It was a working-class district, largely Californio and Mexican, but with other groups living on the fringes, including several hundred Chinese, who crowded into the old buildings east of the Plaza, along Negro Alley.

THE FIRST ECONOMIC BOOM in Los Angeles history was accompanied by a significant increase in public violence. That was not exceptional, since disorder often accompanies rapid development, but it was a major disappointment, since there had been a dramatic drop in the incidence of homicide following the war. Many observers credited the extended episode of lynchings in 1862 and 1863 for the decline in violence. "Notwithstanding the usual legal opposition," Benjamin Truman wrote in the *New York Times*, the extralegal executions in Los Angeles "are admitted to have been productive of great good. Since then the pulse of society has beat with less symptoms of irregularity." By the time Truman made that upbeat assessment, however, the pace of homicide in Los Angeles had already picked up considerably. Only two murders were recorded for 1866, the lowest number since the war of conquest, but there were eight in 1867, ten in 1868, fourteen in 1869, and twenty-two in 1870. In 1867, amid rising concern over public violence, Tomás Sánchez was defeated in a bid for a fifth term as county sheriff by James Frank Burns, a former U.S. marshal, who pledged a crackdown on crime. Two years later the common council created two more deputy marshal positions, but still, that meant there were only five men to police a city of nearly six thousand residents. "Scenes occur almost daily in the streets that would disgrace any frontier village," editor Jack King opined in the *News*.

The level of violence increased, but its character remained the same. Tomás Oliveras beat his wife, Juana Inez, to death with a reata. Henry Rice planted an axe in the head of his stepfather, Samuel

Wright. Charles Howard and Daniel Nichols, scions of a former district attorney and a former mayor, exchanged gunfire in the lobby of the Lafayette Hotel, leaving Howard dead and Nichols seriously wounded. Black barber Peter Biggs ended a quarter century of public brawling in a fatal contretemps with a knife-wielding waiter in a Main Street restaurant.

Three murders in the fall of 1870 brought the pot to a boil. After a night of heavy drinking, Thomas Hardy and Daniel Newman, neighbors who lived with their wives and children on hardscrabble farms south of town, fell into a meaningless dispute over who was better at holding his liquor. Hardy grabbed a shotgun, Newman grabbed Hardy, the gun went off, and Hardy fell dead. Felipe García, convinced that his friend José Ramón Sepúlveda was secretly romancing his estranged wife, taunted him into a gunfight. "I'll make a man of you," García exclaimed. He fired, missed, and was shot dead by Sepúlveda. Cyrus Sanford and Enoch Barnes ended a tavern crawl one Saturday afternoon with a political argument over who was the more committed Democrat. "I'll cut your God-damned throat," said Barnes, brandishing a small pocketknife and advancing on Sanford, who pulled a pistol and fired, putting a bullet through his friend's belly. Barnes looked down to see blood soaking his shirt. "Cy, you've shot me," he exclaimed in surprise. "Enoch," said Sanford, "if you were my own brother I could not have helped it, and I'm very sorry for it." Barnes died the following morning.

Newman, Sepúlveda, and Sanford were indicted by the county grand jury. Newman, a nobody, was promptly tried, found guilty of manslaughter, and sentenced to four years in San Quentin. But Sepúlveda was the son of José Loredo Sepúlveda, proprietor of Rancho de los Palos Verdes, and Sanford was the brother-in-law of transportation magnate Phineas Banning. Both were represented by E. J. C. Kewen, who delayed their trials through a series of procedural maneuvers. "A vigilance committee is promised unless some decisive action is speedily taken," a local correspondent reported. In fact, the committee already existed and was simply waiting for a call to action.

When Sanford's case finally came to trial in December 1870, District Attorney Cameron Thom warned the jurors not to be swayed by Kewen's eloquence. "A conviction of the defendant," he declared, "may prevent vigilante committees in our midst." When the jury found Sanford guilty of second-degree murder, the authorities breathed a sigh of relief.

The justice system was operating with newfound efficiency. The boom in property sales and construction drove up the number of civil suits, overwhelming the district court. In 1868 the state legislature carved out a new judicial district for Los Angeles, and the governor appointed Democrat Murray Morrison to the bench. Morrison streamlined operations. In 1869 he tried seven men for murder, and that autumn he was elected to a full term as district judge. In 1870 he tried, convicted, and sentenced five more murderers to terms in San Quentin, while seven more awaited their day in district court. Not a bad record, especially when compared with earlier times.

These statistics should have been known to the men of the press, but an accurate summary of the court's record was never provided to the public. Instead, the *Star* and the *News* continued to harp on "immunity from punishment," in the phrase of Henry Hamilton. "Murders are of frequent occurrence here," he wrote, "yet no one is ever punished for the offense." Hamilton railed against pettifogging lawyers, corrupt juries, and lazy judges. Criticism had turned to cant. With misinformation parading as fact, could the people be blamed for not knowing the truth?

ABOUT SUNDOWN on a mid-December day in 1870, Michel Lachenais shot and killed Jacob Bell during a dispute over property lines. A hired man witnessed the shooting and informed the authorities, and later that evening Lachenais was arrested in a downtown barroom and taken to jail. News of the homicide and arrest spread quickly through town, eliciting a great deal of public excitement. Lachenais was a large, intimidating man, notorious for his aggressive disposition and his hot temper. "He is known to have committed three murders beside this one," reported the *Daily Alta California*.

Armand Michel Josef Lachenais had come to California from France during the Gold Rush. By 1857, at the age of thirty, he was living in Los Angeles, attracted perhaps by the pueblo's large French-speaking community. In 1859 he married María de la Encarnacion Reyes, whose family owned Rancho Las Virgenes in the San Fernando Valley as well as a number of smaller properties closer to town. It was on one of those plots that the couple made their home, a farm and vineyard located in the southwestern corner of the pueblo's corporate limits, near today's Exposition Park. Lachenais played an active role in the French community, and it was a lethal conflict with one of his countrymen that first brought him to public notice.

That first homicide took place at a drunken wake one night in 1861. The mourners, all of them French, had been drinking for several hours when Lachenais and a man named Henry Delaval got into a heated argument over a trifling matter. Lachenais called Delaval "a shit" and told him to "go to the devil." Delaval responded by slugging Lachenais in the face, which sent him reeling backward. Lachenais drew his revolver and pulled the trigger, but it misfired. He tried a second time, but again the pistol snapped. "What? Do you want to kill us?" one of the men cried. "I have enough for you and him both," said Lachenais, as he reset the percussion caps on his revolver. Delaval raised his cane in a threatening manner. "Come on!" shouted Lachenais, daring him to attack. "Come on, if you're a man!" Delaval charged forward, Lachenais dropped back a step or two, then fired twice, putting two balls into his opponent's belly. Delaval was mortally wounded. "Better to kill the devil than the devil to kill me," said Lachenais. Later that night, after Delaval had died, a mob of Frenchmen descended on Lachenais's ranch, but he had already fled, leaving his wife and an adopted daughter behind.

Lachenais took refuge in Mexico where he remained for five years. In 1866 he finally returned to Los Angeles and surrendered. He would have turned himself in earlier, his attorney told the court, but "he found the proper legal authorities set at defiance and overawed by a violent, illegal, and irresponsible mob styling themselves a Vigilance Committee." Everyone knew that was true. Concluding that a fair trial would be impossible under the circumstances, Lachenais waited and watched, and "so soon as he was informed that the law in the county had regained its supremacy, he hastened here to deliver himself up." Others believed Lacherais had waited until several key witnesses died or moved away. But his defense—that he had been threatened with a deadly weapon, the cane, and had retreated until his back was against the wall—persuaded the jury, and it acquitted him. The French community was outraged. Felix Signoret took note.

The second murder was committed several months after the trial. An Indian alerted a local justice to the suspicious death of emancipado Pablo Moreno, whom Lachenais had employed as a vineyard worker. The Indian reported that in a dying declaration Moreno had accused Lachenais of beating him about the head with the butt of his revolver. Moreno's body, which Lachenais had secretly buried, was exhumed and found to have a seriously fractured skull. Lachenais was indicted for murder and again brought to trial.

No one had witnessed the alleged attack, but several witnesses testified that the workers at Lachenais's vineyard all said he was guilty. None of them testified in court, however, because Indians were prohibited by statute from giving evidence against white men. Doña María, Lachenais's wife, testified that Moreno had broken into a cask of wine and gotten so drunk that he stumbled and struck his head on a rock. "We did everything we could for him," she said. But the jury didn't buy it, convicting Lachenais of manslaughter. He was sentenced to three years at San Quentin, but defense attorney E. J. C. Kewen immediately moved for an "arrest of judgment," arguing that although Indian testimony had been excluded from the trial, it had been the basis for the indictment, making it illegal. Judge de la Guerra overruled the motion, Kewen appealed, and Lachenais was released on bond. Some months later the California Supreme Court tossed out the conviction and ordered a new trial. Burdened with other court business considered more important than the death of an Indian vineyard worker, the authorities never got around to retrying the case.

Lachenais had by then developed a reputation as one of the most fearsome men in Los Angeles. When his wife, Doña María, died under suspicious circumstances in 1869, the rumor around town was that Lachenais had killed her. There is no evidence supporting this claim of a third murder, only the gossip, but it shows what Angelenos thought of the man. The following year he was arrested for shooting at a neighbor, but the case apparently never came to trial. A few months later he was convicted of illegally diverting water from the zanja to irrigate his vineyard. Lachenais was an all-around menace.

During the war the common council extended the zanja system to city lands on the southwest of town, opening them for sale in order to generate badly needed revenue. That area became notorious for disputes over property lines, much as the Monte had been in earlier years. When Spanish authorities laid out Los Angeles in 1781, they did not orient it with the points of the compass but at an angle to the sun's arc in an attempt to provide better light and shade for streets and residences. Outside the pueblo's corporate limits, however, the cardinal grid of the national survey system prevailed. Where those two surveys intersected, as they did along the city limits on the southwest—a pattern that remains clearly visible on a street map of today's downtown Los Angeles—there was persistent conflict among owners, often leading to violence. Horace Bell, whose farm was in that area, frequently fought with his neighbors over access to water for crops and grass for livestock. The southern district, observed the *Daily News*, "has been the theater of many deeds of blood."

Lachenais and his neighbor Jacob Bell both claimed a strip of land that ran between their respective properties. On the Wednesday afternoon of December 14, 1870, Bell and his hired man were plowing that strip when Lachenais came up on horseback and began verbally abusing them. The two men retreated to a nearby shed and waited until Lachenais left, then went back to work. But he soon returned, this time with a Colt's revolver in one hand. Lachenais ordered the hired man to "vamoose," which he did, and as he made his way over the rough furrows of plowed ground he heard a gunshot, and turning, saw Lachenais firing at Bell, who was struggling with his own revolver, which had jammed. Bell was hit and he fell dead. At the inquest Lachenais contended that Bell fired first, but his revolver, found on the ground beside his body, was still fully loaded.

JACOB BELL'S FUNERAL, held the following day, was said to be the largest in public memory, although most Angelenos were recent arrivals in the city and the public's memory went back only a few years. Large attendance at the funerals of murder victims was a good indicator of public anger. Afterward groups of men lingered on street corners, and an angry crowd gathered at the jail. Lachenais's arraignment was scheduled for that afternoon, but Sheriff James Burns decided to postpone it until Saturday, hoping that popular excitement would dissipate. That evening the leaders of the vigilance committee assembled for a secret meeting. Horace Bell was invited to attend, but refused, "because as bad as was the administration of law in Los Angeles, I was willing to endure it and bide a better day." Bell, who was unrelated to the murder victim, was outraged by the crime but had only contempt for the vigilantes. "I never did attend one of those meetings, or participate in any of those unlawful transactions," he said. "I was not born that way." In truth, Bell had once been an enthusiastic Ranger, which in Los Angeles was another word for vigilante.

On Thursday evening the vigilante leaders held a mass meeting. There is no contemporary account of it. The local press, which had formerly reported in detail on vigilante proceedings, including accounts of the arguments over the justice of lynch law, declined to provide any particulars. What is known comes from the recollections of participants. "We decided that Lachenais had committed murder too often in Los Angeles," recalled Joseph Mesmer, who was there, although he was only fifteen. "We didn't waste much time in arguing his case." Harris Newmark offered an equally succinct summary.

"Lachenais's record was reviewed and his death at the hands of an outraged community was decided upon," he wrote in his memoirs. The vigilantes agreed they would attempt to seize and hang Lachenais when he was taken from his cell for arraignment on Saturday morning. That would give them all day Friday to build support. "We are no advocate of vigilance committees," wrote Charles E. Beane, a former Confederate officer who was editing the *Daily News* for publisher Jack King. "But we recognize the fact that the good citizen here holds his life at the mercy of any scoundrel who chooses to kill him and can pay for being defended, and we warn the authorities that if the flowing tide of crime which is now sweeping over us is not checked, a terrible vengeance will be meted out. Regret the fact we may, but we cannot shut our eyes to it."

Nor could Angelenos shut their eyes to what was happening on the morning of Saturday, December 17. People began arriving in the pueblo at an early hour, on horseback, by buggy and wagon, afoot. "It was evident that trouble was brewing," the *Daily News* reported. "Men with knit brows and a mysterious air went hurrying to and fro and gradually the sidewalks of the street leading to the jail were crowded with citizens, drawn thither by the rumor of contemplated tragedy." Families found places on the eastern slope of Poundcake Hill, which provided an unobstructed view of the jail below. Sheriff Burns postponed the arraignment and issued a summons for a posse to protect the prisoner, but only two citizens responded. Facing the inevitable, Burns consulted with jailer Frank Carpenter and arranged for a priest from the Plaza church to meet with Lachenais. Serafina Reyes Lachenais, his seventeen-year-old adopted daughter, was allowed to spend several minutes with him. Henrietta Carpenter, the ten-year-old daughter of the jailer, realizing what was about to take place, slipped out of the house and ran to find herself a good spot on the hill.

At ten thirty some two or three hundred vigilantes assembled in the Arcadia Block at the head of Los Angeles Street, organized themselves into companies, then began their march to the jail. The *Daily News*, in its account, provided the names of two leaders. The crowd was "under the superintendence of F. Signoret, P. McFadden and others." Felix Signoret was the prosperous barber who had led the vigilance committee for several years, and Irishman Patrick McFadden was a master mason with a booming business. What about the "others"? One was the Reverend Asahel M. Hough, in the words of one observer "a Methodist preacher with a shotgun," who had come to Los Angeles after a stint in Montana during a period of intense vigilantism and lynch law. Another, according to Horace Bell, was real estate agent Robert M. Widney, one of Hough's most prominent parishioners. "But at the last moment," Bell claimed, Widney "dropped out and left his pastor to do the substantial work." Although he did not take part in the march of the vigilantes that Saturday morning, Widney's participation behind the scenes was widely rumored.

As the vigilantes marched they were joined by scores of unruly bystanders shouting, "Hang him!" And thus the march took on the character of a lynch mob. Arriving at the jail, the leaders pushed past the undersheriff and forced their way into the jail yard. Once again the iron door was attacked with sledges, crowbars, and a large wooden beam, used as a battering ram. Eleven-year-old Henry O'Melveny was outside, watching and listening from the hillside. "We could look right down upon the jail yard," he remembered years later, and "it was quite piteous to hear the cries of the other inmates of the jail, who all feared they were going to be lynched too." Finally the hinges gave way and the mob streamed inside and up the stairs, where they found Lachenais cowering in his cell.

His arms pinioned behind his back and a stiff rope around his neck, he was escorted down and out into the jail yard, surrounded by a detachment of vigilantes. The crowd on the hillside greeted him with shouted epithets and vulgar gestures. "When he first appeared the nether lip of the prisoner quivered for a moment or two," the *Daily News* reported, "but then all traces of emotion passed away, and he walked to his doom with a tread as firm as if he were upon an ordinary walk." Attention to such details exposed the event as the spectacle lynching it was. Hundreds of people were attentive to the manner in which Lachenais would die, and the vigilantes aimed to please by picking a location for the hanging clearly visible to spectators on the hillside. They marched their prisoner two blocks to a large fenced property at the corner of Temple and New High Streets that everyone knew as Tomlinson's old corral, although it was being used as a lumberyard. Over the gate was a heavy crosspiece, some ten or twelve feet high, and this they used as a gallows. The only protest came from a man who mounted a large wooden box and implored the mob to let the law take its course. But the die was cast. He was shouted down, the box repositioned under the crossbeam, and Lachenais lifted onto it.

As the priest prayed beside him, Lachenais asked permission to dictate his will. "He desired to make provision for the education of an adopted child," the *Daily News* reported. "This privilege was not accorded him." He spoke briefly to the crowd. "I am guiltless of murder," he said. "If I had not killed Mr. Bell, whom I liked and esteemed, he would have killed me. It was done in the excitement . . . ." Someone pulled the box from beneath Lachenais before he finished speaking. The drop was not more than two or three feet, and it took an inordinate amount of time before he strangled to death. He was left hanging for an hour, and before he was cut down, William Godfrey, proprietor of the Sun Beam Photographic Gallery on Main Street, set up his camera and photographed the scene. He later did a brisk business selling the prints.

"THERE IS NO DOUBT but what Lachenais deserved hanging," wrote Horace Bell. But "the Courts ought to have been permitted to decide that question. He had no hearing. He was not permitted to speak in his own defense and to hang him was murder." Few Angelenos expressed so forthright an opinion at the time, yet the lynching had plenty of critics. Charles Beane, despite his sympathy for the fears and frustrations of Angelenos, condemned the action in the *Daily News*. "Every good citizen must deprecate this occurrence," he wrote. To be sure, the legal justice system was weak, "but we submit that the remedy lies not in an organization which flouts all law." He hoped that this would be the last of those acts "which, in the minds of those abroad, stamp us as a semi-civilized community."

In the *Star*, Henry Hamilton continued his long practice of equivocating in the face of vigilantism. He was consistently against lynch law—except when he was for it. "We are opposed to mob law—we are opposed to the formation of vigilance committees," he declared, then hedged his bet. "But of late murder has gone so unwhipt of justice that it appeared there was no law against it. . . . Of the numberless murders committed in this city and county, we have recollection of but one case being punished by law." That was a bald-faced lie, but no one stepped forward to challenge Hamilton's facts, and he persisted in criticizing "the weak arm of the law." The authorities, he held, should "take the hint" and begin dealing swiftly and harshly with violent criminals, making it "unnecessary for the people, from whom all the power of the law proceeds, to ever again retake the law into their own hands."

Apparently getting the message, the common council approved a reorganization of law enforcement, voting to hire another two deputy marshals—now termed patrolmen or policemen—for a total force of seven. And it passed an ordinance establishing a "Board of Police Commissioners," composed of several councilmen as well as the city marshal, arming it with the power "to make all appointments, to suspend, discharge, and to have the entire control and regulation of the police force of this city." Adding the new officers was helpful, but the new board actually weakened the authority of the marshal over his men. Not until 1873 would he be provided with the power to appoint and suspend his own officers.

None of this had the slightest effect on the vigilance committee. The leaders had no intention of disbanding. "It was understood," the *Daily News* reported the day following the lynching, "that another meeting was to be held last night, to decide upon the propriety or expediency of lynching other parties." This and subsequent meetings took place at night and in secret, and within days the committee began issuing notices to selected "evil-doers," warning them to leave town or suffer the consequences. In one case a man named John Kelly, awaiting trial on charges of grand larceny, was given until noon the following day to "make himself scarce." He departed on the morning train for Wilmington and caught the steamer for San Francisco.

The leaders of what was termed the Home Guard Vigilance Committee, or the HGVC, as it was known around the pueblo, issued a formal statement of their aims and objectives in the *Star*. They saw a continuing role for themselves in the justice system of Los Angeles. "The red hand of the assassin has been rife among us," read the statement, "and from corruption or mismanagement, criminals have been allowed to go unwhipt of justice." In his editorial of a few days before, Hamilton had used that same Shakespearean phrase, "unwhipt of justice"—from King Lear—and its reappearance suggested a cozy relationship between the vigilantes and the *Star*. "Our object, in thus associating together, is not to inaugurate mob law, but to protect the life and property of innocent persons to the best of our ability," the vigilantes declared. "And wherever, in our judgment—after mature deliberation and without haste—any assassin has been set free, where the evidence should have convicted him—then, and not until then, shall we meddle with the course of the law." They would act in a restrained manner, they promised, but have no doubt, they would act. Vigilantism had triumphed in Los Angeles fifteen years before. Vigilance committees were now part of the county's virtual institutional structure, and vigilantes were not about to give up that power. Hamilton printed the statement without identifying the authors and added his endorsement. "We are of the opinion that a little hanging by the neck for the perpetration of murder would be about as good a remedy as could be suggested."

The following day the *Daily News* published a letter from a reader, responding to the vigilante declaration. "If an honest jury and learned judge mistake the law, is society any safer in the hands of an ignorant association of green grocers? If a learned judge errs, it is not very probable that he will be improved upon by a dealer in old clothes, or that the old-clothes man will be any more honest than a sworn juror." If the vigilantes wished to bring offenders to justice, "they should have organized under the law, and in aid of its administration."

Popular opinion was divided. Early in 1871, when Jose Ramón Sepúlveda was tried and convicted for the murder of Felipe García, defense attorney E. J. C. Kewen challenged several prospective jurors on their support of lynch law. Houston King of the Monte, brother of Jack King and lifelong Democrat, acquitted five years earlier of the murder of Robert Carlisle, said that when horse or cattle thieves were caught red-handed, they ought to be hanged on the spot, but that he "didn't believe in mobs going and breaking open the jail and taking men out and hanging them." Jonathan Tibbetts, also from the Monte, but a combative Republican, agreed with much of what the HGVC had to say in its public statement, but declared that he "never did approve of the hanging of Lachenais, nor in ever going and breaking into a jail and taking a man thence and hanging him." Henry Hammerton, a young farmer from England who lived with his wife and children on a place in Los Nietos, was generally opposed to capital punishment and said he would never take part in a lynching. But, he continued, if a jury found a man not guilty, "and I positively knew he deserved hanging, I believe he should then be hung."

The testimony suggested the contradictory views held by ordinary Angelenos. Yet the HGVC, with its black-and-white perspective, would officially carry the day. County Judge Ygnacio Sepúlveda charged the grand jury with responsibility for the investigation of Lachenais's killers. "Be they few or be they many, if you believe them to be guilty you must indict them," he instructed the jurors. "Be they men of the higher walks of life, or from the lowest levels of our population, they all stand as violators of the law and should be dealt with accordingly." It was critical that all citizens understand "that their safety and happiness greatly depend in yielding obedience to the laws of the land, and in having due respect for constituted authority, [and] that the violation of law only entails to us injustice, cruelty, dissension, anarchy, and immorality."

But the grand jury failed to indict anyone and issued a report exonerating the vigilantes. It held the justice system ultimately responsible for the lynching. "Had the laws been faithfully executed, and had the criminals been punished by the Courts in a thorough and vigorous manner, the disgraceful scene recently enacted in the broad light of day in Los Angeles city would never have taken place." Thus the grand jury, the body that had indicted twelve men for murder during that very year of 1870, helped perpetuate the same dangerous misinformation that had fueled the support of vigilantism. The year 1871—which would prove the single most violent year in the frontier history of Los Angeles—began with vigilantism and lynch law more firmly entrenched than at any other time since the American conquest.

· CHAPTER 28 ·

CHINATOWN

IF VIGILANTISM WAS TO SUCCEED in deterring violence, the history of Los Angeles suggested that it would require more than a single lynching. So the leaders of the vigilance committee kept at the ready. At some point during the year they began referring to themselves as the Law and Order Party and chose real estate agent Robert M. Widney as their leader and spokesman. Their aim, Widney said, was "to cooperate with officers of the law in suppressing violations of the law." A similar declaration had been made by virtually every vigilance organization in the history of frontier Los Angeles.

The year 1871 opened inauspiciously with the double homicide of brothers Hershel and Henry Bilderback, young men from Ohio who worked as woodchoppers, supplying fuel to the rapidly growing domestic market. The firewood business was intensely competitive, and the Bilderbacks' claim to a forested canyon in the San Gabriel Mountains was contested by Allanson Gardner, another firewood supplier, who employed a crew of half a dozen men. After several attempts to warn them off failed, Gardner decided to evict the brothers by whatever means necessary. Accompanied by two men armed with Henry rifles, he came up on them one morning as they were chopping. "If I was you, I would leave this canyon," Gardner shouted. But before the Bilderbacks could respond, before they even had time to spin around, David "Buckskin" Stevenson fired and put a bullet through the back of one of them, killing him instantly. The other brother took off down the canyon, "running like a deer," Gardner later testified. Stevenson jumped on his mare and went in pursuit. Gardner heard the sound of rifle fire, then saw Stevenson come riding back. "I killed the son of a bitch," he said. "Come on, let's cover them up."

Two weeks later a sheriff's posse recovered the bodies from a shallow grave, "far advanced in the first stages of that decay which is the inevitable end of all things mortal," in the words of the *Star*. Stuffed in the breast pocket of the younger brother's coat was a crumpled letter from his mother. "My Very Dear Son," it began, "I have not heard a word from you since you wrote me you were sick. Oh, I feel so uneasy about you—I fear the worst." It concluded, "Oh, Henry, write to me, if but a line." Gardner's employees implicated their boss, and he in turn fingered Buckskin Stevenson, who was tracked down and killed by a bounty hunter. Gardner was indicted for murder, but defense counsel E. J. C. Kewen successfully delayed the trial until negative coverage in the local press had reached fever pitch. "It is rumored," reported the *Star*, "that a vigilance committee is being organized for the purpose of hanging Allanson Gardner." That news item provided Kewen with probable cause for a change of venue, which was granted by District Judge Murray Morrison, Kewen's brother-in-law. After a trial in San Bernardino, which the defense orchestrated as a virtual prosecution of the late Buckskin Stevenson, Gardner was acquitted.

JUDGE MURRAY MORRISON, who was frequently incapacitated by a chronic illness, struggled to keep up with the felony cases prosecuted by District Attorney Cameron E. Thom. If the volume of homicides fell short of the record carnage of the 1850s, it was in part because of a steep decline in the number of murdered Indians. Before the smallpox epidemics of the 1860s there were an average of four or five Indian victims every year, but by the late 1860s the toll had fallen to one or two. The Indian population of the city collapsed as many emancipados fled the smallpox-infested city for the relative safety of backcountry rancherías. Indian migrants continued to travel to the pueblo to work in the vineyards, the stockyards, or the busy commercial district on the eastside; they still gathered on Negro Alley and continued to be arrested and auctioned off to employers. But there were far fewer of them.

As the countryside filled with thousands of Anglo families, the rural homelands of Indians were placed under increasing pressure. Gabrieleños in the San Gabriel Valley protested that they were being forced from their lands by local growers. Luiseños at Temecula, returning from the grape harvest in Los Angeles, found their houses burned and Anglos in possession of their gardens and zanjas. Desert Cahuillas complained that rancheros had taken over their springs and oases for watering livestock. Native lands were "being invaded and their pastures consumed by the stock of white settlers," wrote a government official, "the water turned away from their ditches to irrigate the gardens of those trespassing upon their lands. And they have no redress."

In this context a new leader emerged, a Luiseño named Manuel Olegario, described in the *Star* as "a large, fine looking fellow, almost as black as a Negro, and quite intelligent and much disposed to stand on his rights as a white man." Olegario had lived and worked in Los Angeles, where he earned a reputation as a man of talent and became a leader of the pueblo's Indian community. But during one of the recurrent outbreaks of smallpox he returned to his home in Temecula. There he played a leading role in the struggle to maintain the Luiseño homeland. In 1870 local leaders chose him to be their paramount chief. The Indian agent had handpicked another man for the position, a conflict broke out between the rivals and their followers, and bloodshed occurred. Olegario forged an alliance with Manuel Largo, captain of the Cahuillas, traditional enemies of the Luiseños, raising fears of communal violence. Olegario and Largo—advised by a number of Angelenos, including vineyardist Matthew Keller, attorney

Christopher N. Wilson, and former ranchero J. J. Warner—met with federal officials and assured them of their peaceful intentions. What they required, the Indian leaders insisted, was federal protection of their homelands. "The danger to which they are now exposed," wrote a correspondent for the Sacramento *Daily Union*, "is that Congress, not finding any convenient lands in the south of California whereupon to place them, will propose to remove them to some distant reservation, . . . a separation as hopeless as the barbarous removal of the Acadian farmers immortalized by Longfellow in 'Evangeline.'"

Olegario insisted that the Luiseños still held legal title to their homeland, that it had never been ceded to the United States. Through the influence of Anglo friends, he traveled to Washington, D.C., where he met with President Ulysses S. Grant, who issued an executive order establishing reservations at the sites of several small rancherías. But the struggle was far from over. Some of those reservations were later disestablished and the residents forcibly removed from their homes and the graves of their ancestors.

In 1877, when several hundred acres of prime Luiseño grazing land came under threat of confiscation, Olegario organized his followers to protect them. The land had been leased by Antonio María "Chino" Varela, son of the late José Sérbulo Varela, former Manilla gangster and Confederate war veteran, who had lost a leg while in service to the South. When Varela and his vaqueros arrived with a herd of several hundred sheep, they were met by Olegario and sixty well-armed men, who escorted them off the property. Varela filed a complaint with the local justice, who issued a warrant for Olegario, but the Indians expelled the constable who came to arrest him. A few days later, however, Olegario died in his sleep. The protest collapsed and Varela took possession. The local press reported the cause as apoplexy or heart disease, but Olegario's followers claimed their leader had been poisoned.

The Luiseños continued to suffer from encroachments on their homelands. "These Indians have been badly treated and are subjects of sympathy," wrote the editor of the San Diego *Union*, but "sympathy for the Indians that ignores the right of white property-holders and settlers is the most pernicious thing that can befall the Indians, for the effect is only to postpone action that alone can save them from going to the wall in a hopeless contest with an advancing civilization."

IN THE MEANTIME cheap Indian labor was being replaced by cheap Chinese labor. The growth of the Chinese community—like the surging demand for real estate or the expansion of the domestic fuel market—was another vital indicator of economic activity. Chinese men began moving to the pueblo in significant numbers during the postwar boom. The 1870 census counted 234 Chinese in the county, and 172 in the city, a snapshot of a rapidly expanding community. They came to California with the intention of working, saving, and returning home with a pile of money, a motive widely shared by immigrants of all backgrounds. Attracted to Los Angeles by expanding prospects for employment, they found work as domestics and cooks, farmworkers and common laborers, the kind of low-wage jobs formerly filled by emancipados.

Some brought entrepreneurial skills. Chinese farmers grew vegetables for the domestic market on leased land south of the city, and Chinese vegetable peddlers—their baskets suspended from long bamboo shoulder yokes—soon were a common sight in all neighborhoods. Chinese laundrymen opened the first commercial laundries in the early 1860s and quickly dominated the business, by 1871 operating eleven of the city's thirteen washhouses and employing a quarter of its Chinese residents. A cigar factory, an herb shop, and a restaurant were among other commercial ventures Chinese entrepreneurs aimed at Angelenos. Because Chinese names were recorded in various and inconsistent ways, it is virtually impossible to track the owners of these enterprises. In 1870 the census enumerator recorded most Chinese in Los Angeles by given name only, often with the addition of the honorific title *Ah*, in the original Cantonese conveying intimacy or affection, but in the way it was employed by Americans a term of estrangement, effectively erasing individual identity. One of the few men listed by his complete name was physician Chee Long Tong (or, in the correct sequence, with family name first, Tong Chee Long), who established a traditional Chinese medical practice and treated a number of Anglo patients, who knew him as Dr. Gene Tong.

More than half the Chinese in the city, including Dr. Tong, lived in the sprawling adobes along Negro Alley, divided and subdivided into a warren of low-rent rooms. Over the years, the Coronel adobe, the building that anchored the alley's southwest corner, had been the site of numerous saloons and dives. It was where Sheriff Barton had first proved his mettle in a memorable July Fourth shoot-out with unruly gamblers, where Tom Smith had danced on the monte table before egging Frank Dana into a lethal gunfight, where John Buckley, Pancho Cruz, and Augusta Cañada had played out their lethal ménage à trois. By 1870 the Coronel building housed the Wing Chung general store, Dr. Tong's office and residence, a Chinese rooming house, a barbershop, and a café. Nearby, wedged between saloons and gambling houses, was a small Chinese theater and a temple or "joss house," several little fan-tan parlors and opium dens, as well as numerous brothel cribs. Negro Alley remained the pueblo's preeminent vice district, but it had also become Chinatown.

At first the local press treated the Chinese with bemused condescension, noting the exotic language, hair style, and costume of the "almond-eyed family" from the "Celestial Kingdom." But as the number of Chinese expanded, the tone of the coverage grew darker. The *Star* focused on what it claimed was the destructive competition between "the Chinese worker and the citizen laboring man," ignoring the fact that the Chinese filled jobs Anglos and Californios had traditionally scorned and assigned to Indian workers. The *Daily News*, edited by Jack King, was even more negative, publishing a series of deeply racist and inflammatory editorials on "the Chinese menace." The Chinese were a people "without one single redeeming feature," the *News* declared, "so utterly depraved and debased that no single thought of virtue or honesty ever entered their heads." In a particularly vicious column, a reporter offered his impression of the "pariahs" who resided along "Nigger Alley."

> Within the buildings, herded like beasts, men, women and children dwell together, ignoring all distinctions of sex, and filthy to a degree absolutely appalling. Noisome vapors pervade the air, creating a stench sickening to senses unperverted by daily contact with these loathsome quarters. Here, crimes too horrible to name are undoubtedly matters of ordinary and perhaps daily or nightly occurrence.

With allusions to animals, filth, and unregulated lust, the press coverage portrayed the residents of Chinatown as barely human.

The negative reporting was accompanied by a dramatic upsurge in violence directed at Chinese residents. The records of the city's justice courts, reasonably complete for the 1860s, include no complaints of violence against Chinese individuals before the spring of 1869, when teamster George Enkhardt was found guilty of having "maliciously run his wagon, loaded with brick, into the cart of a Chinaman and smashing it to pieces." It was followed by no fewer than twenty violent attacks over the subsequent two years. Santiago Aguella was charged with "maliciously cutting and beating Ah Loy over the head and face with one wagon whip without cause or provocation." Andy Sharkey was fined for "beating and kicking a Chinaman without provocation." Patrick H. Gleason pled guilty to maliciously assaulting a Chinese man. When Justice William H. Gray asked Gleason whether he had anything to say in extenuation of his offense, he explained that a Chinese man had "called him hard names," leaving him so angry that "he pitched into the first Chinaman he met." He felt such "great antipathy to the Chinamen," Gleason said, he simply could not help himself.

The Chinese responded forcefully to the violence against them, filing complaints in justice court and pursuing the prosecution of their tormenters. Virtually every Chinese resident of Los Angeles was a member of a *huiguan,* or company, a mutual benefit association designed to assist and protect overseas Chinese. Six *huiguan* established headquarters in San Francisco during the 1850s and 1860s, opening branches in other western cities as the need arose. Five of the six *huiguan* had members in Los Angeles, but a majority of the city's Chinese belonged to the Sze Yup Company. The companies assisted their members with employment and lodging, offered them meeting rooms and lounges where they could relax with their countrymen, and provided them with the assurance that in the event of an untimely death in a foreign land their remains would be returned to family members in China.

The companies also hired local lawyers to represent their members in court. California law forbade Chinese witnesses from testifying in cases involving white persons, but when the lawyer for a defendant moved to quash the complaint of a Chinese man on those grounds in 1869, Justice Gray overruled him, rejecting his "ingenious resort to legal technicalities." Thereafter Chinese residents enjoyed full access to Gray's court.

THE REVENUE of the Sze Yup Company came not only from membership fees but from the services it provided its members. Gambling and opium concessions offered lucrative returns. But with Chinese men outnumbering women by a ratio of five to one, the sex trade was the profit center. A handful of the approximately three dozen Chinese women who resided in the city in 1870 were the wives or mistresses of prominent men. The majority, though, were prostitutes, servicing not only their own countrymen but a growing number of Anglo and Latino customers as well.

Near the Plaza late one night, an off-duty patrolman was accosted by a Chinese streetwalker who tugged at his coat and asked him how he liked it. He played dumb, saying he didn't know what she meant. "You fuck me for two bits," she said. When he hesitated, she doubled down. "Me give you two fucks for two bits." Even at low rates like those, the typical Chinese prostitute produced an annual profit of several hundred dollars for her pimp. The sex trade in Chinatown was valued at thirty or forty thousand a year, the equivalent of several million in today's dollars. While the Sze Yup Company did not manage the brothels itself, its members did, and a share of the revenue went to the company in exchange for referrals and protection.

These women were very young and very vulnerable. Some were the victims of kidnappings in China; others had been sold into slavery by their impoverished families. Forcibly transported to the United States, they were indentured to brothel masters, typically for a term of four years, considered the maximum working life of a prostitute. If they complained or resisted, they risked punishment. The record overflows with accounts of Chinese prostitutes beaten, whipped, and sometimes tortured by brothel masters. One evening as two patrolmen made their rounds near Negro Alley they heard a woman's screams. Rushing down a dark corridor they came upon a group of Chinese men standing over a severely beaten woman who was bleeding profusely from cuts about her face and head. Nearby was her master, Sing Lee, headman of the Sze Yup Company. In halting English she told the patrolmen that she had been punished for resisting his plan to sell her to another man. Both Sing Lee and the woman were arrested and taken to jail, where he was released after paying a small fine. But, according to the *Star*, the woman "begged to be allowed to stay, stating that Sing was 'a big Chinaman,' and that, because she had been the cause of his going to jail, the other Chinamen would kill her [and] cut her body into little pieces." Nevertheless, she was turned out to an unknown fate.

Chinese prostitutes sometimes ran away, but when they did their masters often filed false complaints against them for theft, thus enlisting the authorities in their apprehension. Los Angeles patrolmen, easily corrupted with a little cash, proved eager to cooperate. In October 1870, when the Sze Yup Company offered a $100 reward for the return of a particularly valued woman, both City Marshal William Warren and Deputy Joseph Dye jumped into action. Dye learned where the woman was hiding, but it was Warren who made the arrest and collected the reward. He was escorting the woman to jail, trailed by a large crowd of Chinese, when Dye confronted him on Main Street. "Warren, what are you going to do in regard to this matter?" Dye demanded. "I want my money." Warren brushed him aside. "I don't want anything to do with you," he said. "But you have defrauded me," Dye exclaimed. "You're a damned dirty liar," Warren responded. Dye reacted instinctively, raising his walking stick to strike, but Warren had a derringer pistol concealed in his hand, and he fired first. The ball struck Dye in the forehead but miraculously glanced off, leaving him with nothing more serious than a bad bruise and a terrible headache. The two men pulled their revolvers and, in the words of one witness, "the pistol shots commenced coming thick and fast." Three bystanders were struck before Warren was hit in the groin and fell to the ground, mortally wounded. "I'm killed," he cried. He died the following morning. Tried for manslaughter in district court, Dye was released after Judge Morrison declared the homicide a clear case of self-defense and directed the jury to bring in a verdict of not guilty.

Most fugitive prostitute cases ended more prosaically in the courtroom of Justice Gray, who resented the ability of Chinese brothel masters to corrupt the judicial system. Although slavery had been outlawed by the Thirteenth Amendment to the Constitution, few public officials applied the law of the land to the bondage of Chinese women. Justice Gray was the exception. "The law does not recognize slavery," he exhorted the principals at the close of a hearing in which two Chinese masters disputed the ownership of a woman. Yet Gray had to acknowledge that he did not possess the authority to intervene and release her. "The Court," he declared, "regrets its want of power to punish both parties as they deserve, for the violation of the Laws of the Land and for contempt of this Court in attempting to make it a party to the transaction."

AS CHINATOWN GREW, other *huiguan* established branches in Los Angeles, and the Sze Yup Company slipped from its dominant position. A power struggle broke out among headman Sing Lee's top lieutenants, Sam Yuen and Yo Hing, legitimate businessmen but brothel masters as well, both of them fined in justice court for "maintaining and residing in a house of ill fame." Reports of the conflict began appearing in 1868 and continued through the autumn of 1870, when both men resigned from the old company and led their factions into two *huiguan* that had recently established branches in Los Angeles. Sam Yuen became headman of the local Ning Yung Company; Yo Hing assumed leadership of the branch of the Kong Chow Company. With that move the struggle sharpened for control of the Chinatown vice trade. "Sunday evening, extensive preparations for a battle royal were made by the Chinese denizens of Negro Alley," the *Star* reported in January 1871. "Between the lines formed by the two companies were the headmen arguing the point at issue, which appearances indicated could only be settled by an appeal to the law of arms." But "the row was nipped in the bud" by the timely arrival of the newly elected city marshal, Francis Baker.

Sam Yuen quickly negotiated a defensive alliance with his old boss, Sing Lee. But Yo Hing took them both on. About thirty years old, Yo Hing was both charismatic and commanding, "a huge man," in the description of a contemporary, with "a voice that fairly rumbled when he talked." His Los Angeles career had begun several years earlier when he went to work as a cook in the household of Jack King and his family. He quickly worked his way up, leasing land to grow vegetables and investing his profits in a cigar factory and brothels in Chinatown. Yo Hing was fluent in English and maintained good relations with important Anglos. Horace Bell described him as "a fine fellow," and the *Star* praised him as "the best and most favorably known Chinaman in the city."

Yet in his struggle for control of Chinatown, Yo Hing did not hesitate to employ ruthless tactics. In the spring of 1871 his men abducted the wife of a prominent Chinese merchant, an ally of Sam Yuen's, and succeeded in keeping her hidden for several months. Sam Yuen was shamed as a leader unable to protect his own people, and after months of humiliation he decided the time had come to eliminate his rival once and for all. He put a price on Yo Hing's head and arranged for two professional Chinese gunmen to come from San Francisco. In mid-October they arrived on the steamer, intent on collecting the reward. The contract on Yo Hing was common knowledge in Chinatown, and the cadre of the two companies prepared themselves for a battle royal, stockpiling arms and ammunition. The proprietor of a local hardware store reported he had "sold forty or fifty pistols to Chinamen within the last few days."

On the morning of Monday, October 23, as Yo Hing emerged from an apartment at the northern end of Negro Alley, Ah Choy and Yu Tak, the San Francisco hitmen, were waiting for him. "They fired at me," Yo Hing told the *Star*. "I ran into the house. Ah Choy's pistol got out of order, I think a cap caught in the cylinder, and that saved my life. One ball passed through my coat and shirt." The shooters fled and Yo Hing hurried to the office of his attorney, Jack King, where he swore out a complaint charging the two men "with the crime of assault with deadly weapons with intent to kill." They were arrested and jailed. At a hearing in Justice Gray's court the following afternoon, rival boss Sam Yuen posted their bail.

Yo Hing considered himself in mortal danger. "They are bound to kill me," he told a reporter for the *Star*. "They will kill me even if they are killed after. They don't care and will kill anybody who tries to arrest them." Yo Hing was determined to seize the offensive, which he did that afternoon, shortly before sundown. Sam Yuen later provided his version of what happened. The gunman Ah Choy, he said, "was eating his evening meal, at a back part of a house on the east side of Negro Alley, heard a fuss, and went out to the front door. Yo Hing and three others were around with pistols, and one of them shot Ah Choy in the neck." Moments later three or four of Sam Yuen's fighters burst from the Coronel building across the street and began firing at the assailants.

Mounted patrolman Jesús Bilderrain had been warned by Chinese informants to expect "a big China fight." He was a couple of blocks away when he heard the sound of gunfire. "Follow me," he shouted to fellow officer Esteban Sánchez. He sprang into the saddle and spurred his horse toward Negro Alley. As he approached, Bilderrain testified, "I saw six or seven Chinamen about the middle of the street shooting at each other." He charged into them and the gunmen scattered, running into open doors on either side of the alley. Bilderrain jumped down and nabbed one of them. That was when he saw Ah Choy lying in the doorway of an east side adobe, "dying from a shot he had received." Sánchez rode up. "I saw Bilderrain afoot, ahold of a Chinaman," he said. "At the same time I saw another Chinaman shoot at Bilderrain with a pistol in each hand." Sánchez jumped down and pursued the shooter around the corner of the Coronel, but was driven back by sustained gunfire from a group of Ning Yung fighters massing in the corral at the back of the building.

Bilderrain hailed a bystander and requested his assistance in taking his captive to jail. As they hurried along the south side of the Coronel, a Chinese fighter emerged from the Wing Chung store, fired at them, then darted back inside. Handing his prisoner off to the bystander, Bilderrain charged after the man, revolver in hand. He ran through the open door and someone slammed it behind him. "The house was plum full of Chinamen," Bilderrain said. One of them pressed a pistol to his chest, and he instinctively grabbed it with his left hand. The gunman pulled the trigger, but the hammer came down on Bilderrain's finger. "I went to smack him down," he said, "but some of the Chinamen then shot me." The bullet penetrated his right shoulder, disabling his gun hand. "I had no show for my life," as Bilderrain put it, realizing his only chance was to get out. "I thought I was mortally wounded and I was anxious to die outside," he said. He wrenched the door open with his good hand and stumbled out onto the veranda.

Walter Lyon, who operated a shop in the Arcadia Block, just steps away, saw Bilderrain "come running out with three Chinamen at his heels, pistols in each hand and firing promiscuously." A Mexican boy standing nearby was hit in the leg. Patrolman Sánchez charged after the gunmen, who retreated back into the Coronel, leaving the door ajar.

Bilderrain steadied himself against a post and blew several long blasts on his police whistle. Sánchez stepped up on the veranda, approached the open door, and warily peered in. The interior was thick with gun smoke, but through the haze he could see the figure of a man. "He leveled his pistol at me," said Sánchez. "I presented my pistol and we both fired at the same time." Both shots went wide. Sánchez jumped to the right side of the door and pressed himself against the adobe wall. Robert Thompson, a bystander summoned by Bilderrain's whistle, came running up with another man, and they positioned themselves against the wall on the left side. "What's the matter?" asked Thompson. "The Chinamen are shooting," said Sánchez. "They have shot Bilderrain," the other man added. Thompson pulled his revolver, reached around the door jamb, and blindly fired into the room. "Look out, there are two or three in there and they may shoot you," Sánchez warned. "I'll look out for that," said Thompson. Then, stepping directly in front of the threshold, he fired again. The answering fire from inside was instantaneous. Thompson staggered back, clutching his chest. "I'm killed," he said.

AN ANGLO AND TWO LATINOS had been shot by Chinese fighters. From that point on, that was all that mattered. Robert Thompson suffered a mortal wound, and although Bilderrain and the Mexican boy would recover, the rumors coursing through town placed all three at death's door. Nathan King, a security guard at the railroad depot several blocks away, heard that "the Chinese were killing the white men by wholesale in Negro Alley." He grabbed a rifle and a revolver and hurried there along with dozens of others. Groups of curious and confused men milled about the northern end of Los Angeles Street, where it met Negro Alley. Suddenly a burst of gunfire came from the Coronel building. "The Chinese discharged the contents of their revolvers promiscuously among them," wrote one observer, and "the crowd scattered like leaves before the whirlwind." They quickly regrouped with serious purpose. "Almost every man's hand sought the back pocket of

his pants, and a pistol was drawn, cocked and discharged at the Chinamen in less time than it takes to tell." The firing continued as the sun
set behind the western hills and the streets began to darken. Gas street
lamps had been installed on downtown streets the previous year, but
they would not be lit that evening. The gunfire was intended to keep
the attention of the crowd focused on the façade of the Coronel while
most of the company fighters escaped out the back, slipping into the
vineyards and orange groves, only a few steps away.

Finally the firing from the Coronel stopped altogether. But the
crowd in the street kept up an indiscriminate fire at the building for
another ten or fifteen minutes. No one realized that the company
fighters had already fled. Inside the adobe walls of the Coronel were
several dozen terrified Chinese men and women, none of whom had
anything to do with the gunfight. Outside, at the head of Los Angeles
Street, the crowd was intent on wreaking revenge.

It was a situation fraught with peril. Marshal Francis Baker might
have organized his patrolmen and attempted to disperse the crowd,
which at that point numbered fifty or seventy-five men. But he decided
instead to form them into a posse. "I called to citizens to stop shooting," he testified, "and we would put a guard around the house." He
issued orders to surround the Coronel and allow no one to cross the
line. "If any Chinamen come out, let them have it," he told one man.
"Hail any Chinaman attempting to escape," he instructed another,
"and in case he would not stop, shoot him." Sheriff James Burns, who
showed up a few minutes later, endorsed that plan. "Prevent anyone
from going in or coming out," he told the crowd, and if they resist,
"bring them down." This disastrous decision, legitimizing the use of
lethal violence, led directly to the horrible events that took place over
the next several hours.

BAKER AND BURNS had no sooner established their blockade
than a Chinese man bolted from one of the buildings and made a
desperate attempt to escape. "Here's one! Here's one!" someone cried.

The man was swinging a hatchet, attempting to cut his way through the crowd, and several men began pummeling him with canes and clubs. Two patrolmen waded in and grabbed him; assisted by a clerk named Charles Avery, they began marching him toward the jail, four or five blocks away, trailed by a mob of several dozen men shouting, "Hang him! Hang him!" At the corner of Main and Temple, the heart of the city's business district and only a block from the jail, someone struck Avery on the back of the head, and as he fell to the ground the mob closed in around the officers, pinioning their arms and seizing their prisoner. A big, burly man wielding a Colt's Dragoon shouted for a rope, and one of the mob ran into a dry goods store and emerged with a new coil. Benjamin McLaughlin, watching from the veranda of the Downey Block, was appalled and he confronted the man. "I said it was not right," McLaughlin later testified, "and he said I was a damned Chinaman."

"To the hill!" someone shouted, and the crowd took up the chant. The victim was dragged up Temple Street to the gate of Tomlinson's old corral, where Michel Lachenais had been lynched ten months before. The rope was thrown over the same crosspiece and a knot hurriedly fashioned at the other end. "Hoist him up!" cried the big man with the Dragoon. "God damn him, if you don't put that rope around his neck I'll shoot him anyhow." The noose was forced over the victim's head, and he was jerked up by three or four men. The new rope was stiff and the knot wouldn't slip, so one of the men shimmied up a gate post, and steadying himself against the crosspiece jumped up and down on the victim's shoulders several times, breaking both his collar bones. Several others pulled out their revolvers and riddled the swinging body with bullets. Then the mob hurried back to Negro Alley, celebrating its accomplishment.

"That fellow didn't kick over five seconds," Sheriff Burns heard one of the lynchers exclaim on their return. "They've hanged him," he heard another man say. Burns watched as the lynchers began infecting others in the crowd with their blood lust. "Damn it," shouted the man with the Colt's Dragoon, "we'll show them how to hang Chinamen." Several men incited the crowd with incendiary speeches, and there were angry shouts of "*¡carajo la Chino!*"—fuck the Chinamen! Things were spiraling out of control and Burns figured he had just one more chance. At his urging, District Attorney Cameron Thom stepped up on a box and delivered a law-and-order speech that had little effect. Burns himself then mounted a barrel, shouted for attention, and as a group assembled around him, began pleading for calm. Suddenly the top of the barrel collapsed, Burns crashed to the ground, and the crowd roared with laughter. "No attention was paid to his words," lamented Charles Avery. "Many were anxious to put a stop to the affair," testified John M. Baldwin, a prominent local surveyor, "but there was no one to lead."

At 7 PM the local correspondent for the *Daily Alta California* of San Francisco filed a dispatch by telegraph, the first report to the outside world of the disaster taking place in downtown Los Angeles. "The excitement in this city is intense," he wrote.

> Citizens are arming and Negro Alley and the Chinese quarters are in a state of siege. Already upward of 100 men armed with Henry rifles and shotguns guard the street. One Chinaman has just been captured, taken through the main street, and hanged by the citizens on a lot formerly Tomlinson's Corral and Lumber Yard, the same spot where Lachenais was hung by the vigilantes for killing Mr. Bell a few months ago. . . . The sheriff and civil authorities have given up all attempts to restrain the mob, and no one can tell how far they may go.

ROBERT THOMPSON DIED shortly before 7 PM, and the news quickly circulated through the city. Within an hour the crowd at the head of Los Angeles Street had grown to five or six hundred men, a substantial portion of the three or four thousand adult males residing in the city. The Chinese inside the Coronel hunkered down, and the crowd grew restless. About 8 PM a group of men mounted the roof and after chopping holes through the asphaltum began firing down on the people hiding inside. One Chinese man was immediately killed. Another bolted and dashed into the street. The armed crowd did precisely as it had been instructed by the marshal and the sheriff. "It seemed to me five hundred shots were fired at once," one witness testified. The man, hit numerous times, died in the middle of Negro Alley.

Someone threw a burning torch into the Coronel, and soon smoke began billowing from the holes in the roof. The great Chicago fire had taken place only a few weeks before, and everyone was acutely aware of the danger of general conflagration. One of the patrolmen demanded that the would-be arsonist retrieve the torch, and under the threat of the officer's revolver he warily ventured inside and dragged it out. Suddenly realizing that the Chinese inside had put up no defense, dozens of men began pouring into the building. "Half the horror of the scene was shrouded by the veil of night," wrote one observer. "But to the sense of hearing it stood forth more prominently than it could possibly have done during the day, when the busy hum of the wakeful city would have somewhat smothered the noise."

Young Joseph Mesmer also vividly remembered the furor. "My memories of that night of horrors are vivid and indelibly burned into my brain," he later wrote.

> During my youth my curiosity led me to see practically every lynching that took place in Los Angeles, and I had observed many gruesome sights. But the events that transpired that night were the most irresponsible and bloodthirsty I had ever witnessed. . . . What I saw and heard as a boy of sixteen stands before my eyes to this day as a realization of the extent to which maddened human beings can go. Many of the rioters seemed actually inhuman. They were wild-eyed and sweat-grimed. Knives, pistols, and sword-canes were in many hands; and some armed themselves with short iron-pipes and clubs. Nearly all dashed about trying to vent their brutality on the unfortunate Chinamen the moment they were within reach.

At least one more Chinese was shot and killed inside the Coronel. Another man was seen running from the building. "Like hounds sighting their quarry, a hundred men and boys dashed after him and seized his streaming queue, manhandling him roughly," said Mesmer. "A score at once dashed off with him at a run for Tomlinson's corral."

It was approximately 8:45 PM. Four Chinese men had already been killed. Over the next twenty or thirty minutes fourteen more would be lynched in one of the nation's most appalling episodes of collective violence. Four more men were hanged at Tomlinson's, including Dr. Gene Tong, the only one of the victims recognized by the mob. Dr. Tong pled for his life in both English and Spanish, offering the lynchers gold and silver if they would let him go. At the mention of money, someone pulled off the doctor's trousers and began going through his pockets, looking for cash. Finding none, a frustrated lyncher thrust his revolver in the doctor's mouth and pulled the trigger, blowing off the side of his face. He was probably dead before he was hanged. "It was a most heinous and gruesome scene," wrote Joseph Mesmer. "I have seen a good many men hung, both legal and by the vigilance committee, but nothing so revolting as what befell these Chinese."

Back at the Coronel men and women were being pulled from their hiding places. The lynchers ignored the women, but forced nooses over the heads of the men and dragged them down the street to John Goller's wagon shop, where the crossbar of his portico became a makeshift gallows. "I saw them bring a lot of Chinamen to my house," Goller testified, "and I remonstrated with them for bringing them where my little children were." One of the mob pressed the barrel of his rifle against Goller's cheek and cocked it. "Dry up, you son of a bitch," he said. Goller retreated into his house. Seven Chinese were hanged from his porch, pulled up by a group of men and boys on the roof, one of whom danced a quick step and called out to those below, "bring me more Chinamen, boys, patronize home trade."

Young attorney Henry T. Hazard, watched the proceedings with a mounting sense of self-loathing. With Goller's portico crowded with suspended bodies, the mob dragged several more victims to a large freight wagon standing nearby. "Rope, more rope!" someone cried, and a woman who operated a boardinghouse across the street rushed over and offered her clothesline. "Hang them!" she shouted. "Hang them!" As the line was being cut and nooses fashioned, Hazard took a stand. Climbing onto the tongue of the wagon, he shouted to the mob. "Do you know if the man you're hanging is guilty?" There were catcalls. "You better dry up and get down or we'll hang *you*," one man shouted. "But it isn't right," said Hazard. His friends pulled him down as just someone fired a pistol and a bullet whistled past his face. Three more men were hanged from the high sides of the wagon.

LAWYER AND REAL ESTATE AGENT Robert M. Widney, leader of the Los Angeles vigilantes, was walking from his residence in the southern portion of the city to his office in the Downey Block, at the corner of Temple and Main, when he was hailed by Samuel C. Foy, a longtime resident who operated a harness and saddle shop on Los Angeles Street, only a few steps from Negro Alley. Foy was a vigilante from way back, and served with Widney as one of the leaders of the Law and Order Party. "They are killing all of the Chinese off," Foy exclaimed. Widney supposed he was joking. "It's a fact," said Foy, and he explained what was happening. Widney's first concern was that members of their organization might be involved in the violence. Foy assured him that was not the case. Widney told Foy to round up all the "old vigilantes" he could find and bring them to the corner of Temple and Main. He would be back as soon as he retrieved the revolver he kept in his office.

But Widney could not locate his Colt's Navy six-shooter, so when he came out onto the street and came face-to-face with a mob forcing two Chinese men up Temple toward Tomlinson's gate, he was unarmed. "Years of experience as a trapper and hunter and in the early days of Nevada mining camps," Widney later wrote, "had demonstrated that words were useless with such rioters." Not knowing what else to do, he followed them up the hill. At Tomlinson's he ran into John Baldwin, a vocal opponent of Widney's brand of vigilantism, one of the few men who had turned out to help Sheriff Burns protect Michel Lachenais. That night, however, the two found common cause, both circulating through the crowd, remonstrating with the lynchers. One man—Widney described him as a broad-faced Irishman with square-cut whiskers—pushed a revolver in Widney's face and demanded that he shut up. They had important work to do, he said. Widney asked whether he was a vigilante. "Damn it," the man replied, "we are all vigilantes." He paused, then looked directly at Widney. "And there are a lot of white men here who ought to be hanged also." Widney was stunned. "I believe he referred to me." Widney and Baldwin moved off to the side and watched in silence as the Chinese victims were hoisted up.

Afterward Widney returned to the corner of Temple and Main, where he found Sam Foy and a few others, including grocer John Lazzarovich and Widney's brother William. The younger Widney had taken the revolver from the office and also had a single-shot pistol. He handed the Colt to his brother. Now they all were armed. Widney was determined to rescue the Chinese from the hands of the lynchers. He was equally determined to rescue the reputation of the vigilantes from any association with the mob.

"We saw two or three groups coming with Chinamen," he testified. It was do or die. The first group came up, led by the burly man with the Colt's Dragoon. "The cheap labor is done away with now," he shouted. "Every damned Chinaman will be hung by morning!" William Widney confronted him. "What are you going to do with that man?" he asked. "Hang him, by God," the man with the Dragoon replied. Widney thrust his little single-shot pistol in the big man's face as others grappled with him and seized his revolver. "I can get another in two minutes," the man sputtered. But in the face of this simple demonstration of force by a group of determined men, the mob released its victim, and Foy and young Widney quickly escorted the Chinese man down Spring Street to the jail. Within seconds another group of lynchers arrived, dragging a victim. Lazzarovich and the elder Widney waded into the crowd and seized him. The lynchers resisted, and one of them leveled a revolver at Lazzarovich. Widney pressed his Colt against the man's chest. "Get out or I will kill you," he said in a low, threatening voice. The man went pale and moved aside, and as he did so the mob melted away. Lazzarovich and several others took the Chinese victim to the jail. Widney and the others repeated this several times, saving the lives of four or five men.

Their action succeeded in turning the tide, supplying the leadership that the authorities had failed to provide. One or two patrolmen rescued several more Chinese, but their action came late. At about 9:20 PM Sheriff Burns took charge of the armed vigilantes at the corner of Main and Temple and led them back to Negro Alley, where they established an armed guard around Chinatown. The lynchers retreated to the saloons, where they drank and celebrated until early morning. Over the years the vigilantes of Los Angeles had fostered the conditions which allowed this ghastly orgy of mob violence to take place. But give them their due. On that night of horrors they were instrumental in ending the lynchings.

· CHAPTER 29 ·

Imperfect Justice

At the direction of County Coroner Joseph Kurtz, the mangled bodies of the eighteen Chinese victims were taken to the jail yard and laid on the ground in two parallel rows. The reporter for the *Daily News* saw them there early the next morning. "Their countenances were ghastly and distorted," he wrote, "many of them besmeared with blood and pierced with bullets." Among the approximately twenty Chinese successfully escorted to the jail, a number were wounded, some seriously. Many more had fled into the vineyards and orange groves east of Chinatown or found refuge in the homes of Angelenos. In the morning they went to the jail, searching for missing friends and relations. It was with their help that Coroner Kurtz was able to identify the dead, although the various iterations of his list, recorded in court documents or printed in the press, are inconsistent and feature almost no complete names. In addition to Dr. Tong, the victims included cooks, laundrymen, and common laborers. They were affiliated with four separate *huiguan*. Some had lived in Los Angeles for several years, others had just arrived. Kurtz summoned a coroner's jury, and once they had completed the gruesome task of examining the victims, their bodies were placed in redwood coffins and transported to the cemetery on Gallows Hill, to an isolated corner that served as a potter's field. They were accompanied by several dozen of their countrymen, burning joss sticks and scattering small pieces of paper inscribed with Chinese characters. The remains were later exhumed and returned to China.

"Murder! Terrible Outrages! Fiends in our Midst!" screamed the headlines of the morning *Star*. The lead editorial, written by George Washington Barter, filling in for an ailing Henry Hamilton, decried "the horrible assassinations which were perpetrated in our city last night by the brutal, uncivilized barbarians that infest the country." This was not a reference to the lynch mob but to the Chinese gunmen who shot and killed Robert Thompson and wounded Patrolman Bilderrain and the Mexican boy. The story in the accompanying columns reported the murder of the eighteen Chinese, but regarding that horror, Barter simply wrote that "comment is useless." Instead, he took the opportunity to rail at the Chinese presence in Los Angeles, urging his readers to consider "the best mode of ridding ourselves of such a living curse." The *Daily News*, which appeared later that afternoon, condemned the rioters in no uncertain terms. "The fame of our city," wrote editor Charles Beane, "has received a stain which can be wiped out only by a stern and united performance of duty by our officials." Horace Bell had been at home on Tuesday evening, and the first he knew of the event came from the papers. Barter's editorial in the *Star* disgusted him, as it did many Angelenos. "The *Star* was already growing dim," Bell wrote, but "it never shone brightly after the twenty-fifth of October."

The coroner's jury, made up of ordinary citizens, reassembled in the afternoon for the inquest. Over the subsequent four days Coroner Kurtz examined seventy-nine witnesses under oath. In accordance with California statute law, he did not call any Chinese witnesses—but dozens of Chinese observers packed the courtroom. The witnesses, many of whom had taken part in the violence, were "very careful in giving their testimony," reported one correspondent, "fearing to name individuals whom they know to have taken an active part in the lynchings, lest they be similarly dealt with themselves." John W. Brooks, who witnessed the lynchings at Tomlinson's gate, openly admitted his hesitation. "I am afraid to betray them," he said, "lest they should shoot me." Nevertheless, the collective testimony provided an abundance of specifics from which the jury reconstructed the event in considerable detail. "The revelations made of the brutality exercised by the lynchers," reported the *Daily News*, "are really frightful, and present a sad picture for the mind's eye to scan."

One of the issues most debated in the aftermath was the role played by vigilantism. On Wednesday the leaders of the vigilance committee— Widney, Foy, Lazzarovich, Signoret, Watson, and others—met and issued a statement. "The Vigilance Committee had nothing to do with the attack on the Chinese," it asserted. On the contrary, members of the committee "were the ones who took the Chinese from the rioters and who organized to stop the riot." At the inquest, Widney related the story of being challenged by the armed lyncher with the square-cut whiskers who declared "we are all vigilantes." It made dramatic telling, but Widney regretted it almost as soon as the words were out of his mouth. Immediately after the following witness concluded his testimony, Widney asked permission to amend his statement. "The man referred to was not a member of the old Vigilance Committee," he declared. Widney's defense of the vigilantes, as well as his confidence that he knew those who were and were not "old vigilantes," certainly amounted to a prima facie case for his leadership of the committee. But what was notable was his defensiveness.

That was because the critics of vigilantism were on the attack. For years vigilante leaders had justified their actions by arguing that the legally constituted courts were incapable of securing justice, ignoring the improving record of the justice system. "With the law as well administered as it usually is in Los Angeles," the correspondent of the San Francisco *Daily Evening Bulletin* noted, there seemed no reason to doubt that the courts would have taken up the case against the Chinese gunmen "in due time, without the extraordinary uprising."

But the rioters acted on the same premise as those who for years had promoted lynch law. "We have the sequel of that wretched business now," the article concluded, "in the hanging of eighteen Chinese." Charles Beane of the *Daily News* made a similar argument. "The monstrosity of the thing," he wrote, "was in imitation of the Vigilance Committee, in hanging those arrested, or who surrendered, instead of allowing the law to take its own course. The lawless elements of society have been educated to believe that murder could be indulged in with impunity, provided it was committed by a mob instead of a single individual."

For the first time since the public debate between Francisco Ramírez and Henry Barrows in 1857, vigilantism was under fire. A striking piece of evidence appeared in a short notice published in the *Star* two days after the massacre, a report that the posts and crossbeam at Tomlinson's corral had been torn down by the proprietor. "He evidently does not appreciate the use that it has twice been appropriated for, and has at no little cost to himself entirely destroyed it." No one was a vigilante now.

ON OCTOBER 28 the coroner's jury went public with its report. "The mob consisted of all nationalities as they live in Los Angeles," it concluded. Despite the reluctance of witnesses to provide names, the jury compiled a list of several dozen individuals who had taken part "in the destruction of the lives and property of the Chinamen." Eight men were arrested and jailed under warrants issued by Coroner Kurtz. The press withheld publication of the names, "so as not to defeat the ends of justice," as the *Daily News* put it, continuing the editorial practice toward vigilantes established ten years before.

County Judge Ygnacio Sepúlveda impaneled a special grand jury to issue indictments. "Lawlessness has again raised its monster head in our midst," he declared in his charge. "The scenes enacted on the evening of the twenty-fourth of October, when eighteen human beings were mercilessly murdered by a mob, have sent a thrill of horror throughout the State, and a page is marked in the record of Los Angeles forever indelible, making the name of this community a reproach to humanity and civilization." The previous year Judge Sepúlveda had issued a similar charge to the grand jury investigating the Lachenais lynching, but it had refused to act. "We see the bitter consequences which follow impunity," said Sepúlveda, referring to that failure. He asked the jurors to consider their accountability to society. "Act, and be true to your manhood, to morality, and to mankind. You must indict all who, after the hearing of legal evidence, you consider as deserving punishment for crimes committed within the county. Set an example of true courage in the performance of your duty; be faithful to your trust. In this way only can you satisfy an offended God, violated law, and outraged humanity."

Led by their foreman, the indomitable J. J. Warner, the grand jurors spent the month of November digesting the inquest testimony and examining 111 witnesses. Unlike Coroner Kurtz, who had excluded Chinese witnesses from the inquest, Warner actively solicited their testimony. The task of the grand jury, he wrote in the report he delivered to Judge Murray Morrison in early December, was to expose all those "chargeable with disorders and crimes committed upon that night—crimes which must cause Christianity to weep, civilization to blush, and humanity to mourn." The initial responsibility for the riot, Warner argued, rested with the Chinese company fighters, who turned their guns on officers of the law, resulting in the death of one citizen and the wounding of a policeman. That "opened the way," he wrote, "for evil-doers to create a confusion, in the midst of which the worst elements of society, consisting of all nationalities, not only disgraced civilization by their acts, but in their savage treatment of unoffending human beings, [and] their eagerness for pillage and bloodthirstiness, exceeded the most barbarous races of mankind." Accompanying the report was a flood of indictments, holding 8 Chinese men responsible for the deaths of Ah Choy and Robert Thompson, and 25 rioters for the deaths of the 18 Chinese victims.

The report concluded with a scathing condemnation of the conduct of city and county officers. All of them, Warner wrote, had been "deplorably inefficient in the performance of their official and sworn duties during the scenes of confusion and bloodshed which disgraced this city." Not one had attempted to arrest those men "who in their presence were openly and grossly violating the law, even to the taking of human life." Few made any attempt to rescue the victims, yet the evidence clearly indicated that when resolute men confronted the mob "they were successful and met with no overpowering resistance." The majority of the citizens present on the streets that night, Warner argued, would gladly have joined the authorities in preventing "the revolting scenes that were passing before their eyes," if only a "resolute and energetic man, clothed with authority and an average share of ability and judgment" had organized and directed their efforts. Instead, the city marshal and the county sheriff had improperly instructed members of the crowd, who later "excused themselves of criminality by alleging they acted in conformity to the orders given them." Warner's stinging indictment of local law enforcement was right on target.

By early December more than thirty men had been arrested on warrants signed by District Attorney Cameron E. Thom, dangerously overcrowding the jail. Judge Morrison approved the release on bail of a number, and most immediately skipped town. That raised serious doubts about the capacity of the justice system to handle such a big case. The doubts were amplified when Judge Morrison died of a lingering chronic illness in mid-December. Los Angeles County was about to proceed with the most important prosecution in its history, and it was imperative that the state's Republican governor immediately name someone to serve out the unexpired term. Among the several local jurists who pressed for the appointment was Robert M. Widney, who the *Star* claimed was "sending hot shot after the Governor in the form of subsidiary influence and pressure." Widney, still chafing under the charge of vigilante responsibility for the riot, wanted desperately to be the judge who tried the "Chinese riot cases," as they came to be known.

When Widney won the appointment in early January, editor Charles Beane of the *Daily News*, reacted with scorn. Should a man who had led the vigilance committee, a man who had condoned and abetted murder, be elevated to the bench of the county's highest court? In a biting bit of sarcasm, Beane suggested striking a medal in Widney's honor, one side embossed with "the balances of Justice, with one scale superseded by the effigy of a strangling man and above it the motto—'Law,'" and on the reverse the legend *suspendatur per collum*—hanged by the neck. The issue of vigilantism was not going away.

THE FIRST OF THE CHINESE RIOT CASES, the prosecution of two Chinese men, Quong Wong and Ah Sing, for the murder of Ah Choy, took place in February 1872. Several Chinese witnesses had identified the suspects before the grand jury, but during the trial they refused to repeat their accusations, for fear of retaliation. District Attorney Thom was forced to admit that he had failed to make his case, and Judge Widney directed the jury to bring in a verdict of not guilty, which it did. The *Daily News* dismissed the proceedings as "a complete farce." Some months later Sam Yuen would be acquitted of manslaughter in the death of Robert Thompson. None of the Chinese fighters were convicted in the Chinese riot cases.

Vigilantism played no role in those trials, but it came up immediately in the trial of the first rioter charged with murder, which began in February 1872. Leonard "Curly" Crenshaw, a young midwesterner with a thick shock of hair and a reputation as a troublemaker, was charged with aiding and abetting the murder of Dr. Gene Tong. His attorneys, Thomas Chipley and Christopher N. Wilson, interrogated prospective jurors about their association with vigilance committees. "Are you now or have you ever sympathized with such or a like organization?" Several men answered in the affirmative, and the defense moved their dismissal for cause. It was an uncomfortable moment for Judge Widney, but he sustained the motion. He and his "law and order" colleagues had actively opposed the rioters, and the defense would do whatever it could to keep supporters of vigilantism off the jury.

Once a jury was impaneled, the prosecution presented its case.

Witnesses testified that Crenshaw had been one of the first men on the roof of the Coronel, had fired indiscriminately into a crowd of Chinese, and later that night had bragged of lynching three men. In his own defense, Crenshaw testified that the witnesses were all mistaken, that he had been no more than a bystander, had followed the instructions of the officers, and before retiring had gone to Billy Rapp's saloon, where he "took a couple of drinks and went to supper, then to bed." The defense pointed out that none of the testimony placed Crenshaw at Tomlinson's gate, where Dr. Tong's lynching took place. But the prosecution argued that his riotous conduct had aided, abetted, and assisted the murderers, making him a principal to the crime. The case went to the jurors late on the second day of the trial. They returned after only twenty minutes with a verdict of guilty of manslaughter. According to the *Daily News*, their initial vote had been eleven to one for first-degree murder, but unable to reach unanimity on that charge they compromised on the lesser one.

Following the trial District Attorney Thom announced that he would immediately proceed with the prosecution of nine more of the indicted men for complicity in Dr. Tong's murder. The defendants included three Californios, a Mexican, three men from the eastern states, two from Ireland, and one from Prussia. They ranged in age from twenty to thirty-seven. They included shoemaker Alexander Johnston, the burly man with the Colt's Dragoon, whom numerous witnesses identified as one of the ringleaders. The defendants, read the indictment, "did feloniously, unlawfully, deliberately, premeditatedly, and of their malice aforethought, stand by, aid, abet, assist, advise, counsel, and encourage unknown persons to kill and murder one Gene Tong." They were represented by E. J. C. Kewen and James G. Howard, the most distinguished defense team in southern California. The defense requested a single trial for all the defendants, a proposition District Attorney Thom readily accepted, since it would save the county considerable expense.

Jury selection began on February 20. Kewen and Howard aggressively challenged all prospective jurors regarding their past support for vigilantism. "I was a member of the organization that hanged Lache-nais," one man admitted. "I approved of his hanging and do still." He was dismissed for cause. When Thom objected to the intense inter-rogation, Kewen's response surely must have raised Judge Widney's dander. "Everyone who participated in the hanging of Lachenais or the resolutions of the vigilance committee," he declared, "was a mur-derer, just as much as those who killed these Chinese." Two hundred and fifty-five men were examined before a jury of twelve was seated, consisting of eight farmers, three craftsmen, and a merchant.

During the trial, which lasted eight days, twenty-five witnesses for the prosecution provided disturbing and vivid testimony. When it came time for the defense to present its case, Kewen and How-ard moved for dismissal of the charges. "There was no proof of con-spiracy," they argued, "there was no proof of any involvement of the defendants" in Dr. Tong's murder; indeed, "there was no proof of the death of Gene Tong." The indictments, they argued, "failed to establish the *corpus delicti*," that is, they failed to explicitly state that Dr. Tong had in fact been murdered. Judge Widney overruled all those motions. He acknowledged the error in the indictments, but correct-ing it would require convening another grand jury, a risky proposition. Widney cited the legal doctrine that indictments "shall be construed in the usual acceptance in common language," and argued that the fact of Dr. Tong's death was something acknowledged by everyone in the community. Once the defense finished that piece of business— intended to establish the grounds for an appeal—it closed without calling a single witness.

Judge Widney instructed the jury late on the evening of March 26, 1872. It was the court's responsibility, he told the jurors, to inter-pret the law. And according to the law, when individuals engaged in combination with others in riotous conduct "all are responsible for the acts of each if done in pursuance and furtherance of the com-mon design." It was for the jurors, he continued, to determine matters of fact. Specifically, "whether any or all of these defendants did any act or participated by voice or manner with the rioters." The jurors retired and after several hours of deliberation, at approximately two the following morning, they notified Widney that they had reached a consensus. Despite the hour, the courtroom was crowded as the foreman read the verdicts. Two defendants were acquitted. The remaining seven—Alexander Johnston, Refugio Botello, Louis Mendell, Esteban Alvarado, Patrick McDonald, Charles Austin, and Jesús Martínez— were found guilty of manslaughter. Two days later Widney sentenced them, along with Leonard "Curley" Crenshaw, to terms ranging from two to six years in San Quentin.

KEWEN AND HOWARD appealed to the California Supreme Court, and in the spring of 1873 the justices threw out the convictions, ruling that the indictment had been "fatally defective" in failing to state that Dr. Tong was murdered. It was an outrageous decision based on a trivial technicality, but Judge Widney had no choice but to order the release from San Quentin of the men convicted in his court. They returned to Los Angeles and were never retried. "To this most lame and impotent conclusion, has come the great Chinese riot," reported the *Star*. "The convicted parties escape full punishment for their crimes by a quibble, justice is complacent, and the eagle roosts high. Thus it goes."

Despite this lamentable outcome, the justice system of Los Angeles had performed admirably under the circumstances. In the most complicated case in the county's history, eight rioters had been convicted of taking the lives of eighteen Chinese. It was imperfect justice, to be sure. The defendants ought to have been convicted of first-degree murder. Moreover, in accordance with Judge Widney's reading of the law—that every individual engaged in the riot was legally responsible for the acts of all—many Angelenos went unpunished. Not only the lynchers who were never tried, but the bystanders who furnished the rope, the officials who instructed the crowd to "let them have it," the patrolmen who ignored the crimes committed before their eyes, the respectable citizens who stood by and did nothing. "There is no doubt that all those indicted were guilty," wrote Horace Bell. "But there were so many others." Bell's point is well taken. The massacre was a horrendous act of communal violence. But naming, indicting, and finally convicting a long list of perpetrators after years of allowing vigilantes to get away with murder was a breakthrough. The valence of vigilantism had turned negative. The principal vigilante argument had been that the courts were incapable of securing justice. By the late 1860s that was no longer true. If that truth could not be seen in 1870, when Michel Lachenais was lynched, it had become clear by 1872, when the Chinese rioters were convicted.

Bell was one of the few to take the long view. "Ever since that earlier day when the mayor of the town resigned his position in order to go out and lynch a prisoner who was under the protection of the law of the land," he wrote, "Los Angeles was ruled by a lawless mob." Certainly the triumph of lynch law in January 1855, seventeen years before, had marked a signal turning point in the history of frontier Los Angeles. Vigilantism became an institutional feature of Los Angeles life, encouraged by the press and condoned by the authorities. "All this is disagreeable to recall and to record," wrote Bell, "but it is a part of the city's history. The people of Los Angeles made that history. They sowed the wind and reaped the whirlwind. 'As they sowed so did they reap.' The harvest was gathered in on the twenty-fourth of October, 1871."

· CHAPTER 30 ·

FISTS DOUBLED UP

"WHERE IS ALL THIS TO END?" asked John A. Lewis, the *Star*'s first editor, in a column condemning vigilantism published in 1851, twenty years before the Chinese massacre. If Angelenos allowed vigilantism to continue unchecked, Lewis had worried, it would result in the slaughter of innocents, and "the Days of Terror will then come upon us." The same warning was repeated many times over the years by the likes of Benjamin Ignatius Hayes, Manuel Clemente Rojo, James S. Waite, and Francisco P. Ramírez. With the exception of Hayes, who consistently opposed lynch law from the time he arrived in Los Angeles in 1850 until his death in 1877, those critics sometimes wavered in their commitment to the legally constituted justice system. In a frontier community like Los Angeles, with underdeveloped governmental institutions and an extraordinarily high incidence of lethal violence, the immediate satisfactions of summary punishment were difficult to resist. But that made vigilantism nonetheless toxic. The mass violence of October 1871 was a horror foretold.

In the aftermath of the terror, Angelenos frequently expressed concern over the reappearance of vigilantism. An incident that took place only a few weeks after the massacre, in January 1872, stoked those fears.

The twenty-one-year-old daughter of former county judge Agustín Olvera requested her father's consent to marry a Mexican doctor, and when Don Agustín refused to grant his blessing the couple eloped, scandalizing elite Californios. One evening, a day or two after the civil ceremony conducted by a local justice, a messenger appeared at the Lafayette Hotel, where the honeymoon couple were staying, with an urgent appeal that the doctor accompany him to the bedside of a dying man. The doctor grabbed his bag and left in a wagon with the messenger. But on the outskirts of town a group of masked men stopped the horses and seized the doctor. They beat him severely, then covering him in hot tar and feathers. The victim filed charges of kidnapping and assault, and after an initial investigation the authorities arrested a half dozen young men from several prominent Californio families, including two sons of Stephen Clark Foster. For Foster, already suffering the shame of having participated in the defrauding of his niece and god-daughter, Doña Merced, it was all downhill thereafter. He retreated into a world of his own, declining to live with his family, and spent the remainder of his life as one of the city's most notable eccentrics.

"The Sonorans are in a state of exasperation over the late outrage," the *Star* reported, "and talk of lynching the lynchers." E. J. C. Kewen, hired by the families to defend their sons, succeeded in getting the charges dropped for lack of admissible evidence, and soon the excitement faded. But the episode set off alarm bells. "Los Angeles will soon have a reputation for lawlessness if the authorities are unable to check the disposition of the people to take the punishment of alleged offenses into their own hands," declared the San Francisco *Chronicle*. "The recent Chinese riot drew upon that city the animadversions of the press throughout the whole country, and now we have to record a fresh outrage. . . . No community calling itself civilized has a right to allow such things to be perpetrated with impunity."

ROBERT M. WIDNEY proudly embraced the honorable reputation he secured for himself by spearheading the citizen efforts to

rescue Chinese victims and by presiding over the trial of the rioters. But Widney remained highly sensitive about his previous record as a leading vigilante. Some time later, during a legal proceeding in which he was serving as an attorney, the opposing counsel elicited testimony that Michel Lachenais had been hanged "by Judge Widney and some other persons." At those words, Widney jumped from his chair, pulled a pistol from his coat pocket, and charged the witness. "You say I murdered a man?" he exclaimed, his finger on the trigger. "You lie, you perjured villain! I was in the county courtroom trying a case at the time Lachenais was hung and knew nothing whatever about it." The lynching of Lachenais had been witnessed by virtually every resident of Los Angeles, but Widney claimed to have been ignorant of it. The gentleman doth protest too much.

Popular attitudes toward vigilantism and lynch law had changed. But the extent and limit of those changes were suggested by two incidents that occurred two years later, in the spring of 1874. In May, in a desperate shootout several miles west of town, a sheriff's posse captured a notorious outlaw named Tiburcio Vásquez. Wanted for multiple armed robberies and murders in the northern part of the state, Vásquez had fled with his gang to southern California, where they continued their crime spree, earning the leader a reputation as the new Joaquín Murieta or Juan Flores. Vásquez was placed in a heavily guarded jail cell while arrangements were completed for his extradition. "There are some who curse Vásquez's captors for not killing him on the spot," wrote a reporter. "They would like to help drag him from his cell and hang him to the nearest lamp-post."

Yet nothing of the sort took place. Crowds flocked to the jail, not to lynch Vásquez but to gawk at him. In interviews with reporters Vásquez portrayed himself as a persecuted Californio who had acted to defend the honor of his countrymen. He sat for a photographic portrait that sold like hotcakes. Once he recovered from the wounds inflicted during his capture, he was escorted north to San José, where he was properly tried, convicted, and finally executed. "No attempt was made to interfere with the law," wrote Benjamin C. Truman, who had become editor of the *Star*. "A feeling more of relief than of revenge or exultation seemed to be uppermost in the minds of all. If we interpret it rightly, it arose from a firm belief that if convicted of the offenses with which he stands charged, he will receive just punishment."

The capture of Vásquez was celebrated as a significant turning point for law enforcement. And under the tenure of Judge Widney and his successor, former county judge Ygnacio Sepúlveda, the district court's efficiency continued to improve. During the three years following the Chinese massacre, Los Angeles County authorities investigated forty-seven murders. Thirty-seven of them were "cleared," either by the death of the suspect, a determination of justifiable homicide, or an indictment. Twenty-nine men were brought to trial for murder or manslaughter, resulting in twenty convictions. Both the clearance rate (79 percent) and the conviction rate (70 percent) compare very favorably with modern patterns—quite impressive in light of what had come before. Growing public confidence in the legally constituted justice system made a crucial difference.

THE SPIRIT OF VIGILANTISM, however, was not yet dead, as events in the crossroads settlement of Workman's Mill, at the narrows on the east bank of the San Gabriel River, soon demonstrated. The episode began on a June afternoon, not long after Vásquez had been sent north. Rebecca Humphreys Turner, a young wife and mother in the late stages of pregnancy, was sitting on her front porch, rocking her three-year-old daughter, when she observed a young Mexican named Jesús Romo—a stocky man known as El Gordo—ride up to her husband's general merchandise store, some twenty or thirty yards from the house. William Turner prided himself on his good relations with the Mexicans and Californios who made up the majority of his patrons, insisting they were his good friends. "I did not share his confidence," Mrs. Turner wrote in a candid memoir not published until after her death, many years later. "I was afraid of them. They were alien to me, and looking on their swarthy faces I thought of Vásquez—Vásquez the notorious, whose name was a terror throughout the state. I distrusted the whole race." Handing the child to her sister, Mrs. Turner wrapped a shawl about her shoulders and tucked a large revolver into the folds. "I don't like the looks of that Greaser," she announced. "I am going down to the store."

When she entered, her husband was showing Romo his stock of leather boots. As he turned to retrieve another pair, Mrs. Turner saw Romo pull a knife, throw an arm around her husband's neck, and begin slashing at his throat. "I heard my husband utter an unearthly groan as the razor edge sank into his flesh, and I saw him thrust his hands between the knife and his throat, cutting his fingers to the bone." Grabbing the revolver, she jammed it into Romo's back and pulled the trigger, but she had not cocked it and it snapped. She dropped the weapon and jumped onto Romo's back. Mr. Turner broke free and ran outside. Romo shook Mrs. Turner off and went in pursuit. She picked up the revolver again, cocked it, and succeeded in firing a round at his back, but missed. Romo spun around, pulled his own pistol, and fired point blank. Mrs. Turner had already turned to run, and the ball smashed into her back and lodged in her chest. "Oh, I'm killed," she cried as she dropped to the ground. Romo ran back into the store, grabbed some eighty dollars in silver coin, and fled. The couple would recover from their horrible wounds, but he lost the use of his right hand and she lost the baby. "Mrs. Turner is a brave woman," editor James Madison Bassett declared in the *Herald*, a new Los Angeles daily, only a few months old. "The courage and presence of mind which she exhibited in saving the life of her husband would do credit to a Joan of Arc."

Word of the outrage spread through the neighborhood, and soon groups of armed men were gathering at Workman's Mill. Many of her husband's Spanish-speaking customers were among them, led by a local farmer named Francisco Bustamante, who according to Mrs. Turner was "first in the field, proving his friendship by actively organizing and leading the main searching party." Rather than showcasing ethnic cooperation, however, the manhunt greatly exacerbated existing tensions. The night following the attack on the Turners, a group of Monte Boys rode south from Workman's Mill to Pío Pico's El Ranchito, where Romo had once been employed. Shouting and waving their revolvers, they invaded the Pico's bunkhouse and rousted his vaqueros, who responded with angry stares and muttered threats. Romo was not among them.

A constable's posse located the culprit several days later, hiding in a pile of driftwood on the river bottom, less than a mile from the scene of the crime. Romo attempted to run, but was brought down by both loads from a double-barreled shotgun. Seriously wounded, he confessed. He had attacked William Turner to steal his money, he said, and shot his wife to prevent her from shooting him. The men loaded him into the bed of a wagon and drove to Workman's Mill, where the Turners identified him before a large but orderly crowd. The constable then announced he was taking Romo into Los Angeles to hand him over to the sheriff. They had not gone far when he was stopped by a small group of mounted men who seized Romo and dragged him to a nearby oak, from which he was summarily hanged. According to Mrs. Turner, the tree was destroyed not long thereafter by Romo's relations. They "chopped it down and burned it," she wrote, "burned every leaf and branch, and scattered the ashes to the four winds."

Benjamin Truman of the *Star* applauded the hanging. "Swift and terrible as the retribution meted out to this miscreant, we have yet to hear of a single person by whom the act is disapproved," he wrote. "If irregular and extra-judicial punishment for crime was ever warranted in any instance, it was in this." Editor Bassett offered a more nuanced version of the same argument in the *Herald*. "There are instances," he wrote, "where justice can only be attained through unlawful acts. The hanging of El Gordo was one." He had failed in his attempt to murder the Turners but succeeded in killing their unborn child, for which he deserved to die. But since the law did not treat that crime as a homicide, the state would not have executed him, so the people had to. "We may preach law and order as long and as strong as we like, but when the people find the law will not protect them, they will protect themselves," wrote Bassett. "We must protect ourselves—legally if possible, but we must protect ourselves." These arguments had been heard many times before. A correspondent in the San Francisco *Daily Evening Bulletin* offered a starker explanation. "Perhaps the fact that Vásquez has become rather a lion and a hero than a culprit has had something to do in provoking wild vengeance in the case of El Gordo."

The group who lynched Romo, the *Star* reported, included "some of the worthiest and most respected citizens of Los Angeles County." Yet in accordance with editorial custom, none of the local papers identified those men by name, despite the fact that, as Rebecca Turner wrote in her memoir, everyone in the neighborhood knew who they were. The coroner's jury reported they had been "unable to find any indictment in the case, for want of evidence identifying any of the persons who committed the crime." The verdict outraged the Californio and Mexican communities, who packed an angry public meeting held in San Gabriel. Pío Pico, smarting from the invasion of his ranch, cursed the Monte Boys, and swore that he and his vaqueros would "kill the whole damn lot of them." A few days later, an open letter addressed to Pico appeared in the *Herald*. "If, by chance, some one of the vigilantes has a bad end by your hand or your influence or the friends of the late Jesús Romo, may God forgive you," it read. "Neither one nor two will pay the debt. As soon as we begin, God alone can see the end." It was signed "Monte Vigilantes." The 1874 incident at Workman's Mill, ending in threat and counterthreat, pointed to continuing ethnic tensions and the enduring appeal of vigilantism. It is important to note, however, that Jesús Romo was the last man hanged by vigilantes in Los Angeles County.

Not long after the lynching, Francisco Bustamante, the Mexican friend of Mr. Turner's, announced that he and his large family were relocating to another part of the county. "I am now out of favor with my countrymen," he told the Turners. Friendships across ethnic lines raised the suspicions of some of his neighbors, and fearing for his safety

Bustamente had taken to wearing a revolver. "He embraced us both," Mrs. Turner wrote, and "as his big arms enfolded me, the old terror rushed back like a great wave. I shuddered inwardly and felt a knife between my ribs." Mrs. Turner felt a little ashamed of herself. "There was no earthly reason for the fantastic emotion," she wrote, "since Bustamante was loyalty itself. But I couldn't help it to save my soul, and I was glad when his foot was in the stirrup and he was waving his hand from the bend in the road."

"WITH ALL THE HORRORS of a year ago before us," the *Daily News* observed on the first anniversary of the Chinese massacre, "it is gratifying to note that since then the knife and pistol have not been so frequently at work as previously." Not only were county authorities doing a better job of investigating, arresting, and convicting perpetrators, but the frequency of lethal conflict in Los Angeles had fallen dramatically. From 1869 through 1871, the county recorded a total of seventy-one homicides (including the eighteen men slaughtered during the riot), a homicide rate comparable to the dark days of the 1850s. Over the subsequent three years, however, from 1872 through 1874, the number of murders dropped to twenty-three, a decline of nearly 70 percent. A homicide rate of this order of magnitude—a new normal—would continue for the next two decades.

What accounted for the decline? Violence in frontier Los Angeles was overdetermined. A legacy of colonial conquest; antagonistic relations among Indians, Californios, Mexicans, Anglos, and Chinese; conflicts over land and labor; large numbers of transient men; a thriving counterculture of vice and crime; a city awash in wine and aguardiente; and deadly weapons readily at hand—all these factors contributed to the mayhem. By the early 1870s none of them had changed appreciably for the better. Los Angeles continued to be a restless, rowdy, rumble of a town, and would remain so until its transformation into something resembling a middle-class metropolis toward the end of the century. What was different in the early

1870s was the newfound power and authority of the legally constituted justice system. Increased confidence in the possibility of official
justice offers the best explanation for the decline in the level of lethal
violence.

On New Year's Day, 1875, the *Herald* crowed over the reduced rate
of violence. "The criminal record shows that Los Angeles, with its
population of mixed races, is just as orderly as cities of its size on other
parts of the continent." Not quite. Although violence had fallen to
its lowest level since the American conquest, Angelenos continued
to assault and murder one another with far greater frequency than
the residents of most American communities. Over the remainder
of the century the prevailing murder rate in Los Angeles would
remain three times the rate in New York City and 50 percent
higher than the country at large.

OF THE SIX HOMICIDES committed in Los Angeles County
during 1874, two in particular claimed a great deal of public attention. "During the last month," James Bassett reported in the *Herald* at
the end of June, "no less than three or four wife-murders have been
committed in this city and vicinity. Of all the wickedness of which
man is guilty, this is the most beastly and damning." Wife murder
directed the public's attention to what was arguably the root of the
violence problem, the endemic abuse and assault that went on in private homes, preparing men for the slings and arrows of the public
world by training them to employ violence to resolve conflict. Two
of those murders were committed within a few blocks of the Plaza,
only weeks apart.

On Commercial Street, near the railroad depot, John and Eliza
McDonald operated the Shamrock Restaurant, a popular establishment that boasted "the best 25 cent meals to be had in the city."
Immigrants from Ireland in their midtwenties, the McDonalds were
hard workers, and built up a thriving trade. Young Joseph Mesmer
performed small jobs for them and claimed to know both husband

and wife quite well. McDonald could be a reasonable man, Mesmer recalled, but he had a vicious temper and treated his wife brutally. She was "a most comely woman of fine appearance with a loveable disposition," Mesmer said, and her husband was intensely jealous of the attentions paid to her, although it was her charm that accounted for a good deal of the Shamrock's repeat business. McDonald often accused his wife of infidelity, something that would have been difficult for her to pull off, with a public dining room to manage and four children under the age of eight. On several occasions she filed complaints in local justice court, accusing her husband of assault. McDonald was admonished and fined, then went back to battering his wife.

One afternoon, after a confrontation with her husband, Mrs. McDonald fled to the house of a neighbor. McDonald followed her there, but finding the door barred he returned to the Shamrock fuming mad. When his wife returned to the restaurant some time later, he struck her, knocking her to the floor. She retreated to their rooms upstairs, but soon came down with the baby in her arms. McDonald went after her again but was restrained by one of the waiters. While his wife sat nursing the baby, he went back to his counter, where he was slicing bread and cheese with a large knife, muttering curses under his breath. McDonald himself later recalled the next few moments. "She sat there and talked, and said something cross, I don't know what, but it greatly exasperated me. In the heat of passion I threw the knife I held in my hand at her." The knife barely missed the infant and penetrated the mother's side. "I'm dead!" she cried, and dropping the baby she jumped up, ran out the door, and into the street, where she collapsed. McDonald rushed to her side with loud demonstrations of grief. "But she was past hearing him," wrote Mesmer, "and the unsympathetic crowd was not impressed by his tears."

Patrolmen quickly arrested McDonald and hustled him off to jail before the situation got out of hand. The lynching of Jesús Romo was still fresh in the minds of the authorities, and fearing an attack by a mob, the sheriff surrounded the jail with a strong guard. County Judge H. K. S. O'Melveny issued a public statement. "Threats have been made to organize for the purpose of hanging some of the prisoners now in the jail," he wrote.

> This every man who has the honor of this city at heart should at once abandon and oppose. Its effect would be to degrade us in the opinion of mankind elsewhere. The act itself would be a crime. No man can justify the act of taking unarmed men from the custody of the officers of the law and hanging them without a trial. We have laws and men ready to execute those laws and as honorable men we are bound to regulate our conduct in obedience to those laws and assist them to do so according to law, not by violence and disorder.

Los Angeles remained calm.

McDonald was indicted for murder and his trial scheduled for September. But when it began his attorneys, Kewen and Howard, pounced on an error in the indictment, mistakenly naming the victim as "Louisa" rather than Eliza McDonald. They had used a carelessly written indictment as the basis for the reversal of the conviction of the Chinese rioters, and Judge Sepúlveda wasn't taking any chances. He ordered the grand jury to reconvene and prepare a new indictment, which required postponing the trial for several months. James Bassett worried over the consequences in the *Herald*. "People are justified in expressing doubts as to the probity of our laws and the possibility of our courts meting out justice while guided by a code so exact in its requirements," he wrote. "Nothing offers a greater inducement to the people to take the law in their own hands than a consciousness that the law of the land is insufficient for the full protection of life and property." But there were no protests or demonstrations, and in December McDonald was tried, convicted, and sentenced to life in prison at San Quentin.

THE DRAMATIC MURDER of Eliza McDonald occurred in public. The murder of Rafaela Ledesma de Marasovich took place in private, in an old adobe on Bath Street, a block or two north of the Plaza church, a stretch rivaling Negro Alley as a resort of vice and disorder. The victim, a native of Mexico, had been married for fourteen years to Lucas (or Lucca) Marasovich, a Croatian who had come to California during the Gold Rush and by the 1870s owned a stake in a mining and smelting operation in the desert, east of Los Angeles. The couple had no children. Marasovich was away at his mine for much of the time, and his visits home often meant trouble for Mrs. Marasovich, for he was a wife beater, even though she was weak and sickly, said to be suffering from a chronic heart condition.

One Sunday evening, Navio and María Valenzuela, who lived nearby, heard the sound of conflict coming from the Marasovich place. They knew the couple only by sight. "I heard the man quarreling with and abusing the woman," Mrs. Valenzuela testified at the coroner's inquest. "I heard her crying." The Valenzuelas went to investigate, and finding the front door of the Marasovich adobe ajar, they peered inside. "I saw the man standing in front of the woman," Mr. Valenzuela testified. "The woman was crying and asking the man why he was beating her. Then he struck her in the face, knocking her down." Mrs. Valenzuela saw the woman "fall backwards between the wall and the bed. She never spoke afterward. She was dead." Mr. Valenzuela wasn't sure whether the woman was dead or alive. "The side of the door shut her from my view," he said. His eyes were firmly fixed on Marasovich. "He was mad when he struck the woman. He was standing in front of her, abusing her, with both fists doubled up, in the attitude of striking. He struck the woman with his fists."

Marasovich denied that any of this had happened. Why would the Valenzuelas make it up? "Navio Valenzuela is my enemy," Marasovich testified. The truth, he said, was that his wife had been chronically ill. "She has been subject to the heart disease for fourteen years," he said. On the night in question she stumbled "and fell between the wall and bed about 6 o'clock, and died about 1 o'clock the next morning." He had not thought to call a physician. When the authorities arrived, acting on a tip (from the Valenzuelas, perhaps), Marasovich had already placed his wife's body in a coffin. A doctor acting for the coroner conducted a postmortem examination and found "a severe wound over the right eye extending toward the temple, which separated the flesh from the bone or skull," along with "other marks of violence, particularly on the neck, under the chin on the right side." Those wounds alone were probably not mortal, the doctor reported, but he concluded that the beating had "superinduced a natural death."

The coroner's jury ruled that Rafaela Ledesma de Marasovich "came to her death by blows inflicted at the hands of the said Lucas Marasovich." But the grand jury indicted him for manslaughter rather than murder, perhaps because his beating had only "superinduced" the death. The trial jury rejected even that charge, convicting Marasovich of simple assault and battery, and Judge Sepúlveda sentenced him to a year in the county jail. Soon numerous prominent Angelenos were petitioning the governor for his release, arguing that Marasovich "was not guilty of the offense for which he was imprisoned." It had been a family matter, *un asunto de su familia*. The governor issued a pardon and Marasovich was released. He continued to reside in Los Angeles and rose to become a respected authority in the local mining industry. Some things had changed. Some things had not.

FORGIVE ME, I HAVE
KILLED YOUR BROTHER

THE FILE OF THE MARASOVICH CASE does not include the
trial transcript, so the name of the attorney who represented the
accused is not recorded. But it might well have been E. J. C. Kewen.
It was his kind of meat. "Any murderer or horse thief that could get
the impulsive southerner to take his case," an Angeleno recalled years
later, "was as good as acquitted." Kewen continued to practice law
through the late 1870s. But rather than growing milder as he aged,
he became increasingly testy, involved in more than his fair share of
blowups and contretemps.

A disheartening comeupance of a sort came for Kewen in the
spring of 1877. His wife's brother had died prematurely, and since
the man's wife had previously died in childbirth it left their young
son orphaned. In the absence of a will the Kewens petitioned the
court to be appointed legal guardians of their nephew. But the child's
maternal grandmother made the same application, and when the contending parties failed to reach an accommodation, the matter went to
trial. Kewen represented himself. During a hearing in county court,
the opposing attorney, John S. Thompson, introduced evidence "of a

very personal nature" suggesting that Mrs. Kewen "was not a proper guardian." That evidence may have concerned the chronic illness—quite possibly tuberculosis—that had afflicted Frances Kewen for some years. Whatever it was, exposing the evidence in open court outraged Kewen, and he berated Thompson for his lack of chivalry, shaking his finger angrily at the man. When that failed to provide sufficient emotional release, Kewen reared back and struck Thompson in the face. Thompson staggered, then counterpunched, knocking Kewen to the floor. The sons of the two attorneys, young men in their early twenties, jumped into the fray, revolvers were drawn, and there was a near riot before friends succeeded in pulling them apart.

The public exposure of the family conflict and Kewen's own lack of restraint deeply humiliated him. The following day he uncharacteristically apologized to Thompson and to the court, paid a fine of one hundred dollars for contempt, and dropped the suit. Although he officially maintained his practice, Kewen retired to his San Gabriel estate. He may have been suffering from the same disease as his wife, for some months later he suffered a massive hemorrhage of the lungs. He died in 1879 at the age of fifty-one, his wife following him to the grave three years later at the age of fifty-two.

LOS ANGELES LAWYERS remained a fighting lot. In 1872, after reading law and passing an oral examination, Horace Bell was admitted to the bar. He opened an office, beginning a legal career that would last more than a quarter century. Pugnacious and persistent, Bell was noted for defending Spanish-speaking clients, known throughout Sonoratown as *el abogado de los pobres*, the poor people's lawyer. In the meantime he was composing his memoir, *Reminiscences of a Ranger*, which appeared in 1881, the first book published in Los Angeles. The next year he founded a weekly newspaper, the *Porcupine*, and during its run of several years Bell delighted in exposing the corruption of Los Angeles city and county government.

He continued to allow his legal and political battles to descend into personal conflicts. His fighting disposition invited challenge, and he got it in spades. During his campaign against corruption Bell focused his criticism on the Los Angeles chief of police, charging him with corruption, bribery, drunkenness, and indecency. After enduring the scorn of the *Porcupine* for weeks, the frustrated chief finally burst into Bell's office with a cocked revolver, and violence was narrowly averted by the intervention of Bell's eldest son. Bell declined to press charges and the matter was dropped. Some time later Bell took to lambasting the county sheriff in the pages of his paper. After one particularly excoriating editorial, Bell was walking past the courthouse when he heard someone loudly curse him. Turning toward the voice, he saw two men struggling with the sheriff, gripping both his arms to keep him from shooting Bell. Concluding he would "make a two-sided affair of the business," Bell procured a loaded Colt's Dragoon, draped his linen duster over it, and returned to the sheriff's office. For several long seconds the two men stood staring daggers at each other, and when his opponent made no move to draw, Bell turned to leave. If the sheriff remained "bent on human gore," he announced as he departed, he would meet him on the edge of town, "where people would not be disturbed by their foolishness."

VIOLENCE CONTINUED to haunt the lives of many Angelenos. One night in February 1875, Andrés Pico failed to return to his home on south Main Street after an evening on the town. Growing alarmed, the members of his household went in search and found the sixty-five-year-old man lying in a nearby street, bloody, bruised, and unconscious. The authorities concluded that Don Andrés had slipped and hit his head, but the family suspected "foul play." He remained unconscious for several days before dying.

The death shattered Don Pío, and according to family legend he spent a small fortune in a failed attempt to identify his brother's assailant. Don Andrés had never married, but he was a celebrated lover, fathering a host of illegitimate children, all of whom he acknowledged and supported in good spirit, although he legally adopted none of them. He died intestate, and his firstborn son, Rómulo Pico, petitioned to be named executor of the estate. Don Pío contested the application in court, denying that Rómulo was his brother's blood offspring. This ugly case dragged on for several years, split the Pico family, and cost Don Pío plenty. Like many others, he was unable to keep up with the payments on his mortgages, with their ruinous rates of interest. Not only did he lose this suit, but soon thereafter he lost control of most of his property, including Pico House. Don Pío's wife had died childless some years before, but like his brother he had fathered numerous illegitimate children, and with several of them he retired to his last remaining piece of property, El Ranchito on the San Gabriel River, which he had taken from Francisca Pérez de Silvas thirty years before.

There, on a summer evening in 1883, Don Pío's eldest son, Ranulfo Pico, was shot and killed by his lover, María Ygnacia López. They had been living together for some time, and Pico, according to López, had promised her they would marry. But when she told him she was pregnant he admitted that he would never marry her, then callously turned and walked away. López pulled a small revolver from her apron pocket and shot Pico in the back of the head. Hearing the shot, his sibling Alfredo Pico rushed into the room. "Forgive me, I have killed your brother," López exclaimed.

She was arrested but soon released on bond posted by several sympathetic citizens. Public opinion was entirely on her side. "There is little sympathy expressed for the victim," a correspondent reported, "as he was apparently unnaturally heartless in refusing to meet his promises and save the injured girl from exposure." The *Herald* attributed the tragedy to "the denial of justice to the weaker sex." Women in López's position—fearing the expense of a lawsuit, the humiliation of cross-examination, and the scorn of an all-male jury—"have adopted the pistol as their remedy instead of the law. When will justice be done in such cases without violence?" There is no record that María Ygnacia López was ever brought to trial.

As he lay mortally wounded in 1855, Samuel King had challenged his three sons to go after the man who shot him: "If you have any of my blood in your veins you will not let him live." Andrew Jackson King and his brothers went on to cut a violent swath across frontier Los Angeles. Jack King was one of the original Monte Boys, and during the Civil War he served not only as the county's undersheriff but as political chief of the local secessionist majority. But following the 1865 shootout at the Bella Union that claimed the life of one brother, King put down his guns and devoted himself to the more peaceful if no less confrontational pursuit of editing a local newspaper and practicing law. He prospered, and with the able assistance of an accomplished wife raised a family of six children. Their eldest son, George Bloom King, was an emblem of the rising of a new Los Angeles, trained as a civil engineer and employed in a position of responsibility by city government. Young King was "one of the elect," opined the *Los Angeles Times*, the offspring of a pioneer family, scion of a distinguished public servant. But George Bloom King disappointed his parents by refusing to settle down. Into his midthirties he remained single, a frequent habitué of the city's bars and brothels.

In 1898 King became infatuated with a beautiful young prostitute named Teresa Kerr. After months of spending several nights a week in her company at the house of Madame Van on New High Street, he persuaded Kerr to take up residence with him. Once he overcame the opposition of his parents, he promised, they would marry. In the meantime they took rooms at a boardinghouse, where he registered under an assumed name. According to their landlady, the couple lived quietly enough, although she occasionally overheard arguments between them over King's habit of staying out late and spending his earnings on booze, cigars, and cards. After some weeks King grew tired of the relationship. "I don't know what we are going to do for money, sweetheart," he said to Kerr shortly before Christmas. "I think you had better go back," referring to Madame Van's. Kerr was horrified. "I told him that I would rather kill myself than go back to that life."

One day King left for work in the morning but failed to return in the evening. It took several days before Kerr would admit to herself that he had abandoned her. She wrote King notes, but they were returned unopened. She went to his office, but he refused to admit her. Resolving to do something dramatic, she pawned a ring he had given her, purchased a small revolver with the proceeds, then stationed herself in the stairwell of city hall late one afternoon. She caught him unawares as he left work. "What do you mean by acting this way?" she demanded. "Don't make a scene," he admonished. Then he noticed she had something concealed under her cape. "What have you got there?" he asked. "Something to end my suffering," she said, and pulled out the pistol. The gun went off and the bullet tore down through King's guts and lodged in his thigh bone.

He lived long enough to make a dying declaration. Teresa Kerr was "a common chippie," he said. "I got stuck on her like a fool and took her out and kept her. She was so God-damned jealous and her temper was so bad that she led me to disgust life, and I had to quit." Kerr insisted that her intention had been to kill herself in front of King, but that he had gone for the gun and it discharged by accident. King was asked whether that was true. "No," he said, "she has been laying for me." Kerr was indicted for murder in the first degree.

King's accusation, printed in the local papers, did the prosecution little good. "The statement is so coarsely worded," the *Times* pronounced, "it is doubtful whether the prosecution will put it in evidence." Public sympathy was entirely with Kerr, and at her trial, which lasted several days, scores of women packed the courtroom. "Gray haired matrons and young women from the very best society were gathered in imposing numbers to show their sympathy for the defendant," reported the *Herald*. "Sisters all, they felt that Teresa Kerr was deserving of human sympathy and sisterly support."

The prosecution presented a strong case. "Stung by King's desertion," declared the district attorney, Teresa Kerr "had gone to slay him as he came from his office in city hall, and like a good actress, she covered her real motive by studied expressions of grief while her heart was rejoicing in feelings of revenge." But the defense put Kerr on the stand to refute the charge, and she testified at length and in detail about the coldhearted conduct of George Bloom King.

The jury retired after hearing closing arguments and the judge's instructions. Nine minutes later the jurists signaled that they had reached a verdict. Before they were ushered back into the courtroom, the judge made an announcement from the bench. "When the jury comes in, if there is any demonstration here," he said, "I'll have about half of you in the county jail." Nevertheless, when the verdict was read—"Not Guilty"—the courtroom erupted in pandemonium. The judge shrugged his shoulders. "I see these ladies will have their way, and I suppose we'll have to let them have it."

Andrew Jackson King turned sixty-five the year his eldest son was murdered. He lived for another quarter century, but he never spoke in public about his loss. Noted for his lofty carriage and his elegant manners, King practiced law well into his seventies and to the end of his days remained a loyal Democrat. He regularly attended the party's county convention, where he was often asked about old times. During one of those gatherings he pleased the reporter for the *Herald* by recounting tales of the old pueblo, when disagreements among men were settled, as King put it, "by nectar from old Kaintuck and a six shooter." It was easier to romanticize the violence of frontier Los Angeles than to own the burden of its history. The iniquities of the fathers shall be visited on the children. Cold comfort for old men.

NOTES

The following notes list citations by the name of the newspaper, collection, or author and refer to an extensive bibliography available online at the following website: books.wwnorton.com/books/Eternity-Street/.

PREFACE

xi   **I served as a juror:** Thompson 2006, for an account of this trial by another juror.

xii   **comprehensive list of homicides:** Faragher 2014

xiii   **"all violence is an attempt":** Gilligan 1997:11–12.

xiii   **"violence always needs justification":** Arendt 1970:77.

PROLOGUE

1   **"Defend yourself":** *Star* 1852.07.10; "People vs. Joseph Caddick and Charles Norris," 1852.07.07, Box 1, Los Angeles County 1850–1860, "Criminal Court Cases," Seaver Center for Western History Research (hereafter cited as Criminal/Seaver).

1   **"brave but reckless":** Newmark 1916:206–7.

2   **"a terrible place":** *Alta California* 1854.10.19.

2   **Homicides:** Faragher 2014.

2   **New York City:** Monkkonen 2001:59.

3   **Felipe Sebastián Alvitre:** Mason 2004:18–25; Castañeda 1993:22–23.

3   **"an incorrigible rogue":** Crosby 2003:143.

4   **Alvitre offspring:** Northrop 1976:23–29; "Rancho Potrero Chico and Misión Vieja," Spitzzeri 2010–14.

4   **storm of violence:** *Star* 1852.03.20, 1852.08.28.

4   **"on the bare back":** *Star* 1853.09.24; Spitzzeri 2005a:88–89.

5   **"fourteen severe wounds":** *Star* 1854.09.21.

5   **young widow:** *Star* 1855.01.04; DAR 1952.

5   **Charles Moore:** *Star* 1854.09.21.

6   **William Workman:** *El Clamor Público* 1857.03.14, clipping Hayes 1877b 43:146–48.

6 **"Where are your father and mother?":** *Star* 1854.11.02, clipping Hayes 1877b 43:410.

6 **they were discovered:** *Southern Californian* 1854.11.02.

7 **"Porque era Americano":** *Star* 1854.11.30, 1855.01.18.

7 **David Brown:** Chamberlain 1996:350n.

7 **Texas Mounted Volunteers:** Carney 2008.

7 **"committed extensive depredations":** Taylor to Adjutant General, 1847.06.06, Polk 1848b:1178.

7 **John Joel Glanton:** Chamberlain 1996:350n; *Alta California* 1851.01.15; Jeremiah Hill, deposition 1850.05.09, Guinn 1903d:58–60.

8 **San Diego:** William Carr, deposition, 1850.05.09, Guinn 1903:54–55.

8 **Brown in Los Angeles:** q.v. "David Brown," federal manuscript census, Los Angeles County, California (1850), enumeration taken 1851.01.15.

8 **sneak attack:** William Carr, deposition, 1850.05.09, Guinn 1903:54–55.

8 **deputy city marshal:** *Alta California* 1851.01.15.

8 **"Here it is":** "People vs. Dave Brown and Charles Lavellé," 1851.03.17, Box 1, Criminal/Seaver.

9 **"He shot":** *Star* 1851.09.27, clipping Hayes 1877b 43:55.

9 **Brown was acquitted:** *Star* 1852.01.31, clipping Hayes 1877b 49:61.

10 **"We buried":** Hobbs 1875:218–19.

10 **Pinckney Clifford:** *Star* 1854.10.19; *Southern Californian* 1854.12.14.

11 **"one more chance":** *Southern Californian* 1854.10.19; *Star* 1854.10.19; Woods diary, 1854.11.28, Bynum 1941:75.

11 **shackled in irons:** *Southern Californian* 1854.10.26.

11 **Alvitre's trial:** *Star* 1854.11.30.

11 **the courtroom was outfitted:** *Southern Californian* 1854.11.16.

12 **"for the benefit":** Hayes diary, 1854.11.24, Hayes 1929:107.

12 **"It is truly worthy":** *Star* 1854.11.30, clipping Hayes 1877b 43:421.

13 **"every officer":** *Southern Californian* 1854.10.19.

14 **"tone of the press":** *Southern Californian* 1854.11.30.

14 **"duly tried":** Hayes diary, 1854.11.30, Hayes 1929:107–8.

14 **"There is no room":** *Star* 1854.12.07.

14 **"the District Court":** *Southern Californian* 1854.12.14.

14 **stay of execution:** *Southern Californian* 1855.01.04.

14 **"So Alvitre is to be hanged":** *Star* 1855.01.11.

15 **"One happens to be":** *Southern Californian* 1855.01.11.

15 **"The Sheriff is determined":** *Southern Californian* 1855.01.12, reprinted *Alta California* 1855.01.16.

16 **"'Tis strange":** Lord Byron, *Don Juan* (1823):canto xiv, stanza 101.

16 **"manifest destiny":** O'Sullivan 1845.

17 **"no brighter sun":** *Star* 1853.02.26.

CHAPTER 1

21 **"a new era":** Alvarado 1876 3:67–69.

22 **nearly three hundred individuals :** Gonzales-Day 2006.

22 **more than fifty:** Faragher 2014.

22 **Féliz-Villa marriage:** Northrop 1976:128–29; baptism records SG:05612 and SG:04025, ECPP 2006; marriage record, 1829.05.11, MIR 1964.

22 **Charo:** Vega 1877:16.

22 **two children:** Northrop 2004:105–6; baptism records SG:07672 and SG:07785, ECPP 2006.

22 **"*el güilo*":** Botello 1878:21.

23 **"*como Díos manda*":** Hittell 1898 2:494–95.

23 **Alipás brothers:** Beebe and Senkewicz 2006:119–20.

23 **"*Hoy las Féliz mueres*":** Prudon 1836b:4.

23 **"the lost lamb":** Alvarado 1876 3:61.

24 **"peace and harmony":** Botello 1878:21–22.

24 **"make a party":** Alvarado 1876 3:61.

24 **"Why wait":** Prudon 1836b:5.

24 **bid them goodbye:** Botello 1878:22; Alvarado 1876 3:61.

24 **"My heart tells me":** Alvarado 1876 3:62.

25 **disfigured:** Botello 1878:22; death record LA:00268, ECPP 2006.

25 **Several witnesses:** Botello 1878:22.

25 **"the little father":** Kielbasa 1997:93.

25 **Féliz-Cota family:** Northrop 1976:106–26.

25 **"Death to Gervasio":** Prudon 1836b:9.

26 **requiem mass:** Coronel 1994:90.

26 **"We swear:"** Alvarado 1876 3:64.

26 **"Strike, Gervasio":** Prudon 1836b:6.

27 **"Whomsoever":** Guinn 1901a:132–33.

27 **"shed blood":** Prudon 1836b:10.

28 **Jonathan Temple:** Barrows 1894c:40–42.

28 **"I am a foreigner":** Prudon 1836b:1–2.

28 **Prudon, Arzaga, Araujo:** Bancroft 1882–1890 20:62–66.

29 **fifty-five men:** Prudon 1836a:87–88; Bancroft 1882–90 36:62 and McLure 2009:156 assert that the committee was made up mostly of foreigners; González 1993:140 and Casas 1999:212–13 claim the committee was predominantly Mexican; in fact, 40 of the 55 were Californios.

29 **distribution of arms:** Alvarado 1876 3:64–65.

29 **"*salus populi*":** Prudon 1836a:87–88; Bancroft 1882–90 20:418–19; Guinn 1915a 1:183–85; Layne 1934a:220–21.

30 **"An immediate answer":** Layne 1934:221.

30 **"chose not to wage":** Alvarado 1876 3:65.

30 **"You did well":** Alvarado 1876 3:65–66.

31 **firing squad:** Tays 1932:289.

31 **"Both died":** Death record, LA:00271 and LA:00272, ECPP 2006.

CHAPTER 2

33 **five homicides:** "Contra Miguel Sánchez por heridas," 1834.09.12, Los Angeles Ayuntamiento, 1830–50, "Alcalde Court Records" (hereafter cited as ACR) 5:563–67; "Ynformacion sumaria contra Enrique Sepúlveda," 1835.02.17, ACR 5:754–826; "Criminal sobre omicidio [sic] Ygnacio gentil," 1835.08.08, ACR 5:677–705; Prudon 1836a cites two more victims by name, but there are no corresponding case files.

33 **frequency of homicide:** Faragher 2014; the ratio of homicides to population; assuming a population of 2,239 (1836), five murders over three years is a rate of

75/100,000, three times the rate of Oaxaca, Mexico in 1877, Taylor 1979:180–81; cf. Monkkonen 2001, 2003, 2005a, and 2005b, Roth 2009.

34 *"a me no me"*: Alonso 1995:80.

34 **"lax"**: Cunyngham-Cunningham 1898:200.

34 **1830 and 1836 census:** Bancroft 1882–90 19:557; Layne 1936.

34 **migrants from the south:** Reid 1968:98–99; Layne 1936.

34 **"I am disgusted":** Tomas Yorba to José Noriega, 1834.11.22, Phillips 2010:203–4.

35 **"out of control":** Angustias de la Guerra, c1878, Beebe and Senkewicz 2006:265.

35 **violent crime:** 81% of the violent crimes committed by Indians victimized other Indians, but only 18% of the violent crimes committed by Mexicans victimized other Mexicans; data compiled from case file abstracts, 1830–46, Chavez-García 1998.

35 **"There are here":** Antonio Osio to Mariano Vallejo, 1836.02.24, Tays 1932:281.

35 **"taught Christianity":** Carlos III to Carlos Francisco de Croix, 1770.04.08, Monroy 1990:22.

35 **"useful vassals":** Felipe de Neve to Junípero Serra, c1780, Monroy 1990:22.

35 **"Shall we think":** Pedro Font, c1776, Salomon 2010:13.

36 **twenty-five thousand converts:** Geary 1934:162.

36 **"the soldiers":** Serra to Viceroy Antonio María Bucareli y Ursúa, 1773.05.21, Engelhardt 1927:6–7.

37 **spoils of conquest:** Alonso 1995:94; Castañeda 1993:25.

37 **implacable foes:** McCawley 1996:44.

37 **"They had little basis":** Kealhofer 1991:551–52.

37 **ecological crisis:** Hackel 2005:71–75.

38 **"very poor":** Palóu 1926:219.

38 **"usually caught":** Pedro Font, c1776, Caughey and Caughey 1976:62.

38 **rebellions:** Hackel 2003.

39 **fugitivism:** Heizer 1978; McCawley 1996:196.

39 **The lash:** Guest 1983:13–14; Hurtado 1992:380.

39 **"a man of talent":** Reid 1968:76–77, 88.

39 **"He struggled constantly":** César 1878:6.

39 **"reduced to obedience":** Monroy 1990:22.

40 **"The Indian population":** Mariano Payeras, c1820, Archibald 1978:157; see Phillips 1975:33–34; Jackson 1995:172; McCawley 1996:196–97; Hackel 1998:122; Hackel 2005:101–2.

40 **"We entered":** Juan Crespi, 1769.08.02, Bolton 1927:146–48.

41 **José Vicente Féliz:** Mason 2004:19–22.

41 **immediately north:** Nunis 2004:5, 14.

41 **Social mixing:** Rios-Bustamante 1985:92–93.

41 **"the pernicious familiarity:"** Pedro de Fages, c1787, Mason 1984:127.

42 **"a set of idlers":** Isidro Alonso Salazar, c1796, Richman 1911:171.

42 **"should have been":** José Sernán, c1796, Phillips 1980:433–34.

42 **"If there is anything":** Narciso Durán, c1831, Engelhardt 1913 3:398.

43 **"According to the laws":** Diego de Borica, c1796, Guinn 1915a 1:97.

43 **prime objective:** Pubols 2000:333.

43 **initial attempt at secularization:** Bancroft 1882–90 20:103–6; Hutchinson 1969:128–32; Haas 2003:13–17; Ivey 2003.

44 **"remove the yoke"**: Echeandía to José Figueroa, 1833.03.19, Bancroft 1882–90 20:106.

44 **"scheme of spoliation"**: Victoria, 1831.01.19, Hittell 1898 2:127.

44 **Pío de Jesús Pico:** Salomon 2010.

44 **"*la breva aplastada*"**: Layne 1935c:37–38; Login and Login 2010.

45 **"No Mexican citizen"**: Pico 1973:31–34.

45 **"criminal abuse"**: "Pronunciamento de San Diego," 1831.11.29, Bancroft 1882–90 20:202–4n.

45 **"I was determined"**: Pico 1973:122.

46 **"Officers in skirts"**: Osio 1996:182; Pico 1973:50–52.

46 **"Leave that pack"**: Hittell 1898 2:140–41.

46 **"I'm no man"**: Bell 1881:65.

47 **Andrés Pico:** Tays 1932:168.

47 **"men in petticoats"**: Bell 1881:52–53.

47 **Accounts differ:** Osio 1996:108–11; Robinson 1846:120; Bancroft 1882–90 20:206–8; Guinn 1901a:44–45; Hittell 1898 2:140–41; Tays 1932:166–68.

48 **"Let peace return"**: Figueroa, 1833.01.16, Smith 1977:3.

48 **"entrenchments"**: Figueroa, c1834, Hittell 1898 2:183.

CHAPTER 3

49 **"I am not an animal"**: Alvarado 1876 4:126–27; Sánchez 1995:162.

49 **"These Indians"**: Portilla, 1834.12.20, Hittell 1898 2:189–90.

49 **"He was filled"**: Eulalia Pérez, c1877, Beebe and Senkewicz 2006:106–7.

49 **"wasted in behalf"**: Herbermann 1913 13:427.

50 **outpost at San Bernardino:** James 1911:285–87; Beattie and Beattie 1939:30–31.

50 **captive taking:** Coronel 1994:26; Bancroft 1882–90 21:67–68.

50 **"Huge tracts"**: Coronel 1994:16, 22.

50 **Pico exemplified:** Salomon 2007:366.

50 **"I dedicated myself"**: Pico 1973:90.

51 **"Pío Pico"**: César 1878:2–5.

51 **"All that San Luis Rey"**: William Hartnell, c1839, Dakin 1949:230.

51 **brace of pistols:** Pico 1973:92.

51 **the former mission estate:** Eversole 1986:325–29.

52 **"They were the ones"**: Lugo 1950:226.

52 **"*se crió entre los indios*"**: Rojas 1964:24.

53 **"When he walks"**: "Wild Life," *Baily's Magazine of Sports and Pastimes* 2 (1861):387.

53 **"whatever they could afford"**: Lugo 1950:221.

53 **"flying like the whirlwind"**: Loughead 1896:109.

53 **mounted warfare:** Rojas 1964:7.

53 **hombre real:** Alonso 1995:80–81.

53 **"The country has"**: Robinson to Bryant & Sturgis, 1835.03.14, Ogden 1944b:317.

54 **"as one of the wealthiest"**: Newmark 1916:66–67.

54 **Abel Stearns:** Bancroft 1882–90 22:732–33; Wright 1977:4–9; Woolsey 1993:104–5; Barger 254:131–33.

54 **cara de caballo:** Fedewa 1970:270n.

55 **"I firmly believe"**: Stearns to Juan Bautista Alvarado, c1840, Fedewa 1970:37–38.

55   **Jean Louis Vignes:** Bancroft 1882–90 22:762–63; Hittell 1898 3:179–80; Newmark 1916:197; Splitter 1949:115; Jore 1963; Mollno 2008.

55   **"With my knowledge":** Davis 1890:170.

55   **Indian population of Los Angeles:** Eversole 1986:163–67.

57   **"the women excelled":** Bell 1930:3.

57   **"As soon as":** Mariana Richardson de Torres, n.d., Miller 2004:105; see also Salomon 2010:51.

58   **"angry at being treated":** Arnaz 1878:15.

58   **"live far more wretched":** Durán to José Figueroa, 1833.07.03, Geary 1934:137.

58   **Calle de los Negros:** Weaver 1974:26; Gonzalez 1993:43.

58   **Public drunkenness:** Robinson 1938:158; Guillow 1996:59–61; Street 2004:95–96; Phillips 2010:189.

58   **sentenced to forced labor:** Phillips 1980:435–39.

59   *Ranchería de poblanos:* Robinson 1952:15–25; Estrada 2003:48–49; Phillips 2010:185.

59   **de jure segregation:** Robinson 1938:162–69; Guillow 1996:57–63; Guinn 1899c:211; Torres-Rouff 2006a:102–4.

59   **"dirty and filthy":** Los Angeles Ayuntamiento, 1845.01.11, González 1993:202.

59   **twenty-five Indians:** Faragher 2014.

59   **"The sign of Indian murder":** Brent 1926:8; Phillips 1980:440n; ACR 4:1074–82, 7:86–213, 411–*36;* Star 1855.02.08, 1856.01.11, 1856.10.04, 1856.10.18, 1862.03.29.

60   **"abominable monster":** Prudon 1836a:87.

60   **Women were victims:** Faragher 2014.

60   **"He has hit me":** "Sumaria contra Guillermo [Tomás] Urquidez por adulterio," 1842.01.25, ACR 3:127–67, 690–712; Chavez-García 1999:276–77.

61   *"un asunto de su familia":* "Ynformacion sumaria contra Enrique Sepúlveda," 1835.02.17, ACR 5:754–826.

61   *"los linchamientos":* Botello 1878:25.

61   **"He was a man":** José de Jesús Pico, c1878, Miller 1998:41.

61   **Requena's report:** Bancroft 1882–90 20:431.

61   **"scandalous events":** Chico, 1836, Bancroft 1882–90 20:430.

62   **beat a quick retreat:** Osio 1996:137–39.

62   **"free and sovereign state":** José Castro, 1836.11.08, Bancroft 1882–90 20:471.

63   **"do what we do":** Rojo 1972:99.

63   **"The benignity":** Alvarado, proclamation, 1837.07.09, Bancroft 1882–90 20:529n; Miller 1998:54–55, 60–61.

63   **violent criminal complaints:** Woolsey 1996:107n; Langum 1987:74; Chavez-García 1998.

63   **nine Californios:** Faragher 2014.

64   **Nicolás Fink:** "Causa Criminal contra Acensio Valencia," 1841.01.19, ACR 2:102–498.

65   **Alvarado authorized:** Bancroft 1882–90 21:629–30n.

65   **"wickedest town in California":** Layne 1934:227.

65   **"the noted abode":** Simpson 1847 1:402–04.

65   *el pueblo de los diablos:* Peña to Mariano Guadalupe Vallejo, 1839.06.08, Bancroft 1882–90 20:588.

CHAPTER 4

67 **fifty extranjeros:** Bancroft 1882–90 21:14–18; Hittell 1898 2:275.

67 **"We were all crammed":** Camp 1936:126.

68 **Mexican law:** Hittell 1898 2:100.

68 *"malditos extranjeros":* Alvarado, proclamation, 1840.04.26, Robinson 1846:181–82.

68 *los rifleros americanos:* Nunis 1967:3–18.

68 **"a bummer":** Wilson to Savage, 1877.11.30, Churchill 1991:531–32.

69 **"transients":** Layne 1936:11.

69 **lone star flag:** Richter 2006:218.

69 **identical banner:** Bancroft 1882–90 20:468.

69 **"California next!":** Garner and Craig 1970:24.

70 **"very cruel outrage":** Forrest to Alvarado, 1842.06.14, Hittell 1898 2:269.

70 **"vagabonds":** Alvarado to Forrest, c1842.06.16, Hittell 1898 2:271.

70 **"a plump and punchy":** Simpson 1847:349.

70 **"lost all judgment":** Juan Espejo, Miller 1998:35.

71 **"Outrage":** *Philadelphia North American and Daily Advertiser* 1840.08.08.

71 **"smiled graciously":** Farnham 1844:54, 67, 412–13.

72 **Bidwell-Bartleson party:** Nunis 1991.

72 **"To take the country":** Bidwell to Annie Kennedy, n.d., Bidwell and Kennedy 1973:3.

72 **Rowland-Workman party:** Spitzzeri 1998.

73 **"personal donation:"** Rowland 1999:62–63.

73 **Barton:** Guinn 1902a:424 does not list Barton in the 1842 migration, but includes William Perdue (or Perdew), who reportedly came to California with Barton; Rowland 1999.

73 **Barton family:** q.v. "Barton," federal manuscript census, Randolph County, Illinois (1820), and Howard County, Missouri (1830); California State Census, 1852.

73 **"Santiago Barton":** Barton-Rowland marriage record, 1845.04.06, MRI 1964.

73 **"We are all well here":** Rowland to Manuel Alvarez, 1846.02.28, Rowland 1999:86.

74 **"numerous parties":** Vallejo 1875 3:384.

75 **"They presented":** Robinson 1846:207.

75 **"If I told":** Coronel 1994:23–27.

75 **"Without doubt":** Alvarado to Micheltorena, 1842.10.19, Tyler 1843:21–22.

76 **"Would that I":** Micheltorena to Mariano Guadalupe Vallejo, 1842.10.25, Bancroft 1882–90 21:315.

76 **"to protect the interests":** Upshur to Jones, 1841.12.10, Tyler 184345–48.

76 **"That Texas":** Tuthill 1866:148–49.

76 **"war was not only inevitable":** Jones, memorandum, 1842.10.23, Tyler 1843:88–89.

77 **"My approach":** Jones 1960:26.

77 **"Señor Alvarado":** Osio 1996:208–09.

77 **"Although I come":** Jones, "To the Inhabitants of the Two Californias," 1842.10.19, Tyler 1843:31–32.

78 **"I have received":** Jones to Micheltorena, 1842.10.21, Tyler 1843:34.

78 **"require that satisfaction":** Micheltorena to Jones, 1842.10.26, Tyler 1843:36.

79 **"Does Commodore Jones"**: Juan Nepomuceno Almonte to Daniel Webster, 1843.02.07, Tyler 1843:8.

79 **"ardent zeal"**: John Young Mason to Jones, 1845.03.01, Smith 2000:121.

79 **"for beauty"**: Jones 1960:14.

79 **"la bella"**: Fedewa 1970:270n.

79 **"the Eden"**: Davis 1889:168–69.

79 **"preventing it"**: Micheltorena, c. 1843, Jackson 1975:259–60.

80 **"might rattle"**: Hittell 1898 2:325.

80 **"Sir, you have aroused"**: Alvarado to Micheltorena, 1845.01.06, Bancroft 1882–90 21:490.

82 **"Women and children"**: Davis 1889:178–79.

82 **"uniformly preferred"**: Farnham 1844:64.

82 **"I will give you"**: Pío Pico, 1845.02.21, Wilson 1934:99–101.

82 **"to unite the Californians"**: John Coffin Jones to Larkin, 1845.02.25, Larkin 1951–68 3:49.

83 **"The Californians have succeeded"**: Larkin to John C. Calhoun, 1845.03.22, Larkin 1951–68 3:80–81.

83 **"Californians are now free"**: Larkin to Moses Yale Beach, 1845.09.30, Larkin 1951–68 3:371.

83 **"There is little to prevent"**: Duflot de Moras 1937 2:28, 31.

CHAPTER 5

85 **"aside from which"**: Sellers 1957:355.

85 **"reoccupation of Oregon"**: "Democratic Party Platform," 1844.05.27, APP 1999–2014.

85 **"the fulfillment"**: O'Sullivan 1845:5–10.

85 **"is to extend"**: Polk, Inaugural Address, 1845.03.04, APP 1999–2014.

86 **"In the clearest"**: Bancroft to Frémont, 1886.09.02, Frémont 1890:923.

86 **"confidential agent"**: Buchanan to Larkin, 1845.10.17, Bancroft 1882–90 21:597–98.

87 **"the eventualities of war"**: Frémont 1887:422–24.

87 **"secret instructions"**: Polk 1910:83–84.

87 **"the new state of affairs"**: Bancroft to Frémont, 1886.09.02, Frémont 1890:923.

87 **"I am now going to give"**: Hastings to Larkin, 1845.11.09 and 1846.01.22, Larkin 1951–68 4:92, 177.

88 **"sane government"**: Royce 1886:125.

89 **"You and the party"**: Castro to Frémont, 1846.03.05, Kelsey 1910:98.

89 **"I peremptorily refused"**: Frémont 1887:460.

89 **"Bandoleros"**: Castro, proclamation, 1846.03.08, Nevins 1955:229.

89 **"council of war"**: Larkin to William A. Leidesdorff, 1846.04.13, Larkin 1951–68 4:284.

90 **"We find ourselves"**: Revere 1849:25–26, who mistakenly identifies the anti-American speaker as Pío Pico, who was not at the meeting; McKittrick 1944:249–52 identifies Castro as the principal opponent of American acquisition.

90 **"We are republicans"**: Revere 1849:28–30.

91 **"The majority"**: Stearns to Larkin, 1846.06.12, Larkin 1951–68 5:19.

91 **"vast majority"**: Warner to Larkin, 1846.06.16, Larkin 1951–68 5:33.

92   **"bold and chivalrous"**: Gillespie to Bancroft, 1846.04.18, Ames 1938:136–40.

93   **"Mexico has passed"**: Polk, "Special Message to Congress on Mexican Relations," 1846.05.11, APP 1999–2014.

93   **"humiliated and humbled"**: Frémont to Thomas Hart Benton, 1846.07.25, Frémont 1887:545.

93   **"A grand opportunity"**: Frémont 1887:490, 508.

93   **"on their way"**: Frémont to American settlers, 1846.06.06, Ide 1880:112–13.

94   **"He brought war"**: Royce 1886:112.

94   **"completely frustrated"**: Larkin to Buchanan, 1847.01.14, Larkin 1951–68 5:180–81.

CHAPTER 6

95   **attempted to overthrow**: Bancroft 1892:40–42.

96   **"What can I do"**: Phelps 1871:284.

96   **"War is preferable"**: Larkin to Gillespie, 1846.04.23, Larkin 1951–68 4:340–41.

96   **"I have notified you"**: Castro to Pío Pico, 1846.06.08, Larkin 1951–68:9–10.

96   **"I was convinced"**: Pico 1973:133.

96   **"A gang"**: Pico, "Proclamation to the People of California," 1846.06.23, Larkin 1951–68 5:69–71.

97   **"extraordinary indifference"**: Pico to Larkin, 1846.06.29, Larkin 1951–68 5:81–82.

97   **"and still keep untarnished"**: Larkin to Anthony Ten Eyck, 1846.07.04, Larkin 1951–68 5:102.

97   **"We must take the place"**: Larkin, memorandum, n.d., Bancroft 1882–90 22:228n.

97   **"shameful"**: Bancroft to Frémont, 1886.09.03, Nevins 1955:245.

97   **"carry it"**: Sloat, "Proclamation to the Inhabitants of California," 1846.07.07, Polk 1847b:499:102–3.

98   **"with all the respect"**: Sloat to Pío Pico, 1846.07.09, Polk 1849:1013–14.

98   **"prevent the sacrifice"**: Sloat to Castro, 1846.07.07, Polk 1849:1012.

98   **"As he cannot believe"**: Castro to Sloat, 1846.07.09, Polk 1849:1012–13.

98   **"The history of your country"**: Alvarado to Larkin, 1846.07.09, Larkin 1951–68 5:123–24.

99   **"California Battalion"**: Frémont, 1846.07.05, Bancroft 1882–90 22:179–80n.

99   **"are principally backwoodsmen"**: Walpole 1850 1:165–66.

100   **"I know nothing"**: Gillespie, 1848.02.22, "California Claims," 1848: 512:32.

100   **"I acted solely"**: Frémont, deposition, 1848.02.28, "California Claims," 1848: 512:32.

101   **"violated every principle"**: Stockton, "Address to the People of California," 1846.07.29, Bancroft 1882–90 22:255–57n.

101   **"where Commodore Stockton"**: Larkin to Buchanan, 1846.07.29, Larkin 1951–68 5:180–81.

101   **"It does not contain"**: Sloat to Bancroft, 1846.08.10, Polk 1849:1034.

101   **"half way measures"**: Gillespie to Bancroft, 1846.07.25, Ames 1938:278.

102   **"embraced"**: Pico 1973:149.

102   **"No matter how great"**: Pico to Minister of Foreign Relations, 1846.07.13, Pico 1934:109–10.

103   **"I will either take"**: Stockton, 1847.12.07, Polk 1848a:179.

103 **"If you will agree"**: Stockton to Castro, 1846.08.07, Bancroft 1849:5.
103 **"You offer me"**: Castro to Stockton, 1846.08.09, Bancroft 1849:5–6.
103 **"If Stockton had sent"**: Alvarado 1876 5:242; Miller 1998:123.
103 **"I can count on"**: Castro to Pío Pico, 1846.08.09, Bancroft 1882–90 22:273–74.
103 **"If the Spaniards"**: Rojo 1885.
104 **"iniquitous invasion"**: Castro, "Proclamation to the Inhabitants of California," 1846.08.09, Pico 1934:117–18.
104 **"The best thing"**: Coronel 1994:33.
104 **"My friends, farewell"**: Pico, "Proclamation to the People of California," 1846.08.10, Pico 1934:122–23.
105 **"The United States will come"**: Harrison 1953:30.
105 **two dozen like-minded**: Guinn and Barrows 1889:238; Guinn 1901a:94; Krythe 1951:40.
105 **"Receiving so much kindness"**: Wilson 1934:77, 102.
106 **"Tell him"**: Wilson 1934:102.
106 **"web-feet regiment"**: Phelps 1871:308.
107 **"a parade"**: Frémont 1887:566.
107 **"At first the children"**: Phelps 1871:308.
107 **"a Territory"**: Stockton, proclamation, c1846.08.17, Polk 1847a:672.
107 **"That I will not"**: Stockton to Gillespie, 1846.08.18, Box 3, Doc. 23A, Gillespie 1845–1860.
108 **"I should have someone"**: Wilson 1934:104–5.
108 **"All is now peaceful"**: Stockton to Polk, 1846.08.26, Frémont 1970–84 2:194.

CHAPTER 7
109 **"A remarkable fellow"**: Bell 1930:116.
110 **"the Machiavelli"**: Guinn 1901a:50.
110 **"*Los Mexicanos*"**: Rojo 1885.
110 **"fair fight"**: Stockton, 1846.10.05, *Californian* 1846.10.24.
110 **"disgraced the country"**: Rico 1877:24.
110 **Don Sérbulo's marriage**: Brown-Coronel 2011:43–45; Schuele 2012:147–48.
111 **"I swear"**: Rojo 1885.
111 **"some very good men"**: Gillespie to Bancroft, 1847.02.16, Ames 1938:324–25.
112 **"Every means"**: Ibid.
112 **"mutiny, drunkenness"**: Kurutz 2003:121.
112 **handful of hooligans**: Coronel 1994:34–36; Lugo 1950:199–200.
112 **"*Abajo los Americanos*"**: Guinn and Barrows 1889:75.
112 **Barton**: Bancroft 1882–90 22:309; Warner 1876:31.
113 **"aiding the party"**: Kurutz 2003:130.
113 **"*A las armas*"**: Coronel 1994:37–38.
113 **"that even those"**: Rico 1877:26.
113 **"Fellow Citizens"**: "Pronunciamento de Varela y otros Californios contra los Americanos, 24 de Setiembre, 1846," Janssens 1878:14–17.
114 **"There was not a soul"**: Rojo 1885.
114 **José María Flores**: Layne 1935b.

115 *"el pedrero de la vieja"*: Guinn 1899a:265–66.
116 **"I then requested"**: *Alta California* 1858.05.17.
117 **"Gillespie's course"**: Wilson 1934:104.
117 **"rumor was"**: Robidoux to Manuel Alvarez, 1848.05.01, Robidoux 1972.
117 **"They are going"**: Foster 1877:22.
118 **"The majority of them"**: Wilson 1934:106.
119 **"They would have"**: Lugo 1950:205.
119 **"most of whom"**: José Palomares, 1877, Beattie 1942:146.
119 *"Adelante, adelante"*: Rojo 1885.
119 *"Mueran los Americanos"*: Foster 1877:25.
120 *"Incendiar la casa"*: Rojo 1885.
120 **"Don't shoot"**: Wilson 1934:109.
120 **"I am your friend"**: Ibid.
120 **"I told him"**: Lugo 1950:204.
121 **"There's some deviltry"**: Wilson 1934:109.
121 **"Say to him"**: Wilson 1934:110–11.
122 **"I marched out"**: Gillespie to Secretary of the Navy, 1848.07.08, Ames 1938:347.
122 **"only long enough"**: Treaty of capitulation, 1846.09.29, Box 3, Doc. 90, Gillespie 1845–60
122 **"Hoping that my courier"**: Gillespie to Bancroft, 1847.02.16, Ames 1938:332–34.

CHAPTER 8
125 **"our little band"**: Stockton, 1846.10.06, *Californian* 1846.10.24.
125 **"wade knee-deep"**: Shuck 1870:604.
125 **"lawless violence"**: *Californian* 1846.10.17.
126 **"nothing to fear"**: Mervine to Stockton, 1846.10.25, Driver 1969:34.
126 **"for the want of which"**: Duvall diary, 1846.10.07, Duvall 1924:116.
127 **"Let us give"**: Guinn and Barrows 1889:74–75.
127 **"quite as much fatigued"**: Gillespie to Bancroft, 1847.02.16, Ames 1938:337.
127 **"the enemy appeared"**: Duvall diary, 1846.10.07, Duvall 1924:116–17.
128 **"Bejabers"**: Parsons 1870:62.
128 *"Muchachos"*: Rojo 1885.
129 **"Shot after shot"**: Gillespie to Bancroft, 1847.02.16, Ames 1938:337.
129 **"Let's eat some"**: Vega 1877.
129 **"Let us content ourselves"**: Rojo 1885.
129 **"left behind weapons"**: Carrillo to José María Flores, 1846.10.08, Doc. 82, Janssens 1878.
130 **"We presented"**: Duvall diary, 1846.10.09, Duvall 1924:117.
130 **"the Battle of Captain"**: Bancroft 1882–90 22:320n.
130 **"made use"**: Mervine to Stockton, 1846.10.09, Driver 1969:346.
131 **"very bad defeat"**: Stockton to Gillespie, 1847.03.11, Box 4, Doc. 194, Gillespie 1845–60.
132 **"to hoist"**: Stockton to Bancroft, 1846.11.23, Bancroft 1849:9.
133 **"General Kearny is"**: Bryant 1848:428.
133 **"Much must necessarily"**: Marcy to Kearny, 1846.06.03, Polk 1847b:87.
134 **"a leap in the dark"**: Cooke 1878:70.

134 **"The American flag"**: Kearny to Roger Jones, 1846.12.12, *Niles National Register*, 1847.05.15.

134 **"The general feeling"**: Griffin diary, 1846.10.06, Ames 1942:199.

134 **"It surprised me"**: Kearny to Mary Kearny, 1846.12.19, Kearny 1990:192.

135 **"bragging like the devil"**: Griffin diary, 1846.11.23, Ames 1942:209–10.

135 **"We are still to look"**: Emory diary, 1846.12.01, Emory 1848:104.

136 **"Poor fellows"**: Johnston, 1846.11.30, Johnston 1848:612.

136 **"country people"**: Emory diary, 1846.12.03, Emory 1848:107.

136 **"in feudal style"**: Griffin diary, 1846.12.04, Ames 1942:334.

137 **"comfortable and happy"**: Emory diary, 1846.12.02, Emory 1848:105–6.

137 **"stimulated to work"**: Johnston, 1846.12.02, Johnston 1848:613.

137 **"worse by far"**: Griffin diary, 1846.12.02, Ames 1942:220.

138 **"were getting restless"**: Coronel 1994:41.

CHAPTER 9

139 **Barton:** Guinn 1901a:94.

139 **"If you see fit"**: Stockton to Kearny, 1846.12.03, Porter 1909:104–5.

140 **"would send them all"**: White 1956:56.

140 **Cupeño informants:** Johnston, 1846.12.04, Johnston 1848:614.

140 **"received with great pleasure"**: Gillespie to Stockton, 1846.12.25, Box 4, Doc. 140, Gillespie 1845–60.

141 **"*Ellos son mas muchos*"**: Véjar 1877:68.

141 **"Be careful"**: Rojo 1885.

141 **"to dismount them"**: Clarke 1961:198.

141 **"wan, thin"**: Dupont 1885:100.

141 **"No sir"**: Davis 1889:420.

141 **"I then determined"**: Kearny to R. Jones, 1846.12.13 "California Claims," 1848: 514.

141 **"We were on"**: Emory diary, 1846.12.05, Emory 1848:107–08.

142 **"The native Californians"**: Camp 1922:34.

142 **"Californians of Spanish blood"**: Gillespie to Bancroft, 1846.04.18, Ames 1938:136.

142 **"numerous as well as brave"**: Davis 1889:421.

142 **"He did not want"**: Botello 1878:154–55.

142 **"If General Kearny"**: Warner 1876:25–26.

142 **"boots and saddles"**: Griffin diary, 1846.12.11, Ames 1942:335.

143 **"Be steady"**: Gillespie to Stockton, 1846.12.25, Box 4, Doc. 140, Gillespie 1845–60.

143 **"charge as foragers"**: George Pearce, n.d., Munro-Fraser 1880:581.

144 **"Trot"**: Dupont 1885:102.

144 **Johnston resolved:** Harby 2012.

144 **"*Un tiro*"**: Véjar 1877:71.

144 **"like so many alarm bells"**: Gillespie to Stockton, 1846.12.25, Box 4, Doc. 140, Gillespie 1845–60.

144 **"The clouds hung low"**: Roberts 1917:223.

145 **"For God's sake"**: Clarke 1961:209.

145 **"*valiente Morin*"**: Woodward 1946:34–36.

145 **"*Aquí vamos*"**: Davis 1889:423.

146 **"We trembled"**: Roberts 1917:223–24.

146 **"this was no battle"**: Rojo 1885.

146 **"Rally men"**: Gillespie to Stockton, 1846.12.25, Box 4, Doc. 140, Gillespie 1845–60.

146 **"Such an affray"**: Dupont 1885:103.

146 ***"Asi se hace"***: Véjar 1877.

146 ***"Ya es Gillespie"***: Gillespie to Stockton, 1846.12.25, Box 4, Doc. 140, Gillespie 1845–60.

147 *el güero*: Foster 1877:9–10; Osio 1996:240; Rojo 1885.

147 **"Where's the match?"**: Gillespie to Bancroft, 1847.02.16, Ames 1938:344.

148 **"This was an action"**: Griffin diary, 1846.12.11, Ames 1942:335-36.

148 **"it would have been well"**: Dunne, 1878, Clarke 1961:216.

148 **"Another such victory"**: Coy 1921:12.

148 **"without other casualty"**: A. Pico to Flores, 1846.12.06, Janssens 1878:45–46.

149 **"We are without"**: Turner to Stockton, 1846.12.06, Polk 1848a:186.

150 **"the firing with cannon"**: Wilson 1934:113–14.

151 **"Stockton refused to send"**: Griffin diary, 1846.12.11, Ames 1942:337.

151 **Panto**: Smythe 1908:220.

151 **"We could see"**: Woodward 1946:48.

152 **"to vindicate his"**: Stockton, 1847.12.08, Polk 1848a:185–89.

152 **"I have thought"**: Stockton to Turner, 1847.12.07, Cleland 1944:230; cf. original Spanish translation, Doc. 23, Coronel 1817–1894.

153 **"They all had"**: Davis 1889:430-31.

153 **"burned to get"**: Downey 1963:182.

154 **"Our General has"**: Griffin diary, 1846.12.20, Ames 1942:340–41.

154 **"To arms"**: *Californian* 1846.11.28.

155 **"to abstain"**: Frémont to Mervine, 1846.11.27, Frémont 1970–84 2:233.

155 **"I denied nothing"**: J. Pico 1878:72–73.

155 **"a lady"**: *St. Louis Union*, 1847.01.15, Cutts 1847:161.

155 **"You were about"**: Frémont 1887:599.

156 **"The impression"**: John R. Wilson, 1848.02.19, "California Claims" 1848:42.

156 **"Bad weather"**: Frémont to Stockton, 1847.01.02, Frémont 1970–84 2:249.

CHAPTER 10

157 **"We have had"**: Griffin diary, 1846.12.20 and 1847.01.03, Ames 1942:340, 347.

158 **"We made"**: Lugo 1950:208–9.

158 **"Do not wait"**: Castro to Flores, received 1846.12.29, Rojo 1885.

158 **"Destiny's cold hand"**: Rojo 1885.

159 **"Our men"**: Stockton to George Bancroft, 1847.02.05, Bancroft 1849:31.

159 **"We were actuated"**: Downey 1963:200.

159 **"Keep your forces"**: Stockton to Frémont, 1847.01.03, Bancroft 1849:272–73.

160 **"to avoid the useless"**: Flores to Stockton, 1847.01.01, Bancroft 1849:19–20.

160 **"whom I had captured"**: Stockton to John Y. Mason, 1848.02.18, Polk 1849:1051.

160 **"that he was a rebel"**: Stockton to Bancroft, 1847.01.15, Bancroft 1849:20–21.

161 "a general amnesty": Stockton, proclamation, 1847.01.05, Brockmann 2009:203.

161 "Ladies were soon": Emory diary, 1847.01.07, Emory 1848:119.

162 "I want you all": Downey 1963:202.

162 "Before we had fairly": Downey 1963:203–4.

163 "Do or die": Downey 1963:205–8.

163 "There is quicksand": Gillespie to Bancroft, 1847.02.16, Ames 1938:345.

163 "Quicksand be damned!" Guinn and Barrows 1889:76–77.

164 "They aimed chiefly": Coronel 1994:47–48.

164 "Down they came": Downey 1963:208–10.

165 "strange emotions": Warner 1876:23.

165 "no matter who": Downey 1963:214–15.

165 "I thought": Coronel 1994:48.

166 "solely on a point": Warner 1876:23.

166 "We all considered": Emory diary, 1846.01.09, Emory 1848:120–21.

167 "They kept up": Downey 1963:213.

167 "The streets were full": Emory diary, 1846.01.10, Emory 1848:121–22.

168 "No sooner": Downey 1963:215.

168 "All I could do": Juanita de Díos Rendon, 1847.10.29, Torres-Rouff 2006:183–84.

168 "We have marched": Watson 1990:280.

168 "The forces": Colton 1850:167–68.

168 "nothing heard": Griffin diary, 1847.01.11, Ames 1942:353.

169 "We are in possession": Kearny to Frémont, 1847.01.10, Bancroft 1882–90 22:402n.

169 "conquering by clemency": Frémont 1848.01.24, Polk 1848a:379.

169 "The arch-ruffian": Smith 1919 1:345–46.

169 "I no longer flattered": A. Pico to P. Pico, 1847.04.05, Pico 1934:132–34.

170 "as long as": Rojo 1885.

170 "We are ready": Dupont 1885:115.

170 "they would take": McLane 1971:102–3.

171 "return peaceably": Treaty of Cahuenga, 1847.01.13, http://www.militarymuseum.org/Cahuenga.html, accessed 2011.10.07.

171 "I have the honor": Frémont to Kearny, 1847.01.13, Frémont 1970–84 2:257–58.

171 "The junior officers": Griffin diary, 1847.01.14, Ames 1942:41–42.

172 "This was the end": Pico to Pico, 1847.04.05, Pico 1934:132–34.

CHAPTER 11

173 "As long as": Wilson 1934:123.

174 "There is something": Watson diary, 1847.01.14, Watson 1990:284.

174 "I am informed": Kearny to Stockton, 1847.01.16, Taylor 1850:267.

174 "I need say": Stockton to Kearny, 1847.01.16, Taylor 1850:268.

175 "playing a grab game": McLane 1971:104.

175 "to terminate his": Stockton to John Y. Mason, 1848.02.18, Polk 1849:1037–54.

175 "With great deference": Frémont to Kearny, 1847.01.17, Polk 1848a:6.

175 "he would unquestionably": Kearny, 1847.11.04, 39.

175 **"I had contracted"**: Frémont to Thomas Hart Benton, 1847.02.03, Frémont 1970–84 2:284.

175 **"there is, or should be"**: Bancroft 1882–90 22:432.

176 **"I am not recognized"**: Kearny to Adjutant General Roger Jones, 1847.01.17, Polk 1848a:94–95.

176 **"a collision between us"**: Kearny to Stockton, 1847.01.17, Grivas 1961:71, emphasis added.

176 **"I should not"**: Stockton to Mason, 1848.02.18, Polk 1849:1054, emphasis added.

176 **"thus trying to incite"**: Watson diary, 1847.02.02, Watson 1990:290–91, emphasis added.

176 **Duvall recorded gossip:** Duvall 1957:93.

176 **"Frémont has a large force"**: Wilson 1934:124–25, emphasis added.

177 **"Frémont deliberately"**: Coronel 1994:34.

177 **"The young women danced"**: Lugo 1950:212–13.

177 **"Throughout the Californian"**: Frémont to Benton, 1847.02.03, Frémont 1970–84 2:283-84.

178 **"He wears the sombrero"**: Duvall 1957:53–54.

178 **"He gave rowdy balls"**: William Rich Hutton to William Rich, 1849.08.19, Hutton 1942:31.

178 **"Frémont's a low fellow"**: Ord 1978:24.

178 **"harem, publicly established"**: *Star* 1856.09.08.

178 **Geronimo López:** Prudhomme 1932:315.

178 **"You damned rascal"**: Foster 1877:9–10.

178 **"favors the country"**: Gillespie to Larkin, 1847.03.05, Larkin 1951–68 6:37.

179 **"I will, agreeably"**: Kearny to Roger Jones, 1847.01.14, Polk 1848a:80.

179 **"You see how transitory"**: Stockton to John R. Thompson, 1847.02.06, Brockmann 2009:222.

179 **"Viewing my position"**: Frémont to Willard P. Hall, 1847.02.11, Polk 1848a:10–11.

179 **published a circular:** Kearny, "To the People of California," 1847.03.*01*, *Californian* 1847.03.06.

180 **"waiting for something"**: Foster 1888:48.

180 **"My place"**: Foster 1888:48–51.

181 **"unsafe at this time"**: William H. Russell to Cooke, 1847.03.16, Polk 1848a:15.

181 **"I told him"**: Cooke 1878:290–92.

181 **"If these Americans"**: Cooke to H. S. Turner, 1847.03.25, Polk 1848a:124–25.

182 **New York Regiment of Volunteers:** Biggs 1977.

182 **"There were men"**: Walter Murray, 1878, Bancroft 1882–90 22:505.

182 **"the Mormons were cannibals"**: Tyler 1881:276.

183 **"Last night we were"**: Standage diary, 1847.04.25, Golder 1928:219.

183 **"With the prospect"**: Tyler 1881:280.

183 **"when I send"**: Hollingsworth 1923:247.

183 **"so much fuss"**: Foster 1877:19–20.

183 **"None of your insolence"**: Bigelow 1856:205.

184 **"I this morning"**: Kearny to Jones, 1847.05.13, Taylor 1849a:292–93.

184 "Americans Should Rule": Price 1967:68.
184 "Frémont disappointed": Dorrance 1987:167.

CHAPTER 12

185 "a Territory of the United States": Stockton, proclamation, 1846.08.17, Polk 1847a:672.
185 "make all needful rules": Constitution of the United States, Art. IV, Sec. 3.
185 "Foreign countries occupied": Davis, 1846.12.09, Chase 1850:178–79n.
186 "similar to that": William L. Marcy to Kearny, 1846.06.03, Polk 1847b:85.
186 "The possession of portions": John Young Mason to Stockton, 1847.01.11, Polk 1848a:56–58.
186 "This is a military": Mason to L. W. Boggs, 1847.06.02, Taylor 1849b:317–18.
186 "dislike the change": Mason to Roger Jones, 1847.06.18, Taylor 1849a:298–99.
187 "preserved a quiet": Stevenson 1886:29–30.
187 "No doubt": S. C. Rowan to Griffin, 1847.07.28, Warren 1954–55:251.
188 "no Californios came": Stevenson to Governor Mason, 1847.07.13, Stevenson 1974.
188 "belle of the evening": H. H. F. Toye, 1847.07.04, Hollingsworth 1923:239.
189 "danced like a bear": Foster 1877:34.
189 "When this was communicated": Stevenson to Mason, 1847.07.13, Stevenson 1974.
189 "When a man": Foster 1877:34–41.
190 Julien Bartolet: "Averiguacion sumaria para indagar la muerte de Julian Bartelott," 1847.07.10, ACR 7:725–62.
190 "to act with all rigor": "The French People Residing in the City of Los Angeles" to Stevenson, 1847.07.16, Los Angeles County 1834–49, "Los Angeles County Prefecture Records" 2:534–35 (hereafter cited as PR).
190 "the worst of it": Griffin diary, 1847.08.14, Ames 1942:62.
191 "I have a guard": Hollingsworth diary, 1847.08.06, Hollingsworth 1923:242.
191 "Poco tiempo": California Star 1848.01.22; Guinn 1901a:102.
192 "Everything is quiet": Hollingsworth diary, 1847.12.04, Hollingsworth 1923:243.
192 Stevenson received intelligence: Guinn 1897c:147.
192 "As night came on": Hollingsworth diary, 1847.12.09, Hollingsworth 1923:244–46.
193 "the worst class": Stevenson to Mason, 1847.12.19, Bancroft 1882–90 22:626n.
193 "I then knew": Foster, n.d., Guinn and Barrows 1889:91.
193 "But no attention": Foster, 1891, Robinson 1949:321.
193 nine murders: Faragher 2014.
194 "yo establa": "Criminal para indagar la muerte del Capitan Yerbavuena," 1847.04.06, ACR 7:794–830.
194 "motherfucker": "Criminal Contra Pedro Pacheco por la muerte de Jose Maria Machado," 1848.09.04, ACR 5:1184–1221.
195 "deserting rapidly": Hollingsworth diary, 1848.07.18, Hollingsworth 1923:253–54.
195 "The gold fever": Hollingsworth diary, 1848.08.02, Hollingsworth 1923:253–55.

195 **"Americans and Californians"**: Mason, 1848.08.06, Bancroft 1882–90 22:591–92.

196 **"the great law of necessity"**: Buchanan to William V. Voorhies, 1848.10.07, Taylor 1849b:7.

196 **"The pueblo has changed"**: Griffin to Stevenson, 1849.03.11, Griffin 1949:9.

196 **"It is known"**: Bennett C. Riley to W. T. Sherman, 1849.04.16, Taylor 1849a:876.

CHAPTER 13

202 **"Don Pedro"**: Bell 1881:36.

202 **"Nigger Pete"**: Newmark 1916:137–38.

202 **"I remained"**: Hayes diary, 1850.02.05, Hayes 1929:71–72.

202 **"I threw myself alone"**: Hayes diary, 1849.09.10, Hayes 1929:13–14.

203 **"Last night"**: Hayes diary, 1849.09.20, Hayes 1929:17.

203 **"a polite"**: Hayes diary, 1849.10.28, Hayes 1929:28–29.

203 **"surrounded by squaws"**: Hayes diary, 1850.01.23, Hayes 1929:58.

204 **"Rowland is married"**: Hayes diary, 1850.01.31, Hayes 1929:69.

204 **"Twilight had just"**: Hayes diary, 1850.02.01, Hayes 1929:69–70.

204 **"The whole scene"**: Hayes diary, 1850.02.03, Hayes 1929:71–72.

205 **"And thereupon"**: Griffin to J. D. Stevenson, 1849.03.11, Griffin 1949:9.

205 **"held a public meeting"**: Wilson 1934:124–26.

206 **"So little interest"**: Foster, 1878, Barrows 1893a:63.

206 **"It has been the custom"**: Browne 1850:371.

206 **"It was not"**: Browne 1850:11.

206 **"begged leave"**: Browne 1850:22.

207 **"Negro Alley"**: *Star* 1853.01.29, clipping Hayes 1877b 49:119.

207 a group of drunken Americans: "Causa Criminal contra el Americano Santiago Ollin," 1850.01.04, ACR 6:979–89.

208 **"without any provocation"**: "Causa Criminal contra los individuos que atacaron la casa de Don Santiago Monet," 1850.01.07, ACR 6:776–804.

208 **"gringo"**: "People v. James R. Vansand," Box 1, #85, Criminal/Seaver.

208 Patrick Mooney: "Causa Instruida contra Patricio Mune [*sic*]," 1850.02.12, ACR 6:1070–83.

209 **"Our town"**: Foster to Governor Peter H. Burnett, 1850.02.20, PR 2:833–34; also see Foster to Brigadier General B. Riley, 1850.02.25, PR 2:835–36.

209 Stephen Cribbs: "Inventario de los bienes del finado Thomas Cribbs," 1850.02.14, ACR 6:1163–92.

210 **"sons of the sunny South"**: Hayes 1877b 43:4.

210 **"a tall and powerful"**: Brier 1903:463–64.

210 Purdy: Broadstone 1918 1:547, 740; Harrold 1986:36, 42, 51.

210 **"They told me"**: Case 31 [no title], 1850.01.07, ACR 6:766–75.

211 **"Poor Purdy"**: Hayes 1877b 43:5.

211 crusading editor: Buchanan 1956:11.

211 **"Our city has been"**: Foster to Burnett, 1850.03.12, PR 2:840–42.

212 he received a response: J. Hamilton to Foster, 1850.03.28, PR 2:883.

CHAPTER 14

213 **"a secret junta"**: Hayes 1929:186–87.

213 **"punctilious, perhaps"**: Warner 1876:35.

214 **the judicial system:** Bakken 2003; Bacon 1905.

214 **Oliver S. Witherby:** Uberti 1978.

215 **"But notwithstanding":** "Francesca Pérez Silvas vs. Mariano Silvas," 1851.01.06, Box 1, #25, Los Angeles County 1850–79, "District Court. Civil Cases" (hereafter cited as DCC).

215 **"divorce from bed":** Friedman 1984:652–55.

215 **"using offensive words":** "Criminal contra Mariano Silvas por golpes a su mujer," 1844.04.12, ACR 4:892–914; Chavez-García 2004:25.

216 **"gross and abusive":** "Francesca Pérez Silvas vs. Mariano Silvas," 1851.01.06, Box 1, #25, DCC.

216 **"whipped me severely":** "People vs. Miguel Soloma," 1850.11.29, Box 1, #74, Criminal/Seaver.

216 **"He tied me":** "People vs. Martin Duerte," 1850.08.02, Box 1, #30, Criminal/Seaver.

217 **"he gave me":** "People vs. Jose Cerbelo Barilla [sic]," 1850.07.02, Box 1, #65, Criminal/Seaver.

217 **"the peaceable and quiet":** "Francesca Pérez Silvas vs. Pio Pico," 1851.01.04, Box 1, #27, DCC.

218 **Women were victims:** Faragher 2014.

218 **"I cried out":** "People vs. Santiago Olivera, Cura Valdez, Simplicio Valdez, and Esteban Silvas," 1852.02.03, Box 1, #94, Criminal/Seaver; Woolsey 1979:93.

219 **"He shut the door":** "People vs. Thomas Foster," 1853.07.15, Box 2, #128, Criminal/Seaver.

220 **"We congratulate":** *Star* 1856.06.07.

220 **"I am sorry to tell":** Wilson to Margaret Wilson, 1856.08.03, Box 5, Wilson 1836–1941.

220 **Foster suicide:** *Alta California* 1862.01.30.

220 **"violently tore her":** "Marie Jesus Bouchet Blair vs. Nicholas Blair," 1852.09.22, Box 2, #70, DCC.

220 **"We enjoyed ourselves":** Blair to María Jesús Bouchet de Blair, 1852.09.22, Box 10, Stearns 1821–1935.

221 **Blair suicide:** *Sacramento Daily Union* 1852.10.04.

221 **"The California ladies":** Hayes to B. M. Hughes, 1853.01.24, Hayes 1929:91.

221 **Carrillo divorce:** "Francisca Sepúlveda vs. José Antonio Carrillo," 1853.10.02, Box 4, #100, DCC; *Star* 1853.12.10; Chavez-García 2004:119.

221 **"Felipe Rheim":** "People vs. Felipe Reim [sic]," 1850.07.01, Box 1, #15, Criminal/Seaver.

222 **"While laboring":** "Rosaria Dias de Rheim vs. Felipe Rheim," 1857.07.01, Box 13, #440, DCC.

222 **"Violence, like charity":** Gilligan 1997:5.

222 **"gloriously intoxicated":** Newmark 1916:58–59, 64.

222 **"in a manner":** "Rosaria Dias de Rheim vs. Felipe Rheim," 1858.09.11, Box 14, #455, DCC.

223 **This time:** "Rosaria Dias de Rheim vs. Felipe Rheim," 1860.03.09, Box 20, #700, DCC.

223 **Rheim suicide:** *Star* 1860.04.21.

223 **"Even though you love":** Koegel 1994 2:128.

CHAPTER 15

226 **"gentle horses:"** Lewis Granger to Abel Stearns, 1851,02.04, Stearns 1821–1935.

226 **Sonoreños attacked:** "People vs. Antonio Borcamonte and F. Perato," 1850.09.04, Box 1, #53, Criminal/Seaver; *Sacramento Transcript* 1850.09.26.

226 **they escaped:** *Alta California* 1850.11.30.

227 **"sons and assistants":** *Alta California* 1851.01.14.

227 **"by the hands of ":** "People vs. Francisco Lugo, et al.," 1851.01.28, Box 1, #84, Criminal/Seaver.

228 **"Old Man Lugo ":** Bell 1881:174–75.

228 **Agua Mansa:** Vickery 1977:18–32.

229 **"Chief of the Cahuilla":** Phillips 1975:47–48, 50–51, 164.

229 **"pretty as Arabians":** Brent 1926:10–11.

229 **thirty to forty dollars a head:** Cleland 1951:106.

230 **a very large retainer:** Bell 1881:196.

230 **"rapidly rolling":** Brent to Edward Brent, 1851.04.16, Brent 1850–1939.

231 **"Let's kill":** "People vs. Francisco Lugo, et al.," 1851.03.06, Box 1, #84, Criminal/Seaver.

231 **"The witness confessed":** Brent 1926:21.

232 **"It was an impossibility":** Brent 1926:17–18.

232 **married at Council Bluffs:** Hyde 2000:238.

233 **"I spoke to Mrs. Robinson":** "People vs. José María Lugo et al.," 1850.08.03, Box 1, #49, Criminal/Seaver.

233 **"*Qué escándalo es éste*":** "People vs. George W. D. Robinson," 1850.08.14, Box 1, #62, Criminal/Seaver.

233 **"His bearing":** Brent 1926:21.

234 **"race feeling":** Ibid.

234 **"They say that":** *Alta California* 1851.04.05.

234 **"These bands are composed":** *Alta California* 1851.06.17.

234 **"Our boys have been":** Brent 1926:23–26.

235 **Don Antonio had simply ignored:** Star 1851.06.14.

235 **"the sympathy":** Brent 1926:34–36.

236 **"If the men had descended":** Brent 1926:37.

236 **"armed to the teeth":** Warner 1876:35–36.

236 **"A great deal":** Brent 1926:50–51.

237 **"They had threatened":** Star 1851.05.26.

237 **"determined to take":** J. Bankhead Magruder to B. D. Wilson, 1851.05.25, Hanks 2000:246–47.

238 **"They made some inquiries":** *Star* 1851.06.14.

238 **"His offer was":** Lugo 1950:213.

238 **"in military order":** *Star* 1851.06.14.

240 **"as if doomed":** *Star* 1851.11.20.

241 **"They replied":** *Star* n.d., reprinted *New York Spectator* 1851.08.14.

241 **"The Indians first":** *Star* 1851.11.20.

242 **"I saw the bodies":** *Star* 1851.06.14.

242 **"resented the gloating":** Brent 1926:65.

242 **"The volunteers":** *Alta California* 1851.06.17.

242 **"He can return"**: Los Angeles County officials, proclamation, 1851.06.02, *Alta California* 1851.06.28.

242 **"a beautiful sword"**: *Los Angeles Herald* 1899.01.23.

243 **coroner's jury exonerated**: *Star* 1851.06.14.

243 **"lawless and reckless scum"**: *Alta California* 1851.06.17.

244 **"Behind these efforts"**: Brent 1926:65.

244 **"Other American settlers"**: Ibid.

244 **"the most ordinary"**: *Star* 1852.03.06.

244 **refused to settle down**: *Daily Evening Bulletin* 1874.09.12, 1874.11.26, 1877.02.05; *Alta California* 1876.06.14; *Los Angeles Herald* 1876.06.14.

CHAPTER 16

245 **"Let us remember"**: Wilson 1952:23–24.

246 **"Most of our"**: Keller 1859:346–47.

246 **vineyards**: *Alta California* 1851.08.07.

246 **"crowded from morn"**: Bell 1881:47.

247 **"Police Regulations"**: Los Angeles Common Council 1850–74, 1850.07.27, 1:53–55, 61–62 (hereafter cited as Common Council).

247 **"I wish"**: Charles Henry Brinley to Abel Stearns, 1852.08.30, Stearns 1821–1935.

247 **"Los Angeles had"**: Bell 1881:47–48.

247 **"Indians arrested"**: *Star* 1852.10.09.

248 **"unlawful"**: *Star* 1853.12.03; Guillow 1996:137–38.

248 **Juan Pelon, a Cahuilla**: "Causa Criminal Contra el Yndio Juan Pelon," 1850.01.10, ACR 6:874–91.

248 **"took an axe"**: *Star* 1852.12.03.

248 **"drunken frolic"**: "People vs. Juan Chapo," 1854.06.07, Box 3, #173, Criminal/Seaver.

248 **"On Monday"**: *Star* 1852.10.09.

249 **clubs and stones**: *Alta California* 1851.04.04; *Sacramento Daily Union* 1851.04.10.

249 *churchurki*: Reid 1968:46.

249 **"produced enormous excitement"**: Brent 1926:7; *Star* 1851.05.17.

249 **banned the playing of *peon***: Common Council 1851.05.07, 1:165.

250 **"How many of the Indians"**: *Star* 1851.11.01, reprinted *New York Tribune* 1851.12.20.

250 **Juan Antonio arrived**: *Star* 1851.11.08, reprinted *Alta California* 1851.11.13.

250 **"the big men"**: *Star* 1851.07.19, reprinted *Alta California* 1851.07.24.

250 **"Nothing could be"**: *Star* 1851.07.05, reprinted *Alta California* 1851.07.14.

251 **"is regarded by all"**: *San Diego Herald*, 1851.11.27; Hill 1927:139.

253 **"On Saturday morning"**: *San Diego Herald* 1852.01.17; *Alta California* 1851.12.03.

253 **"were in his favor"**: William Marshall, 1851.12.10, Roll 9, Binder 7, "Whaley House Papers."

253 **"The moment has arrived"**: Garra to Estudillo, 1851.11.21, Roll 9, Binder 6, "Whaley House Papers;" Evans 1966:343.

254 **"The tocsin of war"**: Thomas Whaley to Rachel Pye Whaley, 1851.12.02, Roll 9, Binder 5, "Whaley House Papers."

254 **"The native Californians"**: *San Diego Herald* 1851.11.27, reprinted *Alta California* 1851.12.04.

255 **imminent danger of attack**: Williams to Los Angeles County authorities, 1851.11.20, *Alta California* 1851.12.21.

255 **"urgent necessity"**: *Star* 1851.11.29, reprinted *Alta California* 1851.12.12.

255 **"It would strain"**: Bean to Governor John McDougal, 1851.11.30, *Alta California* 1851.12.12.

256 **"If we lose this war"**: Garra to Antonio, c1851.12.01, *Star* 1851.12.20; Phillips 1975:81.

256 **"I have a good strong"**: Garra to Duff Weaver, c1851.12.02, *Star* 1851.12.05.

256 **"he was ready"**: Antonio to Olvera, 1851.12.08, *Star* 1851.12.13; *Alta California* 1851.12.27.

256 **"I am your prisoner"**: *Alta California* 1852.01.06.

256 **"catch bad men"**: *Star* 1851.12.13, reprinted *Alta California* 1851.12.18.

257 **"These prisoners"**: *Alta California* 1851.12.14.

257 **makeshift gallows**: *Alta California* 1851.12.13.

257 **"It was not my intention"**: Statement of William Marshall, 1851.12.10, Roll 9, Binder 7, "Whaley House Papers;" Bibb 1976.

257 **"We shall soon number"**: Whaley to Anne E. Launay, 1851.12.17, Roll 9, Binder 5, "Whaley House Papers."

258 **"To have done less"**: O. M. Wozencraft to Luke Lea, n.d., Phillips 1975:102.

258 **"join with us"**: *Alta California* 1852.01.03.

258 **"owed no allegiance"**: *San Diego Herald* 1852.01.17.

259 **"His whole deportment"**: *San Diego Herald* 1852.01.17.

259 **"What's the use?"**: Smythe 1908:192.

259 **Treaty of Temecula**: Kappler 1928:1124–26.

259 **"They came to collect"**: *Star* 1852.01.24, reprinted *Alta California* 1852.01.28.

260 **"To place upon"**: *Star* 1852.03.13.

260 **"Where will you"**: Journal of the Third Session of the Legislature of the State of California (San Francisco: G. K. Fitch and V. E. Geiger, State Printers, 1852):602–4.

261 **"We have been"**: Cahuillas to Commissioner of Indian Affairs, 1856.05.15, Phillips 1975:135.

261 **"You must remain quiet"**: Beattie and Beattie 1939:236–37, 251.

261 **Cahuilla legend**: Bean 1965:5.

CHAPTER 17

263 **two hundred homicides**: Faragher 2014; an average of 20 homicides per year (1850-59) in a population of 7,341 (the mean of the population for Los Angeles County in 1850 and 1860) is a homicide rate of 272/100,000; cf. Ciudad Juarez, 240/100,000 in 2010, *Washington Post* 2012.08.20.

263 **"Who today"**: *Star* 1851.09.27, clipping Hayes 1877b 47:136.

264 **"We are told"**: *Star* 1851.06.27, clipping Hayes 1877b 43:92.

264 **"to watch over"**: Common Council 1851.07.12, 1:178–79.

265 **a total of eighty-three men**: *Star* 1851.07.12, clipping Hayes 1877b 49:18.

265 **"might be called"**: Bancroft 1882–90 36:486.

265 **"admirably calculated"**: *Star* 1851.07.12, clipping Hayes 1877b 49:18.

265 **"Our views"**: *Star* 1851.10.11.

265 **when two men**: *Star* 1852.07.24.

266 **"In accordance with"**: *Star* 1852.07.31.

267 **"Young men"**: Ibid.

267 **"everyone could see"**: *Los Angeles Herald* 1899.01.23.

267 **"Justice was the goal"**: *Star* 1852.08.07.

267 **"Rico! Rico! Rico!"**: *Star* 1852.12.04.

268 **"His death"**: *Star* 1852.11.13.

268 **"the deceased, Gen."**: *Star* 1852.11.20, clipping Hayes 1877b 43:121.

268 **"even applied torture"**: Coronel 1994:70–71.

269 **"a gang of desperadoes"**: *Star* 1852.11.27.

269 **"father one night"**: *Los Angeles Herald* 1899.01.23.

269 **"I belonged to"**: *Star* 1852.12.04, clipping Hayes 1877b 43:133.

269 **Harry Love**: *Star* 1852.06.19 [misidentified as "Lull"], 1852.06.26 [corrected to "Love"].

270 **"a people's court"**: Bell 1881:41–43.

270 **"launched into eternity"**: *Star* 1852.12.04, clipping Hayes 1877b 43:133.

270 **she implicated yet another**: Ibid.

271 **"I have just shot"**: Bell 1881:24–26.

271 **"Dr. Hope was determined"**: Coronel 1994:70–71.

271 **"The proof in the case"**: *Star* 1852.12.11, clipping Hayes 1877b 43:131.

272 **"bad women"**: Ibid.

272 **"We made a mistake"**: William A. Wallace, n.d., Moore 1886:549.

272 **"inhuman execution"**: *Star* 1853.10.08.

272 **"none of the Californians"**: Hayes 1877b 43:146.

272 **Hayes later learned**: *El Clamor Público* 1857.02.21.

273 **"Heavy clouds over-spread"**: Bell 1881:47.

273 **"white man's rendezvous"**: Packman 1944:75.

273 **"peculiar obstacles"**: *Star* 1853.08.06.

274 **a gang of Californios**: *Star* 1853.10.08.

274 **"one of the most exciting"**: Bell 1881:151–54.

275 **"choked off"**: *Star* 1853.10.08.

275 **"The bad feeling"**: Ibid.

276 **"Are we a people"**: Ibid.

276 **"Should we not"**: *Star* 1853.10.22.

276 ***"No me pude aclimatar"***: *El Vigia* [Ensenada, Baja California, Mexico] 2011.08.27, http://www.elvigia.net/noticia/manuel-clemente-rojo-primera-parte, accessed 2011.11.19.

CHAPTER 18

277 **"So as you see"**: Hayes to David Atchison, 1853.01.12, Hayes 1929:96–97.

277 **"to better order"**: Hayes to B. M. Hughes, 1853.01.24, Hayes 1929:92.

277 **"His health"**: Emily Hayes to "M. E.," 1852.08.26, Hayes 1875a:52.

277 **"I consider myself"**: Hayes to B. M. Hughes, 1853.01.24, Hayes 1929:93.

278 **"I do not think"**: Emily Hayes to sister, 1852.02.08, Hayes 1929:88.

278 *sankey*: Harper 1888:21.

278 **"Today we walked"**: Emily Hayes to "M. E.," 1852.03.01, Hayes 1875a:44–45.

278 **"Ah, no matter"**: Hayes to B. M. Hughes, 1853.01.24, Hayes 1929:91–92.

278 **"the sweetest thing"**: Hayes 1929:101.

278 **"The site of Los Angeles"**: Emily Hayes to sister, 1852.02.08, Hayes 1929:88.

279 **"They were to have"**: Emily Hayes to sister, 1852.07.11, Hayes 1929:90.

279 **"Gallows Hill"**: Bell 1881:100.

279 **"a clever, manly"**: Hayes to B. M. Hughes, 1853.01.24, Hayes 1929:92.

279 **February 22**: "Invitation to a dance at Don Abel Stearns' home," 1853.02.22, item 169, Del Valle Family 1818–1920.

280 **"the better class"**: Brent, "Life in California":13–17, Brent 1869–1940.

280 **"game little fellow"**: Bell 1881:89–91.

280 **"sallied out alone"**: *Star* 1853.02.26.

281 **"Men have become"**: Ibid.

281 **"Always settle them cases"**: Sparks 1870:148.

281 **"It is my habit"**: Brent, "Life in California":13–17, Brent 1869–1940.

281 **"He was the gamest"**: *Los Angeles Herald* 1900.02.25.

282 **"essentially selfish"**: Burnett 1880:90–93.

282 **"Colt's Army and Navy Pistols"**: *Star* 1852.07.24.

282 **"The patrons"**: Bell 1881:22–23.

283 **prohibiting the carriage or discharge**: Common Council 1:79, 88, 90, 118–19, 126.

283 **restrictions on firearms**: Winkler 2011:167.

283 **"the revolver seems"**: Hayes 1877b 43:5.

283 **accusing Cornwall**: *Star* 1852.08.28.

284 **"Clear the way"**: *Alta California* 1852.09.05.

284 **indicted Cornwall**: "People vs. William Cornwall," 1852.12.08, Box 1, no case #, Criminal/Seaver.

284 **"It was a genuine"**: *Alta California* 1852.08.10.

284 **"an out-and-out"**: Bell 1881:105.

285 **"one of us must die"**: *Star* 1854.01.14.

285 **"We got to drinking"**: "People vs. Thomas Smith and Sterling H. Lester," 1854.04.30, Box 2, #168, Criminal/Seaver.

286 **"Each table with its"**: Bell 1881:28.

289 **overpowered the jailer**: *Star* 1854.07.08.

289 **"better order"**: Hayes to B. M. Hughes, 1853.01.24, Hayes 1929:92.

289 **fourteen homicides**: Faragher 2014.

289 **"He was brave"**: *Star* 1853.12.10.

290 **The trial of Ygnacio Herrera**: "People vs. Ygnacio Herrera," Box 2, #149, Criminal/Seaver; *Sacramento Daily Union* 1853.12.29.

290 **"following the will-o'-the-wisp"**: Bell 1881:158–59.

291 **"We surrounded"**: Brent, "Life in California":13–17, Brent 1869–1940.

291 **"they each proceeded"**: *Star* 1854.01.21; Bell 1881:159–60.

291 **"*vivo o muerto*"**: *Star* 1854.01.21.

291 **"I remonstrated"**: Hayes 1929:101.

291 **"The death of these"**: *Star* 1854.01.28, reprinted *Alta California* 1854.02.05.

292 **attempting to sell some of the loot**: *Star* 1854.02.11.

292 **"To me it has fallen"**: *Star* 1854.02.11.

292 **thirty-ninth birthday**: Hayes 1929:104.

CHAPTER 19

295 **"This place will"**: *Southern Californian* 1854.10.26.

295 **"Americans profess":** *Southern Californian* 1854.08.31.

295 **homicides:** Faragher 2014.

296 **"appalled at the frequent":** *Star* 1854.10.19.

296 **"What a selfish creature":** *Star* 1855.11.24.

296 **"What have you done":** Hayes 1877b 43:435.

297 **"seems very indifferent":** Woods diary, 1854.11.12, Bynum 1941:70–71.

297 **"This is a rough country":** Woods diary, 1854.11.12, Bynum 1941:70.

297 **"Our roads are safe":** *Star* 1854.11.02.

297 **"City of Demons":** Woods diary, 1854.11.29, Bynum 1941:74–76

297 **John Ozias Wheeler:** Newmark 1914:38; Guinn and Barrows 1889:694.

297 **"We cannot but":** *Southern Californian* 1854.11.16.

298 **"Is it not incumbent":** *Southern Californian* 1854.10.19.

298 **"We do not agree":** *Star* 1854.11.02, clipping Hayes 1877b 43:416, with claim of authorship.

298 **"We hold that *life*":** *Star* 1854.11.16, clipping Hayes 1877b 47:165, with claim of authorship.

298 **"Lynch law will":** *Star* 1854.10.05.

299 **"It is but":** *Star* 1854.10.19.

299 **"Our only hope":** *Star* 1854.11.30.

299 **"to no longer wait":** *Southern Californian* 1854.10.19.

299 **"We are at a terrible":** *Southern Californian* 1854.11.23.

301 **"done more toward":** *Star* 1854.12.07.

301 **"the desired effect":** *Southern Californian* 1854.12.21.

301 **"Peace and quietness":** *Southern Californian* c1854.12.28, transcription Hayes 1877b 43:444.

301 **King and Johnson clans:** Brackett 1920:71–73; Mahar 1989.

301 **"an old grudge":** *Southern Californian* 1855.01.11.

302 **"I believed":** "People vs. Josiah Hart," 1854.06.04, Box 2, #180, Criminal/ Seaver.

302 **"he did not consider":** *Star* 1855.01.11.

303 **"Boys, he has":** *Southern Californian* 1855.01.11; *Star* 1855.01.18; King 1935:14.

303 **grand jury declined:** *Star* 1855.02.08.

303 **"We had hoped":** *Southern Californian* 1855.01.11.

303 **"Poor woman":** Woods diary, 1855.01.08, Bynum 1941:80.

304 **"Land is a natural":** *Star* 1855.02.01.

304 **"chained up":** Woods diary, 1854.12.21, Bynum 1941:78–79; *Southern Californian* 1854.10.26

304 **"Brown was asleep":** Woods diary, 1855.01.07, Bynum 1941:80.

304 **stay of execution:** *Southern Californian* 1855.01.04, 1855.01.*11; Star* 1855.01.11.

305 **delayed in transit:** Hayes 1929:108.

305 **"inflamed the native":** Warner 1876:38.

305 **"raised a public clamor":** Bell 1930:242.

305 **Francisco P. Ramírez:** Gray 2012.

305 **Pancho:** Warner 1876:46.

306 **"committed crimes":** *Star* 1855.01.11.

306 **"When you start":** Ibid.

306 **"ready to take":** *Southern Californian* 1855.01.11.

307 **"unequivocally proclaimed":** *Southern Californian* 1855.01.12, reprinted *Alta California* 1855.01.16.

308 **call for volunteers:** *Star* 1855.01.18.

308 **"Extensive and determined":** *Southern Californian* 1855.01.12, reprinted *Alta California* 1855.01.16.

308 **"Alvitre was just":** *Star* 1855.01.18.

309 **"*Arriba*":** Warner 1876:28–29.

309 **"half-dead":** Bancroft 188–90 36:496.

309 **"In a moment":** *Star* 1855.01.18.

309 **"Señores":** Ibid.

310 **"*Ahorcar*":** *New York Tribune* 1855.02.08.

310 **"Words fail":** Warner 1876:28–29.

311 **"He evinced":** *Southern Californian* 1855.01.18.

311 **"but if I did":** *Star* 1855.01.18.

311 **"lot of Greasers":** Newmark 1916:140.

311 *cañada de los muertos*: Guinn 1897:146.

311 **"Thus ended":** *Star* 1855.01.18.

311 **"The omnipotence":** *Southern Californian* 1855.01.18.

311 **"wished to see":** *Star* 1855.01.18.

312 **"No man":** "People vs. Lee," 5 Cal. 353 (1855); *Star* 1855.07.21.

312 **"Lee has returned":** *Star* 1855.12.01; Peterson 1956:108–19.

CHAPTER 20

315 **"Within four or five":** *Star* 1855.09.08.

315 **"plain country fare":** Truman 1874a:168.

316 **"large organized band":** *Alta California* 1855.05.28.

316 **"say their prayers":** Ibid.

317 **issued warrants:** Hayes 1877b 43:464–65.

317 **"We the undersigned":** Citizens to Judge Hayes, 1855.05.16, Hayes 1877b 43:464–65.

317 **declined to prosecute:** Spitzzeri 2005a:91.

317 **a different posse:** *Southern Californian* 1855.05.30, clipping Hayes 1877b 43:470; *Star* 1855.06.02.

317 **"We have":** *Southern Californian* 1855.05.23, clipping Hayes 1877b 43:468.

318 **"So the work goes":** *Southern Californian* 1855.05.30, clipping Hayes 1877b 43:468, 470.

318 **"we wish them":** *Star* 1855.05.26.

318 **"lynch law reigns":** *Star* 1855.02.08.

318 **"Law without arms":** *Star* 1855.04.07.

318 **"we must satisfy":** *El Clamor Público* 1856.05.31.

318 **"The editor":** *Alta California* 1855.02.02.

319 **"Our country":** *Star* 1855.02.22.

319 **"devoted exclusively":** *Star* 1855.05.12.

320 **thirty-three murders:** *Sacramento Daily Union* 1855.12.31.

320 **shootout on the Plaza:** *Star* 1855.03.10.

320 **"all persons who":** California Legislature 1855:217.

320 **"A portion of the people":** *Southern Californian* 1855.07.04.

321 **"widens the barriers":** *El Clamor Público* 1855.07.24.

321 **"Though rather distant":** *Daily Evening Bulletin* 1856.06.11.

321 **"*Bien hecho*":** *El Clamor Público* 1856.05.31.

322 **"Cruz was looked upon":** *Star* 1856.07.19.

322 **"We are all linked":** *El Clamor Público* 1856.07.19.

322 **"Por favor":** *El Clamor Público* 1856.07.26.

323 **"Give it to me":** *Star* 1856.07.26.

323 **"sorry for having":** *Star* 1856.07.26.

324 **"He who commits":** Wallace diary, 1855.07.19, Wallace 1854–58.

324 **"making other bellicose:"** *El Clamor Público* 1856.07.26.

325 **"evincing a deep emotion":** Hayes 1877b 43:584–86.

325 **"the Judge did justice":** Ibid.

325 **"The population of the city":** *El Clamor Público* 1856.07.26.

325 **"destroy all the Americans":** William G. Dryden, deposition, 1856.08.04, Hayes 1877b 43:600.

325 **"might be fired on":** Hayes 1877b 43:584–86.

326 **"American graveyard":** *Star* 1856.07.19.

326 **"they should consider":** *El Clamor Público* 1856.08.02.

326 **"In this country":** "People vs. Fernando Carriaga," 1856.07.24, Box 4, #271, Criminal/Seaver.

327 **"Vámonos":** Ibid.

327 **"Quien vive":** Ibid.

327 **"The truth is":** Hayes 1877b 43:584–86.

328 **"disorderly or suspicious":** *Star* 1856.07.26.

328 **"agreeing to their own":** *El Clamor Público* 1856.08.16.

328 **Handlin:** *Star* 1856.08.02; *El Clamor Público* 1856.08.02.

329 **"We will not take":** *Star* 1856.07.26.

329 **"Companies are now":** *Daily Evening Bulletin* 1856.07.29.

329 **"Being myself":** Hayes 1877b 43:584–86.

329 **"without deliberation":** Hayes 1877b 43:620.

329 **"I passed the next day":** Hayes 1877b 43:584–86.

330 **"the first prosecution":** Hayes 1877b 43:605–6.

330 **"it appearing to me":** "People vs. Fernando Carriaga," 1856.07.24, Box 4, #271, Criminal/Seaver.

331 **"further remark":** Hayes 1877b 43:605–06.

331 **"What was her":** *El Clamor Público* 1856.08.23.

332 **"an Indian woman":** María Candelaria Pollorena de Lazos vs. Casimino Lazos, 1855.03.12, Box 6, #184, DCC.

332 **"false in every detail":** *El Clamor Público* 1856.08.23.

332 **declining to indict:** *Star* 1856.08.23.

333 **"Everyone knows":** *El Clamor Público* 1856.07.26.

333 **"Let us work":** *El Clamor Público* 1856.08.16.

333 **"Ruiz is in his":** *El Clamor Público* 1856.08.23; claim of authorship, Hayes 1877b 43:586.

CHAPTER 21

337 **Barton ranch:** "Tract of land belonging to J. Barton," 1854.12.17, SR Box 26 (26).01 and "Plat of Los Nietos Township," 1862, SR Map 0250.01B, Los Angeles City and County 1845–c1910; Cole 1981:28.

337 **"large and flourishing":** *California Farmer* 1856.11.28.

337 **English walnuts:** *Los Angeles Herald* 1898.01.02.

337 **María del Espiritu Santo:** Baptism record, SJC: 04335, ECPP 2006.

337 **acknowledged as his offspring:** Barton, codicil, 1854.08.24, "Legal documents re estate of Sheriff James Barton," "Documents for the History of Nineteenth-Century Los Angeles," 1846–1908.

338 **"He was an uncouth":** Bell 1930:72-73.

338 **"some alleged ill treatment":** Bell 1881:384.

338 *medio indio:* Star 1857.02.07.

338 **Andrés Fuentes:** Bell 1881:390.

338 **siblings:** Baptism records for parents SJC: 02953 and 03279, ECPP 2006.

339 **"Here comes another":** El Clamor Público 1856.10.04.

340 **"whose vile 'Greaser' laws":** El Clamor Público 1856.11.01.

340 **"to produce a rift":** Star 1856.11.15.

340 **"What name will":** El Clamor Público 1856.11.15.

340 **"an ordinary appearing":** San Jose Evening News 1917.10.27.

340 **"a dark complexioned":** Bell 1881:382.

340 **convicted and sentenced:** Southern Californian 1855.04.18.

341 **"whenever he got out":** Coronel 1994:72.

341 **"on condition":** Bell 1881:384.

341 **missed him:** Coronel 1994:72–73.

341 **set out for home:** Daily Evening Bulletin 1857.02.03.

342 **"I looked upon myself":** Meadows 1963:156–57.

342 **"they would kill":** Testimony of Henry Charles, "People vs. Luciano Tapia," 1857.12.14, Box 5, #337, Criminal/Seaver.

342 **"François":** Coronel 1994:72.

343 **set off at a furious pace:** Bell 1930:72–74.

343 **"seized with terror":** Newmark 1916:205.

343 **"down upon the Americans ":** Forster to Cave Johnson Couts, 1857.01.27, CT 732, Couts 1831–1951.

343 **"raised the standard":** Bell 1881:384.

343 **"threatened the extermination":** Bancroft 1882–90 36:498.

343 **"quasi-revolutionary":** Griswold del Castillo 1979:109.

343 **"the Sonoreans and Mexicans":** Daily Evening Bulletin 1857.02.03.

344 **"The robbers use":** Forster to Cave Johnson Couts, 1857.01.27, CT 732, Couts 1831–1951.

344 **"The party made":** Star 1857.01.31.

345 **staged this ambush:** Coronel 1994:72–73.

345 **"There is Juan Flores":** Alta California 1857.02.01; Star 1857.01.31.

345 **"We have got":** Ibid.

345 **Little stopped firing:** Alta California 1857.02.15; Wallace identified as correspondent, Wallace 1854–58.

345 **"Barton fought":** Ibid.

345 **"Now kill me":** Ibid.

346 **"Thus ended":** Bell 1881:386.

346 **the bodies:** Star 1857.01.31, El Clamor Público 1857.01.31.

346 **"I am sadly afraid":** John Forster to Cave Johnson Couts, 1857.01.27, CT 732, Couts 1831–1951.

346 **"His party returned":** Wallace diary, 1857.01.28, Wallace 1854–58.

347 **"We poor Americans":** Daily Evening Bulletin 1857.02.03.

347 **"There is a call":** Alta California 1857.02.01.

347 "Parents, brothers and sisters": *Star* 1857.01.31.

348 Antonio María Varela: *Sacramento Daily Union* 1857.02.02, identified as "Antonio María Bariles."

348 "could not stand": Varela, petition, 1854.11.28, Brown-Coronel 2011:65.

348 "We are bound": *El Clamor Público* 1857.01.31.

349 "In the matter": *Star* 1857.01.31.

349 not once but twice: q.v. "Barton," federal manuscript census, Los Angeles California, 1860 and 1870.

349 registered to vote: California Voter Registers, 1866–98, http://www.ancestry.com.

349 "This is to show": "In the Matter of the Estate of José Santiago Barton, Deceased," Tuttle and Carpenter 1906:538; *Los Angeles Herald* 1878.02.20.

349 a bountiful property: Guinn 1907f 2:1117; *Pacific Rural Press* 1877.12.08; *Los Angeles Herald* 1879.01.12.

CHAPTER 22

351 "When the word came": *Los Angeles Herald* 1899.04.24

352 "most useful man": Warner 1876:42.

353 "came forward:" *El Clamor Público* 1857.03.21.

353 "with a brutality": *El Clamor Público* 1857.02.14.

353 "a number of arrests": *Star* 1857.01.31.

353 "threw themselves": *El Clamor Público* 1857.01.31.

353 "all in favor": *Alta California* 1857.02.15.

353 "Death": *El Clamor Público* 1857.03.21.

354 "an old offender": *Star* 1857.02.07.

354 "Nothing less": *El Clamor Público* 1857.04.04.

354 "We will not forget": *El Clamor Público* 1857.02.07.

355 "Neither did I": White 1956:85–86, 89; also see Barrows 1896b.

355 "I had to adjourn": *Alta California* 1857.02.15.

355 torchlight meeting: *Star* 1857.01.31.

356 "There was really": *Alta California* 1857.02.15.

356 "He entered each house": Ibid.

356 "were there simply": *El Clamor Público* 1857.04.04.

356 "We hope": *El Clamor Público* 1857.01.31.

357 "I want that boy": White 1956:89.

357 fifty-one lanceros: *Star* 1857.02.07.

357 hideout: John Forster to John S. Griffin, 1857.01.30, Box 29, Stearns 1821-1935.

360 "We galloped": "People vs. Luciano Tapia," 1857.12.14, Box 5, #337, Criminal/Seaver.

360 Accounts differ: *Star* 1857.02.07; *El Clamor Público* 1857.02.07; *Alta California* 1857.02.15.

360 "The town is in": *Alta California* 1857.02.15.

361 Precitos Canyon: Arellano 2009.

361 two men guarding the trail: *Star* 1857.02.07.

361 "He rests quietly": *El Clamor Público* 1857.02.07.

362 "He has run": *Alta California* 1857.02.15.

362 summary justice: *Star* 1857.02.07; *El Clamor Público* 1857.02.21, 1857.03.21.

362 **"We, the thieves"**: *Star* 1857.02.14.

363 **"to prove their innocence"**: *Alta California* 1857.02.*15; Star* 1857.02.14.

363 **"honor bound"**: *Star* 1857.02.14.

363 **"threats of violence"**: *El Clamor Público* 1857.02.07.

363 **killed shopkeeper George Pflugardt**: *Alta California* 1857.02.15.

363 **"very respectably connected"**: Coronel 1994:204.

364 **"Let us not"**: *El Clamor Público* 1857.02.14.

364 **"patted on the shoulder"**: *Star* 1857.02.14.

364 **"was the fatal result"**: *Daily Evening Bulletin* 1857.03.02.

364 **"Old Scott rose"**: *Alta California* c1857.02.25, clipping Wallace 1854–58.

365 **"It was of course"**: *El Clamor Público* 1857.02.21.

365 **"before being released"**: *El Clamor Público* 1857.04.04.

365 **"It was generally"**: *Daily Evening Bulletin* 1857.03.02.

365 **"the Americans were for"**: *Alta California* c1857.02.25, clipping Wallace 1854–58.

365 **"shocked and horrified"**: *El Clamor Público* 1857.02.21.

366 **"All who are in favor"**: *Alta California* c1857.02.25, clipping Wallace 1854–58.

366 **"There was nothing"**: *Star* 1857.02.21.

367 **"He was hung"**: *Alta California* c1857.02.25, clipping Wallace 1854–58.

367 **"Those who seek"**: *El Clamor Público* 1857.02.21.

367 **"inasmuch as they"**: *Alta California* 1857.12.26.

368 **"It was a happy day"**: *El Clamor Público* 1858.02.20.

368 **"Considerable uneasiness"**: *Alta California* 1858.03.27.

368 **"There is here"**: *Daily Evening Bulletin* 1858.02.26.

369 **"It will be"**: *Daily Evening Bulletin* 1858.08.24.

369 **"I hope you"**: Hayes diary, 1857.09.17, Hayes 1929:166–67.

370 **"All my life"**: *Sacramento Daily Union* 1858.07.28.

371 **"He rather broke down"**: *Daily Evening Bulletin* 1858.12.06.

371 **"accidentally hung"**: Spitzzeri 2005a:96-97.

372 **"a committee acting"**: *Star* 1858.12.04.

372 **"out of the way"**: *Daily Evening Bulletin* 1858.12.06.

CHAPTER 23

373 **"We can not find"**: *El Clamor Público* 1858.12.04.

373 **"News of the barbaric"**: *El Clamor Público* 1858.12.18.

373 **"a young man"**: *Daily Evening Bulletin* 1858.06.28.

373 **"a great wrong"**: *Daily Evening Bulletin* 1858.12.11.

374 **"It is indeed awful"**: *Daily Evening Bulletin* 1858.06.28.

374 **"would have continued"**: *Daily Evening Bulletin* 1859.01.26.

374 **"We have had quiet"**: *Daily Evening Bulletin* 1858.12.11.

374 **by the numbers**: Faragher 2014; the mean annual homicide rate dropped from 390/100,000 (1850–54) to 109 (1858–62).

375 **"There is the same"**: *Star* 1858.04.17.

375 **"This is an awful "**: Smith to Joseph F. Smith, 1857.03.19, Compton 1997:162.

375 **"There has been"**: *Daily Evening Bulletin* 1859.10.27.

375 **thirty felony indictments**: *Southern Vineyard* 1859.12.22.

375 **"foragers at the public"**: Bell 1930:72.

376 **"somewhat undersized"**: Robinson 1979:164.

377 **"whom I would like"**: Bernard Reid to John C. Reid, 1850.05.30, Reid 1983:198.

377 **"colonel"**: *Sacramento Transcript* 1850.08.16.

377 **younger brothers**: *Alta California* 1851.01.10, 1851.09.21, 1851.09.25, 1853.06.20; *Panama Herald* 1853.08.12, http://www.sfgenealogy.com/californiabound/cb187.htm.

377 **"big guns"**: *Weekly San Joaquin Republican* 1855.12.08.

377 **"a damn Know Nothing"**: *Alta California* 1854.11.09.

378 **"drove him almost"**: *Los Angeles Herald* 1879.11.27.

378 **"new fields of glory"**: *Star* 1855.12.15.

378 **"Look here"**: Harrison 1953:50.

378 **"the spirit of conquest"**: Bell 1881:212.

378 **"a Whig of olden time"**: *Star* 1856.09.20.

379 **"a fighter from way back"**: Bell 1930:12.

379 **"The greater portion"**: *Alta California* 1858.09.13.

379 **"My daughter was"**: Bell 1930:102–03.

379 **"promenading the parlor"**: *Star* 1858.09.18.

380 **"I was sitting"**: Bell 1930:102–03.

380 **"Dorsey, I have"**: *Star* 1858.09.11; *Alta California* 1858.09.13.

380 **"It had to be"**: Brackett 1920:84-85.

381 **"the citizen corporal"**: *Southern Vineyard* 1859.06.10.

381 **"sneaked into a country"**: *Southern Vineyard* 1859.08.10.

381 **"so notoriously corrupt"**: *Star* 1859.07.30.

382 **"I am a Republican"**: *Star* 1895.07.09.

382 **"It is unbelievable"**: *El Clamor Público* 1859.12.24.

382 **formal challenge**: *Star* 1859.07.09.

382 **"Dueling, shooting "**: *Star* 1859.09.24.

383 **"It places the district"**: *Star* 1860.04.14.

383 **"Here is the maiden"**: Barrows 1893b:56.

384 **"Whatever disaster"**: *Star* 1860.11.10.

384 **"We are on the highway"**: *Star* 1861.01.05.

384 **"southern from nature"**: Hayes to Emma Thompson, 1861.02.14, Hayes 1929:256.

384 **"sick at heart"**: Hayes to Edward M. Samuel, 1861.02.11, Hayes 1929:253.

385 **"This grim catastrophe"**: Benjamin 1956 2:101.

385 **"They would be put"**: Ridley to General William C. Kibbe, 1861.03.09, Armistead 2003.

385 **"To all of them"**: *Los Angeles Herald* 1880.10.13.

385 **"go South"**: *Los Angeles Herald* 1884.11.27.

386 **"Chino" Varela**: Smith 1977:121, 123; Brown-Coronel 2011:75; Bancroft 1882–90 24:204n.

386 **"The deceased was"**: *Star* 1860.09.08.

386 **"more danger of disaffection"**: Sumner to Lieutenant Colonel E. D. Thompson, 1861.04.30, United States War Department 1880–1901 I 50/1:474 (hereafter cited as OR).

386 **"There are people here"**: Hancock to Major W. W. Mackall, 1861.05.04, OR I 50/1:477–78.

387 **"We were ready"**: Cooney 1924:59–60.
387 **"There need be"**: Hancock to Maj. W. W. Mackall, 1861.05.14, OR I 50/1:486.
387 **"Secessionists are"**: Dimmick to General E. V. Sumner, 1861.08.08, OR I 50/1:559.
387 **"Until very lately"**: *Daily Evening Bulletin* 1861.09.04.

CHAPTER 24
389 **plagues of biblical proportion**: Rowland 1999:153–55.
389 **"As misfortunes come"**: *Alta California* 1863.05.29.
390 **"Gardens or orchards"**: *Star* 1863.06.06.
390 **"Coronel pointed out"**: Hayes to George A. Pendleton, 1863.01.28, Hayes 1929:284.
390 **"the only constitutional"**: Barrows to Col. J. H. Carleton, 1862.04.09, OR I 50/1:993–94.
390 **"In what country"**: Barrows to General George Wright, 1862.04.10, OR I 50/1:996–98.
391 **"Pistols were flourished"**: *Los Angeles Herald* 1879.11.27.
391 **"abused and menaced"**: *Star* 1862.09.13.
391 **"Secesh has carried"**: *Daily Evening Bulletin* 1862.09.09.
391 **"Arrest a score"**: *Daily Evening Bulletin* 1862.10.11.
392 **"no demonstration"**: *Alta California* 1863.07.12.
392 **"a very feverish"**: James F. Curtis to R. C. Drum, 1863.07.12, OR I 50/2:521.
393 **"should be maintained"**: Hayes announcement of candidacy, 1863.10.21, Robinson 1977:44.
393 **"Hayes is no"**: Griffin to Wilson, 1863.07.29, Box 9, Wilson 1836–1941.
393 **"not secretly"**: *Daily Evening Bulletin* 1861.09.04.
393 **"it is difficult"**: Hayes diary, 1862.01.10, Hayes 1929:261–62.
394 **a dramatic increase in homicides**: Faragher 2014.
394 **"The people decided"**: *Star* 1861.05.04.
394 **"I touched her"**: Lenz 1954:195.
395 **"Bring him out"**: *Star* 1861.20.19.
395 **"showered him"**: "The Killing of Mrs. Leck," Box 2, folder 7, Mesmer 1860–1914.
396 **"Verily the soul"**: *News* 1861.10.18.
396 **"We have ever been"**: *Star* 1861.10.19.
396 **"It is supposed"**: *Star* 1862.03.29.
397 **"You do not"**: "People vs. John Buckley," 1863.07.25, Box 3, Part C, #701, Los Angeles Criminal Cases, 1861–79, Huntington Library (hereafter Criminal/Huntington).
397 **"I understand you are"**: Graves 1927:410
398 **"Lawyers do abound"**: *Alta California* 1863.11.23.
398 **"aid and protection"**: Hayes to Col. James F. Curtis, 1863.11.20, "People vs. Pablo Valdenegro," 1863.11.14, Box 2, #683, Criminal/Huntington.
398 **"old timers"**: "Cold Blooded Slaying," Box 2 Folder 7, Mesmer 1860–1914.
398 **"emphatically opposed"**: *Star* 1863.11.28.
399 **"For the last year"**: *Alta California* 1863.11.24.
399 **"It occurred to me"**: *Star* 1863.12.19.
399 **"I have killed"**: Bancroft 1887 1:509–11.

400 **indictment:** "People vs. Charles Wilkins," 1863.12.16, Box 2, #667, Criminal/Huntington.
400 **"In reply to your":** R. C. Drum to King, 1863.12.16, OR I 50/2:699.
401 **"The people were":** Barrows 1894c:42–44.
401 **"In looking back":** *Los Angeles Times* 1887.05.12.
401 **"It cleared the atmosphere":** Barrows 1894c:42–44.

CHAPTER 25
403 **"Married":** *Star* 1858.04.24.
404 **"We miss thee":** "We Miss Thee at Hom*e,*" *Star* 1857.09.12.
404 **"The long, low vale":** "Retrospect (in Los Angeles)," Coolbrith 1895:24.
405 **"She might easily":** Stoddard 1889:313.
405 **Carsley:** "The Ahnentafel of Anthony Michael D'Agostino," http://toncxjo .tripod.com/ahnentafel.html.
406 **"Oh, balm, and dew":** "Fragments from an Unfinished Poem," Wentworth 1867:343.
406 **"I want to hear":** "Josephine Donna Carsley vs. Robert Carsley," 1861.12.10, Box 24, #853, DCC.
408 **intimate violence:** 91 (40%) of 228 Los Angeles divorce cases included accusations of violence against at least one of the spouses, DCC.
408 **"wholly unfit":** "Thomas C. Swigart vs. Serena Swigart," 1870.05.18, Box 55, #1642, DCC.
408 **"Swigart & Huber":** *Los Angeles Herald* 1874.07.31, 1876.05.03.
410 **"cruel and inhuman":** "Mary Ellen Culberson vs. William C. Culberson," 1872.05.25, Box 74, #1994, DCC.
410 **"only the exercise":** "Bridget Carmona vs. Joseph G. Carmona," 1874.04.29, Box 94, #2464, DCC.
410 **"a woman of the most":** "María Elizalde de Rubio vs. Andrés Rubio," 1871.06.23, Box 65, #1830, DCC.
411 **"He called me":** "Augustina Varela de Emerson vs. Hiram Emerson," 1872.07.01, Box 74, #2011, DCC.
411 **Following the wedding:** *San Francisco Morning Call* 1873.12.07.
411 **"keep up his passions":** "William M. Stoddard vs. Mary A. [Neal] Stoddard," 1874.03.28, Box 92, #2398, DCC.
413 **granted her petition:** "San Francisco Divorces," http://www.sfgenealogy .com/sf/sfdiv75.htm.
413 **"Yes mother":** "Rebecca M. Palmer vs. Nathan A. Palmer," 1873.02.18, Box 81, #2156, DCC.
415 **"He told me":** "Eleanor Jane Johnson vs. William Johnson," 1871.09.22, Box 66, #1865, DCC.
415 **justice court:** Los Angeles County 1863–1874 (Still/Gray) 1869.08.30, 1870.01.10,
416 **"Stand back":** "William Johnson vs. Eleanor Jane Johnson," 1873.11.15, Box 88. #2328, DCC.
417 **married an enterprising rancher:** Vandor 1919 1:937–38.
417 **"He threatened":** "Malvina [sic] Prater vs. John B. Prater," 1872.10.17, Box 77, #2064, DCC; "People vs. J. B. Prater," Box 10, #1211, Criminal/Huntington; *Daily Evening Bulletin* 1873.02.20.

418 **"flood of tears"**: Los Angeles County 1863–74 "Justice of the Peace Minute Books" (Gray) 1870.10.13 (hereafter cited as JP).

CHAPTER 26

419 **"It is generally"**: Charles Robinson Johnson to Abel Stearns, 1862.11.28, Stearns 1821–1935.

420 **"the most perfect"**: Bell 1881:302.

421 **"John Rains was"**: Bell 1881:237.

421 **"look of love"**: Jonathan R. Scott, 1862, Black 1975:67.

421 **"a rancho girl"**: Bell 1930:257.

421 **"All the young men"**: Wallace diary, 1857.01.12, Wallace 1854–58.

422 **"If you don't"**: Black 1975:63–64.

423 **Doña Merced's assets**: Black 1975:281–84.

424 **"a striking-looking fellow"**: Marryat 1855:46.

424 **"a dashing Hotspur"**: Bell 1881:115.

424 **"high words"**: Hayes to Couts, 1862.11.26, CT 1015, Couts 1831–1951.

425 **"habitually or frequently"**: Hayes to Couts, 1862.12.10, CT 1020, Couts 1831–1951.

425 **"I am as innocent"**: José Ramón Carrillo to Julio María Carrillo, 1864.05.30, Black 1975:100–1.

425 **"the people of the State"**: *Star* 1863.04.18.

425 **"extra-judicial"**: Hayes to Couts, 1865.07.06, CT 1036, Couts 1831–1951.

425 **"Some *enemies*"**: Hayes to Couts, 1862.12.08, CT 1019, Couts 1831–1951.

426 **"deceived by said Rains"**: Black 1975:83.

427 **"I did not abandon"**: José Ramón Carrillo to Julio María Carrillo, 1864.05.30, Black 1975:100–101.

427 **"band of cutthroats"**: *News* 1863.12.02.

427 **"all the charms"**: Browne 1869:41–42.

428 **"When I learned"**: José Ramón Carrillo to Julio María Carrillo, 1864.05.30, Black 1975:100–101; *Alta California* 1864.05.30.

428 **"by fraud"**: *Star* 1864.03.05.

428 **"published by instigation"**: *Star* 1864.03.12.

429 **"He seemed to be"**: Bell 1930:115.

429 **"He does not do"**: José Ramón Carrillo to Julio Carrillo, 1864.05.30, Black 1975:100–101.

429 **"Well, Uncle Bill"**: Bell 1930:115–16.

429 **"Don't let him fall"**: Black 1975:101.

430 **"Don't bother"**: Bell 1930:116.

430 **"You have little idea"**: Hayes to John Brown, 1864.05.30, Beattie and Beattie 1939:164.

431 **"I desire"**: Julio María Carrillo, *Sonoma Democrat* 1864.06.11, clipping Hayes 1877b 50/2:249.

431 **"We are sure"**: María Merced Williams de Rains to Benjamin Hayes, 1864.05.27, Black 1975:112.

431 **"There were a good"**: Bell 1930:102–4.

432 **"I really believe"**: Henry Wilkes to Benjamin Hayes, 1864.06.20, Black 1975:288.

432 **"If I was justified"**: Hayes to Colonel J. F. Curtis, 1864.05.27, Black 1975:285–86.

432 **"It appears"**: Walker 1971:70.

433 **"Rarely has a woman"**: Hayes to María Merced Williams de Rains, 1864.06.06, Beattie and Beattie 1939:161.

434 **"Merced's only alternative"**: Black 1975:118.

434 **"a woman of impulsive"**: Black 1975:93.

434 **"If a receiver"**: Hayes to C. B. Younger, 1865.05.23, Black 1975:138.

434 **"further violence"**: Hayes to P. Monday, 1865.05.23, Black 1975:149.

434 **"Jack King is"**: Hayes to Couts, 1865.07.06, CT 1036, Couts 1831–1951.

435 **"Your time has come"**: *Alta California* 1865.07.15.

436 **"I hardly think"**: Hayes to Couts, 1865.07.06, CT 1036, Couts 1831–1951.

437 **"one of the most"**: *Daily Evening Bulletin* n.d., reprinted *Sacramento Daily Union* 1866.02.01.

437 **"This was a quick"**: Hayes to Couts, 1865.07.06, CT 1036, Couts 1831–1951.

CHAPTER 27

440 **"Call us traitors"**: *News* 1865.11.24.

440 **"six million"**: *News* 1866.12.25.

440 **an adventure worthy:** Gresham 1919:78–91; Money 1921:287–97; Harrison 1953:75–85.

441 **"My reception"**: Bell 1930:77-79.

442 **many street fights:** JP (Shore) 1867.02.20, 1868.06.05, 1868.09.08, 1868.09.17.

442 **"I never did"**: Harrison 1953:171–72.

442 **acquitted of murder:** "People vs. Horace Bell," 1867.03.26, Box 4, #793, Criminal/Huntington; *Star* 1868.08.08.

442 **"I want this community"**: *Los Angeles Herald* 1874.09.11.

443 **successfully defended their claims:** Clay and Troesken 2005:65–66.

443 **"A great many ranches"**: *New York Times* 1868.04.05.

443 **"Not a day passes"**: *Star* 1868.12.19.

443 **"Real estate"**: *Alta California* 1868.12.03.

444 **substantial buildings with metropolitan pretensions:** *Daily Evening Bulletin* 1867.05.05.

445 **"Notwithstanding the usual"**: *New York Times* 1868.04.23.

445 **the pace of homicide:** Faragher 2014.

445 **"Scenes occur"**: *News* 1868.09.22.

445 **Oliveras:** "People vs. Thomas Oliveras," 1866.01.19, Box 4, #742, Criminal/Huntington.

445 **Rice:** *Star* 1870.05.07; *News* 1870.05.07.

446 **Howard:** *Star* 1869.02.20; Newmark 1916:383–84.

446 **Biggs:** *News* 1869.05.08; *Star* 1869.05.08; "People vs. Victor Lamorie," 1869.05.06, Box 5, #888, Criminal/Huntington.

446 **Newman:** *Star* 1870.09.03; *News* 1870.09.10; "People vs. Daniel Newman," 1870.09.04, Box 7, #994, Criminal/Huntington.

446 **Sepúlveda:** *Star* 1870.11.09, 1870.11.10, 1870.11.12, 1871.01.14, 1871.01.18, 1871.01.24, 1871.03.12.

446 **"I'll make"**: "People vs. Ramón Sepúlveda," 1870.11.05, Box 7, #1012, Criminal/Huntington.

446 **Sanford:** *Star* 1870.09.10, 1870.11.20, 1870.11.23, 1870.12.02, 1870.12.14.

446 **"I'll cut":** "People vs. Cyrus Sanford," 1870.09.08, Box 7, #993, Criminal/Huntington.

447 **"A vigilance committee":** *Sacramento Daily Union* 1870.11.21.

447 **"A conviction":** "People vs. Cyrus Sanford," 1870.09.08, Box 7, #993, Criminal/Huntington.

447 **"immunity from punishment":** *Star* 1870.12.02.

448 **"He is known":** *Alta California* 1870.12.16.

448 **farm and vineyard:** "Lachenais, Armand Michel Josef—parcel," n.d., SR Box 29 (22).01, Los Angeles City and County, 1845–c1910.

448 **"go to the devil":** "People vs. Michel Lachenais," 1861.11.04, Box 3, #741, Criminal/Huntington.

449 **"he found the proper":** "People vs. Michel Lachenais," 1861.11.04, Box 4, #741, Criminal/Huntington; "Cold Blooded Slaying," Box 2, folder 7, Mesmer 1860–1914.

449 **"We did everything":** "People vs. Michel Lachenais," 1866.10.29, Box 4, #775, Criminal/Huntington; Tuttle 1875:433–36.

450 **Lachenais had killed her:** *Star* 1870.12.18.

450 **shooting at a neighbor:** *Star* 1871.03.14.

450 **illegally diverting water:** "Michel Lachenais, Malicious Mischief," 1870.06.22, Box 6, #954, Criminal/Huntington.

450 **"has been the theater":** *News* 1870.12.15; Nadeau 1965:20.

451 **"vamoose":** *Star* 1870.12.16.

451 **"because as bad":** Bell 1930:178–79.

451 **"I never did attend":** Bell, "Saddle & Sword," HM 39787, Bell 1829–90.

451 **"We decided that Lachenais":** *Los Angeles Times* 1927.05.15.

452 **"Lachenais's record":** Newmark 1916:420.

452 **"We are no advocate":** *News* 1870.12.17.

452 **"It was evident":** *News* 1870.12.24.

452 **Henrietta Carpenter:** "Jails of Pioneer Days," Box 2, folder 7, Mesmer 1860–1914.

452 **"under the superintendence":** *News* 1870.12.21.

453 **"a Methodist preacher":** *Los Angeles Herald* 1895.03.02.

453 **"But at the last moment":** Bell 1930:180.

453 **"Hang him":** *Alta California* 1870.12.18.

453 **"We could look":** Clary 1966:22–23.

453 **"When he first":** *News* 1870.12.18.

454 **"He desired":** *News* 1870.12.24.

454 **"I am guiltless":** *Star* 1870.12.18.

454 **"There is no doubt":** Bell, "Saddle & Sword," HM 39787, Bell 1829–90.

454 **"Every good citizen":** *News* 1870.12.18.

455 **"We are opposed":** *Star* 1870.12.18.

455 **"Board of Police Commissioners":** *News* 1870.12.31; *Star* 1871.01.07; McPherson 1873a:10, 21, 29, 34, 35, 38.

455 **"It was understood":** *News* 1870.12.18.

456 **"evil-doers":** *Alta California* 1870.12.21.

456 **"make himself scarce":** *Star* 1871.01.22.

456 **Home Guard Vigilance Committee:** *Star* 1870.12.24.

456 **"We are of the opinion"**: Ibid.

456 **"If an honest jury"**: *News* 1870.12.25.

457 **"didn't believe in mobs"**: "People vs. José Ramón Sepúlveda," 1870.11.05 [testimony dated 1871.03.04], Box 7, #1012, Criminal/Huntington.

457 **"Be they few"**: Bell, "Saddle & Sword," HM 39787, Bell 1829-1890.

457 **"that their safety "**: *Star* 1871.11.09.

458 **"Had the laws been"**: *Star* 1871.01.14.

CHAPTER 28

459 **"to cooperate with officers"**: Widney 1921.

460 **"I killed the son"**: *Star* 1871.09.03.

460 **"My Very Dear Son"**: *Star* 1871.09.05.

460 **"It is rumored"**: *Star* 1871.09.06.

461 **"being invaded"**: D. A. Dryden, c1871, Carrico 2008:137.

461 **"a large, fine"**: *Star* c1874, Carrico 2008:120.

462 **"The danger to which"**: *Sacramento Daily Union* 1875.11.19.

462 **died in his sleep**: Carrico 2008:122; Phillips 2014:210.

462 **"These Indians have been"**: Phillips 2014:208.

462 **by given name only**: Louie 1998:95–104.

464 **"almond-eyed family"**: *Star* 1861.08.17.

464 **"the Chinese worker"**: *Star* 1870.09.28.

464 **"without one single"**: *News* n.d., Zesch 2012:94.

465 **"pariahs"**: *News* 1870.08.24.

465 **"maliciously run"**: JP (Still/Gray) 1869.05.18.

465 **twenty violent attacks**: Zesch 2012:95–99.

465 **"maliciously cutting"**: JP (Gray) 1870.10.01.

465 **"beating and kicking"**: JP (Gray)1871.12.05.

465 **"called him hard names"**: JP (Gray)1871.05.27.

466 **"ingenious resort"**: JP (Still/Gray) 1869.07.21.

466 **"You fuck me"**: Armond 2000:70; Zesch 2012:66–67.

466 **annual profit**: Hirata 1979:16–18.

467 **"begged to be allowed"**: *Star* 1871.07.19.

468 **"Warren, what are"**: "People vs. Joseph F. Dye," 1871.01.12, Box 7, #1006, Criminal/Huntington; *Star* 1870.11.01, 1870.11.02.

468 **"The law does not"**: JP (Gray) 1872.10.09.

469 **"maintaining and residing"**: JP (Shore) 1866.09.08.

469 **"Sunday evening"**: *Star* 1871.01.29.

469 **"a huge man"**: Graves 1927:275.

469 **"a fine fellow"**: Bell 1930:170.

469 **"the best and most"**: *Star* 1871.10.30.

470 **"sold forty or fifty"**: "Wing Chung Co. vs. Mayor and Common Council of the City of Los Angeles," 1872.02.20, Box 70, #1941, DCC.

470 **"They fired at me"**: *Star* 1871.10.30.

470 **"with the crime of assault"**: JP (Gray) 1871.10.23.

470 **"They are bound"**: *Star* 1871.10.30.

470 **"was eating his"**: *Star* 1871.10.31.

470 **"a big China fight"**: "Wing Chung Co. vs. Mayor and Common Council of the City of Los Angeles," 1872.02.20, Box 70, #1941, DCC.

471 **"I thought I was"**: *News* 1872.04.02.
471 **"come running out"**: *Star* 1871.10.26.
472 **"He leveled his pistol"**: "Wing Chung Co. vs. Mayor and Common Council of the City of Los Angeles," 1872.02.20, Box 70, #1941, DCC.
472 **"I'm killed"**: *News* 1872.03.31.
472 **"the Chinese were killing"**: *Star* 1871.10.27.
472 **"The Chinese discharged"**: *New York Times* 1871.11.10.
473 **"I called to citizens"**: *Star* 1871.10.26.
473 **"If any Chinamen come out"**: *Star* 1871.10.27.
473 **"Hail any Chinaman"**: *News* 1871.10.27.
473 **"Prevent anyone from going"**: *News* 1871.10.29.
474 **"Here's one"**: *News* 1871.10.28.
474 **"I said it was"**: *News* 1871.11.04.
474 **"To the hill"**: Dorney 1886:232.
474 **"Hoist him up"**: *Star* 1871.10.27.
474 **"That fellow"**: *News* 1871.11.04.
475 **"*carajo la Chino*"**: Dorney 1886:232.
475 **"No attention was paid"**: *News* 1871.10.28.
475 **"Many were anxious"**: *Star* 1871.10.27.
475 **"The excitement"**: *Alta California* 1871.10.25.
476 **"It seemed to me"**: *Star* 1871.10.27.
476 **"Half the horror"**: *New York Times* 1871.11.10.
476 **"My memories"**: "Massacre of Chinese," Box 2, folder 6, Mesmer 1860–1914.
477 **"It was a most heinous"**: "Massacre of Chinese," Box 2, folder 6, Mesmer 1860–1914.
477 **"I saw them bring"**: *News* 1871.11.04.
477 **"bring me more"**: *Star* 1871.10.27.
477 **"Rope, more rope"**: Dorney 1886:233.
478 **"Hang them"**: *News* 1871.11.04.
478 **"Do you know"**: *Star* 1871.10.26.
478 **"You better dry up"**: *News* 1871.10.26, 1872.02.18.
478 **"They are killing"**: Widney 1921a, Foy misidentified as "Fay."
478 **"Years of experience"**: Widney 1921a.
479 **"Damn it, we are all vigilantes"**: *Star* 1871.10.*28*, *News* 1871.10.28.
479 **"We saw two"**: *Star* 1871.10.28.
479 **"The cheap labor"**: *News* 1871.11.04.
479 **"I can get another"**: *Star* 1871.10.27.
480 **"Get out or I"**: Widney 1921a.

CHAPTER 29
481 **"Their countenances"**: *News* 1871.10.28.
481 **the dead**: *News* 1871.10.*26*; *Star* 1871.10.26; Box 7–8, #1067–85, 1089, Criminal/Huntington; Zesch 2012:129–44, passim, provides the most reliable list of victims, but it includes few family names—Ah Cut, Ah Long, Ah Loo, Ah Waa, Ah Wing, Ah Won, Chang Wan, Chee Long Tong, Day Kee, Ho Hing, Jueng Burrow, Leong Quai, Lo Hey, Tong Won, Wah Sin Quai, Wan Foo, Wing Chee, Wong Chin.
482 **"Murder"**: *Star* 1871.10.25.

482 "The fame of our city": *News* 1871.10.25.

482 "The *Star* was already": Bell 1930:175.

482 "very careful in giving": *Alta California* 1871.10.27.

483 "I am afraid": *News* 1871.10.28.

483 "The revelations made": *News* 1871.11.04.

483 "The Vigilance Committee": *Alta California* 1871.10.*26*; *Star* 1871.10.26.

483 "The man referred to": *Star* 1871.10.28.

483 "With the law": *Daily Evening Bulletin* 1871.10.25.

484 "We have the sequel": *Daily Evening Bulletin* 1871.10.27.

484 "The monstrosity": *News* 1871.10.28.

484 "He evidently does": *Star* 1871.10.27.

484 "The mob consisted of": *News* 1871.10.29.

484 "Lawlessness has again": *Star* 1871.11.09; *Sacramento Daily Union* 1871.11.10.

485 "chargeable with disorders": *Star* 1871.12.09.

486 "deplorably inefficient": Ibid.

486 "sending hot shot": *Star* 1871.12.22.

486 "Chinese riot cases": District Court, Minute Book No. 11, 1871.12.08, DCC.

487 "the balances of Justice": *News* 1872.01.03.

487 "a complete farce": *News* 1872.02.15.

487 "Are you now": Spitzzeri 2008:198–200.

488 "took a couple": *News* 1872.02.18.

488 "did feloniously": Spitzzeri 2008:206

489 "I was a member": District Court, Minute Book No. 11, 1872.03.05, DCC.

489 "Everyone who participated": "People vs. L. F. Crenshaw et al.," 1871.11.29, Box 8, #1084, Criminal/Huntington.

489 "there was no proof": "People vs. Louis M. Mendell et al.," 1871.11.28, Box 9, #1115, Criminal/Huntington.

489 "failed to establish": Spitzzeri 2008:197.

489 "all are responsible": "People vs. L. F. Crenshaw et al.," 1871.11.29, Box 8, #1084, Criminal/Huntington.

490 "fatally defective": Ibid.

490 "To this most lame": *Star* 1873.06.11.

490 "There is no doubt": Bell 1930:176.

491 "Ever since that earlier": Bell 1930:166.

CHAPTER 30

493 "Where is all this": *Star* 1851.06.27, clipping Hayes 1877b 43:92.

494 "The Sonorans are": *Star* 1872.01.27.

494 "Los Angeles will soon": *San Francisco Chronicle* 1872.01.25.

495 "by Judge Widney": *Sacramento Daily Union* 1877.08.18.

495 "There are some who": *San Francisco Chronicle* 1874.05.19.

495 "No attempt was made": *Star* 1874.05.15.

496 forty-seven murders: Faragher 2014.

496 "I did not share": Turner 1960:141.

497 "I don't like the looks": Turner 1960:152–54.

497 "Mrs. Turner": *Los Angeles Herald* 1874.06.04.

497 **Francisco Bustamante:** Spitzzeri 1999:297; q.v. "Francisco Bustamante," federal manuscript census, Los Angeles County, 1870.
497 **"first in the field":** Turner 1960:158.
498 **"chopped it down":** Turner 1960:162.
498 **"Swift and terrible":** *Star* 1874.06.07.
498 **"There are instances":** *Los Angeles Herald* 1874.06.09.
499 **"Perhaps the fact":** *Daily Evening Bulletin* 1874.06.06
499 **"some of the worthiest":** *Star* 1874.06.07.
499 **"unable to find any":** *Los Angeles Herald* 1874.06.13.
499 **"kill the whole":** Newmark 1916:470–71.
499 **"If, by chance":** *Los Angeles Herald* 1874.06.10.
499 **"I am now":** Turner 1960:173.
500 **"With all the horrors":** *News* 1872.10.29.
500 **frequency of lethal conflict:** Faragher 2014.
500 **new normal:** Monkkonen 2005a and 2005b.
501 **"The criminal record":** *Los Angeles Herald* 1875.01.01.
501 **three times the rate of New York City:** Monkkonen 2005b:172.
501 **"During the last month":** *Los Angeles Herald* 1874.06.30.
501 **"the best 25 cent meals":** Ritchie 1963:xvii.
502 **"a most comely woman":** "McDonald Uxoricide," Box 2, folder 7, Mesmer
1860–1914.
502 **"She sat there":** *San Francisco Chronicle* 1874.07.02.
502 **"I'm dead":** *Los Angeles Herald* 1874.06.30.
502 **"But she was past":** Joseph Mesmer, "McDonald Uxoricide," Box 2, folder 7,
Mesmer 1860–1914.
502 **"Threats have been made":** *Los Angeles Herald* 1874.07.01.
503 **"People are justified":** *Los Angeles Herald* 1874.10.01.
504 **Lucca Marasovich:** *Alta California* 1872.12.07; Eterovich 1979:67–68.
504 **"I heard the man":** "People v. Lucca Marasovich," 1874.05.10, Box 11,
#1194, Criminal/Huntington.
504 **"Navio Valenzuela is":** *Star* 1874.05.13.
505 **"a severe wound":** "People v. Lucca Marasovich," 1874.05.10, Box 11, #1194,
Criminal/Huntington.
505 **"was not guilty":** *Sacramento Daily Union* 1875.04.13.

EPILOGUE
507 **"Any murderer":** *Los Angeles Herald* 1904.09.18.
507 **"of a very personal":** *Sacramento Daily Union* 1877.06.20.
508 *el abogado de los pobres:* Harrison 1953:180.
509 **"make a two-sided affair":** Harrison 1953:202–5, 241–42.
509 **"foul play":** *Los Angeles Times* 1895.11.27; Salomon 2010:152–54.
510 **"Forgive me":** *Los Angeles Herald* 1883.08.31.
510 **"There is little sympathy":** *Sacramento Daily Union* 1883.08.31.
510 **"the denial of justice":** *Los Angeles Herald* 1883.08.31; Cole 1978:89–94,
511 **"one of the elect":** *Los Angeles Times* 1899.01.01.
511 **"I don't know what":** *Los Angeles Herald* 1899.02.17.
512 **"What do you mean":** *Los Angeles Times* 1899.01.03; *Los Angeles Herald*
1899.02.17.

512 "a common chippie": *Los Angeles Herald* 1899.02.16.

512 "The statement is so": *Los Angeles Times* 1899.02.14.

512 "Gray haired matrons": *Los Angeles Herald* 1899.02.18.

512 "Stung by King's desertion": *Los Angeles Herald* 1899.02.17.

513 "When the jury": *Los Angeles Herald* 1899.02.18.

513 "nectar from old Kaintuck": *Los Angeles Herald* 1902.10.29.

ACKNOWLEDGMENTS

THE RESEARCH AND WRITING of this book benefited from the support and assistance of many individuals and institutions. Yale University provided sabbatical leave and research funds. The Department of History and the Program in American Studies offered the opportunity to test my ideas in the classroom. I thank the many students who participated in several iterations of my freshman seminar, "Violence and Justice in America." I relied on the holdings and services of Yale's excellent libraries. Gregory Eow, former Kaplanoff Librarian for American History at Sterling Memorial Library, helped me gain access to many sources, including a large number of nineteenth-century newspapers on microfilm.

During the decade I worked on this project the Howard R. Lamar Center for the Study of Frontiers and Borders at Yale served as my primary intellectual home. Special thanks go to my dear friends associated with the Center, including Howard R. Lamar, Jay Gitlin, and George Miles. The Beinecke Rare Book and Manuscript Library generously supported a succession of visiting Senior Research Fellows in Western Americana, including Martha A. Sandweiss, David M. Wrobel, Clyde A. Milner II, Carol A. O'Connor, the late David J. Weber, Virginia Scharff, and William F. Deverell. I also want to thank the graduate students with whom I worked during that period: Gerry Cadava, Benjamin Madley, Barry Muchnick, Rebecca McKenna, Katherine Unterman, Ryan Brasseaux, Katherine Gin, Catherine McNeur, Taylor Spence, Christine DeLucia, Jayne Ptolemy, Ashley Riley Sousa, Todd Holmes, Allison Milo Gorsuch, Andrew Offenburger, Mary

Greenfield, Ryan Shaw, Ryan Hall, Isaiah Wilner, Sarah Koenig, Arielle Gorin, Allyson Brantley, and Alyssa Zucher Reichardt.

I conducted much of the research for this history at the Huntington Library and the Seaver Center for Western History Research at the Natural History Museum of Los Angeles County. I benefited from the assistance of Roy Ritchie, Bill Frank, and Peter Blodgett at the Huntington, John M. Cahoon and Betty L. Uyeda at the Seaver Center. Paul R. Spitzzeri of the Workman and Temple Family Homestead Museum provided important source material and expert advice. Scott Zesch generously shared sources and notes. I benefited from the research assistance of Monica Pelayo, Christian Paiz, Daniel Lynch, David Tamayo, and Jeremiah Sladeck.

The ideas behind this book were greatly stimulated by my collaboration with Stephen A. Aron, professor of history at the University of California, Los Angeles, and founding Executive Director of the Institute for the Study of the American West at the Autry National Center, who enlisted me in the Autry's public project on the topic "Violence and Justice in the West."

At W. W. Norton my editor Maria Guarnaschelli again provided encouragement delivered at precisely the right moments. Her former assistant Melanie Tortoroli, now an editor at Viking/Penguin, helped me to see the forest as well as the trees. Sophie Duvernoy helped with the technical details. Otto Sonntag provided excellent copyediting. Adrian Kitzinger drew the maps. Gerard McCauley, my literary agent, again made it all possible.

Danny Faragher, Jimmy Faragher, Tommy Faragher, and David Armstrong read early versions of several chapters, and their enthusiasm for the project kept me going. Elliott West and Michael Magliari, two distinguished western historians, generously took the time to read the entire manuscript and offered constructive criticism.

Every historical project is an expedition to another time and place. Michele Hoffnung, my wife, life partner, and best friend, was by my side through virtually every step of this long, fascinating journey. We visited many historic sites in Los Angeles and southern California and took pleasure in introducing our west coast friends to the unexpected historical treasures of the region. We spent hours discussing the trials and travails of nineteenth-century Angelenos. She listened as I read every chapter aloud and gave me excellent advice on storytelling. This book could not have been written without her support, and I dedicate it to her.

PERMISSIONS

The publisher and author make grateful acknowledgment for permission to reproduce the following illustrations.

FIRST INSERT

Charles Koppel, Los Angeles, from *Reports of Explorations and Surveys to Ascertain the Most Practicable and Economical Route for a Railroad from the Mississippi River to the Pacific Ocean* (1856), 12 vols., 5:35.

William M. Godfrey, Plaza view from Fort Hill, Huntington Library.

Los Angeles Plaza from Fort Moore Hill, Charles C. Pierce Collection, Huntington Library.

Ferdinand Deppe, Mission San Gabriel, reproduced courtesy the Laguna Art Museum.

Emancipated Indian, from Alexander Forbes, *California: A History of Upper and Lower California from Their First Discovery to the Present Time* (1839):6.

Old Indian women of San Fernando Mission, Charles C. Pierce Collection, Huntington Library.

Los Angeles Mission and Plaza before 1869, Charles C. Pierce Collection, Huntington Library.

William M. Godfrey, Hill Street looking north, Seaver Center for Western History Research, Los Angeles County Museum of Natural History.

Old town grocery store, Charles C. Pierce Collection, Huntington Library.

Lugo Family, Seaver Center for Western History Research, Los Angeles County Museum of Natural History.

Execution Scene, Special Collections, Charles E. Young Library, University of California, Los Angeles.

William M. Godfrey, witnessing a vigilante hanging, Seaver Center for Western History Research, Los Angeles County Museum of Natural History.

William M. Godfrey, hanging of Lachenais, Huntington Library.

Samuel Calvert Foy Saddlery, Huntington Library.

Chinatown, Marchessault and Los Angeles Streets, Seaver Center for Western History Research, Los Angeles County Museum of Natural History.

Chinese massacre victims, Security Pacific National Bank Collection, Los Angeles Public Library.

William M. Godfrey, scene of the Chinese riot, Huntington Library.

S. Lazard & Co. dry goods store, Seaver Center for Western History Research, Los Angeles County Museum of Natural History.

Kuchel & Dressel's California Views, Los Angeles, California, Huntington Library.

SECOND INSERT

Pío Pico with wife and two nieces, Seaver Center for Western History Research, Los Angeles County Museum of Natural History.

General Andrés Pico, Charles C. Pierce Collection, Huntington Library.

Benjamin Ignatius Hayes, the Bancroft Library, University of California, Berkeley.

Henri Penelon [?], Emily Chauncey Hayes and son Chauncey, author's collection.

Andrew Jackson King, author's collection.

Stephen Clark Foster, Seaver Center for Western History Research, Los Angeles County Museum of Natural History.

James S. Waite, the San Bernardino Public Library.

Francisco P. Ramírez, Huntington Library.

John O. Wheeler from Harris Newmark, *Sixty Years in Southern California, 1853–1913* (1916).

Juan Bautista Alvarado from *The Century Monthly Illustrated Magazine* 41 (1891):523.

José Castro, the Bancroft Library, University of California, Berkeley.

Raphaela Cota de Temple, Jonathan Temple, and Gregorio de Ajuria, Seaver Center for Western History Research, Los Angeles County Museum of Natural History.

Manuel Requena, California Historical Society Collection, University of Southern California.

José Antonio Carrillo, from Luther A. Ingersoll, *Ingersoll's Century History, Santa Monica Bay Cities* (1908):54.

Antonio F. Coronel, from James M. Guinn, *Historical and Biographical Record of Los Angeles and Vicinity* (1901):953.

Abel Stearns, Huntington Library.

Jean Louis Vignes, Special Collections, Charles E. Young Library, University of California, Los Angeles.

Edward Hereford, Margaret Hereford Wilson, Benjamin D. Wilson, and Thomas Hereford, Huntington Library.

David Alexander and William Workman, Security Pacific National Bank Collection, Los Angeles Public Library.

John Rowland, Alberta Rowland, and child, California Historical Society Collection, University of Southern California.

John C. Frémont from C. Edwards Lester, *Gallery of Illustrious Americans* (1850):40.

Robert F. Stockton, Seaver Center for Western History Research, Los Angeles County Museum of Natural History.

Stephen Watts Kearny from *Graham's American Monthly Magazine* 35 (1849).

John Strother Griffin, Seaver Center for Western History Research, Los Angeles County Museum of Natural History.

Jonathan Drake Stevenson, courtesy William Schultz.

Richard Barnes Mason, U.S. Army Signal Corps.

Henri Penelon, Antonio María Lugo, Seaver Center for Western History Research, Los Angeles County Museum of Natural History.

Francisco de Paula Menito Lugo, Seaver Center for Western History Research, Los Angeles County Museum of Natural History.

Joseph Lancaster Brent, Huntington Library.

Major Horace Bell, Seaver Center for Western History Research, Los Angeles County Museum of Natural History.

James Alexander Watson, author's collection.

William "Uncle Billy" Rubottom, courtesy Pomona Public Library, Pomona, CA.

Henry D. Barrows, California Historical Society Collection, University of Southern California.

Henry Hamilton and William McKee, Huntington Library.

Ina Coolbrith, the Oakland Public Library, Oakland, CA.

Melvina Prater, author's collection.

Tomás Sánchez and John Wilson, Huntington Library.

Edward John Cage Kewen from Winfield J. Davis, *An Illustrated History of Sacramento County* (1890):369.

Phineas Banning, Huntington Library.

Charles Wilkins, courtesy William Secrest.

María Merced Williams, Margarita Chata Bandini, Francisca Williams, Seaver Center for Western History Research, Los Angeles County Museum of Natural History.

John Rains, Luther A. Ingersoll Collection, Los Angeles Public Library.

Robert Carlisle, Seaver Center for Western History Research, Los Angeles County Museum of Natural History.

José Ramón Carrillo, Autry National Center, Los Angeles.

Juan Largo and Jonathan Trumbull Warner with a group of Indians, California Historical Society Collection, University of Southern California.

Manuel Olegario, National Anthropological Archives, Smithsonian Institution.

Henry T. Hazard, James Francis Burns, Robert M. Widney, and Ygnacio Sepúlveda from Harris Newmark, *Sixty Years in Southern California, 1853–1913* (1916).

INDEX